Mortgage Lending, Racial Discrimination, and Federal Policy

JOHN GOERING
RON WIENK
Editors

Mortgage Lending, Racial Discrimination, and Federal Policy

THE URBAN INSTITUTE PRESS
Washington, D.C.

THE URBAN INSTITUTE PRESS
2100 M Street, N.W.
Washington, D.C. 20037

Library of Congress Cataloging in Publication Data

Mortgage lending, Racial Discrimination, and Federal Policy/Edited by John Goering and Ron Wienk.

1. Discrimination in mortgage loans—United States—Congresses.
2. Mortgage loans—Government policy—United States—Congresses.
3. United States—Race relations—Congresses. 4. Discrimination in mortgage loans—Law and legislation—United States—Congresses.
I. Goering, John I. II. Wienk, Ronald E.

HG2040.2.M67 1996 96-15612
332.7′22—dc20 CIP

ISBN 0-87766-656-3 (cloth, alk. paper)

Printed in the United States of America.

Distributed in North America by
University Press of America
4720 Boston Way
Lanham, MD 20706

THE URBAN INSTITUTE is a nonprofit policy research and educational organization established in Washington, D.C., in 1968. Its staff investigates the social and economic problems confronting the nation and public and private means to alleviate them. The Institute disseminates significant findings of its research through the publications program of its Press. The goals of the Institute are to sharpen thinking about societal problems and efforts to solve them, improve government decisions and performance, and increase citizen awareness of important policy choices.

Through work that ranges from broad conceptual studies to administrative and technical assistance, Institute researchers contribute to the stock of knowledge available to guide decision making in the public interest.

Conclusions or opinions expressed in Institute publications are those of the authors and do not necessarily reflect the views of staff members, officers or trustees of the Institute, advisory groups, or any organizations that provide financial support to the Institute.

Dedication

from John,
To Danny, and all the Fabillon family.

from Ron,
To his very supportive, very tolerant parents.

ACKNOWLEDGMENTS

We wish to express deep gratitude to our colleagues at the Technical Assistance Training Corporation (TATC), who provided essential design, planning, and logistical support for the "Home Mortgage Lending and Discrimination: Research and Enforcement Conference," sponsored by the U.S. Department of Housing and Urban Development (HUD) and held in Washington, D.C., on May 18–19, 1993. Papers from that conference serve as the foundation for the current volume.

In particular, Irene Bocella at TATC provided invaluable help in managing the myriad details of the conference. In addition, Alan Skvirsky, President of TATC, and Jaynelle Ketchum provided support and management expertise at key points. Other staff at TATC who provided consistent support were Wynette Fouche-Gibson, Chaulka Creasy, and Marie Parette. We also express sincere thanks to all of the session moderators who helped to coordinate the conference.

Robert Avery, of Cornell University, Charles Finn, of the University of Minnesota, Zina Greene, an independent consultant, and Sandra Wilmore, of the Federal Trade Commission, served as advisers for the conference and offered highly useful advice on content. In the last several years a number of colleagues, some of whom are contributors to this volume, have graciously provided their comments, as well as data, on a number of fair lending issues. These individuals include George Galster, Calvin Bradford, Glenn Canner, Stuart Gabriel, John Yinger, John Simonson, Jonathan Brown, and Deborah Goldberg. Their generous help notwithstanding, the views expressed within the introductory chapters in this volume are those of the authors alone.

We express our appreciation to Steven Cross, at the Office of the Comptroller of the Currency, who facilitated obtaining the financial support of the Comptroller for the conference. Steve also provided substantive advice on conference design issues. In the Office of Fair Housing and Equal Opportunity at HUD, Laurence Pearl was an unfailing supporter and ally throughout the conference and during the preparation of this volume; Susan Forward offered advice during the final stages of conference preparation; and Peter Kaplan has given valuable guidance and opinions about current fair lending enforcement concerns, including legislative and regulatory issues.

HUD's former Assistant Secretary for Policy Development and Research (PD&R), John Weicher, provided initial funding for the fair lending conference. Both Assistant Secretary for PD&R, Michael Stegman, and Deputy Assistant Secretary Margery A. Turner, have subsequently provided important support and encouragement to complete this volume. In addition, a number of PD&R staff helped to guide the final stages of preparation for both the conference and this volume, particularly the late Heather Aveilhe, as well as Valery Dancy and Katherine O'Leary in the Division of Research Utilization. Staff at Aspen Systems Corporation provided expert editorial assistance. We would also like to thank Scott Forrey of the Urban Institute Press, and Molly Ruzicka, who copy-edited the chapters in this volume, for all their great professional assistance. Dan Fabillon was a consistent source of support.

The conclusions and opinions expressed in this volume are those of the authors and do not necessarily represent the views of the U.S. Department of Housing and Urban Development, the Federal government, or the Urban Institute.

John Goering and Ron Wienk, *Editors*

CONTENTS

FOREWORD

Whether or not there is discrimination in the mortgage lending market, this issue is one of the most extensively debated in the civil rights arena. Statistically persuasive national estimates of direct housing rental and sales discrimination have been produced, and similar evidence of discrimination in the entry-level job market has been documented in several cities. Much of the work in both areas has been done at the Urban Institute.

But more than 25 years after the Fair Housing Act, no such definitive research has been conducted in the fair lending arena. Because many early studies were flawed and the results misinterpreted on both sides of the debate, there is as yet no agreement as to the next essential steps in either research or enforcement. As the volume editors put it, "too much debate has occurred while needed research has been left undone, and too much polemic has occurred because only a thin strand of research evidence exists upon which to build national and local policies."

This comprehensive volume seeks to clarify the debate by including rigorous review of fair lending research, applied projects, and enforcement activities to date, as well as recommendations for needed research to resolve unanswered questions. Contributing authors address both measurement issues and investigative techniques.

The analyses contained here shed light on an important and contentious social issue. The intent of the book is to help the housing industry, regulators, advocates, and the research community to better understand, in order to better tackle, the issue of discrimination in an important area of American life—the right to take out a mortgage to buy a home, conditioned only on one's credit-worthiness, not on one's race or ethnic group.

William Gorham
President

Part One

MORTGAGE LENDING DISCRIMINATION RESEARCH

Chapter One

AN OVERVIEW

John Goering and Ron Wienk

I felt discouraged and robbed of my self-worth and esteem, and have given up trying to find other financing.

—Calvin Hicks, quoted in Powers (1993)

I'm not a statistician, but when blacks are getting their loan applications rejected twice as often as whites, and in some cities, it's three and four times as often, I conclude that discrimination is part of the problem. . . .

—Senator Alan Dixon (Senate Hearing 1990)

The personal trauma experienced by Calvin Hicks, a $42,000-a-year security officer, in being rejected for a home mortgage (in Powers 1993) is echoed in the complaints of many families who, after being similarly discriminated against, have filed suit in federal or state court and found monetary relief. George and Elizabeth Green, for example, were awarded $150,000 in 1995 by a California appeals court on the grounds that they had been denied a mortgage loan because they were black (Green v. Rancho Santa Fe Mortgage Co., 706 Cal. App. 1994). In Boston, Shawmut Mortgage Company settled a charge of lending discrimination brought against them by the U.S. Department of Justice by allocating $960,000 to compensate African Americans and Hispanics whose mortgage loan applications had been illegally denied (U.S. vs. Shamut Mortgage Co.). Although accounts of such discrimination are too numerous to be considered anecdotal, social science and policy debate continues to rage about whether—and how much—lending discrimination is actually occurring in American cities ("Housing Discrimination" 1995; Yezer 1995).

This debate formed the core of a May 1993 conference on "Home Mortgage Lending and Discrimination: Research and Enforcement," convened by the U.S. Department of Housing and Urban Development (HUD) in Washington, D.C. The assembled researchers and enforcement agencies sought to answer, although on the basis of dramatically different investigative strategies, two major questions: "What evidence is there of discrimination by mortgage lenders? and If discrimination is occurring, how powerful or significant a force is it?" Papers from the May 1993 conference—updated or revised—form the core of this volume.[1]

From the perspective of housing and civil rights advocates, it may appear an unfortunate sign of the times that HUD would find it necessary to hold a conference and then to prepare a book to discuss the validity of evidence concerning evidence of "discrimination" more than 25 years after enactment of the Fair Housing Act, when all around is living testimony to the racial divisiveness and inequality in American communities and housing markets (Hacker 1992; Massey and Denton 1993; Feagin and Sykes 1994; McCall 1994). Indeed, hearings in the U.S. Senate and House of Representatives on fair lending, held from 1989 through the mid-1990s, purportedly set the stage for rapid progress in the enforcement of federal statutes. Notable improvement in the quality of information collected from the Home Mortgage Disclosure Act (HMDA) also offered the prospects of more definitive action by banking regulators and HUD in enforcing federal fair lending laws. (HMDA was enacted in 1975.)

Civil rights enforcement and research have not, however, progressed in neat linear, irreversible stages. Instead, advocates on both sides have engaged in a social dialogue in which they have debated the evidence concerning lending discrimination and have raised substantial political doubt about the methods of enforcement and research that have been used to uncover "proof" of discrimination. This dialogue has constituted one of the most extensive social science and policy debates in any civil rights arena, with the possible exception of busing and affirmative action.

The lending community has, for decades, argued that it cares only about the color of a person's money and not his or her skin. Listokin and Casey (1980: 10), for example, reported on the "clash" between bankers and advocates in the mid-1970s: "Lenders stress the hegemony of economic criteria, while community and civil rights organizations argue that financial institutions are guided by racial as well as economic policies." The core and spirit of this same tension persist today and form the backdrop for many of the analyses in this volume.

That the lending community does not speak in one voice is signaled by the willingness of numbers of lenders to voluntarily sign and enforce "best practices" agreements in fair lending (Listokin and Casey 1980: 173). These agreements frequently address issues such as better marketing to minority communities, second reviews of loan applications, the strategic location of new offices, hiring practices, and assessing lending standards. The agreements may also address underwriting standards that may adversely affect those with nontraditional sources of income, those with disabilities, and those who wish to finance small loan amounts. Some lenders have also begun to use mystery shoppers or testers, in addition to analyzing their own loan rejection data, to assess fair lending compliance.

Such exceptions notwithstanding, each "stage" in the analysis of research data has been accompanied by new—and often more strident—protests by the banking community that discrimination is not a major problem among lenders in the United States or that there is no good evidence to the contrary. Many of these criticisms have been warranted and have constituted the basis for additional studies to address specific shortcomings. In fact, the evolving concern about the state of lending discrimination has been accompanied by suggestions for improving the conduct of basic social science research on the subject. However, the overall lack of enthusiasm for such research is partially responsible for the continuing rhetoric and debate about whether or not there really is a smoking gun of lending discrimination. This volume seeks to clarify that debate by including fundamental analyses of crucial fair lending research to date, as well as recommendations for needed research to resolve unanswered questions (see Yinger [chapter 2], Tootell [chapter 4], and Galster [chapter 8]).

Without this vitally important research, the pattern of critiques may appear as though no progress has been made over the last several decades, and that major banking institutions are merely opposed to serious enforcement of fair lending statutes. Opposition to additional or innovative forms of research and investigation has remained relatively constant as banking trade groups and some regulators have sought to dispel the notion that there is valid proof of widespread discriminatory irregularities. Considerable effort has been expended to rebut each new study on lending discrimination and, more recently, to diminish the data collected by banking regulators that address fair lending—effort that could better be spent researching definitive answers to whether, how much, and what forms of lending discrimination occur at the national or local levels. This volume's papers address these basic questions.

In the 1990s, hostility toward and skepticism about research and enforcement may, once again, slow the momentum of antidiscrimination agencies (Isaac 1995; Lindsey 1995). Although for some skeptics this is yet another sign of the "inevitable exercise of power by white institutions" (Bell 1992: 373), alternative explanations can be found for the ebbs and troughs of fair lending enforcement. For some analysts, "race fatigue" has settled upon the country (Steele 1990: 23). "The country's conscience is exhausted," stated Delgado (1992: 530–

31), with many whites "tired of feeling guilty about the black community's misfortunes. . . . With all these remedial statutes on the books—assuring fair treatment in housing, education, the workplace, and credit—if blacks are still unsuccessful, still miserable, still complaining, well, what can be done?"

Another area of difficulty involves the enormous methodological problems associated with assembling data to determine whether either intentional or "disparate-impacts" discrimination is occurring in U.S. lending institutions. These methodological problems are underscored each time a study has been undertaken, addressing what, to the outsider, may appear to be a black hole of problematic issues (Listokin and Casey 1980: 31, 159; Schill and Wachter 1993: 272; Caskey 1994).

Statistically persuasive national estimates of direct housing rental and sales discrimination have been produced, based on auditing the behavior of real estate and rental property agents (Turner, Struyk, and Yinger 1991; Turner 1992). Such research has effectively resolved doubts as to the existence or virulence of such discrimination, and has substantially altered subsequent policy and legislative debate. No such definitive, behaviorally based research has been conducted in the fair lending arena, however. As a result, banking trade associations and lending institutions have continued to argue that no smoking gun of discrimination has been found. Because many early studies were flawed, with evidence misconstrued by advocates on both sides, no agreement has been reached as to the next essential steps in research and enforcement.

Some banking industry analysts have recently contended that "while it is nice to have these ideas that you can do things for minority groups, the evidence shows that whatever you do doesn't work" (Seiberg 1995a: 3). A recent *Wall Street Journal* headline (Karr 1995) reads: "Federal Drive to Curb Mortgage-Loan Bias Stirs Strong Backlash." And the editor of an American Bankers Association compendium (Yezer 1995: VI) has suggested what we regard as the unlikely possibility that the reason researchers focus on fair lending is to get "publicity" rather than to accurately assess evidence. Yezer (1995) furthermore charges that false-positive results have been the norm because mortgage lending is so complex, requiring complicated statistical techniques to accurately measure lending bias.

This volume has been prepared because too much debate has occurred while needed research has been left undone, and too much polemic has occurred because only a thin strand of research evidence exists upon which to build national and local policies.

PURPOSE OF THIS VOLUME

This volume assembles evidence and argument concerning the existence or nonexistence of mortgage lending discrimination by depository and nondepository lending institutions. For the first time, a comprehensive review is provided of current research studies, applied projects, and enforcement activities in fair lending.[2] The core questions that the contributing authors seek to answer are those of whether mortgage lending discrimination exists; if so, how much; in what forms; and what investigative research techniques are most useful in uncovering proof of discrimination. The authors review state-of-the-art policy research addressing conventional and Federal Housing Administration (FHA)-insured mortgage lending processes and practices as they may discriminatorily affect minorities, especially African Americans. The findings are designed to be used by both private- and public-sector fair lending researchers and agencies.

Whereas the May 1993 HUD conference that served as the platform for this book was conceived shortly after issuance of the first "new" Home Mortgage Disclosure Act (HMDA) data in 1991, planning for the conference began in earnest just as the results from the Federal Reserve Bank of Boston's now-famous study on lending discrimination (known as the "Boston Fed" study—Munnell et al. 1992), and the details of the consent decree from the equally well-known Department of Justice case against Decatur Federal Savings and Loan, in Atlanta, were emerging. This volume benefits greatly from analysis and debate on these two major research and enforcement projects.

The 1993 HUD conference was designed to stimulate discussion of overlapping and distinctive research and investigative projects. Although substantial differences exist in the objectives and methods of academic versus enforcement institutions, the intersection of these groups' interests is obvious in that both researchers and advocates use data from similar sources to aid in establishing "proof" and are motivated (or frustrated) by the need to provide convincing evidence about the behavior and intentions of members of lending institutions, most of whom do not appear to practice overt racial bias against minorities. This volume furthermore aims to identify priorities for future policies and research in fair lending enforcement.

There are even more important linkages between "fair lending" research and enforcement. It has been research studies and analyses of HMDA data that have forged many critically debated policy questions; more specifically, the ever-present limitations of research have prompted rhetorical charges and countercharges that tend to undermine the credibility of the fair lending policy process. In fact, until quite recently, the spartan nature of fair lending research and enforcement commitments has frustrated effective cooperation and dialogue between the academic and nonprofit research communities and the institutions and agencies that are responsible for either adhering to or enforcing the law. The vigorous debate at the 1993 HUD conference may not have reduced barriers to cooperation, but it provided a forum for an unusually diverse set of viewpoints, as well as useful suggestions for research and enforcement, which are reflected in this volume.

FOUR STAGES OF FAIR LENDING RESEARCH

With enactment of the Fair Housing Act in 1968, initially only a modest level of either research or enforcement activity was engaged in to establish "proof" of discrimination by mortgage lending institutions (Listokin and Casey 1980). A 1974 survey of over 100,000 loan applications, for example, found that blacks were more than twice as likely to be rejected for a loan as whites (Listokin and Casey 1980: 57–58), but the survey lacked needed information on the characteristics of the applicants and the properties for which mortgages were sought.

In 1976, William Taylor, then director of the Center for National Policy Review, testified before Congress on the need for statistical information on lending (quoted in Listokin and Casey 1980: 57):

> Almost every federal agency with statutory duties to protect civil rights has understood the necessity of collecting racial data as an aid to enforcement. While statistical disparities in the benefits accorded to particular racial groups do not constitute conclusive proof of discrimination, the courts in various contexts have held that they can create a presumption that the law has been violated, shifting the burden to defendants to establish that their practices are free from the taint of illegality. In such areas as lending where discrimination often takes subtle forms and where the victim himself may not be aware that he has been discriminated against, such data [are] indispensable.

The argument that assembling data on general racial impacts was an essential first step to enable courts to litigate claims of discrimination constitutes the heart of the disparate-impacts charge and is a persistent requirement for fair lending investigations.

The inertia affecting both the research and enforcement communities (Fishbein 1993) was undoubtedly partially attributable to the enormous difficulties of addressing pressing complaints of discrimination in parts of the housing market aside from lending—that is, rentals and sales—as well as to the obdurate and, at the time, irrefutable argument that the lending industry put forth: bankers care only about the color of money and not about the race or color of the person seeking mortgage credit. At the same time, much of the momentum for both research and enforcement activity in regard to credit allocation biases is due to the increased availability of critically important databases on the number of loans made or loan applications filed with lenders. The most important of these databases, and a fundamental platform for the conduct of race disparity research and enforcement action, has been the Home Mortgage Disclosure Act (HMDA), originally enacted in 1975 and amended in 1989. HMDA, a virtual census of mortgage loans made in metropolitan areas, is unique to the United States and is a vital tool for measuring differential treatment to minority individuals and neighborhoods. That this tool has been and remains flawed is part of the dilemma facing researchers and policymakers alike.

Roughly four stages in the evolution of research and civil rights enforcement have occurred since passage of the Fair Housing Act in 1968. These stages may be demarcated by the special character of the research or enforcement information available, and reflect a crude trajectory of change in the questions asked and the availability of data to answer them. The following sections highlights these stages and indicate how research limitations have continually raised the ante in "proving" the existence of lending discrimination.

Stage One: The "Old" HMDA Studies

As stated, at first only limited research and data collection, largely tied to the 1975 Home Mortgage Disclosure Act, measured compliance with the Fair Housing Act and the Community Reinvestment Act (CRA). HMDA's potential to assist in identifying possible discriminatory lending patterns and enforcing antidiscrimination statutes was in its infancy. Research and analysis soon demonstrated HMDA's limitations in establishing evidence that either individual acts or patterns of discrimination were occurring at the hands of banks, savings and loans, mortgage bankers, or other lenders.

HMDA initially required a variety of depository institutions to disclose by census tract or county name the number and dollar amount of both home mortgage and home improvement loans on a calendar year basis. The statute then, and now, exempts depository institutions with less than $10 million in assets, those covered by equivalent state laws, and those located outside metropolitan statistical areas.

Following passage of HMDA, approximately 300 HMDA analyses were prepared by researchers and community groups aimed at producing action by local or federal banking regulators under the CRA, the Equal Credit Opportunity Act, or the Fair Housing Act. These analyses were facilitated by the preparation and release, after 1980, of standard HMDA tables by the Federal Financial Institutions Examination Council (FFIEC) of loan origination data on conventional, Federal Housing Administration (FHA)/Veterans Administration (VA)/ Farmers Home Administration (FmHA), and home improvement loans by census tract. These "old" HMDA studies typically revealed the distribution of lending within metropolitan areas over time, focusing on the relative allocation of credit to whites versus blacks in suburban versus central city neighborhoods (Stegman 1972; Greeston, MacRae, and Pedone 1975; Leven et al. 1976: 37–50; Hammer, Siler, George Associates 1979; Weicher 1979: 223–25; Canner 1982; Morrow-Jones 1986).

Such analyses, conducted by community groups and other organizations such as the Center for Community Change and the Woodstock Institute, typically concluded that there had been redlining or disinvestment in a particular area or metropolitan center. There was also some analysis of the effect of specific types of loans, such as FHA loans, in fostering inner-city neighborhood decline as well as rapid racial change or "arbitrage" (Bradford and Rubinowitz 1975; Schlay 1985; Squires and Velez 1987; Schlay 1988; Kentucky Commission 1989a). These analyses were used in federal court to assert violations of the federal Fair Housing law. The major case involving HUD and VA was the *Jormon* case in Chicago (Jorman v. Veterans Administration, 654 F. Supp. 748 (N.D. Ill. 1986)), in which plaintiffs alleged that the FHA and VA fostered rapid racial change in the Marquette Park neighborhood (Eagan, Mott, and Roos 1981).

Perhaps the most publicized analysis of "old" HMDA data was the report "The Color of Money" by Bill Dedman, published in a four-part series in May 1988 by the *Atlanta Journal-Constitution*. Using six years of HMDA data for Atlanta lenders, supplemented with information on loan applications, the study found that mortgage loans were made in predominantly white middle-income census tracts at approximately five times the rate in predominantly black middle-income neighborhoods. "Whites receive five times as many home loans from

Atlanta's banks and savings and loans as blacks of the same income, and that gap has been widening each year,'' argued Dedman. The five-to-one (redlining) ratio is made after adjusting for the number of owner-occupied housing units in the tracts under study. HMDA data were supplemented by information on loan applications from a small number of lenders—information that proved crucial to the arguments made.

Dedman's (1988) study was, at the time, subjected to detailed critiques by both local lenders and banking regulators, with reports prepared for the U.S. Senate Banking Committee. According to Dedman (1988: 1):

> Senior bank executives [stated that] any lending differences most likely are caused by factors beyond their control, including poor quality housing and lack of home sales in black neighborhoods, fewer applications from blacks, and limitations in federal lending data. They also pointed out that lending patterns are influenced by real estate agents, appraisers, and federal loan programs.

Although HMDA data permitted a limited analysis of the distribution of home purchase and/or home improvement loans within census tracts, the data were unable to answer questions concerning the practice of discrimination. HMDA redlining studies, argued Canner (1982: 10), failed "to incorporate information on mortgage demand, loan risk, and mortgage contract characteristics, [which] substantially weakens their usefulness for assessing the redlining issue.'' The thrust of these arguments set high hurdles for establishing proof of discriminatory behavior. Economists argued that a variety of supply and demand factors would need to be incorporated into explanations of discrepancies in lending patterns including lack of demand for mortgage loans in the area; adequate measures of equity; external risks that threatened property value or increased the chance of nonpayment; and decisions by entities outside the control of lenders, such as real estate agents and appraisers (Jaffey 1976; Listokin and Casey 1980). In partial reply, some sociological analysts responded that there can be no ideal measure of active housing demand, since the lack of mortgage money (real or perceived) from a lender may in turn reduce demand for sales (Schlay 1989: 211).

Early HMDA studies also were unable to reveal the extent to which home purchase credit needs in minority and moderate income neighborhoods were being met by other types of lenders *not* covered by HMDA. In Atlanta, for example, banking regulators estimated that half the home purchase loans were extended by lenders not covered by

HMDA. The absence of data on nondepository lenders, especially mortgage bankers, was recognized as a major shortcoming in assessing the allocation of credit within an entire jurisdiction or neighborhood, and formed the basis for amending HMDA. There were also a number of known sources of error and missing data in the original HMDA data (JRB Associates 1980; Ryker, Pol, and Guy 1984; Schlay 1985: 6).

Despite the numerous limitations of the "old" HMDA data, they nevertheless provided a useful, standardized monitoring tool for assessing the size of lending disparities by tract (Schlay 1989: 211), and became widely used by bank examiners looking for Fair Housing Act and Equal Credit Opportunity Act (ECOA) violations during compliance examinations (Squires and Velez 1987: 219; Kluckman 1989; Schlay 1989: 217).

The foregoing limitations, as well as the *Atlanta Journal-Constitution's* documentation of loan application information, were a source of interest for Congress when it amended HMDA in 1989, forming the basis for the next stage in "fair lending" inquiries.

Stage Two: The "New" HMDA Data

Major amendments to HMDA occurred with Section 1211 of the Financial Institutions Reform, Recovery, and Enforcement Act of 1989 (FIRREA), including the requirement that information be reported on the race, gender, and income of mortgage loan applications completed after December 31, 1989. This statute provided the basis for the new HMDA disclosure laws and for heightened interest in the treatment of racial minorities by permitting comparisons of the treatment of loan applicants by racial group. By 1992–93, substantial progress was being made in taking full advantage of the "new" data as well as in finding innovative means for supplementing or combining the data with other methods of investigation and analysis. Some of these innovative projects are described for the first time in this volume.

Of particular significance, the new HMDA required expanded coverage of large mortgage lenders not affiliated with depository institutions, such as mortgage companies. This change, accompanied by clarifying language, has resulted in the addition of up to 4 million loans from roughly 1,000 lenders to the new HMDA database. The 1994 data covered 12.2 million loan applications from over 3,000 depository and nondepository lenders. Application information from the first full year of private mortgage insurers was also available for the first time in the 1994 HMDA data.

HMDA regulations now require that all covered institutions must report information on a loan application register, or LAR (C of the Federal Reserve Board; 12 CFR Part 203, cited in Kluckman 1989). The benefits and limitations of LAR data have constituted the major data transformation in both fair lending research and investigations. New HMDA data permit, for the first time, the calculation of loan acceptance and rejection rates by racial grouping.

The data revealed that the rejection rates for African Americans were twice as high as those for whites—rates comparable to those found over 20 years earlier (Listokin and Casey 1980: 58) and virtually identical to the disparities found in 1994 HMDA data. These disparities quickly became the subject of a short, but intense, period of congressional oversight and a variety of industry and fair lending actions.

FIRREA's amendments created a spate of new HMDA analyses regarding the level and characteristics of demand for conventional and FHA loans, as well as the characteristics of individuals denied such credit, using tract as well as individual characteristics of applicants versus those of loan recipients. New HMDA data suddenly raised the stakes in arguments about the race neutrality of bank lending practices, since the data appeared to suggest that there was a systematic pattern of denying loans to African Americans.

Soon after issuance of the first new HMDA data, George Galster (1991), on behalf of the American Bankers Association, issued a report detailing the reasons why the new HMDA data "cannot support conclusive findings of illegal discrimination. . . ." Galster concluded:

> It must be emphasized that studies based on the new HMDA data will not—and indeed cannot—be definitive about whether any lending patterns represent illegal discrimination. The reasons that this assertion can be made so strongly is that the new data do not include information on certain factors that are critical in credit decisions, including . . . characteristics of the property in question and the financial record and condition of the applicant. The data that are omitted from HMDA are precisely those that, if taken into account statistically, would narrow (if not completely eliminate) any differences in dispositions of loan applications that might appear to be related to race and/or gender. (P. 4)

HMDA analyses, Galster argued, cannot establish direct and probative evidence of credit discrimination, because such proof typically requires substantial additional information on the lending or underwriting criteria of the bank; the wealth/debt levels of the applicant; the credit history of the loan applicant; and information about the property serving as collateral. Galster contended that unless such care were exercised, the stage would be set for "irresponsible rhetoric, unjustifiable complacency and the formulation of wrong-headed public policy" (p. 1).

Galster recommended then, and continues to advocate in this volume (see chapters 8 and 27), the following:

> Congress or a regulatory agency should commission a comprehensive, definitive study of mortgage markets. This study should not only statistically investigate data from loan application files of a broad sample of lenders but should also use testers to investigate the pre-application stages before a "paper trail" is created. Only then will we know the extent to which differential treatment discrimination is occurring. The highest social-scientific standards would be required. The cost of such a study would be trivial compared to the cost of either ignoring a potentially severe social problem or wasting resources in a vain attempt to solve a minuscule one. (Galster 1992: 10).

As Galster has noted, it is widely recognized that HMDA data provide no information on the extent of discrimination prior to submission of a written application. No information is available from HMDA or even bank records on the extent to which lenders may actively try to discourage a minority individual (protected class member) from filing an application. Such discriminatory treatment constitutes a probable violation of the Fair Housing Act and has been an issue of concern to fair lending enforcement agencies for years (Schafer and Ladd 1980: ch. 2, p. 1). Recent prescreening testing projects conducted in a number of jurisdictions are discussed in the second part of this volume.

There are, therefore, a number of recognized impediments to using HMDA data to analyze discriminatory credit decisions affecting minority households or neighborhoods. The limitations of the original statute were only partly corrected by FIRREA amendments. Despite the recognized limitations of HMDA, banking regulators began to focus on methods for employing the data to assist in their fair lending and Equal Credit Opportunity Act (ECOA) examinations. A variety of automated targeting, screening, and analysis tools began to be developed for use by loan examiners (LaWare 1993).

Stage Three: Acceptance and Rejection of Loan Applications by Minorities

The third phase of research—the analysis of loan acceptances and rejections—has involved careful statistical specification of additional information collected to supplement the known weaknesses even of "new" HMDA data. This phase of research and investigation includes the 1992 Boston Fed study on mortgage lending (Munnell et al. 1992, 1996), addressed in this volume by Tootell (chapter 4) and Rodda and Wallace (chapter 20), and the massive research effort associated with the *Decatur Federal* case in Atlanta, also included in this volume (see Ritter, chapter 15; Siskin and Cupingood, chapter 16; and Alexander, chapter 17).

As many readers of this volume are aware, the Boston Fed study "Mortgage Lending in Boston: Interpreting HMDA Data" was the first major attempt to supplement new HMDA data with sufficient information to test whether lenders were correct in asserting that they only used legitimate economic considerations in evaluating the creditworthiness of loan applicants, whether black or white. Research staff from the Boston Federal Reserve Board met with Boston area lenders and underwriters, national banking regulators, and HUD staff to obtain their review and approval of the basic survey design and of a list of additional data to be collected. Thirty-eight variables were included in the list of information requested from Boston area lenders, the results of which, it was assumed by Reserve Board staff, would convincingly demonstrate that race was not a determining factor in loan decisions. As Tootell, one of the authors of the Boston Fed study, states in chapter 4 of this volume: "It is difficult to find a variable systematically related to the mortgage lending decision and collected by the lender that the Boston Fed did not gather."

The Boston Fed study's startling finding that race was indeed a fairly powerful influence in lending decisions initially stunned banking regulators and subsequently led to a variety of industry self-examination and fair lending enforcement initiatives. Shortly thereafter, a wholesale media and social science assault was launched on the study's credibility, with all sorts of reasons found to discredit the data and analysis. As a result, extensive reanalyses of the project data were undertaken; however, most analysts confirmed the initial findings of a strong race effect.

Tootell (in chapter 4, this volume) offers the first major reassessment of these criticisms and follow-up studies; he outlines the limitations of some earlier criticisms, as well as the unusual advantages of the Boston Fed study. Many of the studies that critique the merits of the Boston Fed study are furthermore referenced in Rodda and Wallace (chapter 20, this volume), who also confirm that there is a "smoking gun" race effect in making loans to marginally qualified white but not to comparably qualified black borrowers.

A question that comes to mind immediately in regard to the Boston Fed results is whether such racial differences in lending patterns occur in other areas of the country. Although no one has to date replicated the Boston Fed study, Avery, Beeson, and Sniderman (in chapter 3, this volume) address whether there are similarities in racial differences in lending across the country. After carefully controlling for as much information as is provided in the "new" HMDA data, they find racial differences in denial rates across all markets and for all loan types, even after controlling for lender, neighborhood, and applicants' economic characteristics. They further report that these effects are not due to property location or neighborhood, thus causing them to wonder whether differences in how lenders act toward minorities could be an important explanation. They, like others, also encourage research on loan performance or risk outcomes—as exemplified in this volume by Gabriel (chapter 5) and by Berkovec and colleagues (chapters 6, 7, and 10). Research aimed at understanding the higher rates of FHA mortgage lending to minorities is also needed. Minority households may actively seek or prefer mortgages from sources other than banks and thrifts because they perceive that other lenders discriminate (Shear and Yezer 1985: 293). FHA mortgage loans also may be sought more frequently by homebuyers in predominantly minority/middle-income areas because of lower down-payment requirements or easier underwriting standards than those available from conventional lenders. In addition, real estate brokers may illegally refer or steer minorities to such mortgage bankers; there is some evidence that this has occurred in both Chicago and Atlanta (Squires and Velez 1987: 230).

Gabriel (chapter 5, this volume) highlights the difficulties of obtaining clear answers to these questions. The appearance of steering and the differences in treatment of blacks and Hispanics clearly warrant further research that is sensitive to both the history and circumstances of the FHA program and the cities studied. The existence of discrimination in the earliest stages of application for mortgage credit has been discussed as a potentially powerful obstacle to fair credit allocation. Study of such pre-screening is a critical component of any comprehensive examination of the extent and determinants of credit discrimination; indeed, research on pre-screening has been identified as important for some time (Schafer and Ladd 1980; Canner 1982: 6, 10; Shear and Yezer 1985: 293). Testing to examine allegations of discrimination has received periodic support from banking regulators, although few use formally trained testers in the application stage of mortgage lending.

Testing procedures can also be utilized to investigate the level and forms of discrimination in later parts of the credit review and allocation process. Such techniques have been adopted by a small number of fair housing investigations, and a manual for testing for credit discrimination was prepared under a HUD/FHEO (Fair Housing and Equal Opportunity) contract (Kentucky Commission 1989b; Galster 1993).

Recent experiences with lender testing (see chapter 23, by Smith and Cloud, and chapter 24, by Lawton, in this volume) address a number of questions: How many fair housing groups are conducting lender or appraiser testing? What prompts such testing efforts? What, in general, has the testing uncovered, and what actions have been taken in response to the findings? "Self-testing" for lenders is also being encouraged. Barry Leeds and Associates, for example, outlined their approach at the 1993 HUD conference on "Home Mortgage Lending and Discrimination." A host of questions remain about such efforts, including: What types of institutions have been doing self-testing? and What actions have lenders taken in response to findings of testing efforts? Conducting a national audit or testing project has been long debated within HUD and federal banking regulators. While such a testing project would be complicated to design, and national-level estimates of credit discrimination would be expensive to provide, it is an essential research need.

Lenders are not, of course, the only entities involved in the long process of purchasing and financing a home. Sales brokers, appraisers, private mortgage insurers, home insurers, credit reporting agencies, loan holders, and secondary market intermediaries (e.g., Federal National Mortgage Association [Fannie Mae] and Federal Home Loan Mortgage Corporation [Freddie Mac]) all play various roles. As stated earlier, only a slim amount of social science and legal research has probed the extent of lending discrimination and who is causing it. Two pathbreaking papers in this volume address, first, evidence and legal arguments concerning race and the secondary market (Van Order, chapter 11) and, second, racial discrimination in the appraisal industry (Schwemm, chapter 12). Van Order notes the importance of understanding the extent to which underwriting guidelines issued by secondary markets can either be too rigid or can disproportionately affect minorities. Using a simple analysis of loans originated by different racial groups in the primary market, Van Order finds few differences among those loans purchased. The findings are thin, he reports, and suggests that research is needed on underwriting guidelines and their application by lenders. Like Avery et al. (in chapter 3), Van Order also advocates the analysis of "loans made to those discriminated against to see if they perform better." He furthermore encourages research on lender testing as well as greater care in conducting risk-based pricing.

Schwemm's discussion in chapter 12 represents one of the few systematic attempts to integrate the handful of legal analyses (six in all) on discrimination in the appraisal industry. None of these cases resulted in a conviction, suggesting that the subjective nature of appraising could serve as a legitimate defense against an allegation of discrimination. The absence of a clear legal basis for arguing that a discriminatory effect has occurred also tends to obscure future progress. Schwemm contends that education, training, and care by the secondary markets can be helpful. His study underscores the need for ethnographic research into appraisal industry operations, as well as careful attention to constructing and performing sensitivity analyses for disparate-"impacts" thresholds.

Stage Four: Racial Discrimination and Defaults

> *A new Federal Reserve Board study takes aim at the widely held view that banks discriminate against marginally qualified loan applicants. The study contends that the exact opposite is true. . . .*
>
> —Seiberg (1995a)

A small number of researchers have noted the scanty amount of research on the relationship between the risk and default of mortgage loans and the income and racial characteristics of individuals and neighborhoods (e.g., Canner, Gabriel, and Wooley 1991). A decade ago, Shear and Yezer (1985: 294) cautioned that "interest rates and rejections vary directly with the probability of default and the loan-to-value ratio. These forms of differential treatment are to be expected and should not be confused with discrimination." Quercia and Stegman (1992) and Van Order, Westin, and Zorn (1993) have also explored these complex issues, raising questions about overall theoretical and methodological concerns.

Although not so clearly demarcated a stage of research, since it draws heavily on lessons for acceptances-rejections research, the fourth and latest phase in research on lending discrimination includes analysis of mortgage performance or defaults, as represented in this volume by Berkovec et al. (chapters 6 and 7). Based partly on encouragement by governors of the Federal Reserve Board, Berkovec and colleagues began a multiyear effort to examine the probability that minorities' mortgage loans perform differently than those of whites—specifically, that such loans default more often than those to whites and are therefore a poorer risk. Using data supplied by HUD,[3] Berkovec et al. examined how lenders behave toward marginally qualified minority familes whose home mortgage loans were insured by FHA between 1986 and 1989. The authors assumed that if there were any lending discrimination, then African Americans would be held to *higher* standards of creditworthiness than white applicants and would, as a result, default *less* often than whites. However, the authors found that African Americans default more frequently than do whites, and that their losses are higher than those of whites; these findings represented small but statistically significant differences. Berkovec et al. see this higher loss for African American borrowers as supporting the contention that African Americans and whites are treated equally in the default process because, after all, economically rational lenders would not discriminate if it were against their economic interest to do so. The *Wall Street Journal*, one of several publications in the media that have reported on this study, shared Berkovec et al.'s view, stating: "A Federal Reserve Board study challenges a widely held contention that banks and other lenders discriminate against minorities by making it harder for them to qualify for loans" (Jan. 26, 1995).

The finding of higher default rates among African American borrowers shows clearly the conditions necessary for discrimination: lenders can benefit from using results for the *group* to predict the prospects of default for an individual applicant. If African Americans as a group are more likely to experience financial crises, then lenders have economic incentives to use *race* as a predictor of default risk. This is exactly the form of "statistical discrimination" that the Federal Reserve researchers did not study and that is clearly illegal under the Fair Housing Act.

Berkovec et al. acknowledge the many limiting assumptions of their study and the shortcomings in their data. They also admit that they have no "proof" that systematic discrimination has been eliminated. Thus, although their study represents a careful, serious effort to understand why defaults occur in the FHA loan process, it does not prove that there is no longer any racial discrimination in lending.

Berkovec et al.'s analysis in this volume and in earlier work is the subject of two commentaries in this volume, by Galster and Ross (chapters 8 and 9, respectively), following which Berkovec et al. respond to these critiques in chapter 10. The commentaries highlight the disagreement over whether FHA loan performance data show no widespread systematic discrimination in mortgage lending due to lender prejudice. Major concerns are also raised about omitted variables and the bias this introduces, as well as the limitations of the default approach compared to loan-approval-based studies, such as that by the Boston Federal Reserve researchers. Whether or not Berkovec et al.'s study proves the absence of lender prejudice remains hotly debated.

It is now increasingly argued that both loan approval and mortgage default studies are necessary (see, for example, Tootell [chapter 4, this volume] and Van Order and Zorn 1995). Needed research in this area includes supplementing HMDA data to relate loan denials to default rates, as well as more rigorous research aimed at understanding lenders' behavior as they accept, reject, modify terms, and otherwise manage the process of minimizing risk and maximizing profit.

FINAL RESEARCH AND POLICY COMMENTS

After the Federal Reserve Board released the 1994 HMDA data, Jaret Seiberg (1995b: 1), director of regulatory affairs at the American Bankers Association, pronounced the virtual "cresting" of the lending discrimination debate. However, like the announcement of Mark Twain's death, this declaration was a bit premature. As the discussions in this volume underscore, debate and research needs continue to press the policy agenda.

The information and research experience assembled here constitute comprehensive assessment of credit discrimination as of mid-1995, as well as a useful reference in fair lending. Given the rate at which methodology and policy priorities change, this compendium may well not be the last. It is hoped that scholars will benefit from this benchmarking of the field, and that advocates and interest groups will profit from the previously unpublished descriptions of methods and strategies by fair lending enforcement groups.

A host of important social science and policy research issues have emerged as a result of, and in the wake of, the May 1993 HUD conference. How to better measure lending discrimination—in the pre- or post-application stage—remains a core concern, and is closely linked to two other questions: If discrimination exists, what is causing it? and Why is it happening? A number of elementary questions furthermore persist, including: If no differential treatment or disparate impacts are occurring, then why do the denial rates for blacks in the United States remain twice as high as for whites, from the earliest study in 1974 until the 1994 HMDA data (released in July 1995)? If study after study confirms the accuracy of the Federal Reserve Board of Boston's findings, why do bank officials continue to question the obduracy of racial differentials? And why is there so little support for replicating both this study and the Decatur Federal Savings examination, using even better data and analytical methods?

Moreover, if there is no discrimination, why have over 1,500 complaints of such discrimination been lodged, with over 600 of these cases settled in conciliation? Conversely, for the enforcement agencies, if lending discrimination is a common practice, why have there been so few cases in which HUD has found reasonable cause that discrimination has occurred? These issues are embedded in evaluation research that is needed to assess how well enforcement agencies investigate and settle allegations of lending discrimination, either as disparate-treatment or disparate-impacts charges. How effective are agencies in gathering, assessing, and prosecuting the evidence they receive to achieve voluntary compliance, consent decrees, or litigated settlements?

Reviving theories of lending disparities is an even more critically needed task today than when such theories were first espoused nearly two decades ago (Listokin and Casey 1980). Issues that warrant examination are mortgage lending practices and marketing strategies that lenders use to attract minority homebuyers and to avert discrimination in mortgage lending. Research is needed that is both institutional and historical in character, as pointed out by both Galster (chapter 27) and Ritter (chapter 15). HUD is beginning to research those practices. Although there is evidence that minority households tend to do business exclusively with the same lenders (or brokers) in their neighborhood and are reluctant to venture outside their immediate communities to seek mortgages, it is not known what approaches have been successfully tried by lenders to increase mortgage access to underserved communities. The objective is to learn more about lender strategies, including whether lenders employ minorities, train employees in cultural sensitivity issues, locate branch offices in minority and low-income neighborhoods, offer government-backed loan programs, advertise in media outlets with large minority audiences, solicit real estate agents in minority neighborhoods, and perform other functions that expand minority business.

Other unknowns include: Do different lenders use different approaches for specific minority groups, and which approaches are most productive? Which individuals file applications in response to special marketing techniques, and what are their household characteristics? What difficulties do lenders face in minority lending markets and how do lenders overcome them?

Closely connected to issues of lending practices and marketing strategies is the need to identify those stages of searching for a home and for residential mortgage assistance during which discrimination is most likely to occur. There is little systematic information on the housing and credit search process of minority and nonminority households and the extent to which fears or expectations of discrimination may alter the behavior and choices of minorities (Wienk 1992: 237). To what degree, and in what contexts, do minority housing seekers perceive conventional lenders as potentially discriminatory (Feagin and Sykes 1994)? Is there self-steering by applicants for nonracial or racial reasons to specific lenders, or discouragement at a preapplication stage of inquiry? The lack of systematic auditing or testing of mortgage lending facilities, comparable to the huge testing projects of real estate firms in the 1970s and 1980s, illustrates a crucially needed area of research, despite the obstacles to conducting an effective national audit (Turner et al. 1991). Galster (chapter 27) emphasizes this point in his concluding suggestions.

Resistance and opposition to civil rights research and enforcement is, of course, nothing new. As stated at the outset of this chapter, policymaking and social science research projects in civil rights enforcement have not progressed in a straightforward, linear fashion; periods of retrenchment and backlash are a well-noted problem. Nevertheless, the fair housing and fair lending mandates will continue, as will the need for industry, regulators, advocates, and researchers to reach consensus and proceed to conduct the research required to identify and eliminate any vestiges of racial discrimination in lending in America.

Notes

1. A number of papers and comments included in the 1993 HUD conference do not appear in this volume due to space limitations. Copies of the complete set of conference papers are available from HUD's report distribution service, HUD USER (telephone 800-245-2691).

2. In 1979, the Office of Policy Development and Research at HUD published a review of social science research in regard to housing discrimination and then listed the major research priorities. The second priority (out of a total of 18) was for research on discrimination in lending. No action was taken to address this gap at HUD until years later (Yinger, Galster, Smith, and Eggers 1980).

3. Copies of this "Default Data base" are available, at cost, from HUD USER (see telephone number in note 1). The data base currently consists of 14 data files organized

as a single SAS file. Glenn Canner and his staff at the Federal Reserve Board of Governors provided copies of their edited files for use by other analysts.

References

Applebome, Peter. 1989. "U.S. Investigates Possible Bias by Atlanta Lenders." *New York Times*, April 30: 26.

Berry Leeds and Associates, Inc. 1993. "Testing for Discrimination during the Pre-application and Post-application Phase of Mortgage Lending." Paper presented at conference on "Home Mortgage Lending and Discrimination: Research and Enforcement," sponsored by U.S. Department of Housing and Urban Development," May 18–19, Washington, D.C.

Bell, Derrick. 1992. "Racial Realism." *Connecticut Law Review* 24 (Winter): 363–79.

Black, Harold, R. Schweitzer, and L. Mandell. 1978. "Discrimination in Mortgage Lending." *American Economic Review* 68 (May): 186–91.

Boyer, Brian. 1973. *Cities Destroyed for Cash: The FHA Scandal at HUD*. Chicago: Follett.

Bradford, Calvin, and Leonard Rubinowitz. 1975. "The Urban-Suburban Investment-Disinvestment Process: Consequences for Older Neighborhoods," *The Annals of the American Academy of Political and Social Sciences*, 422: 77–86.

Bradbury, Katharine, K. Case, and C. Dunham. 1989. "Geographic Patterns of Mortgage Lending in Boston, 1982–1987." *New England Economic Review* (September/October: 3–30).

Bradley, Donald. 1979. "FHA Mortgage Foreclosures in Decatur-South DeKalb: An Analysis of the problem." Office of Program Planning and Evaluation. Atlanta: U.S. Department of Housing and Urban Development, Region IV. Photocopy.

Bratt, Rachael, and W. Dennis Keating. 1993. "Federal Housing Policy and HUD: Past Problems and Future Prospects of a Beleaguered Bureaucracy." *Urban Affairs Quarterly* 29 (September): 3–27.

Canner, Glenn. 1982. "Redlining: Research and Federal Legislative Response." Staff Study 121. Washington, D.C.: Board of Governors of the Federal Reserve System.

Canner, Glen, S. Gabriel and M. Wooley. 1991. "Race, Default, and Mortgage Lending: A Study of the FHA and Conventional Loan Markets." *Southern Economic Journal* 58 (July): 249–61.

Carlin, Barbara. 1976. "Documentation of the 1974 Master Statistical File on FHA Activity." Urban Institute Report 1104–03. Washington, D.C.: Urban Institute.

Carr, James, and Isaac Megbolugbe. 1993. "The Federal Reserve Bank of Boston Study on Mortgage Lending Revisited." *Journal of Housing Research*. 4(2): 277–313.

Caskey, John. 1994. "Bank Representation in Low-Income and Minority Urban Communities." *Urban Affairs Quarterly* 29 (June): 617–38.

Dedman, Bill. 1988. "The Color of Money: Home Mortgage Practices Discriminate against Blacks." *Atlanta Journal-Constitution*, May 1–16.

Delgado, Richard. 1992. "Derrick Bell's 'Racial Realism': A Comment on White Optimism and Black Despair." *Connecticut Law Review* 24 (Winter): 527–32.

Eagan, John, J. Carr, A. Mott, and J. Roos. 1981. "Avoiding Another Marquette Park." In *Housing and Public Policy: A Role for Mediating Structures*, edited by John Eagan, John Carr, Andrew Mott, and F. John Roos (41–74). Cambridge: Ballinger.

Feagin, Joe, and Melvin Sykes. 1994. *Living with Racism: The Black Middle-Class Experience*. Boston: Beacon.

Financial World Publications. 1989. *The Mortgage Market Statistical Annual for 1989*. Washington, D.C.: Author.

Fishbein, Allen. 1993. "'The Trail of Tears': A Chronology of Fair Lending Enforcement." In *Problems in Community Development Banking, Mortgage Lending Discrimination, Reverse Redlining, and Home Equity Lending* (570–73). Hearings before U.S. Senate Committee on Banking, Housing, and Urban Affairs. Washington, D.C.: U.S. Government Printing Office, February.

Gabriel, Stuart, and Stuart Rosenthal. 1989. "Credit Rationing, Race, and the Mortgage Market." Division of Research and Statistics. Washington DC: Board of Governors of the Federal Reserve System. (Also 1991, *Journal of Urban Economics* 29 (May): 371–79.)

Galster, George. 1991. "A Statistical Perspective on Illegal Discrimination in Lending." Washington, D.C.: American Bankers Association.

________. 1992. "The HMDA Prescription." *Partners* 2 (1): 1, 7, 9–10. Atlanta: Federal Reserve Bank of Atlanta.

________. 1993. "Use of Testers in Investigating Discrimination in Mortgage Lending and Insurance." In *Clear and Convincing Evidence: Measurement of Discrimination in America*, edited by Michael Fix and Raymond J. Struyk. Washington, D.C.: Urban Institute Press.

Greeston, Peter, C.D. MacRae, and C. Pedone. 1975. "The Effects of FHA Activity in Older, Urban, Declining Areas: A Review of Existing, Related Analyses." Urban Institute Report No. 220-1. Washington D.C.: Urban Institute.

Hacker, Andrew. 1992. *Two Nations: Black and White, Separate, Hostile, Unequal*. New York: Charles Scribner's Sons.

Hammer, Siler, George Associates. 1979. "The Role of the Real Estate Sector in Neighborhood Change." Final report prepared for Office of Policy

Development and Research. Pub. No. HUD-PDR–380. Washington, D.C.: U.S. Department of Housing and Urban Development.

Hays, R. Allen. 1985. *The Federal Government and Urban Housing*. Albany: State University of New York.

Hilzenrath, David. 1989. "Median Home Prices in D.C. Area Increase Modest 7 Percent." *Washington Post*, November 14: B8.

"Housing Discrimination: Are Minorities Treated Unfairly?" 1995. *CQ Researcher* 5 (February 24): 169–92.

ICF. 1989. "The Characteristics of HUD-Processed and Direct Endorsement Mortgages." Draft Report for Office of Policy Development and Research, U.S. Department of Housing and Urban Development. Fairfax, Va.: Author.

Isaac, William. 1995. "Epilogue." In *Fair Lending Analysis: A Compendium of Essays on the Use of Statistics*, edited by A. Yezer (167–75). Washington, D.C.: American Bankers Association.

Jaffey, Dwight. 1976. "Credit for Financing Housing Investment: Risk factors and Capital Markets." In *Housing in the Seventies Working Papers* (491–511). National Housing Policy Review. Washington D.C.: U.S. Government Printing Office.

JRB Associates 1980. "Analysis of Home Mortgage Act Disclosure Data from Three Standard Metropolitan Statistical Areas: Accuracy of Disclosure Statement Preparation." Report prepared for the Federal Home Loan Bank Board. U.S. Senate Committee on Banking, Housing, and Urban Affairs. Washington D.C.: U.S. Government Printing Office.

Karr, Albert. 1995. "Federal Drive to Curb Mortgage-Loan Bias Stirs Strong Backlash." *Wall Street Journal*, February 7: 1.

———. 1995. "Federal Study Challenges Notion of Bias Against Minorities in Mortgage Lending." *Wall Street Journal*, January 26: A16.

Kentucky Commission on Human Rights. 1989a. "Louisville Lenders Slightly Improve Poor Home Mortgage Lending Record in Black and Desegregated Neighborhoods of Jefferson County, 1987–1988." Staff Report 89–10. Louisville: Author.

———. 1989b. "Manuals for Testing for Credit Discrimination." Draft report from Center for Community Change. Louisville: Author.

Ketron, Inc. 1977. "An Examination of State Laws Prohibiting Sex and Marital Status Discrimination in Housing and Home Finance." Final report prepared for Office of Policy Development and Research. Washington, D.C.: U.S. Department of Housing and Urban Development.

Kluckman, Jerauld. 1989. "Compliance Examinations Take Hold." *Office of Thrift Supervision Journal* 19 (October): 12–15.

Kushner, James. 1992. "Federal Enforcement and Judicial Review of the Fair Housing Amendments Act of 1988." *Housing Policy Debate* 3 (2): 537–99.

Lamb, Charles, and Jim Twombley. 1995. "Decentralizing Fair Housing Enforcement during the Reagan Presidency." In *Presidential Leadership and Civil Rights Policy*, edited by James Riddlesperger and D. Jackson. Westport, Conn: Greenwood.

LaWare, John. 1993. "Statement." In *Problems in Community development Banking, Mortgage Lending Discrimination, Reverse Redlining, and Home Equity Lending*. Hearings. U.S. Senate Committee on Banking, Housing, and Urban Affairs. (February 24, 526–31). Washington, D.C.: U.S. Government Printing Office.

Leigh, Wilhelmina. 1983. "The Housing Finance System and Federal Policy: Recent Change and Options for the Future." Washington, D.C.; U.S. Congressional Budget Office.

Leven, Charles, J. Little, H. Nourse, and R. Read. 1976. *Neighborhood Change: Lessons in the Dynamics of Urban Decay*. New York: Praeger.

Lindsey, Lawrence. 1995. "Foreword." In *Fair Lending Analysis: A Compendium of Essays on the Use of Statistics*, edited by A. Yezer (IX–XIV). Washington, D.C.: American Bankers Association.

Listokin, David, and Stephen Casey. 1980. *Mortgage Lending and Race: Conceptual and Analytic Perspectives on the Urban Financing Problem*. New Brunswick: Rutgers University Press.

MacRae, Duncan, M. Turner, and A. Yezer. 1982. "Determinants of FHA Mortgage Insurance in Urban Neighborhoods." *Housing Finance Review* 1 (January): 55–71.

Massey, Douglas, and Nancy Denton. 1989. "Hypersegregation in U.S. Metropolitan Areas: Black and Hispanic Segregation along Five Dimensions." *Demography* 26 (August): 373–91.

________. 1993. *American Apartheid*. Cambridge, Mass.: Harvard University.

McCall, Nathan. 1994. *Makes Me Wanna Holler: A Young Black Man in America*. New York: Vintage.

McKay, David. 1977. *Housing and Race in Industrial Society*. London: Croom Helm.

Miller, Ted. 1987. "Where the Money Flows: A Review of a Report by the Woodstock Institute." Washington, D.C.: Urban Institute. Photocopy.

Morrow-Jones, Hazel. 1986. "Neighborhood Change and the Federal Housing Administration: Some Theoretical and Empirical Issues." *Urban Studies* 23 (October): 419–28.

Munnell, Alicia H., Lynn E. Browne, James McEneaney, and Geoffrey M. B. Tootell. 1992. "Mortgage Lending in Boston: Interpreting HMDA Data." Federal Reserve Bank of Boston Working Paper 92-07. Boston: Federal Reserve Bank of Boston, October.

Munnell, Alicia H., Geoffrey M. B. Tootell, Lynn E. Browne, and James McEneaney. 1996. "Is Discrimination Racial or Geographic?" Photocopy. Federal Reserve Bank of Boston.

National Training and Information Center (NTIC). 1979. "A Guidebook: Home Mortgage Disclosure Act and Reinvestment Strategies." Office of Policy Development and Research. Pub. No. HUD-PDR-452. Washington, D.C.: U.S. Department of Housing and Urban Development, July.

Powers, William. 1993. "The Story of a Dream Denied: Discrimination Is Theme as Banking Panel Visits Pr. George's." *Washington Post*, September 25: C1.

Quercia, Roberto G., and Michael A. Stegman. 1992. "Residential Mortgage Default: A Review of the Literature." *Journal of Housing Research* 3(2): 341–79.

Ryker Randy, L. Pol, and R. Guy. 1984. "Racial Discrimination as a Determinant of Home Improvement Loans." *Urban Studies* 21 (May): 177–82.

Schafer, Robert, and Helen Ladd. 1980. "Equal Credit Opportunity Accessibility to Mortgage Funds by Women and Minorities." Final report prepared for Office of Policy Development and Research. Pub. No. HUD-PDR-551-1. Washington, D.C.: U.S. Department of Housing and Urban Development, May.

Schill, Michael, and Susan Wachter. 1993. "A Tale of Two Cities: Racial and Ethnic Geographic Disparities in Home Mortgage Lending in Boston and Philadelphia. *Journal of Housing Research* 4 (2): 245–75.

Schlay, Ann. 1985. "Where the Money Flows: Lending Patterns in the Washington, D.C.–Maryland–Virginia MSA." Chicago: Woodstock Institute.

________. 1988. "Not in That Neighborhood: The Effects of Population and Housing on the Distribution of the Mortgage Finance within the Chicago SMSA." *Social Science Research* 17: 137–63.

________. 1989. "Financing Community: Methods for Assessing Residential Credit Disparities, Market Barriers, and Institutional Reinvestment Performance in the Metropolis." *Journal of Urban Affairs* 11 (3): 201–23.

Seiberg, Jaret. 1995a. "Fed Study Challenges Claims of Loan Bias." *American Banker* (January 25): 1, 3.

________. 1995b. "Greenspan Says Banks Reaching Out to Minorities." *American Banker* (July 20): 1.

Shear, William, and Anthony Yezer. 1985. "Discrimination in Urban Housing Finance: An Empirical Study across Cities." *Land Economics* 61 (August): 292–302.

Squires, Gregory, and William Velez. 1987. "Neighborhood Racial Composition and Mortgage Lending: City and Suburban Differences." *Journal of Urban Affairs* 9 (3): 217–32.

Steele, Shelby. 1990. *The Content of Our Character: A New Vision of Race in America*. New York: St. Martin's Press.

Stegman, Michael. 1972. *Housing Investment in the Inner City*. Cambridge, Mass.: MIT Press.

Turner, Margery. 1992. "Discrimination in Urban Housing Markets: Lessons from Fair Housing Audits." *Housing Policy Debate* 3 (2): 185–215.

Turner, Margery, R. Struyk, and J. Yinger. 1991. *Housing Discrimination Study: Synthesis*. Pub. No. HUD-1318-PDR. Washington, D.C.: U.S. Department of Housing and Urban Development, October.

U.S. Congress Senate. 1990. "Discrimination in Home Mortgage Lending." Hearing before Subcommittee on Consumer and Regulatory Affairs, Committee on Banking, Housing, and Urban Affairs, October 24. Washington, D.C.: U.S. Government Printing Office.

U.S. Department of Housing and Urban Development. 1995. *Empowerment: A New Covenant with America's Communities: President Clinton's National Urban Policy Report*. Washington, DC.: U.S. Department of Housing and Urban Development, July.

U.S. Department of Housing and Urban Development, Office of Financial Management. 1989. "Survey of Mortgage Lending Activity: Annual Tables for 1989." Washington, D.C.: Author, March 31.

U.S. Department of Housing and Urban Development, Office of Policy Development and Research. 1983. "Report to Congress on Housing Counseling." Pub. No. HUD-PDR-736. Washington, D.C.: Author, June.

Van Order, Robert, and Peter Zorn. 1995. "Testing for Discrimination Combining Default and Rejection Data." In *Fair Lending Analysis: A Compendium of Essays on the Use of Statistics*, edited by A. Yezer (104–112). Washington, D.C.: American Bankers Association.

Van Order, Ann-Margaret Westin, and Peter Zorn. 1993. "Effects of the Racial Composition of Neighborhoods on Default, and Implications for Racial Discrimination in Mortgage Markets." Paper presented at meetings of American Economics Association, Jan. 8, Anaheim, Calif.

Wachter, Susan. 1980. "The 1968 Congressional Amendments to the National Housing Act: Their Impact on Urban Areas." In *The Urban Impacts of Federal Policies*, edited by Norman Glickman (462–48). Baltimore: Johns Hopkins University Press.

Walton, Hanes. 1988. *When the Marching Stopped: The Politics of Civil Rights Regulatory Agencies*. New York: State University of New York.

Weicher, John. 1979. "Government Urban Policy and the Lender." Urban Institute Report 252-0000-1-7. Washington, D.C.: Urban Institute.

Wienk, Ron. 1992. "Discrimination in Urban Credit Markets: What We Don't Know and Why We Don't Know It." *Housing Policy Debate* 3 (2): 217–40.

Yezer, Anthony, ed. 1995. *Fair Lending Analysis: A Compendium of Essays on the Use of Statistics*. Washington, D.C.: American Bankers Association.

Yinger, John, G. Galster, Barton Smith, and F. Eggers. 1980. "The Status of Research into Racial Discrimination and Segregation in American Housing Markets." *Occasional Papers in Housing and Community Affairs* 6 (July). Pub. No. HUD-497-6-PDR. Washington, D.C.: U.S. Department of Housing and Urban Development.

Chapter Two

DISCRIMINATION IN MORTGAGE LENDING: A LITERATURE REVIEW

John Yinger

Release of the 1990 Home Mortgage Disclosure Act (HMDA) data initiated a dramatic surge of interest in the behavior of mortgage lenders, especially regarding the possibility that lenders discriminate against African American, Hispanic, and other minority applicants.[1] This chapter explores the recent literature on mortgage discrimination and offers recommendations for future research. Rather than attempting an exhaustive literature review, I develop a conceptual framework for the topic, highlight some key studies, and raise several important issues that the literature has not yet resolved.

By way of preview, the existing literature reveals that lender behavior has many facets and that it occurs in a complex market setting. Although several excellent studies address some aspects of lender discrimination, the complexity of the problem leads to a number of methodological obstacles. Because mortgages are so important for minority access to housing, much more research on these issues is needed.

This chapter is organized into five major sections plus a conclusion. The first section presents a framework for analyzing a lender's approval or rejection of a loan application. This framework leads to precise definitions of discrimination and redlining. The second section reviews the literature on loan approval and on defaults, with a focus on the recent study by Munnell and colleagues (1992, 1996). The third section proposes directions for future research on discrimination in loan approval and, in particular, examines neglected aspects of lender behavior that need to be considered before we can accurately estimate the extent of discrimination. The fourth section turns to discrimination in other types of lender behavior, such as outreach, application processing, and mortgage terms. The final substantive section briefly explores discrimination by other actors in the mortgage market, including real estate brokers and insurers. Finally, section six reviews my main conclusions.

FRAMEWORK FOR CONCEPTUALIZING DISCRIMINATION IN LOAN APPROVAL

Discrimination in the approval of mortgage loan applications is the most dramatic type of lender discrimination, with the most obvious consequences for minority access to housing. It is also the behavior that has received the most study and is highlighted by the HMDA data. This section presents a conceptual framework for the decision to lend, as a basis for defining discrimination and redlining in mortgage lending. This framework, which is similar to the approach of many existing studies, proves valuable in later sections of the chapter that discuss existing research and future research needs.

Decision to Lend

A mortgage is an investment by a lender, who makes profits by selecting investments with a high rate of return. The decision to make a loan, like many other discrete economic decisions, is appropriately modeled by focusing on the probability that a particular choice is made. In this case, the probability that a loan application will be rejected increases as the expected rate of return on that loan falls.[2]

An idealized model of lender behavior therefore focuses on the relationship between the probability that a loan is rejected, R, and the expected rate of return, r. In symbols,

$$R = f^{I}(\mathrm{r}), \tag{2.1}$$

where f^{I} is a function describing this idealized relationship.

Discrimination exists whenever loan applications from a minority group are more likely to be rejected than applications from whites, controlling for the expected return.[3] Similarly, redlining exists, in an analytical sense, whenever loan applications for houses in certain types of neighborhoods, such as largely black neighborhoods, are more likely to be rejected than applications from other neighborhoods, controlling for expected return. Bringing these possibilities into a model of lender behavior leads to

$$R = f(\mathrm{r}, M, N), \tag{2.2}$$

where M indicates that the applicant belongs to a minority group, N indicates that the house in question is located in a certain type of neighborhood, and f is another function. Precise definitions of discrimination and redlining follow directly; analytical discrimination (redlining) exists when the impact of M (N) on R is positive.

The problem for empirical research on this topic is that r is difficult to observe. However, many researchers have recognized that the expected return on a loan depends on the terms of the loan, such as the interest rate and the loan-to-value ratio; the probability that the loan will go into default; and the impact of default on the return. In more formal terms, the expected return is the probability that the loan will not go into default multiplied by the expected return without default plus the probability that the loan will go into default multiplied by the expected return with default.[4] In general, therefore, one can write:

$$r = g(D, C, T), \tag{2.3}$$

where D is the probability of default; C is the cost of default, which can be positive or negative; T stands for the loan terms; and g is another function.

Equation (2.3) is not the end of the story, however, because both the probability and the cost of default are themselves difficult to observe. Thus, another stage is required. The probability of default depends on the characteristics of the applicant, A, the characteristics of the property and its neighborhood, P, and the terms of the loan, T.[5] For example, an applicant with a good credit history is less likely to default, and either rapid expected housing appreciation or a low loan-to-value ratio strengthens a borrower's incentive not to default by raising the equity in the house. With h defined as another function, the probability of default can be written as:

$$D = h(A, P, T). \tag{2.4}$$

Finally, the expected cost of default depends on the difference between the expected value of the property and the amount of the loan. Lenders are more likely to lose money if a house's value is expected to decline and the loan-to-value ratio is high. This relationship can be written as follows:

$$C = k(P, T), \tag{2.5}$$

where k is yet another function.

The equations for the probability and cost of default, (2.4) and (2.5), can be substituted into the equation for the expected return, (2.3), to obtain an expression for r as a function of A, P, and T. To be specific,

$$r = g[h(A, P, T), k(P, T), T] \tag{2.6}$$

or

$$r = \tilde{g}(A, P, T). \tag{2.7}$$

Finally, substituting equation (2.6) or (2.7) into equation (2.2), one finds that the probability of rejection depends on applicant, property, and loan characteristics and, if there is discrimination or redlining, on the minority status of the applicant or on neighborhood characteristics not associated with the rate of return. In symbols,

$$R = f[\tilde{g}(A, P, T), M, N], \tag{2.8}$$

which can be simplified to

$$R = \tilde{f}(A, P, T, M, N). \tag{2.9}$$

Equation (2.9) gives the form used by several studies, which are reviewed below, to estimate discrimination in mortgage lending.

Analytical and Legal Definitions of Discrimination

Using the logic of equation (2.9), the basic analytical or economic definition of discrimination, which was given earlier, can be restated by saying that discrimination exists if minority applicants are more likely to be rejected for a loan than are white applicants, controlling for the applicant, property, and loan characteristics that influence the loan's return. Similarly, this equation indicates that, by the analytical definition, redlining exists whenever a loan is more likely to be turned down in a minority than in a majority neighborhood, controlling for the applicant, property, and loan characteristics that influence its return.

These definitions refer to applicant and property characteristics than can be *observed* by a lender (or to returns expected on the basis of observed characteristics). In fact, lenders may not be able to observe some characteristics that influence the return on a loan (or the probability or cost of default). Lenders are unlikely to know, for example, whether an applicant has friends or family who will lend him money if he runs into financial trouble. Lenders may believe, based on past experience, that minority applicants have poorer unobserved qualifications than others on average, but using this belief to deny a loan to a minority applicant is a form of discrimination, called statistical discrimination.[6] In other words, it is discrimination to turn down a loan to a minority applicant on the basis of information that is valid for minorities on average, but which may not be valid for that individual. This type of behavior may be economically rational, but it still is discrimination.[7]

In formal terms, the minority status variable, M, may influence the dependent variable in equations (2.4) and (2.5) even when all observable applicant and property characteristics have been included.[8] For example, equation (2.4) can be rewritten as

$$D = \hat{h}(A, P, T, M). \tag{2.10}$$

The coefficient of the minority status variable measures the impact on default of the average minority disadvantage in unobserved qualifications. When this equation and the analogous one for the costs of default are substituted into equation (2.3), which then goes into equation (2.2), the new minority status terms are subsumed into the minority status term in equation (2.9). In other words, adding M to equations (2.4) and (2.5) does not change the interpretation of the coefficient of M in equation (3.9); this coefficient still is a measure of discrimination.

As expressed in existing laws against discrimination in mortgage lending, namely the Fair Housing Act of 1968, the Equal Credit Opportunity Act (ECOA) of 1974, and the Civil Rights Act of 1866, the legal definition of discrimination is the same as the analytical one, at least in spirit. The principal law against this type of discrimination, the ECOA, reads in part: "It shall be unlawful for any creditor to discriminate against any applicant, with respect to any aspect of a credit transaction: 1. on the basis of race, color, religion, national origin, sex or marital status, or age (provided the applicant has the capacity to contract)" (quoted in Schafer and Ladd 1981:1). This language contains all the elements of the analytical definition. In particular, the phrase "provided the applicant has capacity to contract" corresponds to the notion of loan return based on an applicant's observable characteristics. Because few cases have been brought to court on the basis of these laws, however, it is difficult to know exactly what type of evidence courts would require to prove that discrimination exists.[9]

As several authors have pointed out, the equivalence of analytical and legal definitions does not hold in the case of redlining. Although evidence to support the analytical definition might help to establish that redlining exists from a legal point of view, the 1977 Community Reinvestment Act defines redlining in terms of the flow of funds to different types of neighborhoods, as well as in terms of decisions on individual loans. Thus, lenders who are not practicing redlining by the analytical definition given here may still be practicing redlining as defined by the law. For a thorough discussion of this topic, see

Barth, Cordes, and Yezer (1979) or Bradbury, Case, and Dunham (1989).

This chapter presents some results concerning redlining by the analytical definition, but does not review studies, such as Bradbury et al. (1989), that examine the flow of funds. For a comprehensive review of the redlining literature, see Schill and Wachter (1993). In focusing on the behavior of individual lenders and on the analytical definitions of discrimination and redlining, this chapter also does not consider how lending practices affect neighborhoods.

EVIDENCE ON DISCRIMINATION IN LOAN APPROVAL

This section reviews several recent studies of discrimination in mortgage loan acceptance. These studies all estimate a version of equation (2.9) using a sample of loan applications. I first discuss the key methodological problem that any study of loan acceptance confronts, namely that of adequate controls. This section also addresses an alternative approach to measuring mortgage discrimination, namely focusing on differences in the probability of default between minority and white loan recipients.

The Key Issue: Adequate Controls

A key methodological problem in estimating equation (2.9) arises because many elements of *A* and *P* are negatively correlated with *M* and *N*, at least for most minority groups and neighborhood definitions of concern. In other words, minority applicants (and applicants in minority neighborhoods) tend to have poorer credit qualifications. This correlation is a problem because it implies that incomplete data for *A* and *P* can result in serious omitted-variable bias in the coefficients of *M* and *N*. This omitted-variable bias is widely recognized in the literature (see, for example, the discussion in Galster 1992).

To be more specific, if an omitted variable, say an applicant's wealth, has a negative impact on the dependent variable (the probability of loan denial) and a negative correlation with minority status, then the coefficient of minority status will reflect some of the impact of minority's relatively low wealth on loan denial. It follows that if key elements of *A* and *P* are omitted, the coefficients of *M* and *N* are likely to be biased upward. Because these coefficients are the estimates of discrimination and redlining, respectively, researchers with inadequate controls may conclude that there is discrimination or redlining when in fact there is none or may overstate the magnitude of this discrimination.

This methodological problem is, of course, the major reason why the HMDA data cannot be used to obtain estimates of discrimination in mortgage lending. Although these data do contain several of the variables in *A* and *P*, such as income and urban area, they do not include several other variables, such as wealth or credit history, that are likely to affect loan returns and to be correlated with minority status. Moreover, for mortgages in the secondary market, one-third do not indicate the race of the applicant and almost half do not indicate applicant income or urban area.[10]

This is not to say that the HMDA data are useless. As several studies, including Canner and Gabriel (1992) and Avery, Beeson, and Sniderman (chapter 3, this volume), have shown, careful examination of these data provide a variety of insights into lender behavior and a few intriguing hints about possible discrimination.[11] Avery et al., for example, show that, controlling for the neighborhood, the lender, and available economic characteristics of the applicant, blacks are far more likely than whites to be denied home purchase, refinancing, and home improvement loans. They point out that the black-white differentials for the latter two types of loans are unlikely to be due to omitted credit variables, because all applicants for such loans already received a home purchase loan, thereby demonstrating their creditworthiness, and obviously have not yet defaulted. Nevertheless, the possibility of omitted variables cannot be ruled out and, without supplementation, these data cannot be used to obtain formal estimates of discrimination or to test hypotheses about it.

Recent Studies

Studies that have estimated discrimination in mortgage lending using a form of equation (2.9) include Black, Schweitzer, and Mandell (1978), King (1980), Schafer and Ladd (1981), Maddala and Trost (1982), and Munnell et al. (1992; 1996).[12] This chapter's review focuses on the two studies with the best data, those of Schafer and Ladd, and Munnell et al.[13]

Schafer and Ladd (1981) took advantage of the fact that California and New York require state-regulated lenders to keep records on mortgage applications. They obtained detailed data on loan applications for state-regulated S&Ls in California in 1977–78 and for commercial banks, mutual savings banks, and S&Ls in New York in 1976–78. Their data set covered 32 metropolitan areas in California and 10 in New York. The control variables in California included applicant income, income relative to requested loan, the LTV ratio, income of secondary earners, age of applicant, age of property, and several neighborhood (census tract or zip code) characteristics, such as income, population change, average sales price, and vacancy rate. The control variables in New York included "income, net wealth, years at present occupation, requested loan amount in relation to current income, and the ratio of the requested loan amount to the appraised value of the property" (p. 187), as well as applicant age and several neighborhood variables such as "income of residents, changes in income and population, and mortgage foreclosure and delinquency rates" (p. 188). Schafer and Ladd were unable to obtain data on applicant credit history in either state.

One unique feature of Schafer and Ladd's (1981) study is that the authors used multinomial logit analysis to treat the loan decision as a four-way choice. In California, the four choices were: "approved as applied for, approved after increasing the requested loan amount, approved after decreasing the requested loan amount, and denied" (p. 132). A somewhat different set was used in New York: "approved as applied for, approved with modifications, denied, and withdrawn" (p. 187).

Schafer and Ladd (1981) found considerable evidence of discrimination against blacks in the loan denial decision.[14] They wrote:

> Black applicants have significantly higher chances of denial than whites in similar circumstances in eighteen of the thirty-two California study areas and six of the ten New York study areas. Moreover, the differences are large; black applicants are 1.58 to 7.82 times as likely to be denied as are similar white applicants. (Pp. 287–89).

Although this study was carefully conducted, the lack of any information on credit history suggests that the results may be affected to some degree by omitted-variable bias.

The most recent study of loan denial is that of Munnell et al. (1996), which originally appeared in 1992. This study estimated versions of equation (2.9) using a sample of over 3,000 loan applications for conventional mortgages in the Boston area in 1990. The sample includes all applications (about 1,200) by blacks and Hispanics in that year and a random sample of white applications. As Munnell et al. pointed out, this study improved on earlier ones by including a more comprehensive list of applicant and property characteristics and by covering all types of lenders, instead of a restricted set.

To minimize the probability of omitted-variable bias, Munnell et al. (1996) supplemented the HMDA data with 38 additional variables. "These variables were selected based both on expectations of what should be important and on numerous conversations with lenders, underwriters, and others familiar with the lending process about what they believe is important" (p. 8). In the end, the authors collected "every variable mentioned as important" in these conversations (p. 23). The final data set includes variables in four categories: probability of default, costs of default, loan characteristics, and personal characteristics. (Although this is a different organizing scheme than the one presented in the preceding section of this chapter, it is entirely consistent with the framework that leads to equation [2.9].) Because the credibility of a study depends on the quality of its controls, the list of key control variables from this study is reproduced in table 2.1.

The list of controls in table 2.1 is more extensive than that in any previous study. Some of these variables are standard for a study of this kind, whereas others are innovative. For example, Munnell et al.'s (1996) consumer and mortgage credit variables measure the seriousness of previous credit problems, ranging from no "slow pay" accounts or late payments to serious delinquencies or extensive late payments. The "public record" variable indicates any record of past credit problems, and the "probability of unemployment" variable is the previous year's unemployment rate in the applicant's industry. Future research may reveal that some factors that lenders consider and that are correlated with minority status have been left off this

Table 2.1 CONTROL VARIABLES USED BY MUNNELL ET AL. (1996)

Probability of Default	*Loan Characteristics*
Housing expense/income	Two- to four-family house
Total debt payments/income	Lender ID
Net wealth	
Consumer credit history	
Mortgage credit history	
Public record history	
Probability of unemployment	
Self-employed	
Loan/appraised value—low	
Loan/appraised value—medium	
Loan/appraised value—high	
Costs of Default	*Personal Characteristics*
Denied private mortgage insurance	Race
Census tract dummies	

Source: Munnell et al. (1996: table 2)

list, but the list is comprehensive enough, and the results for the control variables plausible enough, to give me confidence that Munnell et al. have virtually complete controls for *A*, *P*, and *T*, or in their terms, for the probabilty and costs of default and for loan and personal characteristics.

Munnell et al. (1996) estimated equation (2.9) using logit analysis, which is appropriate for analyzing discrete choices such as the decision to deny a mortgage application. In their preferred specification, Munnell et al. found that the probability of loan denial is 8.2 percentage points higher for blacks and Hispanics than for whites, controlling for the probability and costs of default and for loan and personal characteristics. Since the rejection rate for white applicants is 10 percent, this result, which is highly significant statistically, implies that the rejection rate for minorities is 82 percent higher for minorities than for whites with comparable property and personal characteristics. In my judgment, this result provides strong evidence that lenders discriminate against blacks and Hispanics.

Incidentally, Munnell et al. (1993) tested for redlining by including the racial composition of a census tract in a logit regression with controls similar to those in table 2.1. This variable was not statistically significant.

Munnell et al. (1996) also estimated a variety of different specifications to determine the robustness of their result. They added measures of census tract characteristics, such as the rate of housing appreciation; they added additional loan characteristics, such as whether a grant contributed to the down payment; they added age, gender, and family status of the applicant; they developed a more elaborate method for predicting the probability of unemployment;[15] they dropped the private mortgage insurance variable and excluded cases in which this insurance was denied; they treated application withdrawals as a third discrete outcome; they ran separate regressions for single-family houses, condominiums, and multi-family units; they examined various interaction terms; they ran separate regressions for lenders that specialize in loans to minorities; and they ran separate regressions for minority and white applicants. These alternative specifications have remarkably little impact on their estimate of discrimination, and none of them weakens the conclusion that discrimination exists.

The Munnell et al. (1996) study has received much scrutiny from scholars and commentators. Liebowitz (1993) and Horne (1994) have claimed that the data used for the study are full of errors and contend, or at least imply, that the results should not be taken seriously. However, Munnell et al. used great care in assembling the data set and no one has provided credible evidence that the results of the study are influenced by data errors.[16] Moreover, Carr and Megbolugbe (1993) and Glennon and Stengel (1994) provided independent examinations of the Munnell et al. data that include detailed error-checking procedures and extensive exploration of alternative specifications. Both of these studies support the principal conclusions of the Munnell et al. study.[17]

Overall, Munnell et al. (1996) have advanced the state of the art considerably. Their study is not the last word on this topic, but it is an excellent study in which the authors have made extensive reasonable efforts to show that their principal finding is not based on the specific set of variables they include or on the specific form of their equation. As discussed in the upcoming section on "Directions for Future Research," I believe that several important methodological issues have not been addressed by this or any other research on mortgage discrimination, but I also believe that the Munnell et al. study establishes a strong presumption that lenders discriminate against blacks and Hispanics in providing mortgage loans.

Default Rates as Indicator of Discrimination

Several scholars and commentators have proposed an alternative way to test for discrimination in mortgage markets by examining a key loan outcome, namely default[18] (see columns by Becker 1993, Brimelow 1993, Brimelow and Spencer 1993, and Roberts 1993, as well as more scholarly presentations of this approach by Peterson 1981, Van Order, Westin, and Zorn 1993, and Berkovec et al. 1994).

The so-called default approach seems plausible. Assuming that lenders rank applicants by their creditworthiness, discrimination in loan acceptance against minorities implies that the last white applicants whose loans are approved are less qualified than the last minority applicants whose loans are approved. As a result, the argument goes, the probability of default should be higher for the least-qualified whites than for the least-qualified minorities.

As it turns out, on average, black loan recipients have higher default rates than white applicants (see Quercia and Stegman, 1992, or Berkovec et al., 1994). By combining this fact with the previous argument, Becker (1993), Brimelow (1993), Brimelow and Spencer (1993) and Roberts (1993) concluded that there cannot be any discrimination against blacks.[19] Some observers also have interpreted scholarly work on defaults, such as that by Berkovec et al. (1994), as proof that discrimination no longer exists.[20] For three reasons, this conclusion simply does not follow.[21] The first two reasons are discussed here; the third, discriminatory foreclosure practices, is presented in the upcoming subsection titled "Lender Influence on Default." These three reasons are all mentioned in Berkovec et al. (1994), but have been ignored in popular interpretations of the study's results.[22]

First, and most important, if the average Anglo applicant is a very low credit risk and the average minority applicant is a moderate credit risk, then the *average* creditworthiness of minority loan recipients could be below that of whites even if minorities must meet a higher hurdle to get a loan. The leap to average default rates makes sense only if majority and white loan applicants have similar distributions of creditworthiness, which is clearly not the case (see Peterson [1981] for a careful discussion of this issue).

Some scholars, including Berkovec et al. (1994), have argued that this problem can be solved by controlling for credit characteristics. They recognize that differences in minority and white average default rates cannot be an indication of discrimination, but they claim that discrimination will lead to lower default rates for minority than for white borrowers at any given level of creditworthiness. Berkovec et al. argued, on a formal level, that discrimination should lead to a negative coefficient on the minority status variable in a logistic version of the loan default equation (2.10). Because Berkovec et al. found higher default rates for minorities than for whites, controlling for credit characteristics, they hinted, but never actually stated that discrimination does not exist.[23]

This approach, like an examination of loan denial, is subject to omitted-variable bias, but now the bias works in the opposite direction. As explained earlier, leaving key credit characteristics out of a loan denial regression biases upward the coefficient of the minority status variable and therefore leads to an overstatement of discrimination. Leaving these same variables out of a default regression also leads to an upward bias in the coefficient of the minority status variable, but now a larger coefficient, that is, a higher default rate for minorities, is associated with less discrimination.[24] Because all existing default studies omit key credit variables, such as the applicant's credit history, it seems likely that they all systematically understate discrimination.[25] Berkovec et al. (1994) recognized this possibility when they stated: "to the extent that they [determinants of default that are not accounted for] are correlated with race or ethnicity, biased estimates will result" (p. 287).

Formal models of default include a random error term and therefore recognize that lenders may not be able to observe all of an applicant's credit characteristics. As noted earlier, a lender may not be able to observe, for example, whether an applicant has relatives who will bail him out if he has trouble meeting his mortgage payments. However, these unobserved characteristics undermine this approach if, as seems likely, they are correlated with minority status. In particular, minority borrowers probably have less favorable *unobserved* credit characteristics, on average, than do white borrowers. It follows that they also may have higher default rates even when discrimination exists and one has controlled for all *observed* credit characteristics. To repeat the point made earlier [with appropriate additions], "if [at a given level of observable characteristics] the average white applicant is a very low credit risk and the average minority applicant is a moderate credit risk, then the *average* creditworthiness of minority loan recipients [at that level of observable characteristics] could be below that of whites even if minorities must meet a higher hurdle to get a loan." Thus, a failure to find lower default rates for minority than for white borrowers may be an indication of minorities' relatively poor unobserved credit characteristics instead of evidence that discrimination does not exist. Although the earlier-cited caveat by Berkovec et al. (1994) covers this possibility, their formal model assumes away this possibility. Specifically, it assumes that the error term is not correlated with the borrower's race. However, this assumption simply hides the problem. By definition, one cannot determine whether unobserved characteristics are correlated with race, so the default approach is inherently incapable of separating the impact on default of discrimination from that of credit factors that cannot be observed. This problem does not arise in a study of loan approval.

Moreover, a minority-white disparity in unobserved credit characteristics could itself be a cause of lender discrimination. Lenders cannot observe all credit characteristics for each applicant, but they can observe whether some classes of borrower have higher default rates. If they observe higher default rates for minorities, they can lower their risk by using minority status as a signal for poor unobserved credit characteristics. The result will be a higher rejection rate for minority applicants than for white applicants with identical creditworthiness based on factors the lender can observe, which is statistical discrimination, as defined earlier. In short, a minority-white disparity in unobserved credit characteristics not only undermines the logic of the default approach, but it also gives lenders an incentive to practice statistical discrimination.

Berkovec et al. (1994) dealt with this issue by distinguishing between discrimination based on lender prejudice, which they call uneconomic discrimination and which is the basis for their model, and statistical discrimination. As they put it (p. 288), their results "relate only to what has been called uneconomic discrimination. Estimation findings are not inconsistent with what has been called statistical or economic discrimination, even if the assumptions underlying the basic prediction hold" (p. 288). In my judgment, however, this is only half the story. With minority-white disparities in unobserved characteristics, the default approach needs statistical discrimination to eliminate the impact of these characteristics on default, on average, before it can isolate the impact of uneconomic discrimination.[26] Consider the irony here: *One must assume that statistical discrimination exists before one can obtain evidence about the existence of discrimination based on prejudice.* This point has been lost in popular interpretations of default studies.

The second flaw in the default approach is that, as the conceptual framework in the first main section of this chapter makes clear, the risk of default is not the same thing as the expected loss on a mortgage. Lenders care about losses, not defaults as such, and the expected loss on a mortgage equals the probability of default multiplied by the loss when default occurs. Thus, the expected return on loans to blacks could be higher than the expected return for whites, even if the probability of default for blacks is higher. Moreover, lower costs associated with default for minorities might not just be a coincidence. Anecdotal evidence presented in the upcoming subsection on "Lender Influence on Default" indicates that some lenders are more likely to foreclose on black than white borrowers who are equally behind in their payments. In this case, foreclosure on whites will occur only in the worst cases, that is, only when the losses are high.

Berkovec et al. (1995) acknowledge this problem and conduct an analysis of losses upon default. This analysis is summarized in chapter 7 of this volume. They find that losses are higher for black than for white borrowers, controlling for credit characteristics at the time the loan was made and conclude that "these findings do not indicate that the higher likelihoods of default for black borrowers in the default risk analysis are offset by lower losses in the event of default" (1995). This conclusion is highly misleading. First, their study investigates FHA loans, so the losses are borne by the government, not by lenders, and have no clear connection to lenders' returns—or to their incentives to discriminate.[27] Second, their analysis of loan losses suffers from most of the same problems as an analysis of defaults.[28] Higher loss rates for minorities might reflect credit characteristics that could not be observed at the time the loan was granted, instead of discrimination, and loss rates might be lower for minorities once this disparity in unobserved credit characteristics were taken into account. Moreover, biased foreclosure policies by lenders could lead to selection bias in an analysis of loan losses.

In short, studies of loan defaults cannot provide credible evidence about discrimination in loan approval. The impact of discrimination on defaults cannot be isolated from the impact of unobservable credit characteristics, and minority-white disparities in defaults may be offset by lower loan losses associated with default for minorities than for whites. It is incorrect to argue that discrimination inevitably must lead to lower observed default rates for minorities than for comparable whites, and it is irresponsible to claim that default evidence proves that mortgage discrimination does not exist.

DIRECTIONS FOR FUTURE RESEARCH

Although several high-quality studies of discrimination in mortgage lending have been conducted, understanding of this behavior is still limited. Given the clear policy significance of lending discrimination and the high level of interest in it since the release of the 1990 HMDA data, there is a great need for more research on the topic. This section reviews the key questions that future research needs to address.

Replication

To my knowledge, the only recent study of discrimination in mortgage lending with adequate control variables is Munnell et al. (1996). As I said earlier, this is an excellent study, but one study in one location cannot resolve all the questions researchers and policy makers have on this topic.

First, it would be valuable to know whether results that hold in Boston also hold in other metropolitan areas or nationwide. Although the difference between minority and white default rates—controlling for all the variables in the HMDA data—is similar throughout the country (see Avery et al., chapter 3, this volume), it is still uncertain whether credit variables not found in the HMDA data have a different effect in different regions.

Second, even though the set of control variables used by Munnell et al. (1996), which includes every factor that lenders mentioned to them, appears to be complete, perhaps some variables that influence the return on a mortgage and that are correlated with minority status have been left out.[29] Additional studies with additional control variables would strengthen our confidence that the Munnell et al. results are not influenced by omitted-variable bias.

Third, despite the thoroughness with which Munnell et al. (1996) investigated alternative specifications, none of which altered the conclusion that discrimination exists, alternative specifications might still prove useful. A step in this direction has been taken by Carr and Megbolugbe (1993) and Glennon and Stengel (1994), who investigated a variety of alternative specifications using the Munnell et al. data. None of these alternative specifications alters the conclusion that minority applicants face discrimination.

Endogeneity of Loan-to-Value Ratios

All of the studies discussed in the previous section on "Evidence of Discrimination in Loan Approval" assume that mortgage terms, including LTV ratios, are exogenous. Several scholars, including Maddala and Trost (1982) and Yezer, Phillips, and Trost (1994), have argued that this important assumption needs to be tested.[30] If the assumption does not hold, the estimated coefficients from equation (2.9), including the coefficient of the minority status variable, may be biased.[31]

The available evidence casts doubt on the assumption. Schafer and Ladd (1981) expressed the actual LTV ratio as a function of the interest rate; the loan maturity; the requested LTV ratio; financial characteristics of the borrower and the property; neighborhood characteristics, including racial composition; and minority status variables. In estimating this equation, they treated the interest rate and the loan maturity as endogenous.[32] They found that minority borrowers tended to receive loans with higher loan-to-value ratios than comparable Anglos. Black and Schweitzer (1985) obtained the same result for a different data set using canonical correlation analysis.[33]

Because of this evidence, the endogeneity of loan terms needs to be further explored. A key issue is that the direction of the bias in the coefficient of M in equation (2.9), which is the measure of discrimination in loan approval, cannot be determined a priori. Yezer et al. (1994) argued that loan terms are selected by the applicant, and that a higher LTV ratio for minorities reflects unobserved variables in a loan-term's equation that are correlated with minority status. In this case, they showed that the coefficient of M in equation (2.9) is biased upward; that is, it overstates discrimination in loan approval.

It also is possible, however, that loan terms are determined by the lender and in particular that lenders assign higher LTV ratios to minorities than to equally qualified whites.[34] In this case, some portion of lender discrimination is buried in the coefficient of the LTV ratio in (2.9) and the coefficient of *M* is biased downward.[35] In other words, with LTV ratios assigned on a nondiscriminatory basis, the LTV ratios for minorities would decline, the expected return on mortgages they receive would increase, and the share of loan denials left over for the minority status variable to explain would rise.

No currently available evidence reveals which of these possibilities is more likely. Thus, we know that estimates of discrimination in loan approval might be subject to bias when loan terms, particularly the LTV ratio, are treated as exogenous, but we do not know the magnitude or even the direction of this bias.[36] Research that simultaneously estimates the determinants of the loan amount and loan approval clearly is needed.

Are Control Variables Related to Loan Returns?

A third important issue for future research to consider is whether the control variables used to estimate equation (2.9) are in fact related to loan returns. As discussed earlier, discrimination exists if minority applicants are more likely to be denied a loan, controlling for the expected rate of return on the mortgage. Because the expected rate of return cannot be observed, existing studies use the indirect approach of controlling for applicant, property, and loan characteristics. This approach assumes that the estimated impacts of applicant, property, and loan characteristics on loan denial can be interpreted as the impact of the expected rate of return on denial. If this assumption, which has never been tested, does not hold, however, these estimated impacts might themselves reflect discrimination, and the standard approach may yield an overestimate or, more likely, an underestimate of discrimination.[37]

To be more precise, suppose that data on r are available so that equations (2.2) and (2.3) can be estimated directly. Suppose further, for ease of exposition, that these equations are linear; that is, suppose that the rate of return on a loan is determined by

$$r = \sum_i \alpha_i A_i + \sum_j \beta_j P_j + \sum_k \gamma_k T_k + \epsilon, \qquad (2.11)$$

and the probability of rejection is determined by

$$R = \delta r + \mu M + \eta N + e, \qquad (2.12)$$

where ϵ and e are random error terms.[38] In this case, equation (2.9) becomes

$$R = \delta\left(\sum_i \alpha_i A_i + \sum_j \beta_j P_j + \sum_k \gamma_k T_k\right) + \mu M + \eta N + e^*, \quad (2.13)$$

where $e^* = e + \delta\epsilon$.

Another way to express this point, therefore, is to say that the standard approach to estimating discrimination in loan rejection has a set of untested restrictions built into it. To be precise, the form of equation (2.9) in the literature, again expressed as a linear relationship for ease of exposition, can be written

$$R = \sum_i a_i A_i + \sum_j b_j P_j + \sum_k c_k T_k + mM + nN + e^{**}, \quad (2.14)$$

where e^{**} is another random error term. If the standard conceptual framework is correct, the estimated coefficient of A_i in equation (2.14), namely a_i, must equal $\delta\alpha_i$. Similar restrictions apply to the other variables in A, as well as to the variables in P and T. If these restrictions do not hold, then the indirect approach of equation (2.9) is not equivalent to the direct approach of equation (2.2).

These restrictions not only provide a test of the conceptual framework, but they also reveal that discrimination in the denial decision may show up in coefficients other than m in equation (2.14). Researchers have interpreted the coefficient of M as a comprehensive measure of discrimination (given adequate control variables); however, this interpretation is correct only if the restrictions hidden in the standard approach are met. This important point has not been adequately recognized in the literature.

Suppose, for example, that lenders have discovered that some variable A_i, such as delinquency on credit card debt, has a very small impact on the ultimate return on a mortgage loan but is highly correlated with minority status, M. A lender's rule of thumb in which this type of delinquency greatly increased the probability of loan denial would have the effect of excluding a few qualified whites and many equally qualified minorities. By placing a weight greater than $\delta\alpha_i$ on this variable in the denial decision, a lender can therefore discriminate against minorities without placing a positive weight on the M variable itself.[39] This case would show up as an estimated value of a_i that was greater than the value of $\delta\alpha_i$ found by estimating equations (2.11) and (2.12) directly, and the estimated value of m would understate discrimination.

One example of lender behavior consistent with this view appears in Munnell et al. (1996), who found that applications for mortgages on two- to four-unit buildings were more likely to be denied, all else equal, than applications for single-family houses. This higher probability of rejection does not appear to reflect the risk associated with the uncertain income stream from rental units, because standard underwriting procedures require lenders to incorporate this risk into the applicant's income and hence into the ratios of housing expenses and debt payments to income. Once these ratios (and other factors) are accounted for, therefore, as they are in the Munnell et al. regressions, multi-unit loans should yield the same return as others. Moreover, this property characteristic clearly is correlated with minority status: 28 percent of the mortgage applications from minorities were for multi-unit buildings, compared to only 9 percent for whites. Thus, lenders appear to be discriminating against minorities by raising the rejection rate on multi-unit loans.

Other examples of lender behavior that suggest this type of discrimination were uncovered by the New York State Banking Study (Kohn 1993). This study found that four of the ten banks investigated used underwriting standards that were not in line with industry standards and that had a disproportionately severe impact on minority and female applicants. For example, one bank "had a policy of not making loans under $75,000 in certain counties," and "another made no fixed rate loans with maturities over 15 years and made no loans with a greater than 80% loan-to-value ratio" (p. 2). These examples apply to the terms of the loan, called T in the previous equation, not applicant or property characteristics, and do not involve a linear form; however, the absolute rejection of loans for people with low incomes and/or low down payments clearly has a disproportionate impact on minorities.

Whether associated with applicant, property, or loan characteristics, this type of discrimination could occur consciously, as lenders who want to discriminate but do not want to get caught try to avoid a direct connection between their decisions and minority status (M), or it could occur unconsciously as lenders rely on perceptions or rules of thumb. Lenders may honestly believe, for example, that the appropriate weight for A_i in the loan denial decision is a_i, but if the true impact of A_i on loan returns (through defaults) is a smaller number, then the lender's actions constitute discrimination as defined previously.[40]

These examples do not prove that the restrictions implicit in the standard approach are usually violated.[41] Nevertheless, researchers and policymakers should recognize that the indirect approach on which the literature has so far relied has untested restrictions built into it. If these restrictions are not met, discrimination in loan denials could be higher than existing studies claim. Because the impact of observable applicant and property characteristics on loan returns is difficult to estimate, for lenders as well as for researchers, and because substantial anecdotal evidence suggests that lenders, like other people in business, often base decisions on rules of thumb, there is no reason to believe that these restrictions will be met. When they are not met, estimates of discrimination from the standard method may not be accurate.

In my judgment, therefore, testing these restrictions should be a high priority for future research. They cannot be tested, of course, without data on the returns to mortgages. These data are difficult to obtain because returns, like defaults, cannot be observed at the time a loan is made. However, researchers have proved to be resourceful in studying defaults (see Quercia and Stegman 1992), and data for losses on FHA loans are available (see Berkovec et al. 1994). I am confident that data for returns on conventional loans also could be obtained. Estimating some version of equations (2.12) and (2.13) with these data would make it possible to test these restrictions.

Lender Influence on Default

Another major untested assumption in the mortgage discrimination literature is that "defaults" are under the control of the borrower, not the lender. Default is in quotation marks here because a default, which is defined as nonpayment by the borrower, typically is not observed until it becomes a foreclosure, which is defined as the lender claiming legal rights to a property. As a result, many studies treat the terms *default* and *foreclosure* as synonymous, which they are not, and estimate models of "defaults" using data on foreclosures.

Default is heavily influenced by the borrower; many people who have little or no equity in their house and who are in financial trouble decide to stop making payments on their mortgage. But as several studies have recognized, the lender plays a vital role in turning this behavior into an observable default. As Quercia and Stegman (1992) put it, "although it is the borrower who stops payments, it is the lender who decides if default has occurred by choosing whether to work with the borrower or to foreclose" (p. 343).

In fact, lenders can exercise considerable discretion in how to treat people who have missed payments. They can be content to accept penalties for several months, they can negotiate a repayment schedule

to bring the borrower back up to date, or they can start foreclosure proceedings. Even in the case of mortgages in the secondary market, for which default and foreclosure procedures are explicitly spelled out, loan administrators may have considerable discretion in the timing of their actions.

This issue is relevant here because some lenders may take a harsher stance in foreclosure decisions against minority customers than against white ones. This harsher stance implies that defaults will not be as drawn out, and hence not as costly, for minority customers as for comparable white customers. Moreover, in extreme cases lenders may be able to increase their returns by giving loans that encourage defaults, such as loans with high loan-to-value ratios, initiating foreclosure proceedings if any payment is late, and selling the property for a profit.[42] This type of aggressive posture toward defaults, primarily on home-equity loans held by blacks, was described by CBS News in "A Matter of Interest" (*60 Minutes*, November 15, 1992).[43]

Lender influence on defaults causes conceptual difficulties for both the standard approach to loan denial and the alternative approach of focusing on default rates. Loan denial studies are affected because some minority applicants may be accepted only because a loan officer knows that he or she is more likely to foreclose on the minority's property than on the property of equally qualified white applicants, and therefore will face lower costs if minority borrowers default. This type of behavior is another source of downward bias in estimates of discrimination because it implies that lenders' acceptances of minority loans are boosted by this higher probability of foreclosure.[44]

Moreover, this issue can be added to the list of problems confronting the default test for discrimination. Even given all the strong assumptions needed for the default approach to work so that discrimination against minorities seems to imply a lower default rate for the least-qualified minorities than for the least-qualified whites, lender decisions to initiate foreclosure proceedings more aggressively with minority borrowers could lead to higher observed default rates for these minorities. This point only strengthens my conclusion that the default approach is fatally flawed when used to study discrimination in mortgage lending.

Lender Coaching of White Applicants

Another problem with important implications for research was uncovered in a U.S. Department of Justice investigation of Decatur Federal Savings and Loan in Atlanta in 1992. The investigators discovered that the Decatur loan officers helped white applicants make their applications look stronger (by encouraging applicants to pay off credit card debt, for example), and did not even tell black applicants that deficiencies in applications could be resolved (see Turner 1993). Other examples of this type of behavior were uncovered by several pilot studies of lenders' pre-application behavior, discussed in the upcoming subsection on "Discrimination in Outreach and Application Procedures."

Studies of loan approval control for applicant characteristics as stated in the final application, not as stated during the initial inquiry. These studies therefore understate discrimination whenever discriminatory coaching improves the qualifications of white applicants relative to minority applicants. In this case, discriminatory actions of lenders are hidden in the impact of "control" variables on loan denial. To use an example from the Decatur Federal investigation, suppose that white applicants, but not black and Hispanic applicants, are told to retire their credit card debt before they complete their mortgage applications. Because the level of credit card debt has a negative impact on the probability of obtaining a loan and because lender coaching makes it negatively correlated with minority status (even controlling for other factors), the indirect effect of minority status on loan denial through the credit card debt variable is positive, and ignoring it leads to an understatement of discrimination.

In more formal terms, the bias problem arises because the so-called control variables actually are endogenous, that is, influenced by the lender's coaching. This endogeneity leads to bias in the estimated coefficients in equation (2.9), and in particular to a downward bias in the coefficient of the minority status variable, that is, in measured discrimination.

Discriminatory coaching was examined in an analysis of Decatur Federal's lending practices (see Siskin and Cupingood, chapter 16, this volume), and is mentioned by King (1980) and Munnell et al. (1996), but has not been formally considered in a study of loan denial by a sample of lenders.[45] Thus, we do not yet have evidence on the magnitude of the bias in estimates of discrimination caused by lender coaching. Because so many applicant characteristics could be affected, it may prove to be impossible to model this behavior (and to correct for it with simultaneous equations techniques). The only way to fix this problem may be to reexamine the file of each applicant to determine the applicant's characteristics at the time of application. So long as there is no racial or ethnic disparity in the way characteristics are first recorded, initial characteristics are exogenous, and using them as controls does not lead to biased coefficients. Unfortunately, of course, this is an expensive procedure and the information in the file might not be complete enough to capture all the coaching that occurred.

Resampling Rejected Applicants

Studies based on loan applications, including all the studies reviewed in the previous subsection on "Recent Studies," also need to consider that applicants who are rejected by one lender may apply to another lender. This possibility is considered in a conceptual paper by Nakamura (1993), but has not yet been brought into the empirical work on loan rejection.

This problem can be incorporated into the standard framework by recognizing that instead of one choice, namely to accept or deny a loan application, there are three choices: to accept or deny an original loan application (lender choice); to reapply if one's loan application is rejected (borrower choice); and to accept or deny a repeat loan application (another lender choice).[46] Each of these choices is a function of applicant, property, and loan characteristics. Suppose that the probability that an original loan application will be turned down is P_1, the probability that a rejected borrower will reapply is P_2, and the probability that a repeat application will be turned down is P_3. Ignoring cases in which borrowers apply three or more times, a sample of applications will then contain a share of repeat borrowers equal to P_1P_2. In other words, a sample of N applications contains only $N/(1 + P_1P_2)$ different applicants.

Most people interpret existing loan denial studies as estimating P_1 as a function of applicant and property characteristics. In fact, however, these studies estimate an amalgam probability equal to $P_1(1 + P_2P_3)/(1 + P_1P_2)$. This expression is derived by dividing the possibilities for rejection at either the first or second application, $P_1 + P_1P_2P_3$, by the possibilities for rejection or acceptance at either the first or second application, $1 + P_1P_2$. It equals P_1 only if P_1 and P_3 are equal. Thus the standard approach overestimates P_1 if P_3 is greater than P_1 and underestimates P_1 if P_3 is less than P_1.

This problem could bias estimates of P_1 for both minority and white applicants. The key issue here is whether these biases lead to an over- or understatement of discrimination in loan denial. Either outcome is theoretically possible. Suppose, for example, that white applicants who are rejected for loans the first time (with a given set of applicant and property characteristics) have some unobservable characteristic—

a nervous personality, for example—that makes it very likely that they will be rejected the next time they apply. In this case, P_3 exceeds P_1. Suppose further that rejected minority applicants never reapply because they believe that discrimination will prevent them from ever getting a loan. Thus, P_1 is biased upward for whites but accurate for minorities and the difference between these two denial rates, which is the standard measure of discrimination, is underestimated.

This example is purely hypothetical. No existing study provides information that could be used to determine the direction or magnitude of the bias caused by multiple loan application. In principle, this bias could be avoided by restricting the sample to first-time applicants, but it is not clear whether such applicants can be identified in any available data set.[47] In any case, the bias in existing studies caused by multiple loan applications could be severe and further work on this topic clearly is needed.

The Causes of Discrimination

Finally, the existing empirical literature has not addressed a key issue for policy makers: the causes of discrimination in mortgage lending. As many studies have pointed out in other contexts, one cannot design effective policies to combat discrimination unless one knows why it exists (see, for example, Cain [1986] on labor markets, Yinger [1986, 1995] on housing markets, and Ayres and Siegelman [1995] on car sales). Adding this step is unlikely to alter the estimate of discrimination in loan approval, but it may help to determine the circumstances under which discrimination occurs.

One possible cause of discrimination was discussed in the previous subsection on "Analytical and Legal Definitions of Discrimination," namely that the unobservable credit characteristics of minority applicants are less favorable, on average, than those of majority applicants. This type of behavior, called statistical discrimination, has been widely discussed in the literature; indeed, it is the only cause of mortgage lending discrimination that has received extensive attention.[48] Although no study formally shows that statistical discrimination exists, several of the studies cited in Quercia and Stegman (1992), as well as Berkovec et al. (1994, 1995, and chapters 6, 7, and 10, this volume), found that minority borrowers are more likely to default, controlling for their observable characteristics at the time the loan was granted.[49] This result supports the argument that lenders have an incentive to practice statistical discrimination, but does not prove that they do.

It is important to reiterate that statistical discrimination is illegal, even though it is based on profit-maximizing calculations by lenders. In our society, it is legitimate to consider the observable characteristics of a loan applicant that are related to his or her ability to pay back a loan, but it is not legitimate to use the average unobservable characteristics of a group to make inferences about the unobservable characteristics of an individual. Determining whether statistical discrimination exists is, therefore, a vital question for public policy; if lenders discriminate in response to their belief that minority applicants have less favorable unobserved credit characteristics, then strong antidiscrimination laws, with penalties for violators, are needed to alter their incentives.[50]

Statistical discrimination may not be practiced by the many lenders who plan to sell their mortgages in the secondary market.[51] All these lenders care about, one might argue, is whether a borrower meets the underwriting criteria established by the secondary market institutions.[52] Indeed, once an individual loan is sold, the originator may no longer care about default. However, statistical discrimination may still occur if these lenders believe that it is more difficult to provide documentation for minority applicants, or that sales to minorities will lead to so many defaults that secondary market institutions will have to investigate. After all, the originator wants to avoid being audited by the secondary market institution, or even worse, being forced to repurchase a loan.[53]

Brief discussions of the causes of discrimination in mortgage lending also are provided by Shear and Yezer (1985) and Galster (1992). Following Becker's lead (1971), both of these articles point out that, as in many other markets, the personal prejudice of individual decision makers may lead them to discriminate. In other words, people involved in the loan decision may decide to deny loans to some creditworthy minority applicants because of their own prejudice against minorities.[54] Evidence that lender prejudice is at work would indicate that educational and training programs for lenders, as well as antidiscrimination laws, are needed.

Some tantalizing evidence that lender prejudice may be a factor has been provided by Kim and Squires (1995), who combined the HMDA data for Milwaukee with data on the racial composition of each lender's work force and of its managers. If prejudice is at work, black-white disparities in loan approval rates should decline as minority representation increases in either a lender's overall work force or among its administrators. This is exactly what the study found. Unfortunately, however, the study does not provide a statistical test for the significance of this difference. Kim and Squires also hypothesized that thrifts are less likely to discriminate than are commercial banks, in effect because banks are more likely to be influenced by stereotypes: "Because mortgage loans constitute a much higher share of lending activity for thrifts than for commercial banks, we surmise that thrifts may review mortgage applications more carefully and therefore more successfully avoid racial bias" (p. 102). Kim and Squires also pointed out: "For banks, mortgage lending is not a main line of business; it is more likely a courtesy extended to regular customer" (p. 101), most of whom are white. The authors found evidence to support this hypothesis, but again do not present a formal statistical test. More work of this type would be valuable, especially with more complete controls for applicant credit history—and with formal statistical tests of the key hypotheses.

In the housing market, some evidence supports the view that real estate brokers discriminate against minorities to protect their reputation and future business with an established white community (see Yinger 1986, 1995). Because mortgage lenders often work closely with real estate brokers, these incentives may spill forward onto lenders; that is, lenders may discriminate against minority customers, at least in certain neighborhoods, to protect their reputation with the real estate brokers who send them prospective white buyers.[55]

To my knowledge, no study has provided formal tests of these or any other hypotheses about the causes of discrimination in mortgage lending. Because a better understanding of this topic is so important for policy purposes, additional research on this topic, both conceptual and empirical, should receive high priority.

DISCRIMINATION IN OTHER TYPES OF LENDER BEHAVIOR

The process of obtaining a loan involves more than the lender's decision to accept or reject an application. This section cites other types of lender behavior and briefly reviews the literature on the extent to which these other types of behavior involve racial or ethnic discrimination.

Types of Lender Behavior

A lender's actions in making mortgage loans can be divided into five steps. The first step is advertising and outreach. To some extent, lenders use traditional means to advertise loans, such as newspapers and television, but they also advertise by posting signs in their windows. Thus, the location of their offices is an important element of their advertising programs. Some lenders also may make special efforts to reach certain segments of the population in their market area. The second step involves the lender's application procedures. How are people treated when they enter the lender's office to inquire about a loan? Do application procedures discourage minority applicants? The third step is loan acceptance. This step was considered at length in the first part of this chapter. The fourth step, which occurs simultaneously with the third, is the determination of loan terms. As pointed out earlier, there is some evidence that the LTV ratio is different for equally qualified minority and white borrowers. Discrimination might also exist in the determination of interest rates or loan maturities or loan types. The fifth step is loan administration. As discussed earlier, lenders may be more likely to initiate foreclosure procedures with minority borrowers in default than with comparable white borrowers.

Discrimination in Outreach and Application Procedures

Existing knowledge about lender behavior at stages before the loan approval decision comes primarily from several pilot audit studies described by Smith and Cloud (chapter 23, this volume), Lawton (chapter 24), and Galster (1993b). In an audit, two people, one from a minority group and one from the majority, who have been matched to have the same qualifications successively visit a lender to inquire about mortgages. Discrimination is defined as systematically less favorable treatment of the minority auditors in a sample of audits. This technique has been widely used to study discrimination by landlords and real estate brokers, but so far only a few relatively small-scale pilot studies have applied it to mortgage lending.

As Galster (1993b) has made clear, these studies, which were conducted in Pontiac (Mich.), Louisville, Chicago, and Philadelphia, do not meet the standards of study design or reporting required for research purposes, so they do not provide definitive characterizations of lender behavior at this stage. Nevertheless, their findings are intriguing. Lenders often appear to be less interested in giving information to black than to white customers; they urge black customers, but not whites, to go to another lender; or they emphasize to black customers, but not whites, that the application procedures are long and complicated. In many cases lenders also appear to be more helpful to white than to black customers: white customers are told about more options and, as in the Decatur Federal Savings and Loan investigation, are the only ones given tips on how to meet the lender's underwriting standards (see Turner 1993). Moreover, blacks are more likely than equally qualified whites to be told that they do not qualify for a mortgage.

This type of lender behavior potentially could have a large impact on the access of minority household to loans. By putting up extra barriers for minority customers, lenders may be able to discourage some minorities from filling out applications and may, as explained earlier, tilt information on applications in favor of white applicants. These types of discrimination in the provision of mortgage loans do not show up in the behavior researchers can best observe, namely the loan approval decision. Because of the potential importance of this type of behavior and because the existing pilot studies make audits appear feasible, Galster (1993b) and Wienk (1992) recommended full-fledged audit studies of loan application procedures. I agree. As Wienk stated: "An audit study of lenders would reveal whether prospective buyers are treated differently on the basis of race *before* they submit written loan applications" (p. 238).

Lender decisions about the location of their branches also affect minority access to information about loans. An example of lender branching decisions that appears to involve discrimination was uncovered by the Decatur Federal Savings investigation (see Turner 1993). After its founding in 1927, Decatur opened 43 branches in the Atlanta metropolitan area. Only 1 of those branches was placed in a largely black neighborhood. Moreover, the only 2 branches that were closed over this period were in one case, originally located in a largely black neighborhood and, in the other case, located in a neighborhood that had become largely black. An investigation of branching decisions by a sample of lenders would be valuable.

Discrimination in Loan Terms

Lenders decide not only whether to grant a loan but the terms of the loan, including the interest rate, loan fees, maturity, LTV ratio, and loan type (conventional, adjustable rate, FHA, and so on). Studies of the LTV ratio were discussed previously in the subsection on "Endogeneity of Loan-to-Value Ratios," which pointed out that studies of loan terms must consider the simultaneous nature of decisions about

these terms and in some cases must take into account borrower demand.

Several researchers have argued that lenders do not select the interest rate for an individual loan (see Galster 1992; Munnell et al. 1996). The interest rate is posted in the window, the argument goes, and any borrower who comes in on a given day can borrow at that rate. Therefore, no discrimination in interest rates should occur. This argument may be correct, but an alternative view is possible. Different interest rates are charged on different types of loans, and some customers may be encouraged to take the higher rate alternatives. Moreover, interest rates change from day to day, and some customers may be encouraged to lock in a rate when rates are rising or to wait for a lower rate when they are falling. In addition, banks may have different branches with different rates to which different types of customers are steered (either by branch location or by explicit lender recommendation). The possibility of discrimination in interest rates is thus certainly worth investigating, and should not be assumed away.

Several studies have investigated discrimination in interest rates, loan fees, and loan maturities. Schafer and Ladd (1981) found that blacks and Hispanics are charged higher interest rates and higher loan fees than Anglos in several of their study areas, controlling for relevant factors (and using a simultaneous equations procedure). They did not find any evidence of discrimination in loan maturities, however. Black and Schweitzer (1985) also found some discrimination against blacks in the setting of interest rates. These studies are now somewhat out of date, but so far as I can determine, no more recent studies exist.

Discrimination in Type of Loan

Several studies also have examined the probability that a borrower will receive an FHA loan instead of a conventional loan. Both the borrower and the lender have an interest in this choice. FHA loans are insured, which protects the lender, but cost more than mortgages with private mortgage insurance, which raises the cost to the borrower. Moreover, FHA loans have relatively low down-payment requirements, which makes them relatively more accessible to many borrowers.[56]

It is clear that minority borrowers rely more heavily on FHA loans than do white borrowers. As shown by Schnare and Gabriel (chapter 5, this volume) using 1990 HMDA data, for example, FHA loans constitute 56 percent of all qualifying loans to black borrowers, compared to 29 percent for Hispanics and only 27 percent for whites. To some degree this relatively heavy reliance on FHA loans by minority borrowers can be explained by the fact that, on average, minority borrowers have less wealth than whites, which makes FHA's low down-payment requirement attractive, as well as poorer credit qualifications than comparable whites, which makes the FHA insurance appealing to lenders. Several studies have shown, however, that minority borrowers rely more heavily on FHA than do white borrowers, even after borrower and property characteristics have been taken into account.[57]

Shear and Yezer (1985) argued that discrimination in the market for conventional loans will push minorities to alternative loan sources, such as FHA. A finding that minorities are more likely than whites to receive FHA loans, controlling for borrower, property, and loan characteristics, implies, therefore, that there is discrimination in the conventional loan market.[58] Shear and Yezer's logit analysis of FHA participation found this to be the case, and they concluded that there is "evidence of significant differential treatment of black households by the conventional sector" (p. 301).

Gabriel and Rosenthal (1991) and Canner, Gabriel, and Woolley (1991) estimated discrete choice models of the probability of obtaining a conventional loan (as opposed to an FHA loan), controlling for characteristics associated with default risk. Both studies found that household race is highly significant. Gabriel and Rosenthal calculated that, among "high-risk" households, the probability of getting an FHA loan is 86.2 percent for blacks and 70.2 percent for whites. Among "low-risk" households, this probability is 20.6 percent for blacks and 8.5 percent for whites. Canner and colleagues found that white households are two and one-half to three times as likely to get a conventional loan as are blacks for any given set of borrower and neighborhood characteristics. These two studies reached similar conclusions, summarized by Canner et al. (1991) as follows: "Various possible explanations for a significant race effect include differences in preferences for FHA versus conventional financing among differential racial or ethnic groups, the effects of steering by real estate agents, market specialization by mortgage bankers, or lender bias" (p. 259).

Overall, these studies clearly reveal that FHA loan usage reflects racial disparities in conventional mortgage lending. Further research on this topic is needed to pin down the independent role of this important government program.

DISCRIMINATION BY OTHER ACTORS IN MORTGAGE MARKETS

Mortgage lenders are by no means the only actors in the housing and mortgage markets. This section describes the other actors—brokers, appraisers, insurers, and institutions in the secondary mortgage market—and their roles and briefly reviews the literature on the extent to which these actors practice racial and ethnic discrimination.[59] For more complete analysis of the roles of these actors in the housing and mortgage markets, see Galster (1992).

Real Estate Brokers

For many homebuyers, real estate brokers are the primary source of information about available mortgages. Discrimination in the provision of this information, therefore, could have a large impact on the ability of minority homebuyers to obtain the mortgage funds they need. One early fair housing audit study by Feins, Bratt, and Hollister (1981) found that real estate brokers were far more likely to tell white than black customers about both conventional mortgages and opportunities for creative financing.

This type of discrimination also was investigated by the 1989 Housing Discrimination Study (HDS) (Yinger 1991, 1995). This study conducted over 2,000 audits of real estate brokers in a national sample of metropolitan areas. About half of these audits involved black and white teammates, and the other half involved Hispanic and white teammates. The HDS found large differences in the willingness of brokers to help white and minority customers secure financing. In the black-white audits, 13.3 percent of the black auditors were offered assistance in finding a loan compared to 24.4 percent of the white auditors. The comparable figures for the Hispanic-white audits were 18.1 percent and 22.1 percent. In both cases, the minority-white differences are statistically significant.[60]

Moreover, white auditors were far more likely to be told about both fixed-rate and variable-rate mortgages, whereas minority auditors were more likely to be told about FHA loans. To be specific, the difference in the probability that white and black auditors would be told about loans was 21.5 percentage points for fixed-rate mortgages (whites over blacks) and 15.1 points for adjustable-rate mortgages. The comparable figures for the Hispanic-white audits were 14.7 percent and 10.9 percent. In addition, blacks were 6.7 percentage points more likely than whites (and Hispanics were 3.4 percentage points more likely than whites) to be told about FHA loans. All of these differences, except the FHA result for Hispanics, are statistically significant.

Appraisers

Appraisers play a role in the mortgage market because lenders set the value of a house, and hence of the loan collateral, through an appraisal and tie the amount of the loan to the appraised value. The borrower must pay the market value of the house, not the appraised value. Thus, if the ratio of appraised to market value is systematically lower for minority than for white applicants, minorities will be forced to make higher downpayments than comparable whites and may be unable to afford a house at all.

The history of appraisal practices suggests that appraisal bias may occur. Until 1977, appraisal texts approved by the American Institute of Real Estate Appraisers (AIREA), the main trade organization for appraisers, explicitly called for lower appraised values in racially mixed neighborhoods. This practice was eliminated after a successful Justice Department suit against AIREA (see Schwemm, chapter 12, this volume).

Existing research on this topic is limited and does not uncover significant discrimination in appraisals. Schafer and Ladd (1981) estimated the ratio of appraised value to purchase price as a function of many control variables and the race or ethnicity of the applicant.[61] They found no evidence of discrimination in appraisals against blacks in California, but they did find that appraisals are systematically lower for Hispanic loan applicants in some metropolitan areas. The Hispanic-white differences in appraisals are not large, however, with a maximum of 3.6 percent in one metropolitan area. King (1980) performed a similar test and found little evidence of discrimination in appraisals against Hispanics.

Insurers

Insurers play two roles in the mortgage market. They provide insurance on houses, which lenders generally require before issuing a mortgage, and they provide mortgage insurance. In fact, mortgage insurance is required in the secondary market whenever the LTV ratio is above 80 percent. The government serves as insurer, of course, for FHA and Department of Veterans Affairs mortgages.

Discrimination in home insurance could deny minorities access to housing. If a household cannot get home insurance, it cannot get a mortgage and will have a hard time buying a house at all. Galster (1993b) described a pilot study of discrimination in home insurance in Milwaukee that used the audit technique. This study found that insurance agents were more likely to offer a policy over the telephone when the house to be insured was in a white area than when it was in a black area, and that agents gave more stringent inspection standards in black areas than white areas. A more recent audit study, described in Tisdale, Smith, and Cloud (1994), discovered a reluctance of two large insurance companies to provide insurance in largely black neighborhoods in Louisville, Atlanta, and Milwaukee, and in largely Hispanic neighborhoods in Chicago. Although these studies focused on discrimination against minority neighborhoods, not minority households, and must be interpreted with care, they suggest that minority households may face discriminatory barriers in obtaining home insurance. Further research on this topic clearly is warranted.

Discrimination in mortgage insurance also could deny minorities access to housing. Moreover, this type of discrimination could lead to an understatement of discrimination in studies of loan denial. If minorities are denied insurance more often than equally qualified whites, then controlling for the actual insurance denial brings an element of discrimination into one of the "control" variables; as described previously in this chapter, discrimination is not confined to the coefficient of the minority status variable, and estimates of discrimination may be affected by simultaneity bias.

The only existing study of discrimination in private mortage insurance (Munnell et al. 1993) found that minority applicants were more likely than white applicants to be turned down for this insurance, controlling for a set of characteristics similar to those in table 2.1. Although the authors were unable to determine whether this effect was associated with the minority status of the applicant or the location of the property in a largely minority neighborhood, this study provided clear evidence that some type of discrimination occurs in the provision of private mortgage insurance.

Secondary Market Institutions

Because secondary purchasers have become major players in mortgage markets, it is natural to ask whether their behavior involves any discrimination.[62] Although little is known about this topic, recent discussions of it can be found in Galster (1992) and Van Order (chapter 11, this volume). As Galster (1992) pointed out, the starting point for investigating this question is the finding, documented in Canner and Gabriel (1992), that loans in the secondary market are concentrated in higher-income, largely white neighborhoods. This "could imply either that the secondary sector is passively responding to the pattern of origination or that its rules are causing the origination pattern" (Galster 1992: 657). Both Galster and Van Order have pointed out that the secondary market could influence this pattern through its underwriting standard. According to Van Order, "underwriting guidelines might provide rigid limits on payment-to-income ratios, which disproportionately affect minorities, but which do not affect creditworthiness (see chapter 11, this volume). In fact, this argument is equivalent to the previous argument in this chapter in which some discrimination is buried in the impacts of so-called control variables on loan denial. Unfortunately, there exists no empirical work on the possible discriminatory impact of secondary market underwriting standards, so I can only echo Galster and Van Order by saying that more research is needed on these issues.

CONCLUSIONS

Discrimination by mortgage lenders exists when lenders deny loans to minorities (or treat them unfavorably in other ways) after controlling for the factors that influence the returns on a loan. Several studies offer evidence that such discrimination exists. The best of these studies, Munnell et al. (1996), provides strong recent evidence that mortgage lenders in Boston discriminate against black and Hispanic applicants. According to the authors' preferred estimate, black and Hispanic applicants have an 82 percent higher chance of being turned down for a loan than do equally qualified white applicants.

Discrimination in mortgage lending can have a major impact on minority households' access to housing. Despite this potential importance and despite the evidence that some discrimination exists, several aspects of lending discrimination remain largely unexplored. Indeed, there is far less research on this topic than on discrimination in the housing or labor markets. Further research on discrimination in mortgage lending clearly is warranted.

The first task of future research is to expand our knowledge of the most basic type of lender behavior—the decision to lend. This task encompasses three steps. The first step is to determine whether Munnell et al.'s (1996) results hold in other locations and to search for additional control variables or specifications that affect the estimate of discrimination. The second step is to recognize more fully the complexity of the decision to lend. Future studies need to address five possibilities: the endogeneity of LTV ratios, the violation of restrictions that are implicit in the standard approach, lender influence on defaults, lender coaching of white applicants, and resampling of rejected applicants. Although the net bias from ignoring these aspects of lender behavior could work in either direction, the available evidence suggests to me that existing studies understate discrimination, perhaps significantly, because they have not taken these factors into account. The third step is to develop and test hypotheses about the causes of discrimination. This step is needed to design appropriate policies to combat discrimination.

The second task of future research is to expand our understanding of discrimination in other aspects of lender behavior and of discrimination by other actors in mortgage markets. Although several good studies have been conducted on these topics, many questions remain unresolved, and the literature does not yet provide a comprehensive picture of discrimination in mortgage markets. Thus, we do not know the extent to which discrimination in the decision to lend is reinforced by discrimination in other lender decisions or by other actors in mortgage markets.

Many observers of mortgage markets see the increasing sophistication of the participants in these markets and conclude that something as "irrational" as discrimination against minorities could not continue to exist. In fact, however, discrimination need not be irrational, in that it may be supported by economic incentives. Moreover, strong, recent evidence shows that discrimination continues to exist both in the decision to lend and in other types of behavior in mortgage markets. Laws against credit discrimination have been on the books for a long time, but have not yet eradicated this discriminatory behavior. To help strengthen existing laws and perhaps to design better ones, researchers must provide more careful estimates of discrimination in loan approval, enhance understanding of discrimination in other types of behavior in mortgage markets, and determine why this discrimination exists.

Notes

In preparing this chapter, I benefited greatly from conversations with Robert Avery, James Berkovec, James Follain, Stuart Gabriel, George Galster, Helen Ladd, Leonard

Nakamura, Stephen Ross, Geoffrey Tootell, Ron Wienk, Anthony Yezer, and Peter Zorn. Moreover, I received helpful comments from many of the participants in the May 1993 U.S. Department of Housing and Urban Development conference on "Home Mortgage Lending and Discrimination: Research and Enforcement," especially my discussants, Wilhelmina Leigh, Frank Nothaft, and Ann Shlay. The reader should not assume, however, that this chapter reflects the views of these individuals.

1. The Home Mortgage Disclosure Act of 1975 required lenders to provide information on the locations of their loans. Amendments to HMDA included in the Financial Institutions Reform, Recovery, and Enforcement Act of 1989 required lenders to provide information on all loan applications, including the race of the applicant and the location of the property. For more on the history of the HMDA data, see Canner and Gabriel (1992).

2. A lending institution is in the business of maximizing the return on its loan portfolio, but as pointed out to me by Peter Zorn, individual actors in a lending institution may have different objectives. An individual loan officer, for example, may have an incentive simply to avoid defaults over some relatively short-term horizon. These complexities are not considered in this chapter.

3. Throughout this chapter the term *minority* is used to mean African American or Hispanic and the term *white* is used to mean non-Hispanic white. *Black* is used as a synonym for African American. This usage of *white* is a shorthand because many Hispanic Americans have European or white racial backgrounds.

4. A formal statement of this approach can be found in Peterson (1981).

5. If different types of loan, such as home purchase and home improvement, are pooled in the same regression, then a vector of loan type variables also should be included in the equations for D and C.

6. For further discussion of statistical discrimination, see the subsection later in this chapter on "Causes of Discrimination."

7. Some people argue that discrimination cannot exist if lenders are "simply" maximizing profits. Becker (1993) has argued that "discrimination in the marketplace consists of voluntarily relinquishing profits, wages, or income, in order to cater to prejudice." According to most scholars and to the law, however, discrimination is defined as behavior that denies a person, solely because of race or ethnicity, the rights or privileges to which he or she, on the basis of all observable characteristics, is qualified. See, for example, Cain (1986). Hence, discrimination can be defined without reference to its causes and can arise without prejudice. Even in Becker's pioneering book (1971), the prejudice of customers or workers can give an unprejudiced firm an incentive to discriminate to protect its profits.

8. In principle N might belong in these equations, too. The argument in this paragraph also can be applied to N.

9. Although courts have not ruled on evidence required to prove mortgage discrimination, the U.S. Supreme Court has ruled that statistics in general, and regression analysis in particular, are legitimate evidence in labor market discrimination cases (see Ashenfelter and Oaxaca 1987).

10. These figures are from Canner and Gabriel (1992).

11. See also the review of studies using HMDA data by Galster (1993b).

12. Siskin and Cupingood (chapter 16, this volume) estimate a version of equation (2.9) for a single lender; Peterson (1981) examined sex discrimination in consumer lending.

13. A brief review of Black et al. (1978) can be found in Munnell et al. (1995), and brief reviews of King (1980) can be found in both Munnell et al. (1985) and in Schafer and Ladd (1981).

14. Schafer and Ladd (1981) also tested for redlining by determining whether denial rates are higher in neighborhoods in which redlining has been alleged. They found evidence for redlining in a few cases (pp. 292–96).

15. The alternative unemployment variable is based on an analysis of unemployment in an entirely different data set, namely the Panel Study of Income Dynamics. To be specific, this variable represents the predicted probability "that an individual will become unemployed in the next five years" based on the individual's industry, occupation, and other labor market characteristics in his or her mortgage application (p. 8 in manuscript). Although I think this variable is creative, I also think it inappropriately uses race to predict the probability of unemployment. As Munnell et al. (1996) recognized elsewhere in their paper, using the average characteristics of a minority group to make decisions about an individual applicant is statistical discrimination and is illegal. Their approach, in effect, "allows" the employer to practice statistical discrimination in predicting unemployment and therefore may understate discrimination in loan approval. This understatement appears to be very small in this case, however, as estimated discrimination is virtually the same with the unemployment variable in table 2.1.

16. For detailed explanations of the data-checking procedures conducted by Munnell et al. (1996), along with a response to Liebowitz (1993), see Brown and Tootell (1995) and Browne (1993). A detailed response to Horne (1994) is included in Munnell et al. (1996) and in Brown and Tootell (1995). They point out that virtually all of the errors discovered by Horne are either misinterpretations by Horne, are small in magnitude, or are applicable to variables not included in their regression analyses. Moreover, they use a statistical procedure to show that possible (but unverified) errors in the dependent variable (loan rejection) do not influence their results.

17. This is not to say that Carr and Megbolugbe (1993) and Glennon and Stengle (1994) agreed with Munnell et al. (1996) in toto. For example, Glennon and Stengel emphasized (as I do later in this chapter) that some data and specification issues in the study cannot be resolved without further research.

18. Yet another approach to discrimination, which is not reviewed in this chapter, is to determine whether, after controlling for credit characteristics, minority households are more likely to be "credit constrained" than white households. In this context, a household is said to be credit constrained if it indicates that it could not obtain as much credit as it requested or that it did not search for credit because it expected to be turned down. For a discussion and application of this approach, see Duca and Rosenthal (1994).

19. Actually, these four commentators (Becker 1993, Brimelow 1993, Brimelow and Spencer 1993, and Roberts 1993) went considerably farther than this. They all claimed that the Munnell et al. (1996) findings of discrimination are "flawed" or "invalid" because they did not look at defaults. This claim is nonsense. An analysis of defaults may be an alternative way to test for discrimination, but the existence of this alternative does not invalidate the more direct approach used by Munnell et al.

20. See Karr (1995) and Seiberg (1995).

21. For other critical examinations at the default approach, see Galster (1993a), and Tootell (1993).

22. These reasons also are missed in a formal discussion of Berkovec et al. (1994) by Capozza (1994), who went so far as to say that the study "provides evidence of reverse discrimination and it is statistically significant" (p. 295). This claim is totally without foundation.

23. Berkovec et al. (1994: 287) state: "We have sought to test the hypothesis . . . that discrimination in the lending process should under certain circumstances lead to observed default rates that are lower for minority borrowers than for non-minority borrowers, all else equal. We have not found this result for the data available for the study."

As noted earlier, they then added some qualifications. Several other studies have estimated some form of equation (2.10) and obtained the same result (but may not have drawn the same conclusion). See Van Order et al. (1993) and the review by Quercia and Stegman (1992).

24. For further discussion of this issue, see Tootell (1993) and Ross (1995). I find it ironic that some people who reject the loan denial approach because of possible omitted-variable bias embrace the default approach even though it is subject to exactly the same bias—in the opposite direction. One is tempted to conclude that these people are attracted to a method that systematically understates discrimination.

25. The default approach suffers from another, more technical bias, as well. Ross (1995) showed that because it observes only accepted applicants, the default approach inevitably understates discrimination even if it is not subject to omitted variable bias. Tootell (1993) made a similar point.

26. Actually, I am giving the default approach too much credit here. Ross (1995) showed that even "perfect" statistical discrimination does not completely eliminate the impact of unobserved characeristics on loan outcomes and therefore does not completely eliminate the bias in the default approach.

27. The Berkovec et al. analyses (1994, 1995; also chapters 6, 7, and 10, this volume) of default also use FHA data and the results cannot be generalized to the mortgage market as a whole.

28. An additional problem is that missing data, particularly for loan losses and census tract characteristics, greatly cut Berkovec et al.'s (1995; chapter 6, this volume) sample size and might make their remaining sample unrepresentative. Moreover, the full loss includes the lost interest. Berkovec et al. implicitly assume that this is the same for loans to black and white households.

29. Zandi (1993) claimed that Munnell et al.'s (1996) finding of discrimination is nullified if one includes another variable in the HMDA data set, namely whether the applicant conforms to the lender's credit guidelines. As Carr and Megbolugbe (1993) pointed out, however, lenders who discriminate are likely to rationalize this behavior by claiming that minority applicants do not meet their guidelines. In my judgment, Zandi simply estimates a model in which discrimination appears in his credit variable instead of in the minority status variable.

30. For a recent example of an endogeneity test in a discrete choice model, see Greene, Lovely, and Ondrich (1993).

31. This issue has been called the included-variable problem in the literature on discrimination in employment because it involves variables that are included in the regression as opposed to omitted variables. For example, a regression analysis of black-white wage rate differentials might control for an employee's job category, without recognizing that this category is endogenous. See Killingsworth (1993), which describes both the interpretation and bias issues, and Bloom and Killingsworth (1983).

32. Note that Schafer and Ladd (1981) included the *requested* LTV ratio, which they assumed to be exogenous, in their denial regressions. It is not clear whether applicant requests are influenced by the lender, but even if it were, a better procedure would have been to use the requested LTV as an instrument and to treat final LTV ratio as an endogenous right-side variable. Schafer and Ladd also found that higher LTV ratios for blacks were accompanied by higher interest rates. (See upcoming subsection on "Discrimination in Loan Terms.")

33. Maddala and Trost (1982) found that blacks get smaller loan amounts, but this result is not statistically significant. Although Maddala and Trost carefully modeled both the demand and supply of loanable funds and estimated them simultaneously, they did not control for the market value of the house. Incidentally, Maddala and Trost

argued that an equation for the actual loan amount (and by implication the LTV ratio) should include the requested loan amount as a control variable—which was the Schafer/Ladd procedure (1981). Munnell et al. (1995) also found that minorities had higher LTV ratios on average, but did not test for the endogeneity of this variable (but see note 36).

34. Higher LTV ratios themselves may be desirable for minority applicants, who tend to have less money for a down payment than otherwise comparable white applicants. However, these higher LTV ratios may be accompanied by higher interest rates or loan fees and may give lenders a greater ability to foreclose on loans to minorities (see the following two subsections in this chapter).

35. A labor market example of this type of downward bias has been provided by Killingsworth (1993). In his example, an intermediate variable, performance in an interview (the analog of loan amount), influenced the final decision, whether to hire (the analog of loan approval). Treating the intermediate variable as exogenous leads to an understatement of discrimination in the final decision.

36. Munnell et al. (1996) argued that the likely bias is small, at least in their data set. In their footnote 4, they stated that an instrumental variables procedure to account for the possible endogeneity of their LTV variable "has little impact on the size or significance of the coefficient on race." They did not, however, give the details of this procedure.

37. This issue of the role of control variables also arises in studying discrimination in employment. In a regression of the probability that someone will be hired or promoted as a function of the person's characteristics, the coefficient of a minority status variable is usually interpreted as an indicator of discrimination. But if the coefficients of the "control" variables do not reflect expected productivity, then some discrimination may be reflected in the coefficients of those variables, too. For further discussion of this issue in the employment context, see, Killingsworth (1993).

38. The assumption of linear forms simplifies the presentation but is in no way essential. The conclusions in this section still hold, for example, if the decision to lend is specified as a logit or probit equation.

39. In principle, this effect also could work the other way; lenders could use weights for variables correlated with minority status that are lower than the true impact of such variables on loan returns. In this case, which seems unlikely, the standard approach overstates discrimination against minorities.

40. In legal terms, this behavior has discriminatory impact even if it does not have discriminatory intent. Because there have been so few court cases concerning mortgage discrimination, it is not clear whether courts would grant a judgment based on discriminatory impact alone. Court decisions in labor and housing discrimination cases suggest that they would. See Ashenfelter and Oaxaca (1987) and Yinger (1995: chap. 10).

41. Munnell et al. (1996) reported that a majority of the conventional loan applications in Boston in 1990 failed to meet at least one of the underwriting standards used by the secondary mortgage market. Since most applicants receive loans and do not default, this fact provides prima facia evidence that underwriting criteria often do not correspond to creditworthiness.

42. In principle, the borrower can claim any remaining equity in the house by selling it before the bank forecloses. In some neighborhoods, however, an owner may not be able to sell his or her house quickly enough to make this claim.

43. The lender in question was Fleet Finance. On June 14, 1993, the Georgia Supreme Court ruled, with obvious distaste, that Fleet's policy of providing high-interest loans and aggressively foreclosing when possible was legal. Specifically, the court said: "Although we do not condone Fleet's interest charging practices, which are widely viewed as exorbitant, unethical, and perhaps even immoral . . . , we are constrained to hold

that the loans in question are legal" (quoted in Associated Press 1993: B8). This case did not address the issue of racial discrimination.

44. Although the lender role in defaults has been recognized in the literature, none of the studies reviewed in Quercia and Stegman (1993) examined defaults with a simultaneous equations model of borrower and lender behavior.

45. Siskin and Cuppingood (chapter 16, this volume) found that many rejected black applicants would have been accepted if debt and income ratio calculations had been done the same way for them as for whites.

46. I am grateful to Stephen Ross for suggesting the framework presented in this and the following paragraph.

47. Alternatively, to provide information on P_2 and P_3 as well as on P_1, the entire set of probabilities could be estimated simultaneously with, for example, a nested logit analysis.

48. Although the term *statistical discrimination* did not appear in the lending literature until the mid-1980s, the concept was discussed by Canner (1981) and Barth et al. (1983), and can be seen as an application of the theory of rational credit rationing as developed by Stiglitz and Weiss (1981). For a more recent discussion of the concept, see Shear and Yezer (1985).

49. As indicated earlier, however, these studies may all be subject to bias from omitted credit history and other variables.

50. Barth et al. (1983) pointed out that a law prohibiting behavior that is, in a narrow sense, economically rational may impose economic costs on some groups. Such costs are a small price to pay for equal treatment of all citizens.

51. Half of the home loans originated or purchased in 1990 were sold that year on the secondary market (Canner and Gabriel 1992: 267). Adding 1990 loans sold in later years and loans sold by the small mortgage companies that were not covered in the 1990 HMDA data would bring this share well over 50 percent.

52. This implies that the secondary-market criteria play a crucial role in providing credit for minorities. Moreover, these criteria themselves are discriminatory if they include factors that are not related to loan returns but are correlated with minority status.

53. See ICF (1991).

54. Galster (1992) also pointed out that classical price discrimination could be at work in the mortgage market if lenders believe that, because of discrimination by other lenders, minority applicants have fewer options. This theory might explain why minority applicants are offered worse terms (see upcoming subsection on "Discrimination in Loan Terms"), but it cannot explain why minorities are more likely to be denied loans.

55. Shear and Yezer (1985) pointed out that lenders who operate principally in a prejudiced white community also may want to preserve their reputation with their potential clients by discriminating against minorities. They also suggested, however, that this incentive is likely to be weak because most people do not know who gave their neighbors a loan.

56. The low down-payment requirements also cause a problem because they make default more likely. When combined with poor appraisal practices and aggressive foreclosure policies, this requirement has sometimes led to severe neighborhood deterioration. One study found a neighborhood in Chicago, for example, where 85 percent of the single-family homes sold between 1970 and 1975 received FHA mortgages and by the end of 1976 "over 12% of these homes were demolished or abandoned" (Bradford 1979: 329).

57. Preliminary results of this type using 1990 HMDA data are presented by Gabriel (chapter 5, this volume).

58. Anthony Yezer pointed out to me that this argument is not so clearcut today because FHA loans often have such high LTV ratios that they are no longer comparable to conventional loans.

59. Another important actor is the homebuyer. Little is known about homebuyers' behavior in the loan market. For example, little is known about how minority homebuyers respond to actual and anticipated discrimination in mortage markets. Wienk (1992) argued that blacks may not apply for mortgages because they expect to encounter discrimination. He offered some evidence in support of this argument from the 1983 Survey of Consumer Finances (footnote, p. 230), but no careful study of the topic exists. A simulation model by Yinger (1995: chap. 6) showed that discrimination in housing and mortgage markets can induce significant behavioral responses from minority households.

60. These differences are found to be statistically significant using a logit model with fixed effects. This procedure was described in Yinger (1993).

61. This is a conservative methodology. It assumes that the control variables capture valid reasons other than race or ethnicity for differences between appraisals and market values, but it does not test this assumption. If this assumption is wrong, then following the logic of the previous subsection titled, "Are Control Variables Related to Loan Returns?" some of the "control" variables themselves may capture discrimination.

62. Another question one might ask is whether the existence of secondary mortgage markets expands credit opportunities for minorities. For a discussion of this issue, see Van Order (chapter 11, this volume).

References

Ashenfelter, Orley, and Ronald Oaxaca. 1987. "The Economics of Discrimination: Economists Enter the Courtroom." *American Economic Review* 77 (May): 321–25.

Associated Press, The. 1993. "Court Rules Fleet Loans Were Unethical, Not Illegal." *Syracuse Herald-Journal*, June 15: B8.

Ayres, Robert B., and Siegelman, Mark S. 1995. "Race and Gender Discrimination in Bargaining for a New Car." *American Economic Review* 85 (June): 304–21.

Barth, James R., Joseph J. Cordes, and Anthony M.J. Yezer. 1979. "Financial Institution Regulations, Redlining, and Mortgage Markets." In *The Regulation of Financial Institutions*. Conference Series 21 (101–43). Melvin Village, N.H.: Federal Reserve Bank of Boston and National Science Foundation, October.

———. 1983. "An Analysis of Informational Restrictions on the Lending Decisions of Financial Institutions." *Economic Inquiry* 21 (July): 349–59.

Becker, Gary S. 1971 [1957]. *The Economics of Discrimination*, 2nd ed. Chicago: University of Chicago Press.

________. 1993. "The Evidence against Banks Doesn't Prove Bias." *Business Week*, April 19: 18.

Berkovec, James, Glenn Canner, Stuart Gabriel, and Timothy Hannan. 1994. "Race, Redlining, and Residential Mortgage Loan Performance" *Journal of Real Estate Finance and Economics* 9 (November): 263–94.

________. 1995. "Discrimination, Default, and Loss in FHA Mortgage Lending." Working Paper, Federal Reserve Board, Washington, D.C.

Black, Harold A., and Robert L. Schweitzer. 1985. "A Canonical Analysis of Mortgage Lending Terms: Testing for Lending Discrimination at a Commercial Bank." *Urban Studies 22*: 13–19.

Black, Harold A., Robert L. Schweitzer, and Lewis Mandell. 1978. "Discrimination in Mortgage Lending." *American Economic Review 68* (May): 186–91.

Bloom, David E., and Mark R. Killingsworth. 1983. "Pay Discrimination Research and Litigation: The Use of Regression." *Industrial Relations 21* (Fall): 318–39.

Bradbury, Katharine L., Karl E. Case, and Constance R. Dunham. 1989. "Geographic Patterns of Mortgage Lending in Boston, 1982–87." *New England Economic Review* (September/October): 3–30.

Bradford, Calvin. 1979. "Financing Home Ownership: The Federal Role in Neighborhood Decline." *Urban Affairs Quarterly* 14 (March): 313–35.

Brimelow, Peter. 1993. "Racism at Work? *National Review*, April 12: 42.

Brimelow, Peter, and Leslie Spencer. 1993. "The Hidden Clue." *Forbes*, January 4: 48.

Browne, Lynn E. 1993. "Boston Fed Study Shows Race Bias." Letter to the Editor. *Wall Street Journal*, September 21: A23.

Browne, Lynn E., and Geoffrey M.B. Tootell. 1995. "Mortgage Lending in Boston—A Response to the Critics." *New England Economic Review* (September/October): 53–78.

Cain, Glen G. 1986. "The Economic Analysis of Labor Market Discrimination: A Survey," In *Handbook of Labor Economics*, volume 1, edited by O. Ashenfelter and R. Layard (693–785). New York: Elsevier Science Publishers.

Canner, Glenn B. 1981. "Redlining and Mortgage Lending Patterns." In *Research in Urban Economics*, edited by J. V. Henderson. Greenwich, CT: JAI Press, pp. 67–101.

Canner, Glenn B., and Stuart A. Gabriel. 1992. "Market Segmentation and Lender Specialization in the Primary and Secondary Mortgage Markets." *Housing Policy Debate 3* (2): 241–329.

Canner, Glenn B., Stuart A. Gabriel, and J. Michael Woolley. 1991. "Race, Default Risk, and Mortgage Lending: A Study of the FHA and

Conventional Loan Markets." *Southern Economic Journal* 58 (July): 249–62.

Capozza, Dennis R. 1994. "Comments on 'Race, Redlining, and Residential Mortgage Loan Performance.'" *Journal of Real Estate Finance and Economics* 9 (November): 295–98.

Carr, James H., and Isaac F. Megbolugbe. 1993. "The Federal Reserve Bank of Boston Study of Mortgage Lending Revisited." *Journal of Housing Research* 4 (2): 277–313.

Duca, John V., and Stuart S. Rosenthal. 1994. "Borrowing Constraints and Access to Owner-Occupied Housing." *Regional Science and Urban Economics* 24 (June): 301–22.

Feins, Judith D., Rachel G. Bratt, and Robert Hollister. 1981. *Final Report of a Study of Racial Discrimination in the Boston Housing Market*. Cambridge, Mass.: Abt Associates.

Gabriel, Stuart A. and Stuart S. Rosenthal. 1991. "Credit Rationing, Race, and the Mortgage Market." *Journal of Urban Economics* 29 (May): 371–79.

Galster, George C. 1992. "Research on Discrimination in the Housing and Mortgage Markets: Assessment and Future Directions." *Housing Policy Debate* 3 (2): 639–83.

———. 1993a. "The Facts of Lending Discrimination Cannot Be Argued Away by Examining Default Rates." *Housing Policy Debate* 4 (1): 141–46.

———. 1993b. "Use of Testers in Investigating Discrimination in Mortgage Lending and Insurance." In *Clear and Convincing Evidence: Measurement of Discrimination in America*, edited by M. Fix and R. Struyk (287–334). Washington, D.C.: Urban Institute Press.

Glennon, Dennis, and Mitchell Stengel. 1994. "An Evaluation of the Federal Reserve Bank of Boston's Study of Racial Discrimination in Mortgage Lending." Economic and Policy Analysis Working Paper 94-2. Washington, D.C.: Comptroller of the Currency.

Greene, Vernon L., Mary E. Lovely, and Jan I. Ondrich. 1993. "Do Community-Based Long-Term Care Services Reduce Nursing Home Use?" *Journal of Human Resources* 28 (Spring): 297–317.

Horne, David K. 1994. "Evaluating the Role of Race in Mortgage Lending." *FDIC Banking Review* 7 (Spring/Summer): 1–15.

ICF, Inc. 1991. *The Secondary Market and Community Lending through Lenders' Eyes*. Report prepared for Federal Home Loan Mortgage Corp. Fairfax, Va.: Author, February.

Karr, Albert R. 1995. "Study by Fed Challenges the Contention of Minority Bias in Mortgage Lending." *Wall Street Journal*, January 26: A2.

Killingsworth, Mark R. 1993. "Analyzing Employment Discrimination: From the Seminar Room to the Courtroom." *American Economic Review* 83 (May): 67–72.

Kim, Sunwoong, and Gregory D. Squires. 1995. "Lender Characteristics and Racial Disparities in Home Loan Rejection Rates." *Journal of Housing Research* 6 (1): 99–114.

King, Thomas A. 1980. "Discrimination in Mortgage Lending: A Study of Three Cities." Federal Home Loan Bank Board Working Paper 91. Washington, D.C.: Federal Home Loan Bank Board, February.

Kohn, Ernest. 1993. "The New York State Banking Study: Research on Mortgage Discrimination." Paper presented at conference on "Home Mortgage Lending and Discrimination: Research and Enforcement," sponsored by U.S. Department of Housing and Urban Development, May 18–19, Washington, D.C.

Liebowitz, Stanley. 1993. "A Study that Deserves No Credit." Op. Ed. *Wall Street Journal* September 1: A14.

Maddala, G.S., and Robert P. Trost. 1982. "On Measuring Discrimination in Loan Markets." *Housing Finance Review* 1: 245–68.

Munnell, Alicia H., Lynn E. Browne, James McEneaney, and Geoffrey M.B. Tootell. 1992. "Mortgage Lending in Boston: Interpreting HMDA Data." Federal Reserve Bank of Boston, Working Paper 92-07. Boston: Federal Reserve Bank of Boston, October.

Munnell, Alicia H., Geoffrey M.B. Tootell, Lynn E. Browne, and James McEneaney. 1993. "Is Discrimination Racial or Geographic?" Photocopy. Federal Reserve Bank of Boston.

________. 1996. "Mortgage Lending in Boston: Interpreting HMDA Data." *American Economic Review*. Forthcoming.

Nakamura, Leonard. 1993. "Loan Screening within and outside of Customer Relations." Photocopy, March. Federal Reserve Bank of Philadelphia.

Peterson, Richard L. 1981. "An Investigation of Sex Discrimination in Commercial Banks' Direct Consumer Lending." *Bell Journal of Economics* 12 (Autumn): 547–61.

Quercia, Roberto G., and Michael A. Stegman. 1992. "Residential Mortgage Default: A Review of the Literature." *Journal of Housing Research* 3 (2): 341–79.

Roberts, Paul Craig. 1993. "Banks in the Line of Fire." *Washington Times*, March 12: F1.

Ross, Stephen. 1995. "Mortgage Lending Discrimination and Racial Differences in Loan Performance." Working Paper 95-131, Department of Economics. Storrs: University of Connecticut.

Schafer, Robert, and Helen F. Ladd. 1981. *Discrimination in Mortgage Lending*. Cambridge, Mass.: MIT Press.

Schill, Michael H., and Susan M. Wachter. 1993. "A Tale of Two Cities: Racial and Ethnic Geographic Disparities in Home Mortgage Lending in Boston and Philadelphia." *Journal of Housing Research* 4 (2): 245–75.

Seiberg, Jaret. 1995. "Fed Study Challenges Claims of Loan Bias." *American Banker*, January 25: 1, 3.

Shear, William B., and Anthony M.J. Yezer. 1985. "Discrimination in Urban Housing Finance: An Empirical Study across Cities." *Land Economics* 61 (August): 292–302.

Stiglitz, Joseph, and Andrew Weiss. 1981. "Credit Rationing in Markets with Imperfect Information." *American Economic Review* 71 (June): 393–410.

Tisdale, William R., Shanna L. Smith, and Cathy Cloud. 1994. "Discrimination in the Homeowners Insurance Industry." Testimony of the National Fair Housing Alliance before the U.S. Senate Committee on Banking, Housing, and Urban Affairs, May 11.

Tootell, Geoffrey. 1993. "Defaults, Denials, and Discrimination in Mortgage Lending." *New England Economic Review* (September/October): 45–51.

Turner, James P. 1993. "Statement Concerning Mortgage Lending Discrimination." Testimony before the U.S. Senate Committee on Banking, Housing, and Urban Affairs, February 24.

Van Order, Robert, Ann-Margaret Westin, and Peter Zorn. 1993. "Effects of the Racial Composition of Neighborhoods on Default, and Implications for Racial Discrimination in Mortgage Markets." Paper presented at meetings of American Economics Association, Jan. 8, Anaheim, Calif.

Wienk, Ronald E. 1992. "Discrimination in Urban Credit Markets: What We Don't Know and Why We Don't Know It." *Housing Policy Debate* 3 (2): 217–40.

Yezer, Anthony M.J., Robert F. Phillips, and Robert P. Trost. 1994. "Bias in Estimates of Discrimination and Default in Mortgage Lending: The Effects of Simultaneity and Self-Selection." *Journal of Real Estate Finance and Economics* 9 (3 November): 197–216.

Yinger, John. 1986. "Measuring Discrimination with Fair Housing Audits: Caught in the Act." *American Economic Review* 76 (December): 881–93.

———. 1991. "Housing Discrimination Study: Incidence and Severity of Unfavorable Treatment." Washington, D.C.: U.S. Department of Housing and Urban Development.

———. 1993. "Access Denied, Access Constrained: Results and Implications of the 1989 Housing Discrimination in Study." In *Clear and Convincing Evidence: Testing for Discrimination in America*, edited by M. Fix and R. Struyk (69–112). Washington, D.C.: Urban Institute Press.

———. 1995. *Closed Doors, Opportunities Lost: The Continuing Costs of Housing Discrimination*. New York: Russell Sage Foundation.

Zandi, Mark. 1993. "Boston Fed's Bias Study Was Deeply Flawed." *American Banker*. August 19: 13.

Chapter Three

ACCOUNTING FOR RACIAL DIFFERENCES IN HOUSING CREDIT MARKETS

Robert B. Avery, Patricia E. Beeson, and Mark S. Sniderman

Despite the passage of several laws related specifically to racial differences in housing credit availability, data constraints have limited the number of studies of this issue.[1] Most existing studies use census-tract-level or lender-level data collected under the Home Mortgage Disclosure Act (HMDA) to infer racial differences. Although findings from such work are by necessity indirect, there is a persistent inference of substantial differences in the availability of mortgage and other credit across racial groups. Unfortunately, most of this work has been hampered by the inability to separate the effects of the race of the applicant from the racial composition of the applicant's neighborhood. Studies that use detailed applicant level information to examine the direct effects on mortgage denial rates of both property location and the race of the applicant are rare.[2]

The release of individual application data combined with lender and neighborhood data as required by amendments to the HMDA in 1989, offers unprecedented new opportunities to examine the issue of the role of both neighborhood and individual race in credit availability. Early reports based on the post–1989 HMDA data document differences in denial rates on home mortgage credit applications by race and income of applicants, and by the average income and racial composition of neighborhoods (see Avery, Beeson, and Sniderman 1993a; Canner and Smith 1991, 1992). The extent to which objective lending criteria are responsible for these differences, as opposed to discrimination based on income, race, or neighborhood (redlining), has been the subject of much analysis and debate.

This chapter provides a more detailed documentation of racial and neighborhood differences in denial rates than has previously been available. For each of three loan products (home purchase, refinance, and home improvement), we use estimates from a fixed-effects linear probability model to decompose racial differences in application denial rates for the years 1990 and 1991 into five components reflecting the portion attributable to (1) economic characteristics of the applications reported in HMDA (income, loan amount, loan type, etc.); (2) overall denial rates of the lenders receiving the application; (3) the metropolitan statistical areas (MSAs); (4) census-tract locations of the property; and (5) an unexplained residual. We then compare these components across MSAs, across neighborhood types grouped by income and racial composition, across types of lenders, across the two sample years, for government-guaranteed and conventional loans, and for central city and suburban areas. We also compare racial differences in denial rates across applications grouped by predicted denial rates based on all factors except race.

Our objective in conducting this analysis is two-fold. First, we are interested in determining whether racial differences in credit approvals reflect activity in a small subset of markets or whether they are endemic to most markets. Although the media has paid significant attention to the issue of race and mortgage lending, preliminary studies using the HMDA data have been limited in scope, restricted either to individual cities or specific loan products. For example, in a study that has received wide publicity in the media (Munnell et al. 1992, 1996) the Federal Reserve Bank of Boston conducted an expanded survey of loan applications in the Boston area and concluded that even when controlling for an extensive list of individual applicant characteristics, black and Hispanic applicants were significantly more likely to be denied loans than were white applicants. This study, however, was limited to one loan product (home purchase loans), one city, and one year. Thus, it is not clear whether Munnell et al.'s (1992, 1996) conclusions can be generalized or are specific to certain areas. Second, as stated previously, we are interested in determining whether racial differences in lending stem from variations in applicant characteristics (other than race), differences in the neighborhoods in which properties are located, or racial differences that cannot be explained by these factors.

By way of preview, we find that denial rates for minority applicants are consistently higher than those for white applicants with otherwise identical attributes (as reported in the HMDA data) and who are applying for loans with the same lenders, and for properties located in the same neighborhoods. We also find significant neighborhood effects that differ across racial groups: blacks, in particular are more likely to apply for loans for properties in neighborhoods with higher denial rates, ceteris paribus, than are white applicants. On average, these neighborhood effects are less pronounced than are individual effects, although they are almost equal for home improvement loans.

We find a remarkable degree of consistency in these conclusions across geographic markets and loan products, indicating that the observed racial differences in denial rates are widespread and cannot be attributed to a small subset of markets. Although our analysis reveals substantial and consistent differences in denial rates related to the race of the applicant, even after controlling for a number of applicant characteristics, we emphasize that the HMDA data do not contain enough relevant information about the loan applications to draw any firm conclusions regarding the reasons behind these phenomena. These residual differences may be due to credit histories, employment histories, loan-to-value (LTV) ratios, other factors considered in the loan evaluation process that are not included in the HMDA file, or differential treatment based solely on the race of the applicant.

The remainder of this chapter is organized as follows. The next section presents a simple framework and empirical model for analysis. The third section provides a brief description of the HMDA data and summary sample statistics. The fourth section summarizes our results; and the final section contains concluding remarks.

FRAMEWORK AND EMPIRICAL MODEL

Consider the following simple, yet fairly general, framework in which to evaluate the empirical findings of this study. Assume that the risk of each loan application given all available ex-ante information can be expressed as a risk score, *RS*. Assume, further, that each lender decides to approve or deny an application based on a comparison of its risk score and the lender's maximum acceptable risk. If the risk score is above a cutoff, *c*, the loan is denied; otherwise the loan is accepted. Note that this abstracts from the issue of price by assuming either that lenders price all loans equally or, because of problems of moral hazard and adverse selection, that lenders have a maximum risk acceptable at any price.

This model of lender behavior is deterministic, but in reality, error is likely to enter the process. First, lenders may not know or use all available information in computing risk scores. In this case, *RS* would be their *estimate* of the applicant's risk given the information they use, and the loan-granting decision would still be made deterministically, but based on a different set of information. To a researcher attempting to quantify lender behavior, this case seems identical to the full information case (assuming the researcher has access to all information used by the lender). A second potential source of error is more relevant for this chapter. Lenders may use the risk score (or their own estimate) and behave deterministically, but an external researcher may only observe the lender's assessment of risk with error. That is, researchers may observe a set of instruments, X, for RS for which they believe:

$$RS = X'\beta + e, \tag{3.1}$$

where e is a stochastic error term. This implies that

$$\begin{aligned} \text{Denial} &= 1 \text{ if } X'\beta + e > c, \text{ and} \\ \text{Denial} &= 0 \text{ otherwise.} \end{aligned} \tag{3.2}$$

To an external researcher, who does not observe e, the evaluation process appears to be probabilistic.

If only the lender action (accept/deny), and not the risk score, is observed, estimation of the parameters in equation (3.1) requires assumptions about the error term, e. If the error in (3.1) is assumed to be uniform, then the probability that a loan application will be denied, given X, is proportional to $X'\beta$ plus a constant, and the parameters in (3.1) will be estimable from a linear probability model. If e is normal, then equation (3.2) gives rise to a probit probability model; and if e is double exponential, then (3.2) gives rise to a logistic probability model. Although the scaling of parameters depends critically on the model form, the relative magnitudes and signs of the parameters are likely to be robust with respect to the model form chosen.

Of particular interest for this chapter is the robustness (and interpretation) of racial shift factors that may appear in $X'\beta$. Racial shifts may appear for several reasons. First, race itself may be a predictor of future behavior and thus enter the risk score directly. This might occur, for example, because minorities face discrimination in labor markets and thus have more variable income. This would appear as different risk scores for otherwise equal applications of different racial groups, or as racial shifts in estimated β's. Note that for reasons of cost, lenders may choose to use estimates of RS rather than fully computing it. In this case, race might be an instrument for the variables they do not use.

Second, lenders may practice overt discrimination, and set a lower cutoff, c, for minorities. To an observer who looks only at the accept/deny process, this case would be observationally equivalent to the first case. Overt discrimination may also take the form of lenders (or a subset of lenders) randomly denying a fixed percentage of minorities. This also produces a racial shift.

Third, lenders may in fact not use race, and there may not be any racial shifts in the true risk scores. However, race may be correlated with the omitted variables in the error term, *e*, in equation (3.1). Minority applications could differ from others in the expectation of *e* given *X*. To the external researcher measuring *RS* with error, racial shifts would show up in the estimated β's, making this observationally equivalent to the first two cases, even though race is not used by lenders and does not enter *RS*. Note that the better that *X* is specified, the less this effect should matter.

One might also observe a combination of these effects. For example, only a subset of lenders might have lower risk thresholds for minority applications. In this instance, racial shifts would represent the average lender effect. Moreover, they would also imply consistent residual differences across lenders in overall denial rates (one would expect differences across lenders for other reasons, such as price or preferences for risk). One might also observe combinations of different racial cutoffs and variations in the expected values of the omitted variables, *e*. Again, a measured residual difference correlated with race would represent a combination of effects.

The important point to emphasize here is that each of these sources of racial shifts, with very different policy implications, is likely to produce observationally equivalent results. Moreover, the estimated shifts will be sensitive to the econometric model form chosen. Unfortunately, there is little other than computational convenience to argue for a particular form (we actually employ a linear probability model for this reason). Thus, despite the obvious value in quantifying racial shifts in denial functions, these estimates, regardless of what they are, will be incapable of distinguishing among competing causal models.

Empirical Model

Our empirical specification follows the framework just outlined. We assume that each mortgage application's risk can be represented as a function of the economic characteristics (such as income), neighborhood, market, lender, and race of the applicant. As noted previously, we have no basis on which to select a particular econometric model specification. However, the size of the data set dictates that, in practice, we assume a linear-probability model specification. We thus estimate a model in which the probability of a random loan application being denied is linear in the following terms:

$$\begin{aligned}\text{DENIAL}_{iMTL} = {} & \beta_A \text{AC}_i + \beta_R \text{RACE}_i + \beta_M \text{MSA}_M \\ & + \beta_T \text{TRACT}_T + \beta_L \text{LENDER}_L + e_{iMTL},\end{aligned} \tag{3.3}$$

where DENIAL is one if the *ith* application using the *Lth* lender in the *Mth* MSA and *Tth* census tract is denied, and zero otherwise. MSA, TRACT, and LENDER are dummy variables indicating, respectively, which MSA, census tract, and lender the application relates to, and e is a residual. AC is a vector of application characteristics, other than race, reported in the HMDA data, and RACE is a set of variables indicating the race of the applicant and coapplicant. The model is specified and estimated separately for *each* of three types of loan applications—home purchase, refinance, and home improvement—and for each of two years, 1990 and 1991.

We allow for a considerable degree of nonlinearity in the effects of individual characteristics, AC and RACE, in estimating equation (3.3).[3] Gender, marital status, owner occupancy, and federal loan guarantee (Federal Housing Administration [FHA] or U.S. Department of Veterans Affairs [VA]) are entered as dummy variables. Income and loan amount are entered as linear spline functions with seven knots each (dummies are used for small loan requests for home improvement loans), and the ratio of income-to-loan amount is entered as a series of six dummy variables. Moreover, a five-knot linear spline for income is interacted with marital status and FHA/VA loan status. FHA/VA status is also interacted with a five-knot linear spline of loan amount and the six dummy variables indicating ranges of values for the ratio of income-to-loan amount. Dummy variables for the month of the action date are included as a crude proxy for interest rates and other market conditions.[4] We also include dummy variables for six applicant and two co-applicant racial categories, and interactions between the racial dummies and FHA and VA loan variables and income.

DATA

All commercial banks, savings and loan associations, credit unions, and other mortgage lending institutions (primarily mortgage bankers) that have assets of more than $10 million, that receive at least one mortgage loan application, and that have an office in an MSA are required to report on *each* mortgage loan purchased and loan application made during the calendar year.[5] They must report the loan amount, the census tract of the property (if in an MSA), whether the property is owner-occupied, the purpose of the loan (home purchase, home improvement, or refinancing), loan guarantee (conventional, FHA, VA), action taken (loan approved and originated, application approved but withdrawn, application denied, or application withdrawn before approval), the race and gender of the loan applicant (and coapplicant, if any), and the income relied upon by the lending institution in making the loan decision.[6]

In total, 9,333 financial institutions filed HMDA reports for 1990 on 6,595,089 loans. In 1991, 9,366 institutions filed on 7,939,107 loans. Our analysis focuses on the 7,938,438 loan applications in the two years for one- to four-unit residential properties that were acted upon (denied or approved) by the lenders.[7] Of these, 4,072,158 were for home purchase loans, 2,216,810 were to refinance an existing mortgage loan, and 1,649,470 were for home improvement loans (generally second or third mortgages).[8] These applications were received by 8,745 separate institutions operating in 40,008 census tracts in all 341 of the MSAs defined as of 1990. For our analysis, we define lender at the MSA level; thus, an institution reporting applications for two different MSAs is treated as two different lenders. There are 23,248 such lenders in our sample.

Combined descriptive statistics for the applications reported for 1990 and 1991 under HMDA are presented in table 3.1. Statistics are given separately for home purchase, refinancing, and home improvement loan applications. Clearly, housing credit applicants are a select group of American families. Applicants' median income ($49,000) is substantially higher than the median income of families in MSAs ($37,918) as reported in the 1990 decennial census.[9] The racial composition of the study sample also appears to differ from that of all U.S. families. Blacks filed 7.4 percent of the HMDA applications for the three loan types, yet headed 11.4 percent of the MSA households and were 7.7 percent of the homeowners in the 1990 decennial census. Asian loan applicants (5.2 percent), however, were overrepresented compared with their numbers in the census (2.5 percent of MSA household heads and 2.2 percent of homeowners). The percentage of applicants who were white (81.9 percent) or Hispanic (7.5 percent) is approximately representative of their numbers (78.1 percent of household heads and 84.8 percent of homeowners for whites and 7.5 percent of household heads and 5.0 percent of homeowners for Hispanics).[10]

It is also apparent that denial rates differ substantially by race for all three types of loans (see table 3.2). Denial rates for black applicants are about twice as high as those for white applicants, and for Hispanic

Table 3.1 CHARACTERISTICS OF MORTGAGE APPLICATIONS, NATIONAL SAMPLE, 1990 AND 1991 HMDA

	Home Purchase			Refinance			Home Improvement		
	Percent Sample	Percent Loan$	Denial Rate	Percent Sample	Percent Loan$	Denial Rate	Percent Sample	Percent Loan$	Denial Rate
Race of Applicant									
Native American	.5%	.5%	20.2%	.5%	.5%	23.4%	.8%	.9%	25.8%
Asian (or Pacific Islander)	4.4	6.4	15.5	5.0	7.2	22.5	2.5	5.5	33.1
Black	6.1	4.7	29.2	4.1	3.3	31.6	10.4	5.9	46.1
Hispanic	6.4	6.2	23.2	6.6	6.5	29.1	7.1	6.2	40.0
White	81.9	81.2	13.6	82.9	81.4	16.1	78.4	80.7	22.2
Other	.7	1.0	20.2	.8	1.1	27.9	.7	1.0	36.6
Race of Co-applicant									
No Co-applicant	28.7	24.3	18.1	24.7	23.2	22.3	37.5	28.6	32.2
Same Race as Applicant	69.3	73.4	14.2	73.4	74.6	16.6	60.9	69.2	22.8
Different Race than Applicant	2.0	2.3	15.5	1.9	2.2	20.5	1.6	2.2	23.7
Income of Applicant									
Less than $25,000	13.2	5.4	29.0	8.1	3.2	26.5	24.6	10.5	36.2
$25,000 to $50,000	39.9	28.0	15.0	32.1	19.2	18.1	40.4	28.8	25.9
$50,000 to $75,000	24.5	26.0	11.5	28.2	24.9	15.8	21.0	25.0	20.2
$75,000 to $100,000	10.1	14.1	11.5	13.8	16.0	16.3	7.5	13.1	19.2
More than $100,000	12.3	26.6	12.4	17.8	36.7	19.3	6.5	22.5	15.7
Loan Request									
Less than $50,000[1]	25.0	7.8	23.9	23.3	6.1	17.0	46.0	9.0	28.1
$50,000 to $75,000[1]	21.8	13.7	12.9	18.9	10.0	14.4	29.4	20.0	27.2
$75,000 to $125,000[1]	29.9	29.6	11.0	26.7	22.6	15.8	13.5	19.9	22.1
More than $125,000[1]	23.3	48.9	13.9	31.2	61.2	23.1	11.1	51.1	21.9
Gender									
Male Applicant, Female Co-applicant	64.0	68.3	13.7	69.4	71.0	16.2	55.1	64.6	21.9
Female Applicant, Male Co-applicant	4.3	4.1	18.9	3.6	3.2	21.3	5.8	5.0	29.2
Male Applicant and Co-applicant	1.9	2.1	17.7	1.3	1.6	22.9	.9	1.1	32.2
Female Applicant and Co-applicant	1.3	1.2	19.8	1.0	.9	25.2	.8	.8	34.1
Single Male Applicant	16.9	15.6	18.9	13.4	14.1	23.6	19.6	16.0	31.3
Single Female Applicant	11.8	8.7	16.9	11.3	9.1	20.8	17.9	12.6	33.1
Owner-Occupied	93.6	94.6	15.3	92.1	93.0	17.8	96.5	95.4	26.3

Loan Type									
Conventional	74.7	82.3	15.5	96.3	97.9	18.1	94.9	97.1	25.6
FHA	20.1	13.8	14.4	2.7	1.5	17.3	5.0	2.6	41.8
VA	5.1	3.9	16.2	1.0	.6	15.0	.1	.3	16.5
FmHA	.02	.02	28.4	.0	.0	8.7	.0	.0	19.4
Lender Action									
Loan Denied	15.3	14.0		18.1	22.0		26.4	23.6	
Loan Accepted and Withdrawn	2.7	3.2		3.0	4.0		3.6	3.4	
Loan Originated	82.0	82.7		78.9	73.9		70.1	73.0	
Loan Kept by Originator (% of originations)	42.9	45.1		52.4	52.7		92.9	82.5	
Loan Sold to FNMA (% of originations)	15.2	15.2		17.1	15.3		2.1	5.8	
Loan Sold to GNMA (% of originations)	11.0	8.0		2.1	1.4		.2	.4	
Loan Sold to FHLMC (% of originations)	9.4	9.4		14.8	13.4		1.0	3.6	
Loan Sold Elsewhere (% of originations)	21.5	22.4		13.6	17.2		3.8	7.7	
Reasons for Denial (of Loans Denied)[2]									
No Reason Given	31.3	28.7		22.8	21.5		29.9	30.0	
Debt-to-Income Ratio	17.1	19.3		20.8	20.9		23.3	22.5	
Employment History	4.2	3.1		2.3	1.8		2.7	2.1	
Credit History	26.3	21.9		24.8	20.8		33.9	24.1	
Collateral	8.3	9.4		17.3	20.7		10.5	12.9	
Insufficient Cash	4.1	4.5		1.9	2.1		.8	1.3	
Unverifiable Information	2.9	4.2		3.7	4.6		2.2	3.8	
Application Incomplete	3.0	4.3		3.5	4.3		1.1	1.6	
Mortgage Insurance Denied	.9	1.0		.6	.6		.1	.1	
Other	14.5	17.5		17.4	19.0		11.2	17.6	
Memo Items:									
Median Income ($1,000s)		$48			$57			$39	
Median Loan Request ($1,000s)		$78			$86			$10	
Number of Loans		4,072,158			2,216,810			1,649,470	

[1]Loan categories for home improvement loans are 1) under $10,000, 2) $10,000–$25,000, 3) $25,000–$50,000, and 4) over $50,000.
[2]Up to three reasons for denial could be given, and answers were voluntary. Each category gives the percent of all denials that gave that reason as one of the three.
Source for all tables: Authors.

Table 3.2 CHARACTERISTICS OF MORTGAGE APPLICATIONS, BY RACE, NATIONAL SAMPLE, 1990 AND 1991 HMDA

	Home Purchase			Refinance			Home Improvement		
	Black	Hispanic	White	Black	Hispanic	White	Black	Hispanic	White
Income of Applicant									
Less than $25,000	23.8%	17.8%	12.4%	16.2%	10.2%	7.8%	43.3%	40.8%	21.2%
$25,000 to $50,000	44.9	41.4	40.2	36.3	38.8	32.2	38.9	35.7	41.5
$50,000 to $75,000	19.0	23.9	24.7	25.9	29.2	28.1	12.5	15.4	22.3
$75,000 to $100,000	6.4	8.1	10.2	11.5	10.8	13.7	3.4	4.8	8.0
More than $100,000	5.9	8.8	12.5	10.3	11.1	18.2	1.8	3.3	7.0
Loan Request									
Less than $50,000[1]	37.1	26.0	24.9	31.3	18.3	24.2	66.7	48.9	44.2
$50,000 to $75,000[1]	24.0	18.5	22.5	18.7	14.4	19.9	22.2	29.9	30.2
$75,000 to $125,000[1]	25.6	29.3	30.3	27.1	32.1	26.4	6.8	12.0	14.1
More than $125,000[1]	13.4	26.2	22.3	22.9	35.2	29.4	4.3	9.1	11.4
Gender									
Two Applicants	56.1	78.3	71.7	58.9	78.0	75.8	42.7	63.3	64.7
Single Male Applicant	20.5	13.7	16.9	16.5	10.9	13.5	23.9	19.9	19.1
Single Female Applicant	23.4	8.0	11.4	24.6	11.1	10.8	33.4	16.9	16.2
Owner-Occupied	94.5	93.2	93.8	88.2	90.6	92.5	96.2	95.4	96.7
Loan Type									
Conventional	50.6	70.0	76.0	92.1	96.4	96.3	89.4	92.6	95.8
FHA	38.4	26.5	18.9	5.7	3.1	2.7	10.5	7.3	4.0
VA	11.0	3.5	5.1	2.2	.6	1.0	.1	.1	.1

Lender Action									
Loan Denied	29.2	23.2	13.6	31.6	29.1	16.1	46.1	40.0	22.2
Loan Accepted and Withdrawn	2.8	3.1	2.6	5.7	4.6	2.6	4.2	3.6	3.4
Loan Originated	68.1	73.7	83.9	62.7	66.3	81.2	49.6	56.4	74.4
Loan Kept by Originator (% of originations)	35.5	45.2	43.0	54.6	48.7	53.0	94.9	92.3	93.0
Loan Sold to FNMA (% of originations)	9.5	11.3	15.7	14.9	17.0	17.1	1.4	1.8	2.1
Loan Sold to GNMA (% of originations)	21.1	13.9	10.5	4.8	2.4	2.0	.3	.3	.2
Loan Sold to FHLMC (% of originations)	5.7	11.0	9.3	12.1	20.5	14.1	.6	1.6	.9
Loan Sold Elsewhere (% of originations)	28.2	18.6	21.5	13.6	11.4	13.8	2.8	4.0	3.8
Reasons for Denial (of Loans Denied)[2]									
No Reason Given	27.7	31.2	31.8	24.0	18.9	22.8	27.0	35.1	29.4
Debt-to-Income Ratio	14.7	17.7	17.3	18.7	20.7	21.0	21.8	21.9	23.9
Employment History	3.3	3.5	4.5	1.4	2.0	2.5	2.2	2.7	2.9
Credit History	39.5	24.7	25.3	35.1	27.6	24.2	44.8	32.8	31.8
Collateral	5.5	9.5	8.6	14.4	21.0	17.1	7.5	7.9	11.7
Insufficient Cash	4.4	4.6	4.1	1.6	2.2	1.9	.4	.8	.9
Unverifiable Information	2.2	4.8	2.7	2.7	4.9	3.6	1.8	2.2	2.2
Application Incomplete	2.8	4.3	2.8	2.9	4.5	3.5	1.3	.8	1.1
Mortgage Insurance Denied	.7	1.0	.9	.4	.5	.6	.2	.1	.1
Other	11.2	15.1	14.6	13.8	16.6	17.6	7.9	14.8	11.3
Memo Items:									
Median Income ($1,000s)	$37	$44	$48	$48	$50	$57	$28	$30	$41
Median Loan Request ($1,000s)	$62	$83	$77	$74	$100	$83	$5	$10	$10

[1]Loan categories for home improvement loans are 1) under $10,000, 2) $10,000–$25,000, 3) $25,000–$50,000, 4) over $50,000.

[2]Up to three reasons for denial could be given, and answers were voluntary. Each category gives the percent of all denials that gave that reason as one of the three.

applicants the rate is about 50 percent higher than for whites. Other racial differences are also apparent, particularly with respect to black applicants. Black applicants are more likely to be single and are more likely to apply for federally guaranteed loans. In addition, a larger portion of loans originated to black applicants is subsequently sold, and credit history is given as a reason for denial more often. Furthermore, whereas the median income and loan amounts for black applicants are considerably lower than those for white applicants, the ratio of the two is fairly similar. In contrast, the ratio of median loan amount to median income is consistently higher for Hispanic applicants than for the other two racial groups.

RESULTS

The parameter estimates for the denial rate regressions, equation (3.3), are reported in tables 3.3, 3.4, and 3.5.[11] To reduce the computing requirements, the actual estimation was done in two stages. In the first stage, equation (3.3) was estimated with the individual application characteristics (AC and RACE) and separate intercepts for *each* lender/census-tract combination included as single-component fixed effects.[12] The MSA, lender, and tract effects are thus intertwined in these intercepts. In the second stage, an iterative procedure (equivalent to regressing the fixed-effects intercepts against MSA, census tract, and lender dummies) was used to identify the MSA, tract, and lender effects. By construction, the MSA effects were normalized to have overall sample means of zero; and within each MSA, lender and tract means were normalized to zero. In cases where lender and tract effects were not identified (e.g., a lender was the only lender in a tract and did all of its business there), the effect was assigned to the tract.

A positive coefficient in the denial rate regressions can be interpreted as the expected increase in the probability that an applicant's loan will be denied, resulting from a one-unit increase in the independent variable, holding all other variables constant—specifically, the applicant's MSA, census tract, and lender. Thus, the coefficients on race, for example, represent the expected difference in the probability that a white applicant and a black applicant with the same income, gender, FHA/VA status, loan amount, MSA, census tract, and lender will have their loan applications denied. Thus interpreted, the estimated 1990 and 1991 black–white (0.104 and 0.106, respectively), Hispanic–white (0.038 and 0.052) and, to a lesser extent, the Native

Table 3.3 LINEAR PROBABILITY MODEL OF LOAN DENIAL (1) OR ACCEPTANCE (0), HOME PURCHASE

	1990		1991	
	Coefficient	Standard Error	Coefficient	Standard Error
Owner-occupied (Dummy)	.00649***	.00132	.00979***	.00136
Race (Dummies, "White" Is Base Group)				
Native American Applicant	.02636***	.00703	.04332***	.00685
Asian Applicant	.00171	.00472	.01180*	.00467
Black Applicant	.10385***	.00478	.10552***	.00474
Hispanic Applicant	.03841***	.00463	.05226***	.00461
Other Race Applicant	.03043***	.00432	.05425***	.00426
Mixed Race, Minority Co-applicant (Dummy)	.00764**	.00268	.00047	.00258
Mixed Race, Non-minority Co-applicant (Dummy)	−.02324***	.00294	−.03102***	.00286
Income, Interacted With Race				
Native American Applicant	−.00983***	.00034	−.01060***	.00037
Asian Applicant	−.00974***	.00034	−.01061***	.00037
Black Applicant	−.00986***	.00034	−.01074***	.00037
Hispanic Applicant	−.00981***	.00034	−.01068***	.00037
White Applicant	−.00983***	.00034	−.01065***	.00037
Other Race Applicant	−.00982***	.00034	−.01073***	.00037
Income Splines ($1,000's)				
Income Spline at $20,000	.00604***	.00038	.00644***	.00042
Income Spline at $40,000	.00283***	.00015	.00305***	.00015
Income Spline at $60,000	.00063***	.00015	.00033*	.00015
Income Spline at $80,000	.00013	.00017	.00062***	.00017
Income Spline at $100,000	.00012	.00014	.00002	.00014
Income Spline at $150,000	−.00003	.00010	.00006	.00010
Income Spline at $200,000	.00011	.00006	.00012*	.00006

(continued)

Table 3.3 LINEAR PROBABILITY MODEL OF LOAN DENIAL (1) OR ACCEPTANCE (0), HOME PURCHASE (*continued*)

	1990		1991	
	Coefficient	Standard Error	Coefficient	Standard Error
Loan Amount ($1,000's)				
Loan Amount	−.00191***	.00020	−.00213***	.00020
Loan Amount Spline at $20,000	.00027	.00027	.00104***	.00027
Loan Amount Spline at $40,000	.00179***	.00018	.00107***	.00018
Loan Amount Spline at $60,000	−.00019	.00016	.00037*	.00016
Loan Amount Spline at $80,000	.00038*	.00016	.00015	.00016
Loan Amount Spline at $100,000	−.00020	.00011	−.00024*	.00010
Loan Amount Spline at $150,000	.00022***	.00006	.00047***	.00006
Loan Amount Spline at $200,000	−.00029***	.00004	−.00059***	.00004
Loan-to-Income Ratio (Dummies, Less than 1.5 is Base Group)				
Ratio of 1.5 to 2.0	−.01012***	.00105	−.01661***	.00106
Ratio of 2.0 to 2.25	−.01158***	.00141	−.02318***	.00142
Ratio of 2.25 to 2.5	−.01176***	.00163	−.02301***	.00163
Ratio of 2.5 to 2.75	−.00713***	.00187	−.02103***	.00185
Ratio of 2.75 to 3.0	.00362	.00227	−.00979***	.00224
Ratio over 3.0	.05105***	.00207	.05014***	.00210
Applicant Gender (Dummies, Female Applicant, No Co-applicant Is Base Group)				
Male Applicant, Female Co-applicant	−.01875*	.00763	−.02737***	.00811
Female Applicant, Male Co-applicant	−.00726	.00772	−.00902	.00819
Male Applicant and Co-applicant	−.00354	.00787	−.00281	.00838
Female Applicant and Co-applicant	−.00984	.00800	.00750	.00845
Male Applicant, No Co-applicant	.02815***	.00109	.02549***	.00106
Income, Interacted With No Co-applicant				
Income	−.00332***	.00042	−.00409***	.00045
Income Spline at $20,000	.00514***	.00049	.00581***	.00052
Income Spline at $40,000	−.00051*	.00024	−.00059*	.00024
Income Spline at $60,000	−.00137***	.00030	−.00052	.00031
Income Spline at $80,000	.00049	.00036	.00028	.00037

Race and Marital Status, Interacted With VA Loan				
Native American Applicant	.05046*	.02211	−.05608**	.02089
Asian Applicant	.02433	.01766	−.00575	.01671
Black Applicant	−.00559	.01470	−.01431	.01470
Hispanic Applicant	−.00742	.01548	−.02767	.01527
White Applicant	−.01859	.01428	−.03088	.01436
Other Race Applicant	.02077	.02727	.01728*	.02360
No Co-applicant	−.00617*	.00311	−.01267***	.00276
Race and Marital Status, Interacted With FHA Loan				
Native American Applicant	.00605	.01708	−.01909	.01743
Asian Applicant	−.02650	.01490	−.04396	.01502
Black Applicant	−.01816	.01446	−.03974**	.01457
Hispanic Applicant	−.04093**	.01446	−.05980**	.01454
White Applicant	−.03139*	.01424	−.04720**	.01435
Other Race Applicant	−.01913	.01735	−.05510**	.01715
No Co-applicant	−.01235***	.00164	−.01477***	.00162
Income, Interacted with VA or FHA Loan				
Income	−.00171**	.00054	−.00117*	.00056
Income Spline at $20,000	.00297***	.00058	.00243***	.00060
Income Spline at $40,000	−.00033	.00024	−.00059*	.00024
Income Spline at $60,000	−.00130***	.00034	−.00018	.00032
Income Spline at $80,000	.00197***	.00052	.00070	.00048
Income Spline at $100,000	−.00158***	.00034	−.00125***	.00031
Loan Amount, Interacted With VA or FHA Loan				
Loan Amount	.00359***	.00053	.00399***	.00050
Loan Amount Spline at $20,000	−.00249***	.00069	−.00324***	.00068
Loan Amount Spline at $40,000	−.00230***	.00034	−.00156***	.00035
Loan Amount Spline at $60,000	.00067*	.00027	−.00015	.00027
Loan Amount Spline at $80,000	−.00043	.00027	−.00000	.00026
Loan Amount Spline at $100,000	.00058*	.00026	.00078**	.00024

(continued)

Table 3.3 LINEAR PROBABILITY MODEL OF LOAN DENIAL (1) OR ACCEPTANCE (0), HOME PURCHASE (*continued*)

	1990		1991	
	Coefficient	Standard Error	Coefficient	Standard Error
Loan-to-Income Ratio, Interacted With VA or FHA Loan				
Ratio of 1.5 to 2.0	−.00335	.00222	.00305	.00223
Ratio of 2.0 to 2.25	−.00521	.00299	.00351	.00299
Ratio of 2.25 to 2.5	−.00625	.00347	.00089	.00345
Ratio of 2.5 to 2.75	.00011	.00397	.00355	.00392
Ratio of 2.75 to 3.0	−.00476	.00475	−.00044	.00464
Ratio Over 3.0	−.00744	.00492	−.00935	.00484
Month of Decision (Dummies, December Is Base Group)				
January	.01867***	.00159	.03988***	.00154
February	.02085***	.00155	.03658***	.00152
March	.01328***	.00143	.03091***	.00140
April	.01376***	.00142	.03169***	.00135
May	.00954***	.00139	.01819***	.00131
June	.00382**	.00138	.00538***	.00130
July	.01062***	.00140	.02486***	.00133
August	.00796***	.00137	.01600***	.00132
September	.01078***	.00143	.01816***	.00137
October	.01498***	.00142	.01921***	.00136
November	.00740***	.00146	.00893***	.00140
Memo Items				
Number of Observations	1,984,688		2,087,470	
Mean Denial Rate in Regression Sample	.148		.157	
Number of Tract/Institution Dummies	607,631		662,571	
R Squared (Including Tract/Institution Dummies)	.457		.478	
R Squared (Variation around Tract/Institution Means)	.022		.025	

*Significant at the 5 percent levels.
**Significant at the 1 percent levels.
***[illegible]

Table 3.4 LINEAR PROBABILITY MODEL OF LOAN DENIAL (1) OR ACCEPTANCE (0), REFINANCE

	1990		1991	
	Coefficient	Standard Error	Coefficient	Standard Error
Owner-occupied (Dummy)	.00012	.00223	−.03180***	.00162
VA Loan (Dummy)	−.01603	.00979	−.00333	.00478
Race (Dummies, "White" Is Base Group)				
Native American Applicant	.02245	.01292	.04939***	.00857
Asian Applicant	.04053***	.00906	.02509***	.00562
Black Applicant	.06370***	.00915	.08023***	.00593
Hispanic Applicant	.04342***	.00879	.06279***	.00552
Other Race Applicant	.03812***	.00831	.07412***	.00520
Mixed Race, Minority Co-applicant (Dummy)	.00340	.00570	.00665	.00354
Mixed Race, Non-minority Co-applicant (Dummy)	−.02737***	.00630	−.03567***	.00381
Income, Interacted With Race				
Native American Applicant	.00131*	.00053	−.00475***	.00053
Asian Applicant	.00128*	.00053	−.00466***	.00053
Black Applicant	.00138**	.00053	−.00469***	.00053
Hispanic Applicant	.00135*	.00053	−.00476***	.00053
White Applicant	.00128*	.00053	−.00474***	.00053
Other Race Applicant	.00129*	.00053	−.00484***	.00053
Income Splines ($1,000's)				
Income Spline at $20,000	−.00419***	.00063	.00250***	.00060
Income Spline at $40,000	.00217***	.00028	.00150***	.00019
Income Spline at $60,000	−.00007	.00027	.00034*	.00016
Income Spline at $80,000	.00115***	.00031	.00020	.00018
Income Spline at $100,000	−.00035	.00024	.00009	.00015
Income Spline at $150,000	.00016	.00016	.00005	.00011
Income Spline at $200,000	−.00016	.00009	.00001	.00006

(continued)

Table 3.4 LINEAR PROBABILITY MODEL OF LOAN DENIAL (1) OR ACCEPTANCE (0), REFINANCE (*continued*)

	1990		1991	
	Coefficient	Standard Error	Coefficient	Standard Error
Loan Amount ($1,000's)				
Loan Amount	−.00338***	.00030	−.00122***	.00026
Loan Amount Spline at $20,000	.00281***	.00042	.00036	.00035
Loan Amount Spline at $40,000	.00080**	.00030	.00122***	.00020
Loan Amount Spline at $60,000	.00014	.00031	−.00021	.00018
Loan Amount Spline at $80,000	−.00009	.00031	.00043*	.00016
Loan Amount Spline at $100,000	.00011	.00021	.00009	.00012
Loan Amount Spline at $150,000	.00040***	.00011	.00125***	.00007
Loan Amount Spline at $200,000	−.00067***	.00006	−.00172***	.00004
Loan-to-Income Ratio (Dummies, Less than 1.5 is Base Group)				
Ratio of 1.5 to 2.0	−.00241	.00200	.00335**	.00120
Ratio of 2.0 to 2.25	.00433	.00266	.01505***	.00167
Ratio of 2.25 to 2.5	.00667*	.00301	.02254***	.00191
Ratio of 2.5 to 2.75	.01452***	.00324	.03102***	.00209
Ratio of 2.75 to 3.0	.02524***	.00375	.05599***	.00247
Ratio over 3.0	.08519***	.00326	.13278***	.00223
Applicant Gender (Dummies, Female Applicant, No Co-applicant Is Base Group)				
Male Applicant, Female Co-applicant	−.09152***	.01394	−.03405*	.01344
Female Applicant, Male Co-applicant	−.08392***	.01415	−.01847	.01354
Male Applicant and Co-applicant	−.06548***	.01466	.01502	.01384
Female Applicant and Co-applicant	−.08076***	.01512	.03541*	.01392
Male Applicant, No Co-applicant	.02499***	.00251	.03062***	.00163
Income, Interacted With No Co-applicant				
Income	−.00493***	.00080	−.00245***	.00074
Income Spline at $20,000	.00492***	.00100	.00253**	.00086
Income Spline at $40,000	.00078	.00055	.00086*	.00035
Income Spline at $60,000	−.00013	.00062	−.00045	.00039
Income Spline at $80,000	−.00059	.00068	.00072	.00045

Interactions With VA or FHA Loan				
Native American Applicant	.06556	.04937	.04740	.02902
Asian Applicant	.02625	.02657	.00366	.01586
Black Applicant	.11632***	.01851	.00897	.01150
Hispanic Applicant	.06928***	.01948	.00757	.01179
White Applicant	.08100***	.01268	.02499***	.00751
Other Race Applicant	.04074	.05014	−.01650	.03068
No Co-applicant	.00306	.00835	−.02022***	.00481
Income	.00005	.00009	.00017***	.00003
Loan Amount	−.00025	.00015	−.00010	.00009
Month of Decision (Dummies, December Is Base Group)				
January	−.02674***	.00299	.04361***	.00199
February	−.02489***	.00294	.04639***	.00186
March	−.02567***	.00280	.03852***	.00157
April	−.03137***	.00282	.01968***	.00146
May	−.02573***	.00284	.01591***	.00151
June	−.02640***	.00290	.01517***	.00161
July	−.01995***	.00290	.01479***	.00164
August	−.01890***	.00281	.02448***	.00171
September	.01829***	.00288	.03167***	.00168
October	−.00363	.00282	.02561***	.00148
November	.01590***	.00293	.01167***	.00140
Memo Items				
Number of Observations	716,595		1,500,215	
Mean Denial Rate in Regression Sample	.181		.181	
Number of Tract/Institution Dummies	326,536		563,380	
R Squared (Including Tract/Institution Dummies)	.552		.512	
R Squared (Variation around Tract/Institution Means)	.021		.039	

*Significant at the 5 percent levels.
**Significant at the 1 percent levels.
*** Significant at the .1 percent levels.

Table 3.5 LINEAR PROBABILITY MODEL OF LOAN DENIAL (1) OR ACCEPTANCE (0), HOME IMPROVEMENT

	1990		1991	
	Coefficient	Standard Error	Coefficient	Standard Error
Owner-occupied (Dummy)	−.00311	.00356	−.06323***	.00311
VA Loan (Dummy)	.23181***	.02285	−.11939***	.03181
Race (Dummies, "White" Is Base Group)				
Native American Applicant	.00376	.01285	−.04581**	.01387
Asian Applicant	.07089***	.01073	.09999***	.01071
Black Applicant	.08473***	.01008	.11062***	.01001
Hispanic Applicant	.07295***	.01060	.10532***	.01020
Other Race Applicant	.08060***	.00980	.06489***	.00946
Mixed Race, Minority Co-applicant (Dummy)	−.00124	.00602	−.00220	.00576
Mixed Race, Non-minority Co-applicant (Dummy)	−.04638***	.00701	−.07233***	.00655
Income, Interacted With Race				
Native American Applicant	−.00235***	.00039	−.00749***	.00042
Asian Applicant	−.00256***	.00038	−.00736***	.00039
Black Applicant	−.00258***	.00038	−.00739***	.00039
Hispanic Applicant	−.00274***	.00038	−.00744***	.00039
White Applicant	−.00256***	.00038	−.00728***	.00039
Other Race Applicant	−.00256***	.00040	−.00734***	.00040
Income Splines ($1,000's)				
Income Spline at $20,000	−.00124**	.00046	.00338***	.00047
Income Spline at $40,000	.00109***	.00024	.00121***	.00025
Income Spline at $60,000	.00217***	.00028	.00176***	.00028
Income Spline at $80,000	.00034	.00038	.00098**	.00037
Income Spline at $100,000	.00044	.00033	.00049	.00033
Income Spline at $150,000	−.00027	.00027	−.00076**	.00027
Income Spline at $200,000	.00002	.00016	.00023	.00016

Loan Amount ($1,000's)				
$1,000 or $2,000 Loan (Dummy)	−.02452***	.00275	−.02259***	.00276
$3,000 or $4,000 Loan (Dummy)	−.02099***	.00260	−.01357***	.00260
$5,000 or $6,000 Loan (Dummy)	.01104***	.00263	.01179***	.00260
$7,000 or $8,000 Loan (Dummy)	−.00100	.00302	.00873**	.00298
$9,000 or $10,000 Loan (Dummy)	.02937***	.00274	.02719***	.00272
Loan Amount Spline at $10,000	.00109***	.00021	−.00036	.00022
Loan Amount Spline at $25,000	.00089**	.00029	−.00021	.00030
Loan Amount Spline at $50,000	.00068***	.00018	.00130***	.00020
Loan Amount Spline at $100,000	.00007	.00024	−.00082***	.00023
Loan Amount Spline at $150,000	−.00011	.00038	.00189***	.00035
Loan Amount Spline at $200,000	−.00045	.00024	−.00179***	.00023
Loan-to-Income Ratio (Dummies, Less than 1.5 is Base Group)				
Ratio of 1.5 to 2.0	.01924***	.00405	.02399***	.00411
Ratio of 2.0 to 2.25	.04139***	.00663	.04586***	.00646
Ratio of 2.25 to 2.5	.02468**	.00921	.03351***	.00832
Ratio of 2.5 to 2.75	.04842***	.00893	.03972***	.00851
Ratio of 2.75 to 3.0	.08086***	.01259	.08290***	.01104
Ratio over 3.0	.03781***	.00620	.07892***	.00667
Applicant Gender (Dummies, Female Applicant, No Co-applicant Is Base Group)				
Male Applicant, Female Co-applicant	−.11149***	.00815	.01397	.00802
Female Applicant, Male Co-applicant	−.07509***	.00829	.06173***	.00816
Male Applicant and Co-applicant	−.04764***	.01018	.07199***	.00956
Female Applicant and Co-applicant	−.08031***	.01002	.06688***	.00961
Male Applicant, No Co-applicant	.03643***	.00196	.03618***	.00186
Income, Interacted With No Co-applicant				
Income	−.00472***	.00048	.00066	.00047
Income Spline at $20,000	.00430***	.00062	−.00111	.00062
Income Spline at $40,000	.00203***	.00045	.00203***	.00045
Income Spline at $60,000	−.00118	.00065	.00001	.00064
Income Spline at $80,000	−.00068	.00084	−.00196*	.00083
Income Spline at $100,000	.00026	.00047	.00033	.00047

(continued)

Table 3.5 LINEAR PROBABILITY MODEL OF LOAN DENIAL (1) OR ACCEPTANCE (0), HOME IMPROVEMENT (*continued*)

	1990		1991	
	Coefficient	Standard Error	Coefficient	Standard Error
Interactions With VA or FHA Loan				
Native American Applicant	−.08982*	.03697	.00094	.03303
Asian Applicant	−.11795***	.02371	−.10587***	.01796
Black Applicant	−.17913***	.01179	−.07636***	.00897
Hispanic Applicant	.12198***	.01368	−.08123***	.01177
White Applicant	−.09718***	.00898	−.00750	.00746
Other Race Applicant	−.05892	.04607	−.08987**	.03262
No Co-applicant	−.01994**	.00704	−.02748***	.00536
Income	.00029*	.00012	.00005	.00009
Loan Amount	.00111***	.00026	.00125***	.00023
Month of Decision (Dummies, December Is Base Group)				
January	−.00419***	.00341	.02959***	.00232
February	−.01345***	.00319	.03449***	.00316
March	−.02339***	.00291	.03268***	.00292
April	−.02735***	.00282	.01830***	.00277
May	−.03709***	.00276	.00513	.00276
June	−.03645***	.00278	.00391	.00280
July	−.02804***	.00282	.01010***	.00280
August	−.02454***	.00281	.00025	.00282
September	−.02145***	.00290	.00545	.00290
October	−.01238***	.00284	.01282***	.00285
November	.00227	.00296	.01298***	.00300
Memo Items				
Number of Observations	787,952		861,518	
Mean Denial Rate in Regression Sample	.238		.287	
Number of Tract/Institution Dummies	267,159		285,605	
R Squared (Including Tract/Institution Dummies)	.474		.477	
R Squared (Variation around Tract/Institution Means)	.029		.028	

*Significant at the 5 percent levels **Significant at the 1 percent levels *** Significant at the .1 percent levels

American–white (0.026 and 0.043) and other race–white (0.030 and 0.054) differences for conventional home purchase loans are quite significant. Differences are similar for 1990 and 1991 FHA loans (black–white, 0.117 and 0.113, respectively; Hispanic–white, 0.029 and 0.040; Native American–white, 0.064 and 0.071; and other race–white, 0.043 and 0.046). There is little residual difference between Asian and white denial rates on home purchase loans (0.002 and 0.012). Racial interactions with income appear to be small, with little impact on the overall gap between the races.

Significant racial differences also exist for denial rates on refinance and home improvement loan applications. Compared with home purchase applications, the 1990 and 1991 black–white difference is somewhat smaller for conventional refinance (0.064 and 0.080, respectively) and home improvement (0.085 and 0.111) loan applications. The same is true of the Native American–white differences. However, for Hispanic, Asian, and other race applicants, differences from white denial rates for refinance and home improvement applications are larger than for home purchase applications. Interestingly, whereas there is little residual difference between Asian and white denial rates on home purchase loan applications, the disparity is sizable for refinance (0.041 and 0.025, respectively) and home improvement (0.061 and 0.100) applications—comparable to the Hispanic–white differences.

There is some evidence that marital status may have some impact on denial rates. The denial rate difference between male-female couples and single applicants ranges from 0.019 to 0.053, respectively, when home purchase loans comparisons are made. The range in the gap is even wider for refinance loans (0.034 to 0.117) and home improvement loans (0.014 to 0.148). Interestingly, single males are 0.025 to 0.036 times more likely to be rejected than single female applicants.

The remainder of this section focuses on aggregate racial differences in denial rates. Gross denial rate differences are expressed as the sum of components representing differences in applicant characteristics (AC), neighborhood (TRACT), market (MSA), lender (LENDER), and an unexplained residual. In presenting figures for various applicant groups, components are averaged over all group members and expressed as percentages (by multiplying by 100) instead of fractions. By construction, these components must add up. Thus, for example, if 30 percent of an applicant group were denied, then the sum of the average AC, MSA, TRACT, and LENDER components and the average unexplained residual must equal 30 percent. Similarly, the difference in the percentage denial rates for two groups must equal the sum of the differences in their components.

Neighborhood, MSA, and lender effects are taken directly from the estimated components, TRACT, MSA, and LENDER. The component reflecting each applicant's economic characteristics, AC, is computed using the coefficients from equation (3.3), assuming his or her race is white. The unexplained residual is then computed for each applicant as the difference between the lender's action, DENIAL (1) or ACCEPT (O), and the predicted lender action based on the sum of AC, MSA, TRACT, and LENDER.[13] It should be remembered that MSA, TRACT, and LENDER are *normalized to have a mean of zero*. Since the applicant characteristics, AC, are formed assuming the applicant is white, these normalizations imply that the unexplained residual for white applicants will be approximately, but not exactly, zero due to nonrandom distributions of white applicants across tracts, lenders, and MSAs. In most cases, combined data from 1990 and 1991 are presented. In these cases, the combined data represent a weighted average for the two years, with the weight determined by the number of applications for that type of loan.

Racial Differences in Denial Rates—All Neighborhoods, Both Years

The average applicant, lender, MSA, neighborhood, and residual effects for black, Hispanic, Asian, Native American, other race, white, and total applicants are reported in column one of tables 3.6, 3.7, and 3.8. Because of the normalizations, these numbers by themselves are not particularly meaningful; it is the differences between the racial groups that are of interest. For home purchase and refinance loan applications, the unexplained residual comprises most of the racial differences in percentage denial rates. The residual accounts for two-thirds of the 15.6 percentage point difference between black and white percentage denial rates on home purchase loan applications, and somewhat more than one-half of the 15.5 percent difference for refinance applications. Whereas the Hispanic–white percentage denial rate differential is smaller (9.6 and 13.0 percentage points on home purchase and refinances, respectively), the residual still accounts for about four-tenths of the difference. The same is true for the other racial groups. Census-tract locations also contribute to the racial differences in percentage denial rates on home purchase and refinance applications, but the contribution is much less than the residual associated with the race of the applicant.

For home improvement loan applications, the picture is somewhat different. Whereas the residual still accounts for over a third of the difference, disparities in applicant characteristics (including lender and MSA) account for a sizable portion of the difference between white percentage denial rates and those for blacks and Hispanics. Moreover, census-tract location accounts for a large share of the black–white differential.

There are some other notable differences across the three types of loans. First, racial differences in percentage denial rates are least pronounced for refinance loan applications. Second, for black applicants, the home purchase residual is larger than the refinance and home improvement residuals, whereas the opposite is true for Hispanic and Asian applicants. Finally, although the Asian percentage denial rate is virtually indistinguishable from the white percentage denial rate on home purchase applications, there are significant and largely unexplained differences between Asian and white percentage denial rates for the other loan products.

Racial Differences in Denial Rates by Neighborhood Income and Racial Composition

We now examine racial differences in percentage denial rates within and across census tracts, grouped on the basis of average applicant income: high income (mean income of all applications for loans in the tract of more than $60,000), middle income (mean income between $40,000 and $60,000) and low income (mean income of less than $40,000); and racial composition: primarily white (tracts with less than 10 percent nonwhite applicants), mixed (10 to 30 percent nonwhite applicants), and primarily minority (more than 30 percent nonwhite). Percentage denial rates by neighborhood income and by neighborhood racial composition for black, Hispanic, Asian, and white applicants are given in columns 2–10 of tables 3.6, 3.7, and 3.8. We report the percentage of the applications, the actual percentage denial rate, the portion attributable to applicant characteristics, MSA, lender, census tract, and the unexplained residual, for black, Hispanic, Asian, Native American, white, and other race applicants, in each of the nine types of neighborhoods.

Tables 3.6, 3.7, and 3.8 reveal a remarkable persistence in the unexplained residual. Although the size of the residual varies somewhat across loan type and across tracts that differ in mean income and racial composition, it is always relatively large. For black applicants, the unexplained residual for home purchase loans ranges from 9.0 to

Table 3.6 DIFFERENCE IN AVERAGE PERCENTAGE DENIAL RATES ATTRIBUTABLE TO VARIOUS SOURCES, HOME PURCHASE LOANS, BY NEIGHBORHOOD AND RACE, 1990 AND 1991 HMDA

		High Income[1]			Middle Income[2]			Low Income[3]		
Home Purchase	Total	White[4]	Mixed[5]	Minority[6]	White[4]	Mixed[5]	Minority[6]	White[4]	Mixed[5]	Minority[6]
Black Applicants										
Percent of Blacks	100.0%	5.0%	9.5%	14.2%	5.8%	11.1%	19.7%	2.4%	7.2%	25.2%
Actual Denial Rate	29.2	23.3	24.5	24.1	27.2	28.2	28.0	34.2	35.5	34.5
Applicant Economic Characteristics	16.0	13.6	13.8	13.6	15.0	15.4	14.9	18.1	19.5	18.8
MSA Effect	−.3	−1.0	.2	−.4	−.7	−.3	.2	−.2	−.2	−.5
Overall Lender Effect	.2	.4	.2	−.3	.2	−.2	−.4	.5	2.1	.5
Census Tract Effect	2.4	−1.6	−.4	2.1	−.5	.9	3.7	1.4	1.7	5.0
Residual[7]	10.8	11.8	10.7	9.0	13.2	12.3	9.8	14.3	12.2	10.6
Hispanic Applicants										
Percent of Hispanics	100.0	4.7	16.0	25.8	3.8	9.2	22.9	1.2	2.7	13.7
Actual Denial Rate	23.2	17.9	21.1	21.6	21.5	22.8	23.6	25.0	28.0	29.3
Applicant Economic Characteristics	15.5	13.4	13.8	13.9	15.0	15.6	15.3	17.8	19.6	20.5
MSA Effect	2.0	.3	2.3	3.2	−.3	1.4	2.7	−.5	.0	.7
Overall Lender Effect	.0	1.5	.7	−.8	1.1	.3	−.9	.9	1.0	1.1
Census Tract Effect	1.5	−1.3	−.5	1.6	−.2	.9	2.8	.8	2.5	3.1
Residual[7]	4.1	3.9	4.7	3.7	5.9	4.5	3.7	6.0	4.7	3.9
Asian Applicants										
Percent of Asians	100.0	9.3	27.4	37.4	5.2	6.8	9.7	1.2	1.5	1.6
Actual Denial Rate	15.5	11.2	15.1	15.7	13.4	15.2	19.5	15.9	18.6	21.4
Applicant Economic Characteristics	13.7	12.8	13.3	13.6	13.7	14.0	14.0	16.8	17.8	17.6
MSA Effect	1.0	−.7	1.5	1.5	−1.0	.5	1.6	−1.3	−.3	.1
Overall Lender Effect	−.3	−.3	.1	−.5	−.8	−.7	−.4	−.6	−1.1	−.5
Census Tract Effect	−.1	−1.8	−1.3	.3	−.6	.3	2.9	.3	2.0	2.5
Residual[7]	1.2	1.1	1.6	.8	2.0	1.0	1.5	.6	.2	1.6
Native American Applicants										
Percent of Native Americans	100.0	17.0	21.3	10.0	18.1	10.1	6.0	7.8	5.3	4.3
Actual Denial Rate	20.2	14.1	17.7	22.3	18.0	21.4	26.5	24.5	28.5	32.1
Applicant Economic Characteristics	15.0	12.7	13.2	13.6	14.1	14.6	14.8	17.6	18.6	18.9
MSA Effect	.5	−.7	1.6	2.0	−.7	.7	2.1	−.4	.5	.7
Overall Lender Effect	.7	.1	.8	.9	.7	.2	−.3	.8	1.6	3.4
Census Tract Effect	.2	−1.5	−.9	.4	−.4	.4	2.9	1.5	2.1	4.4

Other Race Applicants										
Percent of Other	100.0%	15.9%	28.4%	16.9%	9.7%	9.9%	11.5%	2.5%	2.4%	2.8%
Actual Denial Rate	20.2	15.2	19.1	22.5	16.0	20.2	27.4	22.7	21.5	26.7
Applicant Economic Characteristics	14.4	13.2	13.9	14.2	13.9	14.7	15.7	17.0	18.3	18.6
MSA Effect	1.1	−.3	1.6	2.4	−.8	.6	2.6	−.9	−1.5	.5
Overall Lender Effect	.3	.3	.4	.7	.1	.1	.3	−.1	1.0	−.4
Census Tract Effect	.1	−1.7	−1.1	1.0	−.5	.9	2.5	.7	1.7	4.4
Residual[7]	4.2	3.8	4.3	4.3	3.6	4.0	3.1	6.1	2.3	3.7
White Applicants										
Percent of Whites	100.0	24.2	17.2	4.1	26.8	9.2	2.4	10.5	3.9	1.7
Actual Denial Rate	13.6	9.8	13.4	17.0	12.1	14.6	19.5	18.3	20.9	24.6
Applicant Economic Characteristics	14.1	12.6	13.2	13.5	14.0	14.3	14.3	17.3	18.1	18.0
MSA Effect	−.2	−.9	1.4	2.1	−1.2	.4	1.5	−.8	−.3	.6
Overall Lender Effect	−.0	−.4	−.1	.1	−.1	−.4	.3	.8	1.4	1.4
Census Tract Effect	−.3	−1.6	−1.0	.5	−.4	.5	2.6	1.0	1.9	4.3
Residual[7]	−.0	−.0	−.1	.8	−.1	−.2	.7	−.1	−.2	.4
Total Applicants										
Percent of Applicants	100.0	21.1	17.2	7.6	23.0	9.2	5.2	8.9	3.9	3.9
Actual Denial Rate	15.3	10.2	14.4	18.6	12.5	16.2	22.8	18.6	22.9	29.5
Applicant Economic Characteristics	14.3	12.7	13.2	13.6	14.0	14.5	14.7	17.3	18.4	18.9
MSA Effect	.0	−.8	1.4	1.9	−1.2	.4	1.6	−.8	−.2	.2
Overall Lender Effect	.0	−.4	.0	−.2	−.1	−.3	−.2	.8	1.4	.9
Census Tract Effect	.0	−1.6	−1.0	.9	−.4	.5	2.9	1.0	1.9	4.3
Residual[7]	1.0	.3	.7	2.4	.2	1.1	3.8	.2	1.5	5.2

[1]Tracts with mean applicant income of more than $60,000.
[2]Census Tracts with mean applicant income greater than $40,000 and less than or equal to $60,000.
[3]Census Tracts with mean applicant income of $40,000 or less.
[4]Census Tracts with less than 10 percent minority applicants (Native Americans, Asians, blacks, Hispanics, or other).
[5]Census Tracts with 10 percent or more and 30 percent or less applications from minority applicants.
[6]Census Tracts with more than 30 percent of all loan applications from minority applicants.
[7]The residual is defined as the average difference between the actual denial rate and the sum of the economic, MSA, tract, and lender effects.

Table 3.7 DIFFERENCE IN AVERAGE PERCENTAGE DENIAL RATES ATTRIBUTABLE TO VARIOUS SOURCES, REFINANCE LOANS, BY NEIGHBORHOOD AND RACE, 1990 AND 1991 HMDA

		High Income[1]			Middle Income[2]			Low Income[3]		
Home Purchase	Total	White[4]	Mixed[5]	Minority[6]	White[4]	Mixed[5]	Minority[6]	White[4]	Mixed[5]	Minority[6]
Black Applicants										
Percent of Blacks	100.0%	4.7%	11.2%	28.3%	4.0%	6.1%	26.5%	1.5%	3.2%	14.6%
Actual Denial Rate	31.6	25.8	30.4	30.7	27.5	30.0	32.7	31.5	31.8	36.2
Applicant Economic Characteristics	18.0	17.6	19.2	19.0	15.8	16.4	17.6	17.2	17.6	17.5
MSA Effect	.6	−.8	.8	1.3	−1.7	−.6	1.9	−2.2	−1.4	−1.1
Overall Lender Effect	.9	1.2	1.2	3.0	1.2	1.4	.2	.9	.7	2.7
Census Tract Effect	3.9	−2.1	−.7	3.2	.2	2.1	6.2	2.5	3.8	8.8
Residual[7]	8.2	10.0	9.8	7.0	11.7	10.6	6.9	13.2	10.5	8.0
Hispanic Applicants										
Percent of Hispanics	100.0	4.2	18.8	39.7	2.2	4.6	23.6	.5	.7	5.5
Actual Denial Rate	29.1	25.5	27.7	29.6	24.7	30.7	30.1	30.0	31.8	26.1
Applicant Economic Characteristics	18.8	18.3	19.4	19.5	15.2	16.6	14.7	16.1	16.7	18.0
MSA Effect	2.5	1.7	2.8	2.7	.9	4.4	3.2	.5	2.1	−2.4
Overall Lender Effect	.7	3.0	1.1	.0	3.2	2.5	.2	4.5	3.1	.8
Census Tract Effect	1.8	−2.1	−.7	2.0	.3	1.8	3.5	2.0	4.6	4.5
Residual[7]	5.4	4.6	5.2	5.5	4.9	5.4	5.6	6.2	5.2	5.2
Asian Applicants										
Percent of Asians	100.0	7.1	27.2	51.4	2.6	3.2	7.4	.4	.4	.5
Actual Denial Rate	22.5	18.9	23.5	22.0	15.9	22.1	27.9	21.4	26.2	31.3
Applicant Economic Characteristics	19.8	18.9	21.0	20.2	14.9	16.0	17.5	15.6	16.6	17.1
MSA Effect	−.3	−.3	.9	−1.2	−1.8	.6	1.4	−2.0	.1	1.4
Overall Lender Effect	−.4	.7	−.0	−1.1	.5	.4	−.0	1.0	.2	2.2
Census Tract Effect	.0	−2.8	−1.9	.4	.2	1.0	4.7	2.0	4.5	9.5
Residual[7]	3.5	2.5	3.5	3.5	2.3	3.8	4.2	4.3	5.0	1.6

Native American Applicants										
Percent of Native Americans	100.0	17.7	28.3	17.2	14.0	6.7	6.7	4.8	2.7	1.9
Actual Denial Rate	23.4	20.1	24.7	26.7	19.2	23.1	28.1	21.7	22.1	28.4
Applicant Economic Characteristics	18.1	17.5	19.5	19.4	14.7	15.7	17.6	15.9	16.4	17.4
MSA Effect	.8	−.1	1.7	1.3	−1.5	2.2	3.2	−1.9	−.9	.3
Overall Lender Effect	.4	.8	.6	.3	.6	1.2	−1.7	.2	.4	2.2
Census Tract Effect	.3	−2.2	−1.0	1.5	.2	1.2	4.7	2.1	3.4	4.9
Residual[7]	3.9	3.7	3.5	4.8	4.4	2.4	4.4	5.0	1.5	2.9
Other Race Applicants										
Percent of Other Race	100.0%	15.7%	34.5%	23.8%	7.2%	5.7%	9.0%	1.5%	1.0%	1.5%
Actual Denial Rate	27.9	23.3	28.3	30.2	19.2	28.3	33.8	24.3	31.1	40.5
Applicant Economic Characteristics	19.6	19.5	21.3	20.2	15.6	16.4	18.2	16.4	16.5	16.7
MSA Effect	1.2	.1	1.4	1.3	−1.3	1.7	3.8	−1.7	−.1	1.0
Overall Lender Effect	1.4	2.0	1.8	.9	1.2	2.1	.3	.1	2.1	3.4
Census Tract Effect	.1	−2.7	−1.6	1.3	−.0	1.6	4.7	1.8	5.5	10.9
Residual[7]	5.5	4.3	5.4	6.5	3.7	6.2	6.1	7.5	7.0	8.2
White Applicants										
Percent of Whites	100.0	26.9	22.8	7.4	23.7	6.5	2.6	7.3	1.9	1.1
Actual Denial Rate	16.1	14.1	19.4	21.7	12.2	17.6	24.4	14.5	19.2	24.2
Applicant Economic Characteristics	16.8	17.0	19.3	19.0	14.4	15.4	16.6	15.5	16.1	16.5
MSA Effect	−.2	−.6	1.5	1.6	−2.0	.9	2.9	−2.4	−.7	−.1
Overall Lender Effect	−.1	−.1	−.0	.1	−.2	−.1	.4	−.3	.1	1.2
Census Tract Effect	−.3	−2.3	−1.3	.9	.1	1.5	4.3	1.8	3.9	7.0
Residual[7]	−.0	.0	−.0	.1	−.0	−.2	.1	−.1	−.3	−.2
Total Applicants										
Percent of Applicants	100.0	23.3	22.4	12.8	20.2	6.1	5.3	6.2	1.8	1.9
Actual Denial Rate	18.1	14.5	20.5	24.4	12.5	19.0	28.4	14.8	20.6	28.6
Applicant Economic Characteristics	17.2	17.1	19.4	19.4	14.4	15.6	17.4	15.5	16.3	17.1
MSA Effect	.0	−.6	1.5	1.2	−2.0	1.1	2.7	−2.4	−.7	−.9
Overall Lender Effect	.0	.0	.1	−.1	−.2	.1	.3	−.3	.3	1.6
Census Tract Effect	.0	−2.3	−1.3	1.3	.1	1.6	4.5	1.9	4.0	7.1
Residual[7]	.9	.2	.8	2.6	.1	.7	3.5	.1	.8	3.5

[1] [2] [3] [4] [5] [6] [7] See notes for table 3.6.

Table 3.8 DIFFERENCE IN AVERAGE PERCENTAGE DENIAL RATES ATTRIBUTABLE TO VARIOUS SOURCES, HOME IMPROVEMENT LOANS, BY NEIGHBORHOOD AND RACE, 1990 AND 1991 HMDA

		High Income[1]			Middle Income[2]			Low Income[3]		
Home Improvement	Total	White[4]	Mixed[5]	Minority[6]	White[4]	Mixed[5]	Minority[6]	White[4]	Mixed[5]	Minority[6]
Black Applicants										
Percent of Blacks	100.0%	2.6%	4.4%	9.1%	3.9%	5.9%	17.3%	2.8%	5.6%	48.4%
Actual Denial Rate	46.1	32.3	37.5	45.5	33.3	39.4	47.0	37.0	41.6	50.4
Applicant Economic Characteristics	27.8	24.7	23.9	23.9	26.7	26.8	25.9	29.1	29.4	29.6
MSA Effect	1.3	.5	4.0	6.3	−3.8	−1.7	4.5	−5.1	−4.8	.8
Overall Lender Effect	2.4	.2	.9	3.1	1.2	1.2	2.2	1.5	2.0	2.9
Census Tract Effect	5.9	−3.7	−1.1	4.5	−1.9	1.3	6.4	.3	3.9	8.8
Residual[7]	8.8	10.7	9.8	7.8	11.0	11.6	8.0	11.2	10.9	8.3
Hispanic Applicants										
Percent of Hispanics	100.0	2.9	10.6	18.5	2.8	6.0	17.8	1.2	2.4	37.7
Actual Denial Rate	40.0	30.8	35.9	40.4	32.4	40.1	43.3	32.1	43.6	40.6
Applicant Economic Characteristics	27.8	22.7	22.4	23.1	25.4	25.5	26.1	27.7	28.0	33.4
MSA Effect	2.4	3.5	6.6	8.4	.3	4.5	6.1	−2.0	2.3	3.6
Overall Lender Effect	.7	.8	.9	.9	.8	.8	1.0	.8	.8	.3
Census Tract Effect	1.0	−3.0	−.8	.5	−1.5	.4	1.8	.3	5.0	1.7
Residual[7]	8.1	6.8	6.7	7.2	7.3	8.9	8.3	5.2	8.0	8.9
Asian Applicants										
Percent of Asians	100.0	6.7	25.1	44.6	4.3	1.4	9.1	1.5	1.5	2.1
Actual Denial Rate	33.1	26.4	33.8	31.5	28.8	34.0	40.4	32.1	40.7	50.9
Applicant Economic Characteristics	21.7	21.2	20.4	20.9	24.1	23.9	23.1	27.7	28.4	28.5
MSA Effect	3.5	2.4	6.3	2.9	−2.5	1.9	5.1	−3.8	−1.7	2.6
Overall Lender Effect	1.1	.4	.9	1.2	1.2	1.3	1.1	.5	1.3	2.3
Census Tract Effect	−.1	−3.2	−1.1	−.4	−1.6	.7	3.5	1.0	4.4	8.8
Residual[7]	7.0	5.7	7.2	6.9	7.5	5.8	7.6	6.7	7.9	8.7

Native American Applicants										
Percent of Native Americans	100.0	14.9	18.6	9.0	20.2	9.2	5.4	11.3	5.8	5.5
Actual Denial Rate	25.8	19.8	24.2	29.7	21.0	29.3	35.3	23.6	27.9	45.2
Applicant Economic Characteristics	24.4	22.0	21.2	21.7	24.5	24.4	24.6	27.1	27.7	29.2
MSA Effect	1.0	.7	6.0	7.3	−3.4	2.0	5.6	−4.6	−2.2	.0
Overall Lender Effect	−1.1	−.5	−1.6	−.1	−1.2	−.8	−.3	−1.5	−3.7	.7
Census Tract Effect	−.2	−3.4	−1.3	.6	−1.7	.9	3.6	.1	3.4	7.7
Residual[7]	1.8	.5	1.0	2.0	2.1	2.3	2.3	1.2	2.6	6.4
Other Race Applicants										
Percent of Other Race	100.0%	14.2%	24.4%	16.0%	12.9%	10.1%	9.1%	4.3%	2.9%	6.1%
Actual Denial Rate	36.6	29.3	35.1	40.0	30.8	37.2	45.2	31.3	37.1	52.6
Applicant Economic Characteristics	23.7	22.6	21.4	21.8	25.0	25.0	24.8	27.5	28.2	29.6
MSA Effect	3.3	1.5	5.8	6.6	−2.1	2.0	6.5	−2.4	−.0	2.7
Overall Lender Effect	2.5	2.1	2.3	3.0	2.6	2.6	2.0	1.4	2.3	3.5
Census Tract Effect	.3	−3.3	−1.6	1.2	−1.5	.3	5.3	.2	5.0	8.7
Residual[7]	6.8	6.4	7.1	7.5	6.6	7.5	6.5	4.3	1.6	8.1
White Applicants										
Percent of Whites	100.0	14.2	13.9	4.3	24.2	7.9	2.8	15.5	4.5	3.2
Actual Denial Rate	22.2	18.3	24.7	29.9	18.0	25.4	35.0	20.8	28.3	40.3
Applicant Economic Characteristics	24.0	22.0	21.1	21.7	24.4	24.3	24.4	27.0	27.5	28.1
MSA Effect	−.5	.8	5.8	7.0	−3.7	1.2	4.9	−5.5	−2.8	.3
Overall Lender Effect	−.4	−1.0	−.7	−.1	−.7	−.1	1.4	−.5	.5	3.3
Census Tract Effect	−.9	−3.5	−1.5	.6	−1.9	.5	4.3	−.1	3.4	7.5
Residual[7]	−.0	−.0	−.0	.4	−.0	−.4	.0	−.0	−.3	1.1
Total Applicants										
Percent of Applicants	100.0	11.8	11.7	7.0	23.3	7.5	5.6	12.7	4.4	10.3
Actual Denial Rate	26.4	18.8	26.3	34.4	18.6	27.7	41.1	21.4	30.8	45.4
Applicant Economic Characteristics	24.6	22.0	21.3	22.1	24.5	24.6	25.2	27.1	27.8	30.2
MSA Effect	.0	.9	5.8	6.5	−3.7	1.2	5.1	−5.5	−2.8	−.4
Overall Lender Effect	.0	−.9	−.4	.9	−.7	.1	1.5	−.5	.7	2.3
Census Tract Effect	.0	−3.5	−1.4	1.0	−1.9	.6	4.4	−.0	3.6	6.7
Residual[7]	1.7	.4	1.1	3.9	.3	1.4	4.9	.3	1.6	6.7

[1 2 3 4 5 6 7] See notes for table 3.6.

Table 3.9 DIFFERENCE IN AVERAGE PERCENTAGE DENIAL RATES ATTRIBUTABLE TO VARIOUS SOURCES, BY NEIGHBORHOOD AND RACE, 1990 HMDA

		High Income[1]			Middle Income[2]			Low Income[3]		
	Total	White[4]	Mixed[5]	Minority[6]	White[4]	Mixed[5]	Minority[6]	White[4]	Mixed[5]	Minority[6]
HOME PURCHASE										
Black Applicants										
Percent of Blacks	100.0%	4.8%	9.3%	14.6%	5.6%	10.5%	20.7%	2.4%	6.6%	25.5%
Actual Denial Rate	29.4	22.6	24.2	23.7	27.4	28.4	28.6	33.6	38.3	34.5
Census Tract Effect	2.4	−1.6	−.4	1.7	−.6	.9	3.4	1.2	2.5	5.3
Residual[7]	11.0	11.1	10.6	9.2	13.5	12.7	10.1	14.5	13.9	10.7
Hispanic Applicants										
Percent of Hispanics	100.0	4.4	15.7	27.2	3.6	8.8	23.8	1.1	2.5	12.9
Actual Denial Rate	22.1	17.3	19.2	19.6	20.9	21.9	22.1	25.4	28.8	30.9
Census Tract Effect	1.5	−1.4	−1.5	1.5	−.2	.8	2.6	.7	2.9	3.5
Residual[7]	3.7	4.1	4.1	3.3	5.6	4.2	3.2	6.3	5.1	3.3
White Applicants										
Percent of Whites	100.0	23.6	17.4	4.4	26.6	9.1	2.6	10.6	3.8	1.8
Actual Denial Rate	13.1	9.4	12.4	15.3	11.8	14.2	19.3	17.7	21.5	24.3
Census Tract Effect	−.3	−1.6	−1.0	.5	−.5	.4	2.6	.9	2.3	4.2
Residual[7]	−.0	−.1	−.2	.3	−.1	−.1	.5	−.1	.3	.8
REFINANCE										
Black Applicants										
Percent of Blacks	100.0	4.2	10.5	29.6	3.6	5.3	27.9	1.5	3.0	14.5
Actual Denial Rate	28.8	26.8	28.6	25.6	27.4	32.3	27.9	32.8	32.3	35.5
Census Tract Effect	3.4	−1.5	−.3	2.6	.7	2.0	5.0	2.5	3.6	7.6
Residual[7]	7.5	10.0	9.6	6.3	10.4	11.1	5.9	12.7	10.4	7.6

Hispanic Applicants										
Percent of Hispanics	100.0	3.3	17.3	42.8	1.7	3.7	24.9	.4	.7	5.1
Actual Denial Rate	25.6	24.6	23.8	25.1	25.3	29.4	26.2	.2	1.5	2.9
Census Tract Effect	1.6	−2.0	−.8	1.8	−.2	1.5	2.9	2.0	5.5	4.8
Residual[7]	4.8	5.6	4.7	4.8	5.4	5.5	4.5	10.1	7.3	4.6
White Applicants										
Percent of Whites	100.0	24.7	23.9	8.7	22.1	6.3	3.0	7.9	2.1	1.3
Actual Denial Rate	16.4	14.7	18.1	19.2	13.5	18.3	23.0	15.5	20.6	24.2
Census Tract Effect	−.4	−2.1	−1.2	.7	−.3	1.0	3.6	1.3	3.4	5.7
Residual[7]	−.1	−.1	−.1	.1	−.0	−.3	.6	−.1	−.4	−.3
HOME IMPROVEMENT										
Black Applicants										
Percent of Blacks	100.0%	2.9%	4.6%	9.0%	3.9%	6.0%	17.3%	2.8%	5.4%	48.0%
Actual Denial Rate	43.4	29.8	34.4	42.3	31.5	36.5	43.6	34.7	37.4	48.2
Census Tract Effect	6.3	−3.8	−1.0	5.1	−1.7	1.6	6.5	.2	3.6	9.7
Residual[7]	8.0	9.9	8.6	6.6	10.9	10.8	7.2	10.5	9.7	7.4
Hispanic Applicants										
Percent of Hispanics	100.0	3.7	13.0	22.1	3.5	7.2	20.1	1.6	2.9	25.8
Actual Denial Rate	35.4	27.8	31.0	32.5	30.5	36.5	38.3	29.3	40.8	39.1
Census Tract Effect	1.3	−3.5	−.9	.7	−1.2	.6	2.7	.3	4.7	2.9
Residual[7]	6.2	6.1	6.0	5.3	7.2	7.8	6.7	3.1	6.7	6.4
White Applicants										
Percent of Whites	100.0	19.9	14.0	4.4	28.2	7.8	2.9	15.3	4.4	3.2
Actual Denial Rate	20.3	16.6	20.9	25.6	16.9	23.3	32.4	19.7	26.7	38.4
Census Tract Effect	−.9	−3.5	−1.6	.8	−2.0	.6	4.4	−.3	3.6	7.9
Residual[7]	−.0	−.0	−.1	.6	−.1	−.4	−.0	−.0	−.3	.8

[1] [2] [3] [4] [5] [6] [7] See notes for table 3.6.

Table 3.10 DIFFERENCE IN AVERAGE PERCENTAGE DENIAL RATES ATTRIBUTABLE TO VARIOUS SOURCES, BY NEIGHBORHOOD AND RACE, 1991 HMDA

		High Income[1]			Middle Income[2]			Low Income[3]		
	Total	White[4]	Mixed[5]	Minority[6]	White[4]	Mixed[5]	Minority[6]	White[4]	Mixed[5]	Minority[6]
HOME PURCHASE										
Black Applicants										
Percent of Blacks	100.0%	5.1%	9.7%	13.8%	5.9%	11.8%	18.6%	2.4%	7.8%	24.8%
Actual Denial Rate	29.0	23.9	24.8	24.5	26.9	27.9	27.3	34.8	33.1	34.4
Census Tract Effect	2.4	−1.4	−.3	2.5	−.4	1.0	3.9	1.7	1.4	4.8
Residual[7]	10.6	12.4	10.8	8.9	12.8	11.9	9.4	14.1	10.8	10.5
Hispanic Applicants										
Percent of Hispanics	100.0	4.9	16.4	24.5	4.0	9.6	22.0	1.3	2.8	14.5
Actual Denial Rate	24.3	18.4	23.0	23.7	22.0	23.6	25.1	24.7	27.3	27.8
Census Tract Effect	1.5	−1.1	−.4	1.8	−.2	1.0	2.9	.9	2.3	2.7
Residual[7]	4.5	3.7	5.4	4.2	6.2	4.7	4.1	5.8	4.4	4.4
White Applicants										
Percent of Whites	100.0	24.8	17.0	3.7	27.0	9.2	2.2	10.3	4.0	1.7
Actual Denial Rate	14.0	10.2	14.3	18.9	12.5	15.0	19.8	18.8	20.4	24.9
Census Tract Effect	−.3	−1.6	−1.0	.6	−.4	.5	2.6	1.2	1.5	4.4
Residual[7]	−.0	−.0	−.1	.9	−.1	−.2	.8	−.1	.0	.3
REFINANCE										
Black Applicants										
Percent of Blacks	100.0	5.0	11.7	27.4	4.3	6.6	25.6	1.5	3.3	14.6
Actual Denial Rate	33.6	25.3	31.4	34.4	27.5	28.8	36.2	30.7	31.5	36.6
Census Tract Effect	4.4	−2.4	−.8	3.6	.3	2.3	7.0	2.2	4.7	10.0
Residual[7]	8.6	9.9	9.9	7.5	12.5	10.4	7.6	13.5	10.6	8.2

Hispanic Applicants										
Percent of Hispanics	100.0	4.8	19.7	37.9	2.6	5.2	22.9	.6	.8	5.7
Actual Denial Rate	31.3	25.8	29.8	32.7	24.5	31.2	33.9	27.2	28.6	24.8
Census Tract Effect	1.8	−2.3	−.7	2.1	.6	2.0	3.9	2.1	4.0	4.3
Residual[7]	5.7	4.2	5.4	5.9	4.8	5.3	6.2	4.5	4.0	5.6
White Applicants										
Percent of Whites	100.0	27.8	22.3	6.9	24.4	6.5	2.4	7.0	1.8	.9
Actual Denial Rate	16.0	13.8	20.0	23.2	11.7	17.4	25.2	14.0	18.4	24.2
Census Tract Effect	−.3	−2.4	−1.4	1.0	.3	1.8	4.8	2.1	4.2	7.5
Residual[7]	−.0	.0	−.0	.1	−.0	−.1	−.2	−.1	−.2	−.1
HOME IMPROVEMENT										
Black Applicants										
Percent of Blacks	100.0%	2.4%	4.1%	9.1%	3.9%	5.9%	17.4%	2.7%	5.8%	48.7%
Actual Denial Rate	48.6	35.1	40.7	48.3	34.9	42.0	50.1	39.2	45.1	52.4
Census Tract Effect	5.5	−3.9	−1.0	3.6	−1.9	1.2	6.4	.6	4.3	8.1
Residual[7]	9.6	11.5	11.1	8.8	11.1	12.4	8.7	11.8	11.8	9.0
Hispanic Applicants										
Percent of Hispanics	100.0	2.4	9.1	16.4	2.4	5.3	16.3	1.0	2.1	45.0
Actual Denial Rate	42.8	33.6	40.2	46.9	34.0	43.0	47.0	35.5	46.0	41.2
Census Tract Effect	.8	−2.5	−.6	.4	−1.6	.3	1.0	.4	4.4	1.3
Residual[7]	9.2	7.4	7.3	8.8	7.4	9.7	9.5	7.5	9.2	9.7
White Applicants										
Percent of Whites	100.0	19.0	13.9	4.2	28.6	8.0	2.7	15.8	4.7	3.2
Actual Denial Rate	24.0	19.9	28.2	34.1	19.2	27.4	37.7	21.9	29.8	42.2
Census Tract Effect	−.8	−3.5	−1.4	.5	−1.9	.4	4.2	.1	3.2	7.1
Residual[7]	.0	.0	−.0	.2	−.0	−.3	.2	−.0	−.3	1.4

[1 2 3 4 5 6 7] See notes for table 3.6.

Table 3.11 DIFFERENCE IN AVERAGE PERCENTAGE DENIAL RATES ATTRIBUTABLE TO VARIOUS SOURCES, CENTER CITY, BY NEIGHBORHOOD AND RACE, 1990 AND 1991 HMDA

		High Income[1]			Middle Income[2]			Low Income[3]		
	Total	White[4]	Mixed[5]	Minority[6]	White[4]	Mixed[5]	Minority[6]	White[4]	Mixed[5]	Minority[6]
HOME PURCHASE										
Black Applicants										
Percent of Blacks	100.0%	3.2%	5.5%	9.5%	4.0%	9.8%	22.5%	1.9%	7.3%	36.1%
Actual Denial Rate	31.2	25.3	29.0	28.2	27.8	28.2	29.1	31.5	34.9	34.5
Census Tract Effect	3.1	−1.8	−.2	3.1	−.8	.9	4.0	1.4	2.7	4.8
Residual[7]	11.0	12.9	12.8	9.5	13.9	12.4	9.8	13.5	12.5	10.6
Hispanic Applicants										
Percent of Hispanics	100.0	3.2	11.7	22.5	2.9	8.9	26.8	1.2	3.6	19.3
Actual Denial Rate	24.7	18.5	22.7	22.1	22.1	22.1	24.2	23.9	27.4	31.0
Census Tract Effect	2.2	−1.4	−.4	2.8	−.4	.6	2.9	.8	2.8	3.5
Residual[7]	4.1	3.8	5.5	3.6	6.2	4.5	3.8	6.0	4.4	3.8
White Applicants										
Percent of Whites	100.0	19.4	16.1	4.7	22.9	11.7	4.0	11.4	6.2	3.6
Actual Denial Rate	14.4	10.1	14.4	17.9	11.5	14.3	19.4	17.2	21.6	24.7
Census Tract Effect	−.1	−1.8	−.9	1.2	−.9	.4	2.8	.8	2.6	4.4
Residual[7]	−.0	−.0	−.2	.6	−.1	−.2	.6	−.1	−.2	.6
REFINANCE										
Black Applicants										
Percent of Blacks	100.0	2.6	7.7	25.4	2.3	4.8	32.0	1.0	3.1	21.1
Actual Denial Rate	32.8	26.3	31.9	30.8	27.8	31.6	32.6	32.0	34.6	37.1
Census Tract Effect	5.0	−2.8	−.8	3.5	−.1	2.0	6.2	3.1	4.8	9.1
Residual[7]	7.9	11.0	10.4	6.5	12.0	11.7	6.8	13.4	10.3	8.0
Hispanic Applicants										
Percent of Hispanics	100.0	3.2	17.1	38.5	1.7	4.9	25.4	.6	1.1	7.5
Actual Denial Rate	29.6	26.8	27.5	30.2	24.3	28.6	31.4	26.7	31.1	28.4
Census Tract Effect	2.9	−2.9	−.8	3.7	−.3	1.4	4.4	2.7	4.1	6.2
Residual[7]	5.3	5.8	4.9	5.2	4.8	4.8	5.9	5.4	5.2	5.3

White Applicants										
Percent of Whites	100.0	21.5	24.0	9.1	19.4	8.7	4.5	7.2	3.3	2.4
Actual Denial Rate	17.3	13.8	20.5	23.2	11.8	17.3	24.2	15.5	20.5	24.5
Census Tract Effect	−.0	−3.0	−1.4	2.1	−.2	1.3	4.7	2.3	4.6	7.2
Residual[7]	−.0	−.0	−.1	.3	−.0	−.2	.1	−.1	−.2	−.3
HOME IMPROVEMENT										
Black Applicants										
Percent of Blacks	100.0%	1.2%	2.5%	6.4%	1.8%	3.9%	17.8%	1.7%	4.8%	60.0%
Actual Denial Rate	47.7	31.1	39.1	45.0	32.8	40.1	46.5	38.1	44.6	50.5
Census Tract Effect	7.0	−3.7	−.8	4.3	−1.5	1.9	6.3	.5	5.6	8.9
Residual[7]	8.6	11.0	10.9	7.5	11.3	12.0	7.9	11.4	10.8	8.2
Hispanic Applicants										
Percent of Hispanics	100.0	1.9	9.0	16.5	2.0	6.6	21.3	1.3	3.4	37.9
Actual Denial Rate	41.6	32.2	36.2	42.8	35.3	38.1	42.7	32.5	42.7	43.3
Census Tract Effect	2.0	−3.9	−1.1	2.1	−1.2	−.3	2.2	1.0	5.3	3.1
Residual[7]	7.9	8.2	6.9	7.3	7.9	8.9	8.2	4.3	8.2	8.1
White Applicants										
Percent of Whites	100.0	13.8	13.3	4.8	21.9	10.2	4.7	16.2	8.0	7.0
Actual Denial Rate	24.5	17.2	25.5	32.0	17.8	24.8	35.2	23.3	30.4	41.5
Census Tract Effect	.3	−3.7	−1.5	1.8	−1.7	.2	4.6	.8	4.5	7.9
Residual[7]	.0	−.0	−.0	.6	−.1	−.4	.3	−.0	−.3	1.4

[1 2 3 4 5 6 7] See notes for table 3.6.

Table 3.12 DIFFERENCE IN AVERAGE PERCENTAGE DENIAL RATES ATTRIBUTABLE TO VARIOUS SOURCES, NON – CENTER CITY, BY NEIGHBORHOOD AND RACE, 1990 AND 1991 HMDA

		High Income[1]			Middle Income[2]			Low Income[3]		
	Total	White[4]	Mixed[5]	Minority[6]	White[4]	Mixed[5]	Minority[6]	White[4]	Mixed[5]	Minority[6]
HOME PURCHASE										
Black Applicants										
Percent of Blacks	100.0%	7.3%	14.8%	20.4%	8.1%	12.9%	15.9%	3.0%	7.1%	10.5%
Actual Denial Rate	26.5	22.1	22.3	21.5	26.8	28.1	26.0	36.5	36.2	34.2
Census Tract Effect	1.4	−1.4	−.5	1.4	−.3	.9	3.1	1.3	.4	5.9
Residual[7]	10.6	11.1	9.6	8.7	12.7	12.2	9.6	15.0	11.9	10.9
Hispanic Applicants										
Percent of Hispanics	100.0	6.2	20.6	29.4	4.7	9.6	18.8	1.2	1.8	7.8
Actual Denial Rate	21.6	17.5	20.2	20.7	21.1	23.4	22.7	26.3	29.1	24.7
Census Tract Effect	.8	−1.2	−.5	.6	−.0	1.2	2.5	.8	1.8	2.1
Residual[7]	4.1	3.9	4.3	3.8	5.7	4.5	3.5	6.0	5.3	4.1
White Applicants										
Percent of Whites	100.0	27.1	17.9	3.7	29.2	7.6	1.4	9.9	2.5	.6
Actual Denial Rate	13.1	9.6	12.8	16.3	12.5	14.9	19.7	19.0	20.0	24.4
Census Tract Effect	−.4	−1.5	−1.1	−.1	−.2	.6	2.3	1.2	.9	4.0
Residual[7]	−.0	−.0	−.0	.9	−.1	−.2	.9	−.1	−.2	−.0
REFINANCE										
Black Applicants										
Percent of Blacks	100.0	7.4	15.8	32.1	6.2	7.7	19.2	2.1	3.3	6.0
Actual Denial Rate	30.1	25.6	29.4	30.5	27.3	28.7	32.9	31.1	28.4	32.0
Census Tract Effect	2.6	−1.8	−.7	2.9	.4	2.1	6.2	2.1	2.7	7.1
Residual[7]	8.5	9.4	9.4	7.5	11.6	9.7	7.1	13.0	10.9	7.7
Hispanic Applicants										
Percent of Hispanics	100.0	5.0	20.0	40.6	2.6	4.4	22.3	.5	.5	4.0
Actual Denial Rate	28.8	24.9	27.9	29.1	25.0	32.4	30.5	31.9	33.1	22.8
Census Tract Effect	.9	−1.7	−.7	.8	.6	2.2	2.7	1.4	5.4	2.3
Residual[7]	5.4	4.1	5.4	5.7	5.0	5.8	5.3	6.9	5.0	5.1

White Applicants										
Percent of Whites	100.0	29.5	22.2	6.6	25.8	5.3	1.6	7.3	1.2	.4
Actual Denial Rate	15.6	14.2	18.7	20.8	12.3	17.9	24.7	14.0	17.3	23.2
Census Tract Effect	−.5	−2.1	−1.3	.1	.2	1.8	3.9	1.6	3.0	6.2
Residual[7]	−.0	.0	−.0	−.1	−.0	−.2	.1	−.1	−.3	.1
HOME IMPROVEMENT										
Black Applicants										
Percent of Blacks	100.0%	6.4%	9.2%	16.2%	9.4%	11.0%	16.2%	5.6%	7.7%	18.2%
Actual Denial Rate	42.0	32.9	36.5	45.9	33.6	38.7	48.7	36.2	36.7	49.0
Census Tract Effect	3.0	−3.7	−1.3	4.6	−2.0	.8	6.9	.1	1.1	8.5
Residual[7]	9.6	10.5	9.1	8.1	10.9	11.3	8.4	11.0	10.9	9.1
Hispanic Applicants										
Percent of Hispanics	100.0	3.8	12.1	20.5	3.6	5.5	14.4	1.2	1.5	37.5
Actual Denial Rate	38.5	30.2	35.7	38.5	30.8	42.3	44.1	32.1	45.7	38.1
Census Tract Effect	.1	−2.6	−.6	−.7	−1.7	1.3	1.2	−.3	4.2	.5
Residual[7]	8.2	6.1	6.5	7.1	7.0	8.8	8.4	6.1	7.5	9.5
White Applicants										
Percent of Whites	100.0	22.7	14.3	4.0	32.3	6.5	1.7	15.1	2.5	.9
Actual Denial Rate	20.8	18.7	24.2	28.4	18.1	26.0	34.8	19.3	24.4	35.1
Census Tract Effect	−1.5	−3.4	−1.5	−.2	2.0	.7	3.8	−.6	1.3	5.7
Residual[7]	−.0	−.0	−.1	.3	−.0	−.3	−.2	−.0	−.3	−.1

[1 2 3 4 5 6 7] See notes for table 3.6.

Table 3.13 DIFFERENCE IN AVERAGE PERCENTAGE DENIAL RATES ATTRIBUTABLE TO VARIOUS SOURCES, COMMERCIAL BANKS, BY NEIGHBORHOOD AND RACE, 1990 AND 1991 HMDA

		High Income[1]			Middle Income[2]			Low Income[3]		
	Total	White[4]	Mixed[5]	Minority[6]	White[4]	Mixed[5]	Minority[6]	White[4]	Mixed[5]	Minority[6]
HOME PURCHASE										
Black Applicants										
Percent of Blacks	100.0%	4.2%	6.5%	10.7%	6.6%	8.4%	19.9%	3.7%	8.4%	31.7%
Actual Denial Rate	37.2	26.2	32.3	37.4	32.2	36.9	37.0	40.3	40.0	39.8
Census Tract Effect	3.1	−1.8	−.6	3.1	−.2	1.4	4.0	2.3	2.5	5.6
Residual[7]	12.6	11.2	11.5	10.9	15.1	15.2	11.2	16.6	14.5	12.2
Hispanic Applicants										
Percent of Hispanics	100.0	4.3	12.5	21.0	4.4	7.6	20.2	2.0	3.4	24.6
Actual Denial Rate	32.5	24.6	32.9	31.6	28.9	33.5	34.8	33.9	37.6	32.2
Census Tract Effect	1.7	−1.2	−.3	1.5	.2	1.1	3.1	1.2	3.6	2.3
Residual[7]	7.5	6.4	8.7	7.2	10.0	9.1	8.3	11.0	8.3	5.2
White Applicants										
Percent of Whites	100.0	21.8	11.9	2.9	31.6	6.8	1.8	17.1	4.2	1.9
Actual Denial Rate	16.8	11.5	18.5	23.4	14.5	19.9	25.6	20.6	24.1	25.9
Census Tract Effect	−.1	−1.8	−1.2	.6	−.4	.6	3.0	1.4	2.6	4.8
Residual[7]	−.4	−1.1	−1.6	.3	−.2	.4	1.3	.3	.5	.1
REFINANCE										
Black Applicants										
Percent of Blacks	100.0	4.8	8.9	20.0	6.3	7.8	21.6	2.9	6.3	21.3
Actual Denial Rate	38.1	26.9	36.8	44.5	27.4	33.5	44.2	29.3	28.9	37.6
Census Tract Effect	4.3	−2.2	−.8	3.3	.2	2.2	6.1	1.8	3.4	9.6
Residual[7]	10.8	9.6	11.1	11.0	11.6	12.3	10.8	11.6	9.8	10.2
Hispanic Applicants										
Percent of Hispanics	100.0	4.2	17.9	33.7	2.9	5.5	21.8	1.0	1.2	11.8
Actual Denial Rate	34.8	32.4	34.7	35.9	27.4	38.8	38.6	29.6	36.9	26.1
Census Tract Effect	1.7	−1.8	−.9	1.4	.7	1.9	3.3	2.2	5.9	4.2
Residual[7]	7.3	9.8	6.0	6.6	8.8	9.4	8.3	8.9	8.3	6.5

White Applicants										
Percent of Whites	100.0	24.5	16.1	5.0	29.6	6.0	2.0	13.0	2.7	1.3
Actual Denial Rate	17.0	14.5	24.3	28.2	12.6	20.3	28.1	14.2	19.0	21.6
Census Tract Effect	−.3	−2.5	−1.6	.4	−.0	1.4	3.7	1.6	3.6	6.2
Residual[7]	−.3	−.5	−1.1	.1	.0	.1	.5	.0	.0	−.2
HOME IMPROVEMENT										
Black Applicants										
Percent of Blacks	100.0%	2.5%	4.0%	7.8%	3.8%	5.6%	15.9%	2.9%	5.8%	51.7%
Actual Denial Rate	46.8	34.4	40.2	48.6	35.0	40.3	47.3	37.4	41.1	50.2
Census Tract Effect	6.1	−4.1	−1.1	4.4	−1.9	1.4	6.5	.3	3.9	9.0
Residual[7]	9.6	11.1	10.7	8.9	12.2	12.1	8.8	12.1	11.8	9.0
Hispanic Applicants										
Percent of Hispanics	100.0	2.6	9.5	16.6	2.6	5.5	16.4	1.2	2.2	43.4
Actual Denial Rate	41.2	32.1	37.8	43.0	34.7	42.1	45.4	34.0	46.4	40.4
Census Tract Effect	1.0	−3.3	−.8	.6	−1.2	.7	1.8	.7	5.0	1.4
Residual[7]	8.6	6.2	6.9	7.6	7.5	9.9	9.3	5.4	8.2	9.2
White Applicants										
Percent of Whites	100.0	18.8	13.1	4.0	28.4	7.6	2.6	17.4	4.8	3.2
Actual Denial Rate	22.9	19.3	25.7	31.8	19.2	26.3	35.9	21.1	28.4	38.7
Census Tract Effect	−.9	−3.7	−1.5	.5	−2.0	.4	4.2	−.1	3.4	7.4
Residual[7]	−.1	−.3	−.5	.1	−.1	−.4	.2	−.0	−.3	1.2

1 2 3 4 5 6 7 See notes for table 3.6.

Table 3.14 DIFFERENCE IN AVERAGE PERCENTAGE DENIAL RATES ATTRIBUTABLE TO VARIOUS SOURCES, THRIFT INSTITUTIONS, BY NEIGHBORHOOD AND RACE, 1990 AND 1991 HMDA

		High Income[1]			Middle Income[2]			Low Income[3]		
	Total	White[4]	Mixed[5]	Minority[6]	White[4]	Mixed[5]	Minority[6]	White[4]	Mixed[5]	Minority[6]
HOME PURCHASE										
Black Applicants										
Percent of Blacks	100.0%	5.5%	12.3%	19.4%	5.9%	9.7%	20.8%	2.1%	6.2%	18.3%
Actual Denial Rate	28.1	23.2	26.5	23.4	24.8	27.7	26.7	30.9	45.6	32.5
Census Tract Effect	2.4	−1.6	−.4	2.0	−.3	1.0	4.0	1.4	2.8	5.4
Residual[7]	10.7	12.7	12.1	8.6	13.0	12.7	9.1	14.7	14.4	9.5
Hispanic Applicants										
Percent of Hispanics	100.0	4.6	17.6	35.2	3.1	6.4	25.4	.8	1.3	5.6
Actual Denial Rate	21.2	19.0	20.2	20.3	20.3	22.5	21.9	20.7	26.7	25.5
Census Tract Effect	1.6	−1.3	−.5	1.8	−.3	1.0	3.2	.8	3.1	3.9
Residual[7]	3.4	3.6	3.8	3.2	4.9	4.0	3.3	2.4	4.5	3.1
White Applicants										
Percent of Whites	100.0	24.6	20.5	5.6	27.3	7.6	2.5	8.2	2.6	1.1
Actual Denial Rate	11.8	8.8	12.6	15.5	10.0	13.1	18.0	15.0	21.4	23.1
Census Tract Effect	−.4	−1.6	−1.0	.6	−.4	.5	3.1	1.0	2.5	4.8
Residual[7]	.1	.0	.2	1.0	−.1	−.2	.7	.2	−.3	1.0
REFINANCE										
Black Applicants										
Percent of Blacks	100.0	3.6	10.9	35.4	2.5	4.0	32.0	.8	1.7	9.1
Actual Denial Rate	29.3	24.9	31.2	27.8	27.7	30.8	28.9	35.4	34.5	34.7
Census Tract Effect	4.0	−2.2	−.8	3.1	.6	2.5	6.0	3.0	5.8	9.3
Residual[7]	7.2	10.0	10.6	5.6	13.3	11.9	5.7	16.7	11.9	7.5
Hispanic Applicants										
Percent of Hispanics	100.0	3.8	17.6	43.4	1.9	3.8	26.1	.4	.4	2.6
Actual Denial Rate	29.7	26.1	29.0	29.6	26.8	32.8	30.3	33.7	35.3	29.1
Census Tract Effect	1.9	−2.2	−.7	2.1	.2	1.9	3.6	2.3	3.6	5.4
Residual[7]	5.3	2.6	5.5	5.6	3.5	5.0	5.4	5.7	5.0	4.2

White Applicants										
Percent of Whites	100.0	25.9	25.5	9.4	22.1	6.2	3.2	5.4	1.4	.9
Actual Denial Rate	16.2	13.5	20.0	21.6	11.1	18.0	24.5	13.8	20.2	24.9
Census Tract Effect	−.3	−2.2	−1.2	1.1	.1	1.7	4.6	2.1	4.4	7.2
Residual[7]	.0	.1	.2	.1	−.1	−.3	−.0	−.3	.2	−.8
HOME IMPROVEMENT										
Black Applicants										
Percent of Blacks	100.0%	5.1%	5.4%	13.6%	4.1%	5.6%	26.1%	2.3%	3.5%	36.4%
Actual Denial Rate	49.5	35.4	42.7	46.8	33.7	46.3	49.9	38.2	47.8	55.4
Census Tract Effect	5.8	−3.7	−.7	4.0	−1.6	1.9	6.8	1.3	5.4	9.3
Residual[7]	8.9	12.5	11.5	7.1	10.4	14.8	7.2	10.1	11.6	8.8
Hispanic Applicants										
Percent of Hispanics	100.0	3.9	15.2	30.8	3.3	6.4	25.7	.9	1.6	12.2
Actual Denial Rate	40.8	33.7	37.3	36.4	32.0	45.4	41.5	36.1	49.0	56.0
Census Tract Effect	1.2	−2.4	−.5	.6	−2.0	−.5	1.4	−1.7	5.1	6.9
Residual[7]	7.4	9.1	7.6	6.1	8.3	10.5	6.0	10.9	13.1	9.8
White Applicants										
Percent of Whites	100.0	22.5	16.4	5.5	28.6	7.5	3.7	10.6	2.7	2.5
Actual Denial Rate	23.2	18.9	27.1	29.3	17.6	28.1	36.5	22.0	31.7	47.4
Census Tract Effect	−.9	−3.1	−1.5	1.0	−1.9	.7	4.3	.0	4.0	8.7
Residual[7]	.0	.0	.8	.7	−.5	−.7	−.1	.0	−.1	2.5

[1 2 3 4 5 6 7] See notes for table 3.6.

Table 3.15 DIFFERENCE IN AVERAGE PERCENTAGE DENIAL RATES ATTRIBUTABLE TO VARIOUS SOURCES, MORTGAGE BANKS, BY NEIGHBORHOOD AND RACE, 1990 AND 1991 HMDA

		High Income[1]			Middle Income[2]			Low Income[3]		
	Total	White[4]	Mixed[5]	Minority[6]	White[4]	Mixed[5]	Minority[6]	White[4]	Mixed[5]	Minority[6]
HOME PURCHASE										
Black Applicants										
Percent of Blacks	100.0%	4.6%	9.9%	14.5%	4.7%	11.5%	20.6%	1.8%	6.9%	25.5%
Actual Denial Rate	24.4	19.5	20.8	22.1	22.5	23.5	23.7	26.5	23.0	29.4
Census Tract Effect	2.2	−1.4	−.2	1.7	−.5	.9	3.6	1.1	−.0	5.1
Residual[7]	9.5	10.3	9.0	9.0	12.0	10.3	9.0	12.5	8.8	9.4
Hispanic Applicants										
Percent of Hispanics	100.0	4.3	16.8	23.2	3.2	11.9	24.0	.9	2.6	13.1
Actual Denial Rate	17.4	12.4	17.6	17.6	15.7	17.4	17.8	14.8	20.0	17.6
Census Tract Effect	1.2	−1.1	−.4	1.4	−.5	.9	2.5	.3	1.7	2.2
Residual[7]	2.6	2.0	3.9	2.5	4.4	3.0	1.7	1.5	2.3	2.5
White Applicants										
Percent of Whites	100.0	25.4	20.6	4.8	21.4	11.1	3.1	7.5	4.4	1.7
Actual Denial Rate	11.4	9.3	13.4	17.2	9.0	11.4	16.1	11.7	13.6	19.0
Census Tract Effect	−.4	−1.4	−1.0	.3	−.5	.4	2.2	.6	.2	4.0
Residual[7]	.2	.6	.3	1.0	.1	−.2	.6	−.8	−.2	−.2
REFINANCE										
Black Applicants										
Percent of Blacks	100.0	4.8	13.7	28.8	3.3	6.2	23.2	1.1	1.9	16.9
Actual Denial Rate	29.4	25.8	24.6	28.4	25.9	23.5	31.8	29.0	34.6	35.2
Census Tract Effect	3.6	−2.3	−.8	2.8	.7	2.3	6.3	2.0	3.6	7.9
Residual[7]	6.3	8.6	6.1	7.0	7.8	5.1	6.0	11.7	9.5	4.5
Hispanic Applicants										
Percent of Hispanics	100.0	4.4	22.5	38.6	1.6	4.8	19.9	.3	.6	7.3
Actual Denial Rate	23.0	19.8	19.9	25.3	16.2	19.5	25.6	16.7	16.4	19.6
Census Tract Effect	1.3	−2.2	−.7	1.6	.7	1.5	3.4	.0	3.3	2.4
Residual[7]	3.8	3.8	3.2	4.5	1.7	1.9	3.5	−.3	−4.1	4.3

White Applicants										
Percent of Whites	100.0	27.6	32.5	10.6	14.6	6.6	3.0	2.9	1.3	.8
Actual Denial Rate	16.3	15.8	16.5	18.3	13.8	15.1	20.7	16.7	18.7	25.9
Census Tract Effect	−.5	−2.1	−1.5	.7	.3	1.5	4.2	2.0	4.1	6.9
Residual[7]	.3	.6	.4	.2	.2	−.4	−.1	−.2	−1.4	.7
HOME IMPROVEMENT										
Black Applicants										
Percent of Blacks	100.0%	1.4%	3.1%	9.6%	2.7%	5.2%	18.6%	1.9%	6.4%	51.1%
Actual Denial Rate	71.7	56.4	46.1	54.4	69.7	71.5	67.8	72.0	78.4	77.6
Census Tract Effect	5.7	−2.6	−1.0	4.4	−1.4	2.1	6.8	−.1	4.2	7.4
Residual[7]	2.0	13.0	2.7	.6	10.2	8.7	.8	4.0	5.2	.8
Hispanic Applicants										
Percent of Hispanics	100.0	2.0	10.3	20.3	1.9	8.5	20.1	.8	3.7	32.4
Actual Denial Rate	52.8	36.4	38.4	46.6	43.8	55.5	50.6	68.0	71.8	60.8
Census Tract Effect	2.2	.0	−.0	.6	−1.5	.1	1.9	1.7	4.1	4.7
Residual[7]	4.6	7.4	2.5	9.6	−6.3	3.5	4.8	5.4	1.6	3.2
White Applicants										
Percent of Whites	100.0	14.9	18.9	7.4	15.9	10.2	5.9	9.8	6.9	10.1
Actual Denial Rate	47.0	28.5	30.0	35.0	49.3	49.7	54.1	66.3	66.8	72.5
Census Tract Effect	1.4	−1.8	−.3	1.3	−.9	1.8	6.4	1.3	4.1	8.2
Residual[7]	.8	.6	1.2	1.4	.8	1.7	−.4	1.3	.6	−.8

[1] [2] [3] [4] [5] [6] [7] See notes for table 3.6.

Table 3.16 DIFFERENCE IN AVERAGE PERCENTAGE DENIAL RATES ATTRIBUTABLE TO VARIOUS SOURCES, CONVENTIONAL LOANS, BY NEIGHBORHOOD AND RACE, 1990 AND 1991 HMDA

		High Income[1]			Middle Income[2]			Low Income[3]		
	Total	White[4]	Mixed[5]	Minority[6]	White[4]	Mixed[5]	Minority[6]	White[4]	Mixed[5]	Minority[6]
HOME PURCHASE										
Black Applicants										
Percent of Blacks	100.0%	6.6%	12.8%	18.4%	6.0%	8.6%	20.7%	2.3%	6.5%	18.1%
Actual Denial Rate	30.9	22.3	25.5	27.2	28.4	31.5	30.8	38.1	40.5	37.7
Census Tract Effect	2.3	−1.6	−.5	2.2	−.4	1.3	3.9	1.7	1.6	5.5
Residual[7]	10.4	10.3	10.2	9.3	12.8	12.5	9.4	14.2	11.2	10.1
Hispanic Applicants										
Percent of Hispanics	100.0	5.3	18.8	31.9	3.4	6.7	22.8	.9	1.5	8.7
Actual Denial Rate	24.7	18.1	22.1	22.7	23.4	26.2	26.0	29.4	34.2	35.7
Census Tract Effect	1.5	−1.3	−.5	1.7	−.2	1.1	3.1	.9	3.1	3.4
Residual[7]	4.7	3.4	4.8	4.1	6.3	5.5	4.7	7.3	6.7	5.9
White Applicants										
Percent of Whites	100.0	27.5	19.7	4.7	26.0	7.0	2.1	9.1	2.7	1.2
Actual Denial Rate	14.0	9.8	13.8	17.7	12.5	16.3	21.7	20.5	25.0	28.1
Census Tract Effect	−.4	−1.7	−1.1	.5	−.4	.6	3.0	1.2	2.0	4.9
Residual[7]	.0	−.2	−.1	.8	−.1	.0	1.1	.2	.5	.6

REFINANCE										
Black Applicants										
Percent of Blacks	100.0	4.7	11.6	29.7	3.9	5.5	27.2	1.4	2.9	13.0
Actual Denial Rate	31.9	26.0	30.6	30.8	27.0	31.0	32.9	31.3	31.3	37.5
Census Tract Effect	4.0	−2.1	−.6	3.1	.4	2.4	6.2	2.5	4.6	9.6
Residual[7]	8.2	9.9	9.8	7.0	11.6	11.2	6.9	13.2	9.9	8.3
Hispanic Applicants										
Percent of Hispanics	100.0	4.3	19.2	40.7	2.2	4.4	23.9	.5	.6	4.4
Actual Denial Rate	29.4	25.3	27.9	29.7	25.3	31.6	31.2	30.8	33.0	27.5
Census Tract Effect	1.8	−2.2	−.8	1.9	.3	1.9	3.6	2.2	4.9	5.1
Residual[7]	5.5	4.4	5.2	5.5	5.3	5.6	5.7	6.4	5.7	5.7
White Applicants										
Percent of Whites	100.0	27.3	23.2	7.6	23.6	6.1	2.6	7.1	1.7	1.0
Actual Denial Rate	16.2	14.1	19.4	21.8	12.1	18.0	24.7	14.4	19.5	24.6
Census Tract Effect	−.4	−2.3	−1.4	.9	.1	1.6	4.4	1.9	4.0	6.9
Residual[7]	−.0	−.0	−.1	.1	−.0	−.0	.1	−.1	−.0	−.1

[1 2 3 4 5 6 7] See notes for table 3.6.

Table 3.17 DIFFERENCE IN AVERAGE PERCENTAGE DENIAL RATES ATTRIBUTABLE TO VARIOUS SOURCES, FHA, VA, AND FMHA LOANS, BY NEIGHBORHOOD AND RACE, 1990 AND 1991 HMDA

		High Income[1]			Middle Income[2]			Low Income[3]		
	Total	White[4]	Mixed[5]	Minority[6]	White[4]	Mixed[5]	Minority[6]	White[4]	Mixed[5]	Minority[6]
HOME PURCHASE										
Black Applicants										
Percent of Blacks	100.0%	3.3%	6.1%	10.0%	5.5%	13.7%	18.6%	2.5%	8.0%	32.4%
Actual Denial Rate	27.4	25.2	22.5	18.2	25.8	26.0	24.8	30.5	31.3	32.6
Census Tract Effect	2.5	−1.3	−.1	1.8	−.5	.7	3.2	1.2	2.1	4.7
Residual[7]	11.3	14.9	11.6	8.5	13.6	12.1	10.1	14.5	13.0	10.9
Hispanic Applicants										
Percent of Hispanics	100.0	3.1	9.7	11.7	4.6	15.0	23.2	2.0	5.4	25.3
Actual Denial Rate	19.5	16.7	16.8	14.1	18.2	19.2	18.0	20.6	24.0	24.2
Census Tract Effect	1.5	−1.1	−.1	1.3	−.3	.7	2.0	.7	2.2	2.8
Residual[7]	2.7	5.8	4.2	1.6	5.3	3.5	1.4	4.7	3.5	2.3
White Applicants										
Percent of Whites	100.0	13.8	9.3	2.0	29.4	15.9	3.3	15.2	7.6	3.4
Actual Denial Rate	12.4	9.7	10.7	11.8	11.0	12.2	15.0	14.1	16.2	20.7
Census Tract Effect	.1	−1.1	−.6	.9	−.5	.3	1.7	.7	1.7	3.6
Residual[7]	−.1	.1	.3	.2	.1	−.5	−.0	−.7	−1.0	.2

REFINANCE										
Black Applicants										
Percent of Blacks	100.0	3.7	6.9	12.3	5.9	12.7	17.8	2.4	6.2	32.3
Actual Denial Rate	28.7	24.0	26.4	26.3	31.1	24.8	29.9	32.7	34.5	29.8
Census Tract Effect	4.1	−1.4	−.0	4.5	.7	1.3	5.5	1.4	2.5	6.9
Residual[7]	8.0	10.6	9.1	6.7	13.1	7.5	6.9	13.1	14.1	6.4
Hispanic Applicants										
Percent of Hispanics	100.0	3.0	9.3	14.1	4.7	11.3	18.1	1.8	3.8	34.0
Actual Denial Rate	21.7	30.2	20.7	22.6	18.0	21.0	21.5	20.8	26.8	21.1
Census Tract Effect	1.9	−1.2	.1	2.6	1.1	.8	2.4	1.3	3.1	2.4
Residual[7]	2.7	13.9	2.8	1.5	1.1	3.4	−.2	4.6	2.9	3.5
White Applicants										
Percent of Whites	100.0	15.7	11.7	3.1	27.2	16.1	3.6	11.9	7.0	3.6
Actual Denial Rate	15.0	13.2	15.0	19.4	13.7	13.7	19.3	16.4	17.2	21.5
Census Tract Effect	.7	−1.7	−.3	2.7	.1	.9	3.4	1.7	3.1	5.9
Residual[7]	−.3	.8	.4	.6	−.3	−1.5	−.4	−.5	−1.9	−1.2

[1 2 3 4 5 6 7] See notes for table 3.6.

Table 3.18 DIFFERENCE IN AVERAGE PERCENTAGE DENIAL RATES, NEIGHBORHOODS SORTED BY PERCENTAGE BLACK, 1990 AND 1991 HMDA

		High Income[1]			Middle Income[2]			Low Income[3]		
	Total	White[4]	Mixed[5]	Minority[6]	White[4]	Mixed[5]	Minority[6]	White[4]	Mixed[5]	Minority[6]
HOME PURCHASE										
Black Applicants										
Percent of Blacks	100.0%	10.0%	8.9%	9.7%	6.5%	13.4%	16.6%	2.1%	8.2%	24.4%
Actual Denial Rate	29.2	24.5	24.5	23.3	26.9	28.6	27.8	34.3	34.9	34.5
Census Tract Effect	2.4	−1.0	.5	2.4	.0	1.2	3.8	1.4	1.9	5.0
Residual[7]	10.8	10.8	10.3	9.1	12.0	12.2	9.8	14.8	11.9	10.7
Hispanic Applicants										
Percent of Hispanics	100.0	36.0	8.6	2.0	23.1	9.4	3.3	12.7	3.6	1.3
Actual Denial Rate	23.2	21.0	20.8	23.3	22.4	24.1	25.8	28.6	29.8	28.0
Census Tract Effect	1.5	.2	1.5	4.0	1.1	3.0	5.1	2.5	3.6	4.6
Residual[7]	4.1	4.2	3.8	3.3	4.2	3.9	4.1	4.3	3.7	3.3
White Applicants										
Percent of Whites	100.0	39.8	5.2	.4	30.4	7.2	.8	10.8	4.1	1.2
Actual Denial Rate	13.6	11.7	12.1	17.6	12.8	14.3	18.6	18.5	21.1	24.4
Census Tract Effect	−.3	−1.4	−.1	2.3	−.3	.7	3.4	1.1	1.9	4.6
Residual[7]	−.0	−.0	.1	1.9	−.0	−.2	.9	−.1	−.1	.5
REFINANCE										
Black Applicants										
Percent of Blacks	100.0	14.4	12.1	17.6	5.1	10.4	21.1	1.2	3.7	14.3
Actual Denial Rate	31.6	30.1	30.9	29.5	30.1	30.9	32.4	32.4	33.3	35.8
Census Tract Effect	3.9	−1.1	1.6	3.8	.9	3.7	6.4	3.3	4.2	8.7
Residual[7]	8.2	9.6	9.1	5.9	11.5	8.7	6.9	12.8	11.0	7.9
Hispanic Applicants										
Percent of Hispanics	100.0	51.4	9.0	2.3	20.8	7.0	2.8	5.4	1.0	.4
Actual Denial Rate	29.1	28.3	30.3	32.7	28.9	33.2	34.7	25.2	35.1	31.5
Census Tract Effect	1.8	.4	2.8	4.9	1.9	5.0	6.4	3.5	8.1	7.9
Residual[7]	5.4	5.3	5.2	6.4	5.2	5.7	6.9	5.4	5.1	3.7

White Applicants										
Percent of Whites	100.0	51.1	5.3	.6	27.0	4.9	.8	7.4	2.0	.8
Actual Denial Rate	16.1	17.0	17.9	24.9	13.6	16.4	23.4	15.2	18.0	23.0
Census Tract Effect	−.3	−1.8	.6	4.0	.3	1.9	6.0	2.1	3.5	6.8
Residual[7]	−.0	−.0	−.2	2.5	−.0	−.2	.3	−.1	−.3	−.2
HOME IMPROVEMENT										
Black Applicants										
Percent of Blacks	100.0%	4.8%	4.7%	6.6%	4.0%	7.8%	15.4%	2.2%	6.9%	47.7%
Actual Denial Rate	46.1	34.3	39.9	47.1	35.2	40.4	47.0	38.3	42.2	50.3
Census Tract Effect	5.9	−2.2	.1	5.6	−1.4	2.0	6.6	.8	3.8	8.9
Residual[7]	8.8	9.4	9.8	7.7	10.7	11.0	7.9	10.6	10.9	8.3
Hispanic Applicants										
Percent of Hispanics	100.0	25.8	5.2	1.1	18.6	5.9	2.1	35.0	4.2	2.2
Actual Denial Rate	40.0	36.6	42.7	51.3	38.7	45.9	52.9	38.7	49.6	53.0
Census Tract Effect	1.0	−.9	1.9	5.9	−.3	3.7	7.1	.8	6.7	10.4
Residual[7]	8.1	7.0	7.0	7.4	8.1	8.7	9.1	8.9	7.8	7.0
White Applicants										
Percent of Whites	100.0	33.4	3.7	.5	31.7	6.2	1.2	15.8	5.0	2.5
Actual Denial Rate	22.2	21.3	25.4	39.1	19.5	23.7	38.0	22.2	25.9	40.7
Census Tract Effect	−.9	−2.6	−.5	5.4	−1.7	1.0	6.6	.2	2.8	8.3
Residual[7]	−.0	.0	−.1	1.5	−.1	−.4	.5	−.0	−.4	1.4

[1 2 3 7] See notes for table 3.6.
[4]Census tracts with less than 5 percent black applicants.
[5]Census tracts with 5 percent or more and 25 percent or less applications from black applicants.
[6]Census tracts with more than 25 percent of all loan applications from black applicants.

Table 3.19 DIFFERENCE IN AVERAGE PERCENTAGE DENIAL RATES, NEIGHBORHOODS SORTED BY PERCENTAGE HISPANIC, 1990 AND 1991 HMDA

		High Income[1]			Middle Income[2]			Low Income[3]		
	Total	White[4]	Mixed[5]	Minority[6]	White[4]	Mixed[5]	Minority[6]	White[4]	Mixed[5]	Minority[6]
HOME PURCHASE										
Black Applicants										
Percent of Blacks	100.0%	17.8%	9.3%	1.5%	25.3%	9.1%	2.2%	30.1%	3.6%	1.0%
Actual Denial Rate	29.2	22.3	26.8	28.5	27.2	29.3	30.5	34.8	32.4	37.6
Census Tract Effect	2.4	−.0	1.4	3.1	1.6	3.3	4.3	4.1	3.6	4.1
Residual[7]	10.8	10.3	9.6	9.1	11.8	9.5	9.0	11.3	10.2	12.5
Hispanic Applicants										
Percent of Hispanics	100.0	8.2	21.0	17.4	5.0	12.8	18.1	2.0	3.2	12.3
Actual Denial Rate	23.2	17.9	22.0	21.5	20.6	23.9	23.3	25.0	29.0	29.3
Census Tract Effect	1.5	−1.2	.3	1.7	.1	1.7	2.7	1.6	3.1	3.0
Residual[7]	4.1	4.8	4.3	3.5	5.5	4.5	3.5	4.9	4.9	3.8
White Applicants										
Percent of Whites	100.0	33.4	11.0	1.0	31.9	5.7	.9	14.2	1.5	.5
Actual Denial Rate	13.6	10.4	15.4	18.6	12.3	16.9	21.0	19.2	21.7	25.2
Census Tract Effect	−.3	−1.5	−.4	.7	−.3	1.1	2.0	1.4	2.7	3.6
Residual[7]	−.0	−.0	.0	1.3	−.1	.0	1.1	−.1	−.0	−.1
REFINANCE										
Black Applicants										
Percent of Blacks	100.0	20.4	18.0	5.8	18.7	10.7	7.2	16.8	1.9	.5
Actual Denial Rate	31.6	27.6	32.4	31.6	30.2	34.0	32.1	34.5	38.2	42.7
Census Tract Effect	3.9	.4	2.2	4.3	4.0	5.8	5.8	7.4	7.7	8.0
Residual[7]	8.2	8.4	8.1	6.3	9.3	7.6	5.6	8.7	8.8	11.3
Hispanic Applicants										
Percent of Hispanics	100.0	8.5	28.3	25.9	2.7	7.4	20.4	.7	1.0	5.0
Actual Denial Rate	29.1	24.9	28.9	29.9	23.9	32.3	30.6	30.2	31.8	25.5
Census Tract Effect	1.8	−2.0	.3	2.4	.7	3.2	3.3	3.3	5.4	4.3
Residual[7]	5.4	5.3	5.4	5.2	4.2	5.8	5.6	5.1	5.3	5.3

White Applicants										
Percent of Whites	100.0	26.8	9.8	1.1	33.1	5.1	.9	20.7	1.9	.7
Actual Denial Rate	16.1	15.1	21.3	24.0	12.5	22.4	25.1	15.6	23.1	25.4
Census Tract Effect	−.3	−2.3	−.1	1.8	.3	2.6	3.5	2.5	5.0	7.1
Residual[7]	−.0	.0	−.1	.3	−.0	−.1	.3	−.1	−.3	−.3
HOME IMPROVEMENT										
Black Applicants										
Percent of Blacks	100.0%	10.0%	4.9%	1.2%	19.3%	5.8%	2.1%	50.9%	4.7%	1.2%
Actual Denial Rate	46.1	39.8	43.0	44.7	41.4	48.7	46.6	48.5	51.8	53.3
Census Tract Effect	5.9	1.0	2.6	3.4	3.6	5.6	4.1	7.8	9.4	8.2
Residual[7]	8.8	9.2	8.7	6.0	9.8	8.6	5.9	8.7	8.2	7.9
Hispanic Applicants										
Percent of Hispanics	100.0	5.5	14.9	11.7	3.6	8.6	14.4	2.1	3.5	35.7
Actual Denial Rate	40.0	32.0	38.0	41.0	33.5	43.2	42.3	38.1	45.8	40.2
Census Tract Effect	1.0	−2.2	1.2	.2	−.4	2.1	1.0	3.5	6.5	1.3
Residual[7]	8.1	6.3	6.9	7.5	7.6	8.5	8.4	6.8	6.9	9.0
White Applicants										
Percent of Whites	100.0	26.8	9.8	1.1	33.1	5.1	.9	20.7	1.9	.7
Actual Denial Rate	22.2	19.6	27.4	31.0	18.8	31.0	32.7	23.5	36.4	38.9
Census Tract Effect	−.9	−3.1	−.5	.0	−1.5	1.3	1.5	1.2	5.2	4.4
Residual[7]	−.0	.0	.0	.4	−.1	−.2	.1	.1	.2	.3

[1 2 3 7] See notes for table 3.6.
[4]Census tracts with less than 5 percent Hispanic applicants.
[5]Census tracts with 5 percent or more and 25 percent or less applications from Hispanic applicants.
[6]Census tracts with more than 25 percent of all loan applications from Hispanic applicants.

Table 3.20 NEIGHBORHOOD AND UNEXPLAINED DENIAL RATE RESIDUALS, BLACKS, BY MSA, 1990 AND 1991 HMDA

	Home Purchase				Refinance				Home Improvement			
	Percent Black	Denial Rate	Tract Effect	Residual Effect	Percent Black	Denial Rate	Tract Effect	Residual Effect	Percent Black	Denial Rate	Tract Effect	Residual Effect
All MSAs < 1 Million	5.0%	33.0%	2.2%	12.2%	2.6%	31.8%	3.8%	10.0%	7.7%	40.5%	4.3%	9.6%
All MSAs 1–2 Million	5.9	30.0	2.5	11.2	3.3	33.0	3.6	8.8	10.3	47.5	5.8	9.5
Anaheim	1.1	27.5	.6	9.6	1.0	34.0	.8	11.4	.8	38.9	−.1	10.3
Atlanta	16.1	28.6	4.2	11.6	7.4	28.2	4.6	7.0	21.8	44.0	3.7	10.6
Baltimore	13.4	18.0	−.4	9.3	5.7	23.3	2.9	7.8	28.3	52.2	4.6	9.5
Boston	4.4	33.4	4.6	9.3	2.3	39.9	8.5	9.8	5.4	31.3	4.2	5.7
Chicago	9.3	24.3	4.2	10.3	6.4	40.2	10.2	8.2	21.9	48.5	8.9	6.7
Cleveland	7.9	27.3	3.4	9.9	4.9	38.7	8.6	10.4	21.2	47.0	6.5	8.3
Dallas	6.6	30.3	2.4	12.1	2.8	35.1	6.4	10.1	9.3	59.3	9.7	10.4
Detroit	8.8	25.0	1.7	9.5	3.0	28.2	6.8	7.9	28.7	48.6	9.6	8.5
Houston	6.2	35.9	2.8	12.8	3.3	30.8	4.2	10.5	11.2	59.9	8.6	11.1
Los Angeles	4.7	28.3	1.9	8.2	7.6	30.2	3.0	5.6	7.6	42.0	1.8	5.7
Miami	7.3	25.2	3.1	6.5	5.5	46.5	4.3	12.2	14.6	58.5	5.1	7.5
Minneapolis	1.8	23.1	2.2	10.2	.5	21.4	1.0	9.2	1.7	38.9	8.3	5.7
Nassau/Suffolk NY	6.0	29.1	4.2	8.9	5.5	33.2	4.6	8.0	6.0	41.8	5.6	8.3
New York	15.0	29.8	2.2	8.6	17.0	31.8	3.7	7.8	24.0	42.8	3.7	7.1
Oakland	5.6	25.9	2.6	8.5	8.2	31.2	3.8	7.6	7.8	44.5	3.8	7.5
Philadelphia	9.4	26.8	1.2	9.6	3.7	32.6	5.2	8.7	16.0	59.2	9.7	8.6
Phoenix	1.7	32.3	1.6	12.3	.8	38.6	3.5	11.3	1.5	51.9	−2.1	3.8
Pittsburgh	4.0	33.1	2.0	11.6	1.3	39.0	5.6	13.1	10.2	57.1	11.5	7.6
Riverside CA	4.4	27.1	.5	9.3	3.7	38.9	.6	10.8	3.5	41.4	.2	6.2
St. Louis	8.6	34.1	6.5	12.5	5.9	21.8	3.3	7.2	20.1	51.8	8.6	9.9
San Diego	1.9	24.1	1.4	7.6	2.1	35.4	4.0	7.5	3.1	34.9	1.6	7.7
San Francisco	1.7	28.4	2.6	8.4	3.5	30.6	3.6	6.7	3.9	37.5	2.4	6.3
Seattle	1.4	25.5	.6	9.5	1.4	25.2	3.2	7.4	2.0	35.0	2.7	9.5
Tampa	3.6	32.5	4.3	9.8	2.6	46.8	5.8	13.1	8.1	38.8	2.1	8.3
Washington	16.4	18.0	1.2	9.2	9.6	24.6	3.3	7.9	25.3	47.5	4.7	8.4
Total	6.1	29.2	2.4	10.8	4.1	31.6	3.9	8.2	10.4	46.1	5.9	8.8

Table 3.21 NEIGHBORHOOD AND UNEXPLAINED DENIAL RATE RESIDUALS, HISPANICS, BY MSA, 1990 AND 1991 HMDA

	Home Purchase				Refinance				Home Improvement			
	Percent Hispanic	Denial Rate	Tract Effect	Residual Effect	Percent Hispanic	Denial Rate	Tract Effect	Residual Effect	Percent Hispanic	Denial Rate	Tract Effect	Residual Effect
All MSAs < 1 Million	4.5%	25.1%	1.1%	4.6%	3.5%	26.9%	1.4%	5.4%	7.6%	36.3%	.8%	8.8%
All MSAs 1–2 Million	4.9	24.9	1.8	4.3	4.2	28.2	2.3	4.5	4.8	44.6	2.8	7.9
Anaheim	11.9	23.1	2.3	4.0	10.1	29.5	2.2	5.9	8.5	39.7	.8	7.8
Atlanta	1.0	17.1	.1	3.4	.5	14.3	−.6	2.3	.8	36.1	−1.8	13.7
Baltimore	.9	14.3	.0	5.1	.5	20.5	−1.0	7.3	.5	48.3	1.0	14.3
Boston	1.9	23.0	2.9	5.4	1.5	22.2	3.0	4.9	2.0	39.4	4.8	8.8
Chicago	10.0	13.4	1.4	2.9	5.3	25.3	2.5	5.4	9.2	37.8	.1	5.5
Cleveland	1.1	19.1	2.1	1.6	.4	30.7	1.3	13.1	1.4	38.5	5.6	3.7
Dallas	7.1	21.2	2.0	2.6	3.3	27.7	2.9	6.5	7.0	55.8	5.1	10.6
Detroit	.7	15.9	.4	2.4	.5	14.5	.3	1.7	1.1	34.0	.3	4.9
Houston	9.1	28.3	2.7	5.5	4.2	21.9	3.4	5.2	10.7	53.2	3.7	11.9
Los Angeles	24.5	23.6	2.2	4.1	22.7	30.1	2.0	5.6	20.3	42.3	.1	7.7
Miami	46.3	19.4	−.2	3.2	44.5	29.6	−.4	3.7	47.0	41.7	−1.9	7.5
Minneapolis	.6	14.0	.8	2.4	.3	20.2	1.2	6.8	.4	28.7	2.5	5.0
Nassau/Suffolk, NY	4.2	21.7	2.2	4.2	2.7	34.1	2.3	8.6	4.0	41.0	2.0	7.8
New York	8.2	26.8	2.5	5.9	7.0	31.8	3.3	5.9	9.7	47.8	3.2	8.2
Oakland	8.3	19.3	2.0	3.2	7.5	23.8	1.8	4.1	7.0	36.4	1.5	6.1
Philadelphia	2.6	22.1	−.8	3.9	.7	26.4	3.5	4.2	2.9	56.3	9.1	6.6
Phoenix	8.3	27.6	2.6	3.2	4.8	33.2	3.9	6.1	11.7	53.8	−1.8	4.7
Pittsburgh	.2	10.0	−.6	−4.4	.2	22.7	1.9	4.4	.3	40.6	.6	5.6
Riverside, CA	21.5	22.1	1.0	3.0	15.0	34.3	.7	6.2	17.6	43.8	.4	6.8
St. Louis	.5	22.7	−.1	6.8	.4	13.8	.8	−.1	.4	30.0	.2	3.6
San Diego	10.8	22.6	1.5	5.1	8.4	33.2	2.3	6.5	9.4	34.5	−.0	5.6
San Francisco	7.0	25.3	2.7	6.5	7.9	26.7	2.0	4.6	6.4	34.4	1.5	5.7
Seattle	1.2	22.9	.6	6.2	1.0	17.5	.9	3.7	1.3	28.4	.6	7.2
Tampa	6.7	25.1	1.2	2.6	7.8	33.2	.5	.4	6.1	34.4	−1.0	7.7
Washington	3.9	11.0	−.3	3.8	2.1	18.2	−.0	4.6	2.9	41.5	1.1	10.6
Total	6.4	23.2	1.5	4.1	6.6	29.1	1.8	5.4	7.1	40.0	1.0	8.1

Table 3.22 NEIGHBORHOOD AND UNEXPLAINED DENIAL RATE RESIDUALS, WHITES, BY MSA, 1990 AND 1991 HMDA

	Home Purchase				Refinance				Home Improvement			
	Percent White	Denial Rate	Tract Effect	Residual Effect	Percent White	Denial Rate	Tract Effect	Residual Effect	Percent White	Denial Rate	Tract Effect	Residual Effect
All MSAs < 1 Million	87.3%	14.2%	−.2%	−.1%	90.6%	14.1%	−.2%	−.1%	82.3%	17.8%	−.5%	−.0%
All MSAs 1–2 Million	83.9	12.8	−.3	−.1	86.4	15.6	−.3	.0	81.1	24.4	−.9	−.1
Anaheim	72.7	17.1	−.4	−.1	76.6	21.4	−.3	−.1	77.4	26.3	−.1	−.4
Atlanta	80.0	10.8	−.8	−.2	89.9	12.0	−.4	.1	75.1	19.5	−1.1	−.5
Baltimore	82.4	8.6	.1	.2	91.4	11.1	−.2	.0	69.2	27.9	−1.9	−.1
Boston	89.0	12.4	−.3	.0	93.3	16.2	−.3	−.1	89.5	17.4	−.3	.2
Chicago	74.5	8.3	−.7	.1	83.5	13.0	−.9	−.1	65.9	20.7	−2.9	.0
Cleveland	88.6	9.1	−.3	.1	92.5	12.8	−.4	−.1	75.5	24.0	−1.9	.3
Dallas	81.6	11.9	−.3	.0	90.6	16.9	−.3	−.1	80.7	27.4	−1.5	−.5
Detroit	88.1	11.0	−.2	.2	94.4	10.0	−.2	.0	68.9	22.2	−4.0	.0
Houston	76.2	14.9	−.5	−.3	87.5	13.6	−.3	.1	74.0	29.7	−1.8	−.9
Los Angeles	53.4	19.4	−1.0	.4	55.8	23.9	−1.1	.1	57.7	30.8	.0	.6
Miami	43.7	17.3	−.4	1.8	47.8	27.1	−.1	1.2	34.7	35.3	.5	.2
Minneapolis	95.1	8.2	−.1	.1	97.8	9.5	−.0	−.0	96.1	19.5	−.2	−.0
Nassau/Suffolk NY	83.9	13.3	−.4	.1	87.1	21.8	−.3	−.1	86.6	28.5	−.5	−.1
New York	59.7	16.6	−1.2	.4	65.0	23.7	−1.6	−.1	59.0	37.6	−2.4	.7
Oakland	65.0	14.0	−.6	−.0	67.2	18.5	−.7	.1	70.9	25.2	−.7	.3
Philadelphia	83.9	9.6	−.1	.1	92.9	14.3	−.2	−.0	78.6	29.5	−2.3	.1
Phoenix	87.3	16.2	−.3	.0	92.1	20.0	−.2	−.2	84.6	48.8	.3	.5
Pittsburgh	94.4	14.0	−.1	−.0	97.0	14.2	−.1	−.1	88.2	28.3	−1.3	−.0
Riverside CA	65.5	18.4	−.3	.3	74.8	25.9	−.1	−.4	72.0	32.9	−.1	.1
St. Louis	89.5	13.9	−.6	−.2	92.0	11.0	−.2	.0	78.2	21.5	−2.2	−.3
San Diego	77.9	15.3	−.2	−.0	81.9	22.7	−.4	−.2	77.0	25.4	−.1	.1
San Francisco	65.7	15.9	−.6	−.1	67.1	20.5	−.7	.0	72.1	25.8	−.4	.4
Seattle	86.8	15.3	−.1	−.0	91.2	13.3	−.1	−.1	88.3	19.1	−.1	−.1
Tampa	87.5	18.0	−.3	.2	87.9	25.7	−.2	.2	83.5	27.4	−.2	.1
Washington	72.1	7.8	−.2	.1	82.0	11.5	−.3	.1	66.4	19.0	−1.8	−.3
Total	81.9	13.6	−.3	−.0	82.9	16.1	−.3	−.0	78.4	22.2	−.9	−.0

14.3 percentage points across the nine types of neighborhoods; for refinance and home improvement, the range is only slightly lower—6.9 to 13.2 percentage points. For other minority groups, there is a comparable persistence across neighborhoods in the unexplained residual. The tables also reveal a remarkable persistence in the neighborhood, or census-tract effects, across racial groups. For all racial groups, applications for properties in predominantly minority and low-income neighborhoods have higher percentage denial rates than for those in predominantly white and high-income neighborhoods.

Whereas the overall impression is one of consistency, a few systematic differences are evident. The difference between black and white percentage denial rates is lowest in primarily minority tracts, and in all neighborhoods the unexplained residual accounts for almost all of the difference, though there is a tendency for it to decline with neighborhood income. For Hispanics, on the other hand, the residual difference varies little by the income or race of the neighborhood. We tend to focus on minority–white comparisons, but there are also interesting differences across the minority groups. For example, for most types of neighborhood, our model predicts a lower percentage denial rate for blacks than for Hispanics. This lower predicted percentage denial rate, however, is swamped by the higher residuals for blacks, and as a result the overall percentage denial rates within each type of neighborhood are 5 to 10 percentage points higher for black applicants.

To examine the robustness of these results, a number of other comparisons were made. The sample was restricted to 1990 applications (table 3.9), 1991 applications (table 3.10), center city areas (table 3.11), and non-center-city areas (table 3.12). The sample was restricted by lender type (tables 3.13, 3.14, and 3.15). Loans were divided into conventional (table 3.16) and FHA or VA (table 3.17) applications. Neighborhoods were defined by the percentage of applicants that were black (table 3.18) and Hispanic (table 3.19). Data were also disaggregated by MSA, with results presented for the top 25 MSAs and grouped for smaller ones (tables 3.20, 3.21, and 3.22).

In all cases, the results support the basic findings of tables 3.6, 3.7, and 3.8. The size of the unexplained black residual is remarkably constant. In no neighborhood, MSA, lender, or guarantee type is the home purchase residual less than 6.5 percent or more than 16.6 percent. For refinance loans it is never less than 5.6 percent or more than 16.7 percent. The ranges for home improvement loans are similar. *This suggests that the unexplained black–white difference is not an artifact of one year, one market, or one type of lender, but that it is pervasive.*

Moreover, it is not confined to central-city, low-income, or minority areas. Indeed, the largest gaps occur in white and high-income areas. Tract effects appear to be equally consistent, albeit smaller. The typical black applicant for home purchase and refinance loans appears to have an estimated 3-percent higher probability of denial, because of the neighborhoods he or she is applying in, than the typical white applicant for similar loans. The neighborhood effect is most pronounced for home improvement loans, with the gap being about 7 percent.

Despite the apparent thoroughness of these robustness tests, there remains a concern that the validity of each of these findings rests upon the appropriateness of the same basic denial model, as well as our assumption that the form of this model is linear. To examine this assumption, one final robustness test was employed. Observations were grouped according to their predicted probability of denial based on AC, MSA, and LENDER. This could be considered a nonparametric rank-ordering of observations by risk (except for race and neighborhood). Average differences in the black–white and Hispanic–white unexplained residual and tract effects were then computed for each predicted denial probability group and are presented in tables 3.23 and 3.24. By construction, within each group the sum of the other predicted characteristics is the same for blacks and whites (or Hispanics and whites), so the sum of the residual and tract racial differences must equal the differences in percentage denial rates across races.

The linear probability model assumption implies that the racial differences in denial rates (and the residual and neighborhood subcomponents) should be constant across predicted probability groups. If the underlying model form were logistic or probit, then the differences would be increasing as the denial probability rose from 0 to 50 percent. The results presented in tables 3.23 and 3.24 suggest that whereas the residual and neighborhood group differences do rise when the denial probability increases from 0 to 10 percent, they are fairly constant above that level. Although not an exact match, this result suggests that the linear probability model form may not be any less appropriate than others.

CONCLUSIONS

We find a persistent difference in the denial rates of white and minority applicants, particularly blacks, even after accounting for lender, neighborhood, and applicant economic characteristics (as best we can measure them with the HMDA data). Moreover, we find a remarkable degree of consistency in these conclusions across geographic markets and loan products, indicating that the observed racial differences in denial rates are widespread and cannot be attributed to a subset of markets or type of lender or type of loan.

It is by now well known that the HMDA data do not contain enough relevant information about the loan applications to draw any firm conclusions regarding the reasons for these differences. We cannot determine whether these findings are generated by a process of lender discrimination against minorities, because our residual differences may be due to credit histories, employment histories, LTV ratios, wealth, or other factors that lenders consider in the loan evaluation process but that are not included in the HMDA file. Because our analysis excludes these variables, we cannot conclude that the unexplained residual unambiguously stems from differential treatment based solely on the race of the applicant. There is some evidence in the HMDA data that these variables may be correlated with race, as witnessed by the more prevalent citation of credit history as a reason for denial for minorities (table 3.2). Such a correlation could confound the estimation of the pure racial effect.

Despite this weakness of the HMDA data, our analysis does shed some light on the reasons for observed differences in denial rates across racial groups and neighborhoods. It has been argued that property location is an important source of racial differences in denial rates. Because house value appreciation tends to be lower in low-income and minority neighborhoods, these areas are considered more risky from the lender's point of view. Moreover, some lenders argue that appraisals are harder to conduct and interpret in low-income and minority neighborhoods, because the housing stock is generally older and more heterogeneous, and appraisers are less familiar with these neighborhoods.[14] Our analysis indicates that property location does contribute to racial differences in denial rates, but on average, neighborhood effects are smaller than those stemming from applicant characteristics. Moreover, when comparing similar applicants, racial differences in denial rates still exist and are roughly the same size within neighborhoods, regardless of the type of neighborhood.

Since there are a number of potential explanations for the racial differences we find in our residual denial rates, further study will be necessary to pinpoint the causes. For example, one explanation could be that factors observed by the lenders but not contained in our data are driving the results. If so, one would expect larger residual differ-

Table 3.23 BLACK–WHITE RESIDUALS BY DENIAL PROBABILITY, 1990 AND 1991 HMDA

Denial	Home Purchase				Refinance				Home Improvement			
Probability (percent)	Cumulative Black	Percent White	Residual Gap	Tract Gap	Cumulative Black	Percent White	Residual Gap	Tract Gap	Cumulative Black	Percent White	Residual Gap	Tract Gap
Less than 0	4.5%	4.2%	2.0%	1.5%	6.5%	5.6%	1.7%	2.7%	3.1%	5.7%	0.0%	4.4%
0	7.4	8.3	2.9	1.6	9.5	9.5	3.0	3.3	4.2	8.0	1.2	3.8
1	9.5	11.1	3.8	1.7	11.3	12.0	2.2	3.4	4.8	9.3	3.2	3.6
2	11.8	14.4	4.7	1.6	13.0	14.8	4.6	3.0	5.5	10.8	2.8	4.0
3	14.5	18.1	5.5	1.7	15.0	17.8	5.4	3.3	6.3	12.3	2.2	4.2
4	17.5	22.3	6.6	2.1	17.1	20.9	6.5	4.1	7.1	14.0	2.5	4.0
5	20.8	26.7	7.5	2.0	19.3	24.1	6.1	3.6	7.9	15.7	3.8	4.4
6	24.3	31.2	7.6	1.9	21.7	27.3	7.3	4.1	8.9	17.4	4.0	4.1
7	28.0	35.8	9.1	2.3	24.1	30.6	5.8	4.7	9.8	19.3	6.5	4.0
8	31.8	40.2	9.1	2.4	26.7	33.9	6.2	4.0	10.9	21.2	4.9	3.9
9	35.8	44.6	9.8	2.5	29.6	37.1	7.1	4.0	11.9	23.1	4.8	4.0
10	39.8	48.8	10.4	2.5	32.4	40.4	7.4	4.5	13.0	25.0	7.1	4.8
11	43.7	52.8	11.6	2.6	35.2	43.6	7.9	4.2	14.2	27.1	7.0	4.7
12	47.4	56.6	12.0	2.6	38.0	46.7	8.0	4.3	15.4	29.2	7.9	4.8
13	51.0	60.0	12.1	2.8	40.6	49.7	10.4	4.3	16.6	31.3	7.0	5.0
14	54.5	63.2	12.7	2.8	43.2	52.6	9.6	4.2	18.0	33.4	7.9	5.0
15	57.7	66.2	13.5	2.9	45.8	55.4	9.1	4.3	19.4	35.5	9.4	5.0
16	60.9	69.0	15.0	3.0	48.3	58.0	9.1	4.2	20.9	37.7	9.7	5.7
17	63.9	71.7	13.4	3.3	50.7	60.6	8.9	4.4	22.4	40.0	9.1	5.9
18	66.8	74.1	14.3	3.2	53.1	63.0	9.9	4.7	24.1	42.2	10.7	5.8
19	69.4	76.3	14.5	3.4	55.4	65.3	9.8	5.0	25.8	44.4	11.7	6.9
20	71.8	78.3	14.6	3.5	57.7	67.5	10.3	4.6	27.6	46.7	11.5	6.6
21	74.1	80.1	14.7	3.6	59.9	69.5	9.0	4.2	29.6	49.0	9.2	7.0
22	76.2	81.8	14.2	3.3	62.2	71.6	10.8	4.6	31.6	51.3	10.7	7.3
23	78.1	83.2	14.5	3.4	64.3	73.5	11.5	5.4	33.7	53.7	11.2	7.5

24	80.0	84.6	15.4	3.4	66.4	75.3	12.1	5.4	35.8	55.9	10.7	7.2
25	81.8	85.9	15.1	3.5	68.6	77.1	11.9	4.8	38.0	58.2	10.1	7.6
26	83.4	87.0	15.9	3.6	70.6	78.7	10.1	4.8	40.2	60.5	11.1	8.1
27	84.8	88.0	16.0	3.1	72.6	80.3	10.1	5.5	42.6	62.7	12.2	7.6
28	86.1	89.0	16.4	3.8	74.6	81.8	12.3	5.1	45.6	64.9	11.7	8.1
29	87.3	89.8	13.9	4.1	76.5	83.2	10.6	6.0	47.4	67.1	10.8	8.1
30	88.4	90.6	16.0	3.5	78.1	84.5	9.6	4.8	49.9	69.2	11.4	7.6
31	89.4	91.3	15.8	2.9	79.7	85.7	9.1	5.1	52.4	71.2	10.2	7.6
32	90.2	91.9	13.7	3.1	81.2	86.8	8.4	4.8	54.7	73.2	10.6	7.8
33	90.9	92.4	18.3	3.5	82.6	87.8	10.3	4.7	57.2	75.0	10.1	7.9
34	91.6	92.9	11.6	3.6	83.8	88.7	8.9	4.8	59.5	76.8	10.8	7.8
35	92.2	93.4	15.1	3.5	85.0	89.6	10.0	5.4	61.8	78.5	11.6	7.9
36	92.8	93.8	13.5	3.4	86.1	90.4	10.8	4.4	64.0	80.1	9.1	7.5
37	93.4	94.2	14.6	3.4	87.2	91.1	7.3	5.7	66.2	81.5	9.1	7.4
38	93.8	94.5	11.7	3.7	88.1	91.8	8.4	4.6	68.1	82.9	8.0	7.2
39	94.2	94.9	14.8	3.1	89.0	92.5	11.4	5.6	70.1	84.3	10.6	7.3
40	94.6	95.1	14.8	3.1	90.0	93.1	11.2	3.8	72.0	85.5	11.4	7.4
41	94.9	95.4	11.5	2.9	90.9	93.7	10.9	4.8	73.8	86.6	11.2	7.5
42	95.2	95.7	12.4	3.2	91.7	94.2	8.0	5.7	75.4	87.7	8.9	7.3
43	95.5	95.9	14.1	2.9	92.4	94.7	9.8	4.2	77.1	88.7	11.5	8.2
44	95.7	96.1	14.1	3.6	93.1	95.1	8.1	4.9	78.6	89.6	10.6	7.7
45	96.0	96.4	12.7	2.8	93.7	95.5	13.7	4.5	80.1	90.5	10.6	7.4
46	96.2	96.6	11.8	1.9	94.3	95.9	8.6	5.4	81.4	91.2	9.0	7.7
47	96.4	96.8	11.5	3.3	94.8	96.2	8.7	3.6	82.6	91.9	9.7	7.6
48	96.6	96.9	11.6	3.3	95.2	96.5	14.4	4.8	83.8	92.6	9.1	7.7
49	96.8	97.1	14.4	3.1	95.6	96.8	8.5	5.5	84.9	93.2	11.4	6.4
50	97.0	97.3	7.3	2.5	95.9	97.0	9.6	5.7	85.9	93.7	10.1	7.2
More than 50	100.0	100.0	8.2	1.7	100.0	100.0	7.5	5.0	100.0	100.0	6.4	6.0

Table 3.24 HISPANIC–WHITE RESIDUALS BY DENIAL PROBABILITY, 1990 AND 1991 HMDA

Denial	Home Purchase				Refinance				Home Improvement			
Probability (percent)	Cumulative Hispanic	Percent White	Residual Gap	Tract Gap	Cumulative Hispanic	Percent White	Residual Gap	Tract Gap	Cumulative Hispanic	Percent White	Residual Gap	Tract Gap
Less than 0	4.2%	4.2%	1.5%	.7%	5.3%	5.6%	1.6%	.8%	3.4%	5.7%	1.8%	.1%
0	6.8	8.3	1.0	1.0	7.1	9.5	1.2	1.2	4.4	8.0	2.1	1.2
1	8.4	11.1	1.0	1.1	8.1	12.0	1.8	1.2	5.0	9.3	1.0	1.6
2	10.3	14.4	1.5	1.1	9.2	14.8	3.0	1.7	5.5	10.8	4.3	1.2
3	12.4	18.1	1.6	1.4	10.4	17.8	3.0	1.8	6.2	12.3	2.4	1.7
4	14.8	22.3	1.4	1.6	11.8	20.9	2.5	2.3	6.9	14.0	1.7	1.6
5	17.5	26.7	2.2	1.7	13.3	24.1	2.8	2.0	7.7	15.7	2.8	1.7
6	20.4	31.2	2.1	1.7	14.8	27.3	2.7	1.8	8.6	17.4	3.4	1.6
7	23.2	35.8	2.9	1.7	16.6	30.6	2.6	2.2	9.5	19.3	4.3	2.4
8	26.5	40.2	3.8	1.9	18.5	33.9	2.7	2.1	10.5	21.2	4.8	1.7
9	30.6	44.6	3.6	1.9	20.5	37.1	2.8	2.5	11.5	23.1	4.1	2.5
10	34.8	48.8	2.9	1.8	22.6	40.4	4.0	2.0	12.5	25.0	5.8	2.3
11	38.7	52.8	4.1	1.9	25.0	43.6	5.5	2.6	13.7	27.1	5.0	2.3
12	42.2	56.6	4.2	1.9	27.4	46.7	5.3	2.3	14.9	29.2	4.5	2.1
13	45.5	60.0	5.0	1.8	30.0	49.7	4.7	2.1	16.2	31.3	6.2	2.2
14	48.6	63.2	4.8	2.0	32.8	52.6	5.1	2.0	17.4	33.4	6.2	1.9
15	51.6	66.2	4.1	1.6	35.6	55.4	6.3	2.6	18.7	35.5	7.4	2.2
16	54.7	69.0	4.4	1.8	38.5	58.0	5.6	2.6	20.2	37.7	8.7	2.6
17	57.8	71.7	4.9	1.7	41.4	60.6	4.5	2.6	21.7	40.0	9.2	2.3
18	60.8	74.1	4.5	1.8	44.2	63.0	6.0	2.3	23.3	42.2	8.2	1.9
19	63.6	76.3	5.0	1.8	46.9	65.3	5.4	2.5	24.9	44.4	9.6	2.0
20	66.3	78.3	4.2	2.1	49.6	67.5	5.9	2.8	26.8	46.7	8.6	1.7
21	68.7	80.1	5.6	1.6	52.3	69.5	7.4	2.7	28.8	49.0	7.9	1.6
22	71.0	81.8	5.1	1.7	54.9	71.6	6.2	2.7	31.0	51.3	9.2	2.4
23	73.3	83.2	4.6	1.8	57.6	73.5	7.2	2.6	33.1	53.7	8.6	1.8

24	75.4	84.6	5.7	1.8	60.2	75.3	6.0	2.3	35.3	55.9	9.5	1.7
25	77.5	85.9	6.1	1.7	62.7	77.1	7.4	2.6	37.7	58.2	9.2	1.6
26	79.5	87.0	5.1	1.6	65.2	78.7	6.0	2.5	40.2	60.5	9.0	1.4
27	81.2	88.0	5.9	2.0	67.6	80.3	7.7	2.1	42.7	62.7	9.9	2.0
28	82.8	89.0	5.9	1.9	69.9	81.8	6.4	2.6	45.1	64.9	9.1	1.5
29	84.2	89.8	8.6	2.2	72.1	83.2	7.4	2.4	47.6	67.1	8.7	2.1
30	85.4	90.6	7.9	2.1	74.1	84.5	6.7	2.2	50.2	69.2	9.2	1.5
31	86.6	91.3	6.8	1.8	76.0	85.7	7.6	2.5	52.8	71.2	8.8	1.8
32	87.6	91.9	4.9	2.1	77.7	86.8	7.5	2.5	55.4	73.2	8.8	1.6
33	88.6	92.4	6.7	2.1	79.4	87.8	8.7	2.3	58.0	75.0	10.4	1.6
34	89.5	92.9	4.8	2.1	81.0	88.7	7.8	2.5	60.6	76.8	8.8	1.8
35	90.3	93.4	7.7	1.9	82.6	89.6	6.6	2.7	63.1	78.5	9.9	1.7
36	91.1	93.8	6.3	2.6	84.0	90.4	5.5	2.2	65.5	80.1	10.8	1.3
37	91.8	94.2	7.7	2.7	85.4	91.1	7.0	2.4	67.8	81.5	8.7	1.4
38	92.4	94.5	4.9	1.7	86.6	91.8	5.2	2.1	70.0	82.9	7.7	1.7
39	92.9	94.9	8.7	1.8	87.8	92.5	6.5	2.3	71.9	84.3	9.2	1.7
40	93.4	95.1	5.8	1.8	89.0	93.1	7.9	2.1	73.9	85.5	12.3	2.1
41	93.8	95.4	6.6	2.3	90.1	93.7	3.9	1.5	75.5	86.6	11.1	1.7
42	94.2	95.7	3.8	1.5	91.1	94.2	7.0	2.4	77.2	87.7	9.8	2.5
43	94.5	95.9	7.7	1.6	91.9	94.7	6.7	1.7	78.7	88.7	10.8	2.4
44	94.9	96.1	7.2	1.8	92.7	95.1	8.1	2.4	80.2	89.6	10.4	2.2
45	95.2	96.4	4.1	1.8	93.4	95.5	5.7	1.4	81.6	90.5	7.9	2.1
46	95.5	96.6	6.6	2.0	94.0	95.9	9.0	1.8	82.9	91.2	9.8	2.1
47	95.8	96.8	7.3	1.9	94.5	96.2	8.2	1.8	84.2	91.9	10.9	1.7
48	96.1	96.9	5.5	1.7	94.9	96.5	11.9	2.4	85.3	92.6	10.6	2.0
49	96.4	97.1	8.4	1.9	95.3	96.8	8.1	2.4	86.4	93.2	11.0	2.1
50	96.6	97.3	8.3	1.6	95.7	97.0	5.0	2.3	87.4	93.7	10.2	1.6
More than 50	100.0	100.0	4.5	1.4	100.0	100.0	6.6	2.1	100.0	100.0	6.4	1.7

ences for home purchase loan denials than for refinance and home improvement loans, because the latter applicants are a select group that has already received at least one loan—the original home purchase loan. We find some evidence that this is the case: for black applicants, the residual denial rate is higher for home purchase loans than for refinances. Interestingly, this pattern does not hold for Asian and Hispanic applicants; their residual denial rates are greater for refinances than for home purchase loans. For all minority groups there are sizable unexplained residuals for refinance and home improvement loan applications as well as for home purchase applications, suggesting that having once qualified for a new home loan brings little useful information to the regressions. Exactly what kind of process could generate these outcomes for different credit products requires more investigation.

One possibly fruitful approach would be to pay more attention to the individual lenders and their characteristics. In other work (Avery, Beeson, and Sniderman 1993b, 1994), we have demonstrated that lenders are heterogeneous in terms of their propensities to attract and approve minority applicants, and that there appears to be little consistency either within or between lenders in their actions toward minorities. Theories regarding the operation of housing credit markets should exploit these findings as part of a general explanation of the data-generating process.

Additional studies of the relationship between race and risk outcomes would also appear to be particularly important to shed light on the reasons for observed racial differences in our residuals. If the patterns we observe are due to discrimination by lenders, and such discrimination takes the form of a higher risk threshold for minorities, then we would expect loans granted to black applicants to perform better than those granted to whites, ceteris paribus. Given the findings highlighted in this chapter, such examinations would seem important. At the same time, we are cautious about the power of such hypothesis tests. Several different explanations for significant racial intercepts can be observationally equivalent, making it difficult to claim persuasively that any one process adequately accounts for the variations in the data. Accordingly, careful attention to distinguishing among competing hypotheses through choice of data and modeling strategies seems crucial.

Notes

This chapter is an updated version of Working Paper 93-09, Federal Reserve Bank of Cleveland. We thank Glenn Canner, Stuart Garbiel, Stuart Rosenthal, John Yinger, and Peter Zorn for helpful comments. The views stated herein are those of the authors and are not necessarily those of the Federal Reserve Bank of Cleveland or of the Board of Governors of the Federal Reserve System.

1. See, for example, the Fair Housing Act of 1968 and the Equal Credit Opportunity Act, implemented in 1975, which prohibit lenders from discriminating against individual loan applicants on the basis of race or ethnic origin, gender, and other factors. The latter law also prohibits the explicit use of such variables in credit screening, *even if cost-related*. Also, the Community Reinvestment Act of 1977 requires that depository institutions help meet the credit needs of their communities, including low-income and minority areas, in a manner consistent with safe and sound banking.

2. Two exceptions are the studies by King (1980) and Schafer and Ladd (1981), who found little evidence of neighborhood redlining but some evidence of higher denial rates for black and Hispanic applicants, after controlling for all available information on other factors—such as income and credit history—relevant to the lending decision. Although quite informative, these studies were limited in their geographic coverage and in the number and types of lenders surveyed. In addition, several studies have used household-level data without neighborhood effects. Canner, Gabriel, and Wooley (1991), Gabriel and Rosenthal (1991), and Duca and Rosenthal (1992) study racial aspects of credit rationing and market performance by using data from the Survey of Consumer Finances, which comprises information collected from a sample of households. These studies attempt to infer from the households' experiences and demographic characteristics whether lenders treat people differently as a result of their racial status.

3. The use of nonlinear and interactive effects may help to mitigate the impact of the admittedly arbitrary choice of a linear probability model. With more than 2 million observations, the use of either a logistic or probit model form would have been impractical. However, nonlinear transformations of the independent variables allow for a potential model fit that approximates these forms.

4. Lenders reported the date of both the application and loan action. The application month would be the ideal choice as a proxy for interest rates, since most mortgage rates are locked in at that point. Unfortunately, the filing year is defined by the action date, which is the date of the denial for a denied application, but the closing date for accepted and originated mortgages. Because the closing date is typically a month or two later than the approval date, this creates a systematic bias in the HMDA data in the relationship between the loan action and application dates and the loan's disposition. For example, more than half of the applications made in November or December 1991 that were filed for the 1991 calendar year were denials. Closing dates for accepted applications during those months were likely to extend over the first of the year and thus were filed for the 1992 calendar year. Potentially this problem could be reduced by combining several years of data. However, this raises the issue of changing filing requirements.

5. In 1993 the reporting requirement was expanded to include all mortgage bankers taking 100 or more applications in an MSA regardless of their asset size.

6. Institutions with assets of less than $30 million are not required to report race, income, or gender for loan applicants. In addition, the HMDA filings contain many errors and inconsistencies even after extensive editing by the receiving agencies. We dealt with missing and implausible data by using a "hot deck" imputation procedure similar to that used by the U.S. Bureau of the Census. Applications with missing or implausible data were statistically matched to applications for the same type of loan in the same census tract that came closest to them in reported characteristics (race, loan action, income, and loan amount). Missing values were filled in using the variable value

of the matched observation. Overall, income was imputed for 4.9 percent of the study sample applications, loan amount for 1.5 percent, gender for 4.0 percent, and race for 5.6 percent.

7. The following loan filings were omitted from the sample: (1) loans purchased from other institutions (because they did not require an action by the reporting lender and often were missing geographic information) and applications for properties outside the MSAs in which the lender had an office (5,670,768 loans dropped), (2) applications for multifamily homes (55,703 loans dropped), and (3) applications that never reached the stage of lender action because they were either withdrawn by the applicant or closed for incompleteness (869,287 loans dropped). Overall in 1990 (1991), the sample consisted of 1,984,688 (2,087,470) home purchase loan applications; 716,595 (1,500,215) refinancing applications; and 787,952 (861,518) home improvement loan applications. The final sample includes some mobile home loans and condominium loans, since they were treated as one- to four-family units in the HMDA reporting guidelines.

8. The distinction between loan types may be blurred. Institutions were allowed to report home improvement loans secured by a first lien as either home purchase or home improvement loans. Some home improvement loans may also be reported as refinancings if a new first lien was issued. Some refinancing may not have been reported at all. If a refinancing was undertaken primarily for a purpose other than home purchase or home improvement (such as college expenses or to start a business), then it did not have to be reported. Similarly, unless the borrower specifically noted home improvements as a reason for the loan, lenders did not have to report home equity or second-lien mortgages.

9. In the HMDA data, household income may be slightly understated, as it reflects only the portion of an applicant's income used for mortgage qualification.

10. These figures exclude Puerto Rico, which is included in the figures in table 3.1. If Puerto Rico is included, Hispanics are 8.1 percent of the loan sample.

11. The reported standard errors in tables 3.3, 3.4, and 3.5 are those from a standard regression program. These may be biased due to heteroskedasticity stemming from the fact that the underlying model is a linear-probability model.

12. The model was actually estimated using deviations about the means, which is computationally equivalent to a single-component fixed effect model. For 1990 (1991), the home purchase sample had 1,984,688 (2,087,470) observations located in 607,631 (662,571) unique combinations of 40,008 (39,963) tracts and 20,695 (26,508) lenders spread across 340 (341) MSAs; thus, the average tract had about 15 lenders in each year, each of whom served about 30 tracts per MSA. For the refinancing sample in 1990 (1991), the 716,595 (1,500,215) observations were located in 326,535 (563,380) unique combinations of 37,746 (38,912) tracts and 16,159 (23,284) lenders. For the home improvement loan sample in 1990 (1991), the 787,951 (861,518) observations were located in 267,158 (285,605) unique combinations of 39,219 (39,216) tracts and 12,280 (13,276) lenders.

13. An argument can be made that the basic model should have been estimated only using white applicants, as this would yield estimates of the racial residual differences that are less sensitive to assumptions about the model's parameterization. Although we considered this option, we decided against it because it left too few observations in some of the minority tracts for accurate estimates of the tract effects. Comparisons with some subpopulations suggest that results using the white-only sample would be very similar to those obtained with the full sample.

14. See Lang and Nakamura (1993) or ICF (1991) for more discussion on this point.

References

Avery, Robert B., Patricia E. Beeson, and Mark S. Sniderman. 1993a. "Home Mortgage Lending by the Numbers." *Economic Commentary* (Federal Reserve Bank of Cleveland), February 15.

———. 1993b. "Lender Consistency in Housing Credit Markets." In *Proceedings of the 1993 Conference on Bank Structure*, Federal Reserve Bank of Chicago (339–58). Chicago: Federal Reserve Bank of Chicago. Also, *Working Paper* 93-10. Federal Reserve Bank of Cleveland (August).

———. 1994. "Cross-lender Variation in Home Mortgage Lending." *Economic Review* (Federal Reserve Bank of Cleveland) 30 (4, Quarter 4): 15–29.

Canner, Glenn B., and Delores S. Smith. 1991. "Home Mortgage Disclosure Act: Expanded Data on Residential Lending." *Federal Reserve Bulletin* 77 (November): 859–81.

———. 1992. "Expanded HMDA Data on Residential Lending: One Year Later." *Federal Reserve Bulletin* 78 (November): 801–24.

Canner, Glenn B., Stuart A. Gabriel, and J. Michael Wooley. 1991. "Race, Default Risk, and Mortgage Lending: A Study of the FHA and Conventional Loan Markets." *Southern Economic Journal* 58(1): 249–62.

Duca, John V., and Stuart S. Rosenthal. 1992. "Borrowing Constraints, Household Debt, and Racial Discrimination in Loan Markets." Photocopy.

Gabriel, Stuart A., and Stuart R. Rosenthal. 1991. "Credit Rationing, Race, and the Mortgage Market." *Journal of Urban Economics* 29 (May): 371–79.

ICF, Inc. 1991. *The Secondary Market and Community Lending through Lenders' Eyes*. Report prepared for Federal Home Loan Mortgage Corp. Fairfax, Va.: Author, February.

King, A. Thomas. 1980. "Discrimination in Mortgage Lending: A Study of Three Cities." *Working Paper* 91, Office of Policy and Economic Research, Federal Home Loan Bank Board. Washington, D.C.: Federal Home Loan Bank Board, February.

Lang, William W., and Leonard I. Nakamura. 1993. "A Model of Redlining." *Journal of Urban Economics* 33 (March): 223–34.

Munnell, Alicia H., Lynn E. Browne, James McEneaney, and Geoffrey M.B. Tootell. 1992. "Mortgage Lending in Boston: Intepreting HMDA Data." Federal Reserve Bank of Boston Working Paper 92-07. Boston: Federal Reserve Bank of Boston, October.

Munnell, Alicia H., Geoffrey M.B. Tootell, Lynn E. Browne, and James McEneaney. 1996. "Mortgage Lending in Boston: Interpreting HMDA Data." *American Economic Review*. Forthcoming.

Schafer, Robert, and Helen F. Ladd. 1981. *Discrimination in Mortgage Lending*. Cambridge, Mass.: MIT Press.

Chapter Four

TURNING A CRITICAL EYE ON THE CRITICS

Geoffrey M.B. Tootell

In a 1992 study on lending discrimination for the Federal Reserve Bank of Boston, Munnell and colleagues found that race played an independent role in the mortgage lending decision. Three years later, these authors refined and extended their results (Munnell et al. 1996). The earlier study, however, was subjected to several criticisms, ranging, on a conceptual level, from concerns about the effects of possible omitted variable bias to, on a more mundane level, questions about the specification of the model and the integrity of the data. Whereas any of these criticisms could potentially be important in a study of this sort, this chapter demonstrates that, in fact, none are.

The question of whether or not relevant variables have been omitted from the analysis is addressed thoroughly in Munnell et al. (1996), and is discussed only briefly here. Instead, my critique focuses on the specification of the model for what is now known as the "Boston Fed" study and on the validity of the data.

The first major section of this chapter briefly analyzes the possibility of omitted variable bias. The usefulness of examining mortgage defaults, rather than application denials, is discussed in this context. The second major section considers various specification issues in detail. It is shown that altering the equation or the estimation technique of the original study, as critics have explicitly or implicitly suggested, either has no effect on the results or is not supported by the data. In fact, race remains a significant factor in the mortgage lending decision even if these alternative specifications are used. The accuracy of the data is then examined. Claims about the unreliability of the data, as discussed in the third major section, are shown to be more hyperbole than reality. Although the integrity of the data has drawn the most attention, these criticisms have the least validity. The conclusion briefly discusses how the enforcement of fair lending laws has been affected by the recent debate.

CRITICISMS BASED ON THEORY: OMITTED VARIABLE BIAS

It has been argued that the Boston Fed study finding (Munnell et al. 1992, 1996) that race plays a significant role in the mortgage lending decision suggests that a variable important to the lending decision and correlated with race may have—indeed, some argue, must have—been omitted. If an omitted variable exists that is positively correlated to both minority status and the probability of denial, then the importance of race may be overstated in the statistical analysis. Possible omitted variables fall into two categories, those that are part of the lender's information set and those that are not.

It was widely suspected that the HMDA data omitted variables that were important to the mortgage lending decision, that were correlated with the race of the applicant, and that were part of the information set of the lender. This suspicion motivated the Boston Fed, with the help of the other regulatory agencies, to attempt to collect every piece of information in the lenders' files that could be related to the mortgage lending decision. One undisputed result of the Boston Fed study has been confirmation that the HMDA data do omit important variables that are in the lender's files.

Omitted variables may also exist that are correlated with the race of the applicant and the performance of the loan but are not part of the lender's information set. Phelps (1972), Spence (1974), and Ashenfelter and Hannan (1986), for example, showed that if lenders are aware of these correlations, then they can use race as a signal for the omitted variable's effect on loan profitability. In such a case, lenders would force minorities to higher standards for the variables that lenders do collect and that were used in the Boston Fed study; this is the statistical discrimination alluded to in Becker (1993). Although illegal, the lender's use of race as a signal for these missing variables could be economically rational if enforcement is lax.

Whether the missing variables are in the lender's information set or not, race would appear significant in a denial regression, at least in part owing to the omitted variables. In the former case, a more complete collection of the data in the lender's files would eliminate the bias in the estimation of the effect of race; in the latter case, it would not. The distinction is important when attempting to analyze the problem.

Testing for Omitted Variables

It is easy to assert that omitted variable bias exists, but the assertion is difficult to prove or disprove. Simply examining how well the equation fits the data is one traditional test for the importance of any possible omitted variables. If the equation seems to be predicting well in general, then the possibility of serious omitted variables is small.[1] On the other hand, if race were being used as a signal, the omitted variables would not seriously diminish the equation's goodness-of-fit, since these variables would be accounted for in the regression by the already included signal.

Unfortunately, when the dependent variable is dichotomous instead of continuous, such as whether to grant or deny a loan application, traditional goodness-of-fit statistics like the R^2 become meaningless. Alternative measures are available, but none reveals just how much of the movement in the dependent variable is left unexplained after accounting for a given set of explanatory variables. The goodness-of-fit measures that do exist all imply that the fit of the equations examined in Munnell et al. (1996) is relatively good, certainly relative to the HMDA data, but the measures cannot quantify the importance of any residual error and/or omitted variable. Munnell et al. (1996) discuss this issue in greater detail.

The lack of an absolute measure of the equation's goodness-of-fit requires that researchers postulate what variables could have been omitted and then examine both their importance in the mortgage lending decision and their correlation with race. To examine the importance of possible omitted variables, two sets of questions need to be answered. First, was any variable in the lender's information set omitted from the Boston Fed study's data set, and is there any evidence that this variable is significantly related to both race and loan performance? Second, are variables missing from both the lender's and the researcher's information sets that are, in fact, correlated with race and loan performance and that the lender knows are correlated with race and profitability?

No definitive answer can be given to either set of questions. There is, however, strong evidence that the Boston Fed analysis did not omit any variable significantly related to the mortgage lending decision that was in the lender's information set. For each application the study collected practically all the information on both the standard loan application form and the credit report, as well as the essential information from the property appraisal.[2] Every variable mentioned as important by the loan officers and underwriters we interviewed was collected, plus many others. It is difficult to find a variable systematically related to the mortgage lending decision and collected by the lender that the Boston Fed did not gather.

As a result, it has been postulated that any omitted variables that do exist and are in the lender's information set must be idiosyncratically, rather than systematically, related to the mortgage lending decision. For example, an applicant may have missed several debt payments due to illness. As a result, the lender may choose to ignore this particular imperfection in the applicant's credit history. A regression that fails to account for the cause of this credit market problem, however, would not be as forgiving. Idiosyncratic characteristics of the property, such as whether a condo is in a building with too few owner-occupied units, have also been suggested as possible omissions.

Idiosyncratic variables may be important to a few applications but, by their very definition, would have no systematic effect on the mortgage lending decision. Statistical models quantify idiosyncratic effects as deviations from the predicted consequences of systematic effects. Even if these variables could be collected, each such variable is relevant to so few observations that an accurate measure of its importance to the mortgage lending decision would be impossible; an idiosyncratic variable is essentially a dummy variable for a single observation, which is one reason bank examiners have such a difficult job.[3] Neither a regression nor an examiner could tell if such a variable had been applied fairly.[4]

Moreover, little, if any, evidence has been advanced revealing any correlation between race and these idiosyncratic variables. Unlike the variables missing from the HMDA data, such as credit history, net wealth, and the loan-to-value ratio, there is no evidence that minority status is related to these hypothesized idiosyncratic variables, particularly after accounting for all the other series in the Boston Fed data base. Such variables may be correlated with the location of the property, the applicant's income, and the like, but there is no reason to believe they should be correlated with the race of the applicant once all these other variables are taken into account.

Default Analysis as Test of Statistical Discrimination

Although the Boston Fed study includes every variable in the lender's information set that is systematically related to the mortgage lending decision, lenders may still use race as a signal for important variables they do not possess, if race is correlated with these variables. Whether or not lenders are using race in this way is obviously difficult to disprove definitively. Traditionally, analysis of mortgage defaults has been advocated to examine this issue. Studies of mortgage defaults can help investigate whether important variables have been omitted from a denial regression and whether race plays an independent role in loan performance, but they are not well-designed to uncover taste-based discrimination.[5]

Tootell (1993, 1995) and Yinger (1993) have demonstrated why default regressions are not well-suited for examining taste-based discrimination. The intuition is fairly simple; since these studies only examine accepted applications, they omit the very observations that would indicate whether discrimination does occur, the rejected minority applications. Furthermore, under the most favorable assumptions, default regressions cannot distinguish between discrimination that is taste-based and discrimination that could be statistical. In fact, Tootell (1995) showed that the effects of these two types of discrimination would tend to offset each other in the estimation of the coefficient on race in a default regression. Finally, even if a noiseless measure of race as a signal could be uncovered from default analysis, the coefficient on race in a denial regression would still be required to assess whether minorities were being treated fairly; the height of the hurdle must be correct.[6] Default studies alone cannot determine whether minorities are being treated fairly.

What default analysis can help uncover is whether race plays an independent role in the probability of loan default, given the information set of the lender. If a default regression that contains the complete information set of the lender produces a higher probability of default for minorities, then the foundation for statistical discrimination exists. However, such a finding does not indicate that statistical discrimination is occurring, or that taste-based discrimination is not. Default analysis can help test whether important variables are being omitted from the denial analysis, but it can neither sidestep the problems with omitted variables nor definitively determine whether taste-based discrimination is occurring.[7]

Furthermore, it appears unlikely that statistical discrimination explains the positive coefficient on race found in Munnell et al. (1996). First, to use race as a signal, the lender must be aware of a higher conditional default probability of minorities, one conditional on all the other information that lenders possess. Default studies must, therefore, predate the denial results and incorporate the relevant part of the lender's information set. The most thorough default analyses—Van Order, Westin, and Zorn (1993) and Berkovec et al. (1994)—were conducted after Munnell et al. (1992). The results from these studies are somewhat inconclusive. Van Order et al. (1993) found a positive effect in some areas of the country and a negative effect in others. These authors also have information only on the racial composition of the ZIP code, not the borrower. Perhaps more important, however, they omit the borrower's credit history. Since minorities tend to have weaker credit histories, this omission strongly biases their estimate in favor of finding a positive relationship between the racial composition of the ZIP code and defaults. Berkovec et al. (1994) also omit credit history, thus biasing the coefficient on race upward in their default regressions; they also examine FHA data, not the conventional mortgage loans studied in Munnell et al. (1996).[8] Further, in our discussions with loan officers and underwriters prior to the Boston lending survey, no one mentioned the use of race as a signal of higher loan default probability; if race were used in this way, lenders would know that race would be found to be significant in the mortgage lending regressions.

The evidence on the existence of important omitted variables is not compelling. If any variables are missing from the Boston Fed database, they are probably also missing from the lender's data set. Default analysis can help to uncover whether variables exist that are missing from the lender's information set and correlated with race, but such a finding does not rule out the existence of taste-based discrimination. Furthermore, using statistical discrimination as an explanation for the role of race in the mortgage lending decision requires prior knowledge of the default analysis, which loan officers and underwriters do not appear to have had. At this point, the case for statistical discrimination as the cause of a positive coefficient on race in the denial regression appears weak.

CRITICISM BASED ON ECONOMETRICS: SPECIFICATION OF THE EQUATION

Since the Boston Fed database is the most complete set of variables extant on the mortgage lending decision, much of the debate about the study has revolved around specification issues. Munnell et al. (1996) report a wide range of specifications, and examine many more. Debate about the exact specification, however, has centered on a few central themes. The exclusion of one or two specific variables found in the data set turned out to be the most important criticism empirically. Conceptually, the most important specification issue concerns possible simultaneity in the determination of the loan-to-value ratio.

Omission of Credit History Guidelines Variable

In the extended survey conducted by the Boston Fed, lenders were asked "whether the applicant's credit history met your loan policy guidelines for approval" (Munnell et al. 1996). The answer to this question has been included in much of the later analysis using the Boston Fed data, and its inclusion tends to have some effect on the estimated size of the coefficient on race. The Boston Fed study has been implicitly criticized for not incorporating this variable in its analysis. However, both econometric theory and common sense demand that this variable be omitted from the estimation since the variable is, in fact, a measure of whether the application was actually denied a mortgage, not a determinant of mortgage denials. Including the variable in the analysis reveals a basic misunderstanding of what this survey question is measuring.

The influence of the credit history guidelines variable on the results is shown in table 4.1. Column (1) of the table provides the results of a basic mortgage denial regression that excludes this variable, whereas column (2) gives the coefficients from the same regression once the answer to this question is included as an explanatory variable.[9] The addition of this variable to the analysis causes the coefficient on race to decline by about one standard deviation, although it remains statistically significant well beyond the 1 percent level. The economic impact of race remains significant, explaining about 5 percentage points of the differential denial rates between races. In general, statistical work that includes the credit history guidelines variable in its analysis tends to find a slightly smaller effect for race in the mortgage lending decision.

However, inclusion of the credit history guideline variable in the statistical analysis of the mortgage lending decision makes little sense conceptually and no sense empirically. The answer to the question that produces this variable is not to be found on the loan application; the judgment about whether the applicant's credit history passed the credit history guidelines of the lender was not made before the application was accepted or denied. Instead, the assessment was formed by the lender well over a year after the decision about whether to grant the loan had been made. The answer to the question is not an objective assessment of the applicant's credit history before the decision, but an explanation for the lending decision a year after that decision was made. Conceptually, it is like putting a reason for denial on the right-hand side of the denial regression, which presupposes that a denial

Table 4.1 RESULTS OF ADDING VARIABLES OMITTED FROM BOSTON FED ANALYSIS (MUNNELL ET AL. 1992)

Variable	Denial Equation (1)	Denial Equation with Credit History Guidelines (2)	Determinants of Credit History Guidelines (3)	Denial Regression with Unverified Information (4)
Constant	−7.68	−6.40	−9.37	−7.88
	(−15.20)	(−11.73)	(−14.64)	(−14.64)
Housing expense/income	.48	.37	.64	.49
	(3.13)	(2.06)	(3.34)	(2.93)
Total debt payments/income	.05	.37	.64	.49
	(6.45)	(5.33)	(3.55)	(5.79)
Net wealth	.00009	.00002	.0001	.0001
	(1.17)	(.22)	(1.36)	(1.58)
Consumer credit history	.32	.008	.69	.31
	(9.27)	(.16)	(15.63)	(8.45)
Mortgage credit history	.32	.008	.69	.31
	(2.68)	(.69)	(4.02)	(2.13)
Public record history	1.15	.23	1.86	1.28
	(6.44)	(.98)	(9.36)	(6.77)
Unemployment region	.08	.07	.07	.08
	(2.84)	(2.15)	(1.81)	(2.67)

Self-employed	.52	.58	.24	.50
	(2.74)	(2.71)	(.93)	(2.51)
Loan to value ratio	2.01	1.63	2.23	2.06
	(4.56)	(3.28)	(4.01)	(4.39)
Denied private mortgage insurance	4.54	4.53	2.24	4.54
	(9.16)	(9.00)	(6.65)	(8.99)
Rent to value in tract	.68	.65	.54	.62
	(3.51)	(3.12)	(1.92)	(3.06)
Two- to four-family home	.48	.71	−.12	.51
	(2.90)	(3.74)	(−.54)	(2.83)
Unverified information				3.02
				(13.10)
Credit history guidelines		3.50		
		(15.55)		
Race	.62	.47	.78	.57
	(4.36)	(2.85)	(4.51)	(3.76)
Log of likelihood function	−838.62	−683.04	−537.02	−746.19
Number of observations	2,923	2,923	2,923	2,923

occurred: in short, the credit history guidelines variable is a surrogate measure of the dependent variable.

The credit history guideline variable's relationship to the dependent variable is highlighted in column (3) of table 4.1. All the determinants of loan denials are used to explain the lender's ex post assessment about whether the applicant passed its credit history guidelines. Since the question only refers to the credit history of the applicant, only the credit history variables should be significant in this regression. In fact, the coefficients on almost all the variables in the denial regression are significant in the ex post assessment of the applicant's credit history. Furthermore, the coefficients in the credit history guidelines regression are almost identical to their counterparts in the mortgage denial regression in column (1) of the table. Importantly, race plays a large and statistically significant independent role in whether the applicant was said to pass the lender's credit history guidelines.

The similarity of the two equations indicates that the credit history guidelines variable is actually capturing whether the applicant, particularly a minority applicant, was denied the mortgage and is not representing the ex ante assessment of the applicant's credit history. Holding the applicant's credit history constant, the applicant's race, loan-to-value ratio, obligation ratios, and employment status, for example, should not help explain whether his or her credit history was acceptable; only the three credit history indexes should be relevant. Unless an important variable exists that is correlated with credit history and all these other included variables, and which also happens to produce similar coefficients for these other variables in both a credit history guidelines regression and a denial regression, including the credit history guidelines variable in the denial regression is simply putting the dependent variable on the right-hand side of the equation. The large estimated coefficient on the credit history guidelines variable and its huge *t*-statistic also indicate that this variable is a surrogate measure of the dependent variable.[10]

As a final test of the validity of using the credit history guideline variable, my colleagues and I compared the objective measures of the credit history of applicants in the largest institutions with the answer to the credit history guidelines question and the action taken. Within a given institution, many of the applications that "failed to pass" these guidelines and were rejected for a mortgage actually had credit histories that appeared to dominate, in terms of better consumer, mortgage, and public records histories, other applications that "passed" these guidelines and whose loans were accepted. These cases highlight the fact that the question is a subjective assessment categorizing the denial decision.

Only ex ante objective variables should be in the equation determining the action taken. The empirical exercise attempts to model lenders' subjective decision making as a function of objective variables. If a subjective, ex post, assessment is included as a determinant of the subjective decision, then the decision itself is being used as a determinant of the decision. The credit history guidelines variable fails to capture possible variations in lending standards across institutions, and any analysis that includes it seriously biases the results.

Munnell et al. (1996) did attempt to capture possible differences in lender standards. Subsets of lenders were examined, allowing standards to vary by type of institution, and the results were the same for these subsets; the coefficients were stable across the cuts.[11] Thus, it did not appear that the importance of the determinants of mortgage lending varied over different lenders. Although Stengel and Glennon (1995) asserted that the three lenders in their study do have different standards, they found that altering the regressions to account for different institutional guidelines had little effect on the regression results; the coefficient on race in the institution-specific regressions was almost identical to that in the market regression, and the significance levels of the coefficient on race were basically unaffected.[12] Furthermore, both of the Munnell et al. studies (1992 and 1996) included dummy variables for each lender in the statistical analysis, to ensure that minorities were not simply frequenting "tough" lenders. The race coefficient remained both statistically and economically significant in these regressions. Differing lender standards do not appear to be a problem with the analysis, which makes sense, given that a large portion of loans are sold in the secondary market.

Inclusion of Unverified Information Variable

A similar problem arises with the answer to the question of whether unverified information appears on the application. Column (4) of table 4.1 shows that unverified information also increases the probability of denial and is highly correlated with the dependent variable. The unverified information variable is correlated with race, but to a lesser degree than the credit history guidelines variable. Yet, it too suffers from several problems. First, it could be endogenous. Applications that are rejected outright do not need to have all the data verified. Thus, unverified information cannot be used to explain denials, since the action taken on the loan may explain whether all the information was verified. Second, like the credit history guidelines variable, this is an ex post assessment. The problem is, however, less severe and, as table 4.1 reveals, its effect on the estimate of the race coefficient is negligible.[13]

Possible Simultaneity in Mortgage Lending Decision

Yezer, Phillips, and Trost (1994) asserted that the mortgage application process is more complicated than is assumed in the empirical model in Munnell et al. (1992). Specifically, they used a simulation exercise to show the scope of any potential bias to the estimate of the coefficient on race in a single equation mortgage denial regression, when it is assumed that the loan-to-value ratio is endogenously determined and positively correlated with race. In general, simultaneous determination of the action taken and the loan-to-value ratio could bias the coefficient on race, although the direction depends on the correlation between the race of the applicant and the loan-to-value ratio.

Is the down payment, in fact, partly the lender's decision? The loan-to-value ratio, especially for first-time buyers, is certainly determined by the amount of wealth the applicants have accumulated and the price of the house they wish to purchase. How much flexibility potential borrowers have once they walk through the lender's door is, however, uncertain. Furthermore, for true simultaneity to occur, the applicant must know the approval or denial outcome when the loan-to-value ratio is being determined. The error term in the denial equation must be realized, and affect the loan-to-value ratio, for any bias in the estimated coefficient on race to occur because of simultaneity. In fact, the loan-to-value ratio can be negotiated as a partial function of the determinants of the lending decision—for example, the down payment may be increased because of a poor credit history—but this change in the loan-to-value ratio does not present a simultaneity problem so long as the error term in the lending decision is not a determinant of the loan-to-value ratio.

The lending process has a chronological sequence; the loan cannot be rejected until the application has been completed, and the application is not completed until the loan-to-value ratio is known. Given this chronology, the equations are block recursive, and no simultaneity bias can occur in the denial regression. Perhaps informal application procedures and decisions occasionally occur, introducing potential simultaneity into some decisions, but this simultaneity is not a widespread characteristic of the actual decision-making process.

Even if the two decisions are made simultaneously, the correlation between the loan-to-value ratio and race is vital in determining the bias in the estimate of the race coefficient. The two variables are, in fact, related. To measure the importance of this correlation for the estimate of the coefficient on race, equations (1) and (2) in table 4.2 reestimate the denial equation while constraining the coefficient on the loan-to-value ratio to be two standard deviations above and below the loan-to-value coefficient estimate in equation (1) of table 4.1. The exercise tests the sensitivity of the estimate of the race coefficient to bias in estimating the coefficient for the loan-to-value ratio. In fact, these drastic changes have little effect on the size or significance of the coefficient on race, suggesting that any bias in the estimate of the coefficient for the loan-to-value ratio, due to any endogeneity of the down payment, has little effect on the estimate of the coefficient for race.

Furthermore, if the two decisions are simultaneous, instrumental variables can be used to avoid any resulting bias. Column (3) of table 4.2 estimates a denial equation including an instrumented estimate of the loan-to-value ratio.[14] The instruments, like the applicant's years on the job, profession, and years of education, are each determined before the applicant walks through the lender's door. Instrumenting for the loan-to-value ratio has no effect on the size or significance of the coefficient on race. The significance of the race coefficient is also robust to the instruments selected.

Finally, since most of the loan-to-value negotiations that might occur probably would be marginal changes near the secondary market loan-to-value threshold levels of 80 percent and 95 percent, the equation is reestimated for a subsample well below these cutoffs. As an extreme, the results for the sample of all applications with loan-to-value ratios of less than 60 percent are shown in column (4) of table 4.2. Even with this subsample, race still plays an economically and statistically significant role in the mortgage lending decision. In short, these data provide little evidence to suggest that the conceptually important issue of endogeneity of some of the explanatory variables in a traditional denial equation is empirically important here.

CRITICISM BASED ON INTEGRITY OF DATA: OUTLIERS AND REDUCED SAMPLES

The issue that has received the most attention in the media is not the proper specification of the Boston Fed study model or omitted vari-

Table 4.2 RESULTS OF MEASURING AND CONTROLLING FOR POSSIBLE SIMULTANEITY

Variable	Low Loan-to-Value Coefficient (1)	High Loan-to-Value Coefficient (2)	Denial Equation Instrumenting for Loan-to-Value Ratio (3)	Low Loan-to-Value Subsample (4)
Constant	−6.86	−8.19	−5.55	−6.30
	(−18.36)	(−21.46)	(−4.56)	(−5.29)
Housing expense income	.47	.48	.45	.35
	(3.06)	(3.09)	(2.89)	(.75)
Total debt payments/income	.05	.05	.06	.05
	(6.67)	(6.46)	(6.71)	(2.55)
Net wealth	.00009	.0001	.00007	.00003
	(1.46)	(1.68)	(.85)	(.19)
Consumer credit history	.31	.31	.33	.19
	(9.21)	(9.24)	(9.37)	(1.72)
Mortgage credit history	.33	.29	.39	−.15
	(2.83)	(2.44)	(2.85)	(-.47)
Public record history	1.17	1.14	1.24	1.16
	(6.58)	(6.40)	(6.57)	(1.78)
Unemployment region	.08	.08	.09	.12
	(2.88)	(2.92)	(2.94)	(1.47)

Self-employed	.47	.51	.49	−.68
	(2.51)	(2.68)	(2.57)	(−1.05)
Loan to value ratio	1.00[a]	2.80[b]	−1.43	2.03
			(−.76)	(1.08)
Denied private mortgage insurance	4.57	4.47	4.90	
	(9.32)	(9.00)	(9.28)	
Rent to value in tract			.74	.20
			(3.64)	(.38)
Two- to four-family home	.54	.49	.59	.60
	(3.31)	(2.93)	(3.10)	(1.00)
Race	.70	.62	.84	1.63
	(5.06)	(4.40)	(4.66)	(3.65)
Log of likelihood function	−846.48	−845.58	−814.88	−105.09
Number of observations	2,925	2,925	2,838	498

a. Constrained to be 1.00.
b. Constrained to be 2.80.

ables, but the integrity of the data. This debate soon became centered in the op-ed pages of the media, but since op-ed pieces are designed more to convince than to illuminate, the discussion quickly was marred by misinformation and error. This section analyzes criticisms concerning the accuracy of the data.

Before that analysis, however, it must be emphasized that the Boston Fed did not alter the original data in any way before making the data public. If an apparent mistake in the decimal place of a loan amount or an obligation ratio was present, it was corrected for our analysis but was not altered in the data released.[15] The Boston Fed allowed other researchers to make their own assessment about these observations. The number of such observations was quite small. Since our results including and excluding these applications were identical, we initially reported the full results. In Munnell et al. (1996), the alternative results are reported. The two major analyses of the data are reviewed next, followed by a discussion of other observations.

Carr and Megbolugbe (1994)

Probably the most objective examination of the data is found in Carr and Megbolugbe (1994; henceforth, also CM), who asserted that miscoded data could "undermine the report's credibility," although they concluded that the Boston Fed results are strongly supported by the data. Their concerns about the data fall into nine categories, or, in their words, "criteria," discussed briefly next.

The first group of criteria cited by Carr and Megbolugbe (1994) resulted from decimal errors that were uncorrected in the released data set or that were errors in variables not used in the analysis. The first criterion removes observations with loan-to-value ratios greater than 3; there were five such applications. Munnell et al. (1996) included no observation with a loan-to-value ratio greater than 2; either a decimal error was corrected or the observation was omitted from the sample. The next two criteria remove 47 observations with low and high implied interest rates—applications listing housing expense that appeared too low or too high relative to the mortgage amount and the loan duration. Some of these anomalies were caused by a decimal error in the loan amount or in one of the components of the obligation ratio.[16] In fact, some of these observations had errors in the housing expense variable that were not reflected in the obligation ratios that the lender calculated and were used by us in the analysis; the interest rate implied by the obligation ratio provided by the lender, and used in the regression analysis, was often much more reasonable for these

47 observations than that implied by the original housing expense information.[17] Whether these observations should be removed or corrected was unclear, so we did both.

Yet, reasons besides data errors can explain why the implied interest rate might be significantly higher or lower than the one the applicants would actually be paying. First, a low loan-to-value ratio would leave a higher percentage of monthly housing expense in the form of taxes and insurance, making the calculated interest rate high. Given the large housing price appreciation in Boston over the previous decade, loan-to-value ratios for many applicants could, and did, decline. Second, when assessing loans on multi-unit properties, some institutions subtracted the income earned by the other units in that property from the housing expense, making the implied interest rate appear very low; these institutions used the obligation ratios calculated in this way when considering the loan. As a result, many of the 47 applications with high implied interest rates had low loan-to-value ratios, and many of the applications with low implied rates were multi-unit properties. An abnormal implied interest rate does not necessarily signal an error, because the interest rate is only implied, not actual. Removing these observations would be arbitrary.

CM continued with several criteria that measure errors in the original HMDA data. From the beginning, the Boston Fed chose not to rely on many of the original HMDA variables, since they were known to be prone to errors; owing to the unreliability of these data, alternatives to these variables were collected and used instead in the study. In fact, most critics, Carr and Megbolugbe included, chose to ignore the problems with the original HMDA data once their criticism of that data had been made. For example, CM found 415 observations where HMDA annual income data did not match the implied annual income from the monthly income collected by the Boston Fed. Again, the Boston Fed collected the monthly income because the accuracy of the HMDA annual income data was suspect; if the income variable appeared to be an outlier, it was the monthly income that was verified on the call-back to the lender, not the HMDA income. CM concluded that "the HMDA recorded income data are incorrect," (p. 5) and then went on to include these 415 observations in their analysis. Why they included them as one of their "criteria" is, thus, unclear.

Another HMDA variable that was not used in the Boston Fed study and that had some errors was whether or not the loan was sold. In the HMDA data, 36 observations were categorized as rejected applications but were also listed as sold loans. Is this an error in the action taken, in a variable Munnell et al. (1996) did use, or in the variable indicating whether or not the loan was sold, which Munnell et al. (1996) did not use? The evidence clearly points to the error being in whether the loan was sold, since all these applications appeared to have been rejected. Not only are these applications generally very weak, but they all have reasons for denial attached to them, as required by HMDA for rejected applications. Lending institutions, in general, were much more careful in transcribing the action taken on mortgage applications than they were with information on whether a loan was sold or not. As a result, the Boston Fed retained these applications as rejections. CM concurred. The purpose of this study was to collect the data relevant to the mortgage lending decision, not to clean up HMDA data irrelevant to the mortgage lending analysis. Highlighting these observations as errors in the data used in the Boston Fed study is incorrect.

CM's other major criterion was whether the obligation ratios calculated from the monthly expense and income variables equaled the obligation ratios lenders asserted they actually used in their lending decision. All of these variables were collected by the Boston Fed. Both the obligation ratios and their components were sought because lenders often discount income when they calculate these ratios; for example, bonuses and commissions are frequently discounted, or spousal income is sometimes not needed for the loan and thus not used in the calculation of the ratios. The components of the obligation ratios and the ratios themselves were collected to ensure that this discounting did not disproportionately affect any group. CM found 460 observations where the ratios used by the lender differed from those calculated using the components. In their analysis, CM chose to use the calculated values. The Boston Fed study decided to use the ratios the lenders provided, since these measures should be the best indicators of the actual ratios considered in the lending decision.

A priori, to use the obligation ratios that the lender provided should be superior, since any discounting of risky or variable income done by the lender should be included as a determinant of the lender's decision to grant the loan. Also, some data errors in housing expense, which may appear as "interest rate errors," are avoided by using the lender's obligation ratios. The first two columns of table 4.3 reveal that using one measure of these ratios rather than the other has little effect on the estimate of the coefficient on race. The more precise estimation of the coefficients for the ratios in column (1) indicates that the data suggest the provided, rather than the calculated, ratios explain the mortgage lending decision more closely. When modeling the mortgage lending decision, the obligation ratios used by the lender,

Table 4.3 EFFECTS OF DATA CHANGES AND SAMPLE REDUCTION

Variable	Given Ratios (1)	Calculated Ratios (2)	No Outliers[a] (3)
Constant	−7.71	−6.33	−8.39
	(−15.27)	(−14.46)	(−14.53)
Housing expense/income	.50	.21	.38
	(3.21)	(1.42)	(2.33)
Total debt payments/income	.05	.008	.06
	(6.56)	(2.59)	(6.94)
Net wealth	.0001	.00008	.0001
	(1.33)	(1.31)	(1.22)
Consumer credit history	.32	.32	.32
	(9.32)	(9.59)	(8.97)
Mortgage credit history	.31	.29	.30
	(2.60)	(2.41)	(2.33)
Public record history	1.15	1.24	1.27
	(6.40)	(7.19)	(6.88)
Unemployment region	.08	.08	.08
	(2.83)	(2.83)	(2.82)
Self-employed	.54	.62	.64
	(2.84)	(3.45)	(3.27)
Loan-to-value ratio	2.01	2.25	2.30
	(4.55)	(5.21)	(4.60)
Denied private mortgage insurance	4.55	.50	4.75
	(9.18)	(9.25)	(8.59)
Rent to value in tract	.69	.62	.70
	(3.58)	(3.22)	(3.39)
Two- to four-family home	.48	.31	.47
	(2.89)	(1.91)	(2.64)
Race	.63	.65	.62
	(4.46)	(4.67)	(4.14)
Log of likelihood function	−834.28	−879.04	−766.27
Number of observations	2,917	2,917	2,741

a. Loan-to-value ratio is between 10 percent and 150 percent. Total obligation ratio is between 10 percent and 80 percent. Net wealth is positive.

rather than the calculated ratios, are superior conceptually and empirically.[18]

Finally, Carr and Megbolugbe (1994) raised doubts about the quality of the net wealth numbers. We had the same doubts and spent considerable time on the telephone to lenders attempting to verify many applicants' net wealth. These calls were rarely productive, even though the largest outliers were being checked. Some researchers have even expressed surprise that slightly over 100 observations had negative net wealth. Negative net wealth need not be rare, as human capital is not included in the calculation of the applicant's assets; for example, the liability of a college loan is not formally offset by the asset value of the human capital produced from that loan. In fact, it is this difficulty in valuing and verifying net wealth that causes lenders to discount it when making a mortgage lending decision.[19]

After all these criteria were cited, CM actually excluded only 53 observations as errors. These observations failed their first two criteria, high and low implied interest rates and high loan-to-value ratios. Of these, my colleagues and I agree that 7 observations probably should be dropped; this was done, in fact, in unpublished tests before Munnell et al. (1992) and in Munnell et al. (1996). Several other observations are obvious errors in decimal placement that are easily corrected. Many of the 53, however, either are not clear errors or are errors in variables not used in the analysis. Thus, a figure of 53 overstates the problem significantly, since subjective judgment is involved in the assessment. Outliers are not necessarily errors. This subjectivity is certainly the case for the 47 observations whose "implied interest rates" were "too high" or "too low." Moreover, even if all the observations with high and low loan-to-value ratios, high and low obligation ratios, and negative net wealth are excluded, the coefficient estimates in column (3) of table 4.3 are little affected. In fact, CM reinforced the findings of the study and provided evidence supporting the integrity of the data.

Horne (1994a, b)

The analysis of the data most frequently cited in the op-ed pages is found in Horne (1994a, b). Federal Deposit Insurance Corporation (FDIC) examiners reviewed a sample of applications from several institutions that were included in the Boston Fed study. The examined institutions were limited to those regulated by the FDIC and to those that had both accepted and rejected minority and white applicants. Furthermore, the applications selected for review were the ones that, despite having the lowest probability of rejection, were, in fact, rejected. Given these criteria, 95 applications were examined: 62 rejections of applications by minorities and 33 rejections of applications by whites. Horne (1994a, b) concluded that the examinations produced evidence of serious data errors. A brief analysis of Horne's criticisms appears in Munnell et al. (1996); the remainder of this subsection analyzes his comments in further detail.

My colleagues and I requested the results of the file reviews to test the robustness of the Boston Fed findings. We requested, in particular, the changes in the data outlined in table 1 of Horne (1994a) and the alterations made to the data for the statistical analysis in Horne (1994b). Horne claimed he could not replicate table 1 of his 1994a paper. He did, however, send to us a copy of the program used to alter the data for Horne (1994b). All the alterations analyzed here emanate from that program. Furthermore, we were given a synopsis of the examiner's write-up for each institution, which discusses in some detail the important applications reviewed.

Table 4.4 shows how Horne's alterations in the data affect the estimation of the determinants of mortgage denials. The first two columns of the table show that, using the full sample, Horne's data changes have little effect on any of the estimated coefficients, including that on race. The regression using the Boston Fed data, column (1), produces estimates for all the coefficients, including race, that are similar to those produced using Horne's altered data.[20] Columns (3) and (4) reestimate the equations in the first two columns for only FDIC institutions. This subsample is analyzed strictly for comparability to Horne (1994b), not for any substantive reason.[21] For either sample, the alteration of the data reduces the coefficient on race by only about one-half of one standard deviation of the coefficient estimate, but it remains large and statistically significant in both samples.

Why do these changes have so little effect? One reason is that many of the corrections made by Horne (1994b) to the data, we made also. When a decimal point seemed obviously misplaced, either in the loan amount or the obligation ratio, we altered the data. Again, the "corrected" data were not sent to the general public, so as not to impose our judgment on other researchers.

However, the major reason the alterations in the data have so little effect on the results is that most of Horne's (1994b) changes were very small and were made to variables not relevant to the study. For example, almost 15 percent of Horne's data alterations were made to HMDA income, used by neither the Boston Fed study nor Horne. We knew the variable was measured erratically, which is why we also collected the monthly income data. Furthermore, changing the applicant's proposed housing expense when the obligation ratios remained unchanged has no effect on the results, since only the ratios are included in the regressions. Finally, changing other error-prone HMDA data, such as whether the approved loan was sold into the secondary market, also has no effect on the results of the study, since the variable was not used in any of the analysis.

Many of Horne's (1994b) changes to the variables that were included in the study were also very slight. There are examples where income

Table 4.4 RESULTS OF HORNE'S ALTERATIONS TO DATA

	Full Sample		FDIC Sample	
Variable	Boston Fed Data (1)	Horne Data (2)	Boston Fed Data (3)	Horne Data (4)
Constant	−7.70	−7.83	−7.76	−8.13
	(−15.25)	(−15.40)	(−10.64)	(−10.74)
Housing expense income	.48	.43	.52	.39
	(3.12)	(2.77)	(2.21)	(1.61)
Total debt payments/income	.05	.05	.04	.05
	(6.62)	(6.93)	(4.51)	(4.99)
Net wealth	.0001	.00002	.0001	.00002
	(1.28)	(.47)	(1.47)	(.58)
Consumer credit history	.32	.32	.56	.57
	(9.26)	(8.93)	(5.94)	(5.28)
Mortgage credit history	.32	.32	.56	.57
	(2.69)	(2.60)	(3.15)	(3.04)
Public record history	1.15	1.24	1.23	1.47
	(6.43)	(6.97)	(4.08)	(4.91)

Unemployment region	.08	.08	.06	.05
	(2.85)	(2.80)	(1.25)	(1.16)
Self-employed	.52	.55	.19	.24
	(2.74)	(2.89)	(.66)	(.80)
Loan-to-value ratio	2.01	2.07	1.77	1.98
	(4.53)	(4.59)	(2.62)	(2.80)
Denied private mortgage insurance	4.54	4.59	4.57	4.67
	(9.17)	(9.29)	(6.97)	(7.17)
Rent to value in tract	.68	.72	−.13	.21
	(3.51)	(3.75)	(−.18)	(.37)
Two- to four-family home	.48	.53	.59	.66
	(2.90)	(3.13)	(2.26)	(2.50)
Race	.62	.55	1.06	.91
	(4.37)	(3.78)	(4.96)	(4.08)
Log of likelihood function	−838.84	−817.51	−357.19	−336.77
Number of observations	2,925	2,925	1,379	1,379

Sources: Data based on Horne (1994b) and Boston Fed study by Munnell et al. (1992, 1996).

was altered by $1 and wealth by $100. Obviously, these adjustments will have little effect on the results. About 10 percent of Horne's changes were to measures of wealth, which have little effect on the estimation, since the coefficient on net wealth in the mortgage lending equation is essentially zero; net wealth could, in fact, be dropped from the analysis with no effect on the results. In short, trivial changes in the data have trivial effects on the results.

One way to illustrate the magnitude of the changes in the data is to compare the estimated probability of denial using the independent variables from the Boston Fed data with the estimated probability of denial using the independent variables from the altered data.[22] The change in the predicted probability of denial is one way to weight the importance of Horne's alterations. After removing five suspicious outliers, the mean change in the predicted probability for the 95 examined applications is only 2.7 percentage points, a small value compared to the standard deviation of the estimated probability of denial, which is 20 percentage points for these 95 applications.[23] In fact, the data changes in 60 percent of the 95 examined applications altered the predicted probability of denial of these observations by less than 1 percentage point. This concordance reveals how minor the changes in fact are. Horne seriously overstated the case for errors in the data by counting trivial changes as well as changes to data that neither Munnell et al. (1992) nor Horne himself used in the analysis.

One might expect that even if the changes to the data had been large, these changes would have had a small effect on the results because only 95 out of 2,925 applications were examined. In fact, these 95 applications represent almost 50 percent of all the rejected loans in the FDIC subsample, and well over 50 percent of all rejected minority applications. A sample of such a large percentage of total rejections should be expected to have a large effect on the estimate of race in the denial equation, if the changes made were significant.

Apart from their trivial impact, some of Horne's alterations did not make sense. For example, one applicant's net wealth was increased from $53,000 to $54 million, whereas the applicant's income was less than $2,000 a month; this application was one of the five outliers mentioned previously. Clearly this "correction" is the result of a misplaced decimal point by Horne (1994b). Many of Horne's other changes also did not add up; in some cases, the income of an applicant would remain unchanged while the housing expense fell, but the ratio of the housing expense to income remained unchanged. Finally, the changes were often inconsistent with the data as described in the examiners' write-ups. For example, Horne increased the obligation ratio from 47 percent to 140 percent for another one of the five outliers mentioned previously. But in the HMDA data, high obligation ratios were not given as the reason for denial, and the synopsis of the examiners' review did not even mention this ratio.

We included these changes nonetheless when analyzing the effects of Horne's alterations in the data on the results, but we did not include Horne's programming errors, which were numerous. For example, whenever Horne (1994b) attempted to change the HMDA income amount, which he did on about one-fourth of the reviewed applications, he mistakenly altered the applicant's gender to the HMDA income value. Again, the changes to the HMDA income were irrelevant to the study, since it was not used in the analysis. Horne also mistook the question describing whether the loan had a fixed or adjustable interest rate for another field. Further, when calculating his closing cost dummy variable, it appears that Horne included the missing value indicator of 666,000 in the liquid assets field instead of omitting these observations.

Horne's (1994b) program also makes a serious error in constructing the dummy variable indicating whether the applicant had a public record of defaults. This credit history category has six subcategories covering various types of public records and bankruptcy. Two of these subcategories are "no public records of defaults" and "the information was not used" (in the evaluation of the application), while the other four subcategories are various types of credit defaults. Horne equated "information not used" with bankruptcy, rather than as no problem. This change is another example of alterations Horne made to the data for observations that were not examined.[24] Since the coefficient on the public records dummy variable is so large, this error could seriously affect the results. These programming errors by Horne were not included in the data changes in any of the tables in this chapter.

More fundamentally, however, it is unclear why errors in the independent variables should have any effect on the estimate of the coefficient on race. Such errors are simply transcription errors, which should be uncorrelated with the applicant's minority status. Even if any such errors were, in fact, correlated with some of the independent variables, the bias in the estimate of the coefficient on race would be determined by the multiple correlation of all these independent variables and race. It is not clear, a priori, what the sign of the effect should be, if it is not zero.

Errors in the independent variables are not an effective criticism. What could be more important, however, are Horne's (1994a, b) claims that errors were made in the dependent variable as well. Horne reversed the action taken on five applications, all of them changes from rejection to acceptance, since only rejected applications were examined. According to the examiner's write-up, one application was rejected because there was no market title; clearly this is a rejection, perhaps due to an omitted variable, but certainly not an acceptance. Another application was rejected at a loan-to-value ratio of 95 percent and accepted in a resubmission with a loan-to-value ratio of 89 percent. Horne made both applications acceptances, yet the initial application was clearly a rejection and the second one an acceptance, as coded in the Boston Fed data. Horne repeatedly mistook the issue of simultaneity, and the possible existence of counteroffers, as errors in the dependent variable; they are not.[25] Still another application was rejected by the lender, but the rejection was later overturned by the state mortgage review board. Since the regression attempts to model lender behavior, not that of the review board, coding it as an acceptance, as Horne does, is incorrect. The other two changes do not appear to be corroborated by the examiner's write-up.

Several loan applications were changed from rejections to withdrawals. Yet, all but one of these applications had reasons for denial attached to them, as required by the Home Mortgage Disclosure Act for a rejected application. According to the examiner's write-up, one application was rejected before the applicant called in to withdraw the application. Since we are investigating lender behavior, not borrower behavior, this application should be listed as a rejection. One examiner stated that the lender believed the borrower wanted to be rejected; Horne (1994b) interpreted that rejection as a withdrawal. Most of these other applications are discussed in the examiner's write-up, with no mention of them as withdrawals. The evidence that these actions should be altered appears very weak.

Because errors in a dichotomous dependent variable can cause inconsistent estimation of the coefficients, this can, however, be a serious problem. The hypothesis that random errors occur in the measurement of the dependent variable can be tested. Hauseman and Scott-Morton (1994) have recently calculated a maximum likelihood function that estimates the frequency of errors in the dependent variable and corrects for this inconsistency. Column (2) of table 4.5 shows that the effect of this correction on the race coefficient's size or significance is zero. The estimated coefficients do not change, because the procedure does not find significant error in the measurement of the dependent variable. Since the evidence is so overwhelming that the dependent variable is accurately measured, the regressions in the

Table 4.5 EFFECTS OF POSSIBLE MISMEASUREMENT IN DEPENDENT VARIABLE

Variable	No Correction (1)	Correction for Possible Measurement Error in Dependent Variable (2)
Constant	−7.70	−7.73
	(−15.25)	(−10.81)
Housing expense income	.48	.48
	(3.12)	(2.94)
Total debt payments/income	.05	.05
	(6.62)	(7.22)
Net wealth	.0001	.0001
	(1.28)	(.67)
Consumer credit history	.32	.32
	(9.26)	(7.60)
Mortgage credit history	.32	.32
	(2.69)	(2.72)
Public record history	1.15	1.15
	(6.43)	(6.20)
Unemployment region	.08	.08
	(2.85)	(2.93)
Self-employed	.52	.52
	(2.74)	(2.71)
Loan-to-value ratio	2.01	2.02
	(4.53)	(4.45)
Denied private mortgage insurance	4.54	4.55
	(9.17)	(8.82)
Rent to value in tract	.68	.68
	(3.51)	(3.47)
Two- to four-family home	.48	.48
	(2.90)	(2.79)
Race	.62	.62
	(4.37)	(4.22)
Estimate of share of measurement error in dependent variable		.02
		(.08)
Log of likelihood function	−838.84	−838.74
Number of observations	2,925	2,925

remainder of this chapter consider data that include only Horne's (1994b) changes in the independent variables.[26]

In fact, the results in Horne (1994b) differed from those of the Boston Fed study only when Horne proceeded to remove observations from the sample and included inappropriate variables in the analysis. By throwing out the 1,600 non-FDIC applications, Horne (1994b) removed one-half of the rejected minority observations. He continued to exclude more observations and to alter the equation's specification to test the robustness of the estimated coefficient on race, eventually reducing the number of minority rejections in the sample by about 80 percent. Furthermore, in all his regressions, he included both the credit history guidelines variable and the unverified information variable, both of which should not have been used in the analysis.[27] Tables 4.6 and 4.7 attempt to replicate Horne's other regression results and to clarify how he obtained them. Results for both the full sample and the FDIC subsamples are reported, even though Horne examined only the FDIC subsample.

Horne repeatedly asserted that only two lenders involved in "community outreach" drive the results. Table 4.6 reestimates the equation in table 4.4 with and without these two lenders. A comparison of these equations, with and without Horne's alterations in the data, shows that removing the data for these two lenders reduces the size of the coefficient on race but does not remove its economic or statistical significance. Only when Horne removed an additional 100 observations from the FDIC sample, included the credit history guidelines variable in the regression, and incorporated the apparently groundless changes to the dependent variable in the analysis does the significance of the coefficient on race in this subsample fall below the 5 percent level.

Even so, the justification for omitting these two lenders is flawed. If community outreach results in applications of lower quality, then the independent variables will capture that lower quality. By removing these two lenders, Horne reduced the FDIC sample of rejected minority applications by almost one-half. In fact, in Horne's (1994b) test of the importance of these lenders, only 38 of 192 minority rejections remained from the full sample.[28]

Horne (1994b) proceeded to remove another 100 or so observations from the sample and to alter the model's specification. Over 40 percent of these 100 observations were removed because they have loan-to-value ratios of less than 30 percent. Another 48 of the 100 observations are properties that are not owner occupied; Horne argued that these are investment properties with different lending standards. The 40 or so applications with low loan-to-value ratios were not prima facie errors. When housing prices appreciate faster than the applicant's income, as happened in Boston and California in the 1980s, loan-to-value ratios will decline. This is particularly true for older, wealthier individuals who owned a house during the period of appreciation. In fact, the low loan-to-value applicants were, on average, eight years older than the rest of the sample and three times as wealthy. Furthermore, 80 percent of the non-owner-occupied properties are single units, which can easily represent second homes rather than investment properties. Second homes do not have different collateral requirements.[29] The omission of these 100 observations from the sample is not justified.

Horne (1994b) also altered the specification of the equation. He broke apart the credit history indexes and separated the loan-to-value ratio into three different segments.[30] Horne's change in the specification of the loan-to-value ratio is unexplained. Munnell et al. (1996) divided the loan-to-value ratio into segments; the thresholds for these segments were chosen using the secondary market guidelines of 80 percent and 95 percent. Horne provided no explanation for why he omitted loan-to-value ratios for applications with a ratio below 91 percent, or for the thresholds he used above that number. Further, his separation of the credit history indexes is not supported by the data.[31]

Finally Horne (1994b) changed all rejections for private mortgage insurance into loan acceptances, even though almost all of them were rejected. Horne offered no justification for this change, in which 45 rejections were reversed to acceptances, altering 24 percent of the minority rejections in Horne's subsample and leaving only one-third of the minority rejections in the total sample. Columns (2) and (4) of table 4.7 reveal that even using Horne's specification, his sample, and these data changes, the coefficient on race is still significant in the mortgage lending decision. No matter which variables or sample is used, the coefficient on race is economically and statistically significant.

Horne (1994b) actually succeeded in producing a coefficient on race that was not significant at the 5 percent level using this specification and sample. For several reasons, we do not succeed in this regard. First, table 4.7 does not include Horne's programming errors. Second, the credit history guidelines and unverified information variables are not used. Finally, Horne's alterations to the dependent variable are not included. If all these changes are made, the significance of the race coefficient would fall below the 5 percent level in some of the columns of table 4.7. However, every step required for Horne to produce this result, the alteration of the dependent variable including changing rejected applications that were also rejected for PMI into acceptances, the programming errors, the sample manipulation and reduction, and the use of the credit history guidelines and unverified information variables, is highly suspect or clearly invalid.

When perusing all of Horne's regression, however, it is important to remember that any statistical inference from the samples that in-

Table 4.6 EXCLUSION OF HORNE'S "INFLUENTIAL LENDERS"

	Full Sample Excluding Two Lenders		FDIC Sample Excluding Two Lenders	
Variable	Boston Fed Data (1)	Horne Data (2)	Boston Fed Data (3)	Horne Data (4)
Constant	−8.14	−8.19	−8.80	−8.99
	(−15.10)	(−15.20)	(−10.15)	(−10.27)
Housing expense income	.48	.44	.47	.36
	(2.99)	(2.68)	(1.73)	(1.28)
Total debt payments/income	.05	.05	.04	.05
	(6.26)	(6.63)	(3.96)	(4.56)
Net wealth	.0001	.0001	.0001	.0001
	(1.39)	(1.71)	(1.89)	(1.97)
Consumer credit history	.32	.31	.32	.31
	(9.01)	(8.74)	(5.33)	(4.98)
Mortgage credit history	.29	.29	.51	.51
	(2.37)	(2.34)	(2.67)	(2.64)
Public record history	1.18	1.20	1.34	1.38
	(6.40)	(6.47)	(4.11)	(4.17)
Unemployment region	.08	.08	.05	.05
	(2.78)	(2.75)	(1.00)	(.94)

Self-employed	.59	.58	.42	.36
	(3.06)	(2.96)	(1.39)	(1.15)
Loan-to-value ratio	2.58	2.52	3.29	3.22
	(5.45)	(5.29)	(3.99)	(3.84)
Denied private mortgage insurance	4.66	4.69	4.85	4.91
	(8.39)	(8.47)	(6.00)	(6.06)
Rent to value in tract	.71	.72	−.66	−.55
	(3.65)	(3.71)	(−.57)	(−.48)
Two- to four-family home	.53	.53	.70	.73
	(2.99)	(2.99)	(2.30)	(2.37)
Race	.44	.44	.70	.66
	(2.87)	(2.86)	(2.70)	(2.49)
Log of likelihood function	−771.51	−761.81	−761.37	−281.71
Number of observations	2,799	2,799	1,253	1,253

Sources: Data based on Horne (1994b) and Boston Fed study by Munnell et al. (1992, 1996).

Table 4.7 HORNE'S ALTERATIONS, SPECIFICATION, AND TURNING PMI REJECTIONS INTO ACCEPTANCES

	Full Sample		FDIC	
Variable	Horne's Specification, Boston Fed Data (1)	Horne's Specification, Alterations, and Sample (2)	Horne's Specification, Boston Fed Data (3)	Horne's Specification, Alterations, and Sample (4)
Constant	−4.79	−4.94	−4.59	−4.88
	(−15.31)	(−15.46)	(−10.71)	(−11.00)
Housing expense/income	.42	.37	.43	.27
	(2.63)	(2.24)	(1.68)	(1.02)
Total debt payments/income	.05	.05	.03	.04
	(6.28)	(6.74)	(3.44)	(4.37)
Net wealth	.0001	.0001	.0001	.0001
	(1.93)	(2.28)	(2.54)	(2.77)
Liquid assets	−.07	−.07	−.53	−.57
	(−.49)	(−.51)	(−2.44)	(−2.48)
No consumer credit history	1.14	1.36	.87	1.42
	(4.28)	(5.22)	(1.91)	(3.34)
No mortgage credit history	.13	.10	.49	.36
	(.82)	(.59)	(1.79)	(1.25)

Public record history	1.17	1.25	.80	1.00
	(6.46)	(6.86)	(2.61)	(3.20)
Late mortgage payments	.92	.95	1.75	1.79
	(1.81)	(1.86)	(2.53)	(2.56)
Delinquent credit	1.12	1.14	1.28	1.36
	(5.74)	(5.70)	(4.11)	(4.17)
Bad credit history	1.34	1.34	1.87	1.91
	(7.31)	(7.14)	(6.51)	(6.35)
Loan-to-value ratio, 91%	.30	.32	.48	.57
	(1.36)	(1.46)	(1.47)	(1.69)
Loan-to-value ratio, 96%	1.20	2.58	1.37	3.65
	(1.81)	(4.60)	(1.39)	(5.11)
Loan-to-value ratio, 100%	1.57	1.45	1.49	1.22
	(5.80)	(5.12)	(3.87)	(2.71)
Two- to four-family home	.38	.42	.33	.44
	(2.16)	(2.35)	(1.18)	(1.56)
Race	.63	.54	.86	.64
	(4.30)	(3.60)	(3.72)	(2.63)
Log of likelihood function	−800.19	−767.54	−326.89	−296.99
Number of observations	2,793	2,730	1,313	1,273

Sources: Data based on Horne (1994b) and Boston Fed study by Munnell et al. (1992, 1996).

cludes the data altered by Horne is highly suspect, since a nonrandom sample of applications was examined and altered. Only rejections were examined, and these rejections were disproportionately, roughly two-thirds, minority. Disproportionately altering minority rejections could well bias the estimate of the race coefficient downward. Even if transcription errors are uncorrelated with race, disproportionately sampling minority rejections could make it appear as though these errors were correlated with race.

In short, Horne's (1994a, b) assertions about problems with the data are unsupported by the evidence. The results in Horne (1994b) are suspect because of his errors in the creation of the data, his reliance on the credit guidelines variable, and his arbitrary reduction of the sample. If anything, attempts to replicate Horne's results attest to just how robust the significance of the coefficient on race is.

Influential Observations

Finally, two other studies, Day and Liebowitz (1993) and Rodda and Wallace (1995), have discussed using influence statistics to examine whether only a few important observations were driving the results. Influence statistics were created to capture the effects of potential outliers in the data. For this data set, they are being used to uncover the observations that have the largest effect on the estimation of the coefficient for race. Influence statistics have been used to determine the fewest number of observations needed to be thrown out of the sample in order to eliminate the effect of race from the mortgage lending regression. Basically, these practitioners are removing the minority applications with the lowest probability of denial who were rejected from the sample. The number of such minority rejections is generally asserted to be around 20, over 10 percent of the minority rejections.

It is important to note, however, that the omission from the sample of these 20 observations does not eliminate the statistically significant effect of race from the equation; it simply disguises it. By throwing out the 20 best qualified minorities who were rejected, but not omitting similarly qualified whites who got rejected, the sample is being distorted. A logit regression of mortgage lending over the range of denial probabilities covered by these "influential" minority observations would actually produce a race coefficient that is negative, because no minorities were rejected over this range but some whites were. A logit regression over the sample of observations not covered by these "influential" minority observations would still produce a coefficient on race that is positive and significant. By truncating the sample in this manner, the positive race coefficient in one part of the sample is offset by the artificially manufactured negative coefficient on race in the other part of the sample. If both white and minority rejections are eliminated over the range of denial probabilities covered by "influential" applications, to reduce the problem with the truncation, the number of minority denials needed to be removed to reduce the significance of the coefficient on race below the 5 percent level is over 130, almost 70 percent of the minority rejections in the sample.

CONCLUSION

Munnell et al.'s (1992) Boston Fed study has elicited considerable reaction. Critics have raised serious questions about the quality of the data and the specification of the equation. Most of the analyses about the quality of the data have been inaccurate and misleading, particularly the discussions that have appeared in the media. These critics have either misunderstood the mortgage market, attacked variables not used in the study—such as much of the original HMDA data—or misunderstood the original use of the data. Some errors will occur in any large data set, either due to measurement error or transcription error, but these errors cannot have affected the results. Furthermore, the complaints about misspecification also do not find much support in the data.

The coefficient on race is found to be significant economically and statistically, any way one cuts the data. The important issue is the *interpretation* of this coefficient. Is there an omitted variable? Is race being used as a signal for profitability? Is taste-based discrimination occurring? The answers to these questions are being pursued using default studies, denial regressions, and examiner reviews. Which approach is best suited to uncovering discrimination has important implications for enforcement of the fair lending laws. Problems with default analysis are discussed in Yinger (1993) and Tootell (1993, 1995). Fears of omitted variable bias, and historical accident, have led to reliance on examination procedures for uncovering discrimination. Examiners are, however, asked to do an impossible task. How are they to select the sample of applications? How are they to determine that each independent variable is being applied equally and fairly across all applications? How are they to measure the role of race in the mortgage lending decision? The only answer to all these questions is that they must use statistical analysis, the type of analysis performed in the Boston Fed study.

Notes

1. Of course, any omitted variable's potential correlation with race is not addressed by examining the goodness-of-fit.

2. The study has been accused of omitting many variables that in fact were included. For example, Horne (1994a, b) cited gifts and home equity as omitted variables. Munnell et al. (1992, 1996) did control for whether a gift was included as part of the down-payment, and receiving a gift was found to be insignificant. Home equity was also included in net wealth. Others have actually asserted that liquid assets, credit history, and employment history were omitted, although all are included in Munnell et al.'s analysis.

3. In fact, logistic estimation cannot produce an estimate of the coefficient for a dummy variable on one observation.

4. The importance of these idiosyncratic variables is somewhat contradicted by the size of the secondary market.

5. Furthermore, an economic variable that significantly affects the probability of default is a variable that should be used in the decision about whether to grant a mortgage or not, but it is not necessarily a variable that was used. Thus, its significance and effect in a denial regression are not certain.

6. Again, if minorities did have higher conditional default propensities, a higher hurdle need not, and probably would not, lead to minorities having a negative or zero coefficient in a default regression.

7. In some models, default analysis can not determine whether taste-based discrimination is occurring. In Berkovec et al. (1994) it can, but the power is low compared to equally valid denial regression in their model; see Tootell (1995).

8. FHA data cover exactly the loans one would least expect to be driven by the profit-maximizing behavior that could produce statistical discrimination. Government guarantees on FHA loans are provided to promote social goals other than profit maximization; thus, the coefficients on the right-hand side of a default regression on a sample of FHA mortgages are capturing the effects of these desired subsidizations.

9. The equation in column (1), table 4.1, differs from the base equation in Munnell et al. (1996). The simpler specification presented here is meant to coincide with that used by the critics. For a complete discussion of the choice of these variables, however, see Munnell et al. (1996).

10. The relatively few cases where the application was not rejected even though the applicant failed to pass the credit history guidelines, because of, for example, participation in a special loan program or acceptance of the application for private mortgage insurance, prevent the coefficient from blowing up entirely.

11. Samples were broken down in various ways while attempting to allow enough observations in each cell to examine the coefficient on race. The results were consistent. See Munnell et al. (1996) for an example.

12. Stengel and Glennon (1995) examined three lenders. In only one institution did they conclude that moving the significance level of the race coefficient from about the 1 percent level to almost the 8 percent level changes the result, showing that "it is unlikely that race affects the application outcomes in a systematic way" (p. 17) in that institution. On the contrary, the *p*-value in their preferred institution-specific regression suggests that it is 93 percent probable that race affects the application. Because the regression results are, in fact, so robust, these authors dismissed the estimation results based on examiners' reports, a controversial methodology with which to reject statistical findings.

13. A regression with unverified information as the dependent variable and all the independent variables in the denial regression as explanatory variables looks somewhat like the denial regression. That credit history and the obligation ratios have some effect on whether information was unverified suggests that weaker applications, ones with a higher probability of being rejected, were more likely to have unverified information. Apparently, unverified information was a function of the denial decision, and thus cannot be included on the right-hand side of the denial regression. In fact, when unverified information is instrumented for in the denial regression, the coefficient on race is unaffected. It is important to note that using information that was not verified in the regression is valid if the lender chose not to verify the data.

14. The instruments include all the independent variables in the denial regression except the loan-to-value ratio, plus liquid assets, years on the job, education, marital status, gender, and years in this line of work. These additional variables were selected because they can, and do, affect the loan-to-value ratio but are not significant in the denial equation. The R^2 in the loan-to-value equation is roughly 15 percent. The regression was also tested with instruments for the loan-to-value ratio and both obligation ratios. This procedure had no effect on the size or significance of the race coefficient, or of those of any other coefficient except the loan-to-value ratio. Note that 87 observations were lost performing this test; these observations were missing data in one or more of the additional instruments.

15. Our regressions were estimated with and without the changes and with and without the observations that were changed. It should be noted that whether the data were corrected or not and whether these observations were included or excluded from the sample had no effect on the results.

16. The implied interest rate would depend on the loan amount, the monthly payment, and the term, or duration, of the loan. Errors in interpreting the term of the loan could also cause a problem in the calculation of the implied interest rate. For example, some institutions listed the term as the duration of the fixed-rate portion of the mortgage; a 1-year adjustable-rate mortgage (ARM) was often listed as a 1-year mortgage, and a 7- to 23-year mortgage was listed as a 7-year term. A short duration would make the interest rate appear too low.

17. The Boston Fed requested both the components of the obligation ratios and the ratios used by the lender in the analysis of the application. Because income is often discounted for various reasons, the components need not always equal the lender's ratios. Since we used the lender's ratio, any errors in a component that were not also errors in the lender's ratio would have no effect on the study.

18. It could be argued that the lender changed the discounting of the income after the decision was made, when it provided the Boston Fed with the number. Yet, the difference between the given and calculated ratios was not a function of the other variables in the mortgage lending decision, particularly race. Second, and more important, the ratios from the lender's worksheet were requested, not an ex post calculation.

19. Stengel and Glennon (1995) also failed to find a significant effect of net wealth on the mortgage lending decisions in the institutions they examined.

20. The decrease in the estimate of the coefficient on race in the FDIC subsample is slightly larger in table 4 of Horne (1994b). The difference appears to be caused by our correction of some of his errors, and by his omission in the second column of that table of almost 200 other applications. I attempt to remove these observations later in this analysis. The two operations are done in different stages to clearly assign the effects of each. In no FDIC regression could I exactly replicate his results, suggesting that other changes were made to the data or sample that were not clearly articulated in Horne's program or paper, but these changes did not seem to have a significant effect on the estimate of the coefficient on race.

21. Without explanation, Horne's regressions cover only the FDIC subsample; since he did not, and could not, limit his analysis to examined applications, he might as well have analyzed the entire sample.

22. The coefficients used to calculate the probabilities of denial were estimated from a regression using the Boston Fed data. Since this exercise explores the size of the changes in the data sets, a single set of coefficients was used.

23. Note that all the examined applications were rejections. The five outliers removed seemed to be caused by data or programming errors of Horne's.

24. These changes were not based on examinations, since only 3 of these 36 changes were made to applications that were reviewed.

25. In fact, if all counteroffers are recorded this way, then the system is unquestionably block recursive, as each decision is made after the loan-to-value ratio is decided upon, and simultaneity would not be a problem in the mortgage denial regression.

26. The results are basically the same whether Horne's (1994b) dependent variable is used or the HMDA's. Exceptions are noted when they occur.

27. Horne (1994b) suggested that the credit history guidelines variable "reflects information over and above that contained in the credit history variables, irrespective of race" (p. 16), and thus does not invalidly pick up the race effect. It adds information to the regression because the variable is a surrogate of denials, particularly minority denials. Adding predictive power does not prove that it adds valid information. For example, information that is available only after an event occurs certainly helps predict that the event will occur, but it should not be used to help predict the event beforehand. Reestimation of table 4.4 to include the credit history guidelines variable has little or no effect on the estimate of the size or significance of the coefficient on race in the entire FDIC subsample, but its effect grows as Horne reduces the sample further.

28. My colleagues and I could never exactly replicate Horne's subsamples, so other changes to the sample were made that were not clearly articulated in Horne (1994b). The slight differences in the sample could explain some differences in the results.

29. Logit regressions that allow a different constant term and a different coefficient on the loan-to-value ratio for owner-occupied and non-owner-occupied properties reject that the two are different. The FDIC subsample provided some evidence that the intercept is different, whereas the total sample showed some evidence that the coefficient on the loan-to-value ratio is different. The evidence is not overwhelming that they face significantly different standards. In any event, if one believes the lending standards differ between these types of loans, the proper coefficients should be allowed to differ; the observations should not be omitted.

30. Horne later included education in his regressions. That variable is omitted since it never approaches statistical significance. Its omission has little or no effect on the results.

31. Munnell et al. (1992) examined the constraint imposed by using the credit history index as opposed to dummy variables for every type of credit history response, and the constraint imposed by this index could not be rejected.

References

Ashenfelter, Orley, and Timothy Hannan. 1986. "Sex Discrimination and Product Market Competition: The Case of the Banking Industry." *Quarterly Journal of Economics* 101(1): 149–73.

Becker, Gary S. 1993. "The Evidence against Banks Doesn't Prove Bias." *Business Week*, April 19: 18.

Berkovec, James A., Glenn B. Canner, Stuart A. Gabriel, and Timothy H. Hannan. 1994. "Discrimination, Default, and Loss in FHA Mortgage Lending." Board of Governors of the Federal Reserve System. Photocopy, November.

Carr, James H., and Isaac F. Megbolugbe. 1994. "A Research Note on the Federal Reserve Bank of Boston Study on Mortgage Lending." Federal National Mortgage Association, Office of Housing Research, Washington, D.C. Photocopy.

Day, Ted, and Stan J. Liebowitz. 1993. Mortgages, Minorities, and Discrimination. University of Texas at Dallas. Photocopy.

Hausman, Jerry A., and Fiona Scott-Morton, 1994. "Misclassification of a Dependent Variable in a Discrete Response Setting." Massachusetts Institute of Technology Department of Economics Working Paper 94-19.

Horne, David K. 1994a. "Evaluating the Role of Race in Mortgage Lending." *FDIC Banking Review* (Spring/Summer): 1–15.

———. 1994b. "Mortgage Lending, Race, and Model Specification." Federal Deposit Insurance Corporation, Division of Research and Statistics. Photocopy.

Munnell, Alicia H., Lynn E. Browne, James McEneaney, and Geoffrey M.B. Tootell. 1992. "Mortgage Lending in Boston: Interpreting HMDA Data." Federal Reserve Bank of Boston Working Paper 92-07. Boston: Federal Reserve Bank of Boston, October.

Munnell, Alicia H., Geoffrey M.B. Tootell, Lynn E. Browne, and James McEneaney. 1996. "Mortgage Lending in Boston: Interpreting HMDA Data." *American Economic Review*. Forthcoming, March.

Phelps, Edmund S. 1972. "The Statistical Theory of Racism and Sexism." *American Economic Review* 62: 659–61.

Rodda, David, and James E. Wallace. 1995. "Fair Lending Management: Using Influence Statistics to Identify Critical Mortgage Loan Applications."

Paper presented at meetings of American Real Estate and Urban Economics Association, Abt Associates, May 30.

Spence, A. Michael. 1974. *Market Signaling: Informational Transfers in Hiring and Related Screening Processes*. Cambridge, Mass.: Harvard University Press.

Stengel, Mitchell, and Dennis Glennon. 1995. "Evaluating Statistical Models of Mortgage Lending Discrimination: A Bank-Specific Analysis." Economic and Policy Analysis Working Paper 95-3, Comptroller of the Currency. Washington, D.C.: Comptroller of the Currency.

Tootell, Geoffrey, M.B. 1993. "Defaults, Denials, and Discrimination," *New England Economic Review* (September/October): 45–51.

————. 1995. "Can Studies of Application Denials and Mortgage Defaults Uncover Taste-Based Discrimination?" Federal Reserve Bank of Boston, Department of Research. Photocopy.

Van Order, Robert, Ann-Margaret Westin, and Peter Zorn. 1993. "Effects of the Racial Composition of Neighborhoods on Defaults, and Implications for Racial Discrimination in Mortgage Markets." Paper presented at meetings of American Economics Association, Jan. 8, Anaheim, Calif.

Yezer, Anthony M.J., Robert F. Phillips, and Robert P. Trost. 1994. "Bias in Estimates of Discrimination and Default in Mortgage Lending: The Effects of Simultaneity and Self-Selection." *Journal of Real Estate Finance and Economics* 9 (3, November): 197–215.

Yinger, John. 1993. "Discrimination in Mortgage Lending: A Literature Review and Recommendation for Future Research." Paper presented at "Home Mortgage Lending and Discrimination: Research and Enforcement Conference," sponsored by U.S. Department of Housing and Urban Development, Washington, D.C. May 18–19.

Chapter Five

THE ROLE OF FHA IN THE PROVISION OF CREDIT TO MINORITIES

Stuart A. Gabriel

This chapter presents the results of a study which examined the role of the Federal Housing Administration (FHA) single-family insurance program in the provision of credit to minority borrowers and in predominantly minority neighborhoods. The study is based on loan application and origination data collected as part of the Home Mortgage Disclosure Act (HMDA) of 1975, as amended by the Financial Institutions Reform, Recovery, and Enforcement Act of 1989. The HMDA data contain basic information on the race and income of mortgage applicants, as well as on the location of their properties by census tract.

This study addresses three main questions concerning the use of FHA mortgage insurance by minority borrowers:

- Does the use of FHA mortgage insurance vary by the race or ethnicity of the mortgage applicant or neighborhood?
- Are minorities more likely to receive a loan if they apply for FHA insurance than if they apply for a conventional mortgage?
- Do observed racial and ethnic differences in loan acceptance rates and the use of FHA insurance actually reflect underlying differences in household income, the requested loan amount, or other factors believed to affect the risk of default?

Recent analyses of HMDA data conducted by the Federal Reserve and others have uncovered sizable differences in loan acceptance rates by race and ethnicity.[1] In general, blacks and Hispanics are less likely to be accepted for a mortgage when compared to whites with similar incomes. Much the same patterns are found with respect to the racial composition of the neighborhood. Moreover, whereas the differentials appear to be greatest in the conventional market, they occur for government-backed loans as well. Such patterns have led some observers to suggest the possibility of systematic racial discrimination in the mortgage lending industry.

Unfortunately, the HMDA data do not enable one to control for a host of factors that might affect the underlying degree of risk associated with any loan, including the applicant's credit history, front- and back-end debt ratios, the loan-to-value ratio, and the characteristics of the property itself. A recent study by the Federal Reserve Bank of Boston collected detailed information on factors thought to be critical to the underwriting process for a sample of loan applications drawn from the Boston metropolitan area (Munnell et al. 1992, 1995—known as the "Boston Fed" study). Although such factors in fact explained a large proportion of the observed racial and ethnic differentials, blacks nevertheless experienced higher rejection rates than those of "otherwise similar" whites (16 percent versus 11 percent, respectively).

The apparent importance of omitted variables in explaining observed differences in mortgage acceptance rates poses a significant obstacle to any attempt to document discrimination in the mortgage market. According to the Boston Fed study, apparent racial or ethnic differences revealed by the HMDA data are likely to overestimate significantly the actual effect of race or ethnicity on mortgage acceptance. Although the Boston Fed study was restricted to conventional loans (owing to the lack of FHA activity), it is reasonable to expect that factors that helped to explain a large proportion of observed differentials in that market also affect the acceptance rates of both FHA and conventional loans in other parts of the country.

These same factors also could affect the applicant's choice of a mortgage instrument. Previous studies have shown that blacks are more likely to apply for an FHA mortgage compared to whites with similar incomes (e.g., Gabriel and Rosenthal 1991). However, since factors such as household wealth and the ability to make a large downpayment will obviously play a key role in determining mortgage choice, one cannot necessarily attribute the higher use of FHA loans among blacks to racially motivated steering on the part of the lending community. The observed pattern could just as likely reflect the lower downpayment requirements of FHA loans.

This study examines the impact of FHA insurance on minority lending patterns in a sample of 10 metropolitan statistical areas (MSAs). The sample was chosen to reflect a range of conditions that might affect the treatment of minorities in the mortgage market and the relative reliance on FHA as a source of mortgage finance, including the relative share of the FHA market, the recent default experience of FHA loans, the relative sizes of the black and Hispanic populations, and the overall size of the housing market. The study is limited to FHA loans and conventional mortgages below the established FHA ceiling. The analysis excludes other types of government-sponsored loans (i.e., Veterans Administration [VA] and Farmers Home Administration [FmHA]), since eligibility for such mortgages is restricted to certain borrowers or certain locations.

Table 5.1 lists the selected sites and their key characteristics.[2] As shown in the table, the sample represents a mix of geographic locations and market conditions. Whereas much of the analysis is presented on a site-specific basis, we also derived a series of weights that are used to make inferences about the universe of sites contained in the "eligible" sampling frame. Broadly speaking, these sites include markets with at least some FHA presence (i.e., 1,000 or more applications in 1990) and at least some representation of minority loans (i.e., 200 or more applications from blacks or Hispanics in that year). The 77 metropolitan areas that met these two criteria account for 72 percent of all FHA applications received in 1990, as well as 72 percent of all applications (either conventional or FHA) from blacks or Hispanics.

The analysis is based on information obtained from three different data sets:

- 1990 HMDA data, which are used to describe FHA and conventional mortgage applications and origination patterns in each selected market
- 1986–92 default data on FHA loans, which are used to measure historical patterns of risk at the census-tract level and to estimate market-specific models of default behavior based on the characteristics of the borrower, the mortgage, and the neighborhood
- 1980 and 1990 census-tract data, which are used to describe the characteristics of the property's neighborhood.

The first section of the analysis documents the extent to which a borrower's or neighborhood's race or ethnicity is related to the type of loan selected (conventional versus FHA) and the probability that a loan application is approved. The second part of the analysis takes a closer look at the various patterns observed, and tests the extent to which they can be attributed to borrower or neighborhood socioeconomic or other factors. In particular, we estimate two logistic regression models that attempt to isolate the effects of race and ethnicity from other factors related to the household's choice of a mortgage instrument or to its probability of receiving a loan. The loan choice model examines factors that affect the probability that a mortgage applicant applies for an FHA loan rather than a conventional mortgage. The loan acceptance model identifies factors that influence

Table 5.1 CHARACTERISTICS OF SELECTED METROPOLITAN STATISTICAL AREAS

Selected Sites	Total Number of Loan Applications	Number of Applications by Blacks	Number of Applications by Hispanics	Number of FHA Applications	Default Rate	FHA Share	Population	Percent Black	Percent Hispanic
Atlanta	34,734	5,857	312	13,267	3.6%	38.2%	2.8 million	26.0%	2.0%
Baltimore	33,156	4,045	271	12,353	0.9%	37.3%	2.4 million	25.9%	1.3%
Chicago	75,298	6,502	7,430	13,008	2.5%	17.3%	6.1 million	22.0%	12.1%
Columbus	17,154	911	67	6,013	1.5%	35.1%	1.4 million	11.9%	0.8%
Dallas	26,481	1,522	1,542	10,481	7.9%	39.6%	2.6 million	16.1%	14.4%
Houston	29,557	1,563	2,314	8,676	5.8%	29.4%	3.3 million	18.5%	21.4%
Los Angeles	110,114	4,751	25,936	4,451	1.6%	4.0%	8.9 million	11.2%	37.8%
Memphis	11,207	2,872	35	5,948	3.5%	53.1%	1.0 million	40.6%	0.8%
Sacramento	29,117	813	1,514	3,007	0.5%	10.3%	1.5 million	6.9%	11.6%
St. Louis	31,998	2,777	154	9,856	2.6%	30.8%	2.4 million	17.3%	1.1%

whether a conventional or FHA loan application is accepted or rejected. Both analyses examine the extent to which loan choice and loan acceptance rates are systematically related to the race or ethnicity of the borrower, or to the racial composition of the neighborhood in which the property is located, controlling for other factors that may influence credit risk. Both analyses are restricted to conventional and FHA loans that fall below the FHA ceiling.

Given the limitations of the HMDA data, the analysis necessarily excludes a number of key variables known to affect the household's choice of mortgage instrument as well as the lender's assessment of underlying risk (for example, the borrower's credit history). However, we attempted to control for such factors by directly estimating the risk that an individual would default, based on the recent experience of FHA loans. In particular, we used data available from the U.S. Department of Housing and Urban Development's (HUD's) management information systems to estimate a default model for FHA loans based on the characteristics of the borrower, the neighborhood, and the mortgage. We then used this model to estimate the probability of default for each application in the HMDA file, and included this exogenous estimate of risk in both the loan choice model and the loan acceptance model.[3] We also included a variable measuring the recent default experience of FHA loans in the census tract in which each property was located. Racial or ethnic differentials that persist in the HMDA data after controlling for these effects are likely to be attributable to factors other than individual or borrower default risk.

The remainder of this chapter is organized into four main sections. The first of these presents basic information on variations in the relative importance of FHA by location (central cities versus suburbs), type of lender, size and type of loan, and race and income of both the borrower and the neighborhood in which the property is located. The second major section examines loan acceptance rates by each of these factors, and compares the experience of borrowers applying for both conventional and FHA loans. The third main section attempts to control for differences in loan default risk by specifying a loan default model that is used to predict the probability of default for each loan used in the analysis. The fourth major section then utilizes this analysis of loan defaults to examine the extent to which observed racial and ethnic differences in loan choice and loan acceptance rates continue to hold after controlling for differences in the characteristics of the borrower, the loan, and the neighborhood, as well as for differences in loan default probabilities.

USE OF FHA INSURANCE BY MINORITY BORROWERS

This section examines variations in the relative importance of FHA by location, lender type, size of loan, and the race and income of both the borrower and the neighborhood. The principal objective here is to document the nature and the extent of racial and ethnic differences in the use of FHA insurance by borrowers seeking mortgages for amounts that are below the established FHA ceiling. We begin by examining aggregate data describing variations in the use of FHA across a number of different factors believed to influence the borrower's choice of mortgage instruments. The statistics are weighted to reflect conditions in the universe of markets with significant numbers of minority applicants and FHA loans. The study then takes a closer look at the 10 selected housing markets, and compares and contrasts the racial and ethnic differences observed among the sites.

Aggregate Estimates

Table 5.2 presents information on the proportion of all applications and originations that involve the use of FHA insurance by location (central city versus suburban), lender type, size and type of loan, and the estimated ratio of the monthly mortgage payment to the borrower's monthly income.[4] As noted earlier, the statistics refer only to conventional and FHA loans; since VA mortgages are not available to every borrower, and since FmHA loans are only offered in rural sections of MSAs, such mortgages have been excluded from the analysis.

As a point of reference, the first two columns in table 5.2 depict FHA loans as a proportion of total applications and originations. The second two columns present comparable statistics for the subset of mortgages with initial balances below the applicable FHA ceiling. In 1990 (the year of the HMDA data), FHA insurance was not available for loans above $67,500 in most parts of the country, although federally designated "high cost" areas had ceilings as high as $124,875. As a result, this discussion focuses on the subset of loans that would otherwise be eligible for FHA. For ease of presentation, we refer to these loans as "qualifying" applications.

As shown in table 5.2, FHA is used more often in central cities than in suburban areas, although the differences are not pronounced (for example, 33 percent versus 28 percent for loan applications below the FHA ceiling). Indeed, since the volume of lending activity is higher in suburban areas, the majority of FHA applications (57 percent) in-

Table 5.2 FHA SHARE BY LOCATION, LENDER TYPE, AND LOAN CHARACTERISTICS[1]

	All Loans (%)		Qualifying Loans (%)	
	Applications	Originations	Applications	Originations
I. Location				
Central City	23	23	33	33
Suburban	19	20	28	28
II. Type of Lender[2]				
Savings & Loan	14	14	21	21
Commercial Bank	19	18	26	25
Credit Union	3	3	4	3
Independent Mortgage Bank	43	45	59	60
III. Characteristics of Loan				
A. Loan Amount				
<$25,000	7	6	7	6
$25,000-$50,000	28	26	28	26
$50,001-$67,500	38	38	38	38
$67,501-$75,000	36	36	36	36
$75,001-$100,000	32	33	33	33
$100,001-$125,000	19	20	27	29
>$125,000	0	0	0	0
B. Estimated Payment-to-Income Ratio				
<15%	13	13	16	15
15-20%	24	25	36	36
21-25%	26	27	43	44
25-30%	25	27	47	48
>30%	18	20	39	43
C. Purpose of Loan				
Purchase	26	26	37	37
Refinance	4	4	6	5
IV. All Loans	20	21	30	30

[1]FHA share defined as the number of FHA loans divided by the total number of FHA and conventional loans below the FHA ceiling (excluding VA and FmHA loans).
[2]Including subsidiaries.

volve suburban properties. Significantly larger differentials are related to lender type. Independent mortgage bankers, which have historically specialized in FHA loans, process a higher proportion of FHA applications compared to other types of lenders. However, in terms of total applications received, conventional loans now account for the majority of applications (57 percent) received by mortgage bankers. At the same time, commercial banks and savings and loans, which have historically focused on conventional loans, have entered the FHA market. Since both types of lenders account for a relatively high share of overall lending activity, they come relatively close to the mortgage bankers with respect to their share of the FHA market: 36 percent of all applications for FHA loans are received by mortgage bankers, 32 percent by commercial banks, and 32 percent by savings and loans (S&Ls).

The use of FHA insurance also varies with the size of the loan. For mortgages above $50,000, the use of FHA declines as the size of the loan increases (see table 5.2), a pattern that probably reflects a tendency for borrowers at the upper end of the market to be more likely to meet conventional downpayment requirements and underwriting standards. Since FHA loans tend to be more expensive than conventional mortgages, borrowers who are able to qualify for a conventional mortgage presumably will tend not to use FHA. This same basic factor may also explain the tendency for the FHA share to rise with increases in the estimated payment-to-income ratio of the loan.[5]

At the same time, however, FHA is used less frequently for smaller loans (below $50,000—see table 5.2). Indeed, only about 7 percent of all mortgages below $25,000 use FHA. This pattern may in part reflect the higher incidence of refinancings among these smaller loans.[6] Since borrowers who refinance are more likely to have the equity required for a conventional loan—and presumably to have well-established credit histories—they are probably less likely to use FHA. As shown in table 5.2, only 6 percent of all applications to refinance an existing mortgage use FHA, compared to 37 percent of all qualifying purchase loans.

Table 5.3 presents information on the relative importance of FHA by the race and income of the borrower. Not surprisingly, the use of FHA declines as the borrower's income rises, even for the subset of mortgages that are below the applicable FHA ceiling. For such mortgages, 37 percent of all applicants with incomes below 80 percent of the local median applied for an FHA loan, compared to only 19 percent of all upper-income applicants. Table 5.3 also reveals the importance of FHA financing for black borrowers. For example, some 56 percent of all qualifying applications from blacks were for FHA mortgages, compared to 27 percent for whites. This pattern does not appear to be a function of household income. Although the use of FHA by black applicants declines as their incomes rise, 39 percent of all qualifying loan applications from upper-income blacks involved FHA, compared to only about 19 percent for upper-income whites. In fact,

Table 5.3 FHA SHARE BY RACE AND INCOME OF BORROWER

Borrower Characteristics	All Loans (%)		Qualifying Loans (%)	
	Applications	Originations	Applications	Originations
Race/Ethnicity of Borrower:				
White	18	19	27	27
Black	48	50	56	57
Hispanic	21	24	29	31
Asian	9	10	18	18
Income of Borrower				
80% median or below	36	38	37	39
81-100% median	35	35	36	37
101-120% median	28	29	31	31
>120% median	10	10	19	19
Borrower Income and Race:				
80% Median or Below				
White	30	33	31	33
Black	62	64	62	65
Hispanic	36	40	38	41
Asian	25	26	27	28
81-100% Median				
White	32	33	34	34
Black	59	60	60	61
Hispanic	31	35	33	36
Asian	23	23	26	25
101-120% Median				
White	27	28	29	30
Black	53	55	55	57
Hispanic	23	26	25	26
Asian	15	16	17	18
>120% Median				
White	9	10	19	19
Black	26	28	39	41
Hispanic	8	9	14	15
Asian	4	4	10	10

Note: An FHA share is defined as the number of FHA loans divided by the total number of FHA and conventional loans.

the use of FHA by upper-income blacks (39 percent) is higher than its use among lower-income whites (31 percent).

In contrast, Hispanics appear relatively similar to whites in their use of FHA, at least on an aggregate basis. Hispanics in the lowest-income categories are the one exception to this rule. Although their reliance on FHA is well below the rate observed for blacks with similar incomes (38 percent versus 62 percent of qualifying applications), it is significantly higher than the rate observed for whites (38 percent versus 31 percent) (see table 5.3). In the other income categories, the FHA share for Hispanics is comparable to, or somewhat below, the FHA share for whites.

The use of FHA is consistently lower for Asian borrowers than it is for whites (see table 5.3), regardless of their incomes. Only about 18 percent of all qualifying applications from Asians use FHA, compared to 27 percent for whites. The differential is smaller for low-income borrowers, but the FHA share for Asians in this income category (27 percent) is still below the share for whites (31 percent). For upper-income borrowers, the use of FHA by Asian households is only about half the rate observed for whites (10 percent versus 19 percent).

Table 5.4 presents information on the use of FHA by the racial composition and income of the property's neighborhood (or census tract). As expected, the FHA share declines as neighborhood income rises. For example, for loan applications below the FHA ceiling, the FHA share falls from 33 percent in lower-income census tracts (below 80 percent of the local median) to 25 percent in upper-income tracts (above 120 percent of the local median). However, the relationship between use of FHA and neighborhood income is not as strong as it is for the borrower's income.

Reliance on FHA also appears to rise with increases in the neighborhood's concentration of minorities (defined, for purposes of this analysis, as the percentage of residents in each census tract who are black or Hispanic). For example, FHA represents about 24 percent of all qualifying loan applications in census tracts that are less than 10 percent minority, compared to 38 percent in tracts that are more than 50 percent minority (see table 5.4). The same basic pattern holds when one stratifies the data by both the income and racial composition of the census tract. In tracts with incomes below 120 percent of the local median, the use of FHA is consistently highest in predominantly minority tracts and consistently lowest in tracts that are primarily white.[7]

The relationship between the concentration of minority households and the use of FHA in each neighborhood largely reflects the differences in the types of census tracts that are selected by different types of borrowers. Table 5.5 presents the distribution of loan applications across the different neighborhood types for borrowers of different racial and ethnic groups. As shown in the table, minorities for the most part seek financing for homes in minority neighborhoods. For example, over 62 percent of all black applicants—and 49 percent of

Table 5.4 FHA SHARE BY RACE AND INCOME OF CENSUS TRACT

Census Tract Characteristics	All Loans (%)		Qualifying Loans (%)	
	Applications	Orginations	Applications	Originations
Percentage Minority[a]				
Under 10% minority	15	16	24	24
11-20% minority	22	24	33	34
21-30% minority	23	24	33	34
31-50% minority	25	25	34	33
50% or more minority	31	33	38	39
Income				
80% median or below	28	29	33	33
81-100% median	23	24	30	31
101-120% median	19	19	28	28
>120% median	11	12	25	25
Income and Race				
80% median or below				
Under 10% minority	22	23	24	25
11-20% minority	24	25	28	29
21-30% minority	26	27	31	32
31-50% minority	30	30	35	34
50% or more minority	32	34	38	40
81-100% Median				
Under 10% minority	19	20	23	24
11-20% minority	29	31	38	40
21-30% minority	25	26	36	37
31-50% minority	24	24	35	34
50% or more minority	27	28	37	37
101-120% Median				
Under 10% minority	16	17	24	25
11-20% minority	22	24	35	35
21-30% minority	20	21	33	33
31-50% minority	16	17	28	28
50% or more minority	32	33	44	44
>120% Median				
Under 10% minority	11	11	23	23
11-20% minority	14	15	30	30
21-30% minority	18	20	35	37
31-50% minority	7	8	17	18
50% or more minority	4	5	9	12

Note. An FHA share is defined as the number of FHA loans divided by the total number of FHA and conventional loans.
a. Minority includes blacks and Hispanics only.

Table 5.5 DISTRIBUTION OF QUALIFYING LOAN APPLICATIONS BY RACE OF BORROWER AND PERCENTAGE MINORITY IN TRACT

Percentage Minority in Tract	Race/Ethnicity of Borrower (%)			
	White	Black	Hispanic	Asian
<10 Percent	55	8	10	25
11-20 Percent	20	8	12	24
21-30 Percent	10	8	12	17
31-50 Percent	8	14	17	20
>50 Percent	7	62	49	14
All Tracts	100	100	100	100

Table 5.6 FHA AS PERCENTAGE OF ALL QUALIFYING APPLICATIONS BY RACE OF BORROWER AND PERCENTAGE MINORITY IN TRACT

Percentage Minority in Tract	Race/Ethnicity of Borrower (%)			
	White	Black	Hispanic	Asian
<10 Percent	25	54	32	19
11-20 Percent	35	60	42	21
21-30 Percent	34	61	39	20
31-50 Percent	30	63	39	18
>50 Percent	30	55	25	18

Hispanics—applied for loans in predominantly minority neighborhoods, whereas over 55 percent of all whites applied in neighborhoods that are less than 10 percent minority. Asians were the only group examined who applied for mortgages in a wide variety of neighborhood types, although half of their applications were in census tracts that are less than 20 percent minority.

In contrast, the type of loan selected by a borrower of a given racial or ethnic group is fairly constant across neighborhood types, as shown in table 5.6. For example, about 54 percent of all black borrowers seeking financing in predominantly white neighborhoods used FHA, compared to about 55 percent of all blacks seeking financing in predominantly minority tracts. Thus, the observed relationship between the concentration of minorities and the use of FHA in each neighborhood appears to reflect underlying differences in the loan choice of individual borrowers.

Patterns in Individual MSAs

Table 5.7 presents information on use of FHA insurance by different racial and ethnic groups in each of the 10 selected MSAs. The figures

Table 5.7 FHA AS A PROPORTION OF ALL QUALIFYING LOAN APPLICATIONS BY RACE AND BY MSA

Metropolitan Area	White %	Black %	Hispanic %	Asian %
Atlanta	34	66	51	40
Baltimore	37	65	53	37
Chicago	11	50	32	9
Columbus	26	52	58	21
Dallas	46	64	65	42
Houston	36	54	54	28
Los Angeles	6	4	6	5
Memphis	55	78	70	51
Sacramento	10	21	18	7
St. Louis	24	60	35	25

for blacks, which refer to loan applications for mortgages that are below the FHA ceiling, are consistent with the national estimates in most of the sites, although Los Angeles and, to a lesser extent, Sacramento are notable outliers. In Los Angeles, where 37 percent of all loan applications are below the established FHA ceiling, only a handful of borrowers rely on FHA, regardless of their racial or ethnic group. In the remaining markets, however, blacks are much more likely to apply for an FHA loan compared to whites.

In contrast, the statistics for Hispanics and Asians differ somewhat from the aggregate data. With the exception of Los Angeles, Hispanics are significantly more likely to apply for an FHA mortgage compared to whites (see table 5.7). Although the FHA share for Hispanics is typically below the share for blacks, in two areas with relatively large concentrations of Hispanics—Dallas and Houston—the shares are roughly the same. The use of FHA among Asians varies across the sites, but is typically comparable to that observed for whites. Thus, the aggregate data appear to obscure a significantly higher use of FHA among Hispanics, and give the illusion of significantly lower rates for Asians that do not exist in the majority of sites.

As indicated in table 5.8, the use of FHA increases steadily as the neighborhood's minority percentage rises. However, in Dallas and Houston, the FHA share is relatively low in census tracts that are less than 10 percent minority, but then fairly constant across the other neighborhood types. This pattern probably reflects the relatively high use of FHA loans by Hispanics in these two markets, combined with a somewhat greater tendency among Hispanics to apply for loans in more integrated tracts (as shown in table 5.5).

Table 5.8 FHA AS A PROPORTION OF ALL QUALIFYING LOAN APPLICATIONS BY PERCENTAGE MINORITY IN TRACT: SELECTED MSAS

	Percentage Minority in Tract				
Metropolitan Area	<10%	11-20%	21-30%	31-50%	>50%
Atlanta	36	40	44	46	61
Baltimore	34	44	48	53	62
Chicago	10	14	22	28	39
Columbus	24	41	40	44	42
Dallas	38	53	50	54	53
Houston	28	37	44	41	40
Los Angeles	4	6	10	5	5
Memphis	60	60	44	69	72
Sacramento	6	11	13	16	19
St. Louis	24	33	35	37	51

LOAN ACCEPTANCE RATES

This section examines loan acceptance rates for both conventional and FHA mortgages. Although the analysis explores variations across a number of different factors—including location, lender type, and size of loan—it again focuses on variations that are related to the race or ethnicity of the borrower or of the neighborhood in which the property is located. Previous analyses of the HMDA data revealed significantly lower acceptance rates among blacks and, to a lesser extent, Hispanics for both conventional and government-sponsored loans. This analysis explores the extent to which acceptance rates for minorities may be lower under FHA than for conventional loans—an outcome that could conceivably be caused by the observed higher use of FHA among blacks and Hispanics in most of the markets considered.

The discussion here is intended to set the stage for the causal models of loan choice and loan acceptance that are developed later in the chapter. At the outset, however, it is important to emphasize that lower acceptance rates cannot by themselves be considered evidence of discrimination or more restrictive underwriting guidelines on the part of conventional (or FHA) lenders. If, for example, riskier borrowers are systematically channeled into FHA, then FHA acceptance rates could be relatively low even if the program used less-restrictive underwriting guidelines. Whereas the regression analysis below attempts to measure the treatment of "otherwise similar" borrowers, the many difficulties involved in measuring all of the factors related to the underwriting decision make the findings suggestive at best.

Aggregate Estimates

Table 5.9 presents aggregate data on the proportion of conventional and FHA loan applications accepted by the lender, with results stratified by location, lender type, loan amount and type, and estimated payment-to-income ratio.[8] Acceptance rates are shown for both conventional and FHA mortgages, and are weighted to reflect conditions

Table 5.9 LOAN ACCEPTANCE RATES BY LOCATION, LENDER TYPE, AND LOAN CHARACTERISTICS

	All Loans (%)	All Conventional Loans (%)	All FHA Loans (%)	Qualifying Conventional Loans (%)
I. Location				
Central City	84	84	82	83
Suburban	87	87	87	86
II. Type of Lender[1]				
Savings & Loan	86	86	85	86
Commercial Bank	84	84	83	82
Credit Union	88	89	81	88
Independent Mortgage Bank	87	84	87	88
III. Characteristics of Loan				
A. Loan Amount				
<$25,000	74	74	72	74
$25,000-$50,000	81	83	78	83
$50,001-$67,500	85	87	83	87
$67,501-$75,000	87	88	86	88
$75,001-$100,000	89	89	89	89
$100,001-$125,000	89	90	91	87
>$125,000	86	86	NA	NA
B. Payment-to-Income Ratio[2]				
<15%	84	85	81	84
15-20%	88	89	86	87
21-25%	88	89	87	88
25-30%	86	86	89	86
>30%	75	75	78	73
C. Purpose of Loan				
Purchase	86	87	85	85
Refinance	83	83	77	84
IV. All Loans	86	86	85	85

[1]Including subsidiaries.
[2]Estimated.

in metropolitan areas with an active FHA market and a significant number of minority loans. Again, as a point of reference, we present information on acceptance rates for all types of loans, regardless of size. However, unless otherwise noted, the statistics cited in the text refer to the subset of loans for amounts below the applicable FHA ceiling.

In general, the acceptance rates of conventional and FHA loans are remarkably similar across the various categories identified in the table. Indeed, for loans below the established ceiling, the overall acceptance rate for FHA mortgages is exactly the same as for conventional loans (85 percent). And while some variations arise when one examines subsets of loans defined by location, lender type, or size and type of mortgage, these differences are for the most part very small.

As shown in table 5.9, the probability that a mortgage application is accepted appears to be lower in central city than in suburban locations for both conventional and FHA loans. Acceptance rates also tend to be slightly lower for mortgage applications submitted to commercial banks (regardless of type) and for FHA applications processed by credit unions; the latter, however, account for less than 1 percent of all FHA loans.

Acceptance rates also appear to rise with increases in the size of the loan for both conventional and FHA mortgages. However, the relationship between acceptance rates and the estimated payment-to-income ratio is more complex. On the one hand, acceptance rates are lowest for applications that would result in payment-to-income ratios in excess of 30 percent—an outcome that is consistent with the underwriting standards of both conventional and FHA loans. On the other hand, acceptance rates are also relatively low for applications whose projected payment-to-income ratio is less than 15 percent. This pattern may in part reflect refinancings, which tend to have lower acceptance rates when compared to purchase loans, particularly for FHA mortgages.

Table 5.10 presents loan acceptance rates by the race and income of the borrower. The findings are consistent with earlier analyses of the HMDA data, and reveal relatively large differences by race and ethnicity for both conventional and FHA loans. Although acceptance rates also appear to vary with the borrower's income, the differences observed for income are typically smaller than those observed for race. In general, the acceptance rates of both conventional and FHA loans rise with the income of the borrower. For example, for conventional loans below the FHA ceiling, the acceptance rate is 77 percent for lower-income borrowers (less than 80 percent of the local median)

Table 5.10 LOAN ACCEPTANCE RATES BY RACE AND INCOME OF BORROWER

Borrower Characteristics	All Loans (%)	All Conventional Loans (%)	All FHA Loans (%)	Qualifying Conventional Loans (%)
Race/Ethnicity of Borrower				
White	88	87	89	86
Black	72	72	72	70
Hispanic	80	79	84	79
Asian	85	85	84	85
Income of Borrower				
80% median or below	78	76	80	77
81-100% median	85	84	85	85
101-120% median	87	87	88	87
>120% median	88	88	88	89
Borrower Income and Race				
80% Median or Below				
White	81	78	86	79
Black	67	63	69	64
Hispanic	76	74	81	74
Asian	81	81	82	82
81-100% Median				
White	87	86	89	86
Black	72	71	72	71
Hispanic	82	80	86	82
Asian	85	85	82	87
101-120% Median				
White	89	88	91	89
Black	74	73	75	74
Hispanic	83	81	87	83
Asian	84	84	85	86
>120% Median				
White	90	90	91	90
Black	77	77	77	77
Hispanic	81	80	86	81
Asian	85	85	86	86
All Loans	86	86	85	85

and 89 percent for upper-income borrowers (above 120 percent of the local median). Patterns for FHA loan applications are for the most part similar to those observed for conventional loans, with the highest acceptance rates observed among upper-income borrowers. However, FHA acceptance rates appear to be somewhat higher for lower-income borrowers compared to conventional loans (80 percent versus 77 percent).

Acceptance rates for conventional and FHA loans also vary with the race and ethnicity of the borrower. In general, blacks have the lowest acceptance rates, regardless of income or loan type. Consider the statistics for conventional loans below the FHA ceiling. As shown in table 5.10, such applications have a 70 percent acceptance rate for blacks, compared to an 86 percent rate for whites. Differences in conventional loan acceptance rates for whites and blacks do not appear to be a function of borrower income. Indeed, the acceptance rate for conventional loan applications by upper-income blacks (77 percent) is below the acceptance rate for lower-income whites (79 percent).

In general, blacks appear to do somewhat better under FHA than in the conventional mortgage market, although the differences are not as large as those observed for whites or Hispanics. Seventy-two percent of all applications by blacks for FHA mortgages are accepted, compared to 70 percent for comparably sized conventional loans (table 5.10). Most of this differential appears to be caused by differences in the acceptance rates of conventional and FHA loans for lower-income blacks (64 percent versus 69 percent, respectively). In the remaining income categories, the acceptance rates for blacks are about the same for conventional and FHA mortgages.

Hispanics and Asians also have lower acceptance rates compared to whites in the majority of income categories. However, the acceptance rates for both of these groups are consistently higher than those observed for blacks. Asians, who are relatively infrequent users of FHA, appear to have about the same acceptance rate regardless of the type of loan selected. However, Hispanics appear to have significantly higher acceptance rates under FHA than they do with conventional loans. For example, 84 percent of all FHA applications from Hispanics are accepted, compared to an acceptance rate of only 79 percent for conventional loans (table 5.10). Similar differences are found within each of the income categories, with the largest differences observed among lower-income borrowers.

Finally, whites appear to have the highest acceptance rates regardless of loan type or borrower income. Whites also appear to do somewhat better under FHA than they do with conventional loans. As with blacks and Hispanics, the largest differences in the acceptance rates of conventional and FHA loan applications by whites are found among lower-income borrowers. While the differences for whites (79 percent versus 86 percent) are not as large as those observed for Hispanic borrowers (74 percent versus 81 percent), they are significantly larger than the differences observed for blacks (64 percent versus 69 percent) (see table 5.10).

Loan acceptance rates also vary with the neighborhood's income and concentration of minority households, as shown in table 5.11. In general, the acceptance rates of both conventional and FHA loans rise with the income of the census tract. However, within each tract income category the acceptance rates of conventional and FHA loans are about the same. Thus, whereas lower-income borrowers tend to have higher acceptance rates under FHA compared to conventional loans, similar differentials do not appear to occur in lower-income neighborhoods.

FHA and conventional acceptance rates also appear to fall with increases in the area's concentration of minority households. For example, 76 percent of all FHA loan applications in predominantly minority neighborhoods (those with at least 50 percent minority residents) are accepted, compared to 90 percent in predominantly white census tracts (less than 10 percent minority). A similar pattern is observed for conventional loans. For example, for conventional loans below the FHA ceiling, acceptance rates fall from a high of 88 percent in neighborhoods that are less than 10 percent minority to a low of 76 percent in tracts with the highest concentrations of minority households.

The relationship between the acceptance rates of FHA and conventional loans also appears to vary with the neighborhood's racial and ethnic composition. In general, the acceptance rates of FHA loans are higher than the acceptance rates of conventional loans in census tracts with relatively low concentrations of minority households. For example, 90 percent of all FHA loan applications in predominantly white tracts are accepted, compared to 88 percent for conventional loans. This basic pattern continues to hold when tracts are classified by both income and percentage minority, with the largest differences between conventional and FHA loans observed in low- and moderate-income neighborhoods. In general, the acceptance rates for FHA loans are higher than those observed for conventional loans in areas with low concentrations of minorities, and are lower than those observed for conventional loans in predominantly minority areas.

Table 5.12 presents the acceptance rates of conventional and FHA loans by the race/ethnicity of the borrower and the neighborhood's concentration of minority households. Again, acceptance rates tend to fall with increases in the neighborhood's concentration of minority households for each of type of borrower and loan. However, differences

Table 5.11 LOAN ACCEPTANCE RATES BY RACE AND INCOME OF NEIGHBORHOOD

Neighborhood Characteristics	All Loans (%)	All Conventional Loans (%)	All FHA Loans (%)	Qualifying Conventional Loans (%)
Percent Minority[1]				
Under 10% minority	89	89	90	88
11-20% minority	86	86	88	85
21-30% minority	84	84	85	83
31-50% minority	81	82	79	81
50% or more minority	76	76	76	76
Income				
80% median or below	80	80	80	80
81-100% median	85	85	86	85
101-120% median	88	88	88	88
>120% median	89	89	90	89
Income and Race				
80% Median or Below				
Under 10% minority	85	84	87	84
11-20% minority	84	84	87	83
21-30% minority	83	83	83	82
31-50% minority	80	81	79	80
50% or more minority	75	75	76	75
81-100% Median				
Under 10% minority	88	87	90	87
11-20% minority	86	85	88	85
21-30% minority	84	83	86	83
31-50% minority	83	84	80	84
50% or more minority	78	79	75	79
101-120% Median				
Under 10% minority	90	89	90	89
11-20% minority	87	87	89	87
21-30% minority	85	85	84	85
31-50% minority	81	82	79	81
50% or more minority	78	80	75	81
>120% Median				
Under 10% minority	90	90	91	90
11-20% minority	87	87	88	87
21-30% minority	84	84	87	84
31-50% minority	82	82	83	83
50% or more minority	80	79	95	81
IV. All Loans	86	86	85	85

[1]Minority includes blacks and Hispanics only.

Table 5.12 ACCEPTANCE RATES BY RACE OF BORROWER AND PERCENTAGE MINORITY IN TRACT

Percentage Minority in Tract	FHA Loan Applications (%)				Conventional Loan Applications (%)[a]			
	Black	Hispanic	Asian	White	Black	Hispanic	Asian	White
<10% minority	78	88	87	90	73	83	87	88
11-20% minority	73	86	90	89	69	82	87	86
21-30% minority	76	81	83	87	72	79	86	84
31-50% minority	72	80	77	83	72	78	85	83
>50% minority	70	82	79	85	69	78	80	79

a. Excludes loan applications above FHA ceiling.

in the acceptance rates of conventional and FHA mortgages appear to vary with both the race of the borrower and the racial composition of the neighborhood. In general, blacks seeking financing in neighborhoods with low concentrations of minorities tend to do significantly better under FHA than with conventional loans, whereas FHA and conventional acceptance rates are about the same for blacks applying for loans in more segregated tracts. In contrast, both whites and Hispanics appear to do better under FHA, regardless of the neighborhood's racial composition.

Patterns in Individual MSAs

Table 5.13 presents loan acceptance rates by the borrower's race in each of the 10 selected sites. Data for conventional loans are again restricted to applications for loan amounts below the FHA ceiling. As shown in the table, blacks have the lowest acceptance rates in each of the sample sites for both conventional and FHA loans. In Los Angeles, 78 percent of all conventional loan applications from blacks are accepted—the same rate as observed for Hispanics but still below the comparable rates for Asians or whites (both, 82 percent). In the remaining MSAs, acceptance rates for blacks are below those of any other group, and the differences tend to be relatively large for both conventional and FHA loans. Indeed, acceptance rates for blacks are between 18 and 22 percentage points lower than the acceptance rates for whites in the majority of the sites.

The aggregate data suggest that FHA and conventional acceptance rates are more or less comparable for blacks, whereas whites and Hispanics appear to do somewhat better under FHA. However, this pattern is not as strong when one examines statistics for individual MSAs. Acceptance rates for both Hispanics and whites are higher under FHA in the majority of sites. However, blacks in about half of the sites also experience higher acceptance rates under FHA, and in three of the sites—Baltimore, St. Louis, and Memphis—the differences are relatively large. In each of these sites, however, the acceptance rate for blacks under FHA is well below the acceptance rates observed for the other racial and ethnic groups.

Acceptance rates for loan applications from Hispanics are typically above the rates experienced by blacks, but below the rates achieved by either Asians or whites. In the three areas with the largest Hispanic populations—Los Angeles, Houston, and Dallas—the Hispanic acceptance rates for conventional loans are relatively close to the rates

Table 5.13 LOAN ACCEPTANCE RATES BY RACE OF BORROWER: SELECTED MSAS

Metropolitan Area	White (%)	Black (%)	Hispanic (%)	Asian (%)
Atlanta				
Conventional[a]	86	68	82	88
FHA	90	68	88	84
Baltimore				
Conventional	88	74	84	89
FHA	93	84	87	92
Chicago				
Conventional	91	71	85	86
FHA	90	73	89	84
Columbus				
Conventional	84	69	100	84
FHA	86	72	85	76
Dallas				
Conventional	84	68	70	91
FHA	90	71	83	89
Houston				
Conventional	83	63	68	86
FHA	82	64	71	78
Los Angeles				
Conventional	82	78	78	82
FHA	84	74	84	85
Memphis				
Conventional	82	60	100	96
FHA	87	68	83	91
Sacramento				
Conventional	84	76	80	84
FHA	86	75	80	73
St. Louis				
Conventional	86	64	79	87
FHA	88	70	80	89

a. Data for conventional loans restricted to applications below the FHA ceiling.

experienced by blacks. However, even in these markets, Hispanics did considerably better than blacks when they applied for an FHA loan. In the remaining markets, the acceptance rates for Hispanics were closer to those experienced by whites and were well above the rates observed for the local black population.

Table 5.14 presents site-specific data on the acceptance rates of FHA and conventional mortgage applications by the percentage of minority residents in the census tract. The patterns for the most part reinforce the aggregate statistics, which suggest that acceptance rates are relatively low in neighborhoods with the highest concentration of minority households. This pattern occurs in each of the markets considered

Table 5.14 LOAN ACCEPTANCE RATES BY CENSUS TRACT PERCENTAGE MINORITY: SELECTED MSAS

	Percentage Minority in Tract				
Metropolitan Area	<10%	11-20%	21-30%	31-50%	>50%
Atlanta					
Conventional[a]	87	83	82	79	70
FHA	89	88	84	71	69
Baltimore					
Conventional	89	83	83	83	80
FHA	93	92	91	89	84
Chicago					
Conventional	92	90	88	86	76
FHA	91	88	87	84	76
Columbus					
Conventional	85	78	77	74	69
FHA	84	87	81	85	75
Dallas					
Conventional	87	83	83	76	74
FHA	91	89	87	80	84
Houston					
Conventional	86	85	81	79	73
FHA	86	81	79	74	72
Los Angeles					
Conventional	81	82	81	80	79
FHA	82	82	83	85	81
Memphis					
Conventional	84	80	75	71	71
FHA	89	85	79	75	69
Sacramento					
Conventional	85	85	83	82	80
FHA	86	91	81	74	83
St. Louis					
Conventional	86	84	79	84	68
FHA	88	85	74	79	71

a. Data for conventional loans restricted to applications below the FHA ceiling.

and holds for both conventional and FHA loans. However, the aggregate data suggest that acceptance rates are lower for FHA loans in census tracts with high concentrations of minorities. Although this pattern characterizes a number of sites, it is by no means universal. In addition, the site-specific data do not always exhibit a steady decline in acceptance rates as the neighborhood percentage of minority residents rises. This occurs in many instances, but acceptance rates in more integrated areas are sometimes as high as those observed in areas that are predominantly white. Yet despite this variation, acceptance rates are always significantly lower in tracts that are more than 50 percent minority—where, as noted earlier, the great majority of the loan applications from Hispanics and blacks originate.

EMPIRICAL ANALYSIS OF FHA DEFAULT ACTIVITY

The racial patterns observed in the HMDA data raise the possibility of systematic discrimination in mortgage lending. However, racial disparities in loan choice or loan acceptance may also arise because of unmeasured indicators of borrower default risk that are merely correlated with the race of the applicant or the racial composition of the neighborhood in which the property is located. Because of this, it is important to evaluate racial patterns observed in the HMDA data in a manner that adequately controls for the default risk associated with a given applicant and neighborhood.

Economic analyses of credit rationing suggest that lenders may apply binding constraints in reviewing loan applications because of uncertainty regarding either the timely repayment of the loan or the collateral value of the property.[9] Because of this, empirical evaluations of mortgage default behavior focus on variables representing the borrower's equity in the property, the borrower's ability and willingness to service the loan as scheduled, and any attributes of the property or the neighborhood that may affect the collateral value of the property. These empirical analyses generally follow one of two approaches to explaining default behavior. According to the *equity approach*, the decision to default is viewed as an exercise of the option to put the mortgage back to the lender at the par value of the loan. In this framework the put option would be exercised when the costs of default to the property owner are less than the owner's negative equity in the property. In contrast, the *ability-to-pay approach* focuses on events that "trigger" default, since negative equity is often found to be a necessary, but not sufficient, condition for default. For example, potential trigger events might include loss of job or income, change in marital or health status, or other factors.

Few mortgage data sets include information on borrower income at the time that a mortgage default occurs; instead, most studies of mortgage default behavior employ payment-to-income ratios and measures of borrower income stability derived from the time of loan origination to explain the mortgage default decision.[10] Because this study focuses on the loan choice and loan acceptance decisions, the empirical analysis is based on attributes of the borrower, the property, or the neighborhood that should be apparent to the lender at the time of the loan application and that may be associated with the predicted probability that the borrower will default at some time during the life of the loan. Accordingly, the analysis of default risk described in this chapter focuses primarily on attributes available at the time of the loan application, rather than on factors that may be important in explaining actual default behavior but that are not available at the application stage.

This section presents the results of an empirical analysis of FHA default risk, focusing on the effects of borrower race or neighborhood racial composition on the probability of loan default. Loan default models are estimated separately for each of the metropolitan areas included in the analysis. Based on these estimates, the predicted probability that the borrower will default on the loan is then imputed for each observation in the HMDA sample; this predicted default probability is then included as a regressor in the subsequent analyses of loan choice and loan acceptance presented in the next main section of the chapter.

Overall Activity and FHA Default Experience

Before specifying a predictive model of FHA mortgage default probabilities, it is useful to evaluate overall loan default rates in the FHA program. Table 5.15 shows the cumulative default rates in each MSA included in the analysis by year of loan origination.[11] As shown in the table, and as would be expected, cumulative default rates increase with the age of the mortgage. For the sample as a whole, relatively few mortgages originating in the early 1990s had already resulted in a claim; in contrast, among loans originated in the mid- and late 1980s, the cumulative default rate approaches 10 percent.

Table 5.15 also shows substantial variation in default rates across MSAs, partly reflecting conditions in the housing market and the

Table 5.15 CUMULATIVE DEFAULT RATE FOR FHA-INSURED LOANS BY MSA AND BY YEAR OF ORIGINATION[1]

	Year of Loan Origination (%)						
Metro Area	1986	1987	1988	1989	1990	1991	1992
Atlanta	10.2	9.2	11.9	9.3	6.4	3.1	0.7
Baltimore	2.8	3.7	5.6	5.4	4.3	2.4	0.7
Chicago	7.2	7.5	9.9	7.4	5.7	3.5	1.0
Columbus	5.6	5.3	5.5	4.7	3.4	2.1	0.5
Dallas	21.8	13.6	13.9	10.2	7.4	3.7	0.8
Houston	15.1	6.8	5.8	4.1	3.3	2.1	0.4
Los Angeles	4.1	4.1	6.2	7.7	8.4	5.4	1.7
Memphis	8.5	10.0	13.0	9.8	7.4	5.1	0.9
Sacramento	2.9	1.7	1.8	1.9	2.4	2.6	0.4
St. Louis	8.9	6.1	7.1	5.0	3.9	2.0	0.6
All Loans	9.4	6.8	8.3	6.9	5.5	3.2	0.8

[1]Calculated default rates represent unweighted means of the rates recorded in each MSA. The estimates are calculated from the entire loan file and are downward biased in that they exclude defaults for which the termination date is missing.

general economy prevailing in each metropolitan area. Cumulative default rates are higher in Dallas, for example, than in any of the other sampled metropolitan areas for loans originated in 1986 through 1989, reflecting the pervasive economic weakness in that MSA during the mid- to late 1980s; in fact, cumulative default rates for loans originated in Dallas in 1986 reached nearly 22 percent by the end of 1992. Cumulative default rates in Houston are also relatively high—more than 15 percent for loans originated in 1986—but taper off significantly for later origination years, reflecting the improvement in the Houston economy.

Cumulative default rates in several of the other MSAs—such as Baltimore, Columbus (Ohio), St. Louis, Chicago, and Atlanta—are significantly lower for loans originated in 1986, but show a peak in 1988 reflecting the general economic recession of the late 1980s. Similarly, cumulative default rates in Los Angeles are relatively low for loans originated between 1986 and 1988, but exceed those in all other sampled MSAs for loans originated between 1990 and 1992. This pattern is consistent with the economy-wide and residential real estate market recession in California during the early 1990s.[12]

Table 5.16 shows cumulative default rates across all origination years for FHA mortgages in the 10 sampled MSAs by selected loan characteristics. (That same information with loans grouped by year of origination is available from the author on request.) The first part of

Table 5.16 CUMULATIVE DEFAULT RATE FOR FHA-INSURED LOANS BY METROPOLITAN AREA AND BY LOAN CHARACTERISTICS

	Metropolitan Area									
Loan Characteristic	Atlanta	Baltimore	Chicago	Columbus	Dallas	Houston	Los Angeles	Memphis	Sacramento	St. Louis
I. Loan-to-Value Ratio										
90% or less	3.0%[1]	1.9%	2.9%	1.3%	3.6%	1.5%	3.2%	3.1%	1.1%	1.8%
90-95%	3.7	1.7	3.1	2.3	3.5	2.2	4.4	4.7	1.3	2.4
95-97.5%	3.3	2.1	2.9	2.4	3.4	2.1	6.5	5.6	1.7	1.9
More than 97.5%	5.1	4.1	6.1	3.5	4.9	2.6	8.5	8.0	2.6	3.2
LTV not available[2]	9.6	4.4	7.9	4.6	11.4	5.3	5.5	9.9	1.8	4.3
II. Mortgage Payment-to-Income Ratio										
28% or less	7.5%	3.9%	7.0%	4.4%	10.1%	4.8%	4.9%	8.7%	1.6%	4.1%
28-33%	6.0	3.6	5.0	1.6	9.6	4.3	4.9	6.7	1.9	2.0
33-38%	7.2	2.7	6.4	3.0	9.3	3.5	4.9	7.2	1.3	1.2
More than 38%	7.8	3.7	4.3	6.8	7.0	5.3	5.4	8.1	1.3	3.8
Ratio not available	6.2	3.9	5.5	3.3	7.2	3.8	6.2	7.5	1.9	3.3
III. Total Debt-to-Income Ratio										
28% or less	8.4%	3.9%	7.8%	4.8%	11.4%	5.2%	5.2%	9.6%	1.8%	5.3%
28-33%	5.3	4.0	4.9	2.0	7.1	3.8	4.6	5.4	2.1	2.1
33-38%	3.7	2.3	3.8	1.5	4.7	1.3	4.5	5.3	1.3	1.8
More than 38%	5.1	3.8	4.8	2.8	6.7	2.3	6.0	7.7	1.5	2.8
Ratio not available	6.2	3.9	5.5	3.4	7.3	3.9	6.1	7.5	1.9	3.3
IV. Mortgage Term										
Less than 30 years	3.5%	2.0%	3.6%	2.4%	4.5%	3.3%	2.3%	5.1%	1.2%	2.1%
30 years	6.5	3.9	5.9	3.6	8.1	4.1	6.1	8.0	1.9	3.5
Term not available	0.0	0.0	0.0	0.0	—	—	0.0	0.0	0.0	0.0

[1]Calculated default rates represent unweighted means of the rates recorded in each MSA, cumulated across all loan origination years. The estimates are calculated from the entire loan file and are downward biased in that they exclude defaults for which the termination data is missing.

the table compares the cumulative default rate in each metropolitan area by initial loan-to-value (LTV) ratio. Because loans with a higher initial loan-to-value ratio are more likely than other loans (ceteris paribus) to have negative equity at some time during the life of the loan, it is expected that cumulative default rates will generally be higher for loans with higher initial LTV ratios. As table 5.16 shows, cumulative default rates are indeed somewhat higher among borrowers with little initial equity in the property, as indicated by loan-to-value ratios of 97.5 percent or more. Conversely, in most MSAs, loans with initial LTV ratios of less than 90 percent show the lowest cumulative default rates. The expected positive relationship between default incidence and mortgage loan-to-value holds in several metropolitan areas (including Columbus, Los Angeles, Memphis, and Sacramento), as well as generally in the other areas.

Table 5.16 also shows substantial variation across cities in the magnitudes of default probabilities. In Los Angeles and Memphis, for instance, default rates rise to 8 percent or more among borrowers with loan-to-value ratios in excess of 97.5 percent; in contrast, default rates among these higher loan-to-value borrowers remain below 3 percent in Houston and Sacramento.

The second and third parts of table 5.16 show cumulative default rates by mortgage payment-to-income (front-end) and total debt-to-income (back-end) ratios. Because borrowers may have more difficulty making loan payments on loans with higher payment-to-income or debt-to-income ratios, cumulative default rates are expected to increase with front- and back-end ratios. As the table shows, however, in most cases the expected positive relationships between default rates and front- and back-end ratios do not hold. Indeed, in five MSAs the cumulative default rate is highest for loans with payment-to-income ratios of less than 28 percent, and in three areas the default rate is lowest for loans with the highest payment-to-income ratios. Similarly, seven metro areas show the highest default rates for loans with the lowest debt-to-income ratios. Given the fact that the FHA data do not exhibit the expected patterns for front- and back-end ratios, it seems likely that other considerations, such as borrower characteristics (e.g., whether the borrower is a first-time homebuyer), play an important role in determining mortgage default rates. Finally, table 5.16 also shows higher cumulative default rates among 30-year mortgages than among loans with shorter maturities in every metropolitan area. This result is expected, because shorter-term loans amortize more quickly and hence carry lower levels of default risk.

Table 5.17 presents cumulative default rates by selected borrower characteristics for each metropolitan area included in the analysis. (That same information in greater detail, with loans grouped by year of origination, is available from the author on request.) One of the most striking results shown in table 5.17 is the difference in default rates among borrowers of different racial or ethnic groups. In particular, black borrowers have higher default rates than borrowers of any other racial group in all 10 MSAs. Indeed, the difference in mortgage default rates is quite significant in most cases: for example, in Chicago the cumulative default rate among black borrowers by the end of 1992 was about 11.2 percent, which was more than three times as high as the second-highest rate, that for Hispanic borrowers (3.5 percent). In contrast, Asian borrowers exhibited the lowest default rates of any racial group in every MSA except St. Louis. White and Hispanic borrowers generally show default rates that fall between those for black and Asian borrowers, with Hispanic borrowers showing a slightly higher default rate in most MSAs.

These findings are consistent with the results of numerous other studies suggesting higher levels of credit risk among black borrowers (or in predominantly black neighborhoods), slightly higher risk levels for Hispanic borrowers, and slightly lower risk levels for Asian borrowers relative to white borrowers. It is important to recognize, however, that these simple calculations of cumulative mortgage defaults by borrower race fail to control for borrower financial and locational characteristics, some of which are likely to be correlated with borrower race. In the analysis undertaken below, we estimate a well-specified model of mortgage defaults that controls for a large set of borrower and locational characteristics associated with default risk; this model also accounts for any remaining effects on default stemming from borrower race or neighborhood racial composition.

Table 5.17 suggests that default rates tend to decline as borrower income increases. For example, borrowers with household incomes of less than $30,000 showed the highest cumulative default rates in most of the metropolitan areas included in the analysis. However, the highest-income borrowers (household income $75,000 or more) showed elevated default rates in several MSAs; indeed, the lowest default rates in most MSAs were among borrowers with household incomes between $50,000 and $74,999. The unexpected elevation in default rates for higher-income FHA borrowers—a result that did not arise in the study conducted by the Federal Reserve Bank of Boston (Munnell et al. 1992, 1995)—may indicate the presence of other risk factors; in fact, it is possible that these higher-income borrowers use

Table 5.17 CUMULATIVE DEFAULT RATE FOR FHA-INSURED LOANS BY METROPOLITAN AREA AND BY BORROWER CHARACTERISTICS

	Metropolitan Area									
Borrower Characteristic	Atlanta	Baltimore	Chicago	Columbus	Dallas	Houston	Los Angeles	Memphis	Sacramento	St. Louis
I. Race of Borrower										
Asian	1.8%[1]	1.3%	2.2%	0.4%	3.8%	2.2%	5.2%	4.5%	1.1%	2.5%
Black	8.9	6.8	11.2	6.1	14.6	6.2	7.7	12.0	4.4	5.7
Hispanic	4.7	2.2	3.5	1.7	9.5	4.5	5.3	5.1	1.7	2.7
White	3.9	2.5	2.5	2.7	5.2	2.7	5.3	4.7	1.7	2.1
Other or not available[2]	11.3	5.5	9.0	5.5	12.8	5.5	6.2	11.5	2.0	6.1
II. Household Income										
Less than $30,000	8.4%	4.9%	9.0%	5.0%	12.0%	5.2%	4.6%	10.5%	1.8%	4.7%
$30,000–$49,999	6.2	3.1	4.7	2.3	8.0	4.1	5.8	5.3	1.8	3.2
$50,000–$74,999	5.1	2.2	3.3	2.4	5.4	3.0	5.1	4.6	1.5	1.8
$75,000 or more	10.3	2.5	5.3	4.2	7.6	4.0	4.9	8.5	1.2	3.6
Income not available	6.1	3.8	5.4	3.4	7.2	3.9	6.1	7.4	1.9	3.2

(Continued)

Table 5.17 CUMULATIVE DEFAULT RATE FOR FHA-INSURED LOANS BY METROPOLITAN AREA AND BY BORROWER CHARACTERISTICS (*Continued*)

Borrower Characteristic	Metropolitan Area									
	Atlanta	Baltimore	Chicago	Columbus	Dallas	Houston	Los Angeles	Memphis	Sacramento	St. Louis
III. Other Characteristics										
Borrower Age:										
More than 30 years	5.8%	3.4%	6.2%	3.5%	6.9%	3.7%	4.5%	7.0%	1.4%	3.2%
30 years or less	5.6	2.9	4.3	3.3	8.4	4.0	4.9	7.6	1.6	3.1
Age not available	6.8	4.2	6.1	3.7	8.0	4.1	6.5	8.2	2.0	3.6
Homebuyer Status:										
First-time	6.4%	3.2%	4.9%	2.7%	8.4%	3.8%	6.0%	7.8%	1.9%	3.0%
Not first-time	3.1	1.8	3.1	2.2	4.3	2.7	3.5	4.0	1.3	1.6
Status not available	9.7	5.4	7.8	5.0	10.2	4.9	6.5	11.0	2.1	5.4
Property Status:										
New	5.5%	2.2%	2.5%	1.8%	5.8%	2.8%	5.8%	5.0%	1.4%	3.2%
Existing	6.7	4.3	5.9	4.0	8.3	4.2	5.9	8.3	2.0	3.4
Property Type:										
1 unit	6.4%	3.8%	5.7%	3.6%	7.9%	4.0%	5.8%	7.8%	1.9%	3.4%
2–4 units	9.4	5.0	6.3	3.1	6.3	6.4	5.9	8.8	0.7	4.5
Units not available	—	—	—	—	—	—	—	—	—	0.0
Marital Status:										
Married	6.1%	3.3%	5.0%	3.5%	7.7%	3.7%	4.4%	6.8%	1.6%	2.9%
Not married	4.8	2.8	5.3	2.7	6.3	3.6	4.9	6.9	1.3	2.7
Status not available	6.9	4.1	6.2	3.7	8.2	4.2	6.6	8.4	2.0	3.7

[1]Calculated default rates represent unweighted means of the rates recorded in each MSA, cumulated across all loan origination years. The estimates are calculated from the entire loan file and are downward biased in that they exclude defaults for which the termination data is missing.

[2]Includes borrowers identified as landlords, builders, or escrow.

the FHA loan program because these other risk factors make it more difficult for them to obtain conventional loans.

The third part of table 5.17 presents default rates by several other borrower characteristics. For example, younger borrowers are often considered to present greater credit risk than older borrowers, since they often lack well-established credit or job histories. The table shows, however, that borrowers 30 years old or younger actually show lower cumulative default rates than older borrowers in 5 of the 10 metro areas. On the other hand, first-time homebuyers have higher default rates than other borrowers in all 10 MSAs. Likewise, borrowers purchasing existing properties showed higher default rates than those purchasing new properties in each MSA in the analysis.

Table 5.18 presents cumulative default rates by selected neighborhood characteristics in each of the 10 MSAs. The first part of the table shows that default rates tend to be significantly higher in neighborhoods with larger proportions of minority residents, a pattern that holds consistently in every MSA except Los Angeles. The patterns shown in this table are consistent with other recent studies focusing on the relationship between borrower race and neighborhood racial composition and the incidence of mortgage default. It is important to recognize, however, that neighborhood minority composition is often associated with unrelated neighborhood disamenities that adversely affect loan collateralization.

As would be expected, table 5.18 also shows that cumulative default rates tend to be lower in census tracts with higher levels of median family income, a pattern that holds in every MSA except for the highest-income neighborhoods of Baltimore. These higher levels of median family income are likely to be associated with higher levels of neighborhood amenities (including neighborhood socioeconomic status) that may reduce the risk of mortgage default.

Model Specification

In evaluating the mortgage default rates just presented, it is important to keep in mind that the observed patterns of mortgage default behavior by borrower characteristics (especially race or ethnicity) and by neighborhood characteristics (especially percent minority) may not actually be caused by race-based differences in mortgage default behavior. Instead, the observed differences in mortgage default behavior may be caused not by race or ethnicity but by other factors that are merely associated with race and ethnicity, such as income, wealth, employment or income stability, or neighborhood property value ap-

Table 5.18 CUMULATIVE DEFAULT RATE FOR FHA-INSURED LOANS BY METROPOLITAN AREA AND BY NEIGHBORHOOD CHARACTERISTICS[1]

Neighborhood Characteristics[1]	Metropolitan Area									
	Atlanta	Baltimore	Chicago	Columbus	Dallas	Houston	Los Angeles	Memphis	Sacramento	St. Louis
I. Minority Proportion of Tract Residents										
Less than 10%	4.0%[2]	2.8%	2.5%	2.8%	5.9%	2.9%	6.4%	4.6%	1.6%	2.3%
10–24%	6.1	3.2	—	3.2	7.4	4.1	4.9	5.8	2.4	3.6
25–49%	8.0	5.2	—	6.8	13.9	4.7	5.6	8.1	3.4	4.8
50–79%	10.2	7.0	—	7.2	15.9	8.0	7.2	12.3	—	7.1
80% or more	13.3	10.5	—	8.9	20.6	9.1	6.4	15.8	—	6.7
II. Urban Location										
Central City	6.0%	3.2%	2.4%	3.0%	6.3%	3.5%	6.7%	5.6%	1.8%	3.3%
Suburbs	6.3	2.7	3.2	2.0	6.6	3.7	4.9	4.4	1.4	3.4
III. Census Tract Median Family Income										
Less than $30,000	10.5%	7.1%	—%	5.0%	12.7%	5.0%	6.3%	11.2%	2.0%	4.8%
$30,000–$49,999	6.1	3.4	2.7	2.5	6.8	3.8	5.8	5.6	1.8	2.7
$50,000–$74,999	3.2	2.4	2.0	1.4	3.2	2.1	3.9	3.0	0.5	1.1
$75,000 or more	0.0	5.9	0.9	0.0	0.0	0.0	2.2	—	—	0.0

[1]Characteristics of census tracts are based on the 1990 Census of Population and Housing.

[2]Calculation default rates represent unweighted means of the rates recorded in each MSA, cumulated across all loan origination years. The estimates are calculated from the entire loan file and are downward biased in that they exclude defaults for which the termination date is missing.

preciation. To isolate the effects of borrower race and neighborhood racial composition on mortgage lending patterns, it is important to develop a well-specified model of mortgage default behavior that controls as carefully as possible for these other factors as well as for borrower race and neighborhood racial composition.

The data on FHA-insured mortgages are relatively well-suited to the analysis of mortgage default behavior. For both FHA and conventional mortgage lending programs, the use of formal underwriting criteria in evaluating loan applications implies that observed defaults reflect a population with anticipated defaults less than or equal to some critical value. Although both FHA and conventional mortgage applications are evaluated according to formal underwriting criteria, the FHA guidelines are substantially less strict than those of conventional lenders. For these reasons, the FHA data set is likely to present less possibility of sample selection bias compared to a database of conventional loans.

For each mortgage application included in this analysis, the probability of default was predicted on the basis of a logistic model of mortgage default behavior estimated using data on mortgages originated in the corresponding metropolitan area. The dependent variable in these logit models is a binary variable indicating whether that loan resulted in a claim against the FHA at any time before the end of 1992.[13] The explanatory variables used in the model include borrower, loan, property, and neighborhood characteristics that may affect default risk. The variables included in the logit model of default probability are defined in Appendix A.

The model of cumulative default probability is estimated using the entire data set of available observations on FHA loans originated during the period from 1987 through 1992. Because older mortgages are systematically more likely to have experienced a default than are more recently originated loans, the model includes a set of dummy variables representing the mortgage origination year. In particular, cumulative default probabilities are expected to be significantly lower, ceteris paribus, in the first year after mortgage origination assuming adequate loan underwriting, net positive equity in the property, and the borrower's continued ability to repay the loan as scheduled. Cumulative default probabilities are then expected to increase over the early years of the loan as a result of changes in borrower ability to service the loan as scheduled (that is, employment status or other financial factors), as well as changes in other default risk characteristics. Finally, the rate of increase in the cumulative default probability is expected to decline in later years as a result of improved loan collateralization in the wake of housing price appreciation.

The cumulative default probability model includes variables representing several borrower characteristics, including age, gender, marital status, number of dependents, family income, and first-time buyer status. In general, default probabilities are expected to be higher among younger, unmarried, and first-time homebuyers as well as those with a larger number of dependents or lower family incomes.

The regression analysis also includes several variables measuring borrower assets and income, which should reflect the borrower's ability to repay the loan as scheduled. For example, the model accounts for borrower family income (including all sources of income recognized by FHA loan underwriters at the time of loan qualification), coborrower income, and percentage of borrower income derived from salary sources. Higher levels of borrower and coborrower income—as well as a higher percentage of borrower income from salary sources—should enhance the borrower's ability to service the loan as scheduled and hence should reduce the probability of mortgage default.

The analysis furthermore includes several loan characteristics representing mortgage collateralization and borrower ability to service the loan as scheduled. These mortgage characteristics include loan-to-value ratios, front- and back-end ratios, whether or not the loan is for purposes of refinance, and loan term. Mortgage loan-to-value ratios represent the degree of loan collateralization at the time of loan origination; higher loan-to-value ratios indicate lower levels of borrower initial equity in the property and, hence, higher risks of loan default. Front- and back-end ratios, defined as borrower mortgage payment-to-income and total debt-to-income ratios, typically comprise critical elements of the loan qualification and underwriting process. In this analysis, front-end ratios are defined as total monthly mortgage payments (inclusive of property taxes and insurance) as a percentage of total monthly family income recognized by the FHA underwriters; to calculate back-end ratios, the sum of other monthly debt service obligations is added to the monthly mortgage payment. Higher borrower front- and back-end ratios indicate higher levels of borrower monthly debt burdens and, therefore, reduced borrower ability to service the loan as scheduled in the event of a disruption in the borrower's income. The analysis further distinguishes among loans that are less than or equal to 30 years in duration; shorter-duration loans amortize more quickly and thus should carry lower default risk.

The analysis includes a set of property and locational indicators that should affect expected rates of loan collateralization and, hence, probabilities of loan default. Among property characteristics, the study includes the age, condition, and type of property as well as whether the property is a new house. We expect higher rates of loan collateralization and lower levels of default risk among single-family and newer houses as well as among those structures in better condition.

Among locational indicators, the study includes a substantial number of neighborhood variables derived from the 1980 and 1990 censuses. This set of indicators is largely consistent with those employed in the HMDA loan choice and loan acceptance models described in the next main section of this chapter, and includes tract unemployment, vacancy, and poverty rates; tract median housing price and percentage change in price over the 1980s; tract median household income and percentage change in median income over the 1980s; tract racial composition and percentage change in racial composition during the 1980s; tract housing age, ownership status, and type; and tract FHA default rate over the 1986–92 period. In general, higher levels of tract unemployment, vacancy, poverty, or default—or lower levels of tract income, house prices, or changes in median income and house prices—suggest lower expected rates of loan collateralization and, hence, higher probabilities of default. The analysis also includes an indicator of property location in central city or noncentral city areas; lenders typically expect higher levels of default risk in inner-city neighborhoods.

Finally, the empirical specification accounts for any residual effects of borrower race or neighborhood racial composition in the determination of FHA loan default probabilities. As documented in table 5.17, black and Hispanic borrowers tend to show higher levels of default risk relative to white and Asian borrowers. Moreover, minority households are often concentrated in older neighborhoods subject to lower rates of loan collateralization.

The higher levels of default risk among minority households derive from a variety of factors. For example, minority households may be more likely to experience layoffs or other income shocks, sometimes owing to racial discrimination in job markets. Similarly, minority neighborhoods often are characterized by older and less-desirable inner-city locations, elevated levels of neighborhood unemployment and poverty, and less-robust local markets; these conditions, in turn, imply lower rates of property appreciation and loan collateralization in minority areas. Racial discrimination in housing markets may also play a significant role in the clustering of minority households in less-desirable and higher-risk areas of cities. Whereas each of these factors suggests relatively higher risks of mortgage default among minority borrowers or neighborhoods, it is important to note that the logit model specifies and tests numerous proxies for the borrower, property, and locational risks of default. Given the extensive specification of default risk, any remaining effect of borrower or neighborhood race in the prediction of loan defaults may reflect factors unrelated to default risk, including possible racial bias or redlining in mortgage lending.

Finally, it is important to recognize that the model specification assumes that the effect of each borrower, loan, property, or neighborhood characteristic on the cumulative probability of default remains constant for all mortgages in a given metropolitan area, regardless of the mortgage origination year. Put another way, the fact that the model is estimated on loans across all origination years, with dummy variables representing the year of origination, imposes the implicit constraint that all regression coefficients except for the intercept remain constant across origination years. Alternatively, the model could have been specified either with a separate equation for each year of origination, or with dummy interactive variables enabling the coefficients associated with borrower, loan, property, and neighborhood characteristics to differ across origination years.

Appendix B summarizes a series of analyses that were conducted to determine whether the choice of model specification significantly affects the estimated cumulative mortgage default probability model. In summary, the analyses presented in the appendix suggest that, while the model specification employed may be too restrictive, problems with the data used in the analysis, as well as problems of collinearity among the independent variables employed in the regression analysis, are likely to be of significantly greater importance than the model specification in affecting the quality of the empirical results.

Estimation Results and Imputations

Table 5.19 summarizes the coefficients estimated for selected explanatory variables.[14] As the table suggests, many of the estimated effects have the expected signs; however, relatively few of the estimated regression coefficients are significantly different from zero (at a 95 percent level of confidence), and substantial variation exists in results across metropolitan areas in the sample. The most consistently significant coefficients are those associated with the mortgage origination year; moreover, as table 5.19 shows, the magnitude of the origination year coefficients generally increases steadily over the first few

Table 5.19 SUMMARY OF ESTIMATED COEFFICIENTS OF THE LOAN DEFAULT MODELS

	Metropolitan Statistical Area									
	Atlanta	Baltimore	Chicago	Columbus	Dallas	Houston	Los Angeles	Memphis	Sacramento	St. Louis
Mortgage Origination Year[1]										
1990	**+0.79**	**+0.64**	**+1.15**	+0.57	+0.31	+0.06	+0.34	**+0.59**	+0.62	+0.49
1989	**+0.79**	**+0.96**	**+1.37**	**+1.11**	**+0.60**	**+0.91**	**+0.62**	**+0.98**	+0.99	**+0.90**
1988	**+1.05**	**+1.16**	**+1.65**	**+0.96**	**+0.92**	**+1.25**	+0.34	**+1.15**	+1.04	**+0.72**
1987	—	+0.96	**+1.97**	+1.12	+0.23	**+1.73**	+0.18	—	+0.77	—
Front-End Ratio[2]										
28–33%	−0.3	**+1.8**	+0.5	+0.6	+0.6	+0.5	−0.1	−0.3	−2.1	−0.6
33–38%	+0.5	+1.3	+0.4	+0.5	+1.4	−0.6	−1.4	+0.9	**−4.5**	−2.2
More than 38%	**+2.3**	**+2.2**	−0.2	−1.3	−1.5	−0.4	−0.8	−0.2	−1.8	−0.6
Borrower Income	-5.5×10^{-4}	$+5.2\times10^{-3}$	-4.8×10^{-3}	-9.0×10^{-4}	$+1.6\times10^{-2}$	$+1.2\times10^{-2}$	$+8.4\times10^{-3}$	-1.5×10^{-2}	-1.1×10^{-2}	-3.2×10^{-2}
Borrower Net Assets	$+7.0\times10^{-5}$	$+9.0\times10^{-5}$	-3.2×10^{-4}	-2.4×10^{-3}	$+4.0\times10^{-4}$	-2.8×10^{-3}	-7.0×10^{-5}	-8.4×10^{-4}	-1.0×10^{-3}	-3.7×10^{-4}
Tract Default Rate	**+12.4**	+10.2	−3.3	+4.2	+3.3	**+19.2**	+7.3	+3.8	−22.3	+2.7
Race of Borrower[3]										
Asian	+0.59	—	—	—	—	+0.06	−0.26	—	—	—
Black	−0.02	+0.21	+0.84	+0.24	+0.35	+0.19	+0.07	+0.15	−0.66	+0.66
Hispanic	—	—	+0.15	—	+0.32	+0.17	+0.02	—	+0.21	—
Other	—	—	—	—	—	—	**+2.89**	—	**+3.95**	—
Neighborhood Racial Composition										
Percent Black	+14.7	+22.9	−17.0	+2.1	−4.7	−1.0	+1.6	−6.2	+6.3	**−18.5**
Percent Hispanic	+18.1	+25.5	−15.0	+36.2	−4.8	−1.2	+1.2	+6.8	+6.2	−12.9
Percent White	+15.0	**+22.3**	−13.3	+1.7	−4.7	−2.2	+1.3	−6.4	+6.4	−20.4

[1]Compared to loans less than one year old.
[2]Compared to loans with front-end ratio of 28 percent or less.
[3]Compared to white borrowers.
Note: Coefficients shown in **bold** are significant at the 95 percent level of confidence.

years following loan origination, suggesting the expected time profile of cumulative default risk.

In a few of the metropolitan areas (including Atlanta and Baltimore), the coefficients associated with the mortgage payment-to-income (front-end) ratio is close to the expected pattern of default probability coefficients increasing with the front-end ratio. In 8 of the 10 MSAs, however, the coefficient for front-end ratios exceeding 38 percent is negative, suggesting that loans with high front-end ratios have a lower cumulative default probability than loans with low front-end ratios of less than 28 percent. Moreover, the coefficients are generally not statistically significant, a pattern that also holds for coefficients associated with mortgage loan-to-value and household debt-to-income ratios. These results coincide with the simple cross-tabulations presented previously, suggesting that these common loan underwriting requirements offer less insight into default risk than generally believed.

As expected, higher levels of household income and net assets are often associated with lower default probabilities, although the estimated coefficients are not statistically significant. Also as expected, the default rate on mortgages in the property's neighborhood is positively associated with the borrower's default probability in all but 2 MSAs, indicating that neighborhood default rate constitutes a useful proxy for other neighborhood characteristics that could not be included in the model. Again, however, the estimated coefficients are statistically significant in only 2 of the 10 metropolitan areas.

Finally, after controlling for borrower financial, property, and locational characteristics, the results of the logit analysis suggest that there is little systematic correlation between the borrower's race or ethnicity and the cumulative probability of mortgage default. Although the estimated coefficient associated with black borrowers is positive in almost all metropolitan areas, it is statistically significant only in St. Louis. Similarly, the coefficient for Hispanic borrowers is positive in all five of the MSAs for which it could be estimated, but is not statistically significant in any of them. Moreover, the empirical results suggest that there is no particular relationship between neighborhood racial composition and cumulative default probabilities. For example, the proportion of black residents is associated with default probabilities positively in five MSAs, negatively in the other five MSAs, and not significantly in any of them; the results are similarly inconclusive for percentage Hispanic and percentage white. In general, the estimated coefficients do not provide evidence that the borrower's race, or the racial composition of the borrower's neighborhood, has a significant effect on the likelihood of mortgage default.

In evaluating the results of this model of cumulative mortgage default probability, it is useful to keep in mind the limitations of the data used in the analysis. As noted, observations on one or more of the critical variables are missing for a relatively large proportion of the loans included in the database. Moreover, the database does not include data on several important variables that are likely to be related to mortgage default probability, such as the borrower's credit history. These data problems certainly have some effect on the quality of the default model results.

After having conducted this analysis of default risk, coefficient estimates from the default models were used to impute default probabilities for loan applications included in the HMDA files. This imputation process utilized the default model coefficient estimates in conjunction with applicant and census-tract characteristics as contained in the individual HMDA files. The purpose of imputing default probabilities was to construct a default risk variable so that predicted default risk can be accounted for explicitly in the accompanying HMDA analyses of loan choice and loan acceptance. In this way, the analysis attempts to utilize information from the FHA loan file to surmount well-known limitations of the HMDA data in the analysis of mortgage choice and mortgage acceptance decisions.

It bears emphasizing, however, that the HMDA loan files lack information on a variety of borrower and property characteristics evaluated in the default models, including loan-to-value ratios, front- and back-end ratios, borrower assets and percentage of income derived from salary sources, coborrower income, borrower marital status and dependents, and property age, type, and condition. In these cases, the procedure employed in this analysis was to set missing values from the HMDA files to the mean of borrower subgroup values in each MSA by race/ethnicity and by borrower income class. The predicted probability of default associated with each loan application was then entered into the HMDA loan choice and loan acceptance models as an explanatory variable.

LOAN CHOICE AND LOAN ACCEPTANCE MODEL RESULTS

The preceding two sections of this chapter documented pronounced racial and ethnic differences in the proportion of borrowers applying for FHA-insured mortgages, as well as in the proportion of loan applications that were ultimately accepted by the lender. In general, blacks and, to a lesser extent, Hispanics were significantly more likely to apply for an FHA mortgage than white borrowers, and significantly less likely to have their loan applications accepted. Hispanics fared noticeably better under FHA than in the conventional market, although they still did not match the success rates achieved by whites. In contrast, acceptance rates for blacks were roughly the same for conventional and FHA loans, and were well below the rates achieved by whites.

A variety of factors could contribute to the outcomes observed. This chapter attempts to control for at least some of these factors by developing two regression models using HMDA data.[15] First, we describe a loan choice model developed to estimate the probability that a borrower will apply for an FHA mortgage as opposed to a conventional loan. The analysis is restricted to applications for loans below the established FHA ceiling, and takes loan size as an exogenously determined variable. The model relates the probability that a borrower applies for an FHA loan to selected characteristics of the mortgage, the neighborhood, and the borrower. The loan choice model also includes an estimate of the predicted probability that each borrower will default on the mortgage, with this estimate derived from the analysis of default risk presented previously. While other variables included in the equations also measure credit risk, this "predicted default" variable attempts to reflect the influence of factors that might cause lenders to steer minority borrowers to FHA loans or to view applications from minority borrowers in a less-favorable light.

The second part of the analysis examines the probability that a loan application is accepted, controlling for a series of factors believed to reflect the underlying riskiness of the loan.[16] The model distinguishes between the outcomes that are achieved by different racial and ethnic groups under both conventional and FHA loans. The analysis is similar to the loan choice model just described, and includes a similar set of independent variables including the predicted probability of default estimated from the preceding section. The principal objective of the analysis is to estimate the extent to which racial and ethnic differences in loan acceptance rates can be attributed to factors known to affect the underlying riskiness of the loan, rather than to race or ethnicity per se.

Loan Choice Model

Table 5.20 presents the independent variables that were included in the loan choice model, which was estimated separately for each of the 10 metropolitan areas included in the analysis. The results of the

Table 5.20 EXPLANATORY VARIABLES INCLUDED IN THE LOAN CHOICE MODEL

Variables
I. Location (central city versus suburban)
II. Loan Characteristics Type (refinance versus purchase) Estimated Payment-to-Income Ratio
III. Borrower Characteristics Income (percent of local median) Sex of Applicant Race/Ethnicity of Applicant (white, black, Hispanic, Asian, other)
IV. Census Tract Characteristics Housing Stock • Vacancy Rate (1990) • Age (<10, 11–20, 21–30, 30–50, 50+) • Percent Owner-Occupied (1990) • Percent Single-Family (1-4 units) House Values • Average Value in 1990 (absolute or percent of FHA ceiling) • 1980-1990 Percent Change • Rent/Value Ratio (1990) Racial and Ethnic Composition • Percent Minority in 1990 (<10%, 11–20%, 21–30%, 31–50%, 50%+) • 1980–1990 Increase in % Minority Socioeconomic Status • Percent Unemployed (1990) • Percent Below Poverty (1990)
V. Predicted Probability of Default

regression model are presented in Table 5.21. In general, the estimated parameters had the expected signs and were statistically significant in the majority of sites. For example, the third part of the exhibit shows that borrowers with higher mortgage payment-to-income ratios (higher than 15 percent) were significantly more likely to use FHA in every market compared to borrowers with front-end ratios of 15 percent or less; moreover, the magnitudes of the estimated regression coefficients generally increase steadily as the front-end ratio increases (especially in Baltimore, Memphis, and Sacramento). Borrowers refinancing their existing loans were significantly less likely to use FHA in every market.

Table 5.21 ESTIMATED REGRESSION PARAMETERS FOR THE LOAN CHOICE MODEL

	Metropolitan Statistical Area									
Model Parameter	Atlanta	Baltimore	Chicago	Columbus	Dallas	Houston	Los Angeles	Memphis	Sacramento	St. Louis
R-Squared	26.4%	26.4%	21.9%	27.6%	22.7%	18.5%	8.1%	32.1%	11.7%	22.9%
Borrower Characteristics										
Race										
Asian	−4.32***	−6.54***	−2.36***	−11.27***	−8.42***	−13.10***	0.36	−12.05***	−8.16***	−1.35
Black	18.39***	12.69***	25.50***	14.08***	13.72***	11.04***	1.36***	11.08***	7.43***	24.46***
Hispanic	6.28***	8.88***	10.64***	14.97***	10.20***	9.75***	1.80***	−1.34	3.69***	5.24***
Other	−7.57***	−2.07	−0.77	−2.85	1.21	−9.16***	1.72***	1.68	−1.85*	−0.51
Female	0.00***	−1.90***	−2.93***	−4.22***	−2.78***	−3.83***	−0.92***	−2.52***	−1.01***	−5.02***
Income	0.04***	0.09***	0.03***	0.06***	−0.02***	−0.07***	0.04***	0.08***	−0.01***	0.00
Neighborhood Characteristics										
Racial Composition										
11–20% Minority	3.24***	6.01***	1.64***	8.04***	6.50***	0.66	−3.83***	3.41***	3.27***	3.12***
21–30% Minority	3.88***	9.84***	7.39***	8.80***	9.11***	1.99***	−4.61***	−0.52	1.92***	7.67***
31–50% Minority	3.71***	7.60***	7.37***	8.44***	14.11***	2.73***	−6.01***	−1.99**	4.20***	10.45***
>50% Minority	7.60***	7.10***	10.15***	9.35***	10.06***	5.25***	−7.29***	−0.64	4.93***	16.58***
% Change in Min. Comp.	1.68***	−0.04	2.01***	0.43***	0.74***	1.34***	3.85***	2.40***	3.67***	1.92***
Average Property Value	−7.11***	−17.57***	−10.47***	−9.90***	−8.43***	−6.13***	−5.02***	−27.63***	0.04	−16.16***
% Change in Value	4.16***	1.63***	−1.41***	12.69***	−3.95***	−12.63***	−1.47***	−1.41	−5.13***	14.43***
Median Rent/Value	3,840***	4,152***	698***	4,436***	6,389***	4,218***	763***	1,342***	1,931***	4,552***
Age of Housing										−4.62***
11–20 Years	−3.17***	−7.21***	1.36***	−4.98***	−8.33***	−1.56***	−2.98***	−8.89***	−1.77***	−6.51***
21–30 Years	−8.12***	−9.17***	−0.17	−1.13	−3.83***	−1.64***	−6.59***	−12.19***	−1.37***	−3.20***
31–50 Years	−12.16***	−8.12***	0.79*	−1.27	−9.70***	−7.89***	−7.23***	−4.23***	−1.02**	2.38***
>50 Years	−17.28***	−15.81***	−1.54***	−2.56***	−17.31***	4.99***	−8.38***	−9.49***	−2.47***	0.60*
Central City	−2.45***	4.21***	−4.98***	4.80***	2.12***	0.70*	1.05***	15.57***	0.50	−79.58***
Poverty Rate	−2.16	13.83***	6.51***	−15.23***	−63.39***	−55.02***	4.13**	−46.46***	10.43***	−72.23***
Unemployment Rate	96.65***	−43.01***	51.34***	30.95*	−31.36**	40.02**	2.94	70.69***	−2.36	−17.31***
Vacancy Rate	−14.53**	−84.18***	40.72***	−145.75***	−53.56***	−2.82	33.08***	−131.04***	22.52***	−1.13
% Single-Family (1−4 units)	−26.39***	7.98***	25.53***	8.71***	10.61***	11.27***	−0.88	1.45	−9.12***	8.27***
% Owner-Occupied	29.90***	6.10**	−7.21***	−1.78	−12.40***	−3.04	13.70***	3.09	12.48***	
Loan Characteristics										
Payment-to-Income Ratio										
16–20%	22.51***	17.83***	9.58***	22.43***	25.53***	21.18***	−0.95***	33.71***	5.95***	20.40***
21–25%	31.83***	28.98***	14.91***	35.54***	32.66***	30.77***	0.91***	41.01***	11.20***	27.60***
26–30%	38.27***	39.39***	16.37***	44.76***	35.22***	33.43***	3.15***	43.66***	17.36***	32.69***
>30%	32.21***	42.38***	6.59***	38.81***	30.37***	22.96***	4.02***	44.86***	17.60***	19.60***
Refinance	−28.22***	−31.86***	−14.79***	−25.61***	−22.14***	−17.49***	−6.07***	−26.97***	−11.30***	−18.62***
Predicted Default Probability	−15.12***	−23.38***	−8.90***	20.96*	−3.83**	26.31***	21.00***	13.86***	3.13	−6.46***

***significant at 99% **significant at 95% *significant at 90%

The coefficients associated with neighborhood characteristics variables indicate that borrowers in neighborhoods that are undergoing a change in racial composition ("% Change in Min. Comp.") are significantly more likely to use FHA in virtually every MSA included in the analysis. On the other hand, no consistent pattern was associated with the rate of change of neighborhood average property values. Borrowers in neighborhoods with relatively high average property values were less likely to use FHA, as expected, whereas those in neighborhoods with relatively high rent-to-value ratios were more likely to use FHA. Perhaps the only surprising result for neighborhood characteristics is that borrowers in neighborhoods with a relatively older housing stock were generally less likely to use FHA in every MSA except Chicago. Other neighborhood indicators were more mixed. Finally, the loan choice model suggests that the predicted probability that the borrower would default has no consistent effect on whether the borrower uses FHA or a conventional loan program: the coefficient associated with predicted default probability is significantly positive in four MSAs, and significantly negative in five others.

The primary focus of this analysis, of course, is the effect of race and ethnicity on the probability that the borrower would use FHA as opposed to conventional loan programs. In general, the regression coefficients were consistent with the patterns observed in aggregate data on the use of FHA and conventional loan programs by borrowers of each racial or ethnic group. In particular, binary variables signifying a black applicant were statistically significant in all of the sites, and had the positive signs that would be expected if blacks are in fact more likely to apply for an FHA loan compared to otherwise similar whites. Hispanic borrowers showed virtually the same pattern, although the magnitude of the coefficients was not as great for Hispanic borrowers in most MSAs. In contrast, the negative estimated regression coefficient for Asian borrowers in most MSAs indicates a tendency for Asians to apply for conventional loans rather than FHA loans.

Since blacks and Hispanics (and, to a lesser extent, Asians) are more likely to have other characteristics that are associated with the use of FHA—such as lower incomes, for example—differences in the relative use of FHA by whites and blacks are smaller in the regression results (that is, controlling for income and other characteristics) than they appear on the basis of aggregate data. Because of this, table 5.22 presents a comparison of the differences in FHA participation using the regression results (controlling for differences in other factors) and using aggregate data (taking differences in other factors into account).

Table 5.22 ADJUSTED AND ACTUAL DIFFERENCES IN FHA SHARE OF APPLICATIONS BY RACE OF BORROWER

	Adjusted Difference (%)[a]	Actual Difference (%)
Atlanta		
Black	+18***	+32
Hispanic	+6***	+17
Asian	−4***	+6
Baltimore		
Black	+13***	+38
Hispanic	+9***	+16
Asian	−7***	0
Chicago		
Black	+25***	+39
Hispanic	+11***	+21
Asian	−2***	−2
Columbus		
Black	+14***	+26
Hispanic	+15***	+32
Asian	−11***	−5
Dallas		
Black	+14***	+18
Hispanic	+10***	+19
Asian	−8***	−4
Houston		
Black	+11***	+18
Hispanic	+10***	+18
Asian	−13***	−8
Los Angeles		
Black	+1***	−2
Hispanic	+2***	0
Asian	0	−1
Memphis		
Black	+11***	+23
Hispanic	−1	+15
Asian	−12***	−4
Sacramento		
Black	+7***	+11
Hispanic	+4***	+8
Asian	−8***	−3
St. Louis		
Black	+24***	+36
Hispanic	+5***	+11
Asian	−1	+1

a. Adjusted differences are coefficients of variables indicating race/ethnicity of borrower.

***Significant at 99 percent. **Significant at 95 percent. *Significant at 90 percent.

The first column, labeled "adjusted difference," displays the estimated regression coefficients for the various dummy variables signifying the race or ethnicity of the borrower. These coefficients estimate the marginal impact of race or ethnicity on the probability that a mortgage applicant applies for an FHA loan, using an "otherwise similar" white applicant as the basis of comparison. The second column in the table presents the actual aggregate difference between the FHA share for the group in question and the FHA share for whites. Comparing the "actual" to the "adjusted" difference in the FHA share for a given group shows the combined effects of other factors that appear to affect the borrower's choice of a mortgage instrument.

For example, table 5.7 showed that 66 percent of all black applicants in the Atlanta metropolitan area applied for an FHA loan, compared to 34 percent of whites. Thus, the FHA share for blacks in Atlanta is some 32 percentage points higher than the FHA share for whites. However, when one controls for underlying differences in the characteristics of the borrower, the loan, and the neighborhood, the FHA share predicted for blacks is only about 18 percentage points higher than the predicted share for otherwise similar whites. In other words, more than 40 percent of the observed difference in the use of FHA by whites and blacks in Atlanta can be attributed to nonracial factors, such as borrower income and locational choice.

Patterns for blacks in the other markets are similar to the findings for Atlanta. In general, blacks are significantly more likely to apply for an FHA loan, as compared to otherwise similar whites. However, with the exception of Los Angeles, factors in addition to race help to explain between one-third and four-fifths of the observed differences in the use of FHA mortgages by whites and blacks. Similar conclusions can be reached for Hispanics, although both actual and predicted differences are typically smaller than those observed for blacks. However, in two markets with large Hispanic populations—Dallas and Houston—patterns for blacks and Hispanics are virtually indistinguishable.

In contrast, Asians are significantly less likely to use FHA, as compared to otherwise similar whites. Indeed, with the exception of Los Angeles, differences predicted by the regression analysis are larger than the differences suggested by a simple comparison of means. This outcome is consistent across the sites, and suggests that nonracial factors serve to narrow the gap between Asians and whites in their use of FHA loans. Evidently Asians, like other minority groups, have a number of characteristics that are associated with a higher use of

FHA. However, in the case of Asians, these factors are not sufficiently strong to bring their use of FHA up to the level employed by whites.

The higher use of FHA insurance by blacks and Hispanics suggested by the regression analysis—as well as its lower use by Asians—may reflect a variety of factors that could not be captured with available data. The most notable of these is the borrower's ability to meet the higher downpayment requirements of a conventional mortgage. As noted early in this chapter, the HMDA data do not provide information on the loan-to-value ratio. As a result, the patterns observed for blacks and Hispanics might well reflect their lower levels of wealth at every income level, which would cause them to rely on relatively expensive, low downpayment FHA loans. Likewise, the findings for Asians could conceivably reflect a higher propensity to save (or to pool resources) in comparison to whites. However, without additional information on downpayment levels, it is difficult to assess the extent to which such factors help to explain the observed racial and ethnic differences in the use of FHA—differences that persist even after controlling for a large number of other borrower, neighborhood, and loan characteristics.

Table 5.23 presents a comparison similar to that shown in table 5.22, except that table 5.23 presents adjusted and actual differences in FHA shares across neighborhoods classified according to their concentration of minority households. The first column in the table displays the predicted difference in FHA shares for census tracts with each level of minority concentration, where the base case is an "otherwise similar" tract with a population that is 10 percent or less minority. The second column presents actual aggregate differences in the FHA share for each type of tract, as compared to tracts that are predominantly white.

With the exception of Memphis and Los Angeles, the estimated coefficients of the neighborhood dummies are positive and statistically significant, and suggest that FHA is used more frequently in areas with higher concentrations of minority households. These figures suggest that differences in the racial composition of the borrower's neighborhood explain perhaps 40 to 60 percent of the observed difference in FHA participation among borrowers living in racially mixed or predominantly minority neighborhoods. In general, however, the estimated coefficients are relatively small in comparison to those associated with borrower race, and display no consistent tendency to rise with increases in the percentage minority in the census tract. Given the observed concentration of black and Hispanic applications in predominantly minority neighborhoods—as well as the tendency of whites to apply for loans in predominantly white census tracts—it is admittedly difficult to disentangle the effects of the borrower's and the neighborhood's race. However, based on our analysis, it appears that the race and ethnicity of the borrower is more important than the racial composition of the census tract in explaining choice of loan.

Loan Acceptance Model

Table 5.24 presents the regression coefficients estimated for the loan acceptance model, and table 5.25 summarizes the implications of the model regarding the impact of borrower race on the probability of loan acceptance. Regressions distinguishing between accepted and rejected applications were derived for each of the 10 sample sites using the same basic set of explanatory variables included in the loan choice model (see table 5.20). However, in addition to these variables, the loan acceptance model also included a series of dummy variables, interacted with the race and ethnicity of the borrower, reflecting the type of loan selected (FHA versus conventional).

For the most part, the estimated regression coefficients show the expected signs and are statistically significant. For example, higher-income applicants are significantly more likely to be accepted in every metropolitan area; applicants from neighborhoods with higher average property values show the same pattern, although the effect is statistically significant in only 5 of the 10 MSAs. Applicants are less likely to be accepted if they are in neighborhoods with high poverty, unemployment, or vacancy rates.

The coefficients estimated for applicants with different mortgage payment-to-income ratios are somewhat surprising. The positive and significant coefficients estimated in every MSA for front-end ratios of 16–20 percent and 21–25 percent, and in seven MSAs for ratios of 26–30 percent, suggest that these borrowers are more likely to be approved than borrowers with front-end ratios of less than 16 percent. Although there is a separate variable to indicate applications for mortgage refinancings, it is possible that these coefficients reflect some other loan characteristic in addition to the payment-to-income ratio. In almost every case, however, applicants with front-end ratios greater than 30 percent are less likely to be accepted, as expected. In addition, the magnitude of the coefficients generally declines as the front-end ratio increases, as expected (especially in Chicago and, to a lesser extent, Houston).

Table 5.23 ADJUSTED AND ACTUAL DIFFERENCES IN FHA SHARE OF APPLICATIONS BY PERCENTAGE MINORITY IN TRACT

Percentage Minority in Tract	Adjusted Difference (%)[a]	Actual Difference (%)[b]
Atlanta		
11–20%	+3***	+4
21–30%	+4***	+8
31–50%	+4***	+10
>50%	+8***	+25
Baltimore		
11–20%	+6***	+10
21–30%	+10***	+14
31–50%	+8***	+19
>50%	+7***	+28
Chicago		
11–20%	+2***	+4
21–30%	+7***	+120
31–50%	+7***	+18
>50%	+10***	+29
Columbus		
11–20%	+8***	+17
21–30%	+9***	+16
31–50%	+8***	+20
>50%	+9***	+18
Dallas		
11–20%	+6***	+15
21–30%	+9***	+12
31–50%	+14***	+16
>50%	+10***	+15

(Continued)

Finally, the loan acceptance model indicates that the predicted probability of loan default (estimated on the basis of the analysis presented in the preceding section) generally has the expected negative effect on the probability that the loan application will be accepted. The coefficient for predicted default probability is negative and significant in 6 of the 10 MSAs, and only two MSAs—Columbus and Sacramento—show a positive coefficient for this variable.

Again, however, the primary focus of this analysis is on the effect of the applicant's race or ethnicity, and the racial composition of the applicant's neighborhood, on the probability of loan acceptance. The estimated coefficients of the dummy variables for borrower race and minority proportion of neighborhood residents represent the marginal impact of race on the probability that an FHA or conventional loan application would be accepted relative to a loan application from an "otherwise similar" white applicant. As before, these marginal or

Table 5.23 (Continued)

Percentage Minority in Tract	Adjusted Difference (%)[a]	Actual Difference (%)[b]
Houston		
11–20%	+1	+8
21–30%	+2***	+2
31–50%	+3***	−4
>50%	+5***	−1
Los Angeles		
11–20%	−4***	+9
21–30%	−5***	+16
31–50%	−6***	+13
>50%	−7***	+12
Memphis		
11–20%	+3***	0
21–30%	−1	−22
31–50%	−2**	+9
>50%	−1	+12
Sacramento		
11–20%	+3***	+5
21–30%	+2***	+7
31–50%	+4***	+10
>50%	+5***	+13
St. Louis		
11–20%	+3***	+9
21–30%	+8***	+11
31–50%	+10***	+13
>50%	+17***	+27

a. Adjusted differences are coefficients of variables signifying percentage minority in tract, using tracts that are less than 10 percent minority as the base case.
b. Actual differences are differences between FHA share in a given type of tract (e.g., more than 50 percent minority) and FHA share in tracts that are less than 10 percent minority.
*** Significant at 99 percent. ** Significant at 95 percent. * Significant at 90 percent.

"adjusted" differences can be compared to observed differences in aggregate acceptance rates by racial or ethnic group.

Several broad conclusions can be drawn from the regression analysis. To begin with, after controlling for a number of factors thought to influence the underlying riskiness of the loan—including the applicant's predicted default probability—blacks continue to have a significantly lower probability of loan acceptance compared to whites. This pattern holds in all 10 of the markets for conventional loans, and in 9 of the 10 MSAs for FHA loans (with Sacramento the only exception). In 5 of the metropolitan areas included in the analysis (Atlanta,

Table 5.24 ESTIMATED REGRESSION PARAMETERS FOR THE LOAN ACCEPTANCE MODEL

	Metropolitan Statistical Area									
Model Parameter	Atlanta	Baltimore	Chicago	Columbus	Dallas	Houston	Los Angeles	Memphis	Sacramento	St. Louis
R-Squared	7.8%	4.2%	6.2%	4.5%	5.9%	5.6%	3.3%	9.5%	5.0%	5.7%
Borrower Characteristics										
Conventional Loan										
Asian	2.91***	0.72	−5.38***	−1.30	5.55***	3.27***	0.51	7.53*	−3.86***	0.61
Black	−13.14***	−11.90***	−12.99***	−5.13***	−10.53***	−16.59***	−2.28***	−18.42***	−6.21***	−12.98***
Hispanic	−7.40***	−3.63*	−2.94***	21.52***	−8.67***	−10.88***	−3.59***	15.54**	−3.86***	−5.40***
Other	−1.89	0.47	−1.98***	4.12*	−4.68*	2.62**	−3.00**	−23.12***	−11.22***	−15.63***
FHA Loan										
Asian	−3.86***	−0.83	−5.26***	−13.67***	−0.94	−1.88*	0.81	7.75*	−2.01***	−10.65
Black	−18.31***	−7.18***	−10.58***	−11.70***	−14.18***	17.66***	−9.07***	−14.16***	3.18***	−12.09***
Hispanic	0.34	−6.76***	1.78***	−7.01*	−3.75***	−7.53***	0.99	−5.23	8.80	−8.22***
Other	−7.90***	−11.11***	−7.40***	−6.84*	−4.68***	−11.31***	−2.60	4.02	−5.89	−16.54***
Female	0.77***	1.00***	−0.06	−0.57	0.79**	−0.72*	−0.70*	−0.61	−0.43	−2.53***
Income	0.08***	0.05***	0.02***	0.15***	0.09***	0.08***	0.01***	0.16***	0.03***	0.01***
Neighborhood Characteristics										
Conventional Loan										
11-20% Minority	−1.47***	−3.65***	−0.87***	−4.38***	−1.01**	0.86	−3.34***	3.31***	0.42	0.88*
21-30% Minority	1.29*	−3.41***	−1.76***	−0.68	1.99***	0.73	−1.99	3.60***	−0.95	0.91
31-50% Minority	−0.13	−2.05***	−1.57***	−3.62**	2.25***	−0.24	−3.17**	−0.52	−2.49***	2.82***
>50% Minority	−2.10***	2.67***	−3.75***	−7.76***	1.93**	2.65*	−3.38***	7.05***	−4.07***	3.07***
FHA Loan										
0-10% Minority	2.82***	4.07***	−3.34***	−1.38***	3.47***	3.46***	2.71	6.89***	6.65***	0.13
11-20% Minority	4.68***	4.55***	−5.00***	3.18***	4.54***	−0.96	−0.45	4.00***	10.74***	−0.31
21-30% Minority	2.42***	4.15***	−4.22***	1.94	5.43***	−0.29	2.98	6.58***	1.91*	−7.00***
31-50% Minority	−3.22***	3.22***	−5.85***	4.92***	3.47***	−2.14**	1.20	6.72***	−2.75**	1.21
>50% Minority	3.01***	3.68***	−6.58***	−1.38	6.56***	3.32***	−0.54	7.54***	8.34***	1.21

% Change in Min. Comp.	0.23**	0.31**	0.05***	0.08	−0.41**	0.67***	1.81***	−0.86**	−6.59***	−0.32***
Average Property Value	1.30	4.91***	2.35***	1.62	−0.67	1.06	0.99	4.36**	2.41**	9.02***
% Change in Value	−0.25	−0.61	0.07	0.48	−2.14***	0.46	1.14*	−1.01	−3.14***	−2.64***
Median Rent/Value	−1,049***	−127	54	−1,285***	−1,209***	−717***	−547	−887***	303	−1,185***
Age of Housing										
11-20 Years	0.63**	−1.00**	−0.22	1.01	−1.49***	−0.41	4.85***	−7.10***	−3.66***	1.43***
21-30 Years	0.20	−1.51***	−0.39	−1.06	−1.36***	−2.60***	6.19***	−6.11***	−4.77***	2.63***
31-50 Years	1.12*	−2.14***	0.12	0.69	−3.40***	−4.95***	5.84***	−7.38***	−3.35***	3.09***
>50 Years	4.51***	−1.03	1.63***	0.82	−7.28	0.16	5.22***	−5.99***	−3.22***	2.73***
Central City	−0.81*	2.52***	0.06	0.87*	−1.49***	1.84***	−0.02	7.92***	0.11	0.86***
Poverty Rate	−2.50	−6.78**	−20.20***	−37.21***	−14.65***	−22.06***	−15.58***	10.68**	−8.74***	−23.95***
Unemployment Rate	−10.56	−61.86***	−35.11***	100.63***	−65.04***	−2.34	−17.17	−88.69***	5.27	−42.58***
Vacancy Rate	−33.02***	−2.25	−12.47**	−19.30**	−36.10***	−42.62***	−12.63	−38.57***	−24.02***	−15.45***
% Single-Family (1-4 units)	−9.14***	−0.46	−4.65***	−5.88**	15.88***	6.74***	2.34	25.50***	3.39*	5.50***
% Owner-Occupied	12.33***	−1.07	0.05	2.69	−19.18***	−9.39***	−2.32	−23.96***	−7.11***	−16.70***
Loan Characteristics										
Payment-to-Income Ratio										
16-20%	5.71***	7.14***	0.81***	2.86***	6.14***	3.32***	4.44***	11.10***	1.65***	0.74***
21-25%	5.89***	7.57***	0.54***	2.11***	7.67***	2.31***	5.25***	11.12***	3.33***	1.17***
26-30%	6.31***	5.35***	−1.45***	3.17***	5.82***	0.14	6.03***	9.20***	2.48***	−1.72***
>30%	−3.32***	2.43***	−15.25***	−9.00***	−5.80***	−7.73***	−1.48***	0.32	−7.22***	−9.66***
Refinance	0.33	−0.33	−5.02***	−1.16***	−0.52	4.79	−0.93***	4.34***	−3.54***	4.52***
Type of Institution										
Mortgage Bank	−2.74***	−0.41	3.71***	9.42***	3.48***	7.99***	−3.10***	8.51***	−11.81***	6.69***
Credit Union	1.39	7.87***	5.29***	3.16	−1.73	11.31***	−0.75	17.46***	−0.81	5.28***
Thrift	−5.88***	0.93***	−1.71***	0.79**	0.71**	2.30***	−14.70***	−0.71	−13.54***	−1.91***
Predicted Default Probability	−18.49***	−2.99	−1.04	32.76**	−3.42**	−37.96***	−5.74*	−14.65**	27.94***	−20.20***

***Significant at 99% **Significant at 95% *Significant at 90%

Table 5.25 ADJUSTED AND ACTUAL DIFFERENCES IN THE PROPORTION OF LOANS ACCEPTED BY RACE OF BORROWER

	Black (%)		Hispanic (%)		Asian (%)	
	Adjusted[a]	Actual	Adjusted[a]	Actual	Adjusted[a]	Actual
Atlanta						
Conventional	−13***	−18	−7***	−4	+3***	+2
FHA	−18***	−18	0	+2	−4***	−2
Baltimore						
Conventional	−12***	−14	−4*	−4	+1	+1
FHA	−7***	−4	−7***	−1	−1	+4
Chicago						
Conventional	−13***	−20	−3***	−6	−5***	−5
FHA	−11***	−18	+2***	−2	−5***	−7
Columbus						
Conventional	−5***	−15	+22***	+16	−1	0
FHA	−12***	−12	−7*	+1	−14***	−8
Dallas						
Conventional	−11***	−16	−9***	−14	+6***	+7
FHA	−14***	−13	−4***	−1	−1	+5
Houston						
Conventional	−17***	−20	−11***	−15	+3***	+3
FHA	−18***	−19	−8***	−12	−2*	−5
Los Angeles						
Conventional	−2***	−4	−4***	−4	+1	0
FHA	−9***	−8	+1	+2	+1	+3
Memphis						
Conventional	−18***	−22	+16*	+18	+8*	+14
FHA	−14***	−14	−5	+1	+8*	+9
Sacramento						
Conventional	−6***	−8	−4***	−4	−4***	0
FHA	+3***	−9	+9	−4	−2***	−11
St. Louis						
Conventional	−13***	−22	−5***	−7	+1	+1
FHA	−12***	−16	−8***	−6	−11	+3

a. Adjusted differences are the estimated coefficients of the dummy variable for borrower race, using an otherwise similar white borrower as the base case.
***Significant at 99 percent. **Significant at 95 percent. *Significant at 90 percent.

Columbus, Dallas, Houston, and Los Angeles), blacks appear to have somewhat lower acceptance rates under FHA than in the conventional mortgage market; in the other 5 sites, however, they appear to do somewhat better under FHA than with conventional loans. However, given the limitations of the data, this latter outcome may simply reflect a selection process under which riskier borrowers are systematically steered towards FHA. Whatever the explanation, the analysis suggests that the experience of blacks under FHA is not that different from their experience with conventional loans.

Hispanic applicants also have significantly lower loan acceptance rates than comparable white applicants, although they consistently fare better than blacks.[17] With the exception of Memphis and Columbus—both of which have extremely small Hispanic populations (less than 1 percent of the total population in 1990)—the estimated regression coefficients signifying Hispanic applications for conventional loans were negative and statistically significant. Under FHA, 5 of the sites had statistically significant negative coefficients, and only Chicago showed a significant positive coefficient. Moreover, the estimated coefficients suggest that Hispanics had higher acceptance rates than comparable black borrowers in all 10 metropolitan areas under the FHA program, and in 9 MSAs for conventional loan programs (the only exception being Los Angeles).

Finally, the analysis suggests that Asian applicants generally fare better than either black or Hispanic applicants under both FHA and conventional loan programs; more striking, however, is that Asians seem to fare substantially better under conventional loan programs than in the FHA program. In four markets (Atlanta, Dallas, Houston, and Memphis), Asian borrowers appear to have significantly higher probability of loan acceptance under conventional loan programs than comparable whites; only in Memphis, however, do Asian borrowers appear to do better than whites in the FHA program. Conversely, under the FHA program Asian borrowers in five MSAs (Atlanta, Chicago, Columbus, Houston, and Sacramento) appear to have significantly worse acceptance probabilities than comparable white applicants; only in Chicago and Sacramento, however, do they appear to do significantly worse than white borrowers under conventional loan programs. As noted, this pattern may reflect a tendency to steer higher-risk Asian borrowers to FHA, although the available data do not permit a full analysis of this issue.

Given the consistently strong effect of race estimated in the loan acceptance model, it is somewhat surprising that the effect of the racial composition of the applicant's neighborhood did not show a similarly consistent pattern on the probability of loan acceptance. In general, however, it is notable that the probability of loan acceptance tends to be higher for FHA loans than for conventional loans in all types of neighborhoods.

In summary, then, the results derived from the loan acceptance model suggest that the applicant's race appears to be a consistently important factor in determining the probability that a loan application will be accepted. Black applicants, and Hispanics to a lesser extent, are significantly less likely to be approved for a mortgage than otherwise comparable white applicants, even after controlling for a large number of other borrower, neighborhood, and loan characteristics including the predicted probability that the applicant will default on the loan. The experience of black applicants was essentially no different in the FHA program than under conventional loan programs. Hispanic applicants seemed to fare very slightly better under FHA than under conventional programs, whereas Asians did significantly better in conventional programs than in FHA.

SUMMARY AND CONCLUSIONS

This chapter examined the role of the FHA single-family insurance program in the provision of credit to minority borrowers and in predominantly minority neighborhoods. The study is based on HMDA loan application and origination data for a sample of 10 metropolitan statistical areas (MSAs).

Use of the FHA program is disproportionately high among black borrowers relative to white, Hispanic, and Asian borrowers. For example, 56 percent of all black applicants applying for mortgages below the FHA ceiling apply for an FHA loan, compared to 29 percent of Hispanic borrowers, 27 percent of whites, and just 18 percent of Asians.

Whereas the relative importance of the FHA program tends to decrease as household income increases, black borrowers remain substantially more likely to use the FHA program than white or Asian borrowers at all income levels. Indeed, even higher-income blacks—those earning more than 120 percent of the area median income—rely more heavily on FHA (39 percent) than lower-income whites (31 percent). Reliance on FHA mortgage insurance also declines in higher-income neighborhoods (33 percent of loans in lower-income neighborhoods, compared to just 25 percent in higher-income neighborhoods), and increases in neighborhoods with a higher proportion of minority residents (38 percent of loans in predominantly minority neighborhoods, compared to just 24 percent in predominantly white neighborhoods). These sharply divergent patterns of FHA use by race or ethnicity may reflect a process by which minority borrowers are "steered" to FHA by lenders; alternatively, the observed patterns may simply reflect the different characteristics of borrowers in each ethnic group, for example, accumulated wealth and credit history.

Recent data on mortgage defaults in the FHA program indicate that black and, to a lesser extent, Hispanic borrowers tend to default on their mortgages at considerably higher rates than white or Asian borrowers. As this study shows, these observed patterns may importantly reflect the different circumstances of borrowers of each ethnic group, since higher default rates are evident also among borrowers with lower incomes and among borrowers in low-income and predominantly minority neighborhoods.

To investigate the effect of borrower race and neighborhood racial composition on mortgage lending decisions, three separate models are estimated: models of mortgage default probability, borrower choice between FHA and conventional mortgage programs, and FHA mortgage acceptance probability. The analysis of mortgage default probability focuses on the factors that affect the probability that a borrower will default on the mortgage loan. The default model controls for factors in addition to the borrower's race that might affect default probability, including other borrower characteristics (such as income, assets, marital status, and age); neighborhood characteristics (property values, incomes, and age of the housing stock); property characteristics (condition, location, age); and loan characteristics (mortgage origination year, loan-to-value ratio, payment-to-income ratio, and debt-to-income ratio).

In the case of the 10 metropolitan areas included in the analysis, there does not appear to be any statistically significant relationship between the borrower's race, or the racial composition of the neighborhood, and the probability that the borrower will default on the mortgage. Whereas black and, to a lesser extent, Hispanic borrowers have slightly higher default probabilities than otherwise identical white and Asian borrowers, the estimated race-based differences are not statistically significant.

The analysis of loan choice suggested that black and Hispanic borrowers are significantly more likely to use the FHA loan program than comparable white borrowers, even after controlling for other factors. In fact, race alone appears to account for about half of the observed difference in FHA participation rates for black and Hispanic borrowers. In contrast, Asian borrowers are significantly less likely to use the FHA program than otherwise similar white applicants. It is possible that these patterns reflect some racial steering on the part of lenders, since the racial differences exist after controlling for other factors believed to affect the probability of mortgage default.

An alternative explanation for the greater use of FHA by black and Hispanic borrowers is that they might choose to apply for FHA loans if they experienced a higher probability of loan acceptance in the FHA program compared to conventional loan programs. This analysis of mortgage acceptances in 10 MSAs, however, suggests that black applicants fare no better under FHA than under conventional loan programs: in both cases, blacks are significantly more likely to be rejected than comparable white borrowers. Hispanic applicants show the same pattern, although they consistently fare better than black applicants in both FHA and conventional programs. It should be noted that these results differ from those of previously published studies of mortgage acceptance rates using national 1990 and 1992 HMDA data,[18] which suggested that black and Hispanic applicants are significantly more likely to be accepted under FHA than under conventional loan programs. One possible explanation for this discrepancy in results could be that use of FHA by white borrowers is concentrated in areas where overall denial rates are high.

Also, it is possible that the findings of this study are affected by the lack of data from the HMDA files on several critical variables, including borrower credit history and assets. Low downpayments are one of the key features of FHA loans. Since blacks tend to have fewer assets than whites, even after controlling for income, they may be drawn to FHA because of its low downpayment requirements.

Although it is not possible with the available data to control for all factors that may affect mortgage default, mortgage choice, and mortgage acceptance decisions, the analysis suggests that the observed differences in FHA participation and mortgage acceptance rates between white borrowers and black or Hispanic borrowers cannot be explained fully by factors other than race, including predicted default probability. In particular, the analysis suggests three main conclusions:

- First, black applicants and, to a lesser degree, Hispanic applicants are significantly less likely to have their mortgage applications accepted than otherwise identical white applicants, even after controlling for the predicted probability that the applicant would default on the mortgage.
- Second, acceptance rates in these 10 MSAs for black applicants are no higher under FHA than in conventional loan programs, although Hispanic applicants seem to fare slightly better under FHA than under conventional programs.

- Finally, black and Hispanic applicants are significantly more likely to use the FHA program than comparable white applicants, even after controlling for other factors.

Data limitations prevent us from measuring all of the factors that might affect the underlying riskiness of the loan, such as the applicant's credit history and the loan-to-value ratio. However, the preliminary findings presented in this report suggest that the barriers believed to affect the provision of credit to minorities in the conventional market do not disappear when the mortgage applicant applies for an FHA loan, particularly if the applicant is black.

Notes

1. See, for example, Canner and Gabriel (1992).

2. Additional information on sample selection is contained in Schnare and Gabriel (1993).

3. Key variables not included in the HMDA file, such as the loan-to-value ratio, were set to the mean for subgroups of households defined by race/ethnicity and income.

4. Whereas the HMDA data provide information on the loan amount, they do not identify the terms of the mortgage or the date of loan application or commitment. To estimate the monthly mortgage payment, we assumed a 30-year, fixed-term mortgage and set the effective rate of interest to the annual average for the MSA in 1990, using information obtained from the Federal Housing Finance Board's Mortgage Interest Rate Survey.

5. The only exception to this rule occurs among loans with an estimated payment-to-income ratio of 30 percent or more. This outcome may simply be a product of our estimation procedures, which assume that loans have identical terms. Conceivably, many of the loans in this category could be conventional adjustable rate mortgages (ARMs) with low initial rates, which would make our estimates of the payment-to-income ratio for such mortgages too high.

6. Refinancings accounted for 36 percent of loan applications below $25,000 and 27 percent of loan applications between $25,000 and $50,000. In contrast, only about 20 percent of all applications for loans above $50,000 involved refinancing an existing mortgage.

7. The only exception to this pattern occurs in upper-income minority tracts, where the use of FHA is extremely low (only about 9 percent of all qualifying applications—see table 5.4). However, only half of the sites had observations in this category, and 86 percent of these were in the Los Angeles MSA. As table 5.1 shows, the use of FHA insurance is markedly lower in Los Angeles than in the other MSAs included in this analysis; furthermore, the upcoming table 5.7 shows that this pattern holds in Los Angeles among borrowers of all racial groups. Thus, the figure for upper-income mi-

nority tracts primarily reflects the low use of FHA in Los Angeles, rather than a more general pattern.

8. The loan acceptance rate was derived by eliminating applications that were withdrawn before acceptance or rejection, and then calculating the ratio of the number of accepted applications to the total number of accepted and rejected applications.

9. See, for example, Canner (1981); Stiglitz and Weiss (1981); and Williamson (1986). These studies provide theoretical underpinnings to assessments of rationing in the allocation of mortgage credit.

10. See, for example, Barth, Cordes, and Yezer (1979); Campbell and Dietrich (1983); Foster and Van Order (1984); and Vandell and Thibodeau (1985). Contrary to expectations of a model of mortgage default based on the exercise of the put option, results of these analyses suggest some importance to these nonequity indicators in the estimation of default probabilities.

11. For the purposes of this analysis, cumulative default rates are defined as the number of mortgages endorsed by the FHA in a given year that resulted in a claim on the FHA at any time prior to the end of 1992, relative to the total number of loans endorsed by the FHA in that year.

12. We also calculated cumulative default rates for FHA-insured loans in each of the sampled MSAs by year of origination and by policy age. Results of those analyses similarly illustrate the increase over time in cumulative default rates as loans age. In many of the sampled MSAs, the tables also show variation over time in default rates among similarly aged mortgages, owing in part to fluctuations in the local economic conditions that affect property values, borrower ability-to-pay, and therefore the probability of default. Results of those analyses are available from the authors on request.

13. The model of cumulative default probability used in this analysis differs significantly from the models used in much of the literature on the factors that influence mortgage default behavior. Specifically, this analysis models the probability that there will be a default at any time during the life of the mortgage (through 1992). In contrast, other studies have generally sought to model the probability that there will be a default in a given year. Moreover, this analysis explicitly uses data available at loan origination, since it focuses on the role of predicted default probability on the loan choice and loan acceptance decisions. In contrast, other studies have attempted to use contemporaneous data to model each in a series of repayment/default decisions, and have used data at the time of loan origination only to proxy data that are unavailable contemporaneously.

14. The coefficients for the logit models of the cumulative mortgage default probabilities for each of the 10 MSAs included in the analysis are contained in Schnare and Gabriel (1993).

15. It is worth reiterating that HMDA data do not include several variables that would be useful in modeling loan choice and loan acceptance, as well as in interpreting the empirical results. For example, the HMDA data do not identify loan type (e.g., fixed-rate, adjustable-rate, graduated-payment, etc.). Also, whereas the default probability model presented in the preceding section was estimated using logit regression, the loan choice and loan acceptance models presented in this section were estimated using ordinary least squares (OLS) regression because of constraints on computer resources and the size of the HMDA data set.

16. It is important to note that the loan acceptance model treats loan choice—that is, whether the applicant applied for an FHA loan or a conventional loan—as exogenously determined by the factors included in the loan choice model: borrower characteristics, neighborhood characteristics, loan characteristics, and the predicted probability of default. It is very possible, however, that the loan choice and loan acceptance outcomes are determined simultaneously—that is, that borrowers are steered toward FHA or conventional loan programs based, in part, on the probability that their loan application

would be accepted in each program. This situation would require the use of a simultaneous-equations system for estimating the empirical models to avoid bias in the coefficient estimates. The use of a simultaneous-equations system to estimate loan choice and loan acceptance models jointly constitutes an important area for further empirical research.

17. The only exceptions were for FHA loans in Baltimore, where Hispanics and blacks had comparable acceptance rates (controlling for other factors), and for conventional loans in Los Angeles, where blacks appear to have had a slightly higher adjusted acceptance rate than Hispanics.

18. See, for example Canner, Passmore, and Smith (1994). For an analysis of 1991 HMDA data, see *Federal Reserve Bulletin* (November 1992).

References

Barth, James, Joseph Cordes, and Anthony Yezer. 1979. "Financial Institution Regulations, Redlining, and Mortgage Markets." In *The Regulation of Financial Institutions* (101–43). Melvin Village, N.H.: Federal Reserve Bank of Boston and National Science Foundation, October.

Campbell, T., and J. Kimball Dietrich. 1983. "The Determinants of Default on Conventional Residential Mortgages." *Journal of Finance* 38(5).

Canner, Glen B. 1981. "Redlining and Mortgage Lending Patterns." In *Research in Urban Economics*, edited by J. Vernon Henderson.

Canner, Glen B., and Stuart Gabriel. 1992. "Market Segmentation and Lender Specialization in the Primary and Secondary Mortgage Markets. *Housing Policy Debate* 3(2): 241–332.

Canner, Glen B., Wayne Passmore, and Dolores S. Smith. 1994. "Residential Lending to Low-Income and Minority Families: Evidence from the 1992 HMDA Data." *Federal Reserve Bulletin* 80(February).

Foster, C., and Robert Van Order. 1984. "An Option-Based Model of Mortgage Default." *Housing Finance Review*.

Gabriel, Stuart A., and Stuart R. Rosenthal. 1991. "Credit Rationing, Race, and the Mortgage Market." *Journal of Urban Economics* 29: 371–79.

Munnell, Alicia H., Lynn E. Browne, James McEneaney, and Geoffrey M.B. Tootell. 1992. "Mortgage Lending in Boston: Interpreting HMDA Data." Federal Reserve Bank of Boston Working Paper 92-07. Boston: Federal Reserve Bank of Boston, October.

Munnell, Alicia H., Geoffrey M.B. Tootell, Lynn E. Browne, and James McEneaney. 1995. "Mortgage Lending in Boston: Interpreting HMDA Data." *American Economic Review*. Forthcoming.

Schnare, Ann B., and Stuart A. Gabriel. 1993. "The Role of FHA in the Provision of Credit to Minorities." Report submitted to U.S. Department of Housing and Urban Development. Washington, D.C.: Office of Policy Development and Research, U.S. Department of Housing and Urban Development.

Stiglitz, Joseph, and A. Weiss. 1981. "Credit Rationing in Markets with Imperfect Information." *American Economic Review* (June).

Vandell, Kerry, and Tom Thibodeau. 1985. "Estimation of Mortgage Defaults Using Disaggregate Loan History Data." *Journal of the American Real Estate and Urban Economics Association.*

Williamson, S. 1986. "Costly Monitoring, Financial Intermediation, and Equilibrium Credit Rationing." *Journal of Monetary Economics* 18.

APPENDIX A. VARIABLE DEFINITIONS

AGE1120	Percentage of housing units in census tract that are 11–20 years old
AGE2130	Percentage of housing units in census tract that are 21–30 years old
AGE3150	Percentage of housing units in census tract that are 31–50 years old
AGEGT50	Percentage of housing units in census tract that are more than 50 years old
BANNINC	Borrower total annual effective family income
BASIAN	1, if borrower is Asian; 0, otherwise
BBLACK	1, if borrower is black; 0, otherwise
BDEPS	Number of dependents of borrower
BHISP	1, if borrower is Hispanic; 0, otherwise
BINVEST	1, if investment property; 0, otherwise
BLIQASS	Borrower liquid assets
BMARR	1, if borrower is married; 0, otherwise
BNETASS	Liquid assets available to borrower net of mortgage down payment and closing costs
BOTH	1, if borrower's race is other than Asian, black, Hispanic, or white (primarily Native American); 0, otherwise
BSALINC	Percentage of family income from salary
BWHITE	1, if borrower is white; 0, otherwise
CCITY	1, if property is located in a central city; 0, otherwise
COBOINC	Percentage of family income earned by coborrower
FBUY	1, if borrower is a first-time homebuyer; 0, otherwise

FEMALE	1, if borrower is female; 0, otherwise
LOANTERM	Term of mortgage in months
LTV89	1, if mortgage loan-to-value ratio is at least 80 percent but less than 90 percent; 0, otherwise
LTV915	1, if mortgage loan-to-value ratio is at least 90 percent but less than 95 pecent; 0, otherwise
LTV9675	1, if mortgage loan-to-value ratio is at least 95 percent but less than 97.5 percent; 0, otherwise
LTVGT975	1, if mortgage loan-to-value ratio is 97.5 percent or more
MAGE121	1, if mortgage was originated in 1990; 0, otherwise
MAGE231	1, if mortgage was originated in 1989; 0, otherwise
MAGE341	1, if mortgage was originated in 1988; 0, otherwise
MEDINC90	Median income of census tract households
MEDVAL90	Median value of housing units in census tract
OVER30	1, if age of borrower is over 30 years; 0, otherwise
P1FAM	1, if property has one dwelling unit; 0, if property has two to four dwelling units
PAGE	Age of property in years
PCONDE	1, if property condition is excellent; 0, otherwise
PCONDG	1, if property condition is good; 0, otherwise
PCTDEF	1986–92 census tract FHA default rate
PCTOWNED	Percentage of housing units in census tract that are owner-occupied
PCTSINGL	Percentage of housing units in census tract that are single-family (one- to four-unit) residences
PIB38	1, if borrower total debt-to-income ratio is at least 33 percent but less than 38 percent; 0, otherwise
PIB93	1 if borrower total debt-to-income ratio is at least 28 percent but less than 33 percent; 0, otherwise
PIBGT8	1, if borrower total debt to income ratio is 38 percent or more
PIF38	1, if borrower housing expense-to-income ratio is at least 33 percent but less than 38 percent; 0, otherwise

PIF93	1, if borrower housing expense-to-income ratio is at least 28 percent but less than 33 percent; 0, otherwise
PIFGT8	1, if borrower housing expense-to-income ratio is 38 percent or more
PNEWHOME	1, if property is a new house; 0, otherwise
POV	Percentage if census-tract households are below poverty line
REFINANC	1, if mortgage loan is a refinance; 0, otherwise
TBPOP	Percentage black population in census tract
TCBHPOP	Percentage change in minority (black and Hispanic) population in census tract, 1980–90
TCHHP	Percentage change in median value of housing units in census tract, 1980–90
TCINC	Change in median income of census-tract households, 1980–90
THPOP	Percentage Hispanic population in census tract
TWPOP	Percentage white population in census tract
UNEMP	Unemployment rate in census tract
VACRATE	Percentage of one- to four-family housing units in census tract that are vacant

Note: Unless otherwise noted, census-tract indicators are derived from 1990 U.S. Census.

APPENDIX B. SUPPLEMENTAL ANALYSES OF THE DEFAULT MODEL SPECIFICATION

The regression model of mortgage default behavior presented in this report was estimated separately for each metropolitan area on a combined data set of mortgages originated in the MSAs over all origination years. Since there are strong a priori theoretical reasons to expect that cumulative default rates will be related positively to mortgage age, the model was specified with dummy variables representing mortgage origination year. This choice of model specification placed an implicit constraint on the model: specifically, that the regression coefficient associated with every independent variable *except* mortgage origination year was constrained to be the same across mortgage origination years.

It is possible, however, that this model specification is too restrictive; specifically, it is possible that all regression coefficients should be allowed to vary across mortgage origination years. This unconstrained model can be represented using a model specification in which each independent variable (including the intercept) is interacted with the dummy variables for mortgage origination year, effectively allowing the coefficients associated with every independent variable to vary across origination years.

The justification for this model specification is not based merely on theoretical grounds; rather, it is possible that an incorrect model specification may cause the estimated regression coefficients to differ from their expected relative values. In fact, a few of the estimated regression coefficients presented in this chapter's analysis of default—especially the coefficients associated with loan-to-value ratios—do not show the pattern expected on theoretical grounds. It is possible, therefore, that these counterintuitive results may arise as a result of model specification error—specifically, the use of an inappropriately constrained model.

This appendix presents the results of three types of analysis conducted using data from the Chicago MSA to explore whether a less-restrictive model specification would yield appreciably better results than the constrained model presented in this chapter. The empirical analyses presented in this chapter were estimated on a mainframe computer using the SPSS statistical computing language. Because of the memory constraints associated with conducting logit analysis in SPSS on this computer, the analysis was limited to about 2 percent of the total number of complete observations available for Chicago. Therefore, the first part of the analysis was designed to explore the extent to which the estimated regression coefficients presented in the report may be affected by the sample size constraint, and the extent to which they may be affected by model specification error. To do this, we selected 100 different samples of data, containing about 1,150 randomly selected observations in each sample. We then estimated the constrained and unconstrained versions of the model specification using each of the 100 samples, and employed an F-ratio test of the null hypothesis that the constraints implicit in the model specification employed in this report were appropriate. In formal terms, the null and alternative hypotheses were:

$$
\begin{aligned}
H_o\!: \ & \beta_{187} = \beta_{188} = \beta_{189} = \beta_{190} = \beta_{191} = \beta_{192} \text{ and} \\
& \beta_{287} = \beta_{288} = \beta_{289} = \beta_{290} = \beta_{291} = \beta_{292} \\
& \ldots \text{ and} \\
& \beta_{k87} = \beta_{k88} = \beta_{k89} = \beta_{k90} = \beta_{k91} = \beta_{k92}. \\
H_a\!: \ & H_0 \text{ is not true,}
\end{aligned}
\qquad \text{B.1}
$$

where *k* is the number of independent variables, excluding the intercept. It is important to point out that this comparative analysis was based on ordinary least squares regression rather than logit regression, which is used in this chapter's analysis of default.

To summarize the results of this set of hypothesis tests, the *F* statistic indicated that the null hypothesis could be rejected at the 99 percent level of confidence in 18 out of the 100 samples; at the 95 percent level of confidence in 36 out of 100 samples; and at the 90 percent level of confidence in 45 out of 100 samples.

This set of hypothesis tests, then, provides some evidence that the implicit constraints imposed by the model specification employed in the report is too restrictive. However, the results of the hypothesis tests are not as conclusive as we would expect them to be if model specification were the primary reason for the counterintuitive estimated regression coefficients described in this chapter's analysis of default. This is particularly true given that the sample size of 1,150—although small compared to the total number of complete observations available for analysis in Chicago—is certainly large enough that we would expect a conclusive *F*-ratio test. In short, it is not clear that model specification is an adequate explanation for the observed regression coefficients.

The second analysis was to repeat the comparison of constrained and unconstrained model specifications using the entire data set of 57,341 complete observations in the Chicago metropolitan area. Given the space constraints of the mainframe computer, this analysis was conducted using OLS rather than logit regression; it was also appropriate for the reasons given earlier. Using the *F*-ratio test, the null hypothesis was rejected at a very high level of confidence (greater than 99 percent), again suggesting that the constrained model specification employed in the chapter was not appropriate.

More important, however, than the *F*-ratio test results was the pattern of regression coefficients estimated using both constrained and unconstrained model specifications estimated over the entire data set. Even using the entire data set, as well as the unconstrained model, the coefficients associated with loan-to-value ratio (LTV) do not show the expected pattern. Specifically, while cumulative default rates are expected to increase with LTV ratio, in four of the five mortgage origination years of the unconstrained model (as well as in the constrained model), default rates are estimated to be higher for mortgages with LTV ratios of less than 80 percent than for those with LTV ratios between 80 percent and 90 percent. Moreover, two of the five unconstrained models show default rates higher for 80–90% LTV loans than for 90–95% LTV loans, and one of the five even shows default rates higher for 80–90% LTV loans than for 95–97.5% LTV loans and greater than 97.5% LTV loans. These results suggest that the counterintuitive regression coefficients shown in the chapter may result from some cause other than incorrect model specification.

Finally, the individual regression coefficients estimated using the 100 randomly selected samples (with about 1,150 observations in each sample) were compared to explore how sensitive the estimated regression results were to the sample chosen. Table 5B.1 shows the average of the LTV regression coefficients estimated for the 100 samples using the unconstrained model specification. As this table shows, even taking the average of 100 samples, the pattern of LTV coefficients does not match the expected pattern, which is that all coefficients would be positive, increasing with LTV ratio. For example, all four of the coefficients estimated on mortgages originated in 1991 are negative, as are two of the coefficients estimated on mortgages originated in 1989, one of the coefficients for loans originated in 1988, and one for loans originated in 1987. In addition, the averages of the coefficients do not increase with LTV, as expected.

This comparison of average coefficients suggests that model specification is not the main reason for the counterintuitive pattern of estimated LTV coefficients presented in this chapter. Rather, it appears more likely that the coefficient estimates differ from a priori expectations for one or both of two reasons: (1) data quality issues, and (2) issues of multicollinearity associated with using a large number of independent variables. Each of these potential issues is an appropriate topic for further research.

Finally, table 5B.1 also shows the standard deviation of the LTV coefficients estimated using the 100 samples of loan observations. These figures indicate that there is substantial fluctuation in the estimated coefficients from sample to sample: the coefficient of variation is between 160 percent and 190 percent. This means that the LTV

Table 5B.1 SUMMARY OF MODEL COEFFICIENTS ESTIMATED ON 100 SAMPLES

Loan-to-Value Ratio (LTV)	Unconstrained Model: Origination Year 1991	1990	1989	1988	1987	Standard Deviation
<80%	—	—	—	—	—	—
80–90%	−0.0269	0.0032	0.0020	−0.0020	−0.0092	0.0464
90–95%	−0.0308	0.0084	−0.0094	0.0080	0.0271	0.0490
95–97.5%	−0.0290	0.0188	−0.0014	0.0173	0.0159	0.0549
>97.5%	−0.0285	0.0161	0.0142	0.0098	0.0275	0.0516

coefficient estimates are fairly unstable from sample to sample. Since the memory constraints associated with performing logit analysis on the mainframe restricted the analysis to a sample of about 1,150 observations, this instability in coefficient estimates may be an important consideration in evaluating the empirical results.

Chapter Six

RACE, REDLINING, AND RESIDENTIAL MORTGAGE DEFAULTS: EVIDENCE FROM THE FHA-INSURED SINGLE-FAMILY LOAN PROGRAM

James A. Berkovec, Glenn B. Canner, Timothy H. Hannan, and Stuart A. Gabriel

Recent years have witnessed widespread controversy and policy debate concerning allegations of racial discrimination in mortgage lending. Those allegations derive in part from data assessments resulting from the Home Mortgage Disclosure Act (HMDA), which indicate significantly damped rates of mortgage lending among minority applicants and neighborhoods, even after controlling for applicant income class and neighborhood socioeconomic status.

Although the racial patterns observed in the HMDA data raise the specter of widespread discrimination in mortgage lending, those results may derive as well from unobserved indicators of borrower default risk correlated with applicant race or neighborhood racial composition. As has been argued for some time, evaluation of racial patterns in mortgage lending—including assessment of possible discriminatory lending practices—should be undertaken in a manner that adequately controls for borrower and locational default risk.

Recent contributions to the credit rationing literature (see, for example, Stiglitz and Weiss 1981; Williamson 1986; and Lang and Nakamura 1993) provide the theoretical underpinnings to assessments of default risk in mortgage lending. This literature argues that lenders may apply binding credit constraints to loan applicants due either to uncertainties surrounding timely repayment of the loan or because of factors that may adversely affect the collateral value of the property. In a competitive loan market, it is economically rational for lenders to apply tighter credit conditions to more risky loan applicants, irrespective of whether the risk derives from the attributes of the applicant or from those associated with the neighborhood where the property is located.

Given those formal studies, empirical assessments of default risk focus on variables that represent borrower ability to service the mortgage as scheduled, borrower equity in the property, and transactions costs associated with default (see, for example, reviews of the default literature by Neal 1989 and Quercia and Stegman 1992). Historically, most analyses of default have emphasized factors known to the lender at the time of origination. In these studies, a vector of borrower financial and socioeconomic characteristics typically denotes the likelihood of timely loan repayment. More recently, attention has centered as well on events that may trigger default. In these analyses, borrower equity and ability to pay are sometimes measured contemporaneously. Although recent empirical studies may provide more accurate assessments of events that trigger default, few of those analyses have explicitly examined any residual effects of borrower race or neighborhood racial composition on mortgage loan performance. Further, whereas analysis of triggering events reveals many useful insights, at the time of loan origination, creditors can only assign probability weights to those factors they believe are related to loan performance. Consequently, assessment of creditor behavior at the time of loan origination should focus on information available to the lender at that time.

In a nondiscriminatory world, lenders engage in credit rationing only as required to maximize profits. In that sense, mortgage lenders should be willing to offer credit to those applicants whose loan requests are expected to yield a positive (risk-adjusted) return, and would presumably deny applications that are expected to yield a negative expected return. For the most part, creditors do not ration home purchase loans by varying the price of the credit. Rather, they establish minimum acceptable standards of creditworthiness that prospective buyers and the properties they seek to offer as collateral must meet. The principal exception pertains to the treatment of borrowers seeking loans with high loan-to-value (LTV) ratios. In the conventional loan market, borrowers seeking loans with LTV ratios greater than 80 percent generally pay higher rates because the lenders normally require private mortgage insurance. Private mortgage insurance premiums generally increase in line with increases in the LTV ratio between 80 and 95 percent (the legislative maximum for private insurance). In the Federal Housing Administration (FHA) loan market, borrowers during the period in which the loans in the study we describe here were originated paid a flat insurance premium of 3.8 percent of the loan amount. Given limited variation in the price of FHA mortgage credit, one would expect returns to home lending—

upon accounting for loan amount—to be directly related to losses from default.

As documented in this chapter, minority loan applicants and neighborhoods are often characterized by higher levels of default risk, relative to the applicant pool as a whole. However, to the extent that loan underwriting requirements fully account for borrower and locational default risk, and hence coincide closely with actual loan performance, applicant and neighborhood racial composition should play no residual role in the credit extension decision. Alternatively, as suggested by Peterson (1981) and Van Order, Westin, and Zorn (1993), the prevalence of systematic racial discrimination or redlining may result in lenders' holding minority applicants or applicants from minority neighborhoods to loan qualification standards well in excess of those required by true assessments of default risk. Following Peterson (1981) and others, we refer to this type of discrimination as *uneconomic discrimination*, since it is not in the profit-maximizing interest of the lender to engage in this kind of activity. In this context, uneconomic racial discrimination may be defined as the rejection or discouragement of minority home loan applicants whose credit requests have a positive expected return and/or the acceptance of nonminority applicants whose loan requests have a negative expected return. This kind of discriminatory behavior then would likely result in higher returns to home loans—as evidenced by lower default rates or smaller dollar losses—among minority borrowers or neighborhoods than those observed for nonminority borrowers or neighborhoods.

In contrast to uneconomic racial discrimination, economic racial discrimination, which is also illegal, occurs when creditors use the race of the applicant as a proxy for risk-related characteristics that are either unobservable or costly to obtain. Discrimination of this type may be consistent with profit-maximizing behavior, since race is employed as an indicator of risk. This type of discrimination, as discussed later in this chapter, implies a different relationship between race and observed default rates than that implied by uneconomic discrimination.

The study we conducted evaluates the default risk characteristics and the performance of FHA-insured, single-family residential mortgages. In so doing it assesses any residual effects of borrower race or neighborhood racial composition on the likelihood of loan default. The analysis is undertaken using formerly unavailable individual loan records from the U.S. Department of Housing and Urban Development (HUD), augmented with 1980 census-tract-level data to identify neighborhood locational attributes potentially associated with default risk.

This chapter is organized as follows. The next section places the current study in the context of recent analyses of race, default risk, and mortgage lending. In so doing, we point to methodological or data limitations of previous analyses that are addressed in the current research. The third section provides data and model specification, and the fourth section presents the results of the model's estimation. A summary section concludes the chapter.

RACIAL DISCRIMINATION AND RESIDENTIAL MORTGAGE DEFAULTS

Analyses of mortgage defaults focus fundamentally on variables influencing borrower equity in the property and borrower ability to service the loan as scheduled. Equity is important because default can be seen as the option to return the mortgage to the lender at the par value of the loan. From a strict options perspective, this "put option" would be exercised when borrower negative equity in the property exceeds the homeowner's costs associated with default. In this framework the decision to default is based fully on homeowner loss minimization; the borrower's income and employment situation are taken to be largely irrelevant in that decision. The ability-to-pay approach focuses on events that trigger default, in that negative equity is typically found to be a necessary, but not a sufficient, condition for default.

Unlike early studies, which restricted evaluation of borrower equity to measures available at the time of loan origination, more recent analyses (Campbell and Dietrich 1983; Vandell and Thibodeau 1985) have modeled the mortgage put option using proxies that include estimates of the contemporaneous borrower equity in the property. These studies specify contemporaneous mortgage LTV ratios through variables that measure fluctuations in both the numerator and denominator of that ratio. In Campbell and Dietrich's (1983) study, for example, property value fluctuations were represented using nonquality-adjusted state housing price appreciation rates; borrower equity was further adjusted by the spread between the current market and coupon rate on the mortgage. Vandell and Thibodeau (1985) expanded upon this earlier specification by indexing sample property appreciation rates to those of the region and the census tract where the property was located; those authors further adjusted borrower equity by the percentage difference between the mortgage's current value and its par value, instead of simply calculating the spread between market and coupon rates.

In a more formal option-theoretic approach to mortgage defaults, Foster and Van Order (1984) used FHA data from the 1960s and 1970s to estimate changes over time in LTV ratios and, hence, the portion of loans with negative equity. Their analysis found current and lagged equity variables to be significant to the exercise of the default option. Foster and Van Order also utilized borrower and other loan characteristics to represent transactions costs associated with exercise of the default option; however, those controls added little to their analysis of aggregate default data.

Given borrower negative equity in the property, certain trigger events may adversely affect borrower ability to repay the loan on schedule, and in so doing, may significantly elevate the likelihood of default. Those trigger events might include the loss of employment or income, change in marital or health status, and the like. As might be expected, few mortgage data sets contain contemporaneous information on changes in borrower income; instead, most studies (e.g., Barth, Cordes, and Yezer 1979; Campbell and Dietrich 1983; Foster and Van Order 1984; Vandell and Thibodeau 1985) employ measures of payments-to-income and borrower income stability derived from the time of loan origination. Contrary to expectations of a model of mortgage default based on the ruthless exercise of the put option, results of these analyses suggest some importance to those nonequity indicators in the estimation of default probabilities.

As has been suggested, borrower and neighborhood characteristics may be further useful in evaluating allegations of racial discrimination and redlining in mortgage lending. Typical minority borrowers and neighborhoods may be characterized by higher levels of default risk than their nonminority counterparts (see, for example, Canner, Gabriel, and Woolley 1991). To the extent that estimated default risk—and hence loan underwriting guidelines—inadequately reflect a higher likelihood of default that might be characteristic of minority households or neighborhoods, those loans would be characterized by lower returns to the lender. Racial prejudice among lenders, however, may lead to discrimination against minority households or neighborhoods through the imposition of loan qualification standards that exceed those required to account for the higher levels of default risk. Alternatively, such prejudice may lead to loan standards for nonminority households or neighborhoods that are more lenient than those justified by lower nonminority default risks.

As in Peterson's (1981) discussion of uneconomic discrimination, biased lenders may include a negative discrimination coefficient for minorities or a positive discrimination coefficient for nonminorities in their calculation of the expected present value of loans to minority and nonminority borrowers or neighborhoods. Under these circumstances, minority applicants or applicants from minority neighborhoods would then have to offset that discrimination coefficient through relatively higher levels of loan qualification. Loans to approved minority borrowers would then be likely to be characterized by lower default probabilities, relative to similar loans to nonminority borrowers. To the extent that racial discrimination is systematic among lenders, one would expect relatively lower levels of default and better loan performance among minority borrowers or neighborhoods.

As noted by Peterson (1981), however, a simple comparison of the average loan performance between two groups of borrowers can be misleading if the two groups do not exhibit similar distributions of expected returns. For example, if the proportion of nonminority borrowers who are highly qualified exceeds by a substantial margin the proportion of highly qualified minority borrowers, then default rates of nonminority borrowers, observed without controlling for other determinants of credit quality, would be lower than those associated with minority borrowers. This finding, however, would not necessarily reflect discrimination, but simply the differences in the average creditworthiness of the two groups of borrowers. To avoid this problem, it is necessary to account adequately for other important determinants of loan quality. In the analysis presented here, the data are fully exploited to control for such variations in applicant creditworthiness.

It should be noted that under certain conditions, racial discrimination in lending decisions may not be revealed in differential loan performance. This would be true if discrimination were random rather than affecting only those applicants who are marginally qualified for credit. Also, discrimination may not be revealed in differential loan performance if only some lenders in a local market engage in discrimination and if applicants who are denied home loans on the basis of their race or the location of the property they seek to purchase successfully obtain credit from lenders that do not discriminate. Finally, as discussed more fully later in the chapter, if the discrimination is solely "economic" (i.e., minority status is used as a proxy for risk-related characteristics that are either unobservable or costly to obtain) and if the higher standard of creditworthiness required of minority applicants accurately accounts for this difference, then no default differential between minorities and nonminorities should be observed.

Only a few recent studies (e.g., Barth, Cordes, and Yezer 1979; Van Order, Westin, and Zorn 1993) have expressly attempted to evaluate the effects of individual or neighborhood race on default probabilities. Of those studies, only Van Order and colleagues have explicitly sought to test the Peterson (1981) theory. In all cases, however, shortcomings in available data constrain the interpretability of modeled results. Further, none of those studies is able to test hypotheses associated with both neighborhood redlining and individual-level racial discrimination. Barth et al. (1979) found default rates to be positively associated with black households; however, their various race and gender indicators may well reflect the effects of wealth and other variables omitted from the study. Van Order, Westin, and Zorn (1993) merged information on conventional loans purchased by the Federal Home Loan Mortgage Corporation (Freddie Mac) with decennial census files in estimating a proportional hazard model of mortgage default. Although the database contains information on ZIP code racial composition, the authors' analysis of discrimination effects was limited owing to a lack of critical information on a range of borrower characteristics, including credit history, assets, and, most important, race.

As previously suggested, research to date has failed to adequately specify and test the Peterson (1981) model of credit discrimination in the context of mortgage finance. Although recent studies of default risk apply improved analytical and empirical methods and better specify contemporaneous trigger events associated with default (see, for example, Giliberto and Houston 1989; Kau, Keenan, and Kim 1991; and Quigley and Van Order 1991), these analyses fail to expressly consider the role of racial discrimination and/or neighborhood redlining in mortgage lending. Conversely, the few studies that focus on racial discrimination are inadequately specified and suffer important data limitations.

In a departure from previous work, the current study tests hypotheses concerning both individual-level discrimination and neighborhood redlining in the context of a multivariate statistical model of mortgage defaults. In the process, the research applies both individual-level loan information from the FHA and census-tract-level characteristics from the 1980 decennial census; this information is particularly well suited to the investigation at hand, given the rich array of details concerning borrower attributes and property location. Estimated default probabilities associated with borrower and neighborhood characteristics may further provide new insights concerning the enhancement of existing FHA loan underwriting requirements.

The analysis presented here focuses on default as a measure of expected returns to mortgages. A more accurate measure of expected returns, though, might be expected losses, defined as the default probability multiplied by the expected dollar loss from a default. Although we expect these two measures to be highly correlated, the possibility exists that using a measure of expected losses could result in different conclusions. This would be a particular concern if default costs vary with loan size, which may be correlated with race (see, for example, Evans, Maris, and Weinstein 1984). The relationship between losses and both borrower and neighborhood characteristics will be examined by us in future research.

DATA AND MODEL SPECIFICATION

The principal data utilized in this study are drawn from records pertaining to FHA-insured, single-family mortgage loans originated over the 1986–89 period. Information about the status and characteristics of these loans is drawn from two files maintained by HUD: the F42 EDS Case History File and the F42 BIA Composite File. The former carries information on each FHA-insured loan from its origination through termination. This file is updated regularly and indicates the reason for each termination. The latter contains the loan and borrower characteristics information, and is updated only to append a census-tract identifier from the 1980 Census of Population and Housing.

As suggested earlier, borrower indicators of default risk pertain largely to financial, demographic, and employment information compiled at the time of loan application. Further, many FHA loan files have been geocoded and contain a census-tract indicator; accordingly, each file with such data was matched to neighborhood socioeconomic and housing market indicators for 1980. The census information facilitates evaluation of location-specific factors that may be associated with loan defaults. Further, FHA data on the race of the borrower, and census measures of neighborhood racial composition, enable assessment of any residual effects of discrimination or redlining on the performance of FHA-insured loans.

The FHA-insured data are relatively well suited to the analysis of default, given the inclusion in the program of large numbers of relatively high-risk borrowers. The use of formal underwriting criteria in the loan approval process implies that observed defaults reflect a population with ex ante default risk less than or equal to some critical value. Although both FHA and conventional mortgage applications are evaluated according to formal underwriting criteria, the FHA guidelines are substantially less strict than those of conventional lenders, particularly regarding the level of equity the borrower must have at the time of loan origination and the acceptable levels of housing expense and total debt to income.

To conduct our analysis, a sample was drawn of FHA-insured loans originated during 1986–89. Detailed information on the characteristics as well as the performance of the portfolio of FHA-insured loans was provided by HUD. The main restriction on the sample is that detailed borrower and loan characteristics were recorded by HUD only for a random sample of loans originated in each year. In certain versions of the model, the sample was further restricted (in some cases substantially) owing to the lack of available information on the census-tract location of the property.

The FHA database distinguishes among the variety of instances in which mortgage terminations occur; in this analysis, we evaluate the likelihood of mortgage terminations resulting from borrower default (inclusive of those default outcomes resulting in lender foreclosure, as well as situations in which the borrower conveys title to the property to the lender in lieu of foreclosure).

Sample Characteristics

Definitions of the variables utilized in this study are provided in table 6.1. For the final sample employed, tables 6.2 and 6.3 present selected characteristics of FHA borrowers, the terms of their loans, and census-tract characteristics associated with the FHA loans. Tables 6.4 and 6.5 present cumulative default rates by characteristic for loans originated in each of the four years of the analysis (1986–89). These default rates reflect the proportion of loans originated in each yearly cohort that went into default between the year of origination and the end of the first quarter of 1993.

We discuss here only a few of the more salient results presented in these tables. Note, first, that the vast majority of FHA-insured loans entail very high LTV ratios (table 6.2). This is consistent with objectives of the program to facilitate home ownership among moderate-income borrowers with few assets available for down payment and closing costs. Over 80 percent of the loans in our sample had LTV ratios exceeding 95 percent. Similarly, the debt obligation ratios exhibited by loan applicants are high, averaging about 40 percent for the ratio of total debt payments to income and about 21 percent for the ratio of housing expense payments to income. These averages tend to mask the fact that many FHA borrowers have exceptionally high debt

Table 6.1 VARIABLE DEFINITIONS

RMISSING	1 if borrower race is unknown, 0 otherwise
BLACK	1 if black borrower, 0 otherwise
AMIND	1 if American Indian borrower, 0 otherwise
ASIAN	1 if Asian borrower, 0 otherwise
HISPANIC	1 if Hispanic borrower, 0 otherwise
LTV	Loan-to-value ratio
INVEST	1 if investment property, 0 otherwise
REFIN	1 if loan is a refinance, 0 otherwise
CONDO	1 if property is a condominium, 0 otherwise
DIRECT	1 if insurance approved under direct endorsement, 0 otherwise
URBAN	1 if property located in urban area, 0 otherwise
RURAL	1 if property located in rural area, 0 otherwise
COMP	1 if application indicates "compensating factors," 0 otherwise
FIRSTBUY	1 if borrower is a first-time homebuyer, 0 otherwise
NEW	1 if property is a new house, 0 otherwise
CBUNMARD	1 if borrower is unmarried coborrower, 0 otherwise
DEPNUM	number of dependents (excluding borrower and coborrower)
SELFEMP	1 if borrower is self employed, 0 otherwise
LQASS	Liquid assets available at closing
NOCBINC	1 if no coborrower or coborrower income is zero, 0 otherwise
PCBINC	percent of household income earned by coborrower
LQASS2	Liquid assets squared
AGE<25	1 if borrower is under 25 years of age, 0 otherwise
AGE25-35	1 if borrower is between 25 and 35 years of age, 0 otherwise
AGE35-45	1 if borrower is between 35 and 45 years of age, 0 otherwise
BUYDOWN	1 if mortgage interest rate has been "bought down" by seller, 0 otherwise
INCOME	Total annual effective family income
INCOME2	Income squared
SHRTMOR	1 if mortgage term is less than 30 years, 0 otherwise

ratios. For instance, in most years nearly 10 percent of FHA borrowers had total debt-to-income ratios exceeding 65 percent. Although the average annual incomes of FHA borrowers differ some among the four cohorts, they never exceed $39,000. First-time homebuyers comprise a large proportion of the sample in each year. In 1989, for instance, they accounted for about two-thirds of the FHA-insured loan originations. As indicated in table 6.2, minorities tend to be well represented in each of the yearly cohorts.

As shown in table 6.3, the majority of FHA borrowers reside in predominantly nonminority neighborhoods. About 10 percent of the borrowers reside in neighborhoods in which minorities constitute more than 50 percent of the population. In keeping with the goals of the FHA program, nearly half of the borrowers reside in census tracts

Table 6.1 VARIABLE DEFINITIONS (*continued*)

SINGLEM	1 if borrower is male and there is no coborrower, 0 otherwise
SINGLEF	1 if borrower is female and there is no coborrower, 0 otherwise
HVAL	Appraised value of the property at time of purchase
HVAL2	HVAL squared
POTHINC	Percent of borrower income that is from other (non-salary) sources.
HEI20-38	1 if housing expense to income ratio is between .20 and .38, 0 otherwise
HEI38-50	1 if housing expense to income ratio is between .38 and .50, 0 otherwise
HEI>50	1 if housing expense to income ratio is above .50, 0 otherwise
DTI20-40	1 if total debt-to-income ratio is between .2 and .41, 0 otherwise
DTI41-53	1 if total debt-to-income ratio is between .41 and .53, 0 otherwise
DTI53-65	1 if total debt-to-income ratio is between .53 and .65, 0 otherwise
DTI>65	1 if total debt-to-income ratio is above .65, 0 otherwise
CTBLACK	Black percentage of census tract population
CTAMIND	American Indian/Alaskan Native percentage of census tract population
CTASIAN	Asian percentage of census tract population
CTHISPANIC	Hispanic percentage of census tract population
CTMISS	Percentage of census tract population with race or ethnicity unknown
CTINCOME	Median family income of the census tract as a proportion of the median family income of the metropolitan area as a whole
CTHVAL	Median value of owner-occupied homes in the census tract
CTVACRAT	Percentage of one-to-four family housing units vacant in the census tract
CTMEDAGE	Median age of residential properties in the census tract
CTUNEMP	Unemployment rate of the census tract
CTRENTRATE	Proportion of housing units in the census tract that are rental

whose median family income is less than the median for the metropolitan area in which the census tract is located.

Simple tabulations of default probabilities (tables 6.4 and 6.5) show that default probabilities can differ significantly by characteristics of the loan, borrower, and location. For example, default rates appear to be higher for borrowers with high LTV ratios, smaller loan amounts, lower incomes and home values, and 30-year loans, compared to those with shorter terms to maturity. Among racial and ethnic groups, black borrowers exhibit the highest rates of loan defaults, whereas Asians exhibit the lowest rates of default. As shown in table 6.5, borrowers residing in predominantly minority neighborhoods exhibit higher default rates than those residing in predominantly nonminority neighborhoods. As also indicated, default rates tend to be lower for borrowers in higher-income neighborhoods.

Table 6.2 SELECTED CHARACTERISTICS OF FHA-INSURED LOANS BY YEAR OF LOAN ORIGINATION, 1986–1989 (PERCENTAGE DISTRIBUTION, OR AS OTHERWISE SPECIFIED)

	Year of Loan Origination			
Loan or Borrower Characteristic	1986 percent	1987 percent	1988 percent	1989 percent
All loans (number)	27,671	80,042	101,380	148,801
Loan characteristics				
Loan-to-value ratio				
Less than 90%	10.3	11.3	12.6	14.0
90–95	9.7	10.8	13.4	13.0
96–99	8.6	15.7	26.7	21.9
100–104	49.3	47.3	39.2	46.2
105 or more	22.1	14.9	8.2	5.0
Total	100	100	100	100
Mean (%)	100	99	98	97
Total debt-to-income ratio				
Less than 19%	12.2	11.4	8.6	1.6
20–40	54.1	51.5	46.1	47.5
41–52	17.3	18.2	25.0	43.6
53–64	9.0	10.0	11.6	6.6
65 or more	7.5	8.9	8.6	0.5
Total	100	100	100	100
Mean (%)	37	39	41	41
Housing expense to income ratio				
Less than 19%	45.8	44.8	42.8	56.6
20–37	53.4	54.3	55.9	42.6
38–49	0.7	0.9	1.2	0.7
50 or more	0.0	0.1	0.2	0.0
Total	100	100	100	100
Mean (%)	21	21	22	19
Loan amount				
Mean ($)	58,455	60,614	60,300	64,459
Mortgage term				
Less than 30 year	11.8	8.2	5.7	4.8
30 year	88.2	91.8	94.3	95.2
Total	100	100	100	100
Borrower characteristics				
Race of borrower				
White	78.1	73.5	68.9	79.6
Black	6.4	11.3	18.3	8.1
Hispanic	5.2	7.4	6.7	8.4
Asian	1.4	1.8	1.8	2.0
American Indian	0.2	0.2	0.3	0.2
Unknown	8.7	5.8	4.0	1.7
Total	100	100	100	100

Table 6.2 SELECTED CHARACTERISTICS OF FHA-INSURED LOANS BY YEAR OF LOAN ORIGINATION, 1986–1989 (PERCENTAGE DISTRIBUTION, OR AS OTHERWISE SPECIFIED) (*continued*)

	Year of Loan Origination			
Loan or Borrower Characteristic	1986 percent	1987 percent	1988 percent	1989 percent
Family income				
Less than $30,000	32.1	34.8	36.4	31.2
$30,000–49,999	54.0	51.6	50.4	51.4
$50,000–74,999	11.8	11.5	10.9	14.3
$75,000 or more	2.1	2.1	2.3	3.2
Total	100	100	100	100
Mean ($)	37,293	36,765	36,456	38,732
Age of borrower				
Less than 25	17.5	17.7	20.0	18.7
26–34	53.6	51.2	51.0	50.5
35–44	19.3	20.0	18.9	20.2
45 or more	9.6	11.0	10.1	10.7
Total	100	100	100	100
Mean (age)	33	33	33	33
Marital status				
Single male	9.7	9.3	9.8	12.1
Single female	8.2	7.9	8.6	11.1
Married	80.0	80.1	78.0	63.1
Unmarried coborrowers	2.1	2.7	3.6	13.7
Total	100	100	100	100
Liquid assets				
Mean ($)	10,179	9,723	8,331	11,508
Home value				
Less than $40,000	17.0	15.0	16.3	13.1
$40,000–79,999	68.1	65.5	62.1	57.5
$80,000 or more	14.9	19.5	21.6	29.5
Total	100	100	100	100
Mean ($)	59,010	61,634	62,125	66,781
First-time homebuyer	47.9	51.5	61.9	67.7
Investor	4.8	4.3	1.9	2.0
Refinance	19.6	13.2	3.1	3.1
Condominium	0.2	1.7	4.8	6.2
Direct endorsement	85.0	91.3	96.1	94.7
Self-employed	NA	0.1	0.2	0.1

NA—not available.
Totals may not sum to 100 percent due to rounding.
Source: Department of Housing and Urban Development.

Table 6.3 SELECTED CHARACTERISTICS OF NEIGHBORHOODS WHERE PROPERTY SECURING FHA-INSURED LOAN IS LOCATED, BY YEAR OF LOAN ORIGINATION, 1986–1989 (PERCENTAGE DISTRIBUTION)

	Year of Loan Origination			
Census Tract Characteristics[1]	1986 percent	1987 percent	1988 percent	1989 percent
All loans (number)	828	29,384	80,162	112,510
Racial composition of census tract[2]				
Less than 10%	43.5	52.2	55.7	58.0
10–24	31.8	24.9	25.1	24.1
25–49	14.6	12.7	11.1	10.4
50–79	4.2	5.5	4.4	4.0
80 or more	5.9	4.8	3.7	3.5
Total	100	100	100	100
Income of census tract[3]				
Less than 80%	13.7	15.5	14.1	13.7
80–99	30.6	31.2	31.4	30.8
100–120	29.7	34.2	35.0	34.2
120 or more	26.1	19.2	19.5	21.3
Total	100	100	100	100
Location				
Urban	10.9	22.6	24.1	23.0
Suburban	53.9	44.4	30.5	29.8
Rural	1.3	2.3	2.3	1.8
Unknown	33.9	30.7	43.1	45.4
Total	100	100	100	100

Totals may not sum to 100 percent due to rounding.
1. Characteristics of census tracts are based on the 1980 Census of Population and Housing.
2. Racial composition of census tract is the minority population of a census tract as a percentage of the total population of the census tract.
3. Median family income of census tract as a percentage of the median family income of the metropolitan statistical area where the census tract is located.
Source: Department of Housing and Urban Development and 1980 U.S. Census of Population and Housing.

The Statistical Model

The analysis employs logit regressions to estimate the contribution of the various loan, borrower, and locational characteristics to the likelihood of default. For each of the annual cohorts, we estimate

$$P = exp[bX]/(1 + exp[bX]), \quad (6.1)$$

Table 6.4 CUMULATIVE DEFAULT RATE FOR FHA-INSURED LOANS BY CHARACTERISTIC AND BY YEAR OF LOAN ORIGINATION, 1986–1989[1] (PERCENT)

	Year of Loan Origination			
Loan or Borrower Characteristic	1986 percent	1987 percent	1988 percent	1989 percent
All loans	6.7	4.9	4.2	2.3
Loan characteristics				
Loan-to-value ratio				
Less than 90%	1.6	2.0	2.1	0.9
90–95	4.1	3.3	2.6	1.4
96–99	3.6	4.5	3.8	1.9
100–104	8.2	5.4	4.8	2.6
105 or more	8.2	6.9	8.3	6.8
Total debt-to-income ratio				
Less than 19%	7.9	4.8	4.2	1.8
20–40	6.3	4.8	4.4	2.3
41–52	6.5	4.6	3.7	2.3
53–64	7.3	5.1	4.1	2.6
65 or more	7.5	5.5	4.7	2.3
Housing expense-to-income ratio				
Less than 19%	7.2	4.9	4.1	2.1
20–37	6.3	4.9	4.3	2.5
38–49	3.0	3.9	2.4	2.4
50 or more	9.1	3.2	5.7	6.5
Loan amount				
Less than average	7.9	6.0	5.1	2.7
More than average	5.5	3.8	3.1	1.8
Mortgage term				
Less than 30 year	3.2	2.0	2.5	1.3
30 year	7.2	5.1	4.3	2.3
Borrower characteristics				
Race of borrower				
White	6.2	4.3	3.5	2.0
Black	13.3	9.0	6.2	4.7
Hispanic	6.1	5.1	5.2	2.8
Asian	5.0	3.2	2.7	1.2
American Indian	19.1	6.0	5.2	2.8
Unknown	6.7	4.4	4.8	2.5
Family income				
Less than $30,000	8.5	6.5	5.5	3.1
$30,000–49,999	5.8	4.2	3.7	2.0
$50,000–74,999	5.9	3.4	2.5	1.5
$75,000 or more	6.7	4.1	2.0	1.0

(continued)

Table 6.4 CUMULATIVE DEFAULT RATE FOR FHA-INSURED LOANS BY CHARACTERISTIC AND BY YEAR OF LOAN ORIGINATION, 1986–1989[1] (PERCENT) (*continued*)

Loan or Borrower Characteristic	Year of Loan Origination 1986 percent	1987 percent	1988 percent	1989 percent
Age of borrower				
Less than 25	7.7	5.9	4.3	2.6
26–34	6.2	4.5	4.0	2.1
35–44	7.3	5.3	4.7	2.5
45 or more	6.5	4.2	3.8	2.1
Marital status				
Single male	8.3	5.6	4.7	2.4
Single female	6.3	4.8	3.8	2.0
Married	6.0	4.8	4.2	2.3
Unmarried co-borrowers	6.0	4.0	3.5	2.3
Liquid assets				
Less than average	7.9	5.9	5.1	2.6
More than average	3.6	2.3	1.8	1.4
Home value				
Less than $39,000	9.6	7.9	6.3	3.8
$40,000–79,999	6.6	4.8	4.3	2.3
$80,000 or more	3.9	2.8	2.3	1.7
First-time homebuyer	6.9	5.3	4.4	2.5
Investor	8.4	3.6	1.8	0.7
Refinance	5.6	3.5	3.7	1.5
Condominium	2.9	3.6	2.1	1.8
Direct endorsement	6.3	4.7	4.0	2.1
Self-employed	NA	2.3	2.9	2.3

NA—not available.

1. Cumulative default rate is calculated by computing the number of loan defaults from the year of loan origination through the first quarter of 1993 as a percentage of total loans originated in a given year.

Source: Department of Housing and Urban Development.

where P represents the probability of default for a loan with characteristics X, and X is a vector of the attributes of the loan, including borrower and locational characteristics. The vector of estimated coefficients values, b, indicates the effect of each characteristic on the likelihood of default.

We consider next the expected effects of each of the more important explanatory variables. Loan collateralization at the time of origination represents a critical component of the risk evaluation and underwrit-

Table 6.5 CUMULATIVE DEFAULT RATE FOR FHA-INSURED LOANS BY VARIOUS NEIGHBORHOOD GROUPS AND BY YEAR OF LOAN ORIGINATION, 1986–1989[1] (PERCENT)

	Year of Loan Origination			
Census tract Characteristics[2]	1986 percent	1987 percent	1988 percent	1989 percent
All loans	5.3	5.2	4.3	2.4
Racial composition of census tract[3]				
Less than 10%	3.3	4.2	3.5	1.9
10–24	5.7	5.6	4.5	2.7
25–49	3.3	5.9	5.3	3.0
50–79	8.6	6.3	6.6	3.6
80 or more	8.2	11.5	9.5	4.5
Income of census tract[4]				
Less than 80%	5.3	8.3	6.5	3.8
80–99	7.9	5.6	4.8	2.6
100–120	2.4	4.3	3.7	2.1
120 or more	5.6	3.8	3.1	1.7
Location				
Urban	4.4	6.1	4.5	2.4
Suburban	6.0	4.1	3.3	2.0
Rural	0.0	4.6	3.3	2.3
Unknown	6.2	5.2	4.7	2.5

1. Cumulative default rate is calculated by computing the number of loan defaults from the year of loan origination through the first quarter of 1993 as a percentage of total loans originated in a given year.
2. Characteristics of census tracts are based on the 1980 Census of Population and Housing.
3. Racial composition of census tract is the minority population of a census tract as a percentage of the total population of the census tract.
4. Income of census tract is the median family income of the census tract as a percentage of the median family income of the metropolitan statistical area where the census tract is located.
Source: Department of Housing and Urban Development and 1980 U.S. Census of Population and Housing.

ing process used by creditors; higher LTV ratios are commonly believed to be associated with elevated risks of mortgage default, since even a small adverse movement in property values may put the borrower in a negative equity position. Thus, we expect loans with higher initial LTV ratios to exhibit higher rates of default.

The borrower's anticipated ability to service a loan as scheduled is another important component of risk evaluation. In this vein, creditors assess whether a proposed loan might create an excessive payment burden for the consumer and whether other resources are available to meet payments if unforeseen interruptions in borrower income should arise. Debt obligation ratios are specified in the following two ways: the ratio of housing expense to income (HEI), and the ratio of total debt payment to income (DTI). The former comprises the monthly total mortgage payment (including property taxes and insurance) relative to total monthly effective family income as allowable by the FHA, whereas the latter adds to the numerator the sum of other monthly installment debt payments. Lenders typically devote much attention to the levels of these ratios in the assessment of mortgage credit risk; FHA guidelines regarding insurance endorsements over the period of analysis indicate that an important threshold for the former ratio occurs at 38 percent, whereas the threshold for the latter ratio occurs at 53 percent. We also allow for the possibility of nonlinearities in estimating the relationship between these ratios and the likelihood of default.

The study furthermore tests various other loan characteristics hypothesized to bear importantly on default risk, including loan amount, type, purpose, and term. For example, shorter-term loans—which amortize and build equity more quickly—are hypothesized to carry lower default risk. Since the FHA offers loans with differing terms to maturity, a variable is introduced to indicate a loan that has a maturity of less than 30 years (SHRTMOR). The default literature provides some evidence that refinance loans originated for the purpose of equity takeout have higher default probabilities than do other loans. Although our data fail to distinguish those refinance loans funded for the purpose of equity takeout, the analysis does test for any significant differences in default probability associated with refinance loans (REFIN). Loans taken out by investors (INVEST) may also entail additional risk, since such individuals are likely to exercise the default option more ruthlessly, should equity in the property decline substantially. The distinction between newly constructed and existing properties is also introduced (NEW) to account for the fact that newer units may provide better loan collateral, since they are less likely to require unexpected maintenance outlays by the borrower. In addition, the home value (HVAL) is included as an independent explanatory variable to account for the possibility that loans on higher-valued homes perform differently than loans on lower-valued properties.

In recent years, the vast majority of FHA-insured loans have been processed under the Direct Endorsement program. This program, which began in 1983, allows certified lenders to underwrite FHA loans directly without seeking prior FHA approval. In so doing, the program seeks to avoid the lengthy delays often encountered with HUD processing of loan applications. Previous research suggests that loans directly endorsed consistently experience default rates that are lower than those observed for loans processed by HUD (ICF 1989). Consequently, we include in our analysis a dummy variable indicating whether the loan was directly endorsed (DIRECT).

The empirical analysis further includes a set of borrower characteristics that pertain to the mortgage underwriting process and are hypothesized to affect homeowner ability to repay the loan as scheduled. These characteristics include a vector of borrower sociodemographic characteristics, including borrower age, gender, race/ethnicity, marital status, number of dependents, first-time buyer status, and the like. Also tested are borrower financial characteristics, including total assets, income, income by source, and employment status.

Among borrower sociodemographic characteristics, the age of the borrower (AGE) is captured by categorical variables distinguishing among young, middle-aged, and older borrowers. The analysis also includes dummy variables indicating first-time buyers (FIRSTBUY), single male borrowers (SINGLEM), single female borrowers (SINGLEF), unmarried coborrowers (CBUNMARD), and married borrowers. The number of dependents (children under 18 years of age) is measured by a continuous variable (DEPNUM). Default probabilities are hypothesized to be higher among first-time buyers, since such households are more likely to have little in the way of credit or employment histories; further, those borrowers likely have limited assets with which to maintain loan payments in the case of income disruption. Similarly, households with larger numbers of dependents are expected to have higher default rates, since such borrowers have greater claims on their residual incomes and may be more subject to unanticipated expenditures.

Household balance sheet measures that proxy borrower ability to repay the loan as scheduled include the levels of borrower liquid assets, household income, income by source, coborrower income, borrower type, and self-employment status. Borrower liquid assets (LQASS) comprise funds available to complete the housing transaction at the time of loan settlement; all things equal, higher levels of liquid assets imply reduced likelihood of default as might occur in the context of such "trigger events" as disruptions in income. Borrower income (INCOME) includes all FHA-allowed qualifying income (including base employment income and income from other sources earned by the borrower and coborrower, if any). Higher levels of income suggest concomitantly elevated ability to repay the loan as scheduled, accordingly reducing the probability of default. All things equal, however, higher levels of nonsalary to total borrower income (POTHINC) are hypothesized to elevate the likelihood of default, given the relatively higher levels of volatility surrounding nonsalary income. Also, increased income volatility is associated with self-employed borrowers (SELFEMP), ceteris paribus.

Studies of discrimination focusing on the loan application process have found that credit history is an important determinant of the likelihood of approval of an application (Munnell et al. 1992). Although all borrowers must have acceptable credit history to be granted a mortgage, differences in credit history profiles may be related to the likelihood of default on the part of those granted credit. Although the available FHA data do not provide detailed information on the credit history of each borrower, some information is available on those borrowers deemed to be marginally qualified at the time of application. Specifically, the data contain a variable indicating compensating factors that enabled the loan to be approved for those borrowers that might not otherwise have received credit. Among these factors are indications that the borrower had an excellent credit history, good performance on a previous mortgage loan, and substantial savings. We address the issue of credit history by examining the performance of loans to borrowers assigned a compensation code. More generally, an indication of whether the borrower required a compensating factor (COMP) to receive approval is accounted for in all estimations.

To account for differences in default likelihoods that may be associated with the general location of the property, dummy variables are included that indicate location in the urban part of a metropolitan area (URBAN) and in rural areas (RURAL), with suburban locations representing the omitted category. To account for regional differences in economic conditions, as well as for the potential effects of differing state laws governing foreclosure practices, a dummy variable for each state in which FHA loans were extended is included in all estimations.

In working with the data, we found that census-tract designations were missing for a substantial proportion of all loans and, in particular, for virtually all loans originated in 1986. Because the inclusion of these variables results in a substantial reduction in the size of the sample, estimations without census-tract characteristics are presented in table 6.6 with preliminary estimations that include a number of census tract characteristics following in table 6.7. At this writing,

Table 6.6 LOGIT ESTIMATIONS OF THE RELATIONSHIP BETWEEN THE CUMULATIVE PROBABILITY OF LOAN DEFAULT AND ITS DETERMINANTS

	1986 Loans	1987 Loans	1988 Loans	1989 Loans
INTERCPT	−7.7385***	−5.1035***	−5.9584***	−7.9811***
Loan characteristics				
LTV	6.8356***	3.1341***	3.5185***	6.2932***
HEI20-38	0.0527	0.2564***	0.1709***	0.1873***
HEI38-50	−0.0048	0.6250**	−0.0900	0.2261
HEI>50	1.5981	0.1040	0.2511	1.5840**
DTI20-41	−0.2207**	−0.1086*	−0.0445	0.2041
DTI41-53	−0.1617	−0.1173*	−0.1097	0.2099
DTI53-65	−0.0736	−0.0602	−0.0061	0.3954*
DTI>65	0.0181	0.0573	0.01136	0.2156
REFIN	−0.7786***	−0.4855***	0.2590*	0.3265*
CONDO	−0.5787	0.1399	−0.2102*	0.2241*
BUYDOWN			−0.3215*	0.0884
INVEST	0.8719***	0.3368**	−0.0776	−0.3169
HVAL	−4.9E-5***	−3.6E-5***	−7.231E-6	−2.2E-5***
HVAL2	362.0E-12*	206.0E-12***	36.0E-13	141.0E-12***
DIRECT	−0.1906**	−0.2706***	−0.4515***	−0.6253***
SHRTMOR	−0.7672***	−0.9797***	−0.4822***	−0.4685***
URBAN	0.0534	0.1661***	0.1936***	−0.0407
RURAL	0.1173	0.1778*	0.0863	0.2012*
Borrower characteristics				
COMP		−0.0882	−0.0178	−0.0149
FIRSTBUY	−0.0609	0.1045**	0.2282***	0.1400**
NEW	0.3154	−0.0131	−0.0525	−0.2924***
CBUNMARD	−0.0705	0.0267	−0.0136	0.0116
SINGLEM	0.3016**	0.2136***	0.1759**	0.0662
SINGLEF	−0.2080*	−0.1905**	−0.2552***	−0.3365***
DEPNUM	0.1434***	0.1682***	0.1385***	0.1814***
SELFEMP		−0.6909	−0.5208	−0.1729
LQASS	−0.0395***	−0.0507***	−0.0611***	−0.0266***
LQASS2	0.00023***	0.0003***	0.00041***	0.00015***
NOCBINC	−0.1946*	−0.0003	−0.0690	−0.2129**
PCBINC	−0.00515*	−0.00128	−0.00263*	−0.00547***
AGE<25	−0.0187	0.0915	−0.1178*	−0.0492
AGE25-35	−0.1795*	−0.1766**	−0.1341*	−0.2346***
AGE35-45	0.01106	0.0424	0.0806	−0.0353
INCOME	−0.00234	−0.00584	−0.0132***	−0.0205***
INCOME2	0.00002	0.00008***	0.00007**	0.0001***
POTHINC	0.2477	0.7585***	0.5554***	0.5322***
BLACK	0.8126***	0.6753***	0.4737***	0.6012***
AMIND	0.9070**	0.3807	0.2399	0.1625
ASIAN	0.0178	−0.0925	−0.0814	−0.4405*
HISPANIC	−0.1603	0.00159	0.1192*	−0.0549
RMISSING	0.2335*	0.1181	0.3134***	0.1526
No. of Obs.	27,671	80,042	101,380	148,801

Note: The symbols *, **, and *** denote statistical significance at the 90, 99, and 99.9 percent levels, respectively.

Table 6.7 LOGIT ESTIMATIONS OF THE RELATIONSHIP BETWEEN THE CUMULATIVE PROBABILITY OF LOAN DEFAULT AND ITS DETERMINANTS

	1987 Loans	1988 Loans	1989 Loans
INTERCEPT	−4.9410***	−4.8248***	−6.8573***
Loan characteristics			
LTV	3.4109***	3.5391***	6.3785***
HEI20-38	0.2561**	0.1377*	0.1978***
HEI38-50	0.6260*	−0.0598	0.2165
HEI>50	−0.2972	0.1597	1.7563**
DTI20-41	−0.0932	−0.0833	0.1592
DTI41-53	−0.1970	−0.1829*	0.1822
DTI53-65	−0.1632	−0.0695	0.3346*
DTI>65	0.1828	0.1133	0.1994
REFIN	0.4161**	0.2921*	0.4333**
CONDO	0.7202***	0.2650*	0.4873***
BUYDOWN		0.1722	0.0269
INVEST	−0.0646	−0.0329	−0.3329
HVAL	−8.973E-6	7.70E-6	−0.000018***
HVAL2	92.0E-12*	−4.75E-11	123E-12***
DIRECT	−0.2169	−0.4526***	−0.6907***
SHRTMOR	−0.8434***	−0.4356***	−0.2710*
URBAN	0.2283**	0.1224**	−0.0227
RURAL	0.1455	−0.0586	0.0535
Borrower characteristics			
COMP	−0.0385	−0.1254	−0.0911
FIRSTBUY	0.0738	0.1938***	0.1058*
NEW	−0.0524	−0.1289*	−0.2429***
CBUNMARD	−0.2009	−0.0722	−0.0087
SINGLEM	−0.0494	0.1282*	0.0823
SINGLEF	−0.3207**	−0.3000***	−0.3552***
DEPNUM	0.1910***	0.1338***	0.1733***
SELFEMP	−0.5553	−0.2467	0.0718
LQASS	−0.0625***	−0.0593***	−0.0224***

(continued)

census-tract measures are drawn from the 1980 decennial census and include the racial composition of the neighborhood, as measured by the proportion of the population that was black (CTBLACK), American Indian or Alaskan natives (CTAMIND), Asian (CTASIAN), Hispanic (CTHISPANIC), or other (CTMISS). Other census-tract characteristics controlled for are the neighborhood median family income level as a proportion of the median family income for the metropolitan area as a whole (CTINCOME), the median value of owner-occupied housing units (CTHVAL), the proportion of housing units that were vacant

Table 6.7 LOGIT ESTIMATIONS OF THE RELATIONSHIP BETWEEN THE CUMULATIVE PROBABILITY OF LOAN DEFAULT AND ITS DETERMINANTS (*continued*)

	1987 Loans	1988 Loans	1989 Loans
LQASS2	0.00054***	0.00039***	0.00012***
NOCBINC	0.1183	−0.0452	−0.2401**
PCBINC	0.00014	−0.00235	−0.0071***
AGE<25	0.2233*	−0.0626	−0.0618
AGE25-35	−0.0779	−0.1025	−0.1975**
AGE35-45	0.0614	0.1102	−0.0702
INCOME	−0.00178	−0.0172***	−0.0171***
INCOME2	0.00005	0.0001***	0.00008**
POTHINC	0.4826*	0.5032***	0.5713***
BLACK	0.3696***	0.3415***	0.6398***
AMIND	0.3528	−0.1432	−0.0067
ASIAN	0.1047	−0.0053	−0.3023
HISPANIC	0.0090	0.1372*	0.0741
RMISSING	0.0904	0.2551**	0.2050
Location characteristics			
CTBLACK	0.3001*	0.4891***	−0.1468
CTAMIND	−8.0237	5.3862	−0.1171
CTASIAN	−14.4575**	−6.3791	−7.8146*
CTHISPANIC	−0.6411*	−0.6935***	−0.1903
CTMISS	6.2212	−0.0162	2.3977
CTINCOME	−0.0046*	−0.0025	−0.0060***
CTHVAL	−0.00002***	−0.00002***	−8.15E-6***
CTVACRAT	−0.03490	0.8888*	0.8422*
CTMEDAGE	−0.00556	−0.0053*	0.0003
CTUNEMP	0.9532	−0.5030	−1.4853*
CTRENTRATE	0.1564	−0.1665	−0.3911*
No. of Obs.	29,363	80,135	112,371

Note: The symbols *, **, and *** denote statistical significance at the 90, 99, and 99.9 percent levels, respectively.

(CTVACRAT), the median age of the housing units (CTMEDAGE), the area unemployment rate (CTUNEMP), and the proportion of housing in the neighborhood accounted for by rental units (CTRENTRATE).

ESTIMATION RESULTS

Table 6.6 presents for each of four different loan cohorts the results of logit estimations of the relationship between the probability of default (for the period between the time of origination and the end of the first quarter of 1993) and the determinants of that probability, absent census-tract variables. Columns one through four present results obtained for loans originated in 1986, 1987, 1988, and 1989, respectively. Since the dependent variable may be thought of as the probability of default, a positive (negative) coefficient associated with an explanatory variable implies that the characteristic is associated with an increase (decrease) in the likelihood of default. All four estimations also include as explanatory variables a dummy variable for each state in which loans were made. These are not shown for reasons of space.

Among variables acting as proxies for loan characteristics, the LTV ratio is positive and highly significant in all four annual cohorts. Results indicate, as predicted, that loans with higher initial LTV ratios are more likely to end in default (see table 6.6). This implies, not surprisingly, that requiring borrowers to establish more equity in their properties at the time of loan origination would result in fewer defaults.

We further consider the role of the two obligation ratios (the ratio of housing expenses to income and the ratio of total debt payments to income) in determining the performance of the loan. To investigate the possibility of nonlinearities in the relationship between these ratios and the likelihood of default, each ratio is represented by a series of three dummy variables indicating that the loan falls within specific ranges of the possible values of these ratios. For the ratio of housing expenses to income, HEI20-38 indicates that the value of this ratio falls between 0.2 and 0.38; HEI38-50 indicates that the value of the ratio falls between 0.38 and 0.50; while HEI > 50 indicates a value that exceeds 0.50. Values of this ratio less than 0.2 constitute the omitted category. The variables DTI20-41, DTI41-53, DTI53-65, and DTI > 65 are defined in a similar manner for the ratio of total debt payments to income. Note that these dummy variable categories were structured to reflect the value of 0.38 for the ratio of housing expenses to income and the value of 0.53 for the ratio of total debt payments to income mentioned in FHA underwriting guidelines.

The coefficients of these obligation ratio dummy variables tell a plausible story only in some cases. In general, borrowers with higher ratios of housing expenses to income tend to exhibit higher likelihoods of default. The coefficients of the dummy variables indicating ranges of the ratio of total debt payments to income are not easily interpretable in terms of an overall trend. Since the total obligation ratio includes housing expenses in the numerator, collinearity between these two ratios is a distinct possibility.

The positive and significant coefficients of INVEST in the 1986 and 1987 estimations imply that for originations in these two years, properties purchased as an investment exhibited higher default probabilities, all else equal, than did owner-occupied properties. This relationship, however, is not observed in the 1988 and 1989 estimations.

The relationship between the likelihood of default and a dummy variable indicating that the loan represents a refinance (REFIN) of an existing loan on the same property is also mixed. The negative and significant coefficients for the 1986 and 1987 cohorts indicate that such loans are less likely to result in default, but the significant positive coefficients in the 1988 and 1989 cohorts indicate that such loans were more risky in these later years. A possible reason is that refinancing loans extended in 1986 and 1987 were frequently undertaken to take advantage of the decline in long-term interest rates, whereas loans in 1988 and 1989 may have been undertaken more frequently to extract equity from the property.

A dummy variable indicating that the property is a condominium (CONDO) also fails to show a consistent relationship with default likelihoods over the four cohorts. Note, as well, that a variable indicating that the loan was "bought down" (BUYDOWN) exhibits no consistent relationship with the likelihood of default. In contrast, the coefficients of the dummy variable indicating that the loan was processed through direct endorsement (DIRECT) do indicate a strong and highly significant relationship with default likelihoods. Confirming previous research, the negative coefficients of this variable imply that such loans entail less default risk than loans processed directly through HUD.

The variable SHRTMOR is a dummy variable indicating that the term of the mortgage is less than the traditional 30 years. As predicted, the coefficients of this variable are negative and significant in all four cohorts, implying that, perhaps because of the faster rate at which equity is built, such mortgages entail a lower probability of default than do 30-year mortgages, all else equal.

The value of the property serving as collateral for the loan is also introduced in the analysis through the use of two variables: HVAL indicates the value of the property, whereas HVAL2 is simply the square of this variable. The negative and generally significant coefficients of HVAL and the positive and generally significant coefficients of HVAL2 imply that default likelihoods generally decline with the value of the house; however, this relationship becomes less pronounced for the higher valued houses.

With loans for properties in suburban areas constituting the omitted category, the coefficients of URBAN indicate that, all else equal, loans originated in 1987 and 1988 for properties located in center cities were significantly more risky than loans made for suburban properties. No such relationship is observed, however, for the 1986 and 1989 cohorts. The coefficients of RURAL also suggest that rural loans entailed higher default likelihoods than did similar suburban loans in the 1987 and 1989 cohorts, but this does not seem to be the case for the 1986 and 1988 cohorts.

Among borrower characteristics, the variable COMP is a dummy variable indicating that certain compensating factors (such as an excellent credit history, a long history of continuous employment, or substantial savings) were employed in considering whether to approve the loan. This variable was missing in the 1986 cohort and, as indicated, is not statistically associated with the likelihood of default in the other three cohorts.

Additional regressions were also run using only marginally qualified borrowers; that is, only those borrowers that required compensating factors (as indicated by the compensation codes carried on the FHA data files) for credit approval. These runs revealed that a variable indicating excellent credit history is associated with reduced default rates. Also, the inclusion of this credit-history variable did not alter in any material way the relationship found between minority status and the likelihood of default.

The coefficients of FIRSTBUY indicate first-time home buyers were more likely to default, all else equal, than were other borrowers in the 1987 through 1989 cohorts, but no statistically significant relationship was observed for the 1986 cohort. The coefficients of NEW suggest that loans for newly constructed homes were less likely to default than loans for other homes in the 1989 cohort, but no statistically significant relationship was observed for the earlier three cohorts.

The borrower's marital status is indicated by three dummy variables: CBUNMARD indicates the presence of an unmarried coborrower, whereas SINGLEM and SINGLEF indicate that the borrower is a single male and female, respectively. Married borrowers represent the omitted category. The coefficients of CBUNMARD suggest that unmarried coborrowers are not statistically different from married borrowers in terms of default likelihoods. Single males appear to be more likely to default than married borrowers, while single females appear to be significantly less likely to default in all four cohorts. Next, note that in all four cohorts, default likelihoods unambiguously increase with the number of dependents (other than the spouse) in the borrower's household (DEPNUM). This may result because of the added claims on income associated with higher numbers of dependents in the household. The borrower's status as a self-employed person (SELFEMP), however, does not appear to be significantly related to default likelihoods in the three cohorts for which this information is available.

To account for possible nonlinearities in the relationship between the borrower's liquid assets and the likelihood of default, a variable indicating the borrower's liquid assets (LQASS) and the square of the variable (LQASS2) were both employed. The significant negative coefficient of LQASS and the significant positive coefficient of LQASS2 in each cohort indicate, not surprisingly, that the likelihood of default declines with an increase in the borrower's liquid assets, but that this effect tends to become less pronounced as the amount of the borrower's liquid assets increases.

The variable NOCBINC indicates that there is either no coborrower or that no coborrower income is available for payments on the loan, whereas PCBINC indicates the percentage of the combined income that comes from a coborrower. Whereas the coefficients of NOCBINC are not consistent across cohorts, the coefficients of PCBINC are negative in all cohorts and are statistically significant in all cohorts but 1987. This suggests, in general, that larger percentages of coborrower income entail lower default likelihoods. Diversification benefits associated with the existence of two separate incomes may be a possible explanation.

To capture the relationship between age of the borrower and default likelihoods, dummy variables were defined for three different age ranges: less than 25 years (AGE < 25); between 25 and 35 years (AGE 25–35); and between 35 and 45 years (AGE 35–45), with ages higher than 45 representing the omitted category. Coefficients of these dummy variables suggest that borrowers between the ages of 25 and 35 exhibit lower likelihoods of default, all else equal, than do other borrowers. This finding is contrary to expectations, given the relative lack of credit and employment histories—and hence the higher a priori risk—attached to younger borrowers.

As with liquid assets, we allow for nonlinearities in the relationship between borrower's qualifying income and the performance of the loan. Thus, we introduced in each estimation a variable indicating the borrower's income (INCOME) and a variable indicating the square of that variable (INCOME2). Although results are not identical across cohorts, the negative coefficients of INCOME, together with the typically positive and highly significant coefficients of INCOME2 imply, not surprisingly, that the likelihood of default declines as the income of the borrower rises. However, this relationship becomes less pronounced as income rises.

The variable POTHINC indicates the amount of nonsalary income as a percentage of the total income of the borrower. The coefficients of this variable are positive in all four cohorts and are highly significant in three of them, implying, as hypothesized, that default likelihoods rise with the importance of nonsalary income, all else equal.

Having accounted for an expansive set of borrower and loan characteristics, the remaining individual level variables relate to the borrowers' race. Dummy variables indicating that the borrower is African American (BLACK), American Indian or Alaskan Native (AMIND), Asian (ASIAN), or Hispanic (HISPANIC) are included, with whites representing the omitted category. Because, for a number of loans, information on race was not coded, we also included a dummy variable indicating that the borrower's race is unknown (RMISSING). The positive and highly significant coefficients of BLACK for each of the four cohorts imply that, after controlling for the influence of the other variables in the analysis, black borrowers exhibit a higher likelihood of default than do white borrowers. Further, the inclusion of the other variables in the analysis, as described earlier, has little effect on the differential default rates of whites and blacks. As shown in table 6.4, black borrowers in the 1986 sample have a cumulative default rate of 13.3 percent, over 7 percentage points higher than the default rate for white borrowers in the 1986 sample. The predicted effect of race in the logit model for 1986 is only slightly less, with blacks predicted to have default rates about 6.5 percentage points above that for whites, even after controlling for LTV ratios and other loan and borrower characteristics. Other years show similar results, although cumulative default rates are somewhat lower. Interpretations of these results as they relate to hypotheses of discrimination in mortgage lending are discussed in the subsection following.

The coefficient of the dummy variable indicating that the borrower is an American Indian or Alaskan Native is positive for all four cohorts but is statistically significant only in the case of the 1986 cohort. The coefficient of the dummy variable indicating that the borrower is an Asian American is statistically significant only in the case of the 1989 cohort, with a sign indicating a lower likelihood of default relative to a white borrower, all else equal. The coefficients of the dummy variable indicating a Hispanic borrower imply that Hispanic borrowers are statistically indistinguishable from white borrowers in terms of their likelihood of defaulting on mortgage obligations. The 1988 cohort, however, which exhibits a weakly significant positive coefficient, is an exception. Finally, the coefficients of the dummy variable indicating that the borrower cannot be identified by race are positive for all four cohorts and are statistically significant in the case of the 1986 and 1988 cohorts.

As noted earlier, FHA loans may be underwritten either by HUD or by private-sector lenders under the direct endorsement program. Because these two alternatives involve different types of decision makers in determining who qualifies for a loan, we further investigated the relationship between default likelihoods and race by conducting separate analyses of the performance of loans processed by HUD, as distinct from those processed under the direct endorsement program. This analysis revealed that the signs and statistical significance of the coefficient of BLACK are similar, regardless of whether HUD or a direct endorser processed the loan (results not shown). Thus, the higher likelihoods of default observed for black borrowers apparently are robust to whether the underwriter is a government employee or a private-sector agent.

As a further check on the robustness of the results, we evaluated the impact of urban location on racial default patterns. Specifically, separate models were estimated for borrowers in urban, suburban, and rural locations. The results indicated that default patterns for urban and suburban borrowers are similar. In particular, black borrowers exhibit significantly higher default rates in both urban and suburban locations in each year. The results for rural borrowers, where we had far fewer observations, were less clear.

Although these findings regarding the coefficients of BLACK are not consistent with the prediction implied by models of uneconomic (prejudicial) discrimination as previously outlined, it should be noted that potentially important explanatory variables have yet to be accounted for in the analysis. Important among these are variables describing the rate of housing appreciation in the area in which the property is located, income volatility, and better indications of the borrower's past credit history. Without including improved measures of these effects, we cannot reach definitive conclusions about the implications of this research for the issue of discrimination. Further research will include additional information about loans and borrowers in order to provide a clearer indication of the effect of race and neighborhood location on default.

Finally, as noted earlier, dummy variables indicating the state in which the loan is made were included in all estimations, but not reported. These variables seem to reflect the tendency of states with weaker economies (Texas during the oil bust, for example) to exhibit higher rates of loan default. As mentioned previously, they also may capture important differences in state laws and regulations applying to foreclosure requirements.

Table 6.7 presents the results of logit regressions that differ from those presented in table 6.6, in that 11 variables describing the demographic and economic characteristics of the census tract in which each property is located are added to the list of explanatory variables. These regressions are presented separately, in part because of the substantial number of observations that are lost as a result of including census-tract characteristics.

It is important to note that inclusion of these additional variables (shown at the bottom of table 6.7) for the most part does not appear to change the coefficients of the other explanatory variables in any material way. The most notable exception concerns the coefficients of CONDO, which now suggest a clearer tendency for loans on such properties to exhibit greater likelihoods of default. Also, inclusion of these variables reveals a more consistent tendency for loans used to refinance existing mortgages to perform more poorly.

As for the coefficients of the individual census-tract variables, only a few consistent patterns are found. Focusing first on neighborhood racial composition, we find some evidence of a positive relationship between the proportion of the neighborhood population that is black and the likelihood of default in the 1987 and 1988 cohorts. However, the coefficient of CTBLACK is negative and statistically insignificant in the 1989 cohort. A more consistent pattern emerges in the case of Asians and Hispanics, since the coefficients of CTASIAN and CTHISPANIC are negative in all three cohorts and significant for two of them.

As indicated by the coefficients of CTINCOME, the relative income of the census tract in which the property is located exhibits a highly significant inverse relationship with the likelihood of default, implying that loans on properties located in higher-income census tracts of a metropolitan area are less likely to default. Among the remaining census-tract characteristics, only the median value of owner-occupied properties (CTHVAL) yields consistent and significant results in all years. In particular, the results suggest that properties in neighborhoods with higher median home values perform better over time. This may be due to greater appreciation of properties insured by FHA loans in areas characterized by higher-priced homes. We hope to test this hypothesis in detail when 1990 census tract information is merged into our data files.

Interpretation of Results

This section considers the interpretability of results obtained thus far for the issue of discrimination in mortgage lending. Although some would maintain that evaluation of the relationship between minority status and loan performance can provide a clear indication of the presence of discrimination, the linkage can be fairly complex. To better appreciate the complexities associated with the interpretation of estimation results, table 6.8 presents six possible interpretations of the findings of a mortgage default study.

As table 6.8 indicates, interpreting the findings of a default study such as this one depends on the nature of any existent discrimination as well as the study's ability to control adequately for borrower and locational risk-related characteristics. The taxonomy described in table 6.8 considers, first, the case in which only uneconomic discrimination (or prejudicial discrimination) exists and in which the default study succeeds in accounting for all risk-related characteristics that correlate with minority status. Assuming that minority applicants are subjected to underwriting standards that exceed any objective assessment of default risk, one would expect a loan performance study to find that minority borrowers are less likely to default, controlling for other characteristics. Since we do not find this result in our analysis of FHA loan performance to date, this combination of circumstances should be excluded as a possibility.

The second case described in table 6.8 is consistent with our study finding that blacks are more likely to default, controlling for other risk-related characteristics. In this case, it is assumed that uneconomic discrimination exists, but also that our default study omits variables that correlate positively with both minority status and default. As an example, suppose the default study inadequately accounts for borrower credit history and that, on average, the credit histories of black borrowers are more problematic than those of white borrowers. If this omission more than offsets any reductions in minority default rates owing to discrimination, then minorities would be more likely to default, controlling for those characteristics on which data are available. This explanation may be particularly relevant at this stage of our analysis, in that a number of potentially important variables have yet to be adequately accounted for. Specifically, in future analyses, we will seek to improve the accounting for borrower credit history, borrower income stability, and neighborhood housing price appreciation.

Table 6.8 IMPLIED RESULTS IN MORTGAGE-DEFAULT STUDIES, UNDER VARIOUS SCENARIOS

The Implied Findings for a Default Study Depend on Nature of the Discrimination and the Success of the Study in Accounting for Other Characteristics	
Condition	Implied Default-Study Finding
"Uneconomic discrimination":	
1. "Uneconomic discrimination" (or prejudicial discrimination) exists such that minority applicants are subjected to an underwriting standard in excess of any objective assessment of default risk. The default study accounts for all relevant risk-related characteristics that correlate with minority status.	Minority borrowers are *less* likely to default, controlling for other characteristics.
2. "Uneconomic discrimination" exists, but the default study omits at least one variable that is positively correlated with minority status and default. This omission is important enough to more than compensate for the discrimination-induced lower minority default rates that would otherwise be found. (Less important omissions would not alter case 1.)	Minority borrowers are *more* likely to default, controlling for other characteristics.
No discrimination:	
3. Discrimination does not exist and the default study accounts for all relevant risk-related characteristics.	Minority borrowers exhibit the *same* likelihood of default as do nonminority borrowers, controlling for other characteristics.
4. Discrimination does not exist, but the default study omits at least one variable that is positively correlated with minority status and default.	Minority borrowers are *more* likely to default, controlling for other characteristics.
"Economic discrimination":	
5. "Economic discrimination" exists. This means that the lender uses minority status as a proxy for unobservable (or costly to obtain) characteristics indicating higher default risk. The higher standard required of minorities, however, is not enough to completely account for their higher default likelihoods attributable to these unobservable characteristics.	Minority borrowers are *more* likely to default, controlling for other characteristics.
6. "Economic discrimination" exists. The lender uses minority status as a proxy for unobservable characteristics indicating higher default risk. The higher standard required of minorities accurately accounts for these unobservable characteristics.	Minority borrowers exhibit the *same* likelihood of default as do nonminority characteristics.

The next two cases in table 6.8 pertain to the situation in which discrimination (either uneconomic or economic) does not in fact exist. In the third case, the default study is further presumed to account for all relevant risk-related characteristics that correlate with race. Under these circumstances, a default study should find no significant difference in the default likelihoods of the different racial groups, controlling for other characteristics. Although this case may possibly be relevant to our findings regarding other minorities, it is clearly not applicable in the case of blacks, since blacks are observed to have higher default likelihoods, controlling for other factors. The fourth case similarly assumes no discrimination, but further presumes that the default study omits variables that are positively correlated with both minority status and default. Under these circumstances, a default study should find that minorities are more likely than nonminorities to default, controlling for other factors. This case is similarly consistent with our findings regarding the differences in default likelihoods among white and black FHA borrowers.

The final two cases presented in table 6.8 pertain to the situation in which economic (but not uneconomic) discrimination is present. In the case of economic discrimination, the lender uses minority status as a proxy for unobservable (or costly to obtain) characteristics that correlate positively with both minority status and default risk. In the fifth case, the higher qualification standard required of minorities (because of their higher level of credit risk, controlling for observable factors) is inadequate to completely account for their higher default likelihoods attributable to unobservable characteristics. Under these circumstances, a default study would find that minority borrowers are more likely to default than are nonminorities, controlling for other characteristics. Finally, the sixth case is equivalent to the fifth case, except that the higher standard required of minorities by lenders now completely accounts for the unobservable risk characteristics associated with minority loan performance. In this case, a default study would find no significant differences in default likelihoods after controlling for other relevant factors.

As this list of possible scenarios suggests, results obtained thus far as they apply to black borrowers are consistent with several different possibilities. Specifically, cases two, four, and five in table 6.8 are all potential explanations for our results as they apply to black borrowers. Since these cases are consistent with the alternatives of no discrimination, uneconomic discrimination, or economic discrimination, results obtained thus far do not allow us to draw definitive conclusions regarding the issue of mortgage lending discrimination as it applies to blacks. It is interesting to note, however, that whatever the explanation for the statistical results reported to date, the same pattern seems to hold, regardless of whether the underwriting is done by HUD or the private sector. We hope that future research incorporating more information on potentially important factors related to loan performance will allow us to draw more definitive conclusions regarding discrimination in mortgage lending.

SUMMARY

Some observers have recently argued that alleged discrimination in mortgage lending may be revealed in the performance of loans extended to different racial or ethnic groups. Specifically, it is hypothesized that systematic racial discrimination owing to lender bias may result in lenders holding minority applicants or applicants from minority neighborhoods to loan qualification standards that far exceed those required by objective assessments of default risk. This implies that discriminatory behavior would likely result in higher returns to home loans as evidenced by lower default rates or smaller dollar losses among minority borrowers or neighborhoods than that observed for nonminority borrowers or neighborhoods.

This study evaluates the default risk characteristics and the performance of FHA-insured, single-family residential mortgages. In the context of a multivariate statistical model, the study examines the relationship between a wide variety of loan and borrower characteristics and the default experience of FHA loans. In so doing, it assesses any residual effects of borrower race or neighborhood racial composition on the likelihood of loan default. The analysis is undertaken using formerly unavailable individual loan records from HUD that cover loans originated from 1986 through 1989.

The empirical analysis identifies a number of factors that significantly affect the probability of a loan default. Among the different characteristics of loans examined, higher LTV ratios and longer terms to maturity are associated with higher default rates. Further, loans processed under the Direct Endorsement program appear to be less likely to default than loans processed by HUD. Among the different borrower characteristics, higher amounts of liquid assets, higher house values, fewer dependents, single female borrowers, and borrowers between the ages of 25 and 35 all are associated with lower default probabilities.

In terms of the race or ethnic background of the borrower, preliminary results indicate a higher likelihood of default on the part of black households (compared to white households), whereas the likelihood of default for Hispanic, Asian, and American Indian households does not appear to differ significantly from that of white households. With regard to the neighborhood characteristics included in our analysis to date, we find that loans on properties located in the higher-income census tracts of a metropolitan area and loans in tracts with higher median home values are less likely to default. At this stage of our analysis, we find that the proportion of census-tract populations accounted for by blacks is not strongly and consistently related to the likelihood of loan default, whereas higher population proportions accounted for by Hispanics and Asians appear to be associated with lower likelihoods of default.

As described in table 6.8, the interpretation of findings with respect to the relationship between race and default probabilities as they pertain to discrimination is not straightforward. The results obtained here may or may not reflect discrimination in the mortgage lending process. To further enhance the assessment of discrimination in mortgage lending, our future research will focus on issues related to possible omitted variables and will analyze the actual loss experiences and expected returns to lenders in the FHA loan market.

Note

We are grateful to the Office of Policy Development and Research, U.S. Department of Housing and Urban Development, for providing the FHA mortgage data utilized in this research. Special thanks go to William Shaw, of HUD's Office of Housing, for his assistance. The views expressed here are those of the authors and do not necessarily reflect those of the Board of Governors of the Federal Reserve System or members of its staff.

References

Barth, James R., Joseph J. Cordes, and Anthony M. J. Yezer. 1979. "Financial Institution Regulations, Redlining and Mortgage Markets." In *The Regulation of Financial Institutions*, Conference Series 21 (101–43). Melvin Village, N.H.: Federal Reserve Bank of Boston and National Science Foundation, October.

Becker, Gary S. 1971 [1957]. *The Economics of Discrimination* (2nd ed.). Chicago: University of Chicago Press.

Campbell, T., and J. Dietrich. 1983. "The Determinants of Default on Conventional Residential Mortgages." *Journal of Finance* 38(5): 1569–81.

Canner, Glenn B. 1982. "Redlining and Federal Legislative Response." *Staff Study* (Board of Governors of the Federal Reserve System) 121(October).

Canner, Glenn B., and Stuart A. Gabriel. 1992. "Market Segmentation and Lender Specialization in the Primary and Secondary Mortgage Markets." *Housing Policy Debate* 3(2): 241–329.

Canner, Glenn B., and Dolores S. Smith. 1991. "Home Mortgage Disclosure Act: Expanded Data on Residential Lending." *Federal Reserve Bulletin* 77(November): 859–81.

———. 1992. "Expanded HMDA Data on Residential Lending: One Year Later." *Federal Reserve Bulletin* 78(November): 801–24.

Canner, Glenn B., Stuart A. Gabriel, and J. Michael Woolley. 1991. "Race, Default Risk, and Mortgage Lending: A Study of the FHA and Conventional Loan Markets." *Southern Economic Journal* 58(July): 249–61.

Clauretie, Terrence M. 1987. "The Impact of Interstate Foreclosure Cost Differences and the Value of Mortgages on Default Rates." *AREUEA Journal* 15(3): 152–67.

Clauretie, Terrence M., and Thomas N. Herzog. 1989. "How State Laws Affect Foreclosure Costs." *Secondary Mortgage Markets* (Spring): 25–28.

Dedman, Bill. 1988. "The Color of Money: Home Mortgage Practices Discriminate against Blacks." Parts 1–4. *Atlanta Journal-Constitution*, May 1–16.

Evans, R. D., B. A. Maris, and R. I. Weinstein. 1984. "Expected Loss and Mortgage Default Risk." *Quarterly Journal of Business and Economics* 24: 75–92.

Foster, C., and R. Van Order. 1984. "An Option Based Model of Mortgage Default." *Housing Finance Review* 3(4): 351–72.

Giliberto, S. M., and A. L. Houston. 1989. "Relocation Opportunities and Mortgage Default." *AREUEA Journal* 17(1): 55–69.

ICF, Inc. 1989. *The Characteristics of HUD-Processed and Direct Endorsement Mortgages*. Report prepared for U.S. Department of Housing and Urban Development. Fairfax, Va.: Author, December 18.

Kau, J., D. Keenan, and T. Kim. 1991. "Default Probabilities for Mortgages." Department of Insurance, Legal Studies and Real Estate, Terry College of Business, University of Georgia. Photocopy.

Lang, William W., and Leonard J. Nakamura. 1993. "A Model of Redlining." *Journal of Urban Economics* 33: 223–34.

Munnell, Alicia H., Lynn E. Browne, James McEneaney, and Geoffrey M. B. Tootell. 1992. "Mortgage Lending in Boston: Interpreting HMDA Data." Federal Reserve Bank of Boston Working Paper 92-07. Boston: Federal Reserve Bank of Boston, October.

Munnell, Alicia H., Geoffrey M. B. Tootell, Lynn E. Browne, and James McEneaney. 1996. "Mortgage Lending in Boston: Interpreting HMDA Data." *American Economic Review*. Forthcoming.

Neal, Susan. 1989. "Review of the Mortgage Default Literature." Working Paper, Housing Finance Analysis Division, U.S. Department of Housing and Urban Development, Washington, D.C. Photocopy.

Peterson, Richard L. 1981. "An Investigation of Sex Discrimination in Commercial Banks' Direct Consumer Lending." *Bell Journal of Economics* 12(Autumn): 547–61.

Quercia, Roberto G., and Michael A. Stegman. 1992. "Residential Mortgage Default: A Review of the Literature." *Journal of Housing Research* 3(2): 341–79.

Quigley, J. M., and R. Van Order. 1991. "Defaults on Mortgage Obligations and Capital Requirements for U.S. Savings Institutions: A Policy Perspective." *Journal of Public Economics* 44(3): 353–70.

"Race for Money, The." 1988. *Detroit Free Press*, Parts 1–3, June 24–27.

Stiglitz, Joseph, and A. Weiss. 1981. "Credit Rationing in Markets with Imperfect Information." *American Economic Review* 71(June): 393–410.

Vandell, K., and T. Thibodeau. 1985. "Estimation of Mortgage Defaults Using Disaggregate Loan History Data." *AREUEA Journal* 13(3): 292–316.

Van Order, Robert, Ann-Margaret Westin, and Peter Zorn. 1993. "Effects of the Racial Composition of Neighborhoods on Default, and Implications for Racial Discrimination in Mortgage Markets." Paper presented at meetings of American Economics Association, Jan. 8, Anaheim, Calif.

Williamson, S. 1986. "Costly Monitoring, Financial Intermediation, and Equilibrium Credit Rationing." *Journal of Monetary Economics* 18: 159–79.

Chapter Seven

MORTGAGE DISCRIMINATION AND FHA LOAN PERFORMANCE

James A. Berkovec, Glenn B. Canner, Stuart A. Gabriel, and Timothy H. Hannan[1]

Many recent studies of mortgage lending activity have documented large and persistent racial disparities, including the provision of information to prospective home loan applicants, mortgage loan instrument selection, and the loan application decision process. (See, for example, Board of Governors of the Federal Reserve System 1991; Canner, Gabriel, and Woolley 1991; and Munnell, Browne, McEneaney, and Tootell 1992, hereafter referred to as MBMT). For the most part, findings of those analyses indicate significant race effects that are not well explained by objective factors. Hence the findings have led to allegations of widespread racial discrimination in mortgage lending.

This article seeks to evaluate discrimination in home mortgage originations by examining the performance of mortgage loan portfolios. This approach follows from the theoretical foundations of the economics of discrimination (Becker 1971), which are based on the premise that biased lenders will require higher expected profits from loans to minority applicants. As applied to lending by Richard Peterson (1981), this premise implies that biased lenders may hold minority applicants to more stringent underwriting standards than those required for other applicants.[2] Thus discrimination results in lower expected default costs and higher expected profits for loans originated for marginally qualified minority mortgage borrowers in comparison with those observed for marginally qualified nonminority borrowers.

It is important to note that this theory assumes that discrimination against minorities occurs at the margin, affecting those who are near the borderline for creditworthiness, and excludes the possibility that the discrimination is unrelated to credit risk.[3] The theory predicts that this discrimination changes loan performance at the margin. Thus, inferences about discrimination that are made from loan performance data must distinguish between *average* and *marginal* loan performance. As noted by Peterson (1981) and by Ferguson and Peters

(1995), simple comparisons of average loan performance between two groups of borrowers can be misleading if the groups do not exhibit similar distributions of expected returns in the absence of discrimination. If, for example, the proportion of highly qualified nonminority borrowers is substantially higher than that of highly qualified minority borrowers, default rates of nonminority borrowers—observed without controlling for other determinants of credit quality—would be lower than those associated with minority borrowers. This finding, however, would simply reflect the differences in average creditworthiness for the two groups of borrowers and would not necessarily indicate differential underwriting standards.[4]

Our study employs a rich Federal Housing Administration (FHA) data set to evaluate the determinants of loan performance as measured by both the likelihood of default and the losses that occur in the event of default. The data consist of a large number of individual loan records recently made available by the U.S. Department of Housing and Urban Development (HUD). That information is augmented with 1980 and 1990 census tract characteristics to account for neighborhood location attributes associated with default risk. These data are particularly well suited to the investigation, given the vast array of detail concerning characteristics of loans, borrowers, and neighborhoods in which the homes are located.

The following section of this article presents the theoretical foundations for the tests of discrimination in mortgage loan performance as they apply to the likelihood of default. The section entitled "Discrimination and Loan Performance" provides a description of the data used in the analysis and empirical specifications of the models. The section entitled "Data and Model Specification" presents the results of model estimations, and the final section provides a summary of the findings.

DISCRIMINATION AND LOAN PERFORMANCE

The starting point for our analysis is a simple rationing model of loan origination. One must assume that lenders observe a creditworthiness index (C) for each loan applicant. For our purposes we assume that there is a direct relationship between the level of C for an applicant and the default risk of that applicant. The applicant's default risk is represented by an expected default probability, D(C), where $0 < D(C) < 1$ and $D' < 0$ for all values of C. Default probabilities are assumed to vary only with C. No other observable characteristics of the applicant, including race, affect default risk.

As with most mortgage lending studies, we assume that lenders do not price risk directly but grant loans only when expected default probabilities (or expected default costs) are below a certain level. Loan allocation is then based on observed values of C. Our model allows for three possible outcomes to a request for mortgage credit: Lenders approve conventional loans for the most creditworthy applicants, lenders reject loan requests from the least creditworthy applicants, or lenders allocate FHA-insured loans to applicants whose requests rank among the intermediate values of C.

In this framework, discrimination affects marginal applicants, through the use of a higher loan qualification standard for minorities than for comparable nonminorities. The outcomes of underwriting decisions on loan applications are determined as follows:

$$\text{If: } C > A + B, \text{ Then: CONVENTIONAL LOAN;} \tag{8.1}$$

$$\text{If: } A + B > C > F + B', \text{ Then: FHA LOAN;} \tag{8.2}$$

$$\text{If: } C < F + B', \text{ Then: REJECTED APPLICATION,} \tag{8.3}$$

where A represents the minimum level of creditworthiness required for approval of a conventional loan, and F is the minimum level necessary for an FHA-insured loan. The values of B and B', assumed to be positive, indicate the degree of discrimination faced by the applicant. Discrimination can occur at either one or both of the two margins. Greater values of B represent increased discrimination in the conventional loan market, while higher levels of B' indicate increased bias in the underwriting of FHA loans.

If C were observed directly, discrimination could easily be detected by comparing the minimum levels of C for accepted loans for the borrower groups within each loan type. One could also compare maximum levels of C for conventional loan rejections to identify B', or FHA loans to identify B'.

However, outsiders cannot observe the creditworthiness index directly. Our assumption is that outside analysts observe instead a set of characteristics of the loan and applicant that are related to C. Formally, this is expressed as:

$$C = X\beta + \epsilon, \tag{8.4}$$

where X is a vector of observed characteristics, β is a vector of known constants, and ϵ is an error term observed only to the lender. In this framework borrowers with the same observable characteristics X will have different default risks, and get different receptions from lenders, because of differences in the unobservable ϵ. As lenders observe ϵ, the highest default risk applicants at every level of X will be rejected.

In the presence of discrimination, the rejection probability of an applicant with characteristics X is given by:

$$d(X) = \int_{\epsilon < F - X\beta + B'} f(\epsilon)d\epsilon \tag{8.5}$$

and the probability of approval for an FHA-insured loan is given by:

$$P(X) = \int_{F - X\beta + B'}^{A - X\beta + B} f(\epsilon)d\epsilon \tag{8.6}$$

The observed default rate of FHA borrowers at a given level of X is the probability of default given that the loan was accepted by the lender. This conditional probability is defined by:

$$\begin{aligned} \text{Prob(Default|FHA)} &= \text{Prob(Default and FHA)/Prob(FHA)} \\ &= \int_{F - X\beta + B'}^{A - X\beta + B} D(X\beta + \epsilon)f(\epsilon)d\epsilon/P(X) \end{aligned} \tag{8.7}$$

Let $R(X,B,B')$ represent this conditional probability. It can be shown that R is always decreasing in B and B'.[5] As a result, at every level of observed characteristics X, a group adversely affected by discrimination should, all else being equal, have lower default rates than other borrowers.[6] In the context of this model, if X contains all characteristics that are important in determining default, ex-ante, discrimination results in lower observed default rates at all values of $X\beta$.[7]

The intuition behind this result is straightforward. Bias that results in setting higher creditworthiness standards for conventional loans pushes the minority borrowers with the highest default risk among conventional borrowers into the FHA group where they are now the lowest-risk borrowers. Thus discrimination causes the average value of ϵ, for every value of $X\beta$, to rise in both the FHA and conventional groups. A similar situation occurs at the other margin, where discrimination results in rejections for what otherwise would be the highest-risk minority FHA borrowers. Again, bias results in improving the relative quality of the FHA minority borrower pool.

This result is the basis of our empirical work on default risk. Conditioned on all observable characteristics, discrimination at the margin results in lower average default rates for every quality level of borrower. Assuming that the distributions of unobservable factors are equal, discrimination in underwriting standards should be revealed by lower ex post default rates for the affected group of borrowers.

DATA AND MODEL SPECIFICATION

The principal data utilized in this study are drawn from records of FHA-insured single-family mortgage loans originated during the three-year period 1987–1989. Information about the status and characteristics of the FHA loans is drawn from two files maintained by HUD: the F42 EDS Case History File and the F42 BIA Composite File.[8] The former provides information on the status of each FHA-insured loan through the first quarter of 1993. The Composite File contains information on loan and borrower characteristics.

Our analysis uses a sample of FHA-insured loans originated during the 1987–1989 period. The full set of loans could not be used, because detailed borrower and loan characteristics were available for only a random sample of loans originated in each year. Sample size was further reduced by the omission of loans lacking valid census tract identifiers or those missing other data. The final estimation sample used in this analysis included nearly 220,000 loans.

Although the FHA database distinguishes among a variety of instances in which mortgage terminations occur, in this analysis we evaluate the likelihood of mortgage terminations resulting from borrower default, defined as lender foreclosures and other cases in which borrowers convey title to the lender in lieu of foreclosure. Only defaults that had occurred by the first quarter of 1993 are observed in the data.

The multivariate analysis of default risk employs logit regressions to estimate the contribution of the various loan, borrower, and location characteristics to the likelihood of default. For each of the annual cohorts, we estimate:

$$P = \exp[\gamma X]/(1 + \exp[\gamma X]), \tag{8.8}$$

where P represents the probability of default for a loan with characteristics X, which is a vector of the attributes of the loan, including borrower and location characteristics. The empirical model estimates conditional default probabilities, given that the loan was approved. The underwriting screen used in the loan approval process will, in general, alter the coefficient estimates. Thus the vector of estimated coefficient values, γ, indicates the effect of each characteristic on the conditional default probability, not the "true" underlying default risk. This is consistent with our theoretical model, where discrimination affects the conditional default probability.

A wide variety of loan and borrower characteristics are included in the model (as described in Berkovec et al. 1995). Also included are census tract measures drawn from the 1980 and 1990 decennial censuses. In the estimations presented here, 1980 census data are used to describe levels of neighborhood-specific characteristics, and changes in these characteristics are measured using both 1980 and 1990 census data. Specifically, we consider the racial composition of the neighborhood, as measured by the proportion of the population that was black (CTBLACK), American Indian or Alaskan Native (CTAMIND), Asian (CTASIAN), Hispanic (CTHISPANIC), and other (CTMISS). Other census tract characteristics controlled for are neighborhood median family income level as a proportion of median family income for the entire metropolitan area (CTINCOME), median value of owner-occupied housing units (CTHVAL), proportion of housing units that were vacant (CTVACRAT), median age of housing units (CTMEDAGE), area unemployment rate (CTUNEMP), and proportion of housing in the neighborhood accounted for by rental units (CT-RENTRATE).[9] State-specific dummy variables are also included to further control for the effects of location, including differences in foreclosure laws (Clauretie and Herzog 1989).

EMPIRICAL RESULTS

Definitions of the variables used in the analysis are presented in table 7.1, while information on the means and standard deviations of the variables is presented in table 7.2. Results of the logit analysis are presented in table 7.3.

In keeping with program objectives, the FHA program tends to serve relatively high-risk borrowers, and the vast majority of FHA-insured loans entail very high loan-to-value ratios. More than 80 percent of the loans in the sample had loan-to-value ratios exceeding 95 percent. Similarly, the debt obligation ratios of FHA borrowers in the sample are high, averaging about 40 percent for the ratio of total debt payments to income and about 21 percent for the ratio of housing expense payments to income.

First-time homebuyers and moderate-income borrowers comprise a large proportion of all FHA borrowers. Minorities, particularly blacks and Hispanics, are well represented in each annual cohort. A full 10 percent of FHA borrowers reside in census tracts in which minorities constitute more than one-half of the population, and nearly one-half of FHA borrowers reside in neighborhoods whose median family income is less than the median for the metropolitan area in which the neighborhood is located.

Simple bivariate correlations suggest that default probabilities differ significantly by loan, borrower, and location characteristics. For example, higher default rates appear to be associated with higher loan-to-value ratios, lower incomes and home values, and smaller loan amounts. Among racial and ethnic groups, the highest rates of loan default are associated with black borrowers, while Asian borrowers exhibit the lowest default rates. Default rates are also higher among borrowers residing in predominantly minority neighborhoods.[10]

Table 7.3 presents results of logit estimations of the relationship between the probability of default and a selected subset of independent variables.[11] Results are provided separately for loans originated in 1987, 1988, and 1989.

The primary focus of this study is the effect of race and neighborhood characteristics on default, after controlling for other important determinants of risk. These results are discussed here; other coefficient estimates are discussed in Berkovec et al. (1994, 1995).

The residual effect of borrower race on default is estimated by including a series of dummy variables indicating that the borrower is black (BLACK), American Indian or Alaskan Native (AMIND), Asian (ASIAN), or Hispanic (HISPANIC), with whites representing the omitted category. Because information on race was not coded for a number of loans, a dummy variable indicating that the borrower's race or ethnic status is unknown (RMISSING) was also included.

The main result of the study is that, after controlling for the influence of other variables in the analysis, it was found that black borrowers exhibit a significantly higher likelihood of default than do white borrowers. For example, in the 1987 cohort, black borrowers are predicted to have cumulative default rates that are about 2 percentage points higher than those of white borrowers, all else being equal. This differential is smaller than the observed differential in default rates for the 1987 sample, in which the default rate for blacks is 9.0 percent, compared with a default rate for whites of 4.3 percent. Thus approximately one-half of the differential in observed default rates between whites and blacks can be explained by differences in

Table 7.1 DEFINITIONS OF VARIABLES

RMISSING	1 if borrower race is unknown, 0 if known
BLACK	1 if black borrower, 0 if any other race
AMIND	1 if American-Indian borrower, 0 if any other race
ASIAN	1 if Asian borrower, 0 if any other race
HISPANIC	1 if Hispanic borrower, 0 if any other race
LTV	Loan-to-value ratio
INVEST	1 if investment property, 0 if noninvestment property
REFIN	1 if loan is a refinance, 0 if initial financing
CONDO	1 if property is a condominium, 0 if not a condominium
DIRECT	1 if insurance approved under direct endorsement, 0 if not approved under direct endorsement
URBAN	1 if property located in an urban area, 0 if nonurban
RURAL	1 if property located in rural area, 0 if nonrural
SUBURBAN	1 if property located in a suburban area, 0 if nonsuburban
COMP	1 if application indicates compensating factors, 0 if no compensating factors
FIRSTBUY	1 if borrower is a first-time homebuyer, 0 if not a first-time homebuyer
REPEATBUY	1 if borrower is not a first-time homebuyer, 0 if a first-time homebuyer
NEW	1 if property is a new house, 0 if not a new house
CBUNMARD	1 if borrower is not married to coborrower, 0 if borrower and coborrower are married
DEPNUM	Number of dependents (excluding borrower and coborrower)
SELFEMP	1 if borrower is self employed, 0 if otherwise employed
LQASS	Square of the liquid assets
NOCBINC	1 if no coborrower or coborrower income is zero, 0 if coborrower's income is greater than zero
PCBINC	Percent of household income earned by coborrower
LQASS2	Liquid assets available at closing
AGE <25	1 if borrower is under 25 years of age, 0 if older than 25 years
AGE 25-35	1 if borrower is between 25 and 35 years of age, 0 if younger than 25 or older than 35
AGE 35-45	1 if borrower is between 35 and 45 years of age, 0 if younger than 35 or older than 45
BUYDOWN	1 if mortgage interest rate has been bought down by seller, 0 if interest rate has not been bought down
INCOME	Total annual effective family income
INCOME2	Square of the income

other characteristics. Other years show similar results, although cumulative default rates for all racial groups are lower.[12] Except for blacks, no other racial or ethnic group is found to be consistently different from whites in the likelihood of default, once other factors are taken into account.

Table 7.1 DEFINITIONS OF VARIABLES (*continued*)

SHRTMOR	1 if mortgage term is less than 30 years, 0 if term is greater or equal to 30 years
SINGLEM	1 if borrower is male and there is no coborrower, 0 if there is a coborrower
SINGLEF	1 if borrower is female and there is no coborrower, 0 if there is a coborrower
HVAL	Appraised value of the property at time of purchase
HVAL2	HVAL squared
POTHINC	Percent of borrower income that is from other (non-salary)
HEI 20-38	1 if housing expense to income ratio is between .20 and .38, 0 otherwise
HEI 38-50	1 if housing expense to income ratio is between .38 and .50, 0 otherwise
HEI >50	1 if housing expense to income ration is above .50, 0 otherwise
DTI 20-41	1 if total debt to income ratio is between .2 and .41, 0 otherwise
DTI 41-53	1 if total debt to income ratio is between .41 and .53, 0 otherwise
DTI 53-65	1 if total debt to income ratio is between .53 and .65, 0 otherwise
DTI >65	1 if total debt to income ratio is above .65, 0 otherwise
CTBLACK	Black percentage of census tract population
CTAMIND	American Indian/Alaskan Native percentage of census tract population
CTASIAN	Asian percentage of census tract population
CTHISPANIC	Hispanic percentage of census tract population
CTMISS	Percentage of census tract population with race or ethnicity unknown
CTINCOME	Median family income of the census tract as a proportion of the median family income of the metropolitan area as a whole
CTHVAL	Median value of owner-occupied homes in the census tract
CTVACRAT	Percentage of one-to-four family housing units vacant in the census tract
CTMEDAGE	Median age of residential properties in the census tract
CTUNEMP	Unemployment rate of the census tract
CTRENTRATE	Proportion of housing units in the census tract that are rental
CHGMEDV	The change between 1980 and 1990 in the median value of owner-occupied homes in the census tract
HERF	The Hirschmann-Herfindahl index of market concentration, defined as the sum of squared market shares of the number of home purchase loans of lenders in each MSA

As for the coefficients of the census tract variables, only a few consistent patterns are found. Focusing on neighborhood racial composition, we find some evidence of a positive relationship between the proportion of the neighborhood population that is black and the likelihood of default in the 1987 and 1988 cohorts, but the coefficient

Table 7.2 MEANS AND STANDARD DEVIATIONS OF EXPLANATORY VARIABLES

	1987		1988		1989	
	Mean	Standard Deviation	Mean	Standard Deviation	Mean	Standard Deviation
Default Probability	.053		.044		.024	
Loan Characteristics:						
LTV	.971	.083	.979	.078	.975	.079
HEI 20-38	.611	.448	.579	.494	.443	.497
HEI 38-50	.013	.114	.012	.111	.007	.085
HEI 50	.001	.038	.002	.042	.0005	.022
DTI 20-41	.508	.500	.465	.499	.470	.499
DTI 41-53	.196	.397	.250	.433	.441	.469
DTI 53-65	.111	.314	.116	.320	.068	.251
DTI <65	.095	.294	.086	.280	.006	.074
REFIN	.037	.188	.029	.169	.028	.166
CONDO	.040	.197	.048	.213	.061	.240
BUYDOWN			.006	.074	.058	.234
INVEST	.035	.184	.019	.136	.020	.140
HVAL	62,850	20,837	63,016	21,576	67,627	23,622
HVAL2	4.38E9	2.85E9	4.44E9	2.97E9	5.13E9	2.51E9
DIRECT	.972	.165	.964	.186	.948	.221
SHRTMOR	.052	.223	.046	.210	.039	.193
URBAN	.226	.419	.241	.428	.230	.421
RURAL	.023	.150	.023	.149	.018	.133
SUBURBAN	.320	.467	.320	.466	.319	.466
HERF	528	318	546	347	542	360
Borrower Characteristics:						
COMP	.014	.166	.018	.134	.021	.143
FIRSTBUY	.578	.494	.623	.485	.680	.466
REPEATBUY	.204	.403	.203	.402	.260	.439
NEW	.117	.321	.118	.323	.119	.324
CBUNMARD	.033	.177	.037	.190	.141	.348
SINGLEM	.090	.286	.102	.303	.126	.331
SINGLEF	.078	.268	.089	.285	.115	.320
DEPNUM	.903	1.179	.918	1.240	.881	1.164

of CTBLACK is negative and statistically insignificant in the 1989 cohort.[13] A somewhat more consistent pattern emerges with respect to the Asian and Hispanic populations of a neighborhood, since the coefficients of CTASIAN and CTHISPANIC are negative in all three cohorts and statistically significant—at a very modest level—for two of them.

Despite attempts to exploit the FHA data to the extent possible to control for the major determinants of loan performance that may be

Table 7.2 MEANS AND STANDARD DEVIATIONS OF EXPLANATORY VARIABLES (*continued*)

	1987		1988		1989	
	Mean	Standard Deviation	Mean	Standard Deviation	Mean	Standard Deviation
SELFEMP	.001	.031	.002	.039	.001	.028
LQASS	9,103	12,060	8,335	11,394	11,607	18,142
LQASS2	2.26E5	8.42E5	1.99E5	8.34E5	4.64E5	2.214E6
NOCBINC	.461	.498	.446	.497	.459	.498
PCBINC	22.306	23.286	23.057	24.033	22.548	23.290
AGE <25	.190	.392	.201	.401	.187	.390
AGE 25-35	.507	.500	.511	.500	.506	.500
AGE 35-45	.194	.395	.187	.390	.201	.401
INCOME	36,377	15,388	36,689	15,300	39,006	16,989
INCOME2	1.6E3	1.9E3	1.6E3	1.9E3	1.8E3	2.3E3
POTHINC	.057	.118	.057	.120	.057	.116
Borrower Race:						
BLACK	.178	.383	.190	.392	.091	.288
AMIND	.003	.050	.003	.056	.002	.049
ASIAN	.021	.142	.019	.137	.022	.145
HISPANIC	.067	.251	.066	.248	.075	.263
RMISSING	.059	.235	.042	.201	.017	.128
Location Characteristics:						
CTBLACK	.091	.190	.079	.174	.080	.174
CTAMIND	.006	.008	.005	.009	.005	.010
CTASIAN	.015	.025	.014	.025	.013	.028
CTHISPANIC	.072	.130	.063	.116	.057	.108
CTMISS	.024	.029	.022	.028	.021	.031
CTINCOME	102.257	23.708	102.882	22.830	103.880	23.770
CTHVAL	53.877	20.334	53.391	20.072	53.401	20.263
CTVACRAT	.063	.052	.062	.051	.063	.055
CTMEDAGE	19.461	12.678	19.553	12.884	19.338	12.831
CTUNEMP	.063	.037	.061	.036	.060	.036
CTRENTRATE	.276	.160	.267	.155	.265	.157
CHGMEDV	.620	.454	.577	.425	.581	.441
No. of Observations		29,056		79,304		111,596

correlated with race or ethnic status, the possibility that such a variable has been omitted remains a concern. The most obvious candidate for such a variable is the borrower's credit history, found by MBMT to be important in explaining the likelihood of a loan denial in the application decision process. In terms of the specific results

Table 7.3 LOGIT ESTIMATIONS OF THE CUMULATIVE PROBABILITY OF LOAN DEFAULT

	1987 Loans	1988 Loans	1989 Loans
INTERCEPT	−5.1785***	−4.8171***	−6.74***
Loan Characteristics:			
LTV	4.1089***	3.831***	6.1806***
HEI 20-38	0.2461**	0.1334*	0.1990***
HEI 38-50	0.5846*	−0.0482	0.2176
HEI >50	−0.3095	0.1501	1.7305**
DTI 20-41	−0.0989	−0.0725	0.2008
DTI 41-53	−0.2118*	−0.1649*	0.2192
DTI 53-65	−0.1644	0.1202	0.3684*
DTI >65	0.1671	0.1202	0.2383
REFIN	0.4474**	0.2932*	0.4078**
CONDO	0.8118***	0.3334**	0.4086**
BUYDOWN		0.1482	0.0085
INVEST	0.0114	−0.0368	−0.4373
HVAL	−8.7E-6	6.3E-6	−2.2E-5***
HVAL2	1.3E-12	−3.4E-11	1.3E-12***
DIRECT	−0.2547	−0.4353***	−0.6767***
SHRTMOR	−0.7898***	−0.4298***	−0.2726*
URBAN	0.1576*	0.0749	0.0258
RURAL	0.0823	−0.0717	0.1001
HERF ____	−0.0004***	−0.0004***	−0.0004***
Borrower Characteristics:			
COMP	−0.0878	−0.0879	−0.0585
FIRSTBUY	0.0787	0.1930***	0.0985*
NEW	−0.0338	−0.1231*	−0.2177**
CBUNMARD	−0.1945	−0.0956	−0.0219
SINGLEM	−0.0405	0.1326*	0.0753
SINGLEF	−0.2051*	−0.3015***	−0.3636***
SEPNUM	0.1847***	0.1334***	0.1767***
SELFEMP	−0.5437	−0.2557	0.0915
LQASS	−0.0634***	−0.0571***	−0.0214***
LQASS2	0.00056***	0.0004***	0.00011***

obtained, the concern is that if black borrowers on average have worse credit histories than white borrowers, the greater likelihood of default observed for blacks may be attributable to differences in credit histories and may obscure any differential in default rates due to discrimination.

Although we cannot adequately account for credit history in the FHA data, we do attempt to measure the potential bias introduced by

Table 7.3 LOGIT ESTIMATIONS OF THE CUMULATIVE PROBABILITY OF LOAN DEFAULT (continued)

	1987 Loans	1988 Loans	1989 Loans
NOCBINC	0.1261	−0.0477	−0.2499**
PCBINC	0.00022	−0.0024*	−0.0074***
AGE < 25	0.2040*	−0.0463	−0.0400
AGE 25-35	−0.0788	−0.0922	−0.1839*
AGE 35-45	0.0692	0.1195*	−0.0501
INCOME	−0.00183	−0.0175***	−0.0161***
INCOME2	0.00006	0.00009**	0.00008**
POTHINC	0.4822*	0.4906***	0.5796***
Borrower Race:			
BLACK	0.3453***	0.3345***	0.6390***
AMIND	0.3810	−0.1458	0.0171
ASIAN	0.0469	−0.0098	−0.3062
HISPANIC	−0.0613	0.1340*	0.0559
RMISSING	0.0880	0.2327**	0.1948
Location Characteristics:			
CTBLACK	0.3699*	0.4763***	−0.2042
CTAMIND	−5.3305	6.0712*	0.0685
CTASIAN	−13.5250*	−6.1654	−7.6608*
CTHISPANIC	−0.4441	−0.6878***	−0.2121
CTMISS	5.1072	0.5971	2.3171
CTINCOME	−0.0030	−0.0006	−0.0038*
CTHVAL	−2.3E-5***	−2.2E-5***	−8.39E-6***
CTVACRAT	0.3784	0.9834**	0.7769*
CTMEDAGE	−0.00488	−0.0049*	−0.0004
CTUNEMP	0.9091	−0.4423	−1.2343
CTRENTRATE	0.3022	−0.0332	−0.3064*
CHGMEDV	−0.2823**	−0.1173	0.1966***
No. of Observations	29,056	79,304	111,596

Note: The symbols *, **, and *** denote statistical significance at the 90, 99, and 99.9 percent levels, respectively.

its omission from the model, as described in Berkovec et al. (1994). Our findings suggest that the coefficient of BLACK is systematically biased upward—by as much as 40 percent—by the omission of credit history information. However, this is not enough to reverse the sign of the coefficient or influence its statistical significance.

Further checks on the robustness of the main results are described in Berkovec et al. (1994, 1995). These tests included separating the data into subsamples based on levels of risk or values of exogenous variables, with default models estimated separately for each subsample. The results indicate that the finding of higher default rates for black borrowers is not sensitive to a specific selection of data. Black borrowers exhibit significantly higher default rates in virtually all subsamples.

Data on the dollar value of losses are also examined (Berkovec et al. 1995). These results indicate that loss rates after default also tend to be higher for black borrowers. Differences in loss rates from default do not counteract the racial differences in default rates. Black borrowers appear to have higher overall default costs relative to other borrowers, conditioned on available loan characteristics.

SUMMARY

Recent years have witnessed widespread allegations of racial discrimination in mortgage lending. A model of discrimination in credit markets suggests that discrimination carried out by setting higher qualification standards for minority applicants or applicants from minority neighborhoods may be revealed in differential performance of loans extended to these groups. This predicted effect of discrimination is the basis of the empirical tests used in this analysis.

The empirical results do not support a finding of widespread racial bias in mortgage lending. The main empirical finding is that, after controlling for a wide variety of loan-, borrower-, and property-related characteristics, default rates for black borrowers are higher than those for white borrowers. This finding is the opposite of the prediction of the model for lender bias against black borrowers.

Although the empirical finding of higher default rates for blacks in the FHA data appears to be quite robust, conclusions about discrimination are subject to several important caveats. First, omitted variables may bias the results away from finding the expected performance effects from discrimination.[14] While we have sought to exploit the data as fully as possible in order to account for all relevant determinants of default likelihoods and losses, it is likely that some variables were omitted. We have attempted to estimate the magnitude of bias caused by the lack of credit history information in our data. Results do not appear to be altered substantively by the omission of credit history. However, this conclusion is tentative, and it is still possible that omitted variables, correlated with race or ethnicity, could affect the results.

Another caveat is that the basic theoretical prediction that discrimination results in better observed relative loan performance depends on the assumption that lending bias takes the form of different standards of creditworthiness for different groups. Other forms of discrimination that do not alter the distribution of accepted loans would not be revealed in a performance study such as this.

Finally, it should be noted that the model assumes that underlying "true" default probabilities, conditioned on creditworthiness factors observed by the lender, do not differ by race. Violation of this assumption, so that borrower race remains predictive of default even after controlling for creditworthiness, creates the potential for so-called "statistical" discrimination by lenders. This type of correlation between race and the "true" default rates could explain the empirical findings. Thus the estimation findings are not necessarily inconsistent with the existence of "statistical" discrimination.

Notes

1. The views expressed are those of the authors and do not necessarily reflect the views of the Federal Home Loan Mortgage Corporation, the Board of Governors of the Federal Reserve System, or members of the Board's staff. The authors are grateful to the Office of Policy Development and Research of the U.S. Department of Housing and Urban Development (HUD) for providing the FHA mortgage data utilized in this research. Special thanks go to William Shaw of the Office of Housing at HUD for his assistance.

2. As documented in recent analyses (see, for example, MBMT 1992 and Canner, Gabriel, and Woolley 1991), minority loan applicants and neighborhoods are often characterized by higher levels of default risk, relative to the applicant population as a whole. However, to the extent that loan underwriting requirements fully account for borrower and location default risk, and hence coincide with actual loan performance, applicant and neighborhood racial composition should play no residual role in the credit extension decision.

The settlement reached by the U.S. Department of Justice and Shawmut Mortgage Corporation (December 1993), for instance, noted that Shawmut had discriminated against minorities by holding them to a higher standard than those applied to white applicants. Shawmut was also accused of not giving minorities the same assistance provided to white applicants in overcoming borrowing obstacles. (For further discussion, see *The Wall Street Journal*, December 14, 1993.)

3. Evidence from MBMT appears to support the assumption about bias. The study indicates that, to the extent that differences in decisions about applications are observed, they appear in decisions concerning marginally qualified minority and nonminority applicants. MBMT notes that virtually all well-qualified applicants in their study—minority and nonminority alike—were approved for credit.

4. Commentaries in the media focus on ex post *average* default rates. (See, for example, "The Hidden Clue," Peter Brimelow and Leslie Spencer, *Forbes*, January 4, 1991.) In

doing so, those studies implicitly assume that the risk distributions of minority and majority borrowers are identical. However, evidence from MBMT and Canner, Gabriel, and Woolley 1991 indicates systematic variation in risk distribution among minority and majority borrowers.

5. To see this result, simply differentiate R with respect to B and B' as shown in Berkovec, Canner, Gabriel, and Hannan (1994).

6. It is also important to note that in this model, even though lenders know the true relationship between characteristics X and the probability of default and use the information in their underwriting, observed default rates will still vary with X. This does not necessarily mean that lenders could improve their performance by altering their underwriting rules.

7. This assumes that the distribution of ϵ does not depend on the borrower's race.

8. The specific sections of the FHA mortgage insurance program examined in this study are Sections 203, 234, 244, 248, 296, 303, 348, 503, 534, 548, and 596.

9. An earlier paper assessed the effects of a large number of additional neighborhood change variables on default probabilities and generally found little relationship between these variables and the likelihood of default (Berkovec et al., 1994).

10. A detailed discussion of cumulative default rates by borrowers with these and other characteristics may be found in chapter 6, this volume.

11. The models contain about 100 independent variables. Space considerations preclude presentation of all estimates.

12. This is primarily due to the shorter loan lifetime from origination to the first quarter of 1993.

13. As a further test of the interaction between an individual's race and neighborhood racial composition, the sample was split into quartiles based on the percentage of minorities in the neighborhood, with default models estimated on each quartile separately. These results indicate that black borrowers have higher default rates in each type of neighborhood, since the magnitude of the coefficient of BLACK does not vary substantially among the quartiles and is significantly different from 0 in 10 of the 12 (4 runs each year in 1987–1989) logit analyses.

14. Since minorities tend to have riskier observed characteristics, it is likely that omitted unobserved characteristics for minorities also are riskier on average. The probable effect of omitted variables in a default equation thus is to show higher defaults for minorities, a bias toward finding no evidence of discrimination. In accept/reject studies, such as the one by MBMT, the probable bias of omitted variables goes the other way, toward finding discrimination.

References

Barth, James R., Joseph J. Cordes, and Anthony M.J. Yezer. 1979. "Financial Institution Revolutions, Redlining and Mortgage Markets." *The Regulation of Financial Institutions*, Conference Series No. 21, Federal Reserve Bank of Boston.

Becker, Gary S. 1971. *The Economics of Discrimination* (Second Edition). Chicago: University of Chicago Press.

Berkovec, James, Glenn Canner, Stuart Gabriel, and Timothy Hannan. 1994. "Race, Redlining, and Residential Mortgage Loan Performance." *Journal of Real Estate Finance and Economics*.

———. 1995. "Discrimination, Default, and Loss in FHA Mortgage Lending." Unpublished working paper.

Board of Governors of the Federal Reserve System. 1991. "Feasibility Study on the Application of the Testing Methodology to the Detection of Discrimination in Mortgage Lending." Unpublished staff analysis.

Canner, Glenn B., Stuart A. Gabriel, and J. Michael Woolley. 1991. "Race, Default Risk, and Mortgage Lending: A Study of the FHA and Conventional Loan Markets." *Southern Economic Journal* 58.

Canner, Glenn B., Wayne Passmore, and Dolores S. Smith. 1994. "Residential Lending to Low-Income and Minority Families: Evidence from the 1992 HMDA Data." *Federal Reserve Bulletin* 80.

Clauretie, Terrence M. and Thomas Herzog. 1989. "The Effect of State Foreclosure Laws on Loan Losses." *Journal of Money, Credit, and Banking* 22.

Ferguson, Michael F. and Stephen R. Peters. 1995. "What Constitutes Evidence of Discrimination in Lending?" *Journal of Finance* 50: 739.

Lang, William W. and Leonard J. Nakamura. 1993. "A Model of Redlining." *Journal of Urban Economics* 33.

Munnell, Alicia H., Lynn E. Browne, James McEneaney, and Geoffrey M.B. Tootell. 1992. "Mortgage Lending in Boston: Interpreting HMDA Data." Working Paper No. 92–7, Federal Reserve Bank of Boston.

Peterson, Richard L. 1981. "An Investigation of Sex Discrimination in Commercial Banks' Direct Consumer Lending." *The Bell Journal of Economics* 12.

Tootell, Geoffrey M.B. 1993. "Defaults, Denials, and Discrimination in Mortgage Lending." *New England Economic Review*.

Van Order, Robert, Ann-Margaret Westin, and Peter Zorn. 1993. "Effects of the Racial Composition of Neighborhoods on Default and Implications for Racial Discrimination in Mortgage Markets." Paper presented at the Allied Social Sciences Association meetings in Anaheim, California.

Yezer, A., R. Phillips, and R. Trost. 1993. "Bias in Estimates of Discrimination and Defaults in Mortgage Lending: The Effects of Screening and Self Selection." Unpublished paper. Department of Economics, George Washington University.

Chapter Eight

COMPARING LOAN PERFORMANCE BETWEEN RACES AS A TEST FOR DISCRIMINATION: A CRITIQUE OF THE BERKOVEC ET AL. STUDY

George Galster

The issue of discrimination directed toward applicants for mortgages who are members of racial-ethnic minority groups has received markedly increased public attention during the 1990s. Various sorts of evidence, including disparities observed in Home Mortgage Disclosure Act (HMDA) data, vignettes of blatant discrimination, a smattering of court cases, pilot studies using paired testers, and multivariate statistical analyses of lenders' loan application files, have combined to paint a convincing picture of the problem (for reviews, see Galster 1992; Cloud and Galster 1993; and Yinger, chapter 2, this volume).

More recently, this view has been challenged by an entirely different analytical perspective. First articulated by Peterson (1981) and later expounded by Becker (1993) and Brimelow and Spencer (1993), this position argues that discrimination in the mortgage underwriting process can be deduced by examining the racial-ethnic differences in the performance of loans granted, specifically in the default rates of blacks versus whites. This argument has been articulated several times previously in this volume and is not detailed again here. Suffice it to say that previous critiques of this view have already thoroughly discredited it (Galster 1993; Tootell 1993; and chapter 2, this volume).

I recapitulate only the central criticism here. Although the marginal minority borrower will be better qualified (and thus have a better-performing loan) than will the marginal white borrower in the presence of prejudice-based discrimination, the relationship between the average borrowers cannot be ascertained with any precision without recourse to arbitrary assumptions about the cross-race distributions of creditworthiness among borrowers.

Berkovec et al. (chapter 7, this volume) have attempted to provide a more sophisticated defense of the default approach for testing lender discrimination. Their contribution is to model the creditworthiness,

C, of an applicant as the sum of two sets of factors, one observable both to the lender and to the research analyst and the other observable (or measurable) only to the lender. Berkovec et al. proceeded to argue about prejudiced lenders' behaviors along the lines previously set forth in this volume, except that they further partitioned the underwriting decision into those qualified for conventional mortgages, those qualified only for Federal Housing Administration mortgages, and those unqualified for any mortgages. Higher standards for *C* were established for minorities at both conventional/Federal Housing Administration (FHA) and FHA/no loan thresholds by prejudiced lenders, leading to a somewhat better-qualified pool of minority holders of both conventional and FHA mortgages.

As illustrated by hypothetical data in table 8.1, white applicants require a minimum *C* of 60 to obtain a conventional loan and a minimum of 20 to obtain an FHA loan. Prejudice-based discrimination might lead to higher *C* thresholds for minorities, such as 65 and 25, respectively. Thus, the minority applicant with $C = 61$ is rejected for a conventional loan and relegated to the FHA borrower pool. Similarly, the minority applicant with $C = 22$ is rejected for all loans. Both acts raise the average *C* among minority FHA borrowers.

But note that this is insufficient to produce the result that average *C* for minority FHA borrowers is higher (i.e., default rates are lower, on average) than for whites. As the data in table 8.1 make clear, the average *C* in the minority FHA pool is improved as a result of discrimination, but it need not exceed the average value of whites. To their credit, Berkovec et al. noted that such a comparison of average loan performance across races creates an ambiguous indicator of discrimination.

Instead, Berkovec et al. (chapter 7, this volume) offered a subtle new argument in an attempt to compare the treatment of the marginal applicants. Recall that they assume that some of the elements comprising *C* are not measured (or statistically controlled) by the researcher who is analyzing lenders' loan files. Discrimination should systematically result in these unobserved factors favoring minorities: this is the essence of the higher standards to which minorities are held. Thus, Berkovec et al. argued, if one statistically controls for observable characteristics of the applicant, a finding that minority status (which serves as a proxy for the unobserved characteristics) is associated with better loan performance (lower defaults, for example) would constitute evidence of discrimination. Inasmuch as Berkovec et al. found the opposite in their empirical work, they concluded that prejudice-based discrimination is absent.

Table 8.1 HYPOTHETICAL ILLUSTRATION OF BERKOVEC ET AL. FRAMEWORK

	Creditworthiness Scores of Applicants	
	Minority	Majority
	10	
	16	16
		18
20 = Majority Threshold For FHA Loan	----------	----------
	22	
25 = Minority Threshold For FHA Loan		
	32	32
	42	
		50
		59
60 = Majority Threshold For Conventional Loan	----------	----------
	61	
65 = Minority Threshold For Conventional Loan		
	71	
		74
	81	
		84
		94

	Average Creditworthiness Scores of Applicants	
	Minority	Majority
No Discrimination		
Rejected Pool	13	17
FHA Pool	32	47
Conventional Pool	71	84
Discrimination		
Rejected Pool	16	17
FHA Pool	45	47
Conventional Pool	76	84

Source: Author.

The analysis of whether loan performance provides a valid indicator of lender discrimination depends on how one specifies the factors comprising the index of creditworthiness, *C*, that lenders observe. *C* is assumed to be directly related to loan performance (i.e., to profitability; inversely related to defaults). I argue here that, regardless of how the components of *C* are specified, the Berkovec et al. (chapter 7, this volume) procedure does not yield a valid estimate of discrimination, although the precise reasoning varies in the four cases considered here.

Following Berkovec et al. (chapter 7, this volume), assume that research analysts (who are not the lender) can observe a set of characteristics X of the loan and applicant that are related to C through a vector of coefficients β plus an error term indicating characteristics observable only to the lender ϵ; $C = X\beta + \epsilon$.

Case 1: All components of C are observable ($\epsilon = 0$), and race of applicant R is not a component of X and is uncorrelated with all components of X.

In this case, the research analyst has a completely specified model that is equivalent to "getting inside the head" of the lender. Although the distribution of X (and thus C) may well differ depending on R, a loan performance regression that controls for X cannot help but yield a statistically insignificant coefficient for R. Put differently, if everything that affects C is controlled and R does not, by assumption, affect C, there can only be a zero coefficient for R in the Berkovec et al. (chapter 7, this volume) regressions, regardless of whether the lender was discriminating or not. In terms of the hypothetical data in table 8.1, comparisons of those with the same C could not reveal any independent racial differential. If the lender were discriminating in a fashion as hypothesized by Berkovec et al., one would likely observe lower C values for some whites among those accepted for loans than would be observed for any minorities accepted for similar loans. But recall that this is not the Berkovec et al. statistical test.

Case 2: Not all components of C are observable to the researcher, and race of applicant R is not a component of X and is not correlated with X or ϵ.

In this case, there are omitted variables in the loan performance equation (i.e., components of ϵ), but there is no bias in the R coefficient because R and ϵ are assumed independent. In a nondiscriminatory world, there would be no reason for the R coefficient to be statistically significant. But if there were prejudice-based discrimination by lenders forcing approved minority applicants to possess higher values of unobserved characteristics for any level of observable ones, R would tend to be significant. Yet, if R were significant it would violate the assumption of this case; we cannot begin by making the assumptions of case 2, because a particular finding of the test would violate them.

Case 3: Not all components of C are observable, and race of applicant R is not a component of X but is correlated with ϵ.

In this case, the Berkovec et al. (chapter 7, this volume) regressions will suffer from omitted-variable bias (i.e., the components of ϵ), the degree of which will be proportional to the correlation between R and ϵ. The coefficient of R will be biased and any interpretation of it misleading. Unfortunately, it is precisely such a correlation between R and ϵ that is the essence of the Berkovec et al. test, inasmuch as they assume that the only source of such correlation is lender discrimination that reputedly forces minorities to have superior characteristics among the (unobserved) ϵ. As Galster (1993) and Yinger (chapter 2, this volume) have argued, however, there are persuasive reasons for a high correlation between R and ϵ even in the absence of prejudice-based lending discrimination; thus the Berkovec et al. test cannot be conclusive if one admits these alternative sources. Stated another way, Berkovec et al. assume that discrimination results in unobservable characteristics for minorities being superior to unobservable charactistics for whites; but if other factors skew unobservables in the opposite direction, the net effect will be an empirical matter in which the reputed discrimination effect will be obscured.[1]

Deeper analysis of the foregoing cases reveals a more fundamental conundrum for Berkovec et al. (chapter 7, this volume). The key feature of their test is that it necessitates that some applicant variables be observed by the lender that are not observed (or controlled) by the research analyst; these are the ones that reputedly would appear as "higher hurdles" for minority applicants, erected by the prejudiced, discriminating lender and producing an observed correlation between R and ϵ. Put differently, the Berkovec et al. method *depends* on omitted variables to bias the coefficient of R in a discriminatory regime. Unfortunately, if too many variables are omitted, the model loses probity for other reasons.

To ascertain why this key methodological feature is flawed, consider two extremes of unobserved (that is, omitted from the regression) variables. One of them, embodied in case 1, has no unobserved variables. As shown in case 1, the coefficient of R was statistically insignificant regardless of the absence or presence of discrimination. The other extreme is embodied in simple comparisons of average loan performance of white and minority borrowers as a group. This is equivalent to estimating a regression with R as the only independent variable. For reasons explained earlier in the context of table 8.1, such a test similarly is incapable of providing an indicator of discrimination, as has been demonstrated by Galster (1993), Tootell (1993), and Yinger (chapter 2, this volume).

Now consider beginning at the completely specified model of case 1 and adding one unobserved variable *Z*. According to Berkovec et al.'s (chapter 7, this volume) logic, the *R* coefficient in a loan performance regression should provide an indicator of discrimination if it proves to be correlated with *Z* and thus proves to be statistically significant through omitted variable bias (assuming *Z* is strongly correlated with *C*). Whether this will manifest itself is doubtful, depending not only on the correlation between *R* and *Z* but also on that between *R* and *X* (potential multicollinearity). As one continues this thought experiment by positing relatively more unobserved *Z* (that are more strongly related to *C*) and less observed (controlled) *X* variables, it becomes more plausible that *R* will be more highly correlated with *Z*, but less plausible that such correlation can be attributed to discrimination. The extreme case when all variables are unobserved (and uncontrolled) makes this plain: even with discrimination, accepted minorities as a group could have lower *C* values than whites, as in table 8.1. Thus, at heart, Berkovec et al.'s method is deeply flawed because it cannot extricate itself from a dilemma that renders the test ambiguous: relatively too few[2] unobserved (uncontrolled) variables, and omitted-variable bias is too weak to permit a signal being produced by discrimination; too many[3] unobserved variables, and the signal is strong but meaningless because it cannot credibly be attributed to discrimination.

Case 4: All components of C are observable, and race of applicant *R* is a component of *X*.

This case assumes that race itself is a strong, unique predictor of creditworthiness, perhaps due to lower stability of income or greater likelihood of declining property value associated with minority-occupied neighborhoods. Under such assumptions, rational, profit-maximizing lenders will assess two otherwise identically qualified applicants differently on the basis of *R* because they differ on *C*. In this case, discrimination due to prejudice becomes indistinguishable from discrimination motivated by profit; in neither case is discrimination clearly observable by Berkovec et al.'s method.

Should such an assessment as described in case 4 produce differential treatment, Berkovec et al.'s (chapter 7, this volume) loan performance regression that controls for *X* will observe a statistically significant coefficient for *R*. Note, however, that such is not produced because lenders are erecting higher *C* hurdles for minorities; rather, for the same *X* minorities have lower *C*. If a lender does not discriminate, the statistical result will be the same nevertheless. A larger number of less-qualified minorities may be granted loans than would occur under a discriminatory regime because, although they have identical X values to whites, they have lower C values. Thus Berkovec et al.'s regression would show an identical coefficient for R regardless of whether the lender were discriminating or not. Only the pool of marginally accepted borrowers would distinguish the two behaviors.

To their credit, Berkovec et al. have admitted that their method is not designed to test for discrimination motivated by profit-maximization ("statistical discrimination"), such as posited in case 4. My point here is that profit-motivated discrimination obscures the search for prejudice-motivated discrimination.

To conclude, Berkovec et al. have conducted a careful study of racial-ethnic differentials in the performance of FHA mortgages. Unfortunately, they go too far in asserting that their findings suggest an absence of lending discrimination based on prejudice. Examination of loan performance, even in the sophisticated manner done there, cannot yield unambiguous indications of the absence or presence of discrimination, whether it be motivated by prejudice or by profit-maximization.

Notes

1. Note that this also would follow if there were large numbers of variables correlated with C that were unobserved by both researchers and mortgage lenders.
2. *Few* here refers to number and degree of unobserved variables correlated with C.
3. *Many* here refers to number and degree of unobserved variables correlated with C.

References

Becker, Gary. 1993. "The Evidence against Banks Doesn't Prove Bias." *Business Week*, April 19: 18.

Brimelow, Peter, and Leslie Spencer. 1993. "The Hidden Clue." *Forbes*, January 4: 48.

Cloud, Cathy, and George Galster. 1993. "What Do We Know about Racial Discrimination in Mortgage Markets?" *Review of Black Political Economy* 22(1): 101–20.

Galster, George. 1992. "Research on Discrimination in Housing and Mortgage Markets: Assessment and Future Directions." *Housing Policy Debate* 3(2): 639–83.

———. 1993. "The Facts of Lending Discrimination Cannot Be Argued Away by Examining Default Rates." *Housing Policy Debate* 4(1): 141–46.

Peterson, Richard. 1981. "An Investigation of Sex Discrimination in Commercial Banks' Direct Consumer Lending." *Bell Journal of Economics* 12 (Autumn): 547–61.

Tootell, Geoffrey. 1993. "Defaults, Denials, and Discrimination in Mortgage Lending." *New England Economic Review* (September/October): 45–51.

Chapter Nine

FLAWS IN THE USE OF LOAN DEFAULTS TO TEST FOR MORTGAGE LENDING DISCRIMINATION

Stephen L. Ross

Berkovec et al.'s (1994, 1995) finding that minority borrowers have higher default rates has been frequently cited by mortgage lenders as evidence that lenders do not systematically discriminate against African Americans. Glenn B. Canner, one of the coauthors of the Berkovec et al. studies, cautions, however, that this interpretation is inaccurate because there are forms of discrimination that the study does not address (cited in Karr, 1995). For example, Berkovec et al. admit that the default approach cannot test for statistical discrimination, in which lenders face an economic incentive to discriminate because minority borrowers are more likely to default on loans for reasons that are unobservable at loan approval. Berkovec et al. are, in essence, testing for discrimination due to prejudice in which the lender faces a trade-off between his or her prejudice and bank profits, and only approves minority loans that are very good risks.

This chapter argues that the default approach is not a good test for discrimination that is due to prejudice. The first section argues that the default approach is a poor test if the correlation between unobservables in the loan approval and default equations is small. The second section shows that assumptions made in the default approach are inconsistent with current findings of racial differences in loan approval, such as the results of Munnell et al. (1992, 1996). The third section concludes that a second test conducted by Berkovec et al. (1994, 1995), in which they test for discrimination in loan foreclosure using an analysis of lender loss upon default, suffers from many of the same problems as the default approach and argues that some of those problems could have been avoided. Finally, this chapter raises the possibility that minority loans may be riskier than majority loans after controlling for variables that are observable at loan approval; the fourth section addresses the policy issues arising from this possibility.

CORRELATION ACROSS EQUATIONS

The default approach to test for discrimination is based on the fact that the loan approval process may lead to a selected sample of approved loans. If minorities are held to a higher standard in loan approval, approved minority loans will be higher in quality on characteristics that are observed by the lender at loan approval but are not measured by researchers (unmeasured characteristics). If these unmeasured characteristics are correlated with borrower default, minority loans should have lower default rates than majority loans after controlling for loan characteristics that are observed at loan approval.

By the same argument, however, if there is no correlation between unmeasured characteristics and default, then default rates cannot be influenced by the loan approval process. This correlation may, in fact, be very weak. Loan default is determined by many factors that arise after loan approval, such as changes in local housing and labor markets. These factors may have a much larger effect on the probability of a loan default than unmeasured characteristics, and racial differences in default may result almost entirely from racial differences that arise after loan approval.

A similar argument can be applied to tests for discrimination based on loan approval data. If unmeasured characteristics are correlated with race, the loan approval-based tests may be biased. If the correlation between equations is negligible, however, these unmeasured characteristics must have little effect on default, and the use of these unmeasured variables cannot be justified based on business necessity. Therefore, unexplained racial differences in lender behavior can be interpreted as discrimination, and the existence of unmeasured characteristics does not bias the approval-based tests. Unfortunately, accurate estimates of this correlation are not available. Simultaneous estimations of loan approval and default equations do not exist because no mortgage data set combines both denied loan applications and outcomes for approved loans.

RACIAL DIFFERENCES IN LOAN APPROVAL

As stated, the default approach tests whether minority loans have lower default rates than majority loans and implies that discrimination based on prejudice does not exist if minority loans have the same or higher rate of default. This implication is based, however, on the assumption that minority and majority tendencies toward defaulting are identical if there is no discrimination based on prejudice and after controlling for loan characteristics observable at loan approval.[1] This assumption is not valid. To see why, first assume that there is no discrimination based on prejudice. Then note that Munnell et al. (1992, 1996) found lower loan approval rates for minorities after controlling for observed characteristics.

Since these findings are assumed not to arise from lender prejudice, I propose two alternative explanations: either that the findings result from unmeasured characteristics that are correlated with race and that predict loan default (omitted-variable bias); *or* that the findings result from unobserved characteristics that are correlated with race, explain default, and provide lenders with an economic incentive to discriminate (statistical discrimination).[2]

Assume, first that the Munnell et al. (1992, 1996) findings are due to omitted-variable bias. The resulting distribution of minority and majority unmeasured characteristics is illustrated by figure 9.1 According to these assumptions, minority loan applications are less likely to be approved because the average quality of minority loans is lower on unmeasured characteristics. Since there is no discrimination due to prejudice, observationally identical minority and majority borrowers are held to the same standard (*C*) on unmeasured characteristics, majority loans are more likely to be approved, and the resulting majority loans have a higher average quality level after controlling for observed characteristics. Therefore, majority loans should have lower, not equal, default levels, which contradicts the basic assumption of the default approach and biases it away from finding discrimination due to prejudice.

Alternatively, assume that there are no systematic racial differences in unmeasured characteristics and that the Munnell et al. (1992, 1996) findings are due to statistical discrimination. In other words, there are unobserved characteristics, which create an economic incentive for lenders to hold minorities to a higher standard. This is shown in figure 9.2, in which the distribution of minority and majority loan quality is identical but minority loans are held to a higher standard ($C + D$). Statistical discrimination raises the average quality of approved minority loans, but the unobserved characteristics directly lower the quality of approved minority loans. There is no reason to believe that these two effects cancel, and therefore minority and majority samples of approved loans may not have the same average quality over unobserved characteristics. The assumption that minority and

Figure 9.1 DISTRIBUTION OF UNMEASURED CHARACTERISTICS FOR LOAN APPLICATION QUALITY: CASE OF OMITTED VARIABLE BIAS

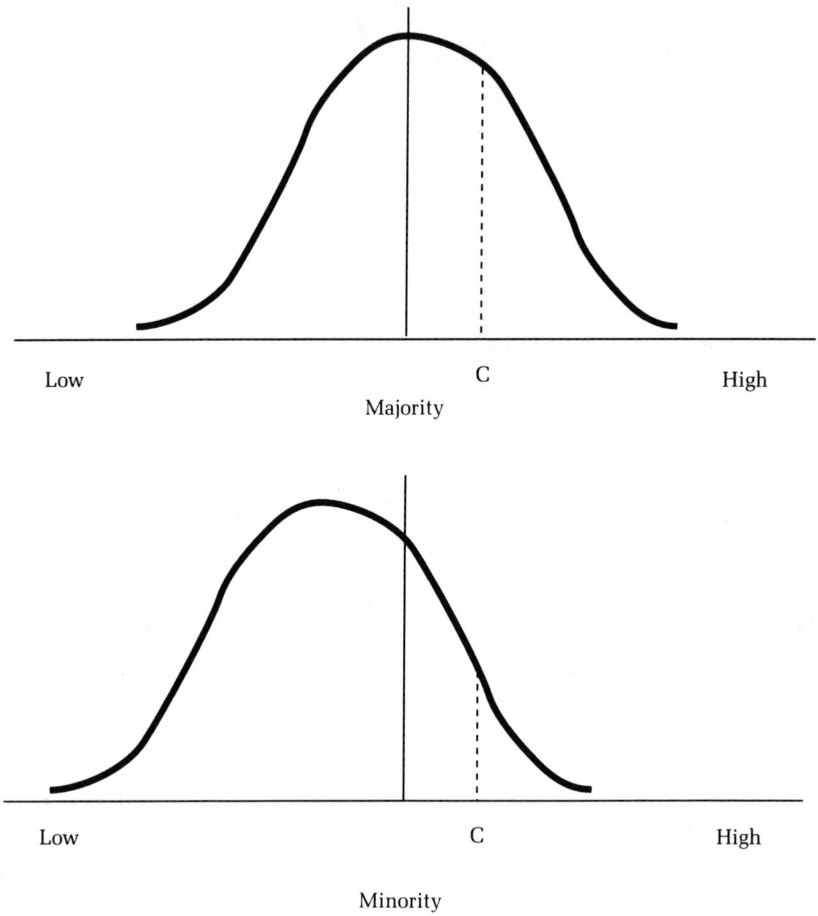

majority default rates are equal when there is no discrimination due to prejudice is again contradicted.

In fact, Ross (1994) examined this possibility for a performance-based test of discrimination using an index of loan profitability rather than loan default. He assumed that lenders are profit-maximizers, and found that the improvement in minority loan profitability resulting from statistical discrimination is smaller than the existing profitability difference resulting from unobservable characteristics. He concluded that performance-based tests of discrimination are biased away from finding discrimination due to prejudice.[3]

Figure 9.2 DISTRIBUTION OF UNMEASURED CHARACTERISTICS FOR LOAN APPLICATION QUALITY: CASE OF STATISTICAL DISCRIMINATION

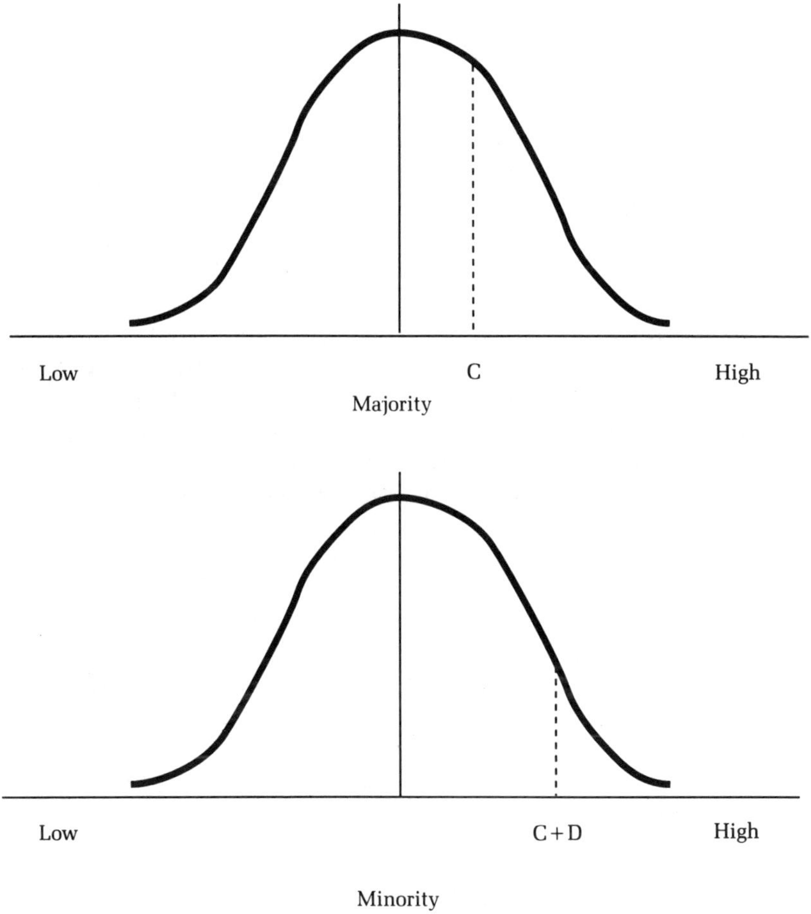

The intuition behind this result is that a profit-maximizing lender holds minority loans to a standard that is just sufficient to exactly cancel out racial differences in loan quality. The racial differences in loan quality, however, affect loan default directly, whereas statistical discrimination affects loan default by creating a selected sample of loans. The two shifts in loan quality are the same size, but one shift enters the default process through a selection bias term. If the unobservables are distributed as normal, the slope of this selection term is less than one, and the effect of statistical discrimination on default is less than the existing racial difference in default due to unobservable characteristics.

FORECLOSURE AND LENDER LOSS

The default approach may also be biased because lenders may act to foreclose minority loans more aggressively than majority loans. Berkovec et al. (1994, 1995) examined this possibility using a "lender loss approach," which is very similar to the default approach. They argued that if lenders foreclose more quickly on minority loans, then minority defaults should exhibit lower lender loss because a quick foreclosure tends to limit losses on defaulted loans. They estimated a model of lender loss, but did not find lower minority losses, and concluded that lenders do not foreclose more quickly on minority loans. In other words, they concluded that lenders do not discriminate against minorities in the loan foreclosure process.

The foreclosure decision, however, is based on all information available to the lender when the loan is actually at risk of default. If lenders discriminate against minorities in foreclosure, minority loans must have lower losses after controlling for all characteristics available at foreclosure. Berkovec et al. (1994, 1995) have estimated the wrong model by only including information available at loan approval. If minorities have worse experiences on average after loan approval, minority defaults may result in larger loan losses. The omission of these observable, postloan approval characteristics biases the lender loss approach away from finding discrimination in the foreclosure process.

In addition, Berkovec et al. (1994, 1995) estimated the race coefficient for the sample of defaulted loans, but the lender loss approach is based on the argument that the default process creates a selected sample of defaulted loans. In the default approach, the effect of the approval process on loan default could not be directly estimated; however, the selection effect in the lender loss equation is estimable. The effect can be found by estimating both the race coefficient in a model of potential lender loss for all approved loans and the race coefficient in a model of actual lender loss for defaulted loans. The selection effect due to the default process is the difference of these two race coefficients, but Berkovec et al. have only estimated the race coefficient for actual lender loss. If minority loans have higher expected lender loss for approved loans, Berkovec et al.'s approach is biased away from finding discrimination in foreclosure.[4]

As discussed earlier, a key problem in any examination of loan default is the inability to distinguish between racial differences in borrower propensity to default and in lender propensity to foreclose. This problem also pervades any attempt to analyze lender loss. It is very difficult to isolate the separate effect of lender and borrower behavior when default by its very nature results from a failed negotiation between the borrower and a loan officer.[5] This problem can only be resolved by a detailed analysis of the behavior of borrowers and lenders when a loan is at risk of default.

FAIR LENDING AND STATISTICAL DISCRIMINATION

This chapter raises the possibility that minorities are more likely to default on loans, and that these defaults may result in larger lender losses upon default. If these possibilities are true, they give lenders an economic incentive to use race as a signal of high-risk loans and to be more restrictive in approving minority loan applications and more aggressive in foreclosing on minority loans. As noted earlier, such behavior is called statistical discrimination and is illegal.

Both the default and lender loss approaches, however, will fail to find evidence of discrimination when lenders have an economic incentive to discrimination. If performance-based analyses such as these are used to justify lender behavior, these lenders may practice statistical discrimination with impunity. This leaves federal regulators with only three short-run policy options: first, to enforce the current statutes that prohibit discrimination for any reason, by examining the loan approvals as is currently being done; second, to allow lenders to use race as a signal of high-default risk and to hold minorities to higher standards; and, third, to subsidize minority loans to compensate lenders for racial differences in loan outcomes, eliminating the economic incentive for discrimination.

If the first option is followed, banks will be forced to incur the additional default cost associated with minority loans. These costs will be passed on to borrowers and possibly depositors in the form of higher mortgage interest rates and lower interest payments on deposits. If the second option is followed, the additional default costs fall primarily on minority households because they will be denied mortgages more often and have those mortgages foreclosed on more rapidly. The third option would spread the cost broadly by using tax dollars to eliminate a lender's economic incentive to discriminate.

I believe that the first option is the only reasonable choice. The third option is not politically feasible, and the second option contradicts a basic principle of equal treatment in our society. It does not matter whether a protected class performs badly on average. An institution cannot exclude an individual based on race, ethnicity, or gender when that individual is qualified based on observable characteristics.

I believe that compromising on this principle would do great harm. A basic notion of fairness in this society is that people should be judged on their accomplishments and not be punished for the actions of others who are similar in appearance to them. In addition, we do not know the cause of racial differences in default. It is possible that these differences arise because of discrimination in other sectors of the economy, which increases the probability of minority borrowers experiencing adverse outcomes after loan approval. If so, is it fair to discriminate against a minority based on unobservable differences that may arise in the future because of expected discrimination? It may seem unfair to force homeowners and depositors to bear the costs associated with more frequent minority loan defaults, but it is our only option unless we as a society are willing to pay for that cost directly with public dollars.

SUMMARY AND CONCLUSIONS

In summary, the correlation between unobservables in the loan approval and default equations is the key to understanding current disagreements over discrimination in mortgage markets. If the correlation is very low, lenders have little excuse for excluding minorities based on characteristics that have not been well specified and do not explain loan performance. If the correlation is high, the sample selection caused by the loan approval process could be substantial, and the default approach may provide insights concerning the nature of discrimination. At present, however, no data set exists that allows the estimation of this correlation.

Even if this correlation is high, the default approach may be a biased test of discrimination due to prejudice. Specifically, discrimination due to prejudice may exist and may be hidden by racial differences in default. These differences may be caused by unmeasured characteristics that are observed by the lender. Alternatively, unobserved racial differences in loan quality may exist. Even if all lenders maximize profits by engaging in statistical discrimination, racial differences in default may remain and hide discrimination due to prejudice.

Finally, this chapter notes that analysis of loan foreclosure using lender loss suffers from the same flaws as the default approach, for the reason that the lender loss approach cannot distinguish between differential treatment in foreclosure and racial differences in propensity to default. Loan default and/or foreclosure is a negotiated process. The significance of racial default differences will remain a mystery until the nature of this negotiation is explored in detail.

The most important result of Berkovec et al. (1994, 1995) is their careful documentation of racial differences in loan default. These differences should concern policymakers because defaults may impose large costs on minority borrowers, and a high minority propensity toward defaulting may create an incentive for discrimination among lenders that government policy may not be able to overcome. Berkovec et al. make no attempt, however, to explain the origin of the default differences; without such an explanation, nothing can be learned from default rates concerning the nature of lending discrimination. This omission is even more disturbing when combined with current attempts to use the Berkovec et al. study as a justification for existing racial differences in loan approval.

Notes

1. Specifically, the default approach assumes that default rates are equal if minority and majority loan applicants are held to the same standard. This is the same as no discrimination due to prejudice so long as prejudice does not result in entirely random actions of denial without regard to borrowers' qualifications. Munnell et al. (1992, 1996) used a statistical framework, which also assumes that discrimination is not random.

2. This discussion is not intended to address the endogeneity issues raised by Rachlis and Yezer (1993).

3. Ross (1994) observed that loan performance approaches are biased for discrete dependent variables, such as loan default, because the approval process affects the estimated coefficients through both the mean and the variance of the error distribution. As a result, Ross examined a performance approach based on a continuous index of loan profitability. If the variance bias identified by Ross is large, the default approach is hopelessly flawed. Alternatively, if the variance bias is small, Ross's analysis for a profitability index also applies to the default approach, and that approach is biased away from finding discrimination due to prejudice.

4. A similar procedure for loan profitability is presented in Ross (1994).

5. The same concern applies to Yezer, Phillips, and Trost (1994), who argued that loan terms are endogenous and concluded that this biases approval-based tests for discrimination toward finding discrimination. This result arises, however, because their approach intrinsically views loan terms as chosen freely by the borrower, rather than as the result of a negotiation between the borrower and loan officer.

References

Berkovec, J., Canner, G., Gabriel, S., and Hannan, T. 1994. "Race, Redlining, and Residential Mortgate Loan Performance." *Journal of Real Estate Finance and Economics* 9 (November): 263–94.

———. 1995. "Discrimination, Default, and Loss in FHA Mortgage Lending." Paper presented at meeting of American Real Estate and Urban Economics Association, January, Washington, D.C.

Karr, A. 1995. "Fed Study Challenges Notion of Bias against Minorities in Mortgage Lending." *Wall Street Journal*, January 26: A12.

Munnell, A., Browne, L., McEneaney, J., and Tootell, G. 1992. "Mortgage Lending in Boston: Interpreting HMDA Data." Federal Reserve Bank of Boston. Working Paper 92-07. Boston: Federal Reserve Bank of Boston, October.

Munnell, A., Tootell, G., Browne, L., and McEneaney, J. 1996. "Mortgage Lending in Boston: Interpreting HMDA Data." *American Economic Review*. Forthcoming.

Rachlis, M., and Yezer, A. 1993. "Serious Flaws in Statistical Tests for Discrimination in Mortgage Markets." *Journal of Housing Research* 4: 315–36.

Ross, S. 1994. "Mortgage Lending Discrimination and Racial Differences in Loan Performance." University of Connecticut Working Paper Series. Photocopy.

Yezer, A., Phillips, R., and Trost, R. 1994. "Bias in Estimates of Discrimination and Default in Mortgage Lending: The Effects of Simultaneity and Self-Selection." *Journal of Real Estate Finance and Economics* 9: 197–216.

Chapter Ten

REJOINDER

James A. Berkovec, Glenn B. Canner
Stuart A. Gabriel, and Timothy H. Hannan

We thank George Galster and Steve Ross (see chapters 8 and 9, respectively, this volume) for their careful readings of our work and appreciate the opportunity to respond to their critiques. It appears to be the opinion of Galster and Ross that loan performance analyses cannot be used to identify discrimination in mortgage lending. We disagree.

Our disagreement with Galster and Ross is that their critiques appear to be focused less on the model and empirical analysis contained in our chapter (hereafter referred to as BCGH) than on the overall role of loan performance studies for evaluating discrimination. The BCGH results do not *prove* that discrimination does not exist; any claim to the contrary is obviously exaggerated. However, *proof* is a very high standard for any empirical analysis. In our opinion, studies of default and loan performance do add value to the debate about mortgage discrimination. Although performance studies may not provide the complete and final answer to all relevant research issues in lending discrimination, they should be an integral part of the overall research program designed to understand discrimination and its effects.

A brief summary of some aspects of the BCGH chapter (chapter 7, this volume) that were not fully discussed by Galster or Ross will be useful. First, and most important, are the empirical findings in the BCGH work. Our primary empirical result is that Federal Housing Administration (FHA) mortgage default rates are higher for black borrowers than for borrowers from other racial or ethnic groups. This result holds even after controlling for all borrower-, loan-, and property-related characteristics available in the data. Furthermore, this result holds for all loan origination years considered in the analysis and for a large variety of subsamples of the data. Thus the finding of higher default rates for black borrowers appears to be very robust.

In addition to default rates, BCGH also examine racial differences in the observed dollar amount of losses resulting from default. Our primary intent is to determine whether losses would give a different pattern of racial differences than default rates would give. In particular, does it seem likely that black borrowers default at a higher rate but have equivalent or lower overall losses when defaults occur? Examination of loss rates given default indicates that this is not the case. On average, black borrowers appear both to default more frequently and to have more severe losses when default occurs. Thus overall default losses, the product of the default probability and the average loss given default, are higher for black borrowers in comparison with other groups of FHA borrowers, after controlling for other available loan characteristics. This finding confirms the results of the default-rate analysis.

The analysis of losses from default also provides limited evidence that the higher default rate for black borrowers is not due simply to differential treatment of delinquent borrowers. The basic argument is that increased forbearance for one group of borrowers would be likely to result in a lower relative default rate, all else being equal, because some delinquent borrowers in the favored group would recover over time. However, the cases in which borrowers eventually default, despite forbearance, should result in higher average losses because their financial circumstances deteriorate. The fact that this pattern of relatively lower losses resulting from default does not occur for black borrowers suggests that differential forbearance policies do not explain the racial differences in default rates. Obviously, our data are inadequate to prove that discriminatory handling of distressed borrowers does not occur. However, results are not consistent with systematic discrimination against blacks in loan resolutions. Improved data that allow for more direct exploration of the process of moving from loan delinquency into default and foreclosure would certainly be desirable. However, such data are not available at this time.

The empirical analysis described in BCGH indicates that black borrowers have both higher observed default rates and higher loan losses on mortgages, after controlling for available indicators of loan quality. Galster and Ross do not dispute this conclusion. Furthermore, it seems unlikely that the performance differentials can be explained by unequal treatment of borrowers after loans are originated. Then the question becomes: What does the evidence on default rates reveal about discrimination in underwriting decisions?

According to the model developed by BCGH, discrimination in underwriting, by holding minorities to higher standards, results in improvements in observed minority FHA loan performance when compared with a nondiscriminatory baseline. Performance effects for FHA loans are shown to occur whether the discriminatory standards are used to evaluate applicants for FHA loans or for conventional loans. The prediction of improved observed loan performance resulting from discrimination follows directly from the assumption that discrimination acts to differentially exclude the weakest applicants of the affected group. Thus discrimination alters the performance of the marginal borrower. This fact does not necessarily imply that discrimination is revealed by comparing average performance among groups, a point that is well established (Peterson 1981) and is repeated by BCGH and Galster and Ross.

The extension in the BCGH study shows that this performance differential from discrimination occurs even after conditioning on observable credit quality characteristics due to a shift in the distribution of unobserved characteristics of accepted borrowers. In the case at hand, unobserved characteristics refer to those factors that are used in underwriting decisions—hence observed by lenders—but do not appear in the data available to outside analysts. This theoretical framework for underwriting decisions is based on the discrete choice models commonly used in accept/reject studies such as the Boston Federal Reserve's analysis (Munnell, Brown, McEneany, and Tootell 1992). Using this framework, discrimination is shown to affect loan performance through a more severe truncation of the unobserved factors at the margin, regardless of the level of observable credit characteristics. The test for discrimination entails looking for the shift in unobservable factors that is induced by discrimination, through a comparison of loan performance in targeted and nontargeted groups, after controlling for observable differences in credit quality.

Discussing his "case 1," Galster notes, in chapter 8, this volume, that the test for discrimination depends on the existence of unobserved factors. This argument is true but basically irrelevant, because without unobserved characteristics discrimination is readily observable by simple comparison of the marginal borrowers, who are easily identified. Furthermore, it is hard to dispute the assertion that unobserved factors are important. In the absence of such factors, a perfect fit of accept/reject models of loan originations should be obtained. Existing models of lending decisions do not come close to explaining all of the variation in loan decisions. Until better explanatory power in these models is achieved, arguments that depend on perfectly observing all factors influencing loan decisions should be discounted. It is our belief that explicit consideration of unobservable factors is an important aspect of the model.

Ross, in chapter 9, notes that the BCGH model requires that unobserved factors (unmeasured characteristics) in underwriting decisions must influence loan performance. This is correct. To the extent that these unobserved factors are simply "random noise" uncorrelated with default, the selection effects associated with underwriting will have no bearing on loan performance. As Ross notes, direct econometric evidence of the effects of the unobserved factors on default does not exist. However, there is ample evidence that many of the observable factors used by underwriters, such as loan-to-value ratio, are strongly associated with loan performance. The BCGH presumption is that underwriting decisions are based on observable and unobservable factors that generally are indicative of loan performance. The relationship need not be perfect; the model predictions are maintained as long as underwriting decisions tend to select the less-risky loans for approval.[1]

According to the BCGH model, discrimination always causes this shift in the distribution of the unobservable component of credit quality and, subject to the discussion above, a corresponding shift in expected loan performance. The remaining issue is the observability of the shift. In other words, when can researchers say that they have found it? The analysis in the BCGH chapter makes two additional assumptions. The first assumption is that the unobservable factors known to lenders are not correlated with race; the second is that the "true" loan performance among racial groups is equal, after controlling for all creditworthiness characteristics observed by lenders. In other words, the influential factors in default that are unobserved by lenders are also uncorrelated with race. Together, these assumptions imply that the performance of loans to all groups, after conditioning for observed loan characteristics, would be equal in the absence of discrimination. In this case, the improved performance of minority loans that is induced by discrimination is revealed by better performance of the affected borrower group relative to identical loans made to other groups. Thus the conclusions in our study reject the joint hypothesis of lending discrimination along with equal "true" loan performance.

Most critiques by Galster and Ross concern the appropriateness of—and effects of violations of—the two assumptions underlying equal observed performance of minority and nonminority borrowers in the absence of discrimination. In the context of the BCGH theoretical model, the relevant assumptions can be termed *no omitted variables* and *no statistical discrimination*. These assumptions will be discussed separately because of their differing implications for discrimination. However, the overall effect of violations of these assumptions on empirical estimates in BCGH will be quite similar, because they introduce a correlation between borrower race and the error term in a default equation, even if race is not used in underwriting decisions.

The first issue is that of omitted variables. In the current context, the implication is that the unobserved factors known by lenders and used in the underwriting decisions (the ϵ term in the BCGH model) are correlated with race. This implication results in a potential omitted variable problem in the BCGH default and loss models because borrower race is correlated with the model error term as a result of the omitted factor. Omitted variables are a potential problem in any empirical study, and this one is no exception. The issue is particularly problematic in discrimination studies since the important measurement is the correlation of race with the model residual.

Because minority groups tend, on average, to have riskier profiles of observable characteristics than non-minorities, it would not be surprising to find the same effects among the unobserved factors. Thus the probable direction of bias from omitted variables in the BCGH analysis is toward not finding discrimination. This is acknowledged in the article, and attempts are made to assess the degree of bias associated with the known important omitted factor, borrower credit history. However, other important omitted factors may also exist. Thus, Galster and Ross are correct in pointing out that the BCGH results are subject to potential bias from omitted variables.

It is important to recognize, however, that the same potential problem with omitted variables occurs in other discrimination studies. In particular, accept/reject studies of mortgage origination are equally subject to omitted variables bias when important factors are omitted from the empirical model. However, in the case of accept/reject studies, the bias is in the opposite direction: toward a finding of discrimination where none exists. It is incorrect to argue that there is a fundamental problem with omitted variables in default studies that does not exist in accept/reject studies. If one believes in the existence of important omitted variables correlated with borrower race, no matter what data exist, one should never accept a test for discrimination that relies on correlations between race and a model residual. This argument appears to eliminate all statistical tests of discrimination based on observed data.

The second issue is the potential for "statistical discrimination," whereby minorities may actually be worse credit risks on average, even though borrower creditworthiness indicators observed by lenders are equivalent across racial groups. In other words, race remains predictive of loan performance even after controlling for everything—observable and unobservable—that lenders know at the time of loan origination. Lenders, therefore, have incentives to engage in statistical discrimination by using race in underwriting precisely because it is predictive of default. Use of borrower race in underwriting to equalize marginal default rates among racial groups is illegal, but some would question whether it qualifies as discrimination.

The potential for statistical discrimination is one explanation for the results contained in the BCGH analysis. Although this potential is the major focus of the critiques by Galster and Ross, the BCGH chapter makes no claims in regard to the results if this "true" racial difference in loan performance exists.[2] In the BCGH model, this racial difference in loan performance implies that the default rate D(C) will depend on race. Thus at given levels of creditworthiness (C), minority groups will have an expected loan performance that is worse than that of non-minorities. In terms of the model, any requirement of higher creditworthiness standards (based on C) for minorities improves the relative performance of affected groups. However, since the baseline—with a common underwriting standard—shows a poorer loan performance for minorities, more discrimination (a bigger differential standard) is needed before a positive performance differential is observed for the affected group.

In this case, one cannot say whether race is used in underwriting unless the baseline performance differential can be quantified. Even if one assumes that lenders make full use of statistical discrimination and equate marginal default rates among racial groups, default rates conditioned on observable characteristics could differ between groups. Full statistical discrimination is consistent with higher, equal, or lower conditional default rates for minorities, depending on assumptions about the distributions of unobservable factors and "true" default differences. Thus, without imposing considerably more structure on the problem, it is difficult to say much about the existence or extent of statistical discrimination. All we can really say is that some degree of bias beyond the statistical level would be revealed as better performance for the affected group. Thus the BCGH results indicate that the extent of bias is not large enough to overwhelm any "true" differential in expected loan performance.

This basic point is made in various ways in both critiques. There does not appear to be any substantive disagreement about the analytic effects of potential statistical discrimination in the BCGH model or results. However, Galster and Ross believe that the possibility that "true" default rates may depend on race invalidates the approach of using loan performance data to investigate discrimination. Again, we strongly disagree.

One reason for disagreement is our belief that loan performance studies *do* have the potential to identify the practice of statistical discrimination by lenders. To the extent that statistical discrimination is a result of correlations between race and performance factors that can be observed after loans are made, performance studies can detect the potential and actual use of statistical discrimination in underwriting. For example, suppose that "true" default rates for minorities were elevated because of a greater unmeasured risk of future unemployment—perhaps due to labor market discrimination. Then lenders might have incentives to statistically discriminate and impose higher standards on minorities to compensate for this increased risk. Analysts may measure the increased unemployment risk after the fact—perhaps by using actual employment experience—and include this factor in a loan performance study. If race is strongly related to loan performance through unemployment risk, inclusion of an actual unemployment risk variable should strongly influence the measured effect of race on loan performance. If, in the absence of information about unemployment risk, lenders were using race to statistically discriminate, then after controlling for unemployment risk the affected group should exhibit improved performance relative to other racial groups. Such an outcome is consistent with the prediction of the BCGH model. If, however, the potential existed but lenders were not statistically discriminating, inclusion of unemployment risk should remove an adverse effect of race on loan performance. This type of augmented loan performance study should be able to distinguish situations of actual and potential statistical discrimination from discrimination based on bias or no discrimination at all.

The BCGH analysis has not been interpreted as an augmented loan performance study, even though some variables such as the 1990 census measures and state-level dummy variables are partially ex post observations. Clearly, there is potential for using improved data in a loan performance study to get better identification of the factors used in loan underwriting. An integrated effort to collect data on loan applications, approvals, and performance, along with borrower characteristics appropriate to monitor default decisions (as suggested in the chapter by Ross), would clearly aid this endeavor. Having said that, we do not believe that the lack of such a model and data indicates that the "default approach is a fatally flawed method for studying discrimination."

Furthermore, loan performance studies have value even if they are only able to determine whether statistical discrimination rather than lender bias is the major issue in lending discrimination. Galster and Ross seem to indicate that statistical discrimination is the cause of much of the observed disparity in mortgage lending rejection rates. However, this has not been the focus of much of the public discussion about the issue nor the basis for enforcement actions. Greater consensus regarding the importance of statistical discrimination would allow research and policy efforts to be better focused on identifying, measuring, and eliminating discrimination in mortgage lending. Whether or not statistical discrimination is the reason for disparities in mortgage lending may be an open question, but it is hard to see how this issue can be resolved without studies of loan performance.

Our interpretation of the BCGH results is limited: our conclusion is that FHA loan performance data do not support a finding of widespread systematic discrimination in mortgage lending due to lender prejudice. The results of our research do not *prove* that there is no discrimination; no single study could do that. Some forms of lending discrimination would not affect loan performance. The BCGH results may be driven by omitted variables and/or a higher "true" default rate for black borrowers, potentially masking a limited amount of lender bias. The indication from BCGH, however, is that omitted variables and/or varying default risks—and not systematic racial bias—are the major factors in lending differentials.

Notes

1. A comparison of the financial and credit-related attributes of denied and accepted applicants in the Boston Federal Reserve study supports the view that underwriting decisions tend to exclude the least creditworthy applicants.

2. Here *true* simply refers to expected default rates of the applicant population conditioned on lender observations of creditworthiness prior to screening by lenders. It is not meant to imply that race is the causal factor but rather that a variable influential in determining defaults is correlated with race but unobserved by the lender.

References

Munnell, Alicia H., Lynn E. Browne, James McEneaney, and Geoffrey M.B. Tootell. 1992. "Mortgage Lending in Boston: Interpreting HMDA Data." Federal Reserve Bank of Boston Working Paper 92-07. Boston: Federal Reserve Bank of Boston, October.

Munnell, Alicia H., Geoffrey M.B. Tootell, Lynn E. Browne, and James McEneaney. 1996. "Mortgage Lending in Boston: Interpreting HMDA Data." *American Economic Review*. Forthcoming.

Peterson, Richard L. 1981. "An Investigation of Sex Discrimination in Commercial Banks' Direct Consumer Lending." *Bell Journal of Economics* 12(Autumn): 547–61.

Chapter Eleven

DISCRIMINATION AND THE SECONDARY MORTGAGE MARKET

Robert Van Order

Racial discrimination in mortgage markets can be defined as treating equally creditworthy borrowers differently on the basis of race. Discrimination can be investigated at the levels of the individual lender or the system as a whole. This chapter examines the issue from a perspective somewhere in between: specifically, the effect of the secondary market on discrimination. Although related to some of the issues involving low-income housing and community lending, discrimination and the secondary market is a separate concern. It can be against affluent borrowers in affluent neighborhoods; moreover, concerns about community lending and affordable housing may be unrelated to race. The focus here is on whether the secondary market makes it more or less likely that discrimination, as just defined, will occur. Research and methodological issues are also addressed, including a consideration of what sort of research can (and cannot) provide fair tests of discrimination. The discussion centers on the conventional secondary market, provided by the Federal National Mortgage Association (FNMA, Fannie Mae) and the Federal Home Loan Mortgage Corporation (FHLMC, Freddie Mac), while largely ignoring the role of the Government National Mortgage Association (GNMA, Ginnie Mae) and the private label secondary market for conventional loans.

Testing the effects of the secondary markets on discrimination is a formidable task. To date, little research has been done. Indeed, the ability of research to shed light on the topic is limited, and it is not clear that convincing research (in the sense of being capable of changing anyone's mind either pro or con) will be done in the near future. In this respect, this chapter reflects a pessimism that can be seen in recent reviews of research issues in discrimination in mortgage markets by Galster (1992) and by Wienk (1992). The research issues in secondary markets are probably more daunting than those in primary markets. Methodologies that appear to be promising in testing for discrimination in the primary market, such as use of accept-reject data supplemented with measures of credit risk (Munnell et al. 1992, 1996) and direct testing by sending similar applicants to lenders to see if treatment varies by race, are not feasible to test the separate effects of the secondary market. From a research point of view, we are left mainly with looking at the relationships among secondary market underwriting guidelines, default risk, and minority loan applications, which it may only be possible to examine at a fairly aggregate level. Difficult conceptual issues are also involved that require an understanding of the secondary market and of how the risks of the leading institutions—Fannie Mae and Freddie Mac—differ from those of traditional portfolio lenders. Research so far suggests that the major factors used in underwriting (down payment, payment burden, and credit history) are, indeed, related to default.

From a policy perspective, not everything requires research. Underwriting guidelines, for instance, should be continually evaluated to identify elements that do not (even if they once did) make sense. Although it is not possible to conduct detailed research on all of the elements of underwriting standards, it is possible to ask whether standards make sense in light of existing research. For example, much research suggests that homeowner equity is a major factor in default. Guidelines concerned with borrower equity are likely to be sensible. Other guidelines that cannot be plausibly connected with credit risk should be adjusted. Much can be (and has been) done to revise standards and clarify what constitutes a reasonable risk for secondary market institutions. Both Fannie Mae and Freddie Mac have recently dramatically altered the language in their guidelines to make it easier for creditworthy minority loans to be sold into the secondary market, and changes in this regard are continuing. Both are also undertaking massive efforts at credit scoring and automated underwriting, which will have major effects on mortgage markets.

The role of the secondary market can be investigated on either a broad macro level or a more detailed micro level. At the macro level, the issue is whether or not the existence of the secondary market has increased the flow of funds to minority borrowers. Of perhaps more importance, however, are the micro questions, which concern underwriting guidelines and standards and whether or not they treat equally creditworthy borrowers differently (see Ohls 1980; ICF 1991; Schnare 1992; Wienk 1992). The micro issue is whether or not creditworthy minorities are getting full advantage from the efficiencies of the secondary market. Even if minorities are benefitting in a macro sense, there may be ways in which the secondary market can provide better and more equitable service.

The next section presents a macro model of a mortgage market, segmented by race, into which a secondary market is added. The model discusses conditions under which a secondary market might help or hurt minority borrowers. After presenting this model, the chapter focuses on micro issues. The third section describes the evolution of the secondary market and incentive issues with which it must cope. The fourth section reiterates this chapter's definition of discrimination and how discrimination might operate in the secondary market. The fifth section looks at empirical evidence that may potentially reveal discrimination, including examining Home Mortgage Disclosure Act (HMDA) data to compare loans sold into the secondary market with all loans originated, as well as analyzing credit risk. Because measuring discrimination requires controlling for credit risk, it is important to look closely at the determinants of credit risk so that we can hold creditworthiness constant. The sixth section concludes the chapter.

A MACRO MODEL

Secondary mortgage markets have the effect of increasing the flow of funds into mortgage markets. For instance, if a bank sells mortgages into the secondary market, it can use the money to make new loans without having to attract new deposits. The loans sold into the secondary market need not be the same type of loans as the new loans made with the proceeds from the sale. For example, the thrift could sell safer, low loan-to-value (LTV) ratio loans and use the proceeds to buy high LTV ratio loans. The increased flow of funds can be expected to benefit all participants in the markets, not just those whose loans were sold. This sort of analysis can be applied to the effects on minorities of a secondary market. The analysis can, however, be complicated. What follows is a formal model of a segmented mortgage market.

Suppose there are two types of loans, minority and nonminority, and that both are originated and held by traditional portfolio lenders. Assume that lenders are reluctant to lend to minorities, but will do so if minority interest rates are relatively high. Each loan type has its own demand and supply, and because the loans are imperfect substitutes, rates need not be identical. Both markets clear, but minority markets clear at higher interest rates (alternatively, they could clear with tougher requirements, such as lower LTV ratios). Demand curves are given by $D_m(r_m)$ for minorities and $D_n(r_n)$ for nonminorities, where m refers to minority, n to nonminority, and r_m and r_n are interest rates charged to minorities and nonminorities, respectively. Markets clear when demand equals supply in both markets. Supply curves are given by $S_m(r_m, r_n)$ and $S_n(r_n, r_m)$, respectively. The presence of r_n and r_m in S_m and S_n reflects the assumption that lenders will move money from one market to the other if the interest rate is high enough. It is assumed that S_n and S_m respond negatively to r_m and r_n, respectively, and positively to r_n and r_m, but are more responsive in absolute value to their own rate.

The minority market is depicted in figure 11.1, with equilibrium borrowing rate, r_m^0. A decline in the nonminority rate, r_n, is assumed to shift the supply curve outward, lowering r_m to, say, r_m^1. A similar analysis applies to the nonminority market. That the two types of loans are imperfect substitutes for one another means that a 1 percent decline in r_n leads to a less than 1 percent decline in r_m in the minority market, and vice versa in the nonminority market.

Equilibrium requires that both markets clear simultaneously, as shown in figure 11.2. *MM′* represents combinations of r_n and r_m that clear the minority market; its slope is less than 1 because of the assumption of imperfect substitutes. Its slope is positive because of the assumption of increasing costs (rising rates are required to get lenders to switch funds to the minority market). NN′ is the same thing for the nonminority market; imperfect substitution means that its slope is greater than 1. Markets clear at *R*, where r_m is assumed to be greater than r_n.

The secondary market is introduced into the model in a way that is least advantageous to minorities, by assuming that it only purchases nonminority loans, so that it only shifts the equilibrium curve in figure 11.2 that applies to the nonminority market. The secondary market both expands the supply of funds and makes it more elastic. In this case, that means shifting and twisting *NN′* to something like *SS′*, which leads to the new equilibrium at $\overline{S}$. The shift in *NN′* causes both rates to fall. In particular, it causes supply to increase in the minority market. As a result, the interest rate falls and minority lending increases. The model is a formalization of a simple point. Even if the secondary market buys no minority loans, it frees up money for portfolio lenders to make more loans to minorities. This may show up as lower rates to minorities as in figure 11.2, as lower hurdles (such

Figure 11.1 SUPPLY AND DEMAND

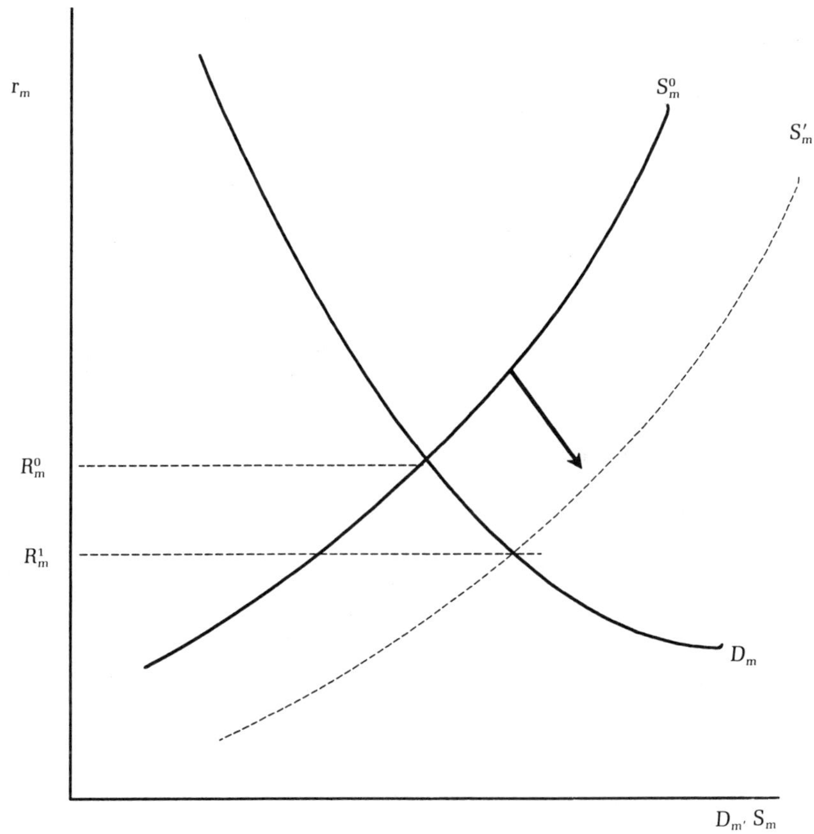

as LTV ratios or credit history), or simply as less rationing. To the extent that the secondary markets buy minority loans, it also shifts and flattens MM' to TT', leading to the equilibrium point $\overline{T}$, which lowers minority interest rates even farther.

An alternate argument would be that there are scale economies for portfolio lenders, and that entry by the secondary market raises costs to these lenders by limiting their ability to take advantage of the scale economies. Hence, in the macro model, secondary markets could have a negative effect on minorities as a whole if there are scale economies and secondary markets buy relatively few minority loans. The importance of scale economies is something about which it is possible to be skeptical given the large number of depository institutions.

Figure 11.2 MULTIMARKET EQUILIBRIUM

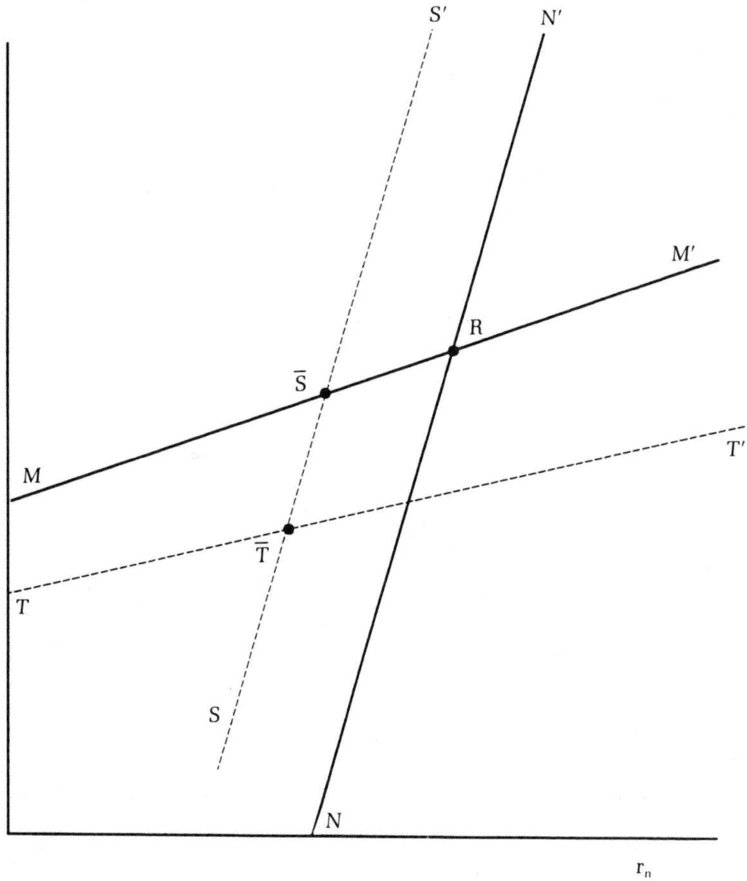

There are other reasons to expect the secondary market to lead to increased credit flows to minorities. The secondary market operates by accepting delivery of all loans that approved sellers deliver, subject to underwriting and other standards discussed later in the chapter. To the extent that discrimination at the originator level derives from perceptions about the risk of minority loans, lenders have an incentive to originate the loans, to sell into the secondary market, and to pass on the risk. To the extent that some of the perceived risks are erroneous, or at least not covered by the underwriting standards, more minority loans will be originated and sold into the secondary market than would have been otherwise. Increased competition, the rise of mortgage bankers and better technology, which have in the past been stimulated by the secondary market, may have also contributed to decreasing discrimination. Wienk (1992), for instance, pointed out that many borrowers apply for loans by telephone, limiting the ability to identify minorities.

All this suggests that it is unlikely that the advent of secondary markets decreases the overall supply of credit to, or raises the interest rate on, loans to minorities. It does not shed light on the question of whether or not secondary markets could better serve minorities.[1] To pursue this issue, the next section discusses the evolution of secondary markets.

EVOLUTION OF SECONDARY MARKET

Most mortgages are now sold into the secondary mortgage market. Virtually all Federal Housing Administration (FHA) and Department of Veterans Affairs (VA) loans become Ginnie Mae mortgage-backed securities. Most conventional mortgages are now sold to either Fannie Mae or Freddie Mac (in 1992 the share was around 60 percent), where they become either mortgage-backed securities (about 70 percent of the time for Fannie Mae and 80 percent of the time for Freddie Mac) or are held in portfolio and financed by debt (typically long term callable debt). There is also a growing "private label" secondary market, largely confined to conventional loans that exceed the Fannie/Freddie loan size limit (currently $207,000 for single family houses), which in the past has done almost as much business (about 10 percent of the market) as FHA/VA.

The modern evolution of the secondary market began in the 1930s with the creation of Fannie Mae as a vehicle to support the then-new FHA program.[2] It grew in the late 1960s with the creation of Ginnie Mae and the restructuring of Fannie Mae as a private corporation. In 1970 Freddie Mac was created to serve the thrifts (and conventional loans) in the way that Fannie Mae served mortgage bankers (and FHA/VA loans). In the 1970s, Fannie Mae moved into the conventional market as Ginnie Mae became the primary vehicle for FHA/VA. Fannie Mae and Freddie Mac are now both government-sponsored enterprises with similar charters and the same regulators.

The evolution of the secondary market has been a product of a variety of factors, many of which are of largely historical interest. For instance, deposit rate ceilings, which limited the ability of thrifts to raise money for mortgage loans, were a major factor in the rising importance of Fannie Mae in the 1960s and 1970s, particularly as a countercyclical device; but deposit rate ceilings are no longer an issue. Similarly, the inability of banks and thrifts to operate nationally was also important, but national deposit markets and liberalized branching rules have limited the importance of this. The main reason, now, for the important role of secondary markets, and particularly for their phenomenal increase in the 1980s, is simply that secondary markets are for the most part a more efficient way of raising money for mortgages than the traditional portfolio-lending thrift institutions.[3] This is primarily because of economies in raising money "wholesale" in the capital markets, in processing the purchase and servicing of large numbers of mortgage loans, and in managing risks through diversification.

Unbundling

The basic services provided by mortgage markets may be described briefly as: originating the mortgage; servicing; accepting the risk of default; and raising money to lend to the borrower. The traditional thrift did all of these. It originated the mortgage, serviced it, took the risk of default (perhaps along with a private or government insurer), and raised money in the deposit market. These functions were performed as one bundle. The secondary market evolved largely by unbundling this package. The major contribution of Ginnie Mae, Fannie Mae, and Freddie Mac has been to facilitate the money-raising part of the bundle by taking on credit risk and packaging mortgages so that they could be sold as relatively homogeneous securities or financed with homogeneous debt in the capital markets.

All four aspects of the mortgage bundle are now unbundled. The market is evolving in the direction of: (1) mortgage originators, who are large in number and small in scale, and who sell to or act as agents for a relatively smaller number of mortgage servicers; (2) mortgage servicers who sell the mortgages into the secondary market and either keep or sell the servicing rights; (3) secondary market institutions and mortgage insurers who take on credit risk; and (4) investors who buy mortgage-backed securities. Indeed, the last function has become further unbundled with the advent of derivative securities (REMICs, CMOs, etc.), which unbundle mortgages into various "tranches" and, as a result, unbundle the risks associated with mortgage prepayment.

This unbundling takes advantage of scale economies where they are important and division of labor, and promotes competition among the suppliers of the various bundles, but these do not occur without cost.

The cost is that the players that focus on one part of the bundle depend on players in other parts of the unbundling to perform services for them as expected (for example, to originate good loans) when it is not always clearly in their interest to do so. That is, there is a principal–agent problem: the principals (for example, the ultimate investors) depend on agents (the institutions originating and servicing the loans) to perform as promised, even though it may be profitable not to do so.

For Fannie Mae and Freddie Mac the major principal–agent issue comes from a reliance on originators and servicers to originate good loans and to service them properly. The major risks are that sellers, with superior information about loans, will adversely select against Fannie Mae and Freddie Mac, keeping good loans and delivering bad loans, or engage in "moral hazard" by actions such as originating and selling loans that are riskier than they appear to be, relaxing monitoring, or underwriting poorly. This is a crucial element of the chain from originators to investors. A fluid secondary market on the scale of the current market requires that investors not have to spend too many resources monitoring the credit risk of the individual borrowers. The ability of Fannie Mae and Freddie Mac to process large amounts of loans rapidly and raise money cheaply requires that they not underwrite individual loans but, instead, set standards for "investment quality" loans and examine only a small fraction of individual loans.

It is not always in the interests of sellers and servicers to perform as expected. For instance, mortgage originators make money based largely on their volume of business. They may have no inherent interest in the quality of the loans they originate once they are sold. This is particularly true for institutions in danger of bankruptcy. Mortgage servicers do have a stake in mortgage performance because delinquent mortgages are more costly to service. However, they benefit from scale economies and therefore have incentives to service lots of loans, and their stake in actual default is small. Hence, to control credit risk, Fannie Mae and Freddie Mac need to do things that align the incentives of a large number of servicers (Freddie Mac currently has over 2,000) with their own. At this time, credit risk is controlled by a combination of mortgage insurance and guidelines and incentives to sellers to sell quality mortgages. One strong incentive for sellers to provide quality mortgages is that they might have to repurchase mortgages for contract violations and may ultimately lose the ability to sell mortgages to Fannie Mae or Freddie Mac.

This is in contrast with the traditional, bundled thrift (portfolio lender) that has all the elements of the bundle under its control and should be less worried that the part of the firm that originates mortgages will take advantage of the part of the firm that evaluates credit risk.[4] Hence, balance between the role of the secondary markets and the role of traditional portfolio lenders depends on the balance between the economies of scale and fundraising that the secondary market brings and the advantages of control over some important risks that the traditional portfolio lender brings.

That this balance has been favorable to the secondary market for single-family mortgages is due primarily to advantageous circumstances in this market, which may not be replicable in other markets. The most important of the favorable circumstances are the ability to use a house as security (this comes from foreclosure laws) and the relatively good information that exists about house values (because houses trade fairly frequently and are relatively, though still imperfectly, easy to appraise). These two factors mean that homeowner equity is a good deterrent to default, and that we have a good idea of homeowner equity at loan origination. As a result, a major concern to institutions that accept credit risk is the probability of equity becoming negative. This risk is subject to some control from diversification (we may not know much at all about how many houses in a particular neighborhood will fall in price by enough to leave owners with no equity, but we have a better idea of how many will on a nationwide basis), and the risk can be analyzed statistically, along with other characteristics such as borrower credit history. The ability to treat houses almost like commodities and default risk almost like a financial option, such as a "put" option that gives the borrower the right to exchange the home for the mortgage (see Foster and Van Order 1984), is a major factor in the success of the secondary market.

These advantages are not common to most other markets. For instance, even multifamily housing is quite different, primarily because it is much more difficult to evaluate multifamily property values. (This is because multifamily properties are much more heterogeneous, they trade less frequently, and incentives for inaccurate appraisals are greater.) Also, incentives to take care of the property are weaker when the owners are not the occupants. It is therefore not surprising that attempts to provide secondary markets for commercial real estate and car loans have not had the success of the secondary-mortgage market for single-family loans, given the big differences between these markets and single-family housing markets.

Although single-family housing has great informational advantages, it is also clear from both experience and research that there is much more to credit risk than simply down payment, equity, and exercising a financial option. As discussed later in the chapter, risks vary by neighborhood, borrower characteristics, and other factors. Hence, even given initial down payment, much potential remains for surreptitiously passing risks through to the secondary market. For the secondary market to thrive, it must control other hard-to-measure sources of risk, so that default risk can be treated in a simple and quantitative manner. For instance, this probably means trying to avoid risks that involve serious information asymmetries.

The underlying choice issues for both buyers and sellers in the secondary market can be summarized as follows. The secondary market has to worry about the principal–agent issues discussed previously. Fannie Mae and Freddie Mac publish guidelines to specify what is clearly acceptable, while allowing lenders to use their judgment to go outside the guidelines when some compensating factor enables the credit risk to remain unchanged (in other words, when the loans are still of investment quality). The potential punishment to lenders who go outside the guidelines and deliver excessively risky loans is that they may have to repurchase loans and eventually may not be allowed to sell mortgages to Fannie Mae and/or Freddie Mac.

The lender must choose between either selling standard mortgages (which it will almost certainly not have to repurchase) or selling nonstandard mortgages (for which there is some risk of repurchase). Not selling (or not originating) nonstandard loans is safer, but at the cost of missing some profitable business. Good underwriters can choose to sell nonstandard mortgages at relatively low risk of repurchase. A further choice, of course, is either to violate the rules deliberately or to be overly aggressive about what is creditworthy and make money from origination and servicing fees until caught. This choice involves adverse selection (such as when the lender sells the bad loans but keeps the good ones) or moral hazard. That entry into and exit from the mortgage origination business is relatively easy may make this a tempting strategy in some circumstances (for example, when firms are in financial trouble and are "gambling for resurrection"). The advent of mortgage brokers and other third party originators with no stake in servicing has increased this risk.

For most lenders, at least some risk of repurchase is inevitable, because no single set of guidelines can provide a perfect measure of credit risk. Local lenders are capable of using their local information to make creditworthy loans. Hence, Fannie Mae and Freddie Mac need to be flexible and to delegate some decisions to lenders (and mortgage insurers). However, this need to delegate inevitably raises the principal–agent problem just discussed. The risk is best controlled by requiring that lenders have some stake in the outcome of their decisions.

This stake currently consists of the risk that lenders will have to repurchase bad loans. The asymmetry of information means there may be no way that lenders who sell into the secondary market can both have discretion to be outside the guidelines and avoid repurchase risk. The task of the guidelines is to be as clear as possible about what is a "safe harbor" and, in particular, to avoid language that discourages safe loans. The test of whether discrimination then results involves looking at data to see if the interaction of guidelines and lender behavior rule out minority loans that are in fact creditworthy. Unfortunately, rigorous tests are quite difficult. We do not, for instance, have accept/reject data relevant to the secondary market or detailed data on creditworthiness like the data used in the Federal Reserve Bank of Boston study (hereafter, the "Boston Fed" study, Munnell et al. 1992, 1996).

For the secondary market to survive and take advantage of the available economies, it must confront the principal–agent problem. The key public policy issue is whether we have the right balance between standards and discretion. The key research issue is how to create tests that can separate discrimination from valid credit control issues.

DISCRIMINATION

As stated at the outset of this chapter, racial discrimination in mortgage markets can be defined as unequal treatment of equally creditworthy borrowers on the basis of race.[5] This definition requires a focus on two issues: What is unequal treatment, and what constitutes equal creditworthiness? A simple example is the rejection of profitable loans to minorities, where profitability is measured by the expected net present value of profits (risk-adjusted). This is a separate (but related) issue from affordable housing and community reinvestment. Discrimination can as easily occur against a minority member with a high income applying for a loan in a credit-saturated neighborhood as it can occur against someone with a low income in an inner-city area in dire need of capital improvements. Although discrimination may be correlated with income and location, the emphasis here is on unequal treatment of equally creditworthy borrowers.

Most recent research on discrimination in mortgage markets has not been very illuminating. The only recent study that provides a real test of discrimination is the Boston Fed study (see Munnell et al. 1992, 1996), which used HMDA data, supplemented with data from loan files, to analyze accept/reject decisions by race for Boston area lenders, using proxies such as LTV ratio and credit history to control for creditworthiness. The study found that about a third of the raw differences in rejection rates between minorities (28 percent rejection rate) and nonminorities (11 percent rejection rate) could be explained by race, rather than creditworthiness; about two-thirds could be explained by variables such as LTV ratio and credit history. The main criticism of Munnell et al.'s study has been whether the effect from race is in fact due to race or to other variables correlated with race that the authors could not measure (see also chapter 4, this volume). Munnell et al. (1992, 1996) discussed secondary markets in the text but did not present any statistical work that might shed light on the role of the secondary market. Although there has been some discussion of the role of the secondary market, it has largely been confined to anecdotal evidence about underwriting guidelines or to the sort of loans that Fannie Mae and Freddie Mac do or do not buy (see Schnare 1992 for a brief survey).

The mechanism through which discrimination, as just defined, would most likely work in the secondary market is through underwriting standards. For instance, underwriting guidelines might provide limits on payment-to-income ratios, which disproportionately affect minorities but do not affect creditworthiness or are overly strict. Both Fannie Mae and Freddie Mac have published underwriting guidelines, and both argue that their guidelines are intended to be flexible and that a large share of their business is outside some of these guidelines. The research question is whether the system results in minority loans that, on average, would be profitable if not sold into the secondary market.

The next section looks at some of the available data. I first examine HMDA data, comparing loans sold into the secondary market with those made in the market as a whole. I then look at preliminary results of some research on credit risk. The question is whether the secondary market's standards are inadvertently tougher on characteristics that are associated with minority borrowers.

WHAT CAN BE DONE WITH RESEARCH?

If the question is whether the underwriting guidelines are too rigid and, as a result, inadvertently discriminate by screening out profitable loans to minorities, then three issues need to be addressed: first, the rigidity of the standards and whether the rigidity is appropriate, given the adverse selection problems faced by the secondary market; second, the extent to which standards disproportionately affect minorities; and, third, the extent to which underwriting standards are actually related to credit risk.

The first issue has been the focus of much debate. In a study sponsored by Freddie Mac, ICF (1991) invited representative lenders from 12 metropolitan areas to a series of focus groups to discuss the effect of the secondary market on community lending. Whereas it was agreed that lenders did not overtly discriminate, representatives expressed concern that racial and ethnic stereotypes affect lending and that some underwriting standards were too rigid. Rigidity is hard to quantify. The Boston Fed study (Munnell et al. 1992, 1996) indicated that about half of the accepted loans in its sample excluded the secondary market guidelines on payments relative to income, and viewed this as an indication of flexibility. Fifty percent is a larger share than is typical of most regions, probably because Boston has very high housing prices, requiring higher-than-average payment burdens. Fannie Mae and Freddie Mac data suggest a share that is closer to 20–25 percent on average.

The second issue can be analyzed by exploiting HMDA data and comparing loans sold to Fannie Mae/Freddie Mac versus all loans originated. Such as analysis paints with a broad brush; it does not look at individual metropolitan areas or neighborhoods, or at subgroups of minorities. It does, however, make some general comparisons. As discussed earlier, it is not necessary for the secondary market to buy the same mix of loans as the market as a whole in order to be helpful to everyone, but a significantly different mix would suggest further consideration.

The third issue can be addressed by looking at the historical risks associated with characteristics identified in underwriting guidelines. Such as analysis attempts to evaluate whether, in a broad sense, the borrower and property characteristics that underwriting standards try to restrict are really associated with credit risk.

HMDA Data

Information derived from 1991 HMDA data about neighborhood characteristics of secondary market mortgage purchases shows that the secondary market closely mirrors the primary market.[6] Table 11.1 compares secondary market institutions with primary market institutions in terms of income, racial composition, and the central city location

Table 11.1 NEIGHBORHOOD CHARACTERISTICS: SECONDARY MARKET VERSUS PRIMARY MARKET INSTITUTIONS (PERCENTAGE OF TOTAL)

	Freddie Mac	Fannie Mae	Primary Market
Percentage in low-income census tracts	9.3	8.0	9.4
Percentage in minority census tracts	6.9	5.6	6.2
Percentage in central cities	34.8	34.9	35.1

Sources: HMDA data for 1991 on conventional, single-family originations and 1980 census. Note that the HMDA sample misses some loans outside metropolitan areas and hence does not represent the universe of loans.

Table 11.2 BORROWER CHARACTERISTICS: SECONDARY MARKET VERSUS PRIMARY MARKET (PERCENTAGE OF TOTAL)

Borrower Characteristics	Freddie Mac	Fannie Mae	Conforming Primary Market
Asian	6.6	4.8	4.3
Native American	0.4	0.4	0.4
African American	2.2	2.5	2.9
Hispanic	5.6	4.6	4.9
White	84.4	86.8	86.7
Other	0.8	0.8	0.7

Source: HMDA data for 1991 on conventional, single-family originations.

Table 11.3 BORROWER INCOME: SECONDARY MARKET VERSUS PRIMARY MARKET

Percentage of MSA Median Family Income	Freddie Mac	Fannie Mae	Primary Market
0–50	2.0	2.1	3.5
51–80	10.4	10.5	11.4
81–100	12.5	12.5	11.8
101–120	14.3	14.6	12.8
121–150	20.0	19.8	17.3
150	40.5	40.8	43.3

Source: HMDA data for 1991 on conventional, single-family originations.

of neighborhoods (census tracts) where the loans are located. Table 11.2 shows the distribution across racial and ethnic groups for Freddie Mac, Fannie Mae, and primary market borrowers. Both tables show that loans purchased by Freddie Mac and Fannie Mae have largely the same characteristics as the conventional, conforming, primary market as a whole. Table 11.3 presents income distributions for borrowers whose loans were bought by Freddie Mac and Fannie Mae, and for borrowers in the primary market overall. Income categories are based on the borrower's income relative to the median family income of the metropolitan statistical area (MSA). The primary market has a higher proportion of borrowers in the lowest income category (at or below 50 percent of local median income); it also has a higher share of borrowers in the highest income category (at least 150 percent of local median income).[7] Across middle-income categories, however, borrowers in the primary and secondary markets are distributed similarly.

Default Data

If the secondary market's underwriting guidelines discriminate by requiring excessive compensating factors for loans that are outside the guidelines and that are also likely to be disproportionately minority loans, then one could expect those minority loans that are accepted to perform better than other, similar loans. This suggests that one should examine the default experience of accepted loans by, for instance, race and neighborhood, as well as the default experience on loans outside the guidelines (such as loans with payment-to-income ratios greater than the "standard" 28 percent). The proposition that loans made to those who are discriminated against should perform better, however, only applies to loans at the margin of being accepted. For instance, nonminority borrowers have, on average, more wealth and may, on average, have 75-percent LTV ratios on accepted loans versus 80-percent LTV ratios for minorities (who have less wealth). Under those circumstances, one should expect the nonminority loans to perform better, on average. Discrimination is more likely to be an issue for 95-percent LTV loans (see discussion in Van Order, Westin, and Zorn 1993). For example, if 95-percent LTV loans in minority neighborhoods were found to perform better than 95-percent loans in nonminority neighborhoods, one might have evidence of discrimination. Hence, if actual results are used to glean insights into discrimination, one needs to look at the performance of marginal loans. Doing so requires careful modeling of credit risk to measure what is marginal.[8]

Table 11.4 reproduces some results from Van Order et al. (1993) that are derived from an estimated default model specifying conditional default rates as a function of initial LTV ratio; the probability of the property having negative equity; borrower and neighborhood (by ZIP code) income; and the payment-to-income ratio and race (measured by percentage black in ZIP code; race of borrower is unavailable) using Freddie Mac data on some 700,000 loans originated from 1975 to 1983,

Table 11.4 PROBABILITY OF DEFAULT BY NEIGHBORHOOD INCOME, QUARTILE, AND RACE FOR 95-PERCENT LTV LOANS

	Black Concentration		
Income Quartile	0–9%	10–24%	>25%
Northeastern Region			
1st Quartile (lowest)	.06	.05	.09
2d	.02	.02	.08
3d	.02	.01	.06
4th (highest)	.01	.02	.06
North Central Region			
1st Quartile (lowest)	.18	.20	.27
2d	.13	.15	.31
3d	.10	.10	.30
4th (highest)	.07	.08	.06
Southeastern Region			
1st Quartile (lowest)	.15	.12	.08
2d	.18	.09	.03
3d	.08	.04	.04
4th (highest)	.09	.08	[a]
Southwestern Region			
1st Quartile (lowest)	.16	.14	.29
2d	.20	.24	.10
3d	.15	.19	.13
4th (highest)	.19	.06	.03
Western Region			
1st Quartile (lowest)	.14	.20	.23
2d	.11	.20	.16
3d	.08	.12	.24
4th (highest)	.06	.03	.07

Source: Data from Van Order et al. (1993).
Note: Probability of defaulting is in first eight years.
a. Too few data points.

sold to Freddie Mac, and matched with 1980 census data. Details of the estimation model can be found in Van Order et al. (1993).

Table 11.4 presents estimates of the probability of default over the first eight years for marginal loans, meaning loans with LTV ratios of 95 percent. We estimated separate models for five geographic regions. In general, loans in low-income neighborhoods (the first quartile) performed relatively poorly, and in three of the five regions, high racial concentration was positively associated with default. The southeastern region consistently showed better performance in black neighborhoods, which suggests racial discrimination; the southwestern region was ambiguous. The other regions suggested either no racial discrimination or an inability to distinguish among competing hypotheses (because we had some of the same omitted-variable problems as other researchers, such as no data on credit history). The results in the Southeast, however, are particularly interesting in light of the higher rejection rates for minorities in that region found in subsequent HMDA data.

Although these results, particularly those for the Southeast, may be illuminating, they are inconclusive with respect to the secondary market. The loans were primarily originated by thrift institutions at a time when the secondary market was relatively small, so it is difficult to separate the effects of the thrifts' standards from those of the secondary market, because the loans were probably not originated with the intention of selling them. It would also be useful to have data on the loans that were not sold.

The data do suggest, however, that default is complicated and needs to be investigated to understand discrimination. For instance, one of the variables that researchers have found to be important in explaining default is the probability of negative equity. Van Order et al. (1993) estimated the probability that each borrower's mortgage balance would be 10 percent or more than the house price by using Freddie Mac housing price data, which can be broken down by race and income of the neighborhood, and exploiting the standard deviation of housing price changes that comes out of the process of estimating average house price. Estimates of the average probability of negative equity, which is a measure of the riskiness of the property (relative to the loan size), are shown by region in table 11.5 by LTV ratio, neighborhood income, and racial concentration. It was found that, looking at unadjusted data, high racial concentration is associated with increased property risk, but the relationship is not causal. Breaking down the data, as is done in the table, reveals that the relationship has nothing to do with race per se; rather, it has to do with black neighborhoods being associated with low down payments and low neighborhood income, both of which are factors in explaining property risk. Holding these two things constant, race has either no significant effect or is found actually to decrease property risk.[9]

Much further research needs to be done. Although we have a good understanding of why low down payments are associated with default, we know much less about why neighborhood income is correlated with default. Income is probably a proxy for numerous characteristics, such as age, location of property, and other neighborhood aspects, that affect property values. The point is that a nondiscriminatory policy that controls for default risk by controlling for both LTV ratio and whatever is behind neighborhood income effects might appear to be discriminatory when it is not. This makes it difficult to determine the impact of underwriting standards on discrimination without careful analysis of default risk.[10]

These are not new results. The Boston Fed study made much the same point; applying unbiased standards to blacks would, in its analysis, mean higher rejection rates for minorities than nonminorities mainly because of differences in down payment and credit history. The Boston Federal Reserve was fortunate to have a data set that allowed control for most objective underwriting criteria, permitting them to estimate how much of the actual difference in rejection rates is and is not related to minority status.

Test of Payment-to-Income Ratios

An important aspect of underwriting guidelines is the ratio of mortgage payment-to-income ratio. Assume that the "true" default model is given by

$$d = F(x, z), \tag{11.1}$$

where d is the conditional default rate, x is a vector of things we can measure, and z is a vector of things we cannot measure. The payment-to-income ratio (P/Y) is one of the elements of x. Because z and x are probably correlated, a regression of d on x will probably give biased estimates of the effects of x on d, holding z constant. This bias should be especially pronounced for values of x outside the guidelines, because the guidelines are intended to cause z to vary such that when x is outside the guidelines, d does not change.

Consider P/Y. The true relationship between d and P/Y is assumed to be upward sloping. For safe loans that are well inside the guidelines, P/Y can be expected to be independent of z, and the estimated slope will be close to the true slope. As P/Y increases, default risk increases and the likelihood increases that z will be chosen so as to mitigate the risk from P/Y, which should induce a downward bias in the estimated slope of the relationship between d and P/Y. We should expect, ideally, that outside the guideline the estimated slope would be zero.

Figure 11.3 depicts hypothetical relationships between default and the payment-to-income ratio. Inside the guidelines, the estimated curve is upward sloping, as one would expect, representing something close to the true relationship, though the slope declines as one approaches the guidelines. Outside the guidelines, if the lender's off-

Table 11.5 PROBABILITY OF NEGATIVE EQUITY BY LTV, NEIGHBORHOOD INCOME (ZIP MED INC), AND RACIAL CONCENTRATION

LTV Ratio	Zip Med Inc	Percent Black in Zipcode 0–9%	10–24%	> 25%
A. Northeast				
10%–80%	1st Quartile	.005897	.007416	.007953
	2nd Quartile	.003527	.004678	.005853
	3rd Quartile	.003593	.005259	.002080
	4th Quartile	.002498	.002516	.000585
81%–90%	1st Quartile	.065436	.066707	.066554
	2nd Quartile	.048034	.052006	.049798
	3rd Quartile	.017158	.057452	.024476
	4th Quartile	.043197	.029170	.011472
91%–94%	1st Quartile	.088044	.097253	.084680
	2nd Quartile	.061097	.072991	.072880
	3rd Quartile	.066512	.074889	.026213
	4th Quartile	.065995	.939248	.020850
95%	1st Quartile	.138203	.117260	.147541
	2nd Quartile	.094592	.114346	.128204
	3rd Quartile	.108737	.091874	.06551
	4th Quartile	.104618	.067792	.033661
B. North central				
10%–80%	1st Quartile	.019689	.017147	.017136
	2nd Quartile	.015859	.011466	.012643
	3rd Quartile	.010009	.013525	.003856
	4th Quartile	.004375	.003036	.005793
81%–90%	1st Quartile	.171871	.163317	.146156
	2nd Quartile	.138412	.104980	.107570
	3rd Quartile	.084303	.111863	.044362
	4th Quartile	.049337	.035709	.083615
91%–94%	1st Quartile	.238608	.205268	.237795
	2nd Quartile	.218982	.155203	.280300
	3rd Quartile	.141437	.573099	.002505
	4th Quartile	.075768	.003706	.073530
95%	1st Quartile	.333280	.221465	.319242
	2nd Quartile	.274196	.222451	.235121
	3rd Quartile	.183693	.181697	.227228
	4th Quartile	.117899	.084203	.154858
C. Southeast				
10%–80%	1st Quartile	.007323	.007117	.008234
	2nd Quartile	.008097	.003640	.004911
	3rd Quartile	.008218	.002656	.005316
	4th Quartile	.008672	.016987	.002405
81%–90%	1st Quartile	.065048	.050036	.073925
	2nd Quartile	.061915	.027815	.040655
	3rd Quartile	.067585	.021051	.047018
	4th Quartile	.068540	.125442	.013437
91%–94%	1st Quartile	.119698	.984742	.097529
	2nd Quartile	.091519	.041014	.064704
	3rd Quartile	.090936	.048006	.034276
	4th Quartile	.093376	.197381	.058601

Table 11.5 PROBABILITY OF NEGATIVE EQUITY BY LTV, NEIGHBORHOOD INCOME (ZIP MED INC), AND RACIAL CONCENTRATION (continued)

		Percent Black in Zipcode		
LTV Ratio	Zip Med Inc	0–9%	10–24%	> 25%
C. Southeast *(cont'd.)*				
95%	1st Quartile	.153016	.123710	.142055
	2nd Quartile	.141151	.058598	.085499
	3rd Quartile	.137552	.059475	.092783
	4th Quartile	.153954	.230691	.042910
D. Southwest				
10%–80%	1st Quartile	.039648	.084187	.062438
	2nd Quartile	.035550	.104063	.033223
	3rd Quartile	.036780	.096019	.140920
	4th Quartile	.036859	.085035	.196237
81%–90%	1st Quartile	.112926	.175095	.172444
	2nd Quartile	.100431	.183728	.116268
	3rd Quartile	.100761	.172486	.253240
	4th Quartile	.121481	.162575	.326379
91%–94%	1st Quartile	.211481	.162575	.326379
	2nd Quartile	.273519	.366045	.218254
	3rd Quartile	.207123	.673967	.415452
	4th Quartile	.283036	.365590	.265058
95%	1st Quartile	.228841	.241593	.328818
	2nd Quartile	.228112	.344739	.199600
	3rd Quartile	.183377	.370988	.353740
	4th Quartile	.244140	.296842	.529627
E. West				
10%–80%	1st Quartile	.005638	.001759	.002358
	2nd Quartile	.003455	.001880	.001524
	3rd Quartile	.002852	.000160	.000489
	4th Quartile	.001319	.000756	.000076
81%–90%	1st Quartile	.039107	.022021	.028376
	2nd Quartile	.025552	.010325	.016466
	3rd Quartile	.022168		.011264
	4th Quartile	.012691	.017263	.001822
91%–94%	1st Quartile	.097641	.044850	.070724
	2nd Quartile	.081741	.078873	.200063
	3rd Quartile	.075520		.000001
	4th Quartile	.034701	.045770	
95%	1st Quartile	.111519	.054583	.087881
	2nd Quartile	.086447	.048180	.047554
	3rd Quartile	.078388		.033320
	4th Quartile	.049504	.016868	.002070

Notes: Probability is defined as having equity negative by 10% or more of mortgage balance at some time during first 8 years. Racial concentration is percent black head of household from 1980 census. ZIP MED INC is median income in zipcode in 1980.

Figure 11.3 HYPOTHETICAL RELATIONSHIPS BETWEEN DEFAULT AND PAYMENT-TO-INCOME RATIO

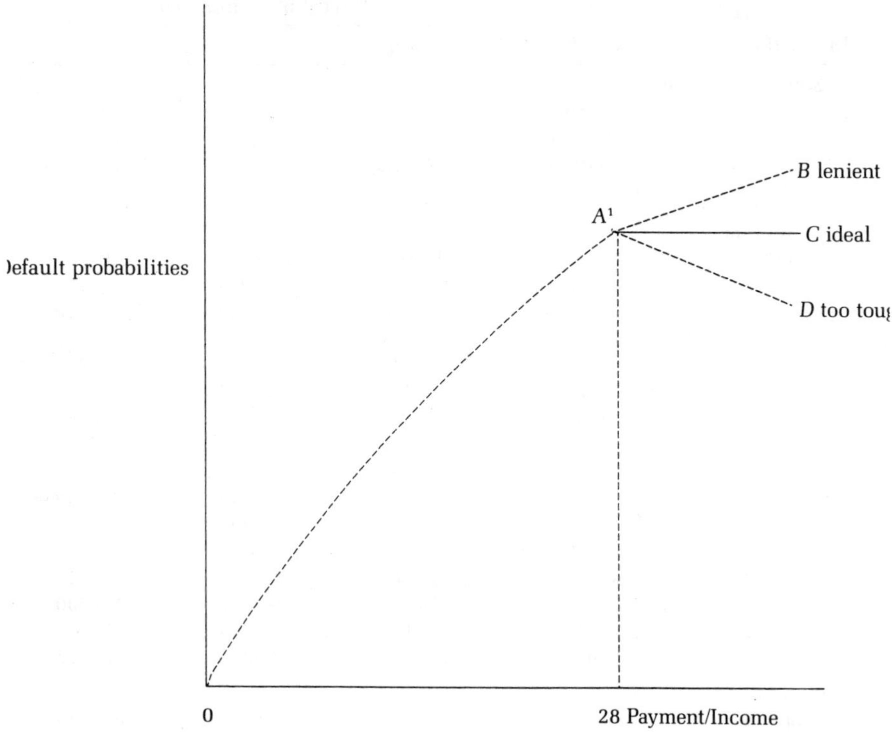

setting factors do in fact offset higher *P/Y*, then default risk will be the same, and the observed relationship should be something like the curve *OAC* (that is, a curve drawn from *O* to *A* to *C*) in the figure; that is, flat outside the guidelines. If the guidelines are too tough, it should look like *OAD* and, if too lenient, like *OAB*. Hence, the role of payment-to-income guidelines can be tested by looking at their relationship with default.

Table 11.6 presents results using the sample of Freddie Mac loans in tables 11.4 and 11.5. My colleagues and I estimated a default model using a proportional hazard model of the form

$$d(t) = a(t)\exp(Bx), \tag{11.2}$$

where $d(t)$ is the conditional default rate, $a(t)$ the baseline time trend, and x the measurable explanatory variables. We estimated the coefficients of x, the Bs, using standard partial likelihood techniques. Estimates of the Bs are presented in the table along with their standard

Table 11.6 MORTGAGE PAYMENT-TO-INCOME RATIO AND DEFAULT

	Region				
Model A	Northeastern	North Central	Southeastern	Southwestern	Western
Coefficient (standard deviation)					
P/Y ≤ 25%[a]	.22	.32	−.02	−1.21	−.44
	(1.00)	(.58)	(.58)	(.20)	(.11)
25% P/Y ≤ 28%[b]	.54	.16	.43	−.36	.17
	(0.54)	(.60)	(.60)	(.22)	(.12)
28% P/Y ≤ 33%[c]	−.22	.26	1.06	−.17	.19
	(1.15)	(.65)	(.61)	(.23)	(.12)

a. Dummy for payment-to-income (P/Y) less than 25 percent (relative to greater than 33 percent).
b. Dummy for P/Y between 25 percent and 28 percent.
c. Dummy for P/Y between 25 percent and 28 percent. Omitted dummy is for P/Y > 33 percent.

	Region				
Model B	Northeastern	North Central	Southeastern	Southwestern	Western
Coefficient (standard deviation)					
P/Y ≤ 25%	.49	−.70	−.17	−.70	−.73
	(1.00)	(.58)	(.58)	(.20)	(.11)
25% P/Y ≤ 28%	.64	.28	.26	−.60	.02
	(1.02)	(.60)	(.60)	(.21)	(.12)
28% P/Y ≤ 33%	−.04	.61	.82	−39	.10
	(1.16)	(.65)	(.61)	(.23)	(.12)
PROB[a]	8.28	4.16	8.79	5.13	5.49
	(0.43)	(.10)	(.35)	(.06)	(.07)
REAL INC.[b]	−0.03	−0.02	.004	.002	.017
	(.005)	(.003)	(.003)	(.001)	(.0006)

a. Probability of negative equity (by at least 10 percent) during first eight years of loan.
b. Borrower's real income.

errors. Part A uses four dummy variables representing four payment-to-income ranges: less than or equal to 25 percent, between 25 and 28 percent, between 28 and 33 percent, and greater than 33 percent. The greater-than-33-percent dummy is omitted. Hence, the coefficients measure the effects of *P/Y* relative to having *P/Y* greater than 33 percent. A negative coefficient means that borrowers in that *P/Y* group default less than those in the greater-than-33-percent group. If the guidelines worked as depicted by *OAC* in figure 11.3, one should see negative coefficients, which are lowest for less-than-25 percent payment-to-income ranges and increase, becoming almost zero in the 28 to 33 percent range. We observed that in the southwestern region, but we saw mixed results elsewhere. The northeastern, north central, and southwestern regions all have coefficients that tended to decline in the range outside the guidelines but were not statistically significant. The West was also ambiguous, with a negative sign in the first group but small positive (though insignificant) signs in the middle groups.

We reran the regressions controlling for other effects. Part B of table 13.6 is a representative example. We added "PROB," the variable representing the probability of negative equity,[11] which is the same variable as depicted in table 11.5 and "REAL INC.," the borrower's real income. Not surprisingly, the variable PROB did most of the work in explaining default, but the coefficients of the payment-to-income variables were similar.

The results are thin for three reasons. First, the loans were originated 10 or more years ago, and guidelines and perceptions of the guidelines have changed. For instance, only about 5 percent of the loans in the sample had payment-to-income ratios greater than 28 percent. Second, the loans were almost all originated by thrifts at a time when the secondary market was small. Hence, it is not clear whose standards one is observing. Third, in the regions where the standards appear to be tough, the coefficients were statistically insignificant. The only significant coefficients for payment-to-income were in the Southwest and West, and their signs were consistent with being lenient outside the guidelines. Hence, the data, such as they are, reject the hypothesis that standards outside the guidelines are too tough.

Clearly, more work with data like these is needed. Freddie Mac has not until recently collected data on race, and stopped collecting income during 1983, though it has started/resumed collecting data on both race and income. Researchers at Freddie Mac have done some preliminary work with data from some mortgage insurers, which so far show a positive relationship between default and debt-to-income ratios even at high levels. The results are, however, quite preliminary.

Understanding the role of underwriting requires first developing a data set that includes a wider range of factors than we now have, and then modeling their effects on default as well as their relationship with race. For the relatively small number of items on which there has been some focus, there is little evidence of bias, but there is also much ambiguity. For instance, guidelines criticized by lenders in ICF (1991) involved elements such as down payment source, documentation of credit history, employment stability, and number of units in the structure. Some empirical work on these has been done at Freddie Mac. This preliminary work suggests that the number of units probably is important (we have had worse experience on two- to four-unit structures than on single-unit ones) and that documentation of credit probably is important because, as research so far indicates, credit history is crucial in predicting default. Employment stability may be a small factor (I suspect that *income* stability is what is important), and we have little information about down payment source (both Fannie Mae and Freddie Mac have relaxed on down payment source).

CONCLUSIONS

Much is still unknown about the role of the secondary market in discrimination. It is probable that the existence of secondary markets has meant more loans to minorities at lower mortgage rates. Research to date does not imply that secondary market standards are overly rigid, but this research remains inconclusive (or nonexistent) about the details.

From a researcher's perspective, recent work on discrimination in primary markets suggests three useful ways of analyzing discrimination:

- Studies like the Boston Fed study (Munnell et al. 1992, 1996) that examine accept/reject data supplemented with data that allow control for creditworthiness;
- Tests that send similarly qualified minority and nonminority borrowers to lenders to see if they are treated differently; and
- Investigations that look at default data to see if minorities are subjected to tougher screening to have a loan accepted.[12]

The first two approaches are not possible in the secondary market. No clear accept/reject decision occurs in the secondary market; instead, a seller decides what to originate and to sell based on a perception of what might have to be repurchased. For the same reason, it is not possible to conduct testing.

This leaves the third approach, investigating the connection between underwriting standards and default, which is a promising line of research. Possible future sources of data are mortgage insurers, enriched data from Fannie Mae and Freddie Mac, and perhaps Federal Housing Administration (FHA) and 1990 census data. There is potential for following the history of recently originated loans (it would be interesting to follow the default history of the loans gathered by the Federal Reserve Bank of Boston), but it will take time to get results.

Unfortunately, problems will always result from the inability to measure compensating factors used in evaluating loans outside the guidelines. Furthermore, because there is likely to be substantial multicollinearity among underwriting criteria, measuring separate effects of individual criteria may be quite difficult.

The risks faced by Fannie Mae and Freddie Mac differ from those faced by most portfolio lenders. In particular, the unbundling of the mortgage process, which is an integral part of the secondary market, means that principal–agent/adverse selection issues are more important in the secondary market. This requires Fannie Mae and Freddie Mac to be concerned about the incentive structure of those who sell and service mortgages, a structure that requires some rigidity in underwriting standards as well as the threat that sellers will have to repurchase loans. Investigating whether this nexus ends up causing creditworthy loans by minorities not to be sold into the secondary market is important; but it is also doubtful that an incentive system that both adequately controls credit risk and completely satisfies everyone concerned with minority lending will be devised soon.

Measures That Might Help

Research may be of limited value, but not all guideline changes require research. Wienk (1992) discussed an example of a 1995 Fannie Mae underwriting guideline involving who was eligible to be a co-borrower. The guideline was clearly outmoded and had no clear theoretical (or empirical) connection with credit risk, so it was revised. More recently, Freddie Mac changed language in its guidelines to emphasize income stability, rather than employment stability of borrowers, and ways to establish creditworthiness without a credit history. Both Fannie Mae and Freddie Mac have endeavored in recent years to purge their guidelines of language that might lead indirectly to discrimination. The intention of these changes is to widen the range of loan characteristics that clearly falls inside the guidelines. Even though research may not give precise answers, theory and common sense can still be useful.

Expanded research on discrimination generally is important. For instance, tests at the lender level may be unable to separate the secondary from the primary market or to uncover all of the secondary market issues. However, this testing should provide some information about discrimination in general, and the knowledge that testing is being done will lessen the probability of discrimination (see Galster 1992 and Wienk 1992).

Despite the sophistication of the capital markets in pricing securities, retail pricing of mortgages could be more sophisticated. In particular, there is little risk-based pricing. Pricing does vary by product (for example, adjustable-rate versus fixed-rate mortgages); however, for most loan products, the only part of the bundle that is explicitly priced according to risk is mortgage insurance, which only covers part of default costs. Not pricing by risk leads to allocation by rationing, which may disproportionately affect minorities—for example, by making it harder to get loans with 95-percent LTV ratios. Minorities have less wealth and generally make smaller down payments (the Freddie Mac data used in the analysis in the fifth section of this chapter confirm generally higher LTV ratios in more racially concentrated neighborhoods), and this contributes (as in the Boston Fed study) to higher rejection rates. One would expect that most applicants would prefer paying, say, an extra quarter percent to not getting a loan at all. Not all dimensions of credit risk are easy to price, but improved pricing should generate some improvements.

Finally, both Fannie Mae and Freddie Mac are moving toward automated underwriting and/or credit scoring. These changes promise to have dramatic effects on underwriting, both because scorecards do not know the race of the applicant and because they make the tradeoffs between various aspects of credit quality (e.g., the tradeoff between down payment and credit history) explicit. Furthermore, a byproduct of the process will be a lot more data, which may shed light on some of the empirical issues discussed above.

Notes

I am grateful to Vanessa Perry and Peter Zorn for their help in preparing this paper, as well as for comments from Michael Bradley, Ann Dougherty, Ed Golding, Tom Holloway, Frank Nothaft, and John Straka. This paper does not necessarily reflect the views of the Federal Home Loan Mortgage Corporation.

1. This analysis also ignores feedback from other markets. For instance, it ignores effects that different rates or credit conditions could have on real estate prices and rents.

2. There was a private secondary market before the 1930s, but it and the private insurers that supported it were wiped out by the Great Depression.

3. A measure of the efficiency of secondary markets is the difference at the retail level between rates on loans above the Fannie Mae/Freddie Mac limit (currently $207,000) and below it. The difference is consistently a quarter to a half of a percent. Although one might argue that this is in part due to Fannie and Freddie's implicit guarantee, that

is not the case. The lenders above the conforming loan limits are primarily depositories, who probably get a much bigger subsidy from their explicit guarantee (deposit insurance).

4. This is not to say that there is no risk. Compensation schemes could induce conflicts of interest inside the firm. The point is that conflicts inside the firm are easier to resolve.

5. The mortgage market works primarily by rationing. That is, loan applications are generally either accepted or rejected, rather than charged different prices according to risk. There is some indirect price rationing because loans with LTV ratios over 80 percent are required to have insurance, which is priced by LTV ratio, and because lenders sometimes adjust loan terms, which is an indirect form of pricing. The focus of discrimination research (Munnell et al., 1992, 1996, for example) has generally been on disparate treatment of equally creditworthy borrowers rather than on charging different prices to similar borrowers.

6. For further analysis, see Nothoff and Perry (1991–92) and Perry (1993).

7. Secondary market institutions are subject to conforming loan limits, which prevent them from purchasing large balance loans. For example, the 1996 maximum loan amount for one-unit properties was $207,000. Loans with larger balances ("jumbo" loans) cannot be purchased by Freddie Mac or Fannie Mae. This is probably the main reason that Fannie Mae and Freddie Mac do relatively less high-income business.

8. The Boston Federal Reserve study has been criticized for not looking at actual defaults on the grounds that minority and nonminority applicants have had similar default rates, indicating (according to the article) that standards were fair. This analysis is wrong, for reasons just cited. In particular, the minority loans accepted in the Boston Fed study (Munnell et al. 1992, 1996) had "worse" characteristics (such as higher LTV ratios and worse credit history) and, absent discrimination, should be expected to default more frequently.

9. This, of course, is not all there is to credit risk. Further research, such as depicted in table 11.6, suggests that individual characteristics (such as credit history) and other loan characteristics (such as payment burden) also matter.

10. Some important, but perhaps subtle, complications should also be noted here. Our model suggests a complicated nexus between race and default. It is apparently legal to "discriminate" on the basis of things like LTV ratios, credit history, and payment burden—which are correlated with race, but which clearly affect default risk. Given that these relationships are complicated, the model presented in this chapter suggests that lenders might be tempted to use race as an instrumental variable. That is illegal. The research problem is that it is hard to tell the difference between different types of discrimination.

11. This is a function of initial down payment and local housing growth.

12. This is not to say there are no other promising routes. For instance, Bentson and Horsky (1991) presented an interesting example of using telephone interviews to get views directly from both house sellers and borrowers. However, their approach required a large number of random telephone interviews to get a rather small sample, and hence, may not be cost-effective.

References

Becker, G. 1971 [1957]. *The Economics of Discrimination*, 2nd ed., Chicago: University of Chicago Press.

Benston, G., and D. Horsky. 1991. "The Relationships between Demand and Supply of Home Financing and Neighborhood Characteristics." *Journal of Financial Services Research* 5: 235–61.

Foster, C., and R. Van Order. 1984. "An Option-Based Model of Mortgage Default." *Housing Finance Review* (October).

Federal Home Loan Mortgage Corp. 1992. "Home Mortgage Eligibility, Appraisal, and Underwriting Requirements." *Seller & Servicers Guide* 1 (January, Bulletin 92-2).

Galster, George. 1992. "Research on Discrimination in the Housing and Mortgage Markets: Assessment and Further Directions." *Housing Policy Debate* 3(2): 639–83.

ICF, Inc. 1991. *The Secondary Market and Community Lending through Lenders' Eyes*. Report prepared for Federal Home Loan Mortgage Corporation. Fairfax, Va.: Author, February.

Munnell, Alicia H., Lynn E. Browne, James McEneaney and Geoffrey M.B. Tootell. 1992. "Mortgage Lending in Boston: Interpreting HMDA Data." Federal Reserve Bank of Boston Working Paper 92-07. Boston: Federal Reserve Bank of Boston, October.

Munnell, Alicia H., Geoffrey M.B. Tootell, Lynn E. Browne, and James McEneaney. 1996. "Mortgage Lending in Boston: Interpreting HMDA Data." *American Economic Review*. Forthcoming.

Nothaft, F., and V. Perry. 1991–92. "Home Mortgage Disclosure Act Data." *Secondary Mortgage Markets* 5 (Winter): 2–8.

Ohls, J. 1990. *Secondary Mortgage Market: Information on Underwriting on Home Loans in the Atlanta Area*. Washington, D.C.: General Accounting Office.

Perry, V. 1993. "Peering into Cities." Secondary Mortgage Markets 10 (1, Winter).

Schnare, Ann B. 1992. "Secondary Market Business Practices and Mortgage Credit Availability." Paper presented at Fannie Mae Annual Housing Conference.

Van Order, Robert, Ann-Margaret Westin, and Peter Zorn. 1993. "Effects of the Racial Composition of Neighborhoods on Default, and Implications for Racial Discrimination in Mortgage Markets." Paper presented at meeting of American Economic Association, Jan. 8, Anaheim, Calif.

Wienk, Ronald. 1992. "Discrimination in Urban Credit Markets: What We Don't Know and Why We Don't Know It." *Housing Policy Debate* 3(2): 217–40.

Chapter Twelve

HOUSING DISCRIMINATION AND THE APPRAISAL INDUSTRY

Robert G. Schwemm

INTRODUCTION

Discrimination in the appraisal of housing is prohibited by a number of laws. The most important of these laws is the federal Fair Housing Act, which was passed as Title VIII of the Civil Rights Act of 1968 and which, as amended by the Fair Housing Amendments Act of 1988, outlaws discrimination in appraising and a variety of other housing transactions on the basis of race, color, religion, national origin, sex, handicap, and familial status.[1]

Although in effect for some 25 years, the Fair Housing Act's ban on appraisal discrimination has produced only a small amount of litigation. Fewer than 10 cases involving Title VIII claims of appraisal discrimination have been reported.[2] The most important of these cases—indeed, the only case designed to bring about major changes in the way real estate appraising is conducted—is *United States* v. *American Institute of Real Estate Appraisers*,[3] in which the U.S. Department of Justice (DOJ) in the mid-1970s successfully challenged the use of appraisal principles that called for lower values in racially mixed neighborhoods.

Most of the other Title VIII appraisal cases have been based on highly individualized fact patterns, although they generally involve the same basic situation. In these cases, a home in which the plaintiff had an interest was appraised too low to qualify for a particular mortgage loan, with the plaintiff alleging that the low appraisal was based on racial considerations and the defendant denying that race played any part in the appraisal. The relative strength of the evidence offered by both sides is generally the key to resolving the case, which means that the court's decision is usually of limited precedential value apart from showing how the judiciary may react to certain types of evidence in an appraisal discrimination case.

The limited nature of Title VIII case law in this area makes it difficult to assess the true role of the appraisal industry in the overall context of the problem of housing discrimination. Obviously, appraisals are an important part of the process of buying, selling, and financing housing. Because lending institutions generally will not approve a home loan unless the loan amount is under a certain percentage of the appraised value of the property (for example, 80 percent),[4] a low appraisal may well result in the denial of a requested loan, which in turn is likely to result in the collapse of the entire deal. As one court recently observed: "An appraisal sufficient to support a loan request is a necessary condition precedent to a lending institution making a home loan."[5]

To acknowledge the importance of appraising in the home buying process does not, however, address the question at issue in this chapter, which is whether illegal discrimination in home appraisals is or is not a major problem requiring a substantial increase in research and enforcement efforts. Representatives of the appraisal industry are likely to argue that the answer is no, based on the dearth of cases in this area and the fact that professional standards now prohibit considering racial factors in appraising neighborhoods. Neither fact is entirely persuasive, however. For example, the number of reported Title VIII cases involving mortgage lending and home insurance is also relatively small, but this hardly means that discrimination in these fields has been eliminated. And with respect to professional standards, the real estate industry, like the appraisal industry, has for some time now endorsed a set of nondiscriminatory principles, but scores of real estate brokers and their agents are accused every year of violating Title VIII and these principles.

Thus, although it may well be that the appraisal industry is generally complying with Title VIII and that only the occasional renegade appraiser behaves in a way that results in litigation, it may also be that the industry has so insulated itself from traditional investigative and research techniques that it is able to engage in widespread discrimination without detection. Or the truth may lie somewhere in between.

While not presuming to resolve this issue, this chapter seeks to provide a basic foundation for addressing it by reviewing housing appraisal discrimination law and the cases dealing with it. The second section of this chapter surveys the applicable laws, with a focus on Title VIII's relevant provisions and a brief comment on the impact of the Financial Institutions Reform, Recovery, and Enforcement Act of 1989 (FIRREA). The heart of this chapter is the third section, which describes and analyzes each of the eight Title VIII cases involving appraisal discrimination that have been reported thus far. A summary of the conclusions derived from these cases and some suggestions for further points of inquiry comprise the fourth section.

LAWS PROHIBITING DISCRIMINATION IN HOUSING APPRAISALS

Overview and Note on FIRREA

As stated previously, the principal federal statute prohibiting discrimination in the appraisal of housing is the Fair Housing Act (Title VIII of the Civil Rights Act of 1968), which, as amended, bans appraisal discrimination on the basis of race, color, religion, national origin, sex, handicap, and familial status.[6] Racial discrimination in the appraisal of housing may also violate the Civil Rights Act of 1866 (42 U.S.C. §1981–§1982).[7] A discriminatory appraisal that results in the denial of home financing may also violate the Equal Credit Opportunity Act of 1974 (ECOA),[8] which bans credit discrimination on the basis of race, color, religion, national origin, sex, marital status, age, and source of income.[9] Federally chartered financial institutions may be subject to antidiscrimination regulations issued by their governing agencies that prohibit lenders from relying on discriminatory appraisals. In addition to these federal laws, most of the states and many localities have statutes prohibiting discrimination in housing appraisal.

The Fair Housing Act's prohibitions of appraisal discrimination are reviewed in the next subsection. This paper focuses on Title VIII, because it is the federal statute most clearly concerned with discrimination in home appraisals and because, although claims under §1981–§1982, ECOA, and other laws may also be appropriate, no case has ever relied on these other laws to uphold a claim of appraisal discrimination without holding that the defendant's discrimination also violated the Fair Housing Act.

Before turning to Title VIII, mention should be made of FIRREA.[10] Title XI of FIRREA establishes a federal regulatory system for appraisers who deal with federally related real estate transactions. The purpose of Title XI is to protect federal financial and public policy interests in such transactions by requiring that appraisals be performed in accordance with uniform standards by individuals of demonstrated competency whose professional conduct is subject to effective supervision.[11] Although FIRREA itself does not ban discriminatory appraisals, it will likely have a profound effect on the way appraisals are conducted and will, at least indirectly, be a source of policy judgments on appraisal standards.

For example, one of the requirements of Title XI is that all appraisals performed in connection with federally related real estate transactions be performed only by individuals who are certified or licensed pursuant to a federally approved state certification procedure.[12] Title XI also requires that an individual may not be certified pursuant to such a state procedure without passing a suitable examination similar to the Uniform State Certification Examination issued or endorsed by the Appraiser Qualification Board of the Appraisal Foundation.[13] This board develops, publishes, interprets, and amends the Uniform Standards of Professional Appraisal Practice (USPAP), which have been adopted by the major appraisal organizations and are now recognized throughout the United States as the generally accepted standards of appraisal practice.[14] Since their promulgation in the mid-1980s, USPAP have included a standard that requires appraisers to consider "neighborhood trends" in developing a real property appraisal, but cautions that: "In considering neighborhood trends, an appraiser must avoid stereotyped or biased assumptions relating to race, age, color, religion, gender, or national origin or an assumption that racial, ethnic, or religious homogeneity is necessary to maximize value in a neighborhood."[15] As a result of FIRREA's Title XI, the Appraisal Qualification Board's USPAP, including this one prohibiting certain kinds of discrimination in appraising, will undoubtedly be more widely taught and tested, and—it is hoped—observed.

Fair Housing Act

The Fair Housing Act itself contains at least three provisions that outlaw discriminatory appraisals. The most clearly applicable is §805, whose subsection (a) makes it unlawful for "any person or other entity whose business includes engaging in residential real estate-related transactions to discriminate against any person in making available such a transaction, or in the terms or conditions of such a transaction, because of race, color, religion, sex, handicap, familial status, or national origin."[16] The term "*residential real estate-related transactions*" in this provision is defined in §805(b) to mean a number of specified practices, including the "appraising of residential real property" (see discussion upcoming).[17] At the same time, §805 concludes with a subsection (c) entitled "Appraisal Exemption," which provides that nothing in Title VIII prohibits a person "engaged in the business of furnishing appraisals of real property to take into consideration factors other than race, color, religion, national origin, sex, handicap, or familial status."[18]

The other two provisions of Title VIII that have been used to challenge discriminatory appraisals are §804(a) and §804(b).[19] Section 804(a) makes it unlawful to refuse to sell, rent, or negotiate for the sale or rental of housing or to "otherwise make unavailable or deny" housing to any person because of race, color, religion, sex, familial status, or national origin. (A similar provision in §804(f)(1) extends these substantive prohibitions to discrimination against those with handicaps.[20]) Because a discriminatory appraisal may lead to the denial of a home loan and thereby make housing "unavailable," a number of courts have held that this practice would violate §804(a).[21]

Section 804(b) makes it unlawful to "discriminate in the terms, conditions, or privileges of sale or rental of a dwelling, or in the provision of services or facilities in connection therewith, because of race, color, religion, sex, familial status, or national origin." (A similar provision in §804(f)(2) extends these substantive prohibitions to discrimination against those with handicaps.[22]) Because appraising may be included in the "services" provided in connection with the sale of a home, discrimination in the terms or conditions of an appraisal may violate §804(b).[23]

There are some important differences in the prohibitions contained in §805(a), §804(a), and §804(b). As a general matter, §805(a) is broader than the other two. For example, §805(a) covers discrimination in all aspects of the appraisal of residential real property, whereas §804(a) and §804(b) apply only to appraisals in connection with the sale or rental of a dwelling. The need to anchor §804(a) and §804(b) to a particular housing transaction means that these sections might not be available, say, in a suit by current residents who want to challenge appraisal practices that undervalue the homes in their neighborhood, whereas presumably §805(a) would apply in such a case. In addition, §804(a) and §804(b) are subject to the exemptions in §803(b),[24] which include the sale of a single-family home by its owner under certain circumstances, whereas these exemptions do not apply to §805(a).[25] On the other hand, the §805(c) exemption that specifically authorizes appraisers to take into consideration factors other than those condemned by Title VIII applies to all of the statute's prohibitions, including those in §804(a) and §804(b) as well as those in §805(a). It would seem, therefore, that §805(a) covers all of the discriminatory appraisal practices included in §804(a) and §804(b), and some that are not included in these other provisions.

The specific coverage of discriminatory appraisals in §805 is the result of a broadening of this section undertaken by the 1988 Fair Housing Amendments Act.[26] (The 1988 Act did not change §804(a) and §804(b) except by adding familial status and handicap to the list of prohibited bases of discrimination.) The version of §805 that was enacted as part of the 1968 Fair Housing Act outlawed only "[d]iscrimination in the financing of housing" by businesses engaged "in the making of commercial real estate loans."[27] The 1968 law, like the current version, prohibited discriminatory "terms or conditions" as well as outright refusals to deal and included loans for the purpose of "purchasing, constructing, improving, repairing, or maintaining a dwelling,"[28] but coverage did not extend to any business that did not make commercial real estate loans.[29]

The 1988 Fair Housing Amendments Act broadened the coverage of §805. As it now reads, §805 includes any entity that engages in "residential real estate-related transactions," which are defined to include not only the making of housing loans but also the purchasing of or the provision of other financial assistance for such loans, the making or purchasing of loans secured by residential real estate, and the selling, brokering, or appraising of residential real property.[30] Under the amended version of §805, "the nature of discriminatory conduct no longer can be limited to matters relating to the actual provision of financing."[31]

In extending §805's coverage to a broader range of transactions, however, the 1988 Congress also indicated that there were limits to this new coverage. For example, and as noted previously, a new subsection (c) was created that specifically protects appraisers from liability under any provision of Title VIII for taking into consideration factors other than those specifically condemned by the statute.

Despite the significant changes to the language of §805 by the 1988 amendments, the fact remains that the Act's prohibitions against discriminatory appraising essentially only restate what had already been the law prior to 1988. According to interpretive regulations issued by the U.S. Department of Housing and Urban Development (HUD), §805 bars persons and entities engaged in appraising residential real property from discriminating against any person "in making available such services, or in the performance of such services, because of race, color, religion, sex, handicap, familial status, or national origin."[32] Except for the addition of familial status and handicap as illegal bases of discrimination, however, most, if not all, of the appraisal practices proscribed by §805 were also unlawful under the 1968 Fair Housing Act. For example, a discriminatory appraisal that blocked a home sale or the financing necessary for a home sale has long been understood to violate §804(a) and the pre-1988 Act version of §805.[33] For the most part, therefore, the new version of §805 simply clarified Title VIII's existing coverage.

The same is true regarding the exemption for nondiscriminatory appraisals provided for in §805(c). Prior to the enactment of this provision, courts in Title VIII appraisal cases under §804(a) and §805 had made clear that appraisal practices were not unlawful unless they were based on race or some other factor prohibited by the Fair Housing Act.[34] Accordingly, the U.S. House of Representatives Committee on the Judiciary described §805(c) as a provision that merely "clarifies that appraisers may take into consideration relevant and nondiscriminatory factors when making appraisals."[35]

Thus, for the past 25 years the Fair Housing Act has prohibited discriminatory appraisals in housing on the basis of race and certain other specified factors. Yet during this quarter century, Title VIII's ban on discriminatory appraisals has produced only eight reported cases. These cases are reviewed in the next section.

TITLE VIII CASES INVOLVING APPRAISAL DISCRIMINATION

United States* v. *American Institute of Real Estate Appraisers

The most important discriminatory appraisal case to date is the earlier-mentioned *United States* v. *American Institute of Real Estate Appraisers*,[36] in which the Justice Department accused four trade associations of violating Title VIII by promulgating discriminatory appraisal standards and by publishing instructional materials and conducting courses and seminars encouraging the use of such standards. The defendants were the American Institute of Real Estate Appraisers (AIREA), the Society of Real Estate Appraisers (SREA), the U.S. League of Savings Associations, and the Mortgage Bankers Association of America. They were sued in 1976 for, among other things, setting standards that caused appraisers and lenders to treat race and national origin as negative factors in determining the value of dwellings and in evaluating the soundness of home loans.

AIREA, for example, published a widely used textbook, *The Appraisal of Real Estate,* which instructed appraisers that "the value of the property being appraised should be adjusted downward if the ethnic composition of the neighborhood to which it belonged was not homogeneous."[37] This so-called "principle of conformity" continued to be adhered to well into the 1970s, years after passage of the 1968 Fair Housing Act.[38] The United States alleged that these and related practices violated §804(a), §805, and §817 (now §818).

The defendants in the *AIREA* case moved to dismiss the complaint, arguing in general that Title VIII does not apply to appraisers and pointing out in particular that §804(a) and §817 do not mention appraisers or the appraisal process. The trial court rejected this contention, noting that appraisers are not exempted from these provisions and holding that discriminatory appraisals could "otherwise make unavailable or deny" housing in violation of §804(a) and could "interfere" with the rights guaranteed by Title VIII in violation of §817.[39]

After this ruling, AIREA entered into settlement negotiations with HUD and DOJ. The resulting proposed settlement agreement and affirmative action program called for AIREA to adopt the following three fundamental policy statements:

1. It is improper to base a conclusion or opinion of value upon the premise that the racial, ethnic, or religious homogeneity of the inhabitants of an area or a property is necessary for maximum value.
2. Racial, religious, or ethnic factors are deemed unreliable predictors of value trends or price variance.
3. It is improper to base a conclusion or opinion of value, or a conclusion with respect to neighborhood trends, upon stereotyped or biased presumptions relating to race, color, religion, sex, or national origin or upon unsupported presumptions relating to the effective age or remaining life of the property being appraised or the life expectancy of the neighborhood in which it is located.[40]

AIREA agreed that these principles reflected sound appraisal practices, and the United States determined to its own satisfaction that "the policies satisfy the requirements of the Fair Housing Act."[41]

The settlement agreement also called for AIREA to implement these stated policies through specific changes in *The Appraisal of Real Estate* and in its other instructional materials, courses, and seminars. AIREA also agreed to change the rules and commentary relating to certain elements of its code of professional ethics, such as by issuing a new reporting rule that provided in part: "All written appraisal reports relating to residential real estate which state that a neighborhood is undergoing decline or is about to undergo decline must contain the specific facts or reasoning upon which the . . . conclusion . . . is based."[42] AIREA futhermore agreed to expand its recruitment and outreach programs aimed at acquainting women and minority group members with opportunities in the real estate appraisal profession.[43]

When AIREA and DOJ asked the court to enter this settlement order, objections were raised to it by SREA and by an individual appraiser who was a member of AIREA. SREA's objections were based in part on its view that Title VIII did not apply to appraisers, which, as noted previously, the court rejected. In addition, SREA was concerned that approval of the settlement would place a judicial imprimatur on specific theories of appraising, which would stifle the exchange of ideas within the profession and would condemn alternative theories. The court discounted this fear, noting that its acceptance of the settlement would not amount to judicial adoption of the policies agreed to, but only to a determination that the settlement was valid and lawful.[44] The court also noted that approval of the settlement would affect only the claim against AIREA and therefore would not prejudice SREA's defense in this case.[45] Nevertheless, SREA argued that it might be at a competitive disadvantage with the litigation continuing against it but not against AIREA; however, the court considered this concern to be "speculative."[46]

The objections of the individual AIREA member were also rejected. The member had argued that the agreement would infringe on his First Amendment rights, presumably because he would no longer be free to advocate or use appraisal principles inconsistent with those adopted in the settlement agreement. The court noted, however, that the individual was not bound by the agreement; that AIREA, as a private organization, was not subject to the First Amendment; and that the possibility of the individual being sanctioned by AIREA at some later date for violating the newly agreed-to principles was a contingency inappropriate for judicial consideration at that time.[47]

Having determined that the settlement agreement was valid and lawful under the Fair Housing Act and that the objections by the other parties did not justify its rejection, the court approved the agreement and entered it as an order in an opinion issued on November 23, 1977.[48] The individual AIREA member attempted to appeal this decision, but the court of appeals ruled in 1978 that it lacked jurisdiction to hear the matter because the trial court's order was not a final decision in the case or an otherwise appealable order.[49] This ruling meant that the trial court's approval of the settlement order remained intact.

Significance and Impact of *AIREA* Case

The *AIREA* case is significant for at least four reasons. First, it showed that the passage of the 1968 Fair Housing Act did not by itself lead the appraisal industry to abandon reliance on race and other illegal factors—a reliance that was finally successfully challenged only after a major suit brought by the Justice Department. Second, the *AIREA* case settled once and for all that appraisal discrimination is indeed covered by Title VIII, for the trial court's ruling upholding DOJ's position on this issue was never seriously disputed thereafter.

Third, *AIREA* led to fundamental changes in appraisal principles dealing with race, national origin, and other factors condemned by Title VIII, including the abandonment of the "principle of conformity" and the substitution therefore of the principles adopted in the settlement agreement. Not only did AIREA make changes in *The Appraisal of Real Estate*, its code of ethics, and other AIREA publications, but, as SREA predicted, the court-approved settlement eventually forced SREA and similar organizations to follow suit.[50] Indeed, the basic theory of the *AIREA* claim was eventually endorsed by HUD in its proposed regulations interpreting the 1988 Fair Housing Amendments Act's ban on appraisal discrimination, which condemned the practice of "instructing or encouraging any person, either by statement or conduct, or imposing standards requiring any person, to consider any factor which relates to race, color, religion, sex, handicap, familial status, or national origin . . . in making an appraisal of residential real estate."[51]

Finally, the very success of the *AIREA* litigation ultimately made discriminatory appraisal cases much more difficult to win, for once the industry adopted race-neutral policies, allegations of unlawful discrimination had to be based on the aberrational behavior of an individual appraiser as opposed to a professionally dictated practice. Virtually all of the appraisal cases decided after *AIREA* involved such an individual allegation, and none of them has resulted in a victory on the merits for the plaintiff. These cases are discussed later in this section.

Pre-*AIREA* Case

Harper v. Union Savings Ass'n

The only reported Title VIII case involving appraisal discrimination decided prior to the settlement order in the *AIREA* case was *Harper*

v. *Union Savings Ass'n*,[52] a 1977 decision by Judge William J. Thomas of the Northern District of Ohio. The plaintiffs in *Harper* were a black couple who alleged that Union Savings' decision to foreclose on their home loan for late payment was racially discriminatory because the defendant had not been equally aggressive in foreclosing against delinquent white borrowers. Judge Thomas held that this claim stated a cause of action under Title VIII's §805, but he went on to rule for the defendant on the merits because he found that its foreclosure of the plaintiffs' mortgage was "solely for justifiable reasons. Race played no part in Union's foreclosure decision."[53]

As part of the Harpers' effort to prove racial discrimination in the defendant's foreclosure decision, they offered as evidence the appraisal of their home that Union Savings had done in 1972 when the Harper loan was made and that was before the defendant's loan committee when it decided to foreclose on the loan in 1974. The appraisal form included a section headed "Neighborhood," under which were printed three categories: "American," "Mixed," and "Foreign." The word "*Mixed*" was circled on the Harpers' form. The plaintiffs argued that this indicated that Union's appraisal was based in part on the fact that the neighborhood was racially mixed, an interpretation the court found plausible.[54] Nevertheless, Judge Thomas ruled that this evidence did not establish the defendant's racial motivation in foreclosing on the Harper loan, for no connection was shown between Union's awareness of the mixed nature of the neighborhood and its foreclosure decision, and other evidence showed that legitimate financial concerns about the Harpers prompted the foreclosure decision.

Despite his ruling in favor of the defendant in *Harper*, Judge Thomas was critical of the terminology used on Union Savings' appraisal form, and stated that the terms "*American*," "*Mixed*," and "*Foreign*," when used to describe the neighborhood, "created a potential for misuse."[55] The terms had been removed from the defendant's form in late 1975, which the court characterized as a change "long overdue."[56]

Thus, although the defendant escaped liability in *Harper* based on the totality of the evidence, its use of an appraisal form that seemed to call for the characterization of neighborhoods on racial and/or national origin grounds created an inference of discrimination. Put another way, the defendant's eventual decision to abandon this part of its appraisal form, like the reforms provided for in the *AIREA* settlement, would in the future eliminate a source of evidence that at least suggested a reliance on illegal factors in the appraisal process.

Post-*AIREA* Cases

HANSON V. VETERANS ADMINISTRATION

In the 1986 *Hanson v. Veterans Administration* case,[57] the Fifth Circuit Court of Appeals affirmed a trial judge's ruling that the Veterans Administration (VA) did not engage in illegal discrimination in its appraisal of homes in a predominantly black, middle-class neighborhood in Houston, known as the MacGregor subdivision. The plaintiffs in *Hanson* were individuals who sought to buy or sell homes in MacGregor and the West MacGregor Protective Association. They alleged that the VA's appraisal practices relating to its home loan guaranty program caused homes in the plaintiffs' neighborhood to be "underappraised" at a significantly higher rate than in white areas. Each of the individual plaintiffs was a party to a different agreement for the sale of a home in which a VA-guaranteed loan was sought. In each instance, the VA's appraisal was below the price prospective purchasers had agreed to pay for the property, which caused many of the prospective purchasers to reduce their offers or to look elsewhere, in turn allegedly causing an overall diminution in property values in the MacGregor area.

The plaintiffs claimed that the VA's appraisal practices violated Title VIII, §1981–§1982, and the Fifth and Fourteenth Amendments to the Constitution. After a bench trial, the district court ruled in favor of the VA in an unreported decision, relying on various grounds including the fact that it felt the evidence failed to establish either discriminatory intent or discriminatory effect.

The Fifth Circuit Court of Appeals affirmed the ruling in a 1986 decision.[58] The court of appeals began its legal analysis by upholding the plaintiffs' standing to sue.[59] It also ruled that the plaintiffs' claim stated a cause of action under Title VIII's §804(a), because the VA's alleged practices, though not directly involving sales or rentals, might nevertheless interfere with home sales on racial grounds.[60]

On the merits, however, the appellate court held that the evidence justified the trial court's ruling for the VA. This part of the *Hanson* opinion began by noting that the plaintiffs were required to prove intentional discrimination in order to prevail under §1981–§1982 and the U.S. Constitution, but that a violation of §804(a) "may be established not only by proof of discriminatory intent, but also by a showing of a significant discriminatory effect."[61]

With respect to discriminatory intent, the plaintiffs pointed to the facts that (1) VA appraisers had learned to evaluate racially mixed neighborhoods negatively on the basis of the "principle of conformity," which had been taught in *The Appraisal of Real Estate* textbook until the *AIREA* settlement in 1977 and which continued to be used by appraisers thereafter because it had not been formally denounced by the VA; (2) phrases used by appraisers to describe the MacGregor neighborhood—such as "economic depreciation," "changes in the neighborhood," and "lack of pride of ownership"—were code words that reflected racial considerations; and (3) VA appraisals of homes in MacGregor were "riddled with errors" (for example, understating the size of a home or overstating its age), which collectively suggested a racial bias.[62]

The defendant countered with five Houston appraisers who testified as expert witnesses that (1) the phrases used did not have racial connotations; (2) the appraised values of specific homes in MacGregor appeared reasonable (for example, one house's low appraisal was based on the presence of termites, dry rot, and foundation settlement); (3) no Houston appraiser used race to evaluate property any more, because to do so would be unethical; and (4) the VA appraisal form required appraisers to certify that they did not take race into account in doing an appraisal.[63]

The evidence also showed that the basic technique used to appraise homes for the VA was the "market approach" method, a race-neutral technique that sets the value of the subject property on the basis of adjustments to the sales price of three "comparables"—recently sold homes in the neighborhood that are as similar as possible to the subject property. According to the *Hanson* opinion:

> The sales price of these three comparables is used as a starting point to appraise the subject property; the appraiser may adjust the sales price of the comparable property either up or down depending on the perceived difference between the comparables and the home being appraised. In using this appraisal method, the fee appraiser does not take into consideration a sales price that has been agreed to on the home being appraised.[64]

The trial court accepted the testimony of the VA's witnesses and concluded that any appraisal errors that were made with respect to MacGregor properties were the result of "human error" rather than racial discrimination.[65] The Fifth Circuit upheld these findings as not "clearly erroneous," and therefore affirmed the district court's conclusion that discriminatory intent had not been shown.[66]

To support their Title VIII effect claim, the plaintiffs offered a statistical expert who testified that the VA underappraised a much higher proportion of homes in the MacGregor area (80–86 percent) than in a comparable white area (29 percent) and that regression analysis showed that MacGregor homes generally had higher "predicted values" than their VA appraisal values.[67] The VA countered with its own expert who criticized the plaintiffs' expert for failing to "control" the data in comparing MacGregor appraisals to those in the white area, for using samples that were too small, and for failing to consider important nonrace variables, such as crime rate and school quality, in his regression analysis.[68] The defendant's expert also testified that, when the regression analysis was redone properly, it did not reflect any racial impact.[69] Faced with this conflicting evidence, the trial court chose to reject the views of the plaintiffs' expert and therefore concluded that the VA's appraisal practices had not been shown to have resulted in a racially based negative impact on home values in the MacGregor area, a conclusion that the Fifth Circuit held was supported by the evidence.[70]

A number of lessons can be derived from the *Hanson* litigation. One of these underscores the importance of the *AIREA* settlement on future appraisal cases, for the defense in *Hanson* was able to argue that modern appraisals are free from the discriminatory "principle of conformity" that had existed before *AIREA*. It may be the case, as the *Hanson* plaintiffs contended, that some appraisers continue to rely on racial factors and use code phrases to mask their illegal discrimination, but proving this in the absence of the type of "smoking gun" evidence that the principle of conformity provided is likely to be difficult.

This is true even when the plaintiffs are able to produce expert appraisal testimony establishing that the defendant has underappraised homes in a minority area. In *Hanson*, for example, the defendant was able to convince the fact finder that the underappraisals were the result either of "human error" or of legitimate factors, such as defects in a particular home, or the local crime rate, or school deficiencies. Although these factors may well correlate with a high percentage of minority residents in some areas, their use by appraisers is certainly not illegal per se.

Indeed, the basic market approach to appraising, with its reliance on three "comparables," is inherently race neutral. It is true, of course, that some subjective judgments do enter into this process (such as in choosing which "comparables" to rely on and in making adjustments up or down from the comparables to the subject property), all of which may allow for racial considerations to be reflected in the final appraisal. The point is, however, that proving such discrimination is difficult, because it requires demonstrating that the appraiser departed from what appears to be an inherently nondiscriminatory process and engaged in what amounts to aberrant behavior.

Hanson also shows that the availability of the discriminatory effect theory under Title VIII, while perhaps helpful to plaintiffs in some circumstances, is no panacea for the difficult problem of generally having to prove discriminatory intent in appraisal cases. Finally, *Hanson* is a classic example of the fact that, when the plaintiff's proof of discrimination is circumstantial rather than direct and there is conflicting evidence in the record, the key to the case becomes how the trial court views the evidence, with that view being virtually impossible to have overturned on appeal.

JORMAN V. VETERANS ADMINISTRATION

Another case involving appraisals in connection with the VA's home loan guarantee program was *Jorman* v. *Veterans Administration* (1987).[71] In *Jorman*, residents of a southwest Chicago neighborhood that rapidly changed from predominantly white to predominantly black in the mid-1970s sued the VA for contributing to this racial instability by making home loans too readily available in their area. Among the VA practices that the plaintiffs complained about was the use of a technique known as "John Doe appraisals," which allowed sellers to have their homes preapproved for a VA loan if an otherwise qualified buyer appeared. The plaintiffs alleged that this technique tended to hasten sales and that the VA's overall failure to adequately monitor the effects of its home loan program contributed to the resegregation of the plaintiffs' neighborhood in violation of Title VIII.

The plaintiffs also claimed that VA-hired appraisers considered race in their work and that, as a result of this illegal consideration, they set the value of homes in the plaintiffs' neighborhood lower than was appropriate. To support this claim, the plaintiffs produced a number of witnesses, including a former California appraiser who explained the use of the "principle of conformity" prior to the *AIREA* settlement in 1977 and who testified that "an established, ingrained principle" of the appraisal profession was "for appraisers to take into account neighborhood racial change when doing appraisals."[72] The VA countered this evidence by pointing out that (1) VA policy since at least 1953 had been that race is not a factor that may influence property valuation by VA appraisers; (2) the VA appraisal form requires appraisers to certify that they have not been influenced by race or other factors condemned by Title VIII, and no appraiser had been found to have violated this certification since Title VIII was enacted; and (3) the plaintiffs' appraisal expert had no personal knowledge of how VA appraisals were conducted in the subject neighborhood or whether the particular VA appraisers who conducted those appraisals were ever schooled in or adhered to the "principle of conformity."[73]

Although the relevant time period in *Jorman* was 1975–78, the case was not tried until December 1985. Nine months later, the district court ruled against the plaintiffs, holding that they lacked standing to sue because their claimed injury—losing the benefits of living in a stable, integrated area—was not "fairly traceable" to the VA practices complained about nor was it likely to be redressed by the relief requested by the plaintiffs.[74] With respect to the "fairly traceable" issue, the court concluded that there was no evidence "that John Doe appraisals played any role whatsoever in the rapid racial transition of [the plaintiffs' neighborhood]."[75] In addition, the court ruled that the evidence failed to show that any VA appraiser "ever considered the race of the buyer or seller, or the racial composition of [the plaintiffs' neighborhood], in determining the reasonable value of any property in [that neighborhood]" or that the appraisers working there

> adhered to or believed in a principle that racial homogeneity is a factor which adds value to homes in a neighborhood, or even that the VA appraisers read any textbooks concerning or belonged to any organizations that adhered to such a tenet. . . . In sum, the Court has concluded that the evidence presented by plaintiffs to establish a causal connection between plaintiffs' injuries and VA appraisal practices is insufficient to establish such a connection.[76]

The plaintiffs appealed, but the Seventh Circuit Court of Appeals affirmed the ruling in a 1987 decision,[77] agreeing with the trial court that the plaintiffs lacked standing because their injury was not shown to be fairly traceable to the defendant's practices.

Although *Jorman* turned on standing issues rather than on the merits, it still provides some insight into the way courts may respond to claims of discriminatory appraisals. As in *Hanson*, the principal lesson of *Jorman* would seem to be judicial skepticism of such claims, at least to the extent that the claims are predicated primarily on the allegation that pre-*AIREA* principles are so "ingrained" in the profession that they are still being adhered to. To prevail, plaintiffs must produce more compelling and specific evidence of the defendant's reliance on racial factors and not simply claim that appraisers in general have been unable to shed their commitment to pre-*AIREA* practices.

THOMAS v. FIRST FEDERAL SAVINGS BANK OF INDIANA

Thomas v. First Federal Savings Bank of Indiana[78] was a 1987 trial court decision that held that the defendant bank's refusal to make a home loan to the black plaintiffs was not based on racial discrimination in violation of Title VIII, §1981–§1982, or the Equal Credit Opportunity Act.[79] The plaintiffs in *Thomas* were a fair housing organization and a black married couple who lived in a minority neighborhood in Gary, Indiana. In 1984, Mr. and Mrs. Thomas applied for a loan from the defendant bank to be secured by a second mortgage on their home. The loan was for $7,100, which would have brought the total indebtedness secured by the home to $24,100, since the amount still owed by the Thomases on their first mortgage was $17,000. The bank ordered an appraisal of the property, which was done by its own chief appraiser (Mr. Beckham) and resulted in an appraisal of only $22,000. Based on this appraisal, the bank denied the Thomases' loan application on the ground that the loan-to-value (LTV) ratio of over 105 percent ($24,100/$22,000) would far exceed the bank's requirement that the LTV ratio be 80 percent or less.

The plaintiffs alleged that the defendant's low appraisal, and therefore its denial of the loan, was based on the Thomases' race and/or the racial makeup of their neighborhood, but the court held that the evidence did not support these claims. In support of their claim that the bank's practices were motivated by the Thomases' race, the plaintiffs produced only indirect evidence in the form of another appraiser, who testified that he disagreed with some of Beckham's judgments in appraising the Thomas home and that he would have appraised it at $40,000. The court noted, however, that this witness admitted that appraising was an art and not a science; that his appraisal was just another subjective evaluation of the Thomas home; that he was not familiar with the Federal National Mortgage Association (Fannie Mae) or Federal Home Loan Mortgage Corporation (Freddie Mac) appraisal forms and guidelines followed by Beckham; and that Beckham had used the same appraisal techniques in valuing property in a variety of different communities, which indicated that he applied these techniques regardless of the race or neighborhood of the homeowners. Based on this evidence, the court concluded that the plaintiffs had not shown that the Thomases' race contributed in any way to the defendant's appraisal of their home.[80]

The claim that the bank's behavior was based on the racial makeup of the Thomases' neighborhood was based primarily on Mr. Thomas's testimony that Beckham had told him that the Thomas home would be worth $100,000 if it were located anywhere else. Because Beckham had died before the trial and could not give his version of this conversation, the court was dubious about accepting it. In any event, the court ultimately determined that Beckham's statement—even assuming it was made—did not reflect racial considerations, but, rather, the concern that the Thomas home was "overimproved" for its neighborhood.[81]

The plaintiffs also attempted to prove their "neighborhood" claim based on a discriminatory effect theory. The court held that this was an appropriate theory under Title VIII, but that the plaintiffs' evidence (including statistics drawn from the defendant's Home Mortgage Disclosure Act statements showing where it made loans in 1983 and 1984) failed to establish that the bank's loan decisions were based on an area's racial makeup as opposed to legitimate business concerns.[82]

Thomas is similar to many of the other discriminatory appraisal cases in that it involved a loan denial based on a low appraisal of the plaintiffs' home, which the plaintiffs alleged, but were unable to prove, was based on racial considerations. Once again, there was no "smoking gun" or other direct evidence of discrimination. The plaintiffs' circumstantial case was based on establishing through expert testimony that the defendant's appraisal was unjustifiably low and improperly done. However, the court was not persuaded of this, and also found that, even if the appraisal was not done well, it was done in the same way that white property was appraised. Thus, although proof of bad appraising may be the start of a successful circumstantial case, it does not by itself establish that an appraisal is discriminatory. Something more must be shown for the plaintiff to prevail.

Old West End Ass'n v. Buckeye Federal Savings & Loan

Old West End Ass'n v. Buckeye Federal Savings & Loan[83] was a 1987 trial court decision in a mortgage redlining case in which the defendant's refusal to accept a full-price appraisal on the plaintiffs' property was used as evidence of its negative attitude toward making loans in the plaintiffs' neighborhood. In 1985, plaintiffs Michael and Gale Mahaffey agreed to sell their home in the racially integrated Old West End section of Toledo, Ohio, to another couple for $78,500. The buyers applied for a mortgage loan from Buckeye Federal, which requested an appraisal on the property. The appraisal arrived at a value equal to the sales price, although it did note that the predominant value for other homes in the area was $70,000.

Buckeye then turned down the buyers' loan application, giving two reasons for its decision: (1) that the property did not qualify for "maximum financing" under the applicable Fannie Mae underwriting guidelines, and (2) that the appraisal was unacceptably high in comparison to other properties in the neighborhood. The Mahaffeys and the buyers then executed a revised purchase contract, the result of which was that the mortgage loan was reduced to $70,000, which

Buckeye approved. Thereafter, the Mahaffeys, joined by their real estate agent and the Old West End Association, sued Buckeye for violating Title VIII and §1981–§1982 by engaging in redlining—discrimination in the financing of housing based on the racial composition of the neighborhood in which the property is located.[84]

Buckeye moved for summary judgment, arguing that its stated reasons for rejecting the initial loan application were both legitimate and nondiscriminatory. With respect to the second reason, for example, Buckeye claimed that the full-price appraisal was too high because it was based on upward adjustments made to the comparables that exceeded an acceptable percentage of the comparable properties' values. The plaintiffs countered with an expert witness who testified that neither of Buckeye's claimed justifications was based on a proper application of the relevant standards. With respect to the appraisal justification, for example, the plaintiffs' expert testified that the appraiser's use of the comparables was indeed appropriate because it took into account the fact that the Old West End was being rehabilitated. The district court held that the plaintiffs' evidence was sufficient to raise a genuine issue as to whether the defendant had acted for legitimate or discriminatory reasons, and it therefore denied Buckeye's motion for summary judgment.[85]

Old West End is a major redlining decision, but its importance as an appraisal case is limited. Its facts do serve to provide some insight into just how important appraisals can be in the home selling process and into how the work of an independent appraiser may be used by an underwriter at a financial institution that wants to sell its loans in the secondary mortgage market. From a litigation standpoint, the principal lesson of the case seems to be that a plaintiff who alleges that an appraisal has been done or used in a discriminatory manner will, in the absence of direct evidence of discrimination, have to produce an expert witness to establish a circumstantial case by showing that the defendant's claimed "legitimate" reasons for its behavior are in fact not justified by the applicable professional standards.

Cartwright v. American Savings & Loan Ass'n

In *Cartwright v. American Savings & Loan Ass'n*,[86] the Seventh Circuit Court of Appeals affirmed a trial judge's ruling that the defendant had not engaged in illegal redlining or appraisal discrimination in dealing with a loan application for a new house in the urban renewal district of East Hammond, Indiana. Mrs. Cartwright was a black woman who first dealt with American Savings in 1965, when it provided a mortgage loan for her and her first husband on a home in Hammond. In

1980, she and her second husband purchased five contiguous lots in the urban renewal area of East Hammond for $1 per lot and applied to American Savings for a $90,000 loan to finance the construction of a new home on this property.

As part of its loan application procedure, American Savings ordered an appraisal on the proposed home from an independent appraisal firm, Vernon Lee & Associates. The appraisal was delayed because Lee was unable to find appropriate comparables in order to do a market approach appraisal. (Eventually, Lee determined that the lack of comparables made a market approach impossible, and the appraisal was done based on the "cost approach."[87]) While Lee was searching for comparables, American Savings asked Cartwright if she could supply any information on this subject, a request that departed from its normal practice of not obtaining appraisal information of this nature from loan applicants.

There was a dispute at trial as to whether Cartwright agreed to supply this information, with the defendant claiming that she did and Cartwright testifying that she did not. In addition, the defendant claimed that Cartwright also mentioned at this time that she was getting a divorce (a statement the plaintiff also denied making). According to the defendant (whose version of these events was credited by the trial court), the change in Cartwright's marital status and her unfulfilled promise to supply information on comparables led American Savings to delay a decision on whether to approve her loan application. Some six months after Cartwright initially applied, American Savings informed her that her application had "died a natural death," but that she could submit a new application if she wanted to. Some months later she did reapply, and American Savings approved this application, but Cartwright eventually chose to finance her home through another institution.

Based on these facts, Cartwright and a local fair housing organization sued American Savings, alleging that it had refused her initial application because of her race and sex and because of redlining in Cartwright's neighborhood in violation of Title VIII, §1981–§1982, and the Equal Credit Opportunity Act. Specifically, the plaintiffs claimed that American Savings discriminated against Cartwright by requiring that she (unlike other would-be borrowers) provide comparable housing information for the appraisal. In an unreported decision, the trial court disagreed, finding that Cartwright had volunteered to supply such information.[88] The lower court also ruled against the plaintiffs' redlining claim, finding that American Savings "has in fact provided a significant number of loans in this area."[89]

The plaintiffs appealed, but the Seventh Circuit Court of Appeals affirmed in a 1989 decision.[90] The court of appeals held that the issue of why American Savings had not promptly approved Cartwright's application—which included the issue of whether the defendant's delay was based on a discriminatory request for information on comparables—turned on credibility determinations that the trial court had resolved in the defendant's favor and that could not be overturned on appeal.[91] Similarly, the appellate court held that the plaintiffs' redlining evidence was inadequate to require reversal because, although it showed that American Savings had approved far more mortgage loans in white areas than in Cartwright's neighborhood, it failed to provide any basis for comparing the defendant's rejection rates of qualified applicants in white versus black areas.[92]

In addition to these specific rulings, the tone of the appellate opinion in *Cartwright* was decidedly sympathetic to the defendant. For example, the Seventh Circuit opined that Title VIII

> does not require that a lender disregard its legitimate business interests or make an investment that is not economically sound. It seems obvious that a lender must be concerned, for example, about financing a new, $90,000 home in a residential area comprised of homes valued at $60,000 or less. . . . [L]enders may legitimately consider the "present market value of the property offered as security . . . and the likelihood that the property will retain an adequate value over the term of the loan." 12 C.F.R. §31.8(c)(7). . . . If [the defendant] told the Cartwrights that the East Hammond urban renewal area could not "afford" their proposed home, we believe the comment reflected American Savings' legitimate financial concern. . . . American Savings was concerned about financing a large, relatively expensive home in an area lacking other homes of comparable market value and sound economic judgment of this nature cannot be considered as a violation of the Fair Housing Act. . . . [T]here is nothing in the record which leads us to believe that American Savings would have been concerned about the location of the Cartwrights' property had they intended to build a home of comparable value to others in the area.[93]

Like the *Old West End* opinion, the Seventh Circuit's decision in *Cartwright* is an important pronouncement on redlining law, but is only of limited value as an appraisal precedent. The case does demonstrate the problems that may arise if a home must be appraised in an area where the lack of recent comparable sales makes a market approach to appraising difficult or impossible. In addition, *Cartwright* shows how important it is for appraisers and lenders to maintain strict adherence to their standard business practices. In this case, the only basis for the claim of discrimination in the appraisal process was that the lender deviated from its normal procedures by asking Cartwright for appraisal information, thereby opening itself up to a charge of differential treatment once the loan application was not approved. The fact that this request may have been an understandable and even considerate reaction to a difficult situation does not change the fact that it was responsible for providing the plaintiffs with a basis for suspecting discrimination, leading them to litigate what otherwise might have been a relatively simple business misunderstanding.

STEPTOE V. SAVINGS OF AMERICA

The same racially mixed Toledo neighborhood that was involved in the *Old West End* case was also the location of *Steptoe* v. *Savings of America*,[94] in which the district court denied the defendant's summary judgment motion in a case alleging discriminatory appraisal and lending practices. The Steptoes were a black married couple who contracted to buy a home in the Old West End for $115,000. They then applied for a 90 percent loan from Savings of America (SOA), which ordered an appraisal on the property. An in-house appraiser for SOA (Edward Clunk) made an initial appraisal of $115,000, but SOA's chief appraiser (Rollie Morgan) thought this was too high and ordered Clunk to redo the appraisal using different comparables. Morgan also disagreed with Clunk that the home's finished attic added any value. Clunk's new appraisal came in at $94,500. Based on this appraisal, SOA advised the Steptoes that the home would not support their requested mortgage. The Steptoes then offered the seller $95,000, which the seller rejected. A month later the home sold to someone else for $115,000 (another bank financed this purchase, appraising the home at $116,000).

The Steptoes and their realtor then brought suit, alleging that SOA's appraisal and lending practices were racially discriminatory in violation of Title VIII, §1981–§1982, and certain other laws. SOA moved for summary judgment, but the district court denied this motion in a 1992 opinion, finding that there was sufficient evidence of racial discrimination to justify a trial of the plaintiffs' Title VIII and §1981–§1982 claims.[95]

The evidence that the *Steptoe* court found sufficient to establish a prima facie case of discrimination was primarily directed toward showing that the second SOA appraisal was too low and that the SOA appraisers had violated their own internal procedures in conducting this appraisal. The evidence supporting the first point—that the $94,500 figure was too low—included proof that (1) SOA itself continued to use Clunk's original $115,000 appraisal on its list of comparables even after Clunk had lowered it to $94,500 for purposes of the Steptoe loan application; (2) the financial institution that ultimately did finance the loan on this property conducted an independent appraisal that produced a value ($116,000) that was even higher than Clunk's original figure; and (3) an independent appraiser produced by the plaintiffs as an expert witness testified that SOA's ultimate appraisal was defective. The evidence that SOA did not follow its usual appraising procedures included the facts that (1) Morgan did not draw inklines through the items on Clunk's original appraisal that he disagreed with; and (2) no comment was made by the SOA appraisers concerning the substantial deviation between the initial and final appraisal figures.

This is not direct evidence of discrimination, but it is, according to *Steptoe,* sufficient circumstantial evidence to establish a prima facie case and thereby allows a fact finder to conclude that the defendant's acts were based on intentional discrimination. Indeed, one of the important parts of the *Steptoe* opinion is that it attempted to identify the necessary elements of a prima facie case of appraisal discrimination involving the race of a neighborhood. According to *Steptoe,* the elements that a plaintiff must show to establish such a case include the following: (1) that the house for which a loan application was made is located in a minority neighborhood; (2) that the application was not approved despite the fact that the applicants were creditworthy; and (3) that an independent appraisal concluded that the value of the property equaled or exceeded the sale price.[96]

In rejecting the defendant's motion for summary judgment in *Steptoe,* the court also pointed to the plaintiffs' statistical evidence, which compared SOA's lending patterns in the Old West End to its activities in a predominantly white suburban area. The court's opinion did not describe what this comparison showed, but it did conclude that the plaintiffs' statistical analysis "supports their position."[97] The court then concluded that this evidence and the other proof in the record established that "plaintiffs have certainly made out a *prima facie* case that SOA's conduct had, at the very least, a racially discriminatory effect on the Steptoes and, possibly, all other potential borrowers who wished to purchase homes in the Old West End."[98]

This last comment is puzzling, because it indicates that the court was confusing a prima facie case of intentional discrimination with a prima facie case of discriminatory effect. It is true, as the *Steptoe* opinion noted, that the plaintiffs might have prevailed under either theory in pursuing their Title VIII claim.[99] However, all of the plaintiffs' evidence discussed by the court (other than the statistical analysis) was directed toward establishing a prima facie case of intentional discrimination. In addition, the precedents discussed by the court in analyzing this evidence were all cases involving intentional discrimination. Indeed, the fact that the *Steptoe* evidence was primarily designed to establish an intent case is confirmed by the fact that the court went on to hold that this evidence was also sufficient to constitute a prima facie case under §1981–§1982, laws that, unlike Title VIII, outlaw only intentional discrimination.[100]

Thus, *Steptoe* is an important, though somewhat confusing, appraisal precedent. More than any other post-*AIREA* case, it shows how a claim of appraisal discrimination based on circumstantial evidence can and must be proved. A necessary element of such a case is to show that the challenged appraisal is insupportably low, which generally requires an independent appraisal that reaches a much higher value and perhaps expert testimony demonstrating that the defendant's appraisal was done in a defective or at least untraditional manner. Failure of the defendant to follow its own standard appraisal practices can also be persuasive circumstantial evidence of unlawful discrimination. Finally, if the defendant is a lender with a poor record of making loans in minority neighborhoods, this fact may suggest a general predisposition toward undervaluing homes in such areas, although this type of redlining proof, being generally more relevant to Title VIII effect cases, is neither necessary nor sufficient to establish a claim of intentional appraisal discrimination.

SUMMARY AND CONCLUSIONS

The command of the Fair Housing Act to home appraisers and to financial institutions that use their work is clear and simple: "Thou shalt not discriminate on the basis of race, color, religion, sex, handicap, familial status, or national origin." A correlation of this commandment is that Title VIII does not prohibit appraisers from taking into consideration any factors other than those seven specifically condemned by the statute.

The problem in assessing the degree and nature of appraisal discrimination is not in knowing what the law requires, but in trying to gauge whether Title VIII's commands are being complied with. One basis for concluding that they are is that only a handful of Title VIII claims of appraisal discrimination have been litigated in the 25 years that the statute has been in effect. But this dearth of cases is not always a reliable guide to the level of discriminatory problems in an industry, as the mortgage lending field illustrates.

Perhaps the most troublesome aspect of the appraisal industry's record in this field is its largely passive history. At the time of Title VIII's enactment, appraisers as a profession were committed to principles that viewed racial and ethnic integration as a negative factor in evaluating neighborhoods. The industry's principal trade groups maintained this view for years after Title VIII became law and only abandoned it after being sued by the Justice Department in the *AIREA* case, a case that the industry initially opposed vigorously.

Even today the industry's key standard for complying with Title VIII seems clearly inadequate, for it merely cautions against relying on the "principle of conformity" or other biased assumptions based on race, age, color, religion, gender, or national origin in evaluating neighborhood trends.[101] Nothing is said about the need to avoid discriminating against individuals, as well as neighborhoods, on the basis of these factors, even though cases like *Thomas* v. *First Federal Savings* and *Cartwright* v. *American Savings & Loan* show that both individual and neighborhood discrimination are actionable under Title VIII. Moreover, the standard says nothing about handicap or familial status discrimination, even though many years have now passed since handicap and familial status were added to Title VIII's list of prohibited factors by the 1988 Fair Housing Amendments Act.[102]

This is not the record of an industry that inspires great confidence in its commitment to voluntary compliance with the Fair Housing Act. As a result, it is not hard to imagine that many individual appraisers, particularly those schooled in pre-*AIREA* principles, may still be considering illegal factors in evaluating individual properties or neighborhoods, although this is likely to be done with a good deal more subtlety than in the past.

Another noteworthy observation about the few reported appraisal cases is that most of them come from only two locations: Toledo, Ohio, and the greater Chicago metropolitan area. What causes this focusing of cases? Putting aside the possibility that appraisers in these areas are simply more inclined to engage in litigation-producing behavior than their colleagues in the rest of the country, the most likely explanation seems to be that these two areas both have aggressive private fair housing organizations that have made a commitment to prosecuting discriminatory lending and appraisal cases. If this is indeed the correct explanation, it suggests that a comparable enforcement commitment on the part of private and/or governmental agencies in other locales might yield similar results.

Despite all this, however, it is hard to make a strong case for the proposition that conscious appraisal discrimination is still a widespread phenomenon. Only six reported Title VIII cases involving claims of appraisal discrimination have been reported since the *AIREA* settlement, and none of these has resulted in a determination that the defendant violated the statute after a trial on the merits.

Due in large part to the reforms generated by *AIREA*, the evidence of discrimination in all of these cases has been circumstantial rather than direct. A typical case involves a low appraisal of a home in a minority or integrated neighborhood, with the plaintiff's evidence designed to show that the defendant's appraisal was not just low but insupportably so (based, for example, on an independent appraisal or the testimony of an expert witness), and that other suspicious factors were present as well (the defendant's having deviated, for example, from its normal business practices).

Such evidence may be sufficient to establish a prima facie case, but this simply means that the defendant will be called upon to provide some legitimate or at least nonillegal reason for its low appraisal. Any number of such reasons—both objective and subjective—can satisfy a court on this score. If the defendant can point to objective, verifiable difficulties with the property or the neighborhood (such as a high crime rate, the lack of recreation facilities, or inadequate public transportation), as was done in the *Hanson* case, it is hard for a fact finder to conclude that illegal discrimination was involved.[103] This is true even if the negative factors relied upon tend to correlate with higher concentrations of minority residents in, say, an inner-city neighborhood.[104]

In addition, because the courts recognize that appraising is an art and not a science, the defense may simply be that subjective judgments led to the low appraisal. Indeed, even "human error" can be a defense, for Title VIII does not require that appraisers be good at their jobs; it only requires that they not consider unlawful factors.

Another factor that tends to favor defendants in appraisal cases is that the basic technique usually employed (the market approach, based on three or more comparables) appears to be inherently race-neutral. How can an appraiser be accused of racial discrimination for undervaluing a property in an integrated neighborhood, if all other similar homes there are actually selling for equally low prices? Of course, there is ample room for subjective judgments—and therefore for illegal discrimination—in applying the market approach (choosing the comparables and making adjustments to their prices), but a defendant using this method starts out with a judicial presumption that discrimination was not involved in the appraisal.

Judges may also be skeptical of discriminatory appraisal claims because of their belief that conservative valuation techniques are generally appropriate for preloan appraisals. The purpose of such appraisals, after all, is to protect the lender from loss in the event of the debtor's future default, a purpose that might be jeopardized if appraisers did not feel free to err on the low side. The Seventh Circuit's opinion in the *Cartwright* case provides a good example of this judicial attitude, for it not only ruled against the plaintiffs but did so in a way that expressed total sympathy for the defendant's need to protect itself financially.

Thus, the Title VIII cases demonstrate that a plaintiff who undertakes to prove a case of intentional appraisal discrimination faces a difficult task. Nor has the availability of the discriminatory effect theory under Title VIII proved to be of much help in this area, for although the courts have endorsed this theory in principle, no decision has yet relied on it to rule for the plaintiff where there was not also prima facie evidence of unlawful intent.

Additional litigation resources may yet produce successful appraisal cases under Title VIII. Certainly these cases must seem daunting for the individual homeseeker-plaintiff to prosecute, for they require expert witnesses and other resources that are generally beyond the command of an individual litigant. But even a major commitment of additional enforcement resources may not guarantee success in this field. After all, the fair housing organizations in Toledo and the Chicago area that have been primarily responsible for generating the reported appraisal cases have yet to prevail in a single such trial on the merits.

Perhaps the most fruitful area for further effort would be to examine how appraisal standards are developed, promulgated, and taught by the industry's leaders and are learned and applied by individual appraisers. This was the basis for the major reforms wrought by the *AIREA* litigation, and the industry's current standards of practice show that further work needs to be done to fully reflect modern fair housing law. In addition, this may be the most effective way to ensure that the subjective judgments that are the key to the appraiser's art generally do not reflect discriminatory factors. As part of this "education" effort, it might also be helpful if all of the standard appraisal forms, such as those provided by Fannie Mae, required appraisers to certify that the factors condemned by Title VIII played no role in their work, a function that the VA forms fulfilled in the *Hanson* and *Jorman* cases.

The time seems ripe for such an effort. As a result of recent developments such as the coming of FIRREA, the growing influence of Fannie Mae, and the power of HUD to issue Title VIII regulations, the appraisal industry must look to the federal government more than ever before for help in establishing its own basic standards of practice. At the least, these standards should reflect a total commitment to compliance with the Fair Housing Act.

Notes

1. The Fair Housing Act is codified at 42 U.S.C. §§3601 et seq. The particular provisions of the Act that have been held to prohibit appraisal discrimination—§804(a), §804(b), and §805 (42 U.S.C. §3604(a), §3604(b), and §3605)—are discussed in the second section of this chapter.

2. These cases are discussed in the third section of this chapter.

3. *United States* v. *American Institute of Real Estate Appraisers*, 442 F. Supp. 1072 (N.D. Ill. 1977), *appeal dismissed*, 590 F.2d 242 (7th Cir. 1978).

4. See, for example, *Thomas* v. *First Federal Savings Bank of Indiana*, 653 F. Supp. 1330, 1334 (N.D. Ind. 1987).

5. *Steptoe* v. *Savings of America*, 800 F. Supp. 1542, 1546 (N.D. Ohio 1992).

6. See note 1 and accompanying text.

7. See, for example, *Steptoe* v. *Savings of America*, 800 F. Supp. at 1547; *Old West End Ass'n* v. *Buckeye Federal Savings & Loan*, 675 F. Supp. 1100, 1105 (N.D. Ohio 1987); *Thomas* v. *First Federal Savings Bank of Indiana*, 653 F. Supp. at 1342.

8. See, for example, *Cartwright* v. *American Savings & Loan Ass'n*, 880 F.2d 912, 925–27 (7th Cir. 1989); and *Thomas* v. *First Federal Savings Bank of Indiana*, 653 F. Supp. at 1341.

9. 15 U.S.C. §1691(a).

10. Public Law 101-73, 103 Stat. 183 (1989).

11. See 12 U.S.C. §1331.

12. Id., §1348(a)(1).

13. Id., §1345(b).

14. See The Appraisal Foundation, *Uniform Standards of Professional Appraisal Practice*, Foreword (Washington, D.C.: Author, 1993).

15. Id., Standard Rule 1-3(a).

16. 42 U.S.C. §3605(a).

17. Id., §3605(b).

18. Id., §3605(c).

19. Id., §3604(a) and §3604(b).

20. Id., §3604(f)(1). For purposes of this chapter, it is assumed that practices banned by §804(f)(1) are the same as those covered by §804(a), so that references to §804(a) should be understood to include §804(f)(1) if the discrimination involved is based on handicap.

21. See, for example, *Hanson* v. *Veterans Administration*, 800 F.2d 1381, 1386 (5th Cir. 1986); *Steptoe* v. *Savings of America*, 800 F. Supp. at 1545–47; *United States* v. *American Institute of Real Estate Appraisers*, 442 F. Supp. at 1079; As the court in the *American Institute* case stated: "The promulgation of standards which cause appraisers and lenders to treat race and national origin as a negative factor in determining the value of dwellings and in evaluating the soundness of home loans may effectively 'make unavailable or deny' a 'dwelling' [in violation of §804(a)]." The *American Institute* opinion also held that this practice violates Title VIII's prohibition against interference with fair housing rights (now §818) as well as §804(a). *Id.*

22. 42 U.S.C. §3604(f)(2). For purposes of this chapter, it is assumed that practices banned by §804(f)(2) are the same as those covered by §804(b), so that references to §804(b) should be understood to include §804(f)(2) if the discrimination involved is based on handicap.

23. See, for example, *Steptoe* v. *Savings of America*, 800 F. Supp. at 1545–47.

24. 42 U.S.C. §3603(b).

25. Compare 42 U.S.C. §3604, first sentence, with 42 U.S.C. §3605; see, for example, *Laufman* v. *Oakley Building & Loan Co.*, 408 F. Supp. 489, 493 (S.D. Ohio 1976).

26. Public Law 100-430, 102 Stat. 1916–39 (1988). Specifically, §805 was amended by §6(c) of the 1988 Fair Housing Amendments Act. See 102 Stat. 1622.

27. 42 U.S.C. §3605 (1982 and Supp. 1987).

28. Id.

29. For example, in *Dunn* v. *Midwestern Indemnity*, 472 F. Supp. 1106, 1110 (S.D. Ohio 1979): "[Section] 3605 does not contemplate proscription of insurance redlining by an insurance company not engaged 'in the making of commercial real estate loans.' "

30. 42 U.S.C. §3605(a), (b).

31. HUD Preamble, 24 CRF chap. 1, subchap. A, App. I, 54 *Fed. Reg.* 3242 (Jan. 23, 1989).

32. 24 CRF §100.135(a).

33. See, for example, *Hanson* v. *Veterans Administration*, 800 F.2d at 1386 (§804[a]); *Thomas* v. *First Federal Savings Bank of Indiana*, 653 F. Supp. at 1336–39 (§805); *United States* v. *American Institute of Real Estate Appraisers*, 442 F. Supp. at 1079 (§804[a]).

34. For example, *Hanson* v. *Veterans Administration*, 800 F.2d at 1386–89 (§804[a]); *Thomas* v. *First Federal Savings Bank of Indiana*, 653 F. Supp. at 1339 (§805).

35. U.S. House of Representatives, Committee on the Judiciary, *Report 100–711: The Fair Housing Amendments Act of 1988* 31, 100th Cong., 2nd Sess. (1988). At the same time, the committee stated its intention "that the appraisal process not operate to discriminate on the basis of race, color, religion, national origin, sex, handicap or familial status." *Id.* This, too, was consistent with the judiciary's understanding of prior Title VIII law. See, for example, *Thomas* v. *First Federal Savings Bank of Indiana*, 653 F. Supp. at 1339: "[§805] is fairly read to prohibit First Federal and other institutions

from utilizing criteria such as race, color, religion, sex or national origin in appraising a potential loan applicant's home."

36. *United States* v. *American Institute of Real Estate Appraisers* 442 F. Supp. 1072.

37. *Hanson* v. *Veterans Administration*, 800 F.2d at 1387.

38. See, for example, *Harper* v. *Union Savings Ass'n*, 429 F. Supp. 1254, 1269–70 (N.D. Ohio 1977).

39. *United States* v. *American Institute of Real Estate Appraisers*, 442 F. Supp. at 1078–79. The court concluded:

> Given a broad interpretation of these provisions, it becomes clear that the United States has stated a claim for relief under their terms. The promulgation of standards which cause appraisers and lenders to treat race and national origin as a negative factor in determining the value of dwellings and in evaluating the soundness of home loans may effectively "make unavailable or deny" a "dwelling" and may "interfere" with persons in the exercise and enjoyment of rights guaranteed by the Act. When such denial or interference occurs as a result of considerations relating to race or national origin, sections 804(a) and 817 are transgressed. Id., 1079.

40. Id., 1077.

41. Id., 1084.

42. Id., 1077.

43. Id.

44. Id., 1084.

45. Id., 1084–85.

46. Id., 1085.

47. Id.

48. Id.

49. *United States* v. *American Institute of Real Estate Appraisers*, 590 F.2d 242 (7th Cir. 1978).

50. See, for example, note 15 and accompanying text (modern appraisal standard cautioning against relying on the "principle of conformity" and other biased assumptions based on race, age, color, religion, gender, or national origin in evaluating neighborhood trends); also Federal National Mortgage Association, *The Appraisal Guide*, no. 18 (Washington, D.C.: Author, 1992) advising appraisers not to consider racial composition in developing a neighborhood analysis and to avoid using subjective terms such as "pride of ownership" that might serve as a proxy for race.

51. See 53 *Fed. Reg.* 45028 (Nov. 7, 1988) (proposing 24 CRF §100.135[d][3]). This proposed regulation was ultimately removed from HUD's final rule out of concern that it might negatively affect affirmative activities to promote integration. See 24 CFR Ch. 1, Subch. A, App. I, 54 *Fed. Reg.* 3235, 3242–43 (Jan. 23, 1989). However, apart from these prointegration programs, HUD's view is that this "unused" regulation accurately reflects the types of activities that would be unlawful if they result in limitations on housing choice. Id., 3235.

52. *Harper* v. *Union Savings Ass'n*, 429 F. Supp. 1254.

53. Id., 1271.

54. Id., 1270.

55. Id., 1269, n. 5.

56. Id.

57. *Hanson v. Veterans Administration*, 800 F.2d 1381.

58. Id.

59. Id., 1384–86.

60. Id., 1386. According to the Fifth Circuit's opinion: "Section 804(a) does address the claim asserted by [plaintiffs]. Discriminatory appraisal may effectively prevent blacks from purchasing or selling a home for its fair market value. This interferes with the exercise of rights granted by the Fair Housing Act." Id.

61. Id.

62. Id., 1387–88.

63. Id., 1385, 1388.

64. Id., 1383.

65. Id., 1388.

66. Id., 1387–88.

67. Id., 1388–89.

68. Id., 1389.

69. Id.

70. Id.

71. *Jorman* v *Veterans Administration*, 654 F. Supp. 748 (N.D. Ill. 1986), *aff'd*, 830 F.2d 1420 (7th Cir. 1987).

72. Id., 759.

73. Id., 759–60.

74. Id., 763–69.

75. Id., 764.

76. Id., 766.

77. *Jorman v. Veterans Administration*, 830 F.2d 1420 (7th Cir. 1987).

78. *Thomas v. First Federal Savings Bank of Indiana*, 653 F. Supp. 1330.

79. The plaintiffs based their Title VIII claims on both §804 and §805 of the Fair Housing Act. The court, however, held that §804 did not apply, because the Thomases were not seeking to buy or rent a home, but, rather, were complaining about the denial of a second mortgage loan on their already-owned property. Under these circumstances, according to the *Thomas* opinion, only §805 would be applicable. Id., 1337. Once the court made this ruling, its primary concern was to evaluate the evidence concerning the §805 claim. After it found that the plaintiffs had failed to prove unlawful discrimination in violation of §805 (id., 1337–41), the court relied on this finding to dispose of the Thomases' §1981–§1982 and ECOA claims as well. Id., 1341–42.

80. *Thomas v. First Federal Savings Bank of Indiana*, 653 F. Supp. 1339.

81. Id., 1339–40.

82. Id., 1340–41.

83. *Old West End Ass'n v. Buckeye Federal Savings & Loan*, 675 F. Supp. 1100.

84. The complaint also named as a defendant Mortgage Investors Corporation (MIC), which had received the buyers' loan application, transmitted it to Buckeye Federal, and included a claim under 42 U.S.C. §1985(3), which prohibits conspiracies to deny civil

rights. Finding that the decisions and policies challenged by the plaintiffs were exclusively those of Buckeye, the trial court dismissed the claim against MIC and, based on that dismissal, held that the §1985(3) conspiracy claim must also fail. Id., 1106–7.

85. Id., 1105. The court also denied summary judgment with respect to the plaintiffs' Title VIII claim based on discriminatory effect, holding that the statistical evidence, which showed that Buckeye Federal's loan rejection rate in neighborhoods with a significant black population was higher than its rejection rate in predominantly white neighborhoods, was sufficient to allow a reasonable fact finder to conclude that the defendant's loan practices had a racially discriminatory effect. Id., 1105–06.

86. *Cartwright* v. *American Savings & Loan Ass'n*, 880 F.2d 912.

87. Id., 914, n. 4. The "cost approach" is based on the appraiser's estimate of the cost of building the home plus the value of the land. Id.

88. Id., 917.

89. Id., 916.

90. *Cartwright* v. *American Savings & Loan Ass'n*, 880 F.2d 912.

91. Id., 918–22.

92. Id., 922–24.

93. Id., 923–24.

94. *Steptoe* v. *Savings of America*, 800 F. Supp. 1542.

95. Id., 1545–47. The *Steptoe* complaint also included claims under 42 U.S.C. §1985(3) (conspiracy to deny civil rights) and Title VI of the 1964 Civil Rights Act (discrimination in federally funded programs), but the court dismissed these claims, noting that they required proof of additional factors that were not present here. Id., 1547–48.

96. Id., 1546–47. These elements are derived from the five elements that the *Steptoe* opinion set forth, which were:

> (1) [that] the housing sought to be secured was in a minority neighborhood;
> (2) that an application for a loan to purchase the housing located in a minority neighborhood was made;
> (3) that an independent appraisal concluded that the value of the housing equaled the sale price;
> (4) that the buyers were credit worthy; and
> (5) that the loan was rejected.

Id., 1546. The text combines elements (2), (4), and the essential part of (5). The *Steptoe* court, itself, questioned the "rejected" part of element (5), noting that in this case, the loan was never formally rejected because the Steptoes withdrew their application after learning of SOA's low appraisal. This should not serve to defeat a plaintiff's claim, according to *Steptoe*, because a lender could always avoid the rejection step by "purposefully lowballing an appraisal and then doing nothing more." Id.

97. Id., 1547.

98. Id.

99. According to the *Steptoe* opinion: "In a discrimination case brought pursuant to the FHA, a plaintiff need not prove that the defendant acted with a racially discriminative motive; a prima facie case can be made out by showing that the defendant's actions had a racially discriminatory effect." Id., 1546.

100. Id., 1547.

101. See note 15 and accompanying text.

102. It seems likely that, particularly with respect to the handicap requirements of the 1988 Fair Housing Amendments Act, appraisers will need to rethink some of their basic assumptions in order to comply with the law. For example, a number of physical changes will need to be made to dwellings in order to comply with the 1988 Act's handicap provisions, which appraisers presumably must not consider as negative factors in valuing a property. Indeed, in issuing regulations interpreting the 1988 Act, HUD noted that the new handicap provisions should not prevent appraisers from considering "an adaptable physical environment as a positive factor in estimating the value of residential real property." HUD Preamble, 24 CFR chap. 1, subchap. A, App. I, 54 *Fed. Reg.* 3243 [Jan. 23, 1989].

103. See also Id. *Fed. Reg.* 3242, indicating that it would be appropriate for appraisers "to use observable, verifiable data that affect the market value of property in a particular area, such as the proximity of certain facilities and services."

104. Cf. *NAACP* v. *American Family Mutual Insurance Co.*, 978 F.2d 287, 290–91, 298 (7th Cir. 1992), cert. denied, 113 S. Ct. 2335 (1993) (Title VIII prohibits insurance companies from charging higher rates in an inner-city neighborhood based on its racial makeup, but not based on its higher rate of arson or other risks).

Part Two

FAIR LENDING ENFORCEMENT

Chapter Thirteen

AN OVERVIEW

John Goering and Ron Wienk

Federal fair lending enforcement has a short history. Perhaps the most significant attempt to ensure nondiscriminatory treatment of mortgage loan applicants was in 1971. In that year, the National Urban League and 12 other civil rights and public interest groups petitioned the federal financial regulatory agencies—the Comptroller of the Currency, the Federal Deposit Insurance Corporation, the Federal Home Loan Bank Board, and the Federal Reserve System—to issue long-delayed regulations to implement fair lending provisions of the Fair Housing Act of 1968. Among other things the petitioners requested were: the recording of all mortgage loan applications indicating the race of the applicant, the disposition of the application, the reason for rejection if disapproved, and the socioeconomic character of the neighborhood of the property for which financing was sought; the logging of oral inquiries; affirmative action by lenders to inform the public of nondiscriminatory lending policy; designation of a compliance officer for each lending institution; development of a national data collection system on lending practices; and an assessment of underwriting and appraisal criteria to determine whether any practices arbitrarily excluded minorities from fair consideration for mortgage loans. The basic charge underlying the Urban League and others' petition was that the regulatory agencies had failed to monitor lender compliance with fair housing/fair lending law. The remedies sought, however, were strongly resisted by both lenders and regulators.

Although regulations were proposed for comment in 1971, by mid-1976 only one of the agencies (the Federal Home Loan Bank Board) had issued a final regulation, which fell far short of what the Urban League and others had requested. Although the U.S. Department of Housing and Urban Development (HUD) had been requesting action by the financial regulators even before the National Urban League petition, by the mid-1970s many other entities—including the Department of Justice and the Office of Management and Budget—were demanding action by the regulators (U.S. Senate 1976: 5).

In 1974, the four financial regulatory agencies agreed to a pilot project to collect mortgage loan application data from supervised lenders in 18 metropolitan areas (see U.S. Senate 1976 and Comptroller of the Currency 1975). Submission of data was voluntary, but lenders for the most part fully complied with the request. Even after attempts to control for applicant income and other factors, the analysis found that minority applicants had loan rejection rates significantly higher than those of white applicants.

The 1974 pilot study was a significant milestone. First, the study's findings were consistent with analyses of HMDA data conducted much later. Second, the study demonstrated that if the regulators *wanted* to do so, it was possible to collect information that was much more inclusive than that collected under the HMDA (passed the year after the survey). Indeed, data collected for the 1974 survey were not dissimilar to—albeit not as comprehensive as—data collected for the Federal Reserve Bank of Boston Study (known as the "Boston Fed" study; Munnell et al. 1992, 1996), conducted almost 18 years later. Third, the survey underscored the importance of collecting not only information about where loans were made but also data about loans not made and about all applicants, both successful and unsuccessful.

Despite persuasive, if not definitive, evidence of racial disparities in treatment of mortgage applicants, the financial regulators continued to resist larger-scale data collection. Finally, in 1976, the National Urban League brought suit against the regulators (*National Urban League et al.* v. *Office of the Comptroller of the Currency et al.* 1977). Settlement agreements with three agencies were reached in 1977 (the Federal Reserve Board managed to extract itself from the suit).

Typical of the agreements reached was that with the Office of the Comptroller of the Currency (OCC) (*National Urban League* v. *Office of the Comptroller* 1977). The OCC agreed to: special training of examiners in consumer protection laws, including fair lending; specialized consumer affairs examinations; establishment of a Consumer Affairs Division and a system of regional consumer specialists; establishment of a data collection and analysis system applying to applications for loans to finance the purchase of one-to-four-unit residential buildings, including use of race/sex information volunteered by the applicant; periodic review and updating of procedures to investigate mortgage lending discrimination complaints; hiring of a full-time civil rights specialist with full access to the comptroller; a study of the feasibility and value of developing "a system for further meaningful use" of HMDA data; and public release of and access (by plaintiffs and others) to, among other things, data, analysis, and reports produced as part of the proposed data system and statistical and other information related to the OCC's efforts to monitor compliance and to investigate suspected or alleged acts of discrimination.

The plaintiffs clearly thought they had won virtually everything they had sought. However, a closer look at the OCC's data system and a historical overview of the agency's fair lending efforts reveal what was in actuality a hollow victory for the plaintiffs, as well as the extraordinary difficulty of identifying individual discriminatory lenders or acts.

OCC'S FAIR HOUSING HOME LOAN DATA SYSTEM

Even before the settlement agreements were reached, the OCC and other agencies had begun efforts to establish systems for collecting and analyzing data about treatment of mortgage loan applicants. Virtually all of the parties involved, including the plaintiffs, believed that the projected data systems would be, at best, only a "tool" for examiners. It was believed that only through on-site investigation of mortgage application files and other lender records could actual proof of discriminatory behavior be found. Many analysts, including some contributing authors in this volume, still believe that loan application file review is the primary, if not sole, method through which discrimination can be found, particularly individual acts of discrimination.

The relevance of data collection and analysis systems to fair lending enforcement and fair lending behavior cannot be overstated. Although there is almost universal agreement that at least some discriminatory lending practices exist, finding "it" and finding those doing "it" has proven especially difficult. As Yinger observes in chapter 2 in this volume: "One cannot design effective policies to combat discrimination unless one knows why it exists." A companion argument, and one that is clearly important for enforcement, is that the effectiveness of policies and enforcement efforts may be limited if one cannot determine *where* discrimination exists. (Yet another requirement is that discrimination be defined, a subject for which there is hardly universal agreement, particularly with regard to practices and policies that are discriminatory in effect.) The research reported in Part I of this volume addresses discrimination principally by looking at the aggregate outcomes of behavior by lenders (and others), as well as the policies of lenders (and others), either of which may adversely affect individuals and groups of individuals. The chapters in Part II of this book address the issue of *finding* illegal behavior and policies.

To deter discrimination, at least three things are necessary. First, individuals or firms subject to a law or regulation must believe there is a reasonable chance they will be monitored for compliance. This is especially true if individuals or firms, for whatever reason, wish not to abide fully by the law. Second, if a noncomplying individual or firm is monitored, there should be a high chance that noncompliance will be detected. Finally, if noncompliance is detected, the individual or firm must believe that sanctions will be imposed and that appropriate corrective action will be required.

Whether simply tools for examiners or ends in themselves, data systems were originally, and still are, regarded by regulators (and lenders) as a means to identify suspect behavior or apparent outcomes of lender policies that have adverse effects on groups of individual applicants. As specified in the OCC's settlement agreement:

> The data collected will be analyzed in Washington by generally accepted statistical techniques to evaluate race, sex, marital status or age as factors in the bank's lending decisions. The objective of this analysis will not be to establish the actual existence of discrimination but rather to identify institutions which warrant further investigation. The analysis will not only focus on the acceptance or rejection of the loan but also upon terms given to the borrower. If personal characteristics such as race or sex appear to be a factor in the decision, a more detailed investigation will be made by specially trained examiners who will use the analyses prepared in the Washington Office in the investigation. A byproduct of the statistical analysis will be the generation of data on loan applications broken down by race, sex, marital status, age and geographic location and on both approval/reject rates and adverse action. These data should permit observations of trends over time and comparison of geographic areas such as SMSA's. This system will be in effect for a minimum of three years, but is subject to change if the methodology does not prove to provide reliable data. (*National Urban League* v. *Office of the Comptroller* 1977: 3–4)

After extensive development efforts, the OCC finally issued Regulation 27, the Fair Housing Home Loan Data System, in October 1979. The regulation described the data to be collected and why: "The Comptroller believes that a combination of computer-assisted analytical techniques and consideration of the data by bank examiners is essential to the effective enforcement of the fair housing lending laws" (v). Banks receiving 50 or more home loan applications per year (for home purchase, refinance, or construction-permanent loans) were to record and maintain extensive data for all applications, and for each of their decision centers. Among other data required for each application were: amount requested, applicant and coapplicant income, monthly housing (and total debt) payments, appraised value, census tract of property, type of mortgage, whether private mortgage insurance (PMI) was required, loan amount and terms, and action taken (withdrawn before terms were offered, denied, withdrawn after terms were offered, approved). By the time the regulation was released, the OCC also required of covered institutions that they collect and record race/national origin, age, sex, and marital status, even if applicants had not volunteered some of the information. In sum, a data system was to be developed with information far more comprehensive than that collected under then-current HMDA reporting requirements, and in some ways more comprehensive than current (1996) HMDA reporting requirements.

For its time, the Fair Housing Home Loan Data System was not only advanced in information it collected for analysis, but imaginative in the analytic uses to which the data were subject. Using three ratios generally considered critical to the underwriting process—loan to value, monthly housing expense to income, and monthly debt expense to income—a calculation of each application's probability of approval was made. The computer program developed for the effort essentially calculated the apparent relative and collective importance of the three ratios, using the bank's actual treatment of applicants.

Having assigned a probability of acceptance to each loan application based on implicit underwriting criteria (based, in turn, on the three ratios), applications were then grouped into three categories: favorably treated (accepted but "should have been rejected"); neutral (accepted or rejected and "should have been"); or unfavorably treated (rejected but "should have been accepted"). Chi-square analysis was then performed, correlating application outcomes to applicant characteristics for which systematic differential treatment is prohibited by law—sex, marital status, age, race (or minority status)—as well as income and house age. (Arbitrary probability cutoffs were used to define favorable, neutral, and unfavorable.) This part of the analysis, called Phase I by the OCC, allowed identification not only of apparent patterns of applicant treatment that might not comply with fair lending law but also of individual loan files for examiners to review—the "tool" many believed would prove critical to finding violations.

A second component of the analysis (Phase II) focused on approved applications, using a complicated set of computer programs to assess whether terms and conditions given approved applicants evidenced any patterns associated with characteristics of borrowers for which systematic differential treatment is prohibited by law. Armed with computer printouts from Washington, D.C., examiners (presumably well-trained in all aspects of fair lending examination) would then find on-site evidence either corroborating or confirming illegal behavior (or policies and practices with disparate impacts) or find "compensating factors" explaining apparent differential treatment.

The Fair Housing Home Loan Data System became fully operational by about 1981. Plaintiffs in the National Urban League suit were impressed with the OCC's approach, and recommended it to other agencies in the lawsuit. (Despite the recommendation, the Federal Deposit Insurance Corporation and the Federal Home Loan Bank Board developed somewhat different data collection and analysis systems; much later, the Federal Reserve System developed its own data system, for which examiners were expected to enter data and perform analysis with user-friendly software developed by Washington staff.)

In 1983, an internal review (by volume coeditor Ron Wienk, with assistance from others) revealed the system's fatal flaws. For one thing, it was a rare bank for which the volume of loan applications was sufficient to identify patterns of "unfavorable" (let alone illegal discriminatory) treatment. Second, it was clear from comments by examiners and others that almost every lender could explain away any "anomalies" revealed by analysis of the data, both in overall patterns and in treatment of individual applicants. What has been popularized through the Boston Fed study (Munnell et al. 1992, 1996) has long been (quietly) confirmed by examiners: For the vast majority of applicants, and especially for those denied loans, there is almost always a plausible reason that might preclude loan approval. As Greene puts it in chapter 22 (in this volume), it is highly unlikely that a "smoking gun" will be found—by examiners or other investigators.

To our knowledge, no lender has ever been charged with noncompliance with law based primarily on analysis and follow-up examination using the OCC's data system. Its value as an investigative tool seemed rather limited. In a paper at HUD's 1993 conference, Larry Riedman offered several explanations, not least of which were lack of resources and expertise for statistical analyses of even large-volume lenders. As Riedman explained in his paper, even the fairly comprehensive data sets that might be created through the OCC's system, or any similar system, might still not capture information relevant to one particular lender's decision-making. (Somewhat inexplicably, however, Riedman then advocated an even more comprehensive data collection system, to be implemented primarily by examiners on-site.)

Scattered through this volume are arguments either favoring or opposing a "matched pair" approach to reviewing lender records of treating mortgage applicants. This approach essentially identifies pairs of otherwise similar applicants who have been treated differently and for which the only apparent difference between applicants appears to be their race, ethnicity, or other characteristic for which differential treatment is prohibited. In the mid-1980s, use of the OCC's data system was fine-tuned so that in addition to providing examiners with computer printouts and information about overall patterns of lender behavior, staff in Washington, D.C., began to identify pairs, or groups of pairs, of individual files recommended for on-site examiner review. Again, to our knowledge, this fine-tuning of the system did not yield charges of discrimination.

Despite the OCC's limited enforcement success with a sophisticated data collection and analysis system (and similar experiences by other agencies), the system routinely yielded information that, at least, confirmed racial differences in application outcomes. As part of the previously mentioned internal review of the system in 1983, it was determined that although statistical analysis for all but the most high-volume lenders was likely to be of very limited enforcement value, analysis of *aggregate* data for reporting banks showed clear research evidence similar to that commonly found over the years by analysts of HMDA data: in particular, black applicants in the combined data pool for any given year were about two-thirds more likely to be unfavorably treated than were white applicants. (Since the OCC operated the analysis portion of its system by usually requiring banks to report information on all minority applicants, but only for a sample of white applicants, the percentage of minority applicants classified as unfavorably treated under OCC's system is by no means a scientific estimate, but is remarkably similar to estimates revealed through the Boston Fed study a decade later.)

After over a decade of using the system, the OCC has now abandoned it. However, the OCC and many others (not only regulatory agencies) are analyzing HMDA and Loan Application Register information and developing new data systems (e.g., the Federal Reserve Board's "New York Model") that may not fully exploit analytic and enforcement lessons that could be learned from careful assessment of systems operated for some or all of the previous 15 years. (State reporting systems predate federal systems.) Siskin and Cupingood (chapter 16) and Rodda and Wallace (chapter 20) describe "breakthrough" efforts that appear essentially similar to approaches by regulators and others at least a decade ago. Have we entered a new epoch of fair lending enforcement with a new set of analytic tools—designed either for enforcement or research—or are we using essentially the same tools with a somewhat more successful application?

The final chapter of the Fair Housing Home Loan Data System story is that we *can* learn from history that perhaps things have changed over time. As a follow-up to the 1983 review of OCC's data system, in 1984 Wienk checked to see if any of the lenders reporting under the Home Loan Data System for the years 1980 through 1982 had also reported in the 1974 pilot study. Relatively few banks were in both samples. However, although it appeared that denial rates of black mortgage applicants had not changed much between the two time periods, their *application rates* had increased. (This observation is from unreported research that, among other things, used American Housing Survey [AHS] data to estimate prospective home purchasers, and used the estimates to assess whether racial and ethnic differences in loan application rates reflected racial and ethnic differences observed in AHS information about recent homebuyers.) In 1996, the Department of Justice and many others (including lenders themselves) consider increased mortgage application rates to be a positive sign of enforcement efforts (as they may also well be of reporting requirements). Again, there appear unexplored lessons from our past.

RESEARCH, ENFORCEMENT, AND SEARCH FOR OMITTED VARIABLES

The OCC's Fair Housing Home Loan Data System illustrates the convergence of research and enforcement approaches. "Old" HMDA data allowed analysis of patterns in loans made; "new" HMDA data allow analysis of patterns not only of loans made but of application activity; the Boston Fed and other studies described in Part I utilize expanded data sets to help explain differential patterns in treatment. Most research has focused on the outcome of the application process, particularly the accept/reject decision, with each new study attempting to add variables that may affect a lender's decision but that had previously been omitted from earlier analyses. As an examiner's tool, the Fair Housing Home Loan Data System differed little from current and prior research, except that examiners, rather than researchers, were to find the "omitted variables" that might explain observed differential treatment of individual applicants. (The lending community, and frequently the financial regulators, have often explained away apparent discrimination by using what might be called the "omitted variable defense''; see, for example, Yezer 1995.) The search for omitted variables continues, and there are many recommendations in this volume for how to improve the search, as well as how to better model the analytic approach (see, in particular, chapters 2, 4, and 27).

Such a search has for the most part been only a portion of the lengthy and complicated process leading to submission of a written application by a prospective homebuyer. This process starts with the decision to buy or not buy, and includes numerous actors other than lenders: advertisers, sellers, sales agents, appraisers, insurers, secondary market intermediaries, and others. Only recently has research begun shifting to the roles of actors other than loan originators. This shift is an important development, given that observed differences in application rates, particularly racial differences, are frequently of much greater magnitude than observed differences in treatment of those who have submitted written applications. Several authors in this volume, as well as Riedman, note that few lenders subject to HMDA reporting requirements report receiving applications from more than a small number of blacks or Hispanics in any given year. (Indeed, 1990 data for OCC banks reporting under HMDA indicated that 45 percent received no applications from blacks, and 47 percent reported receiving no applications from Hispanics—for any type of housing-related loan, including home improvement loans; see Wienk 1992: 238.) Although application rates by minorities appear to be increasing, there has been relatively little research on stages of the home and credit search process (including the decision to begin a search) that occur prior to submission of written applications to lenders. Numerous ideas are recommended in this volume for future research that, collectively, would considerably broaden the search for omitted variables beyond the relatively narrow component of analyzing information in loan originators' files.

ROLE OF TESTING IN RESEARCH AND ENFORCEMENT

Perhaps the most dramatic evidence indicating that the differential treatment of applicants may be too narrow a research focus has been offered by Avery, Beeson, and Sniderman (1994). Using 1990 HMDA data supplemented with census tract information, the authors investigated the relationships among loan originations, approval rates, and application rates. Their key finding is that ''lender differences in minority approval rates account for only about 10 percent of lender differences in minority loan originations: Differences across lenders in minority application rates account for the remaining 90 percent" (p. 28). This finding suggests that we need to know much more about treatment of prospective purchasers before they submit written loan applications, including whether they are discouraged from doing so and why minorities apply to some lenders and not others.

Testing has a long and rich history as an investigative tool, one used by private and public enforcers, researchers, and private industry (typically termed "shopping"). However, its application for fair lending research or enforcement has been limited. Notable exceptions have been its use by the Federal Trade Commission and the state of Massachusetts and by private fair housing organizations. Exploratory and small-scale testing efforts by private fair housing groups are described by Smith and Cloud (chapter 23) and Lawton (chapter 24), referred to by Greene (chapter 22) and briefly reviewed by Galster (chapter 27).

There is almost universal agreement that testing is perhaps the only way to detect systematic differential treatment of mortgage (and other) credit applicants at stages prior to submission of written loan applications. There is ample evidence that financial screening of prospective buyers begins at least as early as when they encounter real estate agents (see Wienk et al. 1979; Turner, Struyk, and Yinger 1991), who are likely to ask more detailed financial information of minority buyers and are more likely to provide them different information about mortgage sources (e.g., suggesting FHA financing more frequently to minorities than to whites).

Over the years, attempts to fund large-scale, or even relatively modest-scale, testing of lenders have met with little success. For example, in 1979 HUD proposed to members of the Federal Financial Institutions Examination Council that a sizable pilot study in at least three metropolitan areas be conducted with joint funding by HUD, the financial regulators, and the Ford Foundation. After months of consideration, the regulators declined to do so; one of the official reasons cited was that the timing was inappropriate because of the unusually high mortgage rates at the time (rates that rose, and stayed, higher for several years thereafter). Galster (chapter 27) describes the most widely known pilot testing, or auditing, project that was considered by the Federal Reserve Board in 1991 and was again rejected. However, between 1979 and 1991, many other testing projects were considered by the regulators and by HUD, with staff usually arguing in favor of at least a pilot effort and agency principals rejecting the proposals.

Arguments frequently offered against testing of lenders are that testing is difficult, expensive, and may have limited value if the objective is to find particular individuals or particular lenders in violation of law. However, alternatives to testing may be more costly or burdensome. Financial regulators from at least the mid-1970s onward spent millions of dollars on data collection and analysis systems, as well as examiner costs, ultimately to achieve indeterminant results. In 1992, The Urban Institute estimated that a sizable, pilot audit of five metropolitan statistical areas (MSAs) (including up to 1,000 tests) would cost $750,000, and that conducting an audit (with approximately 4,000 tests in up to 25 MSAs) might cost as much as $3 million. (Telephone audits might substantially lower these costs.) Such testing would have provided national estimates of racial discrimination at the inquiry stage of the mortgage application process. The Urban Institute proposed its study to all the financial regulators, the Department of Justice, Fannie Mae, Freddie Mac, and many other potential cofunders, all of whom rejected the proposal for varying reasons. In 1992, HUD's reluctance to fund a pilot research audit of lenders is, in part, explained by its sponsorship, under the Fair Housing Initiatives Program, of a series of testing projects for enforcement purposes, the results of which would be unknown for some time.

About the same time the Urban Institute was promoting an audit for research purposes, the Federal Reserve Bank of Boston study results were released (October 1992, Munnell et al.) As Cole observes (chapter 21), the study was initially viewed by many "as ending the debate on whether discrimination exists in the mortgage lending industry." Of course, shortly after the Boston Fed study was released, the Clinton administration took over and was much more interested in pursuing antidiscriminatory activities than the two prior administrations had been. For example, shortly after assuming office, Comptroller Eugene Ludwig announced his office's intent to pursue a pilot testing project as part of apparently significant new fair lending initiatives. (OCC staff have confirmed that one of the new comptroller's first questions was "Why aren't we testing?") Like HUD's support of testing, the comptroller's efforts were to have an enforcement, not research, objective.

Preliminary results of both HUD's and OCC's enforcement testing efforts are to be released as this book goes to press (May 1996). Smith and Cloud (chapter 23) report that as many as two-thirds of lenders subject to testing under a HUD/National Fair Housing Alliance enforcement testing project may have discriminated against black or Hispanic mortgage applicants, and that evidence gathered through the project was sufficient to initiate action against several lenders. In contrast, results of OCC's pilot testing program reportedly may yield neither estimates of discrimination nor evidence upon which enforcement actions might be pursued, because the effort was smaller in scale than that of HUD's and the methodology much more exploratory. (Although as of this writing neither HUD nor the OCC had released details of their testing efforts, the HUD/National Fair Housing Alliance effort included almost 800 tests, spread among approximately 80 lenders in eight metropolitan areas; the OCC effort as reported in Smith and Cloud was of much smaller magnitude.) As Galster (chapter 27) observes, there appears "dramatic incongruity" between the fair lending research and fair lending enforcement communities. Some researchers now question research evidence of discrimination revealed through various analytic approaches, while "enforcers" (most notably DOJ and private fair housing groups) have succeeded in their pursuits of lenders they believed were illegally discriminating. An accurate assessment of the enforcement value of testing cannot yet be made, but evidence presented in this volume, particularly by Smith and Cloud and by Lawton, suggests that testing may be an especially efficient enforcement tool relative to the analytic approaches used by researchers and regulators.

There is no question that the Boston Fed study, and, several years earlier, the series of articles entitled "The Color of Money" in the *Atlanta Journal-Constitution* (Dedman 1988) significantly raised the level of fair lending research and enforcement, including the use of testing. However, in the last few years the most common use of testing is by private fair housing organizations and lenders themselves, through vendors or direct employees. There has yet to be a large, carefully designed *research* effort to discern the nature and extent of discriminatory treatment by lenders preliminary to prospective borrowers' submission of written applications. Similarly, relatively few studies have been undertaken or completed of other actors in the home purchase/credit search process. (A notable exception is HUD's current exploratory research of discrimination in home insurance, under contract with the Urban Institute, building upon earlier efforts by the National Fair Housing Alliance and by the Association of Community Organizations for Reform Now [Acorn]).

Part of the irony with regard to the underutilization of testing as a research tool is that both private and public resources may be wasted. As noted earlier, effective enforcement policies, including self-regulatory efforts, can be most efficiently designed only after determining why, when, where, and by whom discriminatory treatment occurs. Testing is the premier tool for examining treatment.

DISPARATE IMPACT OF POLICIES

Testing is designed to reveal differential treatment, including differential application of policies. But what about the policies themselves? Clearly, some policies are likely to have differential effects, adversely affecting some individuals and groups more than others. Perhaps the most frequently noted loan policy that adversely affects minorities is that of adopting minimum mortgage loan amounts; however, minimum loan amounts are but one of many loan policies that even if evenly applied would disproportionately affect some individuals more than others. The "effects test" issue has been one of the most difficult areas to address for regulators and others involved with fair lending enforcement. Although policies discriminatory in effect may violate law as much as policies or practices discriminatory by intent, and may have adverse consequences of much greater magnitude, regulatory and enforcement efforts addressing disparate impacts have yet to agree on what constitutes illegal behavior. Policies with disparate impacts are legal if their use can be justified by a business rationale—unless it can be proven that substitute policies serving the same rationale (really, outcome) have fewer adverse, differential effects on bases prohibited by law.

Proof of disparate impacts of policies is difficult enough. But demonstrating alternative policies that would serve a business rationale and have fewer disparate impacts is even more difficult. Regulators have grappled with this problem since at least the 1970s, with various intra- and interagency task forces trying to define what practices would be sufficent prima facie evidence of discriminatory, disparate impacts sufficient to cite a lending institution for violation of law. To our knowledge, no loan policies (including underwriting policies) have been defined by courts as being clear violations of fair lending law. In fact, there have been few attempts to present disparate impact arguments in court.

This volume reproduces both the Decatur Federal Savings and Loan and Chevy Chase Federal Savings Bank consent agreements with the Department of Justice (chapters 14 and 25, respectively), both of which are landmark efforts to address policies and practices with apparent disparate impacts, and require efforts designed to reduce those effects. However, doubt remains (particularly among lenders) as to whether the Justice Department cases, had they run their full courses in court, would have resulted in conclusive legal illumination of what constitutes violation of law. In particular, even financial regulators question how to demonstrate that location of a lender's branch offices, and the loans made from those offices, can provide clear evidence of a pattern or practice of discrimination. (Obviously, the Justice Department was convinced that violations of law had occurred.)

Of the two cases, the Chevy Chase Federal case is in many respects the more interesting, since the remedies sought by the Justice Department were even more wide-ranging than those sought in the Decatur Federal case. But perhaps most important is how the case demonstrates the requirements for effective deterrent policy mentioned earlier: reasonable belief that compliance will be monitored, high probability that noncompliance will be detected, and belief that sanctions will be imposed and corrective actions required. After the Justice Department initiated its investigation, but long before it brought charges against Chevy Chase, the institution's geographic pattern of loan activity underwent an astonishing change. Figures 13.1 and 13.2 provide graphic evidence of Chevy Chase Bank's altered loan activity patterns, illustrating, among other things, a change in the bank's ability to reach out to areas within its metropolitan area that it had barely served before the investigation began.

SANCTIONS AND SELF-REGULATION

Two of the more promising developments in fair lending enforcement in recent years have been efforts within the lending industry to seek better understanding of fair lending and to pursue self-regulation. Much of the impetus for self-regulation has come from increasingly successful challenges under the Community Reinvestment Act by community groups who have long contended not only that individuals, particularly minorities, have been victims of discriminatory treatment, but that entire sections of communities have been underserved or even redlined.

Self-regulation is now taking many forms, but three forms are of particular interest. First, many lenders now undertake self-testing, as already mentioned. At the May 1993 HUD conference on "Home Mortgage Lending and Discrimination," Barry Leeds noted that his firm (Barry Leeds and Associates) was at that time devoting over half its business to testing lenders, an activity he claimed hardly existed a few years earlier. Other firms relate comparable increases in their fair

Figure 13.1 LOAN ORIGINATIONS BY CHEVY CHASE/B.F. SAUL MORTGAGE COMPANY, 1992

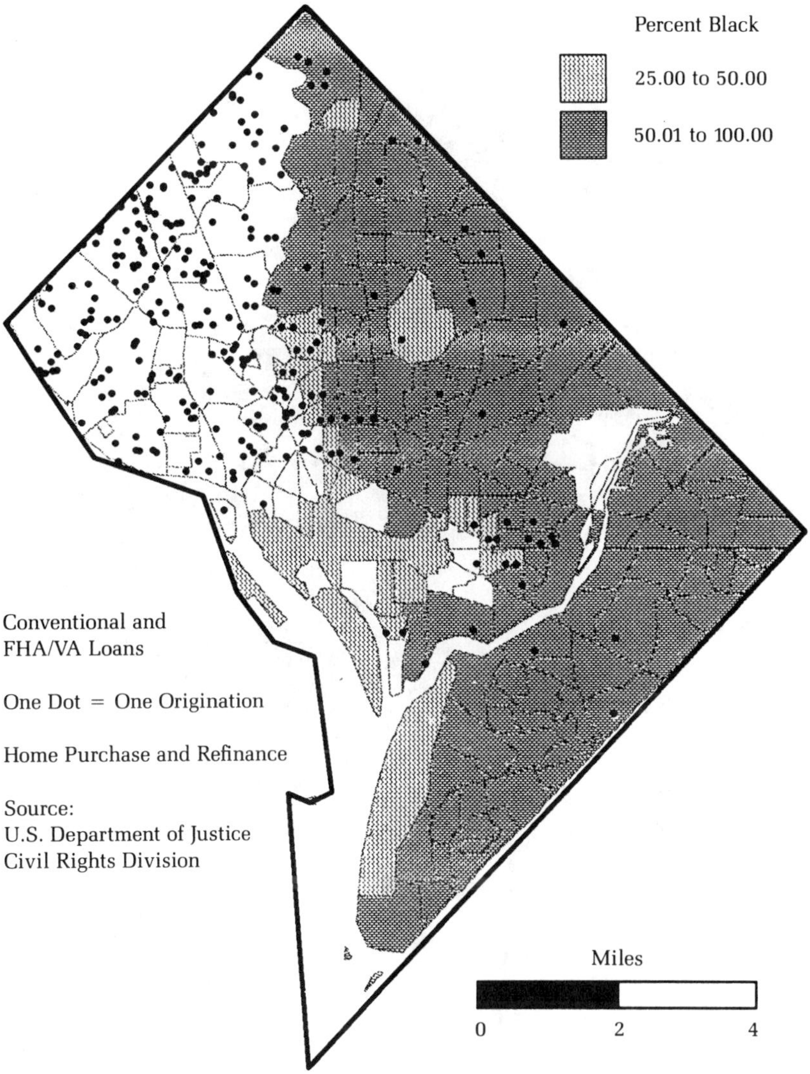

Figure 13.2 LOAN ORIGINATIONS BY CHEVY CHASE/B.F. SAUL MORTGAGE COMPANY, 1994

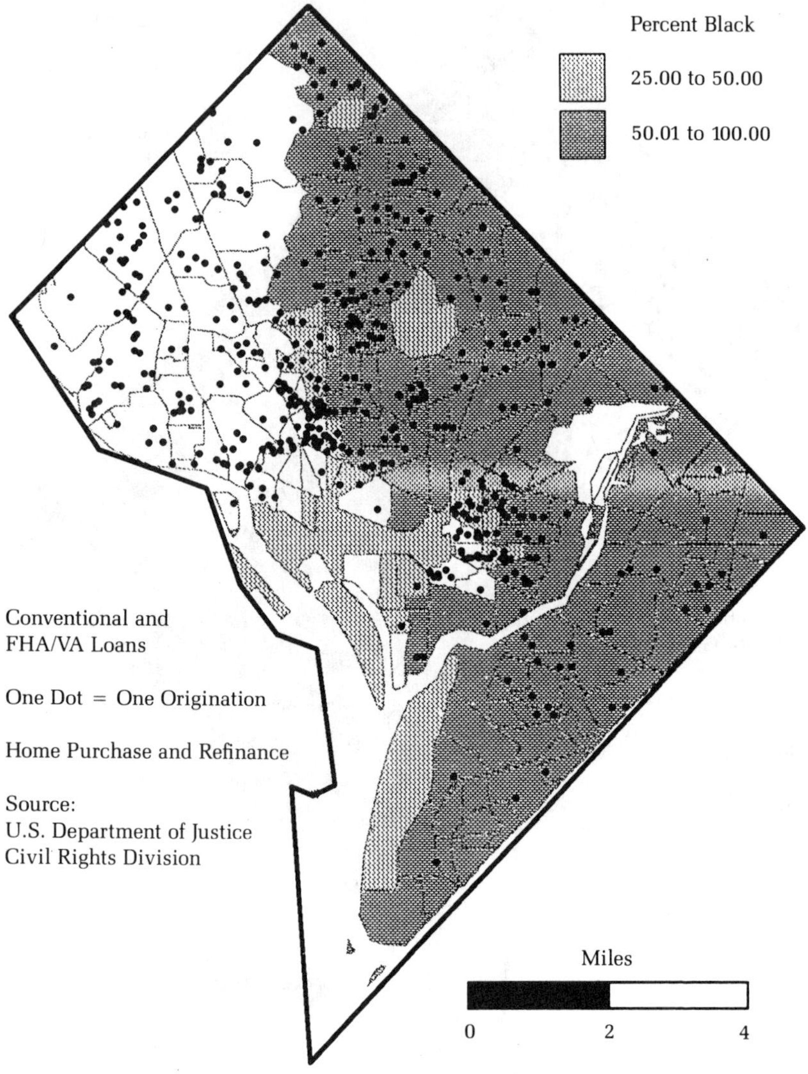

lending consulting and other services provided to the industry. (Interestingly, except through HUD's Fair Housing Initiatives Program, few private fair housing groups—the experts in testing—have been engaged by lenders to conduct testing of their institutions.) Trade organizations, including the American Bankers Association (ABA) and the Mortgage Bankers Association, have come out strongly in favor of self-testing. (The ABA, with help from, among others, Deborah Goldberg of the Center for Community Change, even produced a fair lending compliance videotape demonstrating differential treatment that might be revealed through testing; see American Bankers Association 1990.) Regulatory agencies (e.g., the Federal Deposit Insurance Corporation) and secondary market intermediaries (e.g., Freddie Mac [1994]) have developed self-testing guides. And, of course, the financial regulatory agencies have encouraged self-testing through their 1994 *Interagency Joint Policy Statement on Lending Discrimination.* These pro-testing efforts are positive developments.

A second form of self-regulation is more general self-assessment: investigating policies, their application, and their outcomes. Many lenders, particularly larger ones, are conducting or are about to conduct statistical analyses of their own lending behavior, some as sophisticated as those reported in this volume. (The distinction between "self-testing" and "self-assessment" has left many lenders confused, and nervous, about what regulatory or legal consequences may result from efforts undertaken to discover discriminatory practices or policies on their own. Generally, both the Justice Department and financial regulators appear interested in prospective corrective action, rather than retrospective sanction, for lenders whose self-assessment or self-testing efforts reveal discriminatory policies or practices, although self-testing data need not be disclosed to enforcement agencies.)

A third significant development is what Galster (in chapter 27) has labeled one of two "magic bullets" (the other being testing): scoring systems for mortgage applications. Both Fannie Mae and Freddie Mac have developed and are refining underwriting systems whose applications would significantly automate a process toward which much past criticism has been directed based on the considerable latitude of loan officers and underwriters in treating loan applicants.

Whereas all three approaches to self-regulation are positive developments, it is unclear how widespread the practices are or what effects they are having. Also unclear is the extent to which self-regulation stems from enlightened interest and desire to be nondiscriminatory, or from concern about potential legal sanctions for noncompliance, or both. Alexander (chapter 17) explains that Decatur Federal Savings' fear of costly litigation with the Justice Department was a strong factor, perhaps the primary factor, in its decision to settle the case.

Regardless of motivation, lenders appear far more interested in complying with fair lending law than ever before. Without question, part of that interest stems from the much higher visibility that discrimination issues have received as a result of the efforts of community groups, reporters, researchers, the Justice Department, and HUD and financial regulators. Depository institutions are particularly anxious to avoid negative publicity, fearing, among other things, a loss of deposits and other profit-making opportunities. Charges of discrimination, even if not believed, are to be avoided at virtually any cost.

NATIONAL URBAN LEAGUE ET AL. V. COMPTROLLER OF THE CURRENCY ET AL. RECONSIDERED

Has interest in fair lending enforcement and research peaked? More important, has interest in fair lending compliance peaked? We do not know. However, much can be learned from the National Urban League case and from developments in the intervening years.

A primary reason the Urban League petitioned in 1971 and brought suit in 1976 against the financial regulatory agencies was that the agencies had failed to issue fair lending provisions of the Fair Housing Act of 1968. Ultimately, regulations were released, but not without years of pressure by the petitioners and others, and years of what can generously be called indecision by the regulators. Although recent years have brought about markedly increased regulatory interest in complying with the law by depository and nondepository institutions, there is increasing concern that issuance of regulations related to fair lending compliance by other actors—the insurance industry and secondary market intermediaries—has experienced undue, perhaps irreversible delay. Fair housing advocates are particularly concerned about nonissuance of regulations, partly because they (more than others) fear that discrimination tends to shift to un- or underregulated segments of the overall homebuying, home-financing sector. (There is considerable validity to the argument that, over time, discrimination becomes more subtle.) As more has been learned about behavior by loan originators, interest is shifting to the roles of other actors in the credit market, and to their probable impact on overall outcomes of the lengthy, multiple-actor process.

A second "remedy" sought by the National Urban League was the recording of all loan applications—by race of applicant, disposition of application (and reason for rejection if disapproved), and socioeconomic character of the neighborhood of the property for which financing was sought. For the most part, this objective has been achieved; however, reasons for disapproval have been identified as a major area deserving further research. Can evaluation of credit history, particularly of payment history, be performed in a manner that better (and less discriminatorily) assesses an applicant's ability and willingness to pay? Is failure to obtain private mortgage insurance a legitimate reason for being denied a loan, or an indicator of discrimination by individuals other than loan originators? Similarly, are low appraisals a consequence of discriminatory policies, either by intent or in effect? (And who is "responsible" for failure of an applicant to obtain PMI or a home appraisal sufficient to pass stated underwriting criteria—insurer, appraiser, lender?)

The Urban League and many others assumed that information about applicant treatment would considerably advance knowledge of the nature and extent of discrimination. It has. But we know relatively little about those not appearing in the applicant pool—either by choice or through discouragement. We also know little about those who withdraw from the applicant pool or whose racial/ethnic status is missing from reported data.

A third original objective of the National Urban League petition was to have regulators require lenders to record "oral inquiries" by credit seekers. Although the Comptroller of the Currency did not agree to this recommendation in its settlement with the Urban League, the Federal Home Loan Bank Board did agree to log inquiries, and the logs kept for thrifts under its supervision might be considered the first version of the "new" HMDA data collection and reporting system. In the early 1980s, Home Loan Bank Board staff, both in Washington, D.C., and during examinations, routinely used the logs to assess patterns not only of where loans were made but of where applications were received and their disposition. Tracking inquiries was viewed at the time as an alternative to the more direct technique of testing, which the regulators were not amenable to and which lenders vehemently opposed. But "inquiries" were also difficult to define and to distinguish from "applications." There is relatively little known about the enforcement value of logging and analyzing inquiries, but there is some (largely anecdotal) evidence that Bank Board staff were somewhat successful in persuading thrifts to change lending and marketing outreach efforts based on observed application patterns, particularly vis-à-vis other thrifts within a lender's market area.

Other remedies sought by the National Urban Leaque were also agreed to and implemented, but later quietly abandoned. For example, the OCC agreed to establish a separate cadre of regional consumer specialists; these specialists lasted but a few years. Periodic reports of analytic results of the Fair Housing Home Loan Data System were to be made available to the public, but, with one known exception, never were. Specialized training of examiners in fair lending law and investigation received attention for a while, but slowly and surely evaporated. (One of the low points in fair lending efforts was reached in 1990, when then Senior Deputy Comptroller for Bank Supervision Robert Herrmann requested that timekeeping codes for tracking bank examination not include any codes that might identify the amount of resources devoted to fair lending.) (Currently, the OCC has specialists, again, and also devotes more resources to fair lending training of examiners than it had a few years ago.)

Of equal importance to public policy are careful research and a continuing enforcement commitment grounded in that which is known. As this volume demonstrates, our knowledge of the nature and extent of mortgage credit discrimination is incomplete, as is our knowledge of the means to ensure its absence. Our abbreviated review of the outcomes of the *National Urban League* v. *OCC* settlement suggests that current increased interest in fair lending research and enforcement would benefit by more careful assessment of earlier efforts. For example, are new data systems and analytic approaches significantly different from those developed in the late 1970s/early 1980s? At least one new data system (that of the Federal Reserve System) is not dissimilar to the Fair Housing Home Loan Data System that the OCC has abandoned. Similarly, of what benefit to fair lending enforcement is creation of an examination force specializing in fair lending (or, more generally, consumer protection)? Some agencies (most notably the Federal Reserve System) have long maintained specialization is desirable, while other agencies (e.g., the OCC) have tried, abandoned, and re-tried a specialized examiner approach.

As Part II demonstrates, in recent years there has been a convergence of research and enforcement, and some notable fair lending cases. Two—Decatur Federal and Chevy Chase Savings and Loan—are included in this volume. Assuming that both institutions were discriminatory (there are some who disagree), it remains unclear whether they were more or less discriminatory than other institutions within their markets. Just as Part I chapters illustrate the difficulties of determining the nature and extent of discrimination, Part II chapters illustrate the difficulties of identifying discriminators.

ORGANIZATION OF PART II

Chapter 14 comprises the consent decree in *United States of America* v. *Decatur Federal Savings and Loan Association*. As noted previously, there are very few fair lending legal cases: *Decatur Federal* is the first such case pursued by the Justice Department, and may prove to be the most thorough investigation of a single lender ever undertaken. The *Decatur Federal* case has been described in numerous other forums, but never in so much detail as in this volume. Because of the case's pathbreaking nature, we have included, as chapter 15, a summary by Richard Ritter of a panel discussion of the case held during the May 1993 HUD conference. In chapter 16, Bernard Siskin and Leonard Cupingood provide a technical explanation of the statistical aspects of the investigation. Chapter 17 contains prepared comments in response to the panel discussion by Decatur Federal's lead attorney, Kent Alexander.

It is not an exaggeration to say that the *Decatur Federal* case sent shock waves through the lending community, not so much as a result of the finding of discriminatory treatment (including identification and agreed-upon compensation of individual victims) but more because of the agreed-upon remedies in general. The case also demonstrated the influence of the fourth estate, since the Justice Department's investigation began as a direct result of "The Color of Money" series in the *Atlanta Constitution-Journal* in 1988.

Chapters 18 through 22 present differing perspectives on targeting particular lenders for fair lending investigation as well as on what to examine during an investigation. As Chud and Bonnette, in chapter 18, note, targeting institutions is not a trivial issue, given the limited resources available. The Decatur Federal investigation began with the preliminary investigation of 64 lenders in just one area (Atlanta). Yet federal and state regulatory agencies (including HUD) are collectively responsible for thousands of individual lenders. And despite a history of attempts to thoroughly examine every institution for legal compliance, as well as overall safe and sound operation (usually about once per year), it clearly would be a waste of resources to devote equal attention to each one of them.

Historically, examination efforts have been driven by safety and soundness concerns, not by concern for compliance with fair lending or consumer protection law. Indeed, size of institution, financial condition, and the Gregorian calendar were, and to a great extent still are, the main determinants of examination efforts. Throughout the late 1970s and 1980s, there was considerable debate about whether consumer examinations should be divorced from safety and soundness examinations and whether cadres of specialist examiners were required to maximize lender compliance with consumer protection law. Over the years, financial regulatory agencies have taken varied, and variable, stances on these issues.

Currently, targeting fair lending investigative efforts relies heavily on use of HMDA data supplemented by census data. However, numerous unanswered research questions remain, which, if addressed, might significantly improve fair lending targeting and monitoring and promotion of nondiscriminatory behavior and policy. For example, is size of institution related to fair lending performance? Is competition within a market related to performance? For several years, the OCC operated a compliance program specifically designed to answer these types of questions, but abandoned it before fully assessing its value. (Significantly, one early result of analyzing a huge amount of data collected through the first cycle of examinations under the program was that there appeared to be no statistically significant relationship between bank size and overall compliance performance. Another significant preliminary finding was that banks with above-average performance in complying with consumer protection laws also appeared to have above-average profitability.)

Chud and Bonnette, and Goldstein (chapters 18 and 19 in this volume, respectively) describe initial efforts to target HUD secretary-initiated investigations of lenders using HMDA and census data provided for under the Fair Housing Amendments Act of 1988. Targeting efforts in Philadelphia, as described by Goldstein, also utilized Community Reinvestment Act ratings and public file statements, interviews with Realtors and others, and information from testing data supplied to HUD by the Philadelphia Commission on Human Relations (described further by Lawton, chapter 24). Beyond HMDA and census data, Chud and Bonnette and Goldstein review other information used to select particular lenders for investigation—for example, average processing time (Chud and Bonnette) and cluster analysis using a number of variables to identify groups of institutions behaving similarly, some apparently "worse" than others (Goldstein).

Chud and Bonnette and Goldstein focus on selecting institutions for further investigation, and only briefly address what to do thereafter. However, Chud and Bonnette argue that careful review of a valid sample of application files is "the most important aspect of a lending discrimination investigation," an argument with which Greene (chapter 22) concurs, but takes one step further in contending that a statistician or economist should draw the sample.

Rodda and Wallace, in chapter 20, describe what may become a useful investigative tool—influence statistics—for selecting individual loan application files for more intensive review. Use of influence statistics is an alternative approach to those so far used by financial regulators (e.g., the "matched pair" investigative approach based on differences in probabilities of loan approval, as described in the previous section of the OCC's Fair Housing Home Loan Data System).

Rodda and Wallace present yet another technique through which individual loan application files might be selected for review by examiners, but what examiners *actually do* during their examinations remains ever-evolving, even controversial. At the HUD conference in 1993, Riedman described why the OCC was adopting new fair lending examination procedures at that time, presenting an insider's view not only of the difficulties of conducting fair lending investigations (or examinations) but of how regulators learn from research and prior enforcement efforts. Riedman's presentation also demonstrated how enforcement agencies may differ in perspective; for example, he argued that a bank's compliance program per se may not be particularly important to whether it complies with fair lending law, a position with which Justice Department staff, as revealed through various settlement agreements with lenders, clearly disagree.

Perhaps the most notable innovation in examination procedures described by Riedman in 1993 was the proposed investigation of the "quality of assistance" given mortgage credit applicants by bank personnel. Clearly, this proposed change in examination procedures stemmed directly from observations, first widely publicized upon release of the Boston Fed study, that minorities might not receive advice to overcome obstacles to loan approval equal in value to advice white, Anglo applicants of similar characteristics receive. (Two problems with assessing "quality of assistance" are, first, the frequent lack of a paper trail to enable examiners to review differences in assistance and, second, the difficulty of determining at what point application assistance begins. If application assistance occurs prior to submission of written application, then testing may be the optimal technique for revealing differential assistance.)

By his request, the paper Riedman presented at HUD's conference is not included in this volume. The OCC is about to adopt another set of fair lending examination policies and procedures that may differ from those Riedman described in 1993, and, understandably, neither Riedman nor the OCC would want to mislead readers. Not including Riedman's 1993 paper describing examination procedures about to be (and, on an interim basis, were) adopted because his description may be "out of date" vis-a-vis current (OCC) regulatory policy reflects what might well be considered the state of the art with regard to fair lending enforcement by financial institution regulators: Periodic revisitation of fair lending examination policies and procedures, accompanied by somewhat differing perspectives among the financial regulators. Regulatory policies and procedures on fair lending have for decades been in flux. The principal change in how regulators now approach fair lending monitoring and enforcement compared to how they did so in the past is that regulatory agencies (including HUD, Justice, federal, and state financial regulatory agencies) are much more inclined to revise their regulatory/enforcement efforts based on observations provided through the fair lending research and private fair lending/community development communities. Cole (chapter 21) illustrates both the convergence of research and enforcement information, and how research and enforcement efforts might improve public policy. Many of the fair lending investigation ideas and recommendations Cole presents stem from information first surfaced through research; many others stem from practical experience with regard to how to investigate individual lenders.

Cole describes how an agency with more limited resources than the OCC and other federal regulatory agencies can approach fair lending investigation. One of Cole's more intriguing suggestions is that of interviewing minority applicants if an on-site investigation reveals questionable treatment of minorities vis-à-vis white, Anglo applicants. To our knowledge, applicant interviews are not normally, if ever, part of regulatory investigative techniques. However, investigative reporters routinely interview applicants for articles on discrimination, frequently resulting in compelling descriptions of questionable, if not clearly discriminatory, treatment of minorities. Perhaps applicant interviews may be a much less labor-intensive approach than the detailed reviews of loan files Riedman describes.

Chapter 22, by Greene, the final chapter in this group, contains a step-by-step review and assessment of information commonly found in loan application files. As Greene notes, a single loan file is unlikely to prove discrimination (no smoking guns); comparisons of applicant treatment are a prerequisite for identifying whether discrimination, either by intent or in effect, may have occurred.

The next section of Part II contains two discussions of the use of testing in investigating lenders. Chapter 23, by Smith and Cloud, describes various practical and legal issues with regard to testing. An important point made by the authors is that there is no one correct answer to the question of how many tests are required to "prove" discrimination. Much of the historical resistance by regulators to testing has been based on the perceived necessity of conducting multiple tests not only of the same lender but perhaps of the same loan officer, in order to provide sufficient information to prove discrimination. This viewpoint is uninformed, given that most (federally reported) court cases involving testing for investigating discriminatory treatment in the rental or sale of housing have been successfully litigated with a single test (see Schwemm 1993). Though perhaps more difficult to detect than discrimination by rental or sales agents, discrimination by lending agents might be revealed through a single test.

Chapter 24, by Lawton, describes the results of a testing effort by the Philadelphia Commission of Human Relations. Lawton presents impressive numbers with regard to the enforcement value of preapplication testing. Of 68 lenders tested (some only by telephone), evidence was sufficient to file complaints against 11 of the lenders. At the time of the HUD 1993 conference, 6 of the complaints had been resolved, 3 with formal consent orders. Perhaps the most impressive number presented by Lawton is that the effort cost only $16,000.

The final two entries in Part II are the Justice Department's complaint and consent decree with Chevy Chase Federal Savings Bank, in chapter 25, and Calem's description, in chapter 26, of patterns of residential mortgage activity that appear to have stemmed from the Delaware Valley Mortgage Plan, established in 1977 by a consortium of lenders to increase homeownership in disadvantaged sections of Philadelphia. The mapping of changes in loan originations in the Chevy Chase area, described earlier here, can be compared with Calem's statistical results highlighting differences among Philadelphia lenders who belong to the Delaware Valley plan and those not belonging. Both the Chevy Chase maps and Calem's findings provide convincing evidence that, at a minimum, lenders are capable of serving borrowers throughout their communities.

References

American Bankers Association. 1990. "Fair Lending Compliance: Understanding Equal Treatment." Manual and videotape. Washington, D.C.: Author.

Avery, Robert B., Patricia E. Beeson, and Mark S. Sniderman. 1994. "Cross-Lender Variation in Home Mortgage Lending." *Economic Review* (Federal Reserve Bank of Cleveland) 30 (4): 15–29.

Comptroller of the Currency. 1975. *Fair Housing Lending Practices Pilot Project, Survey C Approach*. Washington, D.C.: Author. Photocopy.

———. 1979. *Fair Housing Home Loan Data System. Regulation 27.* Washington, D.C.: Author.

Dedman, Bill. 1988. "The Color of Money: Home Mortgage Practices Discriminate against Blacks." Parts 1–4. *Atlanta Journal-Constitution*, May 1–16.

Freddie Mac. 1994. "Fair Lending: An Introduction to Self-Evaluation." Washington, D.C.: Author.

Munnell, Alicia H., Lynn E. Browne, James McEneaney, and Geoffrey M.B. Tootell, 1992. "Mortgage Lending in Boston: Interpreting HMDA Data." Federal Reserve Bank of Boston Working Paper 92-07. Boston: Federal Reserve Bank of Boston, October.

Munnell, Alicia H., Geoffrey M.B. Tootell, Lynn E. Browne, and James McEneaney. 1996. "Mortgage Lending in Boston: Interpreting HMDA Data." *American Economic Review*. Forthcoming.

National Urban League et al. v. *Office of the Comptroller of the Currency et al.* 1977. Civil Action 76-0718. U.S. District Court of the District of Columbia: Stipulation of Dismissal, and Settlement Agreement.

Riedman, Larry. 1993. "Perspectives from a Regulatory Agency." Presented at HUD's "Discrimination and Mortgage Lending Research and Enforcement Conference," May, Washington, D.C.

Schwemm, Robert G. 1993. "Fair Housing Cases Involving Testing: A Legal Review of Reported Federal Court Decisions, 1968–1991." Washington, D.C.: Urban Institute.

Turner, Margery A., Raymond J. Struyk, and John Yinger. 1991. *Housing Discrimination Study: Synthesis*. Washington, D.C.: U.S. Department of Housing and Urban Development.

U.S. Senate. 1976. *Report on Fair Lending Enforcement by the Four Financial Regulatory Agencies*. Committee on Banking, Housing, and Urban Affairs. Washington, D.C.: U.S. Government Printing Office.

Wienk, Ronald E. 1992. "Discrimination in Urban Credit Markets: What We Don't Know and Why We Don't Know It." *Housing Policy Debate* 3(2): 217–40.

Wienk, Ronald E., Clifford E. Reid, John C. Simonson, and Frederick J. Eggers. 1979. *Measuring Racial Discrimination in American Housing Markets: The Housing Market Practices Survey*. Washington, D.C.: U.S. Government Printing Office.

Yezer, Anthony M., ed. 1995. *Fair Lending Analysis: A Compendium of Essays on the Use of Statistics*. Washington, D.C.: American Bankers Association.

Chapter Fourteen

THE DECATUR FEDERAL CASE

The text following reproduces the landmark 1992 consent decree entered into by Decatur Federal Savings and Loan and the U.S. Department of Justice, in which Decatur Federal agreed to remedial actions to improve its record of making home mortgage loans to Atlanta-area African Americans.The case was the first "pattern or practice" lawsuit brought by the federal government against a mortgage lender. According to the terms of the consent decree, Decatur Federal was to provide $1 million to 48 black individuals whose home mortgage loan applications had been rejected between 1988 and 1992. Among other major remedial measures stipulated in the decree, Decatur Federal was obligated to expand its lending territory to include most of the city of Atlanta; to advertise extensively in black-oriented news media; to target sales calls to real estate agents and builders in black neighborhoods; to increase pay incentives for the bank's account executives to obtain business in black neighborhoods; to meet the credit needs of low- and moderate-income neighborhoods in branch location decisions; and to open a branch or regional loan office in a predominantly black section of Atlanta. Commentary on this case follows in chapters 15, 16, and 17.

IN THE UNITED STATES DISTRICT COURT
FOR THE NORTHERN DISTRICT OF GEORGIA
ATLANTA DIVISION

UNITED STATES OF AMERICA,
Plaintiff,

v.

DECATUR FEDERAL SAVINGS AND
LOAN ASSOCIATION,
Defendant.

JOINT MOTION FOR ENTRY OF CONSENT DECREE

The parties hereby jointly move the Court for approval and entry of the attached Consent Decree.

For the United States:

JOE D. WHITLEY, UNITED STATES ATTORNEY

JOHN R. DUNNE, ASSISTANT ATTORNEY GENERAL

CURTIS E. ANDERSON
Assistant U.S. Attorney Chief, Civil Division
1800 U.S. Courthouse
75 Spring Street, S.W.
Atlanta, GA 30335
(Georgia Bar No. 016650)
(404) 331-6551

PAUL F. HANCOCK
RICHARD J. RITTER
HOWARD R. GRIFFIN
JEFFREY M. SENGER
Attorneys, Housing and Civil Enforcement Section
Civil Rights Division
U.S. Department of Justice
P.O. Box 65998
Washington, DC 20035-5998
(202) 514-4713

For Decatur Federal Savings and Loan:

KENT B. ALEXANDER
KING & SPALDING
191 Peachtree Street
Atlanta, GA 30303-1763
(Georgia Bar No. 008893)
(404) 572-3430

CONSENT DECREE

The United States files this Consent Decree simultaneously with its Complaint against Defendant Decatur Federal Savings and Loan Association ("Decatur Federal" or "the lender") alleging violations of the Fair Housing Act (Title VIII of the Civil Rights Act of 1968, as amended by the Fair Housing Amendments Act of 1988), 42 U.S.C. §§3601–3619, and the Equal Credit Opportunity Act, 15 U.S.C. §§1691–1691f. The Complaint alleges that Decatur Federal has engaged in policies and practices that discriminated against potential and actual mortgage loan applicants on the basis of race.

Decatur Federal categorically denies all of the allegations in the Complaint and is prepared to show that it has never discriminated on the basis of race and has had in place programs designed to serve all segments of the community, regardless of race.

More specifically, the United States alleges that Decatur Federal has for many years engaged in lending practices that discriminate on the basis of race by conducting its home mortgage loan marketing in a manner that excludes potential black borrowers; by originally defining its customer service area under the Community Reinvestment Act ("CRA") in 1979 so as to exclude most black residents of South Fulton County; by opening virtually all of its branch offices in neighborhoods that were predominantly white at the time and closing branches in neighborhoods that were or became predominantly black;[1] by advertising primarily to potential white customers; by focusing its solicitation efforts in white neighborhoods; by avoiding origination of loan products with particular appeal to black borrowers, such as Federal Housing Administration ("FHA") and Veterans Administration ("VA") loans; and by employing few blacks in key mortgage loan origination positions such as account executive, staff appraiser, and underwriter.

The United States further alleges that Decatur Federal has discriminated against those blacks who did apply for home mortgage loans. It is alleged that in processing loan applications, the lender counseled white applicants about their deficiencies and reworked their applications in order to help them qualify under underwriting guidelines, but did not consistently supply comparable assistance to black applicants. It is also alleged that Decatur Federal rejected qualified black applicants more often than qualified white applicants, even after controlling for all relevant underwriting variables, such as income, credit history, net worth, debt ratios, employment history, and education level.

The parties have agreed that, in order to avoid protracted and costly litigation, this controversy should be resolved voluntarily. To this end, as more specifically described below, Decatur Federal has agreed to continue and expand its affirmative marketing, advertising, and other mortgage lending outreach programs, to revise the delineation of its lending community under the Community Reinvestment Act, to establish and implement criteria to ensure against any discrimination in its branching activities, to ensure the fair and nondiscriminatory consideration of all mortgage loan applicants, and to continue to monitor its own performance to assure a mortgage lending program free of racial discrimination. The Consent Decree is not intended to, and does not, apply to any institution other than Decatur Federal except as provided in paragraph 49, below.

The parties have also agreed that there should be no evidentiary hearing, trial, or other adjudication on the merits, and that the entry of this Consent Decree is not and is not to be construed as an admission by Decatur Federal of the validity of any of the claims asserted in this action.

Now therefore, on the basis of the foregoing representations of the United States and Decatur Federal, it is hereby ORDERED, ADJUDGED, and DECREED as follows:

I. GENERAL INJUNCTIVE PROVISION

1. Decatur Federal, its officials, employees, and agents, as well as successors, as provided in paragraph 49, below, are enjoined from engaging in any act or practice that discriminates on the basis of race in the provision of home mortgages or other real estate-related credit transactions, or in the provision of services or facilities in connection with any such credit transactions; and from imposing on the basis of race different terms or conditions for the availability of home mortgage loans or real estate-related credit transactions. Fair Housing Act, 42 U.S.C. §§3604 and 3605; Equal Credit Opportunity Act, 15 U.S.C. §1691 (a)(1).

II. SPECIFIC INJUNCTIVE PROVISIONS

A. Community Reinvestment Act Delineated Community

2. Decatur Federal will, within one year of the execution of this Consent Decree, expand its delineated community under the Community Reinvestment Act to include all of Fulton County. The lender's CRA Map, as it will be revised, is set forth in Attachment 1 [not included here] (hereinafter referred to as "delineated community").

B. Advertising

3. Decatur Federal will establish an advertising program, as described in this Section, designed to attract qualified applicants for

home mortgage loans from all segments of its community, as defined pursuant to the Community Reinvestment Act and this Consent Decree. The advertising program will include special provisions to target residents of predominantly black neighborhoods.[2]

4. Decatur Federal will place a total of at least 960 column-inches of advertising per one-year period of the Consent Decree in the *Atlanta Tribune*, the *Atlanta Inquirer*, the *Atlanta Daily World*, the *Atlanta Metro*, or comparable black-oriented publications. The lender may vary the size and frequency of advertisements, and the choice of publications for its advertising campaigns, as long as the above overall average is met for each one-year period. These advertisements will be for home mortgage products, and will mention the availability of FHA and VA loans or other products that have comparable advantages.

5. Decatur Federal will create special point-of-sale materials (e.g., posters, brochures, etc.) to advertise products and services of interest to minority home buyers and place the materials in branch lobbies in predominantly black neighborhoods.

6. Decatur Federal will develop a brochure describing its Community Home Buyers Program, its Smart Start pre-qualifying program, its FHA and VA loan programs, and/or comparable programs. The lender will distribute the brochure through such channels as real estate professionals serving black residential areas, church and community groups, and retail outlets in black communities. The lender will distribute at least 2,500 of these brochures per year during the Consent Decree period, and will annually distribute copies of such brochures to each real estate agency that is a member of the Empire Real Estate Board or known to serve black residential areas of the Atlanta Metropolitan area.

7. All of Decatur Federal's advertising for home mortgage loan products will continue to contain an equal housing opportunity logotype, statement, or slogan as described in the Fair Housing Advertising regulations of the United States Department of Housing and Urban Development, 24 C.F.R. Part 109. The lender will continue to follow the guidance of Tables I and II of Appendix I to 24 C.F.R. Part 109 in selecting appropriate type size as well as a slogan, statement, logotype, and other standards for advertising.

8. Decatur Federal's advertising that uses human models in video, photographs, drawings, or other graphic techniques will reasonably represent black as well as white residents of the area which the lender serves. Models, if used, will portray persons in an equal social setting and indicate to the general public that the lender's products are available on a nondiscriminatory basis.

9. Decatur Federal will place a total of at least 360 thirty-second spots per one-year period of the Consent Decree on radio stations WALR, WVEE, WAOK, or comparable black-oriented stations. All of this advertising will be for home mortgage products, and the lender's advertising program will include advertising of the availability of FHA and VA loans and/or comparable loan programs. The lender may vary the frequency of the spots and choice of stations for its advertising campaigns, as long as the above overall total is met for each one-year period.

10. In all television and radio advertisements and promotions for home mortgage loans, the statement "Equal Housing Lender" will continue to be audibly stated. In the alternative, if a television advertisement or promotion for home mortgage loans includes a written statement appearing on the screen, the nondiscrimination statement may so appear; the nondiscrimination must continue to meet the requirements set forth in Appendix I to 24 C.F.R. Part 109 and must appear on the screen as long as any other written statement appears.

11. Decatur Federal representatives will continue to use their test efforts to appear on talk radio and/or television programs aimed at predominantly black audiences at least twice per year during the Consent Decree period to discuss mortgage lending issues.

C. Mortgage Production

12. Decatur Federal will follow a home mortgage loan production program, as described in this Section, designed to increase its origination of home mortgage loans to black borrowers.

13. Decatur Federal will target real estate agents and builders active in neighborhoods in predominantly black census tracts within its delineated community for sales calls. The lender will conduct a study to determine what individuals are active in these neighborhoods by scanning real estate advertisements in black publications, driving through predominantly black residential areas, and seeking input from builders, developers, and other real estate professionals, including representatives of the Empire Real Estate Board.

14. Decatur Federal's current commission pay structure is based on a percentage of the loan amount, so account executives earn larger commissions for originating home mortgage loans in higher dollar amounts. In order to provide account executives and/or mortgage originators with an increased incentive to originate more loans in predominantly black areas and low- and moderate-income census tracts, the lender will implement a special compensation structure for them. Specifically, Decatur Federal will implement a program including increased percentage commissions of 1% of the loan amount, flat-rate

bonuses of $100, and/or other comparable measures designed to operate as genuine incentives for account executives and/or mortgage originators to originate loans in the amount of $50,000 or less. Every six months during the Consent Decree period, the lender will evaluate the effectiveness of the program to determine whether and how changes should be made.

15. Each account executive will continue to maintain a log of all sales calls identifying the name of the real estate agent or agency, builder, or other person or organization contacted for the purpose of home mortgage loan development, and whether the contact was for the purpose of soliciting loan applications in targeted black neighborhoods.

16. Decatur Federal will continue to reserve at least one position for an account executive who will be responsible for soliciting and originating home mortgage loans for Decatur Federal's special loan programs that are geared toward low- and moderate-income neighborhoods. The individual(s) will additionally develop an expertise in these special loan programs, target low- and moderate-income neighborhoods, prepare semi-annual reports on their activities, and serve as a resource to other account executives to encourage the use of Decatur Federal's special loan programs and the origination of more home mortgage loans to black borrowers. The special program account executive(s) and all other account executives will share responsibility for soliciting mortgage applications from the real estate agents and builders identified pursuant to paragraph 13.

17. Decatur Federal will follow up by telephone or letter with all participants in its Community Home Buyers Program and credit seminars within 45 days after the participants' completion of the program to ascertain their interest in applying for home mortgage loans or other Decatur Federal credit products.

18. Decatur Federal will use its best efforts to establish correspondent relationships with financial institutions in its delineated community primarily serving the black community that do not offer competitive long-term home mortgage financing, to expand its lending in black neighborhoods by underwriting applications prepared and submitted by these organizations.

19. Along with the above mortgage production steps, Decatur Federal will conduct additional ascertainment efforts to further understand the home mortgage credit needs of the black community. In this regard, the lender will enter into a contract with an established market research firm or financial institution to determine product needs and effective advertising strategies in black communities. Representatives

of the lender will meet each year with members of at least three black community or civic groups to examine current Decatur Federal loan products, services, and advertising, and discuss ideas for improvements if improvements are necessary.

D. Delivery Network

20. Decatur Federal will develop its delivery network to attract more qualified applicants for home mortgages from predominantly black neighborhoods, as described in this Section.

21. Within one year from the execution of this Consent Decree, Decatur Federal will have a physical presence in South Fulton County from which it will market home mortgage loan products. This presence will be in the form of a regional office or branch where home mortgage loan applicants may apply for loans and submit all documents necessary for approval. This presence will remain in existence at least through the end of the Consent Decree period. Such regional loan office or branch shall be subject to the terms of this Decree.

22. Decatur Federal will follow an objective set of criteria to evaluate future branch openings, closings, and other significant changes in services, and these criteria will incorporate the lender's Community Reinvestment Act obligations. Decatur Federal will pay particular attention to how any proposed changes could affect the lender's ability to meet the credit needs of low- and moderate-income neighborhoods, especially neighborhoods in predominantly black census tracts. Decatur Federal will promptly provide to the United States a copy of any applications or notices to open any branches in its delineated community.

23. Decatur Federal will consider the following alternatives to the closing of a branch in a predominantly black area: maintaining the branch under current conditions; implementing a plan to improve performance through personnel changes, increased marketing efforts, or increased community outreach; reducing the hours of operation of the branch; reducing operating expenses by subleasing space, reducing staffing levels, or other methods; and reducing the services offered by the branch. A branch will not be closed if any of these options could be used effectively. Before making any significant changes in the operation of branch in a predominantly black area, Decatur Federal representatives will meet with leaders of black community and civic organizations to advise them of the proposal, assess its impact on the black community, and discuss alternatives. The provisions of this paragraph will not apply if as a result of a merger or acquisition it is necessary to close branches to avoid duplication of services.

E. Non-discriminatory Treatment of Home Mortgage Loan Applicants

24. Decatur Federal, as further described in this Section, will solicit information necessary to allow for fair evaluation of applications and will assess completed applications from black customers in the same manner and under the same underwriting criteria that it applies to white customers. Nothing in this or any other section of this Consent Decree shall be construed to require Decatur Federal to engage in unsafe or unsound lending practices.

25. Decatur Federal's general home mortgage loan underwriting standards are set forth in Attachment 2 [not included here]. Those standards are based on and incorporate the requirements of the secondary market underwriting guidelines such as the Federal National Mortgage Association's (Fannie Mae) *Selling Guide* and the January 27, 1992, *Bulletin* from the Federal Home Loan Mortgage Corporation (Freddie Mac) describing home mortgage eligibility, appraisal, and underwriting requirements. The parties recognize that the attached Decatur Federal underwriting standards do not purport to identify all of the relevant underwriting criteria and compensating factors that may bear upon the lender's assessment of individual mortgage loan applications, as those are too numerous to incorporate into one document. The parties also recognize that Decatur Federal's underwriting standards incorporate a degree of flexibility and individual assessment risk based on the unique characteristics of individual mortgage applicants, and that this flexibility is especially important to meet the policy objectives of the Community Reinvestment Act.

26. Decatur Federal will require that loan processors and underwriters complete an Application Checksheet, Attachment 3 [not included here], for each applicant, in order to ensure that they solicit information necessary to allow for the fair evaluation of applications consistent with the lender's underwriting standards.

27. Decatur Federal will appoint at least one Review Underwriter who is a supervisor (i.e., underwriting manager or above) or an individual who is a part of a separate reviewing underwriting office with detailed knowledge of the flexibility of the underwriting standards and the various alternative means by which applicants may demonstrate their ability and willingness to repay home mortgage loans. The Review Underwriter(s) will review the loan processing and underwriting for each initially rejected application. The Review Underwriter(s) will certify by signature that the instructions contained in paragraphs 39–41 have been followed and that he/she concurs with or has elected to change (for reasons noted) the initial decision.

28. Decatur Federal will appoint at least one Review Appraiser with experience in appraising properties in black neighborhoods. The Review Appraiser(s) will review all appraisals made on properties lo-

cated in predominantly black census tracts where the appraised value of the property is the deciding factor for not granting the loan on the terms requested by the borrower. The Review Appraiser(s) will form an opinion as to the adequacy and appropriateness of the appraiser's report and conclusions and, if appropriate, will express a different estimate of value, which will be used as the basis for the underwriting decision. The provisions of this paragraph are subject to compliance with applicable regulatory provisions and the Uniform Standards of Professional Appraisal Practice.

29. Decatur Federal will amend the standard adverse action notice to include a reviewer's name and phone number and to encourage the applicant to call the reviewer if the applicant has any questions or believes that Decatur Federal did not possess information that would affect the basis for the action taken. In addition, Decatur Federal will amend the adverse action notice (in cases where the denial is based on credit problems) to encourage the applicant to call if the applicant believes that the credit reporting agency is in error or if the applicant wishes to further explain his/her credit history.

F. Special Programs and Other Remedial Measures

30. Decatur Federal has adopted and implemented a number of special programs and other measures to serve low- and moderate-income and black home buyers, as further described in this Section. Decatur Federal will continue to participate in these programs as they remain available, as described in the following paragraph and in Attachment 4 [not included here], or in similar programs, and will add new programs or alter or modify existing programs, when necessary to serve effectively the credit needs of low- and moderate-income residents in its CRA delineated community.

31. Decatur Federal continues to participate in the Mortgage Bankers Association Lend-a-Hand Program by committing dollars and human resources. This program involves the renovation and refurbishment of homes for low-income owners who would otherwise be unable to upgrade their homes. Decatur Federal's Community Home Buyers Program teaches participants about such topics as managing credit, controlling the household budget, and applying for a home mortgage loan. The lender will use its best efforts to present this Program at least twenty times per year. Upon successful completion of this Program, participants are eligible to receive mortgage loan consideration under more relaxed underwriting standards. The lender conducts regular credit seminars on topics of interest to low-income and black borrowers and funds below-market-rate loans in low-income and minority areas through such programs as the Atlanta Mortgage Consortium and

the Federal Home Loan Bank of Atlanta's Affordable Housing and Community Investment Fund Programs. It additionally participates in the Urban Residential Finance Authority program, the Georgia Housing Finance Authority program, the DeKalb Housing Authority Bond program, and the Department of Housing and Urban Development Section 8 Rehabilitation program. Decatur Federal is and has been heavily involved in acquisition and development, construction, and commercial lending in low- and moderate-income and in black communities. This lending activity represents a major investment in the development and redevelopment of these communities. Decatur Federal is one of several lenders that have pooled resources to provide the financing for a single-room occupancy facility in the City of Atlanta. Decatur Federal has been active with the DeKalb Community Housing Resource Board, a HUD-sponsored volunteer organization comprised of representatives from business, government agencies, non-profit organizations, and colleges and universities. The purpose is to monitor area Boards of Realtors to determine adherence to the Voluntary Affirmative Marketing Agreement and other fair housing-related guidelines.

G. Recruitment

32. Decatur Federal will advertise home mortgage lending job openings on an ongoing basis during the Consent Decree period in a manner that will reach potential black applicants, as further described in this Section, with special emphasis on the following home mortgage lending positions: Account Executive, Underwriter, Loan Counselor, Loan Processor, Staff Appraiser, Assistant Branch Manager, and Branch Manager.

33. Within 45 days after the effective date of this Consent Decree, Decatur Federal will write to the Atlanta office or representative of the National Society of Real Estate Appraisers ("NSREA") to invite their members to apply for inclusion on Decatur Federal's list of approved metro independent fee appraisers. This letter will describe Decatur Federal's current policies and procedures regarding this application process. Any applications received will be processed in accordance with current Decatur Federal policies and procedures regarding the approval of independent fee appraisers. Decatur Federal will additionally notify the NSREA whenever vacancies available to persons outside of the institution occur in the staff appraiser position or whenever there is a need to expand the list of approved metro independent fee appraisers.

34. In fulfilling its obligations under this Section, Decatur Federal will advertise home mortgage lending job openings available to per-

sons outside the institution in black-oriented publications such as the *Atlanta Daily World*, the *Atlanta Tribune*, the *Atlanta Metro Magazine*, and the *Atlanta Inquirer*. The lender will notify predominantly black organizations of openings, such as Fulton Atlanta Community Action, the N.A.A.C.P., the Atlanta Urban League, Inc., the Empire Real Estate Board, DeKalb Economic Opportunity, the Urban Bankers Association, the National Association of Black Real Estate Professionals, and the National Society of Real Estate Appraisers. The lender will solicit referrals from existing black employees, the State of Georgia Minority Business section, and the Atlanta University School of Real Estate. The lender will work with historically black colleges, including Spelman College, Morris Brown College, Clark College, and Morehouse College, to develop and recruit qualified black applicants.

H. Compliance

35. Decatur Federal will maintain Compliance Employees who will monitor the lender's compliance with the Community Reinvestment Act, the Fair Housing Act, the Equal Credit Opportunity Act, and this Consent Decree, as further described in this Section. The Compliance Employees will conduct regular reviews of processing and disposition of mortgage loan applications and the lender's compliance with the specific injunctive provisions of this Consent Decree. The Compliance Employees will review information on denied, approved, and withdrawn loan applications as reflected on its loan tracking system to ensure compliance with this Consent Decree. The Compliance Employees will report any deficiencies to Decatur Federal management and present proposals to correct them.

36. Decatur Federal will enter into a contract(s) with a qualified organization(s) or person(s) to develop and implement a program to test for racial discrimination in Decatur Federal's home mortgage lending. The tester must first submit a proposal to Decatur Federal outlining the methodology and approach to be used. Once the proposal is finalized, Decatur Federal will submit the proposal to the United States for approval, and the approval may not be unreasonably withheld. Decatur Federal will review the testing results with the relevant individual employees and will use the results to determine how to address any concerns with individual employees and whether changes in training are necessary. The United States may conduct independent testing.

I. Training

37. Decatur Federal will provide training to all of its staff with significant involvement in home mortgage lending to ensure their ac-

tivities are conducted in a nondiscriminatory manner, as further described in this Section.

38. Decatur Federal will provide training to its account executives and other loan origination staff on its affirmative marketing programs, including targeted sales calls, and will monitor their activities.

39. Decatur Federal will instruct all its loan processors (employees whose responsibility it is to gather information for an application prior to its submission for an underwriting decision) and loan underwriters that they are required to use their best efforts to obtain and document all relevant information necessary to reach an underwriting decision, and that they will document those efforts in writing in the file on the Application Checksheet, Attachment 3 [not included here]. This instruction will include training sessions regarding the proper completion of each section of Attachment 3 with special emphasis on items 1-8 of the Checksheet.

40. Decatur Federal will instruct all its loan processors and underwriters on the requirements of the secondary market underwriting guidelines with respect to the kinds of information that must be gathered and filed for each applicant and the alternatives and compensating factors allowed by those guidelines.

41. Decatur Federal will instruct its loan processors and underwriters on the provisions of the secondary market guidelines with respect to the various alternative and flexible means described therein by which applicants may demonstrate the ability and willingness to repay their loans.

42. Within 45 days after the entry of this Consent Decree, Decatur Federal will conduct comprehensive training sessions on the applicable provisions of this Consent Decree for every Account Executive, Underwriter, Loan Counselor, Staff Appraiser, Loan Processor, Assistant Branch Manager, and Branch Manager. The lender may conduct specific training sessions for specific groups.

43. Decatur Federal will continue to conduct regular compliance training of its staff with significant involvement in home mortgage lending on the Community Reinvestment Act, the Fair Housing Act, the Equal Credit Opportunity Act, and this Consent Decree. This training will continue to include scheduled training sessions, staff meetings, compliance newsletters, videotapes, regulatory updates, and/or comparable methods. The lender will incorporate cultural diversity and sensitivity training into its training programs given to all managers and customer-contact employees. The lender may contract with outside consultants to provide any of this training.

III. RECORD-KEEPING AND REPORTING BENEFITS

44. During the period of this Consent Decree, Decatur Federal will retain all loan application files submitted for home mortgage loans and all documents and notices relevant to any underwriting decisions, including the Application Checksheets. The lender will also retain all records relating to its obligations under this Consent Decree, including its advertising, mortgage production, branching, special programs, recruitment, and compliance activities.

45. The parties anticipate that as a result of the affirmative marketing procedures set forth in this Consent Decree, the volume of black applicants for home mortgage loans may increase significantly. While this Consent Decree is in effect, if black applicants for home mortgage loans are rejected at significantly higher rates than white applicants, that fact, standing alone, will not be viewed as establishing a violation of this Consent Decree. However, to fairly monitor Decatur Federal's processing and evaluation of home mortgage loan applicants under this Consent Decree, the United States may, from time to time, seek and be provided access to individual home mortgage loan application files, provided such request is reasonable and is upon reasonable notice and in writing to Decatur Federal. The United States will keep all records and information relating to loan applicants confidential to protect the applicants' privacy rights. If the United States identifies any concerns with respect to Decatur Federal's compliance with this Consent Decree in its treatment of home mortgage loan applicants, it will promptly notify Decatur Federal of its concerns and seek to resolve them.

46. Decatur Federal will report its progress under this Consent Decree to the Civil Rights Division of the United States Department of Justice on a semi-annual basis for a period of three years. All reports will be submitted to the United States within 30 days after the close of the semi-annual time period and will include the following information:

a. A report in machine-readable form from its automated loan tracking system for all home mortgage loan applicants. This loan tracking information, though not necessarily final or verified, will include the following:

i. Applicant's application number and date application was received.

ii. Type, purpose, and amount of the loan or application.

iii. Owner-occupancy status of the property to which the loan relates.

iv. The type of action taken on the application and the date.

v. The location of the property to which the loan relates, by state, county, census tract, and Metropolitan Statistical Area.
vi. Race or national origin, and sex of the applicant(s) or borrower(s).
vii. Income relied upon in making the loan decision.
viii. Reason for denial of a loan application (if applicable).

b. A report on all advertising conducted pursuant to this Consent Decree, including the media names, types, and frequencies. The report will include representative copies of all advertising.

c. A report on all Mortgage Production efforts conducted pursuant to this Consent Decree. The report will discuss the targeting of black neighborhoods program as set forth in paragraph 13, and include a list of the individuals determined to be active in those neighborhoods. It will include the Account Executives' sales call logs and the reports from the Account Executives who specialize in originating loans in low- and moderate-income areas detailing their activities. It will analyze the effectiveness of the incentives program in increasing mortgage production in predominantly black areas. It will discuss the correspondent relationships program. It will detail all ascertainment efforts, including the dates, descriptions, and results of all market research; and the dates, groups contacted, and matters discussed in all community outreach meetings.

d. A report on Decatur Federal's branching activity in its delineated community, including detailed explanations of all branch openings, significant service changes, or closings. This report will analyze the effect of all changes on the lender's obligation under the Community Reinvestment Act to meet the credit needs of low- and moderate-income neighborhoods in its service area. The report will detail alternatives considered and/or instituted to avoid closing a branch and the results of any meetings conducted with community organizations regarding the branch.

e. A report of the activities of the Compliance Employees. This report will include a description of all compliance training, the dates held, instructors, content, audience, and the number of individuals who attended. The lender will also preserve the results of the tests described in paragraph 36 above, and report to the United States a summary of the test results and any sanctions or disciplinary actions taken in connection with the test findings.

47. Copies of all notices, correspondence, reports, or documents required to be provided by one part to the other under this Consent Decree will be mailed to the following addresses:

Chief, Housing and Civil Enforcement Section
Civil Rights Division
U.S. Department of Justice
P.O. Box 65998
Washington, DC 20035

Decatur Federal Savings and Loan Association
Risk Management Division/Compliance Department
250 East Ponce de Leon Avenue
Decatur, GA 30030

IV. RELIEF

48. Decatur Federal will place One Million Dollars ($1,000,000.00) in a Decatur Federal Consent Decree Fund to be administered by the United States and distributed to persons whom the United States has identified to Decatur Federal as being allegedly aggrieved persons under the Fair Housing Act and Equal Credit Opportunity Act, all of whom the United States certifies have signed General Releases. The United States has examined the records of Decatur Federal and has informed the lender of the names of all the persons it believes are aggrieved persons as alleged in the Complaint. Funds will be made available to those persons in exchange for signing General Releases. Any balance remaining in the Fund six months after the execution of this Decree shall be returned to Decatur Federal to be used towards paying for compliance with the Consent Decree.

V. SUCCESSOR IN INTEREST

49. The terms of this Consent Decree will bind any successor in interest to Decatur Federal as to employees, branches, and offices now under the control of Decatur Federal, branches subsequently acquired by Decatur Federal, and any branches located in Fulton County and DeKalb County into which Decatur Federal branches are consolidated. The Consent Decree will not apply to any other successor branches or offices, but Part II will apply to any centrally administered functions of the mortgage underwriting and production activities of those other successor branches or offices located in Dekalb and Fulton Counties. It is assumed by the parties that any successor in interest will voluntarily implement the provisions of Part II of this Consent Decree in all successor-in-interest branches located in Dekalb and Fulton Counties, but if any such successor in interest declines to

voluntarily implement Part II in all such branches and offices, it shall present to the United States its proposed plan of operation. If the United States concludes that the proposed plan of operation will hinder the attainment of the goals of this Consent Decree it shall present such concerns to the successor in interest and attempt to resolve the differences voluntarily. Any differences that cannot be resolved by parties may be presented to the court for resolution. No successor is or has been subject to this proceeding, nor has any successor been implicated in this proceeding.

VI. MODIFICATION

50. This Consent Decree may be modified by written agreement of the parties.

VII. RETENTION OF JURISDICTION

51. For the three-year period in which this Consent Decree is in effect, this Court will retain jurisdiction for purposes enforcing this Consent Decree. The parties to the Decree will endeavor in good faith to resolve informally any differences regarding interpretation and compliance with this Consent Decree prior to bringing such matters to the Court for resolution. At any time after three years from the date of the Court's entry of this Consent Decree, Decatur Federal may move for dismissal of the case. Dismissal shall be granted unless, no later than 30 days after receipt of Decatur Federal's motion, the United States objects with particularity to the dismissal. If such objection is made, the Court shall hold a hearing on the dismissal motion and the United States shall have the burden of demonstrating why this Consent Decree should not be terminated. If the United States fails to meet its burden, this Consent Decree shall terminate forthwith and the case shall be dismissed with prejudice.

VIII. COSTS

52. Each party to this litigation will bear its own costs.

It is so ORDERED, ADJUDGED, and DECREED this *17* day of *September*, 1992.

Notes

1. The United States recognizes that Decatur Federal has this year opened its Redan branch, in a location that is surrounded by 55%–84% black census tracts. The lender operates two other branches that serve predominantly black areas.

2. For purposes of this Consent Decree, "home mortgage loans" means one- to four-family dwelling loans and applications originated by Decatur Federal that are required to be reported under 12 C.F.R. Part 203, and "predominantly black" refers to census tracts where black residents constitute 50% or more of the total population based on the 1990 Census.

Chapter Fifteen

THE DECATUR FEDERAL CASE: A SUMMARY REPORT

Richard Ritter

In 1992, the U.S. Department of Justice (DOJ) filed a complaint and an accompanying consent decree (reproduced as chapter 14, this volume) resolving claims that Decatur Federal Savings and Loan, one of the largest providers of home mortgages in the Atlanta area, engaged in a pattern or practice of discrimination against prospective African-American homebuyers when marketing its home mortgage loan products and granting mortgage loans (*United States of America* v. *Decatur Federal Savings and Loan Association* [N.D. Ga. No. 1-92 CV2198] Sept. 17, 1992). The case, which alleged violations of the federal Fair Housing Act and the Equal Credit Opportunity Act, was the first such "pattern or practice" lawsuit that the federal government had ever brought against a major lender.

As delineated in the preceding chapter, the consent decree obligated Decatur Federal to provide $1 million relief to 48 black individuals whose home mortgage loan applications had been rejected between 1988 and 1992; expand its lending territory to include all of Fulton County, which encompasses most of the city of Atlanta; advertise extensively in black-oriented newspapers and radio stations; target sales calls to real estate agents and builders active in black neighborhoods; implement a pay structure to increase incentives for Decatur Federal's account executives to obtain business in these neighborhoods; make future decisions regarding branch locations only after considering the lender's obligations to meet the credit needs of low- and moderate-income neighborhoods; and open a branch or regional loan office in south Fulton County, a predominantly black section of Atlanta.

The decree furthermore required Decatur Federal to retrain all of its mortgage personnel, stipulating that they complete an application checksheet for each loan applicant to ensure that all necessary information was solicited and evaluated fairly. The lender was also to appoint a review underwriter to reexamine each initially rejected application, as well as a review appraiser to reexamine each appraisal that did not support the loan requested.

To ensure future compliance with the law, Decatur Federal was to enter into a contract with an independent testing organization that would arrange for blacks and whites posing as similarly qualified home mortgage customers to visit branch offices to test for racial discrimination. The institution was furthermore enjoined to send regular reports regarding all of its lending activities to the Justice Department for three years.

Three principal participants in the *Decatur Federal* case—Richard Ritter, a DOJ attorney; Bernard Siskin, a forensic economist statistician consultant to DOJ; and Kent Alexander, an attorney for Decatur Federal—contributed to a panel discussion of the case at the May 1993 HUD conference on "Home Mortgage Lending and Discrimination." The participants reviewed the development of the model used by DOJ to prosecute the case; they analyzed its effectiveness; and they speculated on what the model and decree portend for future fair lending enforcement actions. The remainder of this chapter summarizes main points in the discussion.

The impetus for the *Decatur Federal* case was a crucial series of articles in 1988 in the *Atlanta Journal-Constitution* entitled "The Color of Money" (May 1–16). Those articles pointed out widespread disparities in the rates at which the large mortgage lenders in Atlanta were originating mortgage loans in white neighborhoods compared to black neighborhoods. In an initial attempt to discover reasons behind the newspaper's findings, DOJ sent letters to 64 banks and savings and loans in the area, asking for basic information about their underwriting standards and practices. After reviewing this information, DOJ focused on only one lender, Decatur Federal, selected because of its substantial volume of mortgage loans, its large number and high rejection rates of black loan applicants, and its selection of white neighborhoods for loan originations.

In developing its claim that Decatur was redlining black neighborhoods through racially discriminatory marketing practices, DOJ relied on a host of Supreme Court decisions in housing, employment, voting, and school desegregation cases over the past 20 years that establish guidelines for proving purposeful discrimination through circumstantial evidence—most notably, statistics. Statistics showing high levels of unexplained racial disparities in the workplace, schools, housing, and voting are often telltale signs of purposeful discrimination (see, for example, *Teamsters* v. *United States*, 431 U.S. 324 [1976] [employment]; *Columbus Board of Education* v. *Penick*, 443 U.S. 449 [1979] [schools]; *Village of Arlington Heights* v. *Metropolitan Housing Development Corp.*, 429 U.S. 252 [1977] [housing]; *Rogers* v. *Lodge*, 458 U.S. 613 [1982] [voting]).

Another indicator of intentional discrimination is continued adherence to a policy or practice with well-known and predictable racial results, such as arbitrary employment tests that keep minorities out and perpetuate a virtually all-white work force (see, for example, *Washington* v. *Davis*, 426 U.S. 229 [1976]) or drawing voting districts or school attendance zones that perpetuate racial segregation (see, for example, *Thornburg* v. *Gingles*, 478 U.S. 30 [1986]; *Rogers* v. *Lodge*, 458 U.S. 613 [1982]). Finally, evidence of a history of racial discrimination in an industry is relevant to assess whether blatantly discriminatory practices were simply replaced by more sophisticated schemes that accomplish the same intended result—the perpetuation of racial segregation (see, for example, *Rogers* v. *Lodge*, 458 U.S. 613 [1982]; *Hazelwood School District* v. *United States*, 433 U.S. 266 [1977]; *Griggs* v. *Duke Power Co.*, 401 U.S. 424, 427 [1971]).

In applying these principles to Decatur Federal, DOJ found that the bank had operated in the Atlanta area since 1927, and that there was a large black population in and around the white areas where it conducted most of its business that received few, if any, loans from the institution. In examining the histories of both Decatur and Atlanta-area mortgage lending, the Justice Department found, as expected, that many lenders refused to do business with black customers into the 1960s. Even into the early 1970s, many lending institutions were reluctant to make loans in black areas because of overtly discriminatory appraisal theories that viewed the presence of blacks and other minority groups as having "undesirable" influences on property values.

With passage of the Home Mortgage Disclosure Act (HMDA) and the Community Reinvestment Act (CRA) in the 1970s, DOJ was able to pick up the paper trail of lenders like Decatur Federal to determine if racial considerations might still be influencing the bank's lending activities. The HMDA enabled statistical analysis and computer mapping of loan originations in majority white census tracts compared to majority black census tracts. Later amendments permitted statistical analysis of the rates at which minority applicants were rejected for mortgage loans compared to whites. The CRA required lenders to openly declare their lending territories by delineating on maps where they claimed to conduct business.

The HMDA showed that the vast majority (over 97 percent) of Decatur Federal's mortgage loans were made in majority white census tracts. Computer mapping of Decatur Federal's loan originations over a six-year period (1985–90) showed heavy concentrations of loans in white neighborhoods throughout the Atlanta area, but no loans or only a trickle of loans in identifiably black areas. Lenders such as Decatur Federal often contend that these disparities are caused by socioeconomic differences between white and minority neighborhoods. Majority black areas typically include more low-income residents who cannot afford to purchase homes, experience lower population growth, have a higher proportion of rental dwellings, and experience fewer home sales and refinancings than majority white areas. In testing those explanations, DOJ analyzed Decatur Federal's market share of loans in majority white census tracts compared to majority black tracts. This analysis effectively controlled for these explanations because it looked only at loan originations to presumably creditworthy borrowers. The department concluded that it was appropriate to compare Decatur Federal's market share in white and black areas because it was a large-volume lender that could reasonably be expected to compete for loans in black neighborhoods of Atlanta, given their proximity to the white areas in which it had high market share. The market share analysis continued to show severe racial imbalances that were statistically significant and could not have occurred by chance.

Consistent with the Supreme Court's rulings on the role of circumstantial evidence in pattern or practice cases, DOJ looked at other facts that suggested racial considerations influenced the bank's marketing practices. Decatur Federal was found to have arbitrarily excluded most of the black neighborhoods of Atlanta from its loan service area under the Community Reinvestment Act (CRA). This was a classic racial gerrymander in which the bank followed the tracks of a railroad that had historically separated white and black residents of Atlanta. The white areas north of the tracks were included and the black areas south of the tracks were excluded. In its CRA mapping, Decatur Federal chose the law's "political boundary" option for defining its territory to include virtually all of the predominantly white eastern suburbs using county boundaries. On the other hand, in its treatment of majority black Fulton County, the thrift selected the CRA's "effective lending territory" alternative to delineate its service area, incorporating only the areas north of the railroad tracts where it had traditionally made loans. The arbitrary and selective use of these boundary criteria resulted in the exclusion of almost 75 percent of the black population of Fulton County from the bank's recognized service area.

The Justice Department next examined the history of the 43 branches and 8 mortgage offices that Decatur had opened over the years. Only 1 of these had ever opened its doors in a black neighborhood when originally built or located by the institution. That branch (Kirkwood) was a corporate response to the 1968 riots following the assassination of Dr. Martin Luther King. It was an action that the company said was driven by social concern and not profits. Nonetheless, Decatur closed the branch only three years later because company officials said it was losing money. That reason appeared to be a pretext, given the bank's original intentions in opening the branch, but more importantly, DOJ found that it was not unusual for Decatur's newly opened branches to lose money in their first years of operation. Indeed, several that were opened in white neighborhoods in the 1970s remained opened after losing considerably more money than the short-lived Kirkwood branch. The only other full-service branch that Decatur Federal had ever closed in its history was a branch (Glenwood) that was opened in the 1950s when the area was predominantly white and was closed in the mid-1980s after the area had become predominantly black.

The DOJ team next investigated the manner in which Decatur solicited real estate agents and builders for new loan business—the heart of Decatur's marketing strategy. It found they relied on what were described as "Preferred Call Lists," which contained the names of 590 real estate agents and builders in the Atlanta area. Only 1 of these agents/builders was a member of the local association of black realtors, and only 4 had business addresses in black neighborhoods. Interviews with Atlanta-area real estate agents confirmed that Decatur Federal's sales staff (account executives) made solicitations almost exclusively to realtors in white neighborhoods.

One real estate agent who was African American said that when she worked at a real estate agency in north Fulton County, she was called constantly by Decatur Federal's account executives, but when she then went to work for another company in south Fulton County, the contact stopped. A former Decatur Federal account executive told DOJ investigators that she was specifically instructed by the bank not to solicit loans south of Interstate 20, an area that included many of Atlanta's black neighborhoods. Interviews with real estate agents and former bank employees are vitally important in definitively determining the way an institution conducts its marketing strategies.

DOJ also examined Decatur's advertising practices and found that it never used black-owned or minority-directed radio stations or newspapers. The heads of old-line lending institutions in Atlanta, like Decatur Federal, were aware that such advertising is often necessary to dispel the image in the black community that they are "blue chip" lenders that cater to mostly white customers. Indeed, such targeted advertising was a chief recommendation of an Atlanta mayoral commission formed after the "Color of Money" series; that commission found in a report issued in March 1989 that failure to conduct such advertising contributed to the predominantly white flow of credit applicants to these institutions. Decatur Federal received a copy of the commission's report and rejected the advertising recommendations, claiming its advertising in the *Atlanta Journal-Constitution* was sufficient.

Of the "fairly regular" advertising that Decatur Federal did place in the *Atlanta-Journal Constitution*, those ads never mentioned the availability of Federal Housing Administration (FHA) or Department of Veterans Affairs (VA) loans, products Decatur knew were in great demand in black neighborhoods because of their low down-payment requirements and other underwriting standards geared to low-income borrowers. And despite Decatur's being an FHA lender endorsed by the U.S. Department of Housing and Urban Development (HUD), the thrift had only a few applications for those loans—mostly from whites.

Finally, examination of personnel records at Decatur Federal showed that few blacks or other minorities were employed in the key jobs involving mortgage loan solicitation and underwriting, another fact that seemed to reflect the bank's overall strategy to target the white community for loan business. Reviews from that period found no black underwriters, only 1 black on the thrift's 18-person sales force, and only 1 black among 31 appraisers.

In sum, the totality of evidence (historical, statistical, and anecdotal) pointed overwhelmingly in one direction—that Decatur Federal Savings and Loan had for many years pursued a sales and marketing strategy for home loans that intentionally avoided black neighborhoods because of race. This violation of the Fair Housing Act was no different in purpose or result from the classic redlining that existed in some quarters of the banking industry in earlier times when overt discrimination against minorities was openly recognized and espoused. Thus, the Justice Department's marketing discrimination claim against Decatur Federal was not based on novel or extreme legal theories but on well-established principles endorsed by the Supreme Court (not to mention a wealth of lower court precedents) for proving a pattern or practice of discrimination.

Chapter Sixteen

USE OF STATISTICAL MODELS TO PROVIDE STATISTICAL EVIDENCE OF DISCRIMINATION IN THE TREATMENT OF MORTGAGE LOAN APPLICANTS: A STUDY OF ONE LENDING INSTITUTION

Bernard R. Siskin and Leonard A. Cupingood

Home Mortgage Disclosure Act (HMDA) data have revealed substantially higher lending denial rates for black and Hispanic applicants than for whites. The disparities have led to debate about whether discrimination exists in home mortgage lending. Whereas some have argued that the data show evidence of racial discrimination, others have claimed that banks have no economic incentive to discriminate and that the disparities simply reflect true racial differences in the quality of the applications.

In response to the HMDA data, various regulators have attempted to study the relationship between race and mortgage credit decisions. Generally, two types of analyses have been undertaken. One type is nonstatistical in nature and involves a case-by-case comparison of the loan files of a bank. The other type is statistical and studies the loan process in a region across many banks. The New York State Banking Department study, which examined loan decisions at 10 New York banks (Kohn et al. 1992), illustrates the first type. Large samples of accepted applications and almost all of the rejected applications were examined. In total, 972 denials and 1,698 acceptances were reviewed. Each bank was studied separately. The second type of analysis is illustrated by the Federal Reserve Bank of Boston study (Munnell et al. 1992, 1996), which collected data on 3,062 applicants from 131 banks and examined the relationship between race and an application's being rejected. Unlike the New York study, the Boston study was statistical and analyzed the pattern across banks.

In 1992, we were asked to conduct a statistical study of the underwriting practice of Decatur Federal Savings and Loan, in Atlanta, Georgia. The Department of Justice was investigating Decatur Federal for possible racial discrimination in its mortgage lending process under the Fair Housing Act and the Equal Credit Opportunity Act (see preceding chapters 14 and 15). The department requested that we statistically analyze Decatur Federal's loan applications for 1988–89 for any evidence of racial discrimination in the bank's treatment of applicants for mortgage loans. This chapter describes that undertaking and comments upon the differences and similarities between our study and those done by the New York State Banking Department and the Boston Federal Reserve.

POSSIBLE DISCRIMINATION IN UNDERWRITING

Whereas discrimination in the mortgage market can take several forms (such as redlining or discouragement from applying for a loan), our analysis focused primarily on the form of discrimination in which blacks applying for mortgages are not treated the same as similarly situated whites.

Underwriting refers to the process by which the lender determines whether or not to grant an application for a mortgage. It involves assessing the risk to the lender versus the potential return on the transaction. The principal risk to the lender is the possibility of default. The underwriter must consider three principal factors: the amount of money at risk, the borrower's ability to pay, and the borrower's willingness to pay. First, in analyzing the amount of money at risk, the underwriter compares the amount of the loan sought to the appraisal value of the property in question. This is called the loan-to-value (LTV) ratio. Second, the borrower's ability to pay is measured by two ratios: the ratio of housing expenses to the borrower's income and the ratio of the borrower's total monthly debt obligations (housing plus other nonhousing-related obligations) to the borrower's income. If these ratios both fall below stated standards, the applicant is deemed able to pay. If, on the other hand, one or both of these ratios is above the guidelines, the applicant's ability to pay is called into question. These guidelines vary somewhat, depending on the LTV ratio and type of loan. If the obligation ratios exceed the guidelines, the underwriter may look for various compensating or mitigating factors that might indicate the borrower's ability to pay despite the high ratios. Such compensating factors might include a lower-than-normal LTV ratio, the fact that the borrower's income can reasonably be expected to increase significantly, or the fact that the borrower has substantial reserves for contingencies. Finally, a borrower's willingness to pay is judged by the underwriter on the basis of the applicant's past record of debt payment.

In addition, most banks have special rules for special circumstances. For example, a bank may not make a 95 percent LTV loan where secondary financing exists, regardless of the obligation ratios involved; or, a bank may require borrowers to put a certain amount of their own cash down as a condition of the loan, thus assuring that the borrower has an immediate personal financial stake in the property.

At Decatur Federal Savings and Loan, all mortgage loan applicants were required to file a standard residential loan application, which indicated the amount of money the applicant was requesting, the terms of the loan (interest rate and length of loan), and the purpose of the loan. In addition, the applicant was required to provide detailed financial and personal data.

The bank then sought to verify the data on the application, obtain the applicant's credit history, and secure an appraisal of the property. In some cases, the bank asked the applicant to explain past credit problems or discrepancies between the loan application and the verifying data. In other cases, however, the bank did not seek such clarification. Ultimately, the underwriter computed the LTV and obligation ratios, assessed the applicant's willingness and ability to pay, and then made a recommendation to either accept or reject the application.[1] The underwriter's calculations and bases for the ultimate decision were summarized in writing, and the applicant was formally informed of the decision in an acceptance or rejection letter.

Although general written underwriting guidelines existed, the underwriter had wide latitude for discretion. We found from our review of Decatur Federal's loan files that the evaluation and assessment of the applicant's willingness to pay and, to a lesser extent, of his or her ability to pay could be influenced by the underwriter's subjective assessment of the data. It was possible for the underwriter's assessment of an individual's application to involve personal, subjective criteria in addition to the financial data. That is, one applicant might be approved while another applicant with a substantially similar data profile might be rejected.

A second, more subtle, form of disparate treatment may exist where the factual data (such as debt ratios and credit history) are subject to the underwriter's judgment. Although there are general guidelines on what constitutes income or debt, Decatur Federal's underwriters had some latitude in this regard. For example, an underwriter might include overtime wages or proceeds from a rental property as income in one case but not in another. Or, the underwriter might advise one applicant to clear a debt to reduce his or her debt ratio, while rejecting another applicant with a similar debt situation without suggesting a way to ameliorate the problem.

A third, and even more subtle, form of disparate treatment can occur in the interaction between applicant and underwriter. The underwriter may seek an explanation for potentially damaging information (such as poor credit history) in one case, but not seek any such explanation in another case, simply rejecting the application without discussion.

In our initial discussions of the concept of discrimination in mortgage lending, we were asked why a bank would discriminate when there appears to be an economic incentive to make as many good loans as possible. This argument, that discrimination makes no economic sense and therefore should not occur, can be and has been made for other kinds of decisions outside of banking, such as in employment. It has been our experience in other fields, such as employment, that discrimination unfortunately occurs because of incorrect preconceptions and stereotyping. This may also be true in the banking industry. In some cases, the process of assessing loan risk is easy and obvious. Some applicants have no negative factors (in other words, they have an unblemished credit history, low ratios, a low LTV ratio, etc.), whereas others are so negative that any reasonable underwriter would deem the risk too high. However, many applicants fall in the middle, requiring a complex subjective assessment of the negatives and positives (compensating factors). What we observed from our study of Decatur Federal was a tendency for underwriters to have an initial opinion and then develop justifications for this opinion. That is, if the underwriter wanted to make the loan, he or she searched the applicant's file, questioned the applicant more fully, and found ways to interpret the data most favorably to identify compensating factors. Conversely, if the underwriter initially had a negative opinion, he or she did not seek compensating factors as vigorously but, instead, sought rationales for rejection. An applicant's fate was thus often determined by the underwriter's preconceived bias, which was not solely race-based. We saw white applicants who were victims of this bias, and occasionally black applicants were advantaged by it. However, there clearly was a racial correlation with negative factors. Minorities were more likely to be viewed initially as cases for whom the bank found reasons to justify rejection, whereas similarly qualified whites were viewed as cases for whom the underwriters searched for compensating factors to justify acceptance.

POPULATION, SAMPLE, AND DATABASE

Decatur Federal Savings and Loan shared with us how its loan decision process worked and what factors were considered. Each loan file contained the information the bank underwriter received and reviewed, records of telephone conversations with the applicant or other information sources (the appraiser, the employer), a record of the underwriter's calculations, a summary of the underwriter's decision and rationale, and the letter(s) of rejection and/or acceptance.

We coded the following data from Decatur Federal loan files into machine-readable form:

- Loan applications
- Loan underwriting sheets
- Credit reports
- Letters from applicants explaining credit problems
- Mortgage, rental, and loan payment history reports
- Verification of employment
- Verification of deposits
- Appraisal
- Letter(s) of rejection with reasons for adverse action
- Letter(s) of acceptance

We studied three types of loans—conventional fixed-rate, conventional adjustable-rate, and Federal Housing Administration (FHA) loans. The number of complete loan files provided to us for 1988–89 is shown in table 16.1 by type of loan, race, and accept/reject status. Nearly 89 percent of applications from whites for conventional fixed loans were accepted, but only 57 percent of applications from blacks for conventional fixed loans were accepted; for conventional adjustable loans, 88.5 percent of applications from whites were accepted,

Table 16.1 POPULATION OF APPLICATIONS BY TYPE OF LOAN, RACE, AND ACCEPT/REJECT STATUS

	Number of Files		Percentage Accepted		Percentage Rejected	
Type of Loan	White	Black	White	Black	White	Black
	(1)	(2)	(3)	(4)	(5)	(6)
Conventional fixed	1,479	109	88.7	56.9	11.3	43.1
Conventional adjustable	1,431	57	88.5	56.1	11.5	43.9
FHA	117	28	84.6	46.4	15.4	53.6

compared with 56.1 percent accepted from black applicants; for FHA loans, 84.6 percent of white applicants were accepted, as opposed to 46.4 percent accepted from black applicants. Since the number of FHA loans available for study was relatively small, we do not present any detailed results here for FHA loans.

We planned to study all rejected applicants and a matched sample of approximately two accepted applicants for each rejected applicant. We separately studied conventional fixed-rate mortgages and conventional adjustable-rate mortgages. We separated the rejected applicants into various categories based on type of loan and whether their debt and LTV ratios fell within or outside the bank's guidelines. For each group of rejected applicants, we randomly selected up to two accepted applicants with similar LTV and debt ratio characteristics. We also added all accepted black applicants to maximize the number of blacks in our study.

In addition, we reviewed the files in the sample to determine whether there were any special circumstances that would skew the analysis. Such cases were isolated and removed. The types of cases removed fell into two categories. The first category included cases where the bank's underwriting guidelines were not the basis for rejection, such as cases where the loan was not a type accepted by the bank or where the applicant requested to be rejected to nullify a bid on a no longer desired property. The second category comprised cases where normal underwriting standards were clearly waived, such as cases where the bank owned the real estate and had clear justification to make every reasonable effort to make the loan. These cases could not be included in the statistical analysis because they would distort the statistical model. Whether any of the special cases excluded from the study were racially related could not be addressed in the context of a statistical analysis.

Our sampling plan and removal of cases involving special circumstances resulted in our studying 993 applications for conventional fixed-rate mortgages and 997 applications for conventional adjustable mortgages. Table 16.2 shows the number of applications studied by type of loan, race, and accept/reject status. About 13 percent of applications from whites for conventional fixed-rate mortgages were rejected, as opposed to about 44 percent for black applicants, a factor of about 3.4 greater for black applicants. The rejection rates for black applicants were 3.05 times higher than for white applicants for conventional adjustable loans (see table 16.2). Based on the sample design, weights were assigned to each case so that the sample was representative of the loan applicant population being studied.

STATISTICAL MODEL—ADJUSTING FOR OTHER FACTORS

Overview of Modeling Process

Although it was clear that black applicants were rejected at a much higher rate than white applicants, it was not clear to what extent this situation resulted from an inability on the part of black applicants to meet underwriters' guidelines. A statistical analysis of the underlying reasons for this disparity required a comparison of similarly situated white and black applicants.

Whereas it is unlikely that two applicants will be exactly identical in terms of the degree to which they satisfy underwriting guidelines, the statistical technique of logistic multiple regression analysis makes such an analysis possible. Logistic multiple regression analysis is a statistical model that assigns weights to the factors in the underwriting decision-making process that will best predict the outcome event—acceptance of the loan. The weights assigned to each factor (including race) measure the relative importance of that factor in the acceptance of the loan.

The race variable measures the difference in the likelihood of a black applicant's being accepted compared to a white applicant who is similarly situated with respect to the other factors included in the logistic regression analysis. Such an analysis of the bank's mortgage lending decision-making process is, implicitly, an estimate of the bank's scoring of the application. In practice, the bank's system is subjective, as opposed to a formal credit-scoring system, which assigns weights to various indicators of creditworthiness, such as income and employment status, and ultimately derives the creditworthiness of the applicant empirically from these factors. In a best-case scenario, the bank's subjective process would achieve results similar to those derived from an objective, empirical system.

Table 16.2 SAMPLE OF APPLICATIONS STUDIED BY TYPE OF LOAN, RACE, AND ACCEPT/REJECT STATUS

	Number of Files		Percentage Accepted		Percentage Rejected	
Type of Loan	White	Black	White	Black	White	Black
	(1)	(2)	(3)	(4)	(5)	(6)
Conventional fixed	896	97	86.9	55.7	13.1	44.3
Conventional adjustable	946	51	86.5	58.8	13.5	41.2

Whereas the underwriting evaluation of a loan application is, in many instances, subjective, the statistical analysis seeks to replicate the decision process to accept or reject the loan. To the extent that any subjective factors are left out of the model, it is assumed that they are unrelated to race. If, indeed, race plays no role in the process and the valid factors not measured are not race related, the implicit weight given to the "race" factor should not be significantly different from zero.

Factors Studied

We attempted to capture variables in the file that represented the basis on which the underwriter assessed the risk associated with each loan, the applicant's ability to pay, and the applicant's willingness to pay. Here, we accepted as correct the ratio calculations of the underwriters. The complete list of all the variables studied is contained in appendix A, which includes different forms and specifications of the same types of information.

To develop a basic model, we conducted several analyses using all the variables just mentioned except the applicant's race. We developed separate models for the two types of loans studied—conventional fixed-rate and conventional adjustable-rate loans—and we chose the model that best predicted the bank's actual decisions. We deleted variables from the model if their coefficients were inconsistent with economic theory. We then augmented that model with the race variable. Our model for conventional fixed loans predicted 96 percent of the bank's decisions correctly, whereas our model for conventional adjustable loans predicted 95 percent of the bank's decisions correctly. Our analysis demonstrated that black applicants had a statistically significantly lower likelihood of getting conventional fixed-rate and conventional adjustable-rate mortgages than did similarly situated white applicants. Appendix B presents the results of our modeling efforts.

Missing Variables

Our modeling process considered almost every factor for which the bank had information, either through the manual review that eliminated special cases or through the statistical modeling process itself. Two factors, however, were not considered in the model. One was the appraisal results (other than in determining LTV ratios). We did check after the fact to see if the changing characteristics of the neighborhood (declining versus stable) affected our results, and we found they did not.

The other factor not considered in the model is the explanation for credit problems. This is a tricky factor. In some files it was clear that a credit explanation was solicited by the bank, but in other cases there appeared to be no effort to seek an explanation. Also, in many cases after an initial favorable underwriting decision was noted, the applicant was asked to explain his or her credit record. Hence, we felt that in most cases the explanations were used to justify the decision rather than as a factor in the decision-making process. Therefore, the explanations were not included because we felt they would confound the race effect in the analysis. Only in cases where the explanation stated that the credit report was incorrect (for example, where the credit report included items not correctly attributed to the applicant) did we use the data, and in those cases only to correct the credit variables.

"Victims"

We were able to identify potential victims using statistical modeling with a few alternative approaches. First, based on the model described earlier, we identified black applicants who were rejected but who should have been accepted. Second, we also fit a logistic regression model using only white applicants. This white-only model was then used to predict whether or not each black applicant should have been accepted. We identified each black applicant who was predicted to be accepted but was actually rejected as a potential victim.

Recall, also, that within the analysis we accepted the underwriters' calculations of the ratios as unbiased. The debt ratios play an important role in the lending decision. As noted previously, what constitutes debt and income is left, to a significant degree, to the discretion of the underwriter, who can be lenient in cases where he or she wishes to make the loan but where the debt and income ratios do not meet the guidelines. Underwriters may also change the terms of the loan, decreasing the mortgage obligation. In our model, we identified rejected black applicants whose data and ratio computations indicated that they would be rejected. As a third way of identifying potential victims, we determined whether a small change in the debt and income ratio calculations would have made the loan application acceptable. We were able to identify blacks who would have been predicted to be accepted if the ratios had been calculated in a manner similar to that used for white applicants.

It should also be noted that there were cases where the model predicted a rejection, but the applicant was accepted. In a race-neutral system, one would expect to find the proportion of blacks who were accepted but should have been rejected to be the same as the proportion of whites who were accepted but should have been rejected. However, we found that this type of misclassification disproportionately represented white applicants. Thus, some of the blacks who were rejected for whom the model also predicted rejection may also be victims in the sense that not enough exceptions were made for black applicants as compared with white applicants.

Comparison with New York and Boston Studies

In terms of statistical methodology (and findings), our analysis was similar to that used in the Federal Reserve Bank of Boston study (Munnell et al. 1992, 1996); however, we differed somewhat in the variables used because we had more detailed information available. Major differences between our study and the Boston Fed study were that we reviewed the individual files and eliminated special cases where the general modeling would have been inappropriate; and, of course, our analysis was specific to an individual bank.

We differed significantly from the nonstatistical case study approach used in the New York study (Kohn et al. 1992). That study found that the underwriting standards of the 10 banks examined were applied in a generally consistent manner because (1) those applicants accepted either met the underwriting standards or had compensating factors, (2) those applicants denied did not meet the underwriting standards, and (3) the analysis did not indicate any pattern of banks approving loan requests by white applicants while denying loans to minority applicants with similar economic characteristics.

We believe the first two conclusions will be true for most, if not all, banks in the United States. Banks neither accept nor reject applicants without some stated justification. The key issue, of course, is Kohn et al.'s (1992) third finding. Rarely can minority and white applications be exactly matched with respect to economic characteristics. Unless an assessment of the relative weights given to the multitude of negative and positive factors considered in a loan application is obtained, we do not believe a reliable determination of fairness can be made. To determine fairness, a statistical model that can estimate the relative weights being used by each bank must be constructed.

The results of our study are not directly transferable to other banks. The specific variables used and the weights assigned to these variables by the logistic regression model are applicable only to Decatur Federal Savings and Loan during the 1988–89 time period. What is transferable, however, is the logistic regression modeling approach. The specific model must be estimated separately for each bank to fit that bank's underwriting process. It should also be noted that this study was prepared to assist the government in a "pattern or practice" case. We do not purport to suggest that such a study is always necessary to prove discrimination, particularly in individual cases.

Note

1. Occasionally, the decision to reject is made quickly on the basis of a credit report or other special circumstances. In these cases, the appraisal may not be performed and/or the ratios may not be calculated.

References

Kohn, Earnest, Cycil E. Foster, Bernard Kaye, and Nancy J. Terris. March 1992. "Are Mortgage Lending Policies Discriminatory? A Study of 10 Savings Banks." New York State Banking Department.

Munnell, Alicia H., Lynn E. Browne, James McEneaney, and Geoffrey M.B. Tootell. 1992. "Mortgage Lending in Boston: Interpreting HMDA Data." Federal Reserve Bank of Boston Working Paper 92–07. Boston: Federal Reserve Bank of Boston, October.

Munnell, Alicia H., Geoffrey M.B. Tootell, Lynn E. Browne, and James McEneaney. 1996. "Mortgage Lending in Boston: Interpreting HMDA Data." *American Economic Review*. Forthcoming.

APPENDIX 16.A VARIABLES STUDIED

Ability to Pay

EXOB1	Excess of ratio of proposed mortgage to borrower's income over guidelines.
EXOB1SQ	EXOB1 squared (to allow effect of EXOB1 to be more significant the farther away from the guidelines).
EXOB2	Excess of ratio of total debt to borrower's income over guidelines.
LIQASSET	Liquid assets of borrowers.
LIQASRA	Liquid assets of borrowers divided by monthly debt obligation of borrowers.
LIQASSQ	Liquid assets squared.
NETWRTH	Net worth of borrower.
ADJWRTH	Net worth of borrower less automobiles, furniture, and personal property.
EDCOLL	1, if borrower (or coborrower with income) has 16 years or more of schooling (college degree); 0, otherwise.
EDHS	1, if borrower (or coborrower with income) has 12 to 15 years of schooling (high school degree); 0, otherwise.
EDLTHS	1, if borrower (or coborrower with income) has fewer than 12 years of education (less than high school degree); 0, otherwise.
STABJOB	Average number of years in current job, weighted by income of borrower and coborrower in ratio calculation.
STABPROF	Weighted average of borrower's and coborrower's number of years in profession.
MOBILITY	1, if borrower or coborrower is college graduate and is less than 30 years of age (such as a recent college graduate).
MODFACT	Percentage increase (decrease) in proposed housing expense as a result of loan request.
PAYDOWN	1, if loan results in decrease in housing expenses.

RETIRE	If borrower or coborrower has fewer than 2 years on current job and is at least 55 years of age; 1, if both meet condition; 0, otherwise.
STJRG	If borrower or coborrower has graduated school within 2 years and has been on current job fewer than 2 years; 1, if both meet condition; 0, otherwise.
STJRNG	If borrower or coborrower has been on current job fewer than 2 years, has graduated school more than 2 years ago, and is not retired; 1, if both borrower and coborrower meet condition; 0, otherwise.

At Risk

EXLTV80	Amount loan-to-value (LTV) ratio exceeds 80 percent.
EXLTV80S	EXLTV80 squared (to allow effects to be greater for higher LTV ratios).
LTV	Loan-to-value ratio.
LTVLT80	Amount LTV ratio is below 80 percent.
LTVLT80S	LTVLT80 squared (to allow effects to be greater for lower LTV ratios).
EXLTV	Amount LTV ratio exceeds 95 percent.
REXLTV80	EXLTV80 if application is for refinancing (allows effect of LTV ratios being above 80 percent to be greater if application is for refinancing); 0, otherwise.

Willingness to Pay

Number of accounts with late payments by type (M = mortgage; I = installment; C = line of credit; O = open; R = revolving)

LC90	Number of C, I, or M type accounts 90 days late.
LC60	Number of C, I, or M type accounts 60 days late.
LC30	Number of C, I, or M type accounts 30 days late.
LC3060	Number of C, I, or M type accounts 30 or 60 days late.
LC6090	Number of C, I, or M type accounts 60 or 90 days late.
LC306090	Number of C, I, or M type accounts 30, 60, or 90 days late.

LO90	Number of O or R type accounts 90 days late.
LO60	Number of O or R type accounts 60 days late.
LO30	Number of O or R type accounts 30 days late.
LO3060	Number of O or R type accounts 30 or 60 days late.
LO6090	Number of O or R type accounts 60 or 90 days late.
LO306090	Number of O or R type accounts 30, 60, or 90 days late.
L90	Number of C, I, M, O, or R accounts 90 days late.
L60	Number of C, I, M, O, or R accounts 60 days late.
L30	Number of C, I, M, O, or R accounts 30 days late.
L3060	Number of C, I, M, O, or R accounts 30 or 60 days late.
L6090	Number of C, I, M, O, or R accounts 60 or 90 days late.
L306090	Number of C, I, M, O, or R accounts 30, 60, or 90 days late.

Number of accounts rated 30 or 60 days past due (L) or 90, 120, or 150 days past due (I) by type of account.

NRATCIML	Number of C, I, or M accounts currently rated 30 or 60 days past due.
NRATCIMI	Number of C, I, or M accounts currently rated 90, 120, or 150 days past due.
NRATORL	Number of O or R accounts currently rated 30 or 60 days past due.
NRATORI	Number of O or R accounts currently rated 90, 120, or 150 days past due.
NRATL	Number of C, I, M, O, or R accounts currently rated 30 or 60 days past due.
NRATI	Number of C, I, M, O, or R accounts currently rated 90, 120, or 150 days past due.

Serious Credit Problems

SERCREDB	1, if indication of bankruptcy or foreclosure; 0, otherwise.

SERCREDC	1, if indication of any accounts in collection status; 0, otherwise.
SERCREDJ	1, if indication of any judgments, garnishments, or liens in credit history; 0, otherwise.
SERCRED	1, if indication of any bankruptcy, collection, judgment, garnishment, or lien in credit history; 0, otherwise.
NSERCRED	Number of serious credit problems indicated.
NSERCRDB	Number of serious credit problems indicated for bankruptcy or foreclosure.
NSERCRDC	Number of serious credit problems indicated in collection status.
NSERCRDJ	Number of serious credit problems indicated for judgment, garnishment, or lien.
NRENTPST	Number of late rent payments.
NMLATE	Number of late mortgage payments.
NDMLATE	Number of late Decatur Federal mortgage payments.
RNMLATE	Number of mortgage payments past due × REFIN (allows effect of mortgage payment history to be greater for refinance applications).

Other

BLACK	1, if borrower/coborrower is black; 0, otherwise.
REFIN	1, if refinancing; 0, otherwise.
COB	1, if coborrower is present; 0, otherwise.

APPENDIX 16.B LOGISTIC REGRESSION MODEL

1. Conventional Fixed Loans

		Sample	
Variable	Coefficient[a]	Units of Standard Deviation	P-Value
	(1)	(2)	(3)
NRENTPST	−.3200	0.40	.6922
NMLATE	−.0585	0.64	.5247
NDMLATE	−.3417	1.60	.1102
SERCREDB	−.6825	1.62	.1044
NSERCRDC	−1.3209	5.11	.0000
NSERCRDJ	−1.1140	3.51	.0004
RNMLATE	−.5497	3.03	.0025
REXLTV80	−.1522	1.79	.0729
LC90	−.0430	0.15	.8835
LC306090	−.0948	3.79	.0001
LO306090	−.0417	2.43	.0152
NRATCIML	−1.8504	2.83	.0046
NRATCIMI	−.1395	0.13	.9002
EXLTV80	−.2579	3.27	.0011
LTVGT80	−.3015	0.59	.5526
LTVLT80	−.0057	0.28	.7766
EXOB1SQ	−.0072	1.32	.1857
EXOB2	−.3695	7.72	.0000
LIQASSET	+.0043	0.98	.3271
EDCOLL	+.9722	3.90	.0001
ADJWRTH	+.0013	1.10	.2701
STJNRG	−.7763	1.51	.1304
BLACK	−.8032	2.52	.0116
CONSTANT	5.7292	6.96	.0000

a. Model estimates probability that application will be accepted; a positive coefficient indicates variable (or higher levels of that variable) leads to a greater chance of obtaining a loan; similarly, a negative coefficient indicates variable is associated with a lower chance of obtaining the loan.

2. Conventional Adjustable Loans

Variable	Coefficient[a]	Sample: Units of Standard Deviation	P-Value
	(1)	(2)	(3)
NDMLATE	−0.7233	4.01	.0001
SERCREDB	−1.2006	3.03	.0024
NSERCJ	−0.6830	3.89	.0001
RNMLATE	−0.1352	0.88	.3768
REXLTV80	−0.4759	2.69	.0071
LC306090	−0.0500	1.17	.2426
LO306090	−0.0938	3.18	.0015
ASSUMP	−0.7913	2.59	.0096
EXLTV80	−0.2610	6.23	.0000
EXOB1	−0.2091	1.91	.0558
EXOB1SQ	+0.0070	4.26	.0000
EXOB2	−0.3983	6.45	.0000
LIQASSET	+0.00001	1.71	.0876
EDCOLL	+0.9195	3.64	.0003
STJNRG	−0.7233	1.25	.2110
BLACK	−1.0234	2.76	.0057
CONSTANT	+4.4042	5.95	.0000

a. Model estimates probability that application will be accepted; a positive coefficient indicates variable (or higher levels of that variable) leads to a greater chance of obtaining a loan; similarly, a negative coefficient indicates variable is associated with a lower chance of obtaining the loan.

Chapter Seventeen

COMMENTS AND RESPONSE BY DECATUR FEDERAL SAVINGS AND LOAN ASSOCIATION

Kent B. Alexander[1]

This chapter extends the preceding chapters' commentary on the 1992 case of *United States of America* v. *Decatur Federal Savings and Loan Association* by describing the lender's perspective on the Justice Department's (DOJ's) activity in the case. The chapter furthermore addresses various negotiating points in the injunctive relief portion of the consent decree filed in the case, in addition to offering more general comments on other portions of the decree and on DOJ's mortgage lending discrimination initiative.

DOJ'S MORTGAGE LENDING INITIATIVE

"The Color of Money"

As described in previous chapters, the May 1988 series entitled "The Color of Money" that ran in the *Atlanta Journal-Constitution* outlined in detail the allegedly discriminatory practices in home mortgage lending by many Atlanta area lenders. Drawing from statistical data and interviews, the newspaper made the strongest case to date that lending institutions were engaging in what is commonly referred to as redlining. In theory, lenders take a map and literally draw a red line around black[2] areas they wish to avoid. In practice, the newspaper series showed that Atlanta area lenders originated home mortgage loans in white areas at a disproportionately higher rate than in black areas.

Although "The Color of Money" series was controversial, many people in the banking and regulatory community had a difficult time explaining the disparities in the lending statistics. The series attracted national attention, and in 1989 the *Atlanta Journal-Constitution* won a Pulitzer Prize for investigative reporting.

DOJ April 20, 1989, Survey Letter

Based on "The Color of Money" series, DOJ launched an investigation into home mortgage lending practices of Atlanta-area institutions. On April 20, 1989, DOJ mailed letters to 64 Atlanta lenders to survey each of their minority lending practices. In hindsight, the Department was clearly looking for a test case in which to file a "pattern and practice" action involving the Fair Housing Act and the Equal Credit Opportunity Act (ECOA). (DOJ has no enforcement authority under the Community Reinvestment Act of 1977 [CRA]).

DOJ May 20, 1992, Letter to Decatur Federal

Ultimately, DOJ narrowed its list of 64 institutions to 1—Decatur Federal Savings and Loan Association. On May 20, 1992, DOJ informed the lender by letter that a lawsuit alleging violations of the Fair Housing Act and ECOA would be filed unless a settlement could be reached. Negotiations began soon after that.

Although Decatur Federal had a strong record in minority outreach and had lending ratios far from the worst in the city, the thrift was in many ways a logical, strategic choice for a test case. First, it was one of the largest home mortgage lenders in Atlanta, and home mortgage lending was the focus of the investigation. Second, because of Decatur Federal's size, DOJ had a statistically significant number of loan files from which to develop what the Department viewed as reliable statistical analysis. Finally, Decatur Federal had cooperated early on with DOJ, confident that it had never engaged in any discrimination, much less intentional discrimination, and knowing that no discrimination complaints against it had been filed with DOJ. Decatur Federal wrongly assumed that DOJ was obtaining information from it to learn about the mortgage industry in general and to aid DOJ in developing a model for detecting discrimination at other institutions.

By the time DOJ sent its May 20, 1992, demand letter to Decatur Federal, the Department had spent over three years and substantial taxpayer dollars investigating the case. Once Decatur Federal received the notification, there was no question that DOJ would file the complaint. The only question for Decatur Federal was whether to settle or go to trial. Although Decatur Federal retained experts and counsel, and was prepared to defend the case, it ultimately decided to negotiate a settlement for a number of reasons, not the least of which was the extraordinary cost, publicity, and length of the prospective litigation. In addition, Decatur Federal was negotiating a merger with First Union National Bank (First Union), and First Union insisted that DOJ be satisfied with Decatur Federal's compliance prior to any merger.

September 17, 1992, Consent Decree

On September 17, 1992, DOJ and Decatur Federal entered into a consent decree, and DOJ filed its complaint on the same day (*United States v. Decatur Federal Savings and Loan Association*, 92-CV-2198-CAM [N.D. Ga. 9/17/92]). The consent decree reflects considerable negotiation and some very constructive—and some not-so-constructive—ideas to increase home mortgage lending to minority borrowers. Although there is no dispute that minority communities are generally underserved by the banking community, one should also bear in mind that Decatur Federal's minority lending record was no worse, and was probably better, than that of most lenders around the country. Moreover, Decatur Federal categorically denied all charges in the DOJ complaint.[3]

NEGOTIATION OF THE CONSENT DECREE

The consent decree negotiations between DOJ and Decatur Federal stretched over five months. Whereas a line-by-line commentary on the decree would serve little purpose, some of the highlights may be interesting, particularly to institutions subject to mortgage lending discrimination investigations or lawsuits. The points discussed under the following subheadings correlate to the specific injunctive provisions of the decree itself.

"Community Reinvestment Act Delineated Community"

DOJ insisted that Decatur Federal expand the thrift's delineated community under the CRA to include all of Fulton County, Atlanta's largest county, which was 49 percent black. Prior to the decree, Decatur Federal conducted its business primarily in neighboring DeKalb County, which was roughly 42 percent black, and conducted its other business only in a predominantly white portion of Fulton County. Ultimately, Decatur Federal agreed to the expansion, partly because the thrift planned to merge with First Union National Bank and First Union's delineated community already included all of Fulton County.

In the negotiations, DOJ argued that Decatur Federal historically discriminated against blacks and that expanding the CRA-delineated community was warranted. Yet, Decatur Federal never accepted that argument. For instance, DOJ pointed out that Decatur Federal had limited its lending in 1927 to the then nearly all-white DeKalb County. Missing from the analysis was the fact that Georgia law at the time prohibited any lending institution from branching beyond the county in which the institution was based. In fact, Georgia only gradually lifted that prohibition over a period of decades. In the ensuing years, Decatur Federal remained primarily a DeKalb County lender, but did open a very limited number of branches in the affluent northern part of Fulton County and in portions of other counties. Partly because North Fulton County was predominantly white, DOJ inferred discrimination.

In addition, DOJ suggested that Decatur Federal used the Seaboard Coast–Southern Railway Line, which runs east and west through Atlanta's two largest counties—Fulton and DeKalb—as a dividing line for its branching decisions. North of the line, Fulton County is predominantly white; south of the line, Fulton County is predominantly black. Although this scenario makes for an appealing "other side of the tracks" argument, in fact the tracks had no bearing on the thrift's branching decisions. Most of the thrift's branches were located in *DeKalb*, not Fulton County, and the tracks dipped so low into DeKalb County that most of the county—hence, most of the Decatur Federal branches—was on the north side of the tracks.

Moreover, Decatur Federal had complied with the 1979 Community Reinvestment Act when it established its CRA-delineated community. When the CRA went into effect, lenders were asked to define their delineated communities based on their existing branch networks. Decatur Federal, as had all lenders, drew a line around its existing network. Because the thrift was still lending predominantly in DeKalb County, with a smattering of branches in other counties, the CRA lending community covered only DeKalb County and the relevant portions of other counties. Again, partly because North Fulton County was predominantly white, DOJ inferred discrimination.

Lesson: Lenders should reexamine their CRA-delineated communities and consider broadening the community if the CRA territory includes portions of counties that are predominantly white but does not include portions that are predominantly black. There still is a question, however, whether a court would have the authority to order that a CRA-delineated community be expanded.

"Advertising"

DOJ identified increased advertising in the "black" media and in predominantly black areas as a useful way to increase minority lending. The efforts identified in the consent decree include newspaper, television, point of sales, and other types of advertising. The decree also includes "Equal Lender Housing" labeling, which is already required by regulation. Only time will tell how effective the advertising will be, but the efforts should at least help to increase awareness in the black communities that the lender is committed to generating home mortgage loans to borrowers from those communities.

Although generally supportive of the emphasis on advertising, Decatur Federal did observe that DOJ's advertising approach involved a preoccupation with the Federal Housing Administration (FHA) and Department of Veterans Affairs (VA) loan programs. Those programs, once the premier home mortgage minority lending vehicles in the country, are not always as appealing now to minority borrowers as are newer lending programs, particularly in these days of lower interest rates. To DOJ's credit, during the negotiations, the department's attorneys agreed to include the language "and/or comparable loan programs" when calling for advertising of FHA and VA loan programs.

Decatur Federal also pointed out to DOJ that lenders historically do not advertise for home mortgage loans, and DOJ should not *over*emphasize such advertising. In addition, Decatur Federal already advertised in the *Atlanta Journal-Constitution*, by far the most widely circulated newspaper in the Atlanta area.

Lesson: Lenders should consider advertising in the "black" media and in predominantly black areas, rather than relying solely on traditional advertising through large city newspapers, radio stations, and television stations that reach black audiences but are not targeted toward them.

"Mortgage Production"

In targeting mortgage production, DOJ identified a real and practical concern in generating more minority lending: Loan officers are paid a percentage commission for each mortgage origination, so they usually prefer to make loans in affluent white areas where they will make more money on the larger loans. Because homes in predominantly minority areas are often sold at lower values than homes in predominantly white areas, loan officers—black and white—do not find the lower-value loans nearly as attractive. The color at issue is not necessarily black or white, but green.

The consent decree offers several approaches that may provide a partial solution. For instance, Decatur Federal agreed to give loan officers either higher commission percentages or flat rate bonuses for originating loans of $50,000 or less. DOJ's theory is that such added incentives will increase the volume of low dollar loans and make institutions realize that those loans can be profitable. Many in the lending community are skeptical, but DOJ strongly feels that relatively low dollar loans—although not as profitable as high dollar loans—are still profitable, and are necessary under CRA, the Fair Housing Act, and ECOA.

Although some of the steps outlined in the mortgage production section of the consent decree are experimental, they are all designed to increase minority lending. Many of those steps will no doubt become standards in the industry. At the same time, a few of the measures may turn out to be impractical and unprofitable.

Lesson: Recognize the inherent problem in encouraging loan officers to generate low dollar mortgages and experiment with methods to make such lending activity attractive, feasible, and profitable.

"Delivery Network"

The negotiations over the delivery network were tense and almost led to a breakdown in the settlement process. DOJ repeatedly pointed out the dearth of Decatur Federal branches in predominantly black areas. The Department's attorneys not only insisted that the thrift improve its targeted marketing and expand the CRA lending community to predominantly black South Fulton County but also that it open a branch in South Fulton County. In Decatur Federal's view, DOJ was not taking into account the fact that the thrift already operated several branches in other predominantly black census tracts, nor was DOJ considering issues of supply and demand or the costs and regulatory concerns associated with opening a new branch.

There were, moreover, questions of DOJ's legal authority to demand that a branch be built. The nettlesome legal question of whether a court could order a lender to build a branch remains unanswered. Some caselaw suggests that DOJ would not have prevailed in its demand for a new branch had the case gone to trial and DOJ had won.

The court's authority to grant equitable relief pursuant to the Fair Housing Act is limited (see, for example, *Marable* v. *Walker*, 704 F.2d 1219, [11th Cir. 1983] [courts should minimize federal intrusion]; *United States* v. *West Peachtree Tenth Corp.*, 437 F.2d 221 [5th Cir. 1971]; *Smith* v. *Clarkston*, 682 F.2d 1055 [4th Cir. 1982] [local government is not required to construct public housing units]).

Ultimately, DOJ and Decatur Federal settled the new branch issue when Decatur Federal's plans to merge with First Union appeared imminent. First Union did have branches in South Fulton County, and agreed to subject at least one of those branches to all of the terms of the decree.

Lesson: If DOJ insists that a lender build a new branch outside of its existing CRA lending community, take a close look at the legal authority. Lenders should also, however, carefully examine alternatives to closing branches in predominantly black areas if closure would leave the minority borrowing community underserved in any way.

"Nondiscriminatory Treatment of Home Mortgage Loan Applicants"

The DOJ attorneys and Decatur Federal worked together to devise a number of common sense and, one hopes, effective ways to prevent discriminatory treatment of home mortgage loan applicants. The "Treatment" section of the decree offers suggestions that all lenders would find constructive to ensure equal treatment of all applicants. Most notably, the parties designed an application checksheet to ensure that loan officers elicit the same information from every loan applicant, and thus use the same criteria in making all loan decisions. The checksheet is no panacea, but it does provide a common footing for lending decisions.

In addition, a common theme in the consent decree is the idea of using reviewers. The decree calls for "review underwriters" and "review appraisers," who essentially act as safety nets to ensure that the line underwriters and appraisers are making objective determinations of the creditworthiness of borrowers and values of properties. For instance, the review appraiser is responsible for double-checking appraisals of properties in predominantly black census tracts. It is DOJ's hope that the review appraisals will make the lender more sensitive to the valuations of "black" properties which DOJ perceives as artificially low.

In another feature of the consent decree, the "Treatment" section calls for revision of Decatur Federal's standard adverse action notice. By stipulating that the notice include the reviewer's name and telephone number and by inviting the rejected loan applicant to telephone if he or she believes the reason for rejection was unfair, the process makes the lender more accountable to the prospective borrower. In theory, the lender will make decisions more carefully and fairly, so that there should be no reason for a follow-up call from a rejected loan applicant.

Lesson: Lenders should develop underwriting mechanisms to ensure that the same criteria are used for all loan applicants.

"Special Programs and Other Remedial Measures"

Decatur Federal had an impressive array of special programs in place to increase minority lending even before DOJ announced it was bringing action against the thrift. The "Special Programs" section of the decree highlights some of those programs, and the decree commits Decatur Federal to continuing them.

Lesson: An impressive array of special programs will not dissuade DOJ from initiating a Fair Housing Act or ECOA suit against a lender.

"Recruitment"

In the consent decree, Decatur Federal committed itself to seeking more minority job applicants by targeting specific newspapers, colleges, and other organizations. The theory is that a lender with more black employees will attract more black loan applicants. The decree does not, however, bar Decatur Federal from promoting from within the organization. Decatur Federal believed strongly that employee satisfaction and commitment to the thrift would plummet if the employees felt they had no opportunity to advance in their jobs.

Lesson: Lenders seeking to increase minority lending should actively recruit black employees, particularly for mortgage origination positions.

"Compliance"

The "Compliance" section of the consent decree introduced a relatively novel concept of using "testers" to test for mortgage lending discrimination. Although testing to determine customer satisfaction and service quality is commonplace, testing has generally not been used to detect mortgage lending discrimination. Decatur Federal (now First Union) has contracted with Barry Leeds and Associates to develop and implement such a testing program. The program is not described in detail in the decree. It is important to note, however, that mortgage loan determinations are very subjective; thus, designing tester profiles and scenarios that produce useful results may be difficult. Whereas overt discrimination should be easily recognizable, subtle discrimination will not be. For instance, subtle discrimination could occur in the underwriting process, yet for logistical and practical reasons, the testing may end at the preapplication stage. Moreover, statistically significant testing would be prohibitively expensive and impractical. It is too early to tell whether testers can effectively determine whether discrimination exists, so lenders who employ testers may as a cost-effective measure want to consider combining testing for discrimination with testing for customer satisfaction and service quality.

Lesson: Be aware that DOJ views testing as a potentially valuable Fair Housing Act and ECOA compliance tool, and testing should be regarded as a useful means of detecting discrimination. Recognize, however, that the discrimination testing industry is in its infancy.

"Training"

In light of all the affirmative steps required in the consent decree, the decree includes a section outlining training of the lender's employees in the new procedures and requirements.

GENERAL COMMENTS AND CRITIQUES REGARDING DOJ'S APPROACH

The DOJ attorneys at all times during the consent decree negotiations dealt fairly and candidly with Decatur Federal, though there were many differences of opinion on the merits of the case. Aside from the previous comments on the specific injunctive provisions of the decree, the following are some general comments on other areas of the decree and on DOJ's mortgage lending discrimination initiative.

Safe and Sound Lending Practices

The equal lending mandates of the CRA, Fair Housing Act, and ECOA are clearly important and not in dispute. In the consent decree, the parties tried to strike a balance to recognize both those important mandates and the need for lenders to be able to use safe and sound lending practices and to operate at a profit. Specifically, the decree states that nothing in the decree "shall be construed to require Decatur Federal to engage in unsafe or unsound lending practices."

DOJ and the Regulators

There is concern in the lending community that the divisions of responsibility among the Office of the Comptroller of the Currency (OCC), the Office of Thrift Supervision (OTS), the Federal Reserve, and DOJ are becoming blurred and resulting in lenders having to answer to too many masters. Assuming that the new leadership at DOJ chooses to pursue mortgage lending discrimination cases, DOJ should continue its efforts to act in conjunction and coordination with the regulatory agencies in monitoring CRA-related compliance. There is a danger of infighting in this area, if DOJ proceeds unilaterally, and the infighting would lead to uncertainty in the lending community and less-effective CRA compliance.

Reliance on HMDA Data

The Home Mortgage Disclosure Act of 1975 (HMDA) requires that lenders compile and submit data that are useful in evaluating lending patterns and practices, but that the data should not form the sole basis for a determination of discrimination. Indeed, much of the data relevant to the determination of discrimination are not reportable under HMDA.

In the case of Decatur Federal, the thrift had a strong record of acquisition and development loans in predominantly black census tracts, yet that information was not included as part of the HMDA data. Similarly, consumer loans, commercial loans, some home improvement loans, and many deposit-side services are not reported under HMDA. The thrift also had a strong record in minority community involvement and special programming, but that record was not accounted for in the HMDA data.

Proving Discrimination through Statistical Models

Statistical models are useful, and DOJ hired a well-qualified firm to handle the statistical analysis in the Decatur Federal case. There are, however, concerns with the statistical approach.

One problem with basing cases on statistical analyses is that statistical models tend to shift the focus of DOJ toward lenders that originate numerous home mortgage loans, and not necessarily the lenders who have the worst records in minority lending. For instance, Decatur Federal was one of the largest originators of home mortgage loans in the state of Georgia, so the pool of loans from which to draw a statistical analysis was very deep. Meanwhile, other lenders with far worse minority lending records escaped DOJ scrutiny.

Another concern about reliance on statistics is the question of whether mortgage lending decisions can be accurately analyzed using econometric models with logistic regression analyses. Although one would need an econometrician to effectively critique the DOJ analysis, a look at the profile of the borrowers identified by the Decatur Federal analysis as "victims" suggests that the statistical analysis identified borrowers who were rejected because of uncreditworthiness, not discrimination.

Of the 48 Decatur Federal "victims," 20 had back-end ratios (housing payment and other debt/income) at unacceptable levels of over 40 percent. All of the "victims" had bad debt ratios, numerous instances of past and current delinquencies, serious employment history problems, and/or other creditworthiness problems. In short, despite the statistical model identifying these borrowers as victims of discrimination, many lenders exercising safe and sound banking practices would be very reluctant to make loans to any borrowers with the same qualifications. DOJ argued that "marginal black borrowers" were denied loans, while identifying purportedly comparable "marginal white borrowers" who were given loans. In fact, there were many examples of just the opposite. DOJ took the position that Decatur Federal would have to go to trial if it wanted to present the thrift's evidence. For reasons discussed earlier, Decatur Federal decided to settle the case.

The Decatur Federal "victims" received, on average, about $20,833 apiece. To the lender's knowledge, no victim had filed a formal complaint alleging discrimination at the time his or her home mortgage loan application was denied. Not surprisingly, all of the victims fairly quickly agreed to sign general releases to obtain their payments.

"Minorities"

Although the DOJ "minority" lending discrimination initiative is geared toward discrimination against blacks, other minority communities may legitimately ask why they are not included in the initiative.

For instance, Hispanic communities also suffer disproportionate loan declination rates, yet Hispanics are not part of the DOJ initiative.

DOJ's Role

The Justice Department's commitment to root out discrimination in the mortgage lending industry is necessary and commendable, though the question lingers whether the Department should a) rely on regulators with lending expertise and oversight authority to find and refer victims or b) the Department should do it all itself. The Decatur Federal case involved the latter approach, despite comments by John Dunne, the then-Assistant U.S. Attorney General in charge of the Civil Rights Division, in support of the former approach. When interviewed on the television program *Frontline* (June 23, 1992), Dunne stated that the Civil Rights Division would respond to complaints made to the various regulatory agencies, but was not "going to go around the country looking for problems." When asked, "Why not? . . . . Isn't that your job?" Dunne responded: "No, it is not our job. We are not investigators in order to try to dig up cases. We are prosecutors. When a citizen claims that his or her rights have been violated, then we go to court. But we don't just initiate these cases on our own."

Ironically, *Frontline* aired Dunne's comments in the midst of Decatur Federal's negotiations with DOJ. DOJ attorneys have said that Dunne's comments were taken out of context. Moreover, DOJ is now under new leadership. Assuming, however, that regulators are willing to make their FHA and ECOA responsibility a high priority, Mr. Donne's approach may be the right approach.

Notes

1. Kent Alexander is currently the United States Attorney for the Northern District of Georgia. He authored this chapter in 1993, prior to his appointment to that position.

2. Because the DOJ complaint and consent decree use the term *black* instead of *African American*, the term *black* is used here. DOJ focused its investigation only on black applicants and did not address other minorities.

3. "Decatur Federal categorically denies all of the allegations in the Complaint and is prepared to show that it has never discriminated on the basis of race and has had in place programs designed to serve all segments of the community, regardless of race." (Consent decree, p. 1; see also chapter 16, this volume.)

Chapter Eighteen

TARGETING A LENDING DISCRIMINATION INVESTIGATION

Ann Chud and Hal Bonnette

The Fair Housing Amendments Act of 1988,[1] which prohibits, among other things, "discrimination in residential real estate-related transactions,"[2] increased the U.S. Department of Housing and Urban Development's (HUD) enforcement authority by authorizing HUD's secretary to initiate investigations to determine whether a complaint should be filed (referred to as a secretary-initiated investigation), as well as to file a complaint on his or her own initiative (referred to as a secretary-initiated complaint).[3]

An early phase of the secretary-initiated lending investigation process is to conduct a preliminary review of available data on the lender selected for investigation. The purpose of such a review is to help HUD's Office of Fair Housing and Equal Opportunity (FHEO) target its limited resources for the subsequent investigation and analyses to areas and issues of potential discrimination. This targeting process in lending discrimination investigations can be accomplished using Home Mortgage Disclosure Act (HMDA) and census data.

This chapter describes the HUD secretary-initiated enforcement program and the process for targeting a lending discrimination investigation. The methodology section of the chapter explains the utility of HMDA data for targeting purposes, even though the data cannot be used to prove a prima facie case of discrimination.[4]

HUD'S SECRETARY-INITIATED ENFORCEMENT PROGRAM

Legislative Mandate

On September 13, 1988, the Fair Housing Amendments Act of 1988 amended Title VIII of the Civil Rights Act of 1968,[5] becoming effective on March 12, 1989. The amendments increased the time limit for filing a complaint—from not later than 180 days to not later than one year after an alleged discriminatory housing practice has occurred or terminated—and expanded coverage of the act to prohibit discrimination on the bases of handicap and familial status (families with children under 18 years of age) in addition to the previous prohibitions against discrimination on the basis of race, color, religion, sex, and national origin. The secretary's authority was enhanced to include new administrative enforcement authority, to make "reasonable cause" determinations, and to issue a charge if the evidence obtained during an investigation showed that the act had been violated.[6]

As stated, the secretary of HUD also was authorized to initiate investigations to determine whether a housing discrimination complaint should be filed and to file a complaint on his or her own initiative.[7] The prohibitions against discriminatory lending practices were expanded and redefined to cover all residential real estate-related transactions, including the purchasing of loans (the secondary market) and the appraisal of residential real property.[8]

FHEO Response to Mandate

With this new authority, HUD no longer had to wait for someone to file a complaint before taking action to enforce the law. To conduct and manage secretary-initiated investigations and complaints, FHEO created the Systemic/Secretary-Initiated Case Branch (SSICB) in the Office of Investigations.

A major priority of SSICB and FHEO is to be proactive in identifying and investigating incidents of possible lending discrimination. Accordingly, on November 15, 1991, the assistant secretary for Fair Housing and Equal Opportunity entered into a Memorandum of Understanding (MOU) with Federal Financial Institutions Examination Council (FFIEC) member agencies[9] to exchange information and coordinate lending discrimination investigations. In June 1992, FHEO issued and provided FFIEC member agencies with its internal procedures for implementing the MOU. During fiscal years 1993 through 1995, information on 699 complaints had been exchanged between FHEO and the member agencies. In addition, on February 26, 1993, an MOU was executed between HUD's Office of Housing and FHEO, in which the two offices agreed to coordinate their efforts to combat discrimination in lending.[10] This, together with the MOU between HUD and FFIEC member agencies, has promoted an unprecedented spirit of cooperation in the federal effort to combat lending discrimination.

Targeting a Lender

Since 1991, HUD's Office of Housing has provided monitoring information to FHEO when possible instances of lending discrimination have been identified. Most significantly, FHEO is informed when lenders employ a minimum loan requirement in violation of Federal Housing Administration (FHA) requirements, and when FHA's monitors discover evidence of possible race/ethnic redlining or differences in the treatment of white and nonwhite loan applicants. These referrals lead to secretary-initiated investigations similar to the one described in the following section.

METHODOLOGY USED TO TARGET LENDING DISCRIMINATION INVESTIGATION

The methodology presented in this chapter focuses on using HMDA and census tract data to identify, to the extent possible, a lender's policies, procedures, or practices that suggest possible discrimination. Any suggestion of discrimination found during the targeting phase was thoroughly addressed in the later phases of the investigation.

The targeting process involved four stages, beginning with a general examination of the lender's operation and concluding with the identification of individual application files for review. The four stages were as follows:

- Stage one—Reviewed materials submitted by the lender on its policies, procedures, structure, and operating jurisdiction, and examined generally its 1991 HMDA data to gain knowledge of its operation.
- Stage two—Selected metropolitan statistical areas (MSAs) for further review where data suggested the lender was engaged in discriminatory underwriting and redlining.
- Stage three—Studied as closely as data permitted the possible discriminatory behavior identified in stage two.
- Stage four—Identified individual 1992 application files to examine for evidence of underwriting discrimination.

The methodology described here used four types of data: (1) materials submitted by the lender on its policies, procedures, and structure; (2) 1990 census data; (3) edited 1991 HMDA data provided to HUD by the

Federal Reserve Board; and (4) unedited 1992 HMDA data provided by the lender directly to FHEO shortly after March 1, 1993.

Stage-One Analysis

The purpose of the stage-one analysis was to become familiar with the lender's operation by reviewing its policies, procedures, structure, and HMDA data.

Reviewing Materials Provided by the Lender

A review of the materials provided by the lender to FHEO revealed the following information that had to be considered in subsequent analyses:

- The lender is a subsidiary of a nationwide construction company. Its purpose is to process applications from persons wanting to buy a home built either by the parent organization or by another company. Between 1989 and 1991, the percentage of loan applications for homes *not* built by the parent company increased from 24 to 65 percent.
- The lender has approximately 27 branch offices in 11 states covering approximately 40 MSAs. Each branch office has one or more of three purposes: (1) to provide loans to buy homes built by the parent company, (2) to provide loans to buy homes not built by the parent company, and (3) to buy mortgages in the secondary market.
- The lender's authorized lending territories are defined in terms of MSAs and include all counties within each designated MSA.

Reviewing the Lender's 1991 HMDA Data

A general review of the lender's 1991 HMDA data[11] provided more insight into the lender's nationwide operations.

- Fifty-seven percent of the applications received by the lender were for conventional loans, 34 percent were for Federal Housing Administration (FHA) loans, and 9 percent were for Department of Veterans Affairs (VA) loans.
- Seventy-nine percent of the applications were for buying a home, and 21 percent were for refinancing existing loans. No applications were received to improve a home.
- Nearly all of the applications were submitted by persons intending to live in the home being purchased (94 percent).
- Eighty percent of the applicants were white, 7 percent were black, 5 percent were Hispanic, 4 percent were Asian American, 0.2 per-

cent were Native American, and 4 percent were another race or the race was unknown.

- Eighty-three percent of the applicants were male, and 17 percent were female.
- Of the applications received during 1991, 78 percent were approved by the lender, 12 percent were withdrawn by the applicant, 9 percent were denied by the lender, 0.9 percent were not accepted by the applicant, and 0.8 percent were considered to be incomplete by the lender. Oddly, even though the lender claimed to have branch offices that buy mortgages in the secondary market, the lender did not indicate in the 1991 HMDA database that it purchased any loans.[12]

After gaining this information on the lender's operation, the stage one analysis continued by beginning the targeting process. Because of limited resources, FHEO could not investigate each of the lender's branch offices or each MSA in which it does business. Consequently, the investigation had to be focused as narrowly as was possible and practical.

Streamlining Available Information to Simplify Subsequent Analyses

The available information was streamlined by comparing the approval/denial rates of each categorical variable[13] in the HMDA database. This process helped to determine the types of applications that could be deleted from subsequent analyses and the data that could be combined and not examined separately. For example, the approval/denial rates for Native American and Asian American applicants did not differ significantly from those of white applicants, and were dropped from subsequent analyses. However, approval/denial rates of black and Hispanic applicants differed significantly from those for white applicants. Consequently, the remainder of the analyses focused on white, black, and Hispanic applications.[14]

Also, for every gender-specific way that FHEO examined the applicants, no significant differences were found. First, we looked at males in general and females in general and found no significant differences. We then looked at each sex/race combination. Even though we found differences between, for example, white females and black females, the differences were the same as between white males and black males. There was no significant difference between black females and black males. Therefore, the primary difference was still because of race and not sex.

In addition, we looked at the race and sex of applicants and coapplicants to see if mixed-race couples were discriminated against; we found no significant differences in that regard. Lastly, we looked at the sex of the applicant and coapplicant to see if same-sex couples were discriminated against. Again, nothing of significance was found. Based on these analyses, we decided to drop the sex of the applicant from all further analyses.

We also found that the approval/denial rates for applications to buy a home versus to refinance a loan were nearly identical. Consequently, even though most of the applications for refinancing were from whites, we decided to streamline further analyses by not separating out the purpose of the loan.

The approval/denial rates for applicants who would live in the home versus not live in the home were also not significant and were dropped from subsequent analyses.

Even though the approval/denial rates for conventional loans and FHA loans were *not* significantly different, the rates for VA loans were. Because we already knew the lender had a problem with VA loans and because we would examine this issue further during the investigation, we decided not to analyze each type of loan separately in the stage two and three analyses.

As a result of the stage-one analyses, the remainder of the targeting process: (1) focused on applications from whites, blacks, and Hispanics that were approved, denied, or withdrawn; (2) did *not* examine each loan type or purpose separately;[15] (3) did *not* look at applicants who would live in the home being purchased separately from applicants who would not live in the home being purchased; and (4) did *not* examine applications from males and females separately.

Stage-Two Analysis

The purpose of the stage-two analysis was to identify the MSAs where the lender's practices appeared most likely to be discriminatory in preparation for a more detailed review in stages three and four. In stage two, the lender as a whole, each of the MSAs (authorized lending territories) in which the lender did business, and all counties within each MSA were analyzed using several indicators.

Analytical Indicators

Although several indicators were used to analyze the lender's data during stage two, one type of indicator proved to be the most informative. This type of indicator was created by merging 1990 census population data with 1991 HMDA data, and involved comparing the percentage that each race (white, black, and Hispanic) within each MSA constituted of the: (1) population, (2) applications, and (3) loan originations. The idea was that all else equal, the three percentages should be roughly similar. For example, if whites constituted 80 percent of the population in an MSA, then roughly 80 percent of the applications and loan originations also should be from whites.

If an MSA has a sizable black or Hispanic population and the lender has no or few black or Hispanic applications from that MSA, then redlining might be indicated. At the same time, if an MSA has a sizable black or Hispanic population and the percentage of loan originations for blacks or Hispanics is significantly less than the percentage that they constitute either of the area population or of the applications, then this might suggest discrimination in the lender's underwriting procedures.

Two other indicators used to identify MSAs for further analysis were denial rates and average processing times. Denial rates are a useful indicator for targeting an investigation, but one that FHEO uses with caution. As is well known, the problem with denial rates is that they do not consider factors that influence the loan determination, such as the applicant's work and credit history. Denial rates can also hide other problems. For example, during the stage-two analysis, it was found that the lender's branch office in the Chicago area approved all applications for loans from blacks during 1991. An analysis of denial rates alone would have found this branch office possibly to be nondiscriminatory. However, a closer review showed that the branch had only three applications from blacks (0.6 percent of the total), who constitute 22 percent of the population; such a low application rate might indicate redlining.

The average processing time indicator was used in the analysis, but like denial rates, the flaws with this indicator are well known. A high average processing time could indicate that the lender was stalling the application process in hopes of frustrating the applicant into withdrawing the application, or it could indicate that the lender was devoting more time to marginal applications in an attempt to find a way of approving the loan. Average processing times can only be important after a sample of files have been reviewed to determine the reasons for the time used and whether the reasons are discriminatory.

Discrepancies in MSA Data

A comparison of each race's percentage of the population, applications, and originations revealed wide discrepancies in several MSAs.

Table 18.1 shows that lenderwide, whites constituted approximately 71 percent of the population in the lender's jurisdiction, but 84 percent of the applications received and 85 percent of the loan originations. Blacks, on the other hand, constituted about 18 percent of the population, 7 percent of the applications, and 7 percent of the loan originations. Hispanics constituted about 9 percent of the population, 5 percent of the applications, and 4 percent of the loan originations.

Table 18.2 shows that lenderwide, about 8 percent of the white applications were denied, compared to about 17 percent of the black applications and about 14 percent of the Hispanic applications. The table also shows that the lender processed white applications in an average of 51 days, black applications in an average of 57 days, and Hispanic applications in an average of 55 days.

The MSAs are ranked by the four indicators (applications indicator, loan originations indicator, loan denial indicator, and processing time indicator) in table 18.3. From this process, several MSAs were targeted for further review, two of which were Washington, D.C., and Baltimore, Maryland. Even though these MSAs did not rank highly on the applications and loan originations indicators, they did rank highly on the loan denial indicator.

However, the primary reasons that these MSAs were targeted were because: (1) HUD's Office of Housing referred the lender to FHEO initially because of evidence of irregularities in the lender's policies toward VA loans and minimum loan limits in the District of Columbia; and (2) these two MSAs were easily accessible by the investigators out of FHEO's headquarters office in Washington, D.C. Consequently, the stage-three and stage-four analyses presented here use the combined Washington, D.C., and Baltimore MSAs as a model for analyzing other highly ranked MSAs/authorized lending territories.

Stage-Three Analysis

The stage-three analysis examined more closely the MSAs identified in stage two. This analysis used 1990 census data and 1992 HMDA data to review MSAs in terms of lending activity by each branch office and neighborhood (as defined in census tracts).

1991 HMDA Data versus 1992 HMDA Data

The stage-one and stage-two analyses were conducted during fall 1992 when the most-current HMDA data available were for 1991. The decision was made to use the 1991 data during stages one and two for initial targeting, and to wait until the 1992 data were received from

Table 18.1 PERCENTAGE OF 1990 CENSUS, 1991 LOAN APPLICATIONS, AND 1991 LOAN ORIGINATIONS IN THE LENDER'S LENDING TERRITORY BY RACE

	Percentage White			Percentage Black			Percentage Hispanic			Actual Numbers	
MSA	1990 Census	Loan Appl.	Loan Orig.	1990 Census	Loan Appl.	Loan Orig.	1990 Census	Loan Appl.	Loan Orig.	Pop. (000s)	Total Appl.
Lenderwide	**70.8**	**83.6**	**84.9**	**17.5**	**7.4**	**6.6**	**8.9**	**4.7**	**4.4**	**46,463**	**12,697**
Wash., D.C., metro area	62.7	66.8	67.9	26.2	22.7	21.9	5.7	4.1	4.2	3,924	1,191
Baltimore, Md.	71.0	82.9	84.5	25.7	12.3	11.1	1.3	1.2	0.9	2,382	772
Richmond, Va.	68.2	83.7	82.9	29.0	12.7	12.2	1.1	0	0	866	166
Chicago, Ill.	62.3	90.8	91.9	21.7	0.6	0.6	12.1	3.2	2.6	6,070	466
Aurora, Ill.	80.6	93.0	93.2	5.2	3.4	2.6	12.7	1.8	1.7	357	328
Phoenix, Ariz.	77.1	92.1	92.8	3.3	1.7	1.4	16.3	4.0	3.6	2,122	2,262
Tucson, Ariz.	68.2	88.2	89.2	2.9	2.9	2.4	24.5	7.8	7.2	667	102
Las Vegas, Nev.	75.4	82.9	83.9	9.3	5.6	5.2	11.2	7.4	6.6	741	449
Fort Worth, Tex.	75.4	83.5	84.9	10.6	4.1	4.1	11.3	5.8	5.8	1,332	411
Brazoria, Tex.	72.9	87.5	85.6	8.0	2.8	3.6	17.6	6.3	7.2	192	144
Galveston, Tex.	66.6	85.7	91.5	17.2	7.1	3.3	14.2	6.3	4.6	217	224
Dallas, Tex.	66.7	72.9	74.6	15.8	8.3	6.7	14.4	8.4	7.9	2,553	764
Houston, Tex.	56.4	73.6	76.1	18.1	6.3	5.5	21.4	13.8	12.4	3,302	1,064
Atlanta, Ga.	70.1	79.8	81.8	25.8	14.7	12.3	2.0	0.9	0.9	2,834	894
Orlando, Fla.	76.8	77.6	79.9	12.1	5.4	6.3	9.0	11.7	10.3	1,073	205
Tampa, Fla.	83.1	84.9	85.7	8.8	5.8	5.6	6.7	7.6	7.1	2,068	635
West Palm Beach, Fla.	79.1	95.5	94.6	12.0	0	0	7.7	3.0	3.6	864	66
Detroit, Mich.	74.9	90.6	93.3	21.4	2.1	0.7	1.9	2.1	2.0	4,382	234
Denver, Colo.	78.4	92.3	93.0	5.7	1.6	1.1	13.0	4.2	4.0	1,623	645
Boulder, Colo.	89.5	90.6	90.8	0.8	0	0	6.7	3.1	2.8	225	128
Charlotte, N.C.	77.9	81.2	84.7	19.9	15.5	11.8	0.9	0.3	0	1,162	335
Greensboro, N.C.	79.0	84.0	91.4	19.3	10.0	2.9	0.8	0	0	942	50
Raleigh, N.C.	71.8	88.2	90.4	24.8	5.5	4.3	1.2	0.6	0.5	735	525

Note: Includes only metropolitan statistical areas with 50 or more applications.

Table 18.2 LENDER'S 1991 DENIAL RATES AND AVERAGE PROCESSING TIMES BY MSA AND RACE

	White				Black			Hispanic		
MSA	Total Appl.	No. Appl.	% Denied	Av. No. Days	No. Appl.	% Denied	Av. No. Days	No. Appl.	% Denied	Av. No. Days
Lenderwide	**12,697**	**10,619**	**7.6%**	**51**	**937**	**16.7%**	**57**	**602**	**14.1%**	**55**
Wash., D.C., metro area	1,191	796	4.7	56	270	13.0	59	49	12.2	
Baltimore, Md.	772	640	2.2	54	95	11.6	56	9	*	*
Richmond, Va.	166	139	6.5	50	21	14.3	59	0	*	*
Chicago, Ill.	466	423	6.9	51	3	*	*	15	*	*
Aurora, Ill.	328	305	16.1	68	11	*	*	6	*	*
Phoenix, Ariz.	2,262	2,083	8.3	40	39	20.5	44	91	14.3	47
Tucson, Ariz.	102	90	7.8	46	3	*	*	8	*	*
Las Vegas, Nev.	449	372	6.7	63	25	12.0	71	33	18.2	65
Fort Worth, Tex.	411	343	0	62	17	*	*	24	0	70
Brazoria, Tex.	144	126	11.9	53	4	*	*	9	*	*
Galveston, Tex.	224	192	16.2	56	16	*	*	14	*	*
Dallas, Tex.	764	557	0	58	63	0	71	64	0	62
Houston, Tex.	1,064	783	11.4	56	67	25.4	58	147	23.1	54
Atlanta, Ga.	894	713	9.0	32	131	19.1	43	8	*	*
Orlando, Fla.	205	159	5.7	54	11	*	*	24	12.5	59
Tampa, Fla.	635	539	8.2	58	37	13.5	57	48	6.3	64
West Palm Beach, Fla.	66	63	6.4	61	0	*	*	2	*	*
Detroit, Mich.	234	212	12.7	67	5	*	*	5	*	*
Denver, Colo.	645	595	7.6	42	10	*	*	27	14.8	47
Boulder, Colo.	128	116	8.6	52	0	*	*	4	*	*
Charlotte, N.C.	335	272	10.3	57	52	28.9	50	1	*	*
Greensboro, N.C.	50	42	7.1	75	5	*	*	0	*	*
Raleigh, N.C.	525	463	5.2	60	29	17.2	79	3	*	*

Notes: Includes only metropolitan statistical areas with 50 or more applications. Asterisks (*) denote MSA had too few applications (less than 20) for that race to calculate a reliable denial percentage or average processing time.

the lender after March 1, 1993, to conduct the stage-three and stage-four analyses.

One limitation that FHEO works under is the regulatory requirement that a complaint must be filed within one year after the alleged discriminatory act occurred. FHEO does not file an official complaint until after its preliminary investigation indicates a problem with the lender. For the investigation in question, this decision would not be made until 1993; consequently, 1991 data could not be used to help prove discrimination. HUD can only use evidence of discrimination uncovered in the one-year period before a complaint is filed. If, however, problems are found in the 1992 data, then the 1991 data can be used to show a continuing, long-term problem.

Problems in Targeting within Washington, D.C., and Baltimore MSAs

The stage-three analysis focused on the branch[16] operations in the selected MSAs at the census-tract level to determine whether the data suggested that redlining and underwriting discrimination were occurring. At first, we examined the Washington, D.C., MSA separately from the Baltimore MSA. However, after looking at the activity of each of the four branch offices in these two MSAs,[17] we found that the branches did not confine their activity to their own MSA boundaries. The Silver Spring and Greenbelt, Maryland, branches, which are in the Washington, D.C., MSA, processed a large number of applications from persons seeking to purchase homes in the Baltimore MSA. Also, the Towson, Maryland, branch, which is in the Baltimore MSA, processed a few applications from persons seeking to purchase homes in the Washington, D.C., MSA. Because of this cross-boundary activity, we decided to combine the two MSAs and to treat them as one.

Then, in response to an inquiry, the lender provided FHEO with a listing of the applications processed by each branch office for homes built by the lender's parent company and those built by other construction companies. This information revealed that 86 percent of the applications processed by the Silver Spring branch office and 78 percent of the applications processed by the Fairfax, Virginia, branch office, both of which are in the Washington, D.C., MSA, were for homes built by the lender's parent company. On the other hand, 93 percent of the applications processed by the Greenbelt branch office in the Washington, D.C., MSA and 98 percent of the applications processed by the Towson branch office in the Baltimore MSA were for homes *not* built by the lender's parent company.

The situation of a lender processing applications for loans to purchase homes built by the parent organization poses an interesting

Table 18.3 COMPARISON OF WHITE AND BLACK RANKS AND SCORES ON FOUR INDICATORS BY MSA

MSA	Applications Indicator		Originations Indicator		Loan Denial Indicator		Processing Time Indicator	
	Rank	Score	Rank	Score	Rank	Score	Rank	Score
Wash., D.C., metro area	21	1.2	21	1.2	3	2.8	7	+3
Baltimore, Md.	12	2.1	13	2.3	1	5.3	8	+2
Richmond, Va.	10	2.3	10	2.4	6	2.2	4	+9
Chicago, Ill.	2	36.2	2	36.2	*	*	*	*
Aurora, Ill.	18	1.5	16	2.0	*	*	*	*
Phoenix, Ariz.	13	1.9	10	2.4	5	2.5	6	+4
Tucson, Ariz.	22	1.0	21	1.2	*	*	*	*
Las Vegas, Nev.	17	1.7	18	1.8	9	1.8	5	+8
Fort Worth, Tex.	8	2.6	9	2.6	*	*	*	*
Brazoria, Tex.	6	2.9	14	2.2	*	*	*	*
Galveston, Tex.	9	2.4	6	5.2	*	*	*	*
Dallas, Tex.	13	1.9	10	2.4	11	0	2	+13
Houston, Tex.	6	2.9	8	3.3	6	2.2	8	+2
Atlanta, Ga.	16	1.8	15	2.1	8	2.1	3	+11
Orlando, Fla.	11	2.2	17	1.9	*	*	*	*
Tampa, Fla.	18	1.5	20	1.6	10	1.6	10	−1
West Palm Beach, Fla.	1	120.0	1	120.0	*	*	*	*
Detroit, Mich.	3	10.2	3	30.6	*	*	*	*

Denver, Colo.	5	3.6	6	5.2	*	*	*	*
Boulder, Colo.	23	—	23	—	*	*	*	*
Charlotte, N.C.	20	1.3	19	1.7	3	2.8	11	−7
Greensboro, N.C.	13	1.9	4	6.7	*	*	*	*
Raleigh, N.C.	4	4.5	5	5.8	2	3.3	1	+19

Notes: Includes only metropolitan statistical areas with 50 or more applications. Asterisks (*) denote MSA had too few black applications (less than 20) to calculate a reliable denial percentage or average processing time. Therefore, reliable scores could not be determined for these indicators.

"Applications Indicator" is number of times that percentage of MSA black population was greater than percentage of black applicants in that MSA. For example, blacks constituted 26.2 percent of the Washington, D.C., MSA, but constituted only 22.7 percent of applicants in 1991 in that MSA. Applications indicator: 26.2 /22.7 = 1.2.

"Originations Indicator" is the same as applications indicator except that percentage of loan originations that went to blacks was used. For example, once again blacks constituted 26.2 percent of the Washington, D.C., MSA, but only 21.9 percent of the loan originations. Originations indicator: 26.2 / 21.9 = 1.2.

"Loan Denial Indicator" is number of times that black denial rate (percentage) is greater than white denial rate. For example, the white denial rate in the Washington, D.C., MSA was 4.7 percent in 1991, and the black denial rate in that MSA was 13.0 percent. Loan denial indicator: 13.0 / 4.7 = 2.8.

"Processing Time Indicator" is number of days' difference between average processing time for blacks and whites. For example, white applications in the Washington, D.C., MSA were processed in an average of 56 days in 1991, and black applications were processed in an average of 59 days. Processing Time Indicator: black processing time (59) − white processing time (56) = 3. A positive number indicates black processing time is greater than white processing time. A negative number indicates black processing time is less than white processing time.

question concerning redlining. If one of the lender's branch offices processes primarily applications for loans for homes built by the parent company, then by definition the lender has no control over the location of the homes being purchased. Therefore, can the lender be guilty of redlining if the parent company builds its homes in primarily white neighborhoods? This investigation was restricted to the lending activities of the mortgage company and did not examine the building activities of the parent company. Therefore, a decision was made to focus on applications for homes in the Baltimore MSA for redlining purposes because so few of the homes being sought there were built by the parent company, and to review a sample of all application files from both MSAs for underwriting purposes.

Review of Lending Activity in Baltimore MSA

The primary method of reviewing the Baltimore MSA during this stage was to group the census tracts based on their percentage of black households.[18] The four groups used were 0 to 25 percent black households (hereafter referred to as heavily white census tracts), 26 to 50 percent black households (hereafter referred to as moderately white census tracts), 51 to 75 percent black households (hereafter referred to as moderately black census tracts), and 76 to 100 percent black households (hereafter referred to as heavily black census tracts).[19] We then compared the percentages of households, applications, loan originations, and loan denials within each group and across groups.

Analysis of Possible Redlining

Two analyses were designed to determine whether possible redlining was occurring, that is, whether the amount of lending activity decreased in census tracts as the percentage of black households increased. If little or no lending activity occurred in census tracts that were heavily black or in which black households were in the majority, then redlining might be suggested.

The data in tables 18.4 and 18.5 suggest that the lender might be redlining in the Baltimore MSA. Table 18.4 shows that as the percentage of black households increased, the percentage of census tracts with no lending activity also increased dramatically. No applications were received in 27 percent of the heavily white census tracts. However, the percentage of census tracts with no applications steadily increased to 89 percent in heavily black areas.

Table 18.5 looks across the four groups of census tracts by calculating the percentage of total households, applications, loan originations,

Table 18.4 NUMBER AND PERCENTAGE OF CENSUS TRACTS IN BALTIMORE, MARYLAND, MSA BY PERCENTAGE OF BLACK HOUSEHOLDS AND NUMBER OF APPLICATIONS

Percentage Black Households	Number of Applications Received during 1992							
	0	1–5	6–10	11–15	16–20	21–30	31–50	Total
0–25	112	235	49	8	3	2	3	412
	27%	57%	12%	2%	<1%	<1%	<1%	100%
26–50	15	19	2	3	0	0	0	39
	38%	49%	5%	8%	0%	0%	0%	100%
51–75	20	20	1	0	0	0	0	41
	49%	49%	2%	0%	0%	0%	0%	100%
76–100	76	9	0	0	0	0	0	85
	89%	11%	0%	0%	0%	0%	0%	100%
Total	223	283	52	11	3	2	3	577

Table 18.5 NUMBER AND PERCENTAGE OF CENSUS TRACTS, HOUSEHOLDS, APPLICATIONS, AND ORIGINATIONS BY PERCENTAGE OF BLACK HOUSEHOLDS

Percentage Black Households	Households		Applications		Originations		Denials	
	#	%	#	%	#	%	#	%
0–25	648,966	74	1,244	88	1,143	90	41	73
26–50	61,909	7	97	7	80	6	7	13
51–75	54,736	6	52	4	43	3	6	11
76–100	114,534	13	14	1	11	1	2	4
Total	880,145	100	1,407	100	1,277	100	56	101

and loan denials that occurred in each group. The idea is that the percentages within each census tract group should be roughly similar. For example, if 75 percent of the households were in heavily white census tracts, then roughly 75 percent of the applications, loan originations, and loan denials should also occur in this group.

This relationship did not occur, especially in census tracts that were either heavily white or heavily black. The data in table 18.5 contribute to the redlining possibility by showing that 13 percent of the households were in heavily black census tracts; however, only 1 percent of the applications and 1 percent of the loan originations occurred in these tracts. Conversely, 74 percent of the households were in heavily white census tracts, but 88 percent of the applications and 90 percent of the loan originations occurred in these tracts. Coincidentally, the percentage of loan denials in both groups was less than the percentage of households.

Concern with this Type of Redlining Analysis

FHEO has a concern about this type of redlining analysis. The number of households includes those occupied by owners as well as those occupied by renters because we had no method of determining the universe of potential applicants. This type of analysis, therefore, might be skewed.

An examination of the households in the Baltimore MSA in 1990 revealed that the percentage of households that rented increased as the percentage of black households also increased. For example:

- Of the households in heavily white census tracts, 29 percent rented.
- Of the households in moderately white census tracts, 50 percent rented.
- Of the households in moderately black census tracts, 49 percent rented.
- Of the households in heavily black census tracts, 61 percent rented.

It is possible that the reason the percentages of black applications and loan originations were lower than the percentage of black households was because of the large percentage of households that chose to rent instead of own. On the other hand, blacks might rent more than do whites because of lending discrimination. This question could be further examined during the course of the investigation.

Analysis of Possible Underwriting Discrimination

The analyses in this section return to comparing the percentages of white and black households and lending activity within the four groupings of black households. These comparisons were made based on the rough similarities between the percentages in tables 18.6 and 18.8 across the indicators within each black household grouping.

A comparison of the MSA-wide percentages for all four groups combined indicated that the percentages of applications and originations from white applicants were greater than the percentage of white households (89 percent and 90 percent compared to 74 percent, respectively), and that the percentages of applications and originations from black applicants were less than the percentage of black households (8 percent and 7 percent compared to 23 percent, respectively) (see table 18.6). Also, the disparity in the percentages decreased as the percentage of black households decreased and increased as the percentage of black households increased. For example, a closer look at heavily white census tracts revealed that the percentages of white households, applications, and loan originations were nearly the same (91 percent, 92 percent, and 93 percent, respectively) (see table 18.6).

However, as the percentage of black households increased, so did the disparity in the percentages, especially in census tracts where black households were in the majority. For example, in moderately

Table 18.6 PERCENTAGE OF HOUSEHOLDS, APPLICATIONS, ORIGINATIONS, AND DENIALS BY RACE AND PERCENTAGE OF BLACK HOUSEHOLDS

	White Households and Applicants				Black Households and Applicants			
Percentage Black Households	% HH[a]	% Appl.	% Appl. Orig.	% Appl. Denied	% HH	% Appl.	% Appl. Orig.	% Appl. Denied
0–25	91%	92%	93%	80%	7%	5%	4%	17%
26–50	62	71	71	43	35	22	21	57
51–75	37	52	56	33	60	48	44	67
76–100	4	21	18	50	95	79	82	50
Total	74	89	90	70	23	8	7	29

a. HH, households.

white census tracts, the white percentages of households, applications, and loan originations were 62, 71, and 71 percent, respectively (table 18.6); in moderately black census tracts, the white percentages were 37, 52, and 56 percent, respectively; and in heavily black census tracts, the white percentages were 4, 21, and 18 percent, respectively.

It is also of interest that, as the percentage of black households increased, so did the proportion of white applications (table 18.6). For example:

- In heavily white census tracts, whites constituted 91 percent of the households and 92 percent of the applications—a difference of 1 percentage point.
- In moderately white census tracts, whites constituted 62 percent of the households and 71 percent of the applications—a difference of 9 percentage points.
- In moderately black census tracts, whites constituted 37 percent of the households and 52 percent of the applications—a difference of 15 percentage points.
- In heavily black census tracts, whites constituted 4 percent of the households and 21 percent of the applications—a difference of 17 percentage points.

Consequently, even in heavily black census tracts, disproportionate percentages of the applications and originations were from whites. However, it should be noted that the number of applications in heavily black census tracts numbered only 14 (3 from white applicants and 11 from black applicants) (table 18.7).

The final point about the data in table 18.6 is that, as the percentage of black households increased, the percentage of denied applications from blacks also increased. In heavily white census tracts, 17 percent of denied applications were from blacks; in moderately white census tracts, 57 percent of the denied applications were from blacks; and in moderately black census tracts, 67 percent of the denied applications were from blacks. (There were too few applications in heavily black census tracts to calculate a meaningful percentage.)

The last analysis in this section examines the heavily white census tracts more closely, because such a large percentage of applications (88 percent) and loan originations (90 percent) occurred in these tracts (table 18.5). In tables 18.8 and 18.9, the census tracts are grouped into 5 percentage point ranges of black households from 0 to 40 percent. This analysis revealed that the percentage of white households, applications, and loan originations remained remarkably similar within each range up to the 20 percent range of black households (table 18.8).

Table 18.7 NUMBER OF HOUSEHOLDS, APPLICATIONS, ORIGINATIONS, AND DENIALS BY RACE AND PERCENTAGE OF BLACK HOUSEHOLDS

	White Households and Applicants				Black Households and Applicants			
Percentage Black Households	No. HH[a]	No. Appl.	No. Appl. Orig.	No. Appl. Denied	No. HH	No. Appl.	No. Appl. Orig.	No. Appl. Denied
0–25	588,611	1,150	1,066	33	42,217	59	47	7
26–50	38,165	69	57	3	21,404	21	17	4
51–75	20,438	27	24	2	32,933	25	19	4
76–100	4,096	3	2	1	109,273	11	9	1
Total	651,310	1,249	1,149	39	205,827	116	92	16

a. HH, households.

Table 18.8 PERCENTAGE OF HOUSEHOLDS, APPLICATIONS, ORIGINATIONS, AND DENIALS BY RACE AND PERCENTAGE OF BLACK HOUSEHOLDS

	White Households and Applicants				Black Households and Applicants			
Percentage Black Households	% HH[a]	% Appl.	% Appl. Orig.	% Appl. Denied	% HH	% Appl.	% Appl. Orig.	% Appl. Denied
0–5	96%	96%	96%	91%	2%	2%	2%	5%
6–10	89	90	91	71	8	5	4	29
11–15	84	83	84	50	13	13	11	50
16–20	78	78	80	67	18	19	17	33
21–25	72	81	83	80	24	17	15	20
26–30	69	79	82	50	27	21	18	50
31–35	62	55	51	33	33	34	37	67
36–40	58	89	86	100	37	6	7	0

a. HH, households.

Table 18.9 NUMBER OF HOUSEHOLDS, APPLICATIONS, ORIGINATIONS, AND DENIALS BY RACE AND PERCENTAGE OF BLACK HOUSEHOLDS

	White Households and Applicants				Black Households and Applicants			
Percentage Black Households	No. HH[a]	No. Appl.	No. Appl. Orig.	No. Appl. Denied	No. HH	No. Appl.	No. Appl. Orig.	No. Appl. Denied
0–5	375,078	815	758	20	8,103	18	15	1
6–10	97,687	178	169	5	8,595	10	8	2
11–15	52,581	60	54	2	7,821	9	7	2
16–20	30,271	58	52	2	6,906	14	11	1
21–25	32,994	39	33	4	10,792	8	6	1
26–30	14,637	11	9	1	5,758	3	2	1
31–35	10,344	24	18	1	5,481	15	13	2
36–40	5,425	16	12	1	3,506	1	1	0

a. HH, households.

After the 20 percent black household threshold, the disparity between the percentages for whites became increasingly larger. A converse relationship occurred with the percentages for blacks. The only exception was the 31 to 35 percent range of black households. In this range only, the percentages of white applications and loan originations were less than the percentage of white households.

Stage-Four Analysis

The purpose of the stage-four analysis was to identify specific application files to review for evidence of disparate treatment in the loan application and underwriting processes. This identification was possible because the HMDA database comprises data on individual applications. The identifying element for each application is the application number. The application review process taxes an agency's limited resources; however, it is the most important aspect of a lending discrimination investigation. For this reason, a valid sample of files must be chosen for review.

Even though the summary analyses described in stage three pertained to the Baltimore MSA, for reasons previously discussed, the sample of files was selected from both the Baltimore and Washington, D.C., MSAs. This arrangement allowed a review of applications for loans to purchase homes built and not built by the parent company. The files were divided into four strata:

- Applications denied by the lender
- Applications withdrawn by the applicant
- Applications approved in census tracts with 0 to 50 percent black households
- Applications approved in census tracts with 51 percent to 100 percent black households

FHEO decided to review a representative number of applications that were denied, withdrawn, and approved. The four branch offices in the Washington, D.C., and Baltimore MSAs denied only 210 applications; therefore, FHEO decided to review all of them. Because of the large number of applications that were withdrawn by the applicants, FHEO also reviewed a representative sample of those to determine the reason for withdrawal. A sample of 158 files was selected for review from a total of 267 files.

FHEO furthermore reviewed a representative number of applications that were approved, so that the office could check for differences in terms and conditions (such as interest rates or down payments) between the races, especially in census tracts where black households were in the majority. Because of the small number of applications approved in largely black census tracts (143), FHEO decided to review all of them.

Finally, a sample of 324 files was randomly selected for review from the 2,047 that were approved in census tracts that were 0 to 50 percent black.

CONCLUSION

HMDA data are of limited utility in *proving* lending discrimination. However, they are valuable, in conjunction with census data, in *targeting* a lender for investigation and in targeting the investigation itself. HMDA and census data help to indicate the possibility of discrimination against applicants based on their race or gender, and against neighborhoods based on their racial composition. HMDA data also are valuable in choosing a valid sample of application files to review for evidence of discrimination.

This chapter has described the FHEO's use of HMDA and census data to target its investigation of a large, multistate, multibranch lender. FHEO used the data (1) to understand the scope of the lender's operation in terms of the volume of mortgage applications it received and the MSAs in which it did business; (2) to focus the subsequent investigation to particular MSAs and applicant races; (3) to select a valid sample of loan application files for in-depth review; and (4) to formulate questions for interviews of the lender's staff.

Notes

None of the views in this chapter necessarily reflect the views or opinions of the United States Department of Housing and Urban Development or the federal government.

1. PL 100-320 (1988). Fair Housing–Fair Lending (P–H) ¶ 3350 (1988), amending 42 U.S.C. Sections (§§)3601–19, 3631 (1982).

2. 42 U.S.C. 3605, §805.

3. 42 U.S.C. 3610, §810.

4. Although HMDA can show disparities in approval and denial rates of applications by white and nonwhite applicants, FHEO does not believe that these disparities form prima facie evidence of discriminatory lending practices. A determination of whether a lender is engaged in discriminatory activities can and will be made only after a significant sample of loan applications has been reviewed and other specific analyses have been conducted (for example, boundaries of authorized lending territories, location of branch offices, advertisement methods, affect of minimum loan policies, and so forth).

5. 42 U.S.C. §3600–20.

6. 42 U.S.C. 3610, §810. The secretary, in turn, delegated determination authority to the assistant secretary for FHEO and the general counsel (FR-2614).

7. 42 U.S.C. 3610, §810 (a)(iii) allows the secretary to "investigate housing practices to determine whether a complaint should be brought. . . ." Consequently, secretary-initi-

ated investigations are conducted to determine whether there are sufficient grounds for the secretary to file a formal complaint.

8. 42 U.S.C. 3605, §805.

9. FFIEC member agencies are the Comptroller of the Currency, Board of Governors of the Federal Reserve System, Office of Thrift Supervision, National Credit Union Administration, and Federal Deposit Insurance Corporation.

10. A previous joint effort included an FHEO/Office of Housing Monitoring Review of 16 lenders from May through August 1992 using 1990 HMDA data. This review resulted in the identification of two lenders that FHEO has begun investigating through its secretary-initiated investigation program.

11. The stage-one review of this lender began during 1992. Therefore, 1991 HMDA data were the most current data available at that time.

12. The lender never used action code 6 in the HMDA database.

13. Categorical variables have a limited number of established values. For example, the applicant's sex is male or female. Noncategorical variables are dates and variables with unlimited values, such as income or loan amount.

14. At no time during this targeting process did FHEO compare minorities with nonminorities. This type of analysis was not conducted for two reasons. First, to find discrimination ultimately, FHEO has to show that persons were discriminated against because of their particular race or ethnicity, not because they are classified generally as minorities. Second, we found that Asian Americans and Native Americans had denial rates that were equivalent to those of whites and lower than those of blacks and Hispanics. By combining all minority races together, the degree of difference between black/Hispanic denial rates and white denial rates would have been hidden.

15. Even though the loan types and purposes were not analyzed individually in the remainder of the targeting process, they were analyzed further during the investigation, especially during the review of application files.

16. In response to an inquiry, the lender informed FHEO that the branch office designation could be determined from the loan application number in the HMDA database.

17. The lender had three branch offices in the Washington, D.C., MSA. These branch offices are in Fairfax City, Virginia; Silver Spring/Montgomery County, Maryland; and Greenbelt/Prince George's County, Maryland. The only branch office in the Baltimore MSA is located in Towson, Baltimore County, Maryland. The lender had no branch offices in either Washington, D.C., or in Baltimore City.

18. The focus was not on Hispanic households because of the very small percentage of the population that was Hispanic and the small number of applications from Hispanics. In addition, the stage-two analyses used 1990 population data for each race. Beginning in the stage-three analyses, we looked at both 1990 population and household data. The primary focus, however, was on household data, which eliminates any concern that population data are skewed by the possibility of larger families in one race than another. Even though we changed to household data, our research showed that in the Washington, D.C., and Baltimore MSAs, the proportional differences were minuscule.

19. These four groupings were not chosen arbitrarily. We wanted to be able to identify census tracts that consisted heavily of black households, which we defined as 76 to 100 percent black. We also wanted to identify census tracts in which a majority of the households were black, which is 51 percent or more black. To make the analysis of census tracts with the percentage of black households under 50 percent meaningful, we decided to make the first range from 0 percent to the MSA average and the second range from the MSA average to 50 percent. Coincidentally the percentage of black households in the Baltimore MSA is 23 percent. Therefore, we stayed with the four even groups.

Chapter Nineteen

METHODS FOR IDENTIFYING LENDERS FOR INVESTIGATION UNDER THE FAIR HOUSING ACT

Ira J. Goldstein

This chapter presents techniques and analyses of Home Mortgage Disclosure Act (HMDA) data that have been developed by U.S. Department of Housing and Urban Development (HUD) Fair Housing Enforcement Center (FHEC) staff in Philadelphia to identify institutions that may be engaged in a pattern and practice of lending discrimination. In addition to analyzing lending data from the year 1990, HUD FHEC staff collected: Community Reinvestment Act (CRA) statements and evaluations from CRA-regulated institutions; conducted interviews with more than 20 realtors, premortgage counselors, and community advocates in Philadelphia's low-income and minority communities; and compiled preapplication testing data supplied by the Philadelphia Commission on Human Relations.

ROOTS OF SEGREGATED HOUSING IN PHILADELPHIA

Understanding the history of Philadelphia's population and industry in relation to the mortgage lending and appraisal process is essential in approaching the city's lending discrimination problem, which is inextricably bound to relationships among applicants' race, neighborhood racial composition, and availability of credit to finance housing transactions.

Philadelphia is an old industrial city whose residents have tangibly experienced the stress of its economic transformation. In 1921 Philadelphia was a booming manufacturing center, home to 268,000 manufacturing jobs. The demands of World War I had served to reverse a downward trend that had begun around the turn of the century. Replacing some of the manufacturing jobs in Philadelphia were jobs in the postindustrial sector—that is, in the financial, insurance, real estate, and related industries. Middle-income manufacturing jobs gave way to high- and low-income postindustrial-sector jobs. This exacerbated an already unequal distribution of income between black and white workers in Philadelphia (Adams et al. 1991). While this massive economic upheaval was taking place, Philadelphia's population grew from 1.9 million residents in 1900 to a peak of over 2 million in 1950 and then declined to under 1.6 million in 1990. Racially, the black population in Philadelphia grew, in both relative and absolute terms, almost every decade until the present. In 1900 blacks constituted 5 percent of Philadelphia residents; in 1990 the U.S. Bureau of the Census reported that 39.9 percent of the population was black (U.S. Bureau of the Census 1991).

But while the black population was growing in Philadelphia, so too was residential segregation between whites and blacks. In fact, in 1990 Philadelphia was more segregated than it was in 1900 (Goldstein 1985, 1991), making it the fourth most segregated urban county in the nation (Borowski, 1991). Moreover, the segregation of Philadelphia's black residents is in direct contrast to that of every other group, including Hispanics, whose local population increase has been due largely to immigration. Specifically, the residential segregation between blacks and whites increased almost every decade between 1900 and 1990, whereas segregation between whites and other minority groups (such as "old" and "new" European immigrant groups or Hispanics) has tended to decline over time (Goldstein, 1985).

Many explanations for the segregation of Philadelphia and other U.S. cities have been put forth. Some of the arguments are psychological, whereas others are more structural. Some arguments are rooted in the innate predisposition of humans to desire separation, whereas others see segregation as something imposed upon an otherwise communal human nature. The explanation asserted here is that the organization of the urban landscape is largely influenced by the interplay between capital flows, the position of Philadelphia in a larger economic system, the actions of government, and discrimination. Put simply, to understand the current arrangement of land uses and populations, we must have some comprehension of history and the political economy of "space."

An analysis of the development and activities of the Homeowner's Loan Corporation (HOLC), a subsidiary of the Federal Home Loan Bank Board, fits well into this perspective. In 1933 the federal government created HOLC to help bring the housing and finance markets out of the Great Depression. Faced with the problem of generating a cash flow from properties held as collateral (frequently through foreclosure after short-term balloon mortgages could not be refinanced), HOLC restructured the old mortgage instrument and created a long-term mortgage with fixed payments throughout the life of the loan—much like the mortgages common today (see Chudacoff 1975; Bartelt 1984; Jackson 1985; Squires 1992).

One implication of the redesign of mortgages was the need to evaluate not only the creditworthiness of applicants but also the future projected value of the property on which the mortgage was held. HOLC established appraisal guidelines in which the racial composition of areas was explicitly considered. Statements such as "influx of Jewish has discounted value" or "colored has not spread or encroached and is a better grade negro" (cited in Goldstein 1987) or "little or no value today, having suffered a tremendous decline in values due to the colored element now controlling the district" (cited in Squires 1992) were common. With poor ratings, areas were excluded from the traditional sources of housing finance.

Experience in Philadelphia shows that race was not the only factor in a HOLC evaluation. The presence of active industry and/or signs of visible decline of an industrial base were also considered. Bartelt (1984) reported that during the 1930s, both industrial areas and areas of minority concentration received the worst HOLC ratings.

Thus, the deindustrialization of many Philadelphia neighborhoods eroded the foundation of local community stability and provided areas into which Philadelphia's minority population could move. At the same time, these were areas that HOLC determined to be poor risks for the extension of credit because the agency believed that the presence of minorities signaled the decline of an area.

It would be incorrect to suggest that the actions of a single federal agency ought to be held responsible for decades of entrenched residential segregation. The real estate industry itself, through the formal positions of entities like the National Association of Real Estate Boards (NAREB), the Federal Housing Administration (FHA), and the Veterans Administration (VA), also played significant roles (Goldstein 1987; Squires 1992). As HOLC was downgrading urban areas characterized as either racially heterogeneous or homogeneous (with undesirable racial groups) and NAREB was openly promoting steering clients into areas that matched their racial identification, FHA and VA were insuring financing that facilitated the suburbanization of middle-class white households (Chudacoff 1975; Berry and Kasarda 1977; Jackson 1985; Adams et al. 1991; Squires 1992).

Vast areas of many American cities were decimated as a result of these and related practices. And, typically, it was only these areas into which minorities could move. Therefore, a redlined area was destined to decline. As the decline gained momentum, it became perfectly reasonable for lenders to avoid these areas because of the risk that the collateral would never be sufficient to secure the loan. Whereas areas once closed to blacks were opening up, projections of decline, mortgage foreclosures, and the lack of available mortgages destined the established and "new" minority areas to decline (Bartelt 1984; Bartelt et al. 1987). Therefore, the federal government, real estate brokers, and private lenders became key players in a self-fulfilling prophecy of differential urban decline.

Study after study from such diverse fields as journalism, federal agencies, academia, and community groups has demonstrated the relationship between the racial composition of an area and the likelihood that mortgage credit will flow freely into the area. A meta-analysis of post-1980 studies employing HMDA data shows virtual agreement among scholars on the relationship between race and lending. The multiple replications of findings, in different areas and times, lends credence to the conclusion that there is discrimination in the lending industry (Shlay and Goldstein 1993). These studies establish an empirical link between race and lending activity in both local areas (e.g., Bradbury, Case, and Dunham 1989 and Munnell et al. 1992, 1996, for Boston; Dedman 1988, for Atlanta; Goldstein 1987 and 1991, for Philadelphia; Goldstein and Shlay 1988, for New Castle County Delaware; Shlay 1987(b), for Baltimore; Shlay 1987(a), for Chicago; Shlay 1985, for Washington D.C.; and Squires and Velez 1987, for Milwaukee) and nationally (Canner and Smith 1991, 1992; Hula 1992).

At this point, it remains generally undisputed that race plays some role in many lenders' decisions as to where and under what terms and conditions credit to purchase homes will be extended. However, all of the studies just cited examined the activity of all lenders combined. No study to date has broadly and systematically evaluated the role of each lender in the aggregate pattern.[1] The closest one comes to an in-depth analysis of a single lender are studies produced to support a CRA protest (e.g., Goldstein and Shlay 1988). The motivation behind a group's CRA protest has rarely come from a broad-based study of lending activity leading; typically, a lender is challenged because of a group's experiences with that lender.

To enforce the Fair Housing Act (henceforth, the Act) and related laws, the U.S. Department of Housing and Urban Development (HUD) has begun identifying those lenders that contribute most to the unequal pattern of lending. The legal mechanism to do this is the HUD Secretary-initiated investigation. This investigation may lead to the filing of complaints by HUD's secretary against institutions with lending records that indicate a pattern and practice of behavior in violation of the Fair Housing Act. The following is a general description of the methodology and findings of a secretary-initiated examination of Philadelphia lenders.

AGGREGATE LENDING PATTERNS IN PHILADELPHIA

The Secretary-initiated examination of mortgage lending patterns in Philadelphia focused on institutions receiving 50 or more applications for home mortgages on purchases of owner-occupied, one-to-four-unit family homes in the city in 1990. Institutions receiving 50 or more applications accounted for 9,191 total applications. The total number of applications recorded in the HMDA database in 1990 was 10,619. Therefore, this examination accounts for 86.6 percent of all applications in the HMDA database for Philadelphia.

Of the 10,619 loan applications recorded in 1990, 8,587 were approved or were approved and not accepted by the applicant; 1,485 were denied;[2] 487 were withdrawn; and 60 were closed incomplete (see table 19.1). The overwhelming majority of applications were for conventional loans; in 1990, two-thirds of all applications were for conventional loans, 31 percent were for FHA loans, and 2 percent were for other loan types such as VA or FmHA.

To comprehend the extent to which mortgage applications reach white, black, and integrated areas of Philadelphia, Philadelphia census tracts were divided into three types:[3] (1) 75 percent or more white—"white"; (2) between 25 percent and 75 percent black—"integrated"; and (3) 75 percent or more black—"black." The data show that 6,419 applications (60.4 percent of the total) were sought for properties in white census tracts; 2,589 (24.4 percent) for properties in

Table 19.1 ACTION TAKEN ON LOAN APPLICATIONS IN PHILADELPHIA, 1990

Action	Percent of All Applications	Percent of Applications Denied or Approved
Approved/approved but not accepted	81	85
Denied	14	15
Withdrawn	5	—
Closed incomplete	1	—

Note: Percentages in table are based on a total of 10,619 loan applications in HMDA database in 1990. Percentages have been rounded.

integrated tracts; and 1,611 (15.2 percent) for properties in black census tracts.

Similarly, census tracts in Philadelphia were also divided to reflect the presence of Hispanic households.[4] For this examination, tracts were divided into three groups: (1) less than 10 percent Hispanic; (2) from 10 to 20 percent Hispanic; and (3) 20 percent or more Hispanic. The data show that 9,392 applications (88.4 percent of the total) were sought for properties in almost exclusively non-Hispanic tracts; 703 (6.6 percent) were for properties in areas with a small Hispanic population; and 524 (4.9 percent) were for properties in areas with a relatively large Hispanic population.

HMDA data reported for calendar year 1990 were the first such data to contain information on the characteristics of applicants and coapplicants. Prior to 1990, only geographic references were available. The data show that 6,229 (64 percent) of all applicants for whom institutions recorded the race of applicant were white. Black applicants were the next largest group of applicants (20.4 percent), applying for 2,168 loans. Hispanic applicants accounted for 704 applications (6.6 percent). Asians and American Indians accounted for another 543 applications. A total of 869 applications had either no racial identification information reported or the racial identification was other than one of the standard reporting categories.

The mean income reported for applicants was $43,118 (median, $35,000).[5] Applicants below the lowest 25th percentile (i.e., first quartile) of income reported $24,000 or less, and the highest 25th percentile (the fourth quartile) of income reported $48,000 or more. The mean income of approved applicants was $42,429 (median, $36,000).

Another way to look at the issue of income is to divide applicant income into categories, using the median as a point of division. The 30.5 percent of loans denied at the lowest income level (less than 50 percent of the median—see table 19.2), was nearly double the overall denial rate (15.6 percent). At the next highest income level (between half of the median and the median), the percentage of loans denied (17.2 percent) was closer to the expected level. Applicants with income above the median had a substantially lower probability of denial (see table 19.2).

The average income of successful applicants for conventional financing was $43,751, compared to $34,651 for FHA applications and $38,818 for other loan types. The average income of denied applicants for conventional financing was $44,673, compared to $30,883 for FHA loan applications and $36,471 for other loan types. The average in-

Table 19.2 PERCENTAGE OF LOANS DENIED BY APPLICANT INCOME IN PHILADELPHIA, 1990

Applicant Income	Percent of Applicants	Percent Denied
$17,000 and under	11.8	30.5
$18,000–$34,000	38.2	17.2
$35,000–$51,000	29.6	11.2
$52,000–$68,000	10.7	10.0
$69,000 and over	9.8	10.8

come of successful white applicants was $46,716, compared to $31,171 for black applicants and $26,703 for Hispanic applicants. The average income of denied white applicants was $45,862, compared to $28,735 for black applicants and $23,256 for Hispanics.

Overall, the mean amount for which application was made was $59,251 (median, $50,000).[6] The smallest applications (the first quartile) were for $33,000 or less; the largest applications (the fourth quartile) were for $73,000 or more. Approved applications averaged $61,150 (median, $53,000); denied applications averaged $45,190 (median, $35,000).

Approved applications for conventional loans averaged $62,907, compared to $57,588 for approved FHA loans and $63,327 for approved other loan types. Denied applications for conventional financing averaged $44,092, compared to $47,883 for denied FHA loans and $62,260 for denied other loan types.

The data therefore suggest a relationship between the type of loan sought and the amount of the loan.[7] Almost 40 percent of approved conventional loans were under $30,000, compared to 21.9 percent of FHA loans and 27.6 percent of other loan types. FHA loans, in contrast to conventional loans, clustered in the $51,000 through $99,000 range (see table 19.3). On average, successful white applicants received loans for $69,173, compared to $41,480 for black applicants and

Table 19.3 PERCENTAGE OF APPROVED LOANS BY LOAN AMOUNT AND TYPE OF LOAN IN PHILADELPHHIA, 1990

Type of Loan	Under $30,000 (%)	$31,000–$50,000 (%)	$51,000–99,000 (%)	$100,000+ (%)	Total (%)
Conventional	39.8	19.9	29.1	11.2	100.0
FHA	21.9	29.8	44.7	3.6	100.0
Other	27.6	22.7	39.5	10.3	100.0

$35,467 for Hispanics. White applicants who were denied loans averaged amounts denied of $57,329, compared to $35,944 for blacks and $31,320 for Hispanics.

If there is a dual housing market in Philadelphia in which access, value, and quality of housing are linked to the race of the homeowner or the area in which the home exists, an institution's establishment of a minimum loan amount may have a disparate effect on minority group members, minority areas, or both. Overall, 18.3 percent of approved loans were for $30,000 or less; 28.5 percent were for $31,000 through $50,000; 42.2 percent were for $51,000 through $99,000; and 10.9 percent were for $100,000 or more. These percentages vary substantially by race of applicant. Specifically, black and other minority applicants were more likely than whites to have sought and been approved for loans under $30,000. By implication, if all institutions as a matter of policy did not originate loans under $30,000, 10.6 percent of white applicants in the study, 36.5 percent of black applicants, and 49.9 percent of Hispanic applicants would have been unable to obtain financing to purchase their homes (see table 19.4).

One indicator of the equality of treatment of applicants is the final disposition of the loan application (that is, whether the application was approved or denied). White applicants were denied loans about one-third as frequently as black applicants, and half as frequently as Hispanic applicants (see table 19.5).

Disparities in denial rates persist across type of loan sought. Among applicants for conventional loans, one-tenth of white applicants were denied loans, compared to approximately one-third of black applicants and nearly one-fourth of Hispanic applicants. The relative differences across racial groups were similar among applicants for other loan types, although absolute denial rates tended to be lower for FHA-insured loans (see table 19.5).

Table 19.4 PERCENTAGE OF APPROVED LOANS BY LOAN AMOUNT AND RACE OF APPLICANT IN PHILADELPHIA, 1990

Race of Applicant	Percentage Under $30,000	$31,000–50,000	$51,000–99,000	$100,000+
White	10.6	23.9	51.6	13.9
Black	36.5	38.7	21.8	3.0
Hispanic	49.9	33.0	15.4	1.6
Total[a]	18.3	28.5	42.2	10.9

a. Included in total are loans for which no race of applicant was reported by the originating institution.

Table 19.5 LOAN DENIAL RATES BY LOAN TYPE IN PHILADELPHIA, 1990

Race of Applicant by Loan Type	Percent Denied
All Loans	
White	9.2
Black	27.5
Hispanic	18.5
Conventional	
White	10.6
Black	33.3
Hispanic	22.9
FHA	
White	6.0
Black	19.7
Hispanic	10.7
Other	
White	7.9
Black	21.6
Hispanic	9.1

By themselves, denial rates express a very incomplete picture of disparate treatment, especially when inequalities exist throughout American society.[8] One meaningful statistical control for the creditworthiness of an applicant is the applicant's income. This control can be applied not only for the applicant's race but also for the racial composition of the area in which the collateral property is located.

Data on denial rates show that at every income level, whether the analysis is of the applicant's race or the racial composition of the area around the collateral property, the percentage of loans denied is higher for blacks/black areas and Hispanics/Hispanic areas than for whites/white areas (see table 19.6). The data also show that denial rates for black and Hispanic applicants at higher income levels exceed denial rates for white applicants of lower income levels. Similarly, denial rates for higher-income individuals seeking mortgages in black and Hispanic areas are higher than those for lower-income individuals seeking mortgages in white areas. Since by empirically equalizing income we explain many of the differences between applicants, any controlled difference in denial rates observed across racial or ethnic groups more reasonably suggests discrimination than raw differences in denial rates.

The HMDA database released to the supervisory agencies includes the date application was made and the date final action was taken. Of

Table 19.6 PERCENTAGE OF LOANS DENIED BY RACE AND RACIAL COMPOSITION OF CENSUS TRACTS WITHIN WHICH COLLATERAL PROPERTIES ARE LOCATED, IN PHILADELPHIA, 1990

Applicant Income	Applicant Race			Racial Composition of Area around Subject Property		
	% White	% Black	% Hispanic	White	Black	Hispanic
$17,000 and under	25.5	34.9	24.2	24.7	37.5	28.1
$18,000–$34,000	11.0	26.7	19.6	12.5	30.3	22.8
$35,000–$51,000	7.5	23.5	17.3	8.7	20.5	17.6
$52,000–$68,000	6.4	20.2	20.0	9.0	17.6	N.A.
$69,000 and over	7.7	34.8	N.A.	8.9	24.2	N.A.

Notes: N.A. denotes fewer than 25 applications approved or denied. Hispanic areas in this table are census tracts with 20 percent or more Hispanic population.

10,619 applications, the average time to process an application was 71.9 days (median, 62 days). The fastest 25 percent of applications took 43 days or less to process, and the slowest 25 percent took 89 days or more. Approved applications took an average of 74.8 days; denials came much faster—51.1 days. Applications for conventional loans took an average of 68.8 days, whereas FHA loans averaged 78.3 days to process.

Among applications made by whites, the average processing time was 70.3 days (median, 61 days). Approved applications from whites took an average of 71.5 days; denials were faster, on average, at 51.2 days. Applications for conventional loans by whites took an average of 69 days to process; FHA loans averaged 73 days.

Applications submitted by blacks, compared to those of whites, took, on average, 11 days longer to process. The average processing time for applications from blacks was 81.2 days (median, 74 days). Applications from blacks that were approved took, on average, 90.4 days; denials for black applicants, like those of whites, were faster, taking an average of 55.5 days. Applications for conventional loans by black applicants took, on average, 74 days; FHA loans took, on average, 90.9 days.

Among Hispanic applicants, applications took an average of 75.8 days to process (median, 70.0 days). Applications from Hispanics that were approved took 81.5 days; denials came much faster, averaging 53.1 days. Applications for conventional credit from Hispanics took an average of 73.5 days to process; FHA loans averaged 80.0 days.

METHODS FOR IDENTIFYING INSTITUTIONS MOST LIKELY TO BE VIOLATING THE ACT

The first section of this chapter underscored the extent to which past decisions of lenders and appraisers in Philadelphia dramatically influenced the settlement patterns of blacks and whites in Philadelphia. From the perspectives of both fair housing enforcement and public policy, it is impossible to look at these patterns and not seek systemic explanations and resolutions. Yet, we cannot investigate every institution, nor can we presume that every institution contributes equally to the aggregate problem. Therefore, it is necessary to summarize the behavior of each lending institution in a meaningful way, leading to the identification of institutions that may be violating various Fair Housing laws. Section 805(a) of the Fair Housing Act ("the Act"), as amended in 1988, states:

> (a) In General.—It shall be unlawful for any person or other entity whose business includes engaging in residential real estate–related transactions to discriminate against any person in making available such a transaction, or in the terms or conditions of such a transaction, because of race, color, religion, sex, handicap, familial status, or national origin.

The Act defines "residential real estate–related transactions" as loans that are for the acquisition, construction, improvement, repair, or maintenance of dwelling units or loans that are secured by real estate.

Section 810(a)(1)(A)(i) of the Act authorizes the Secretary of HUD to file complaints "on his own initiative." In addition, Section 810(a)(1)(A)(iii) authorizes the Secretary to conduct an investigation to determine whether a complaint should be filed. The regulations implementing the Act at Section 103.200(a)(3) make clear that the investigation leading to the filing of a complaint must "develop factual data necessary for the General Counsel to make a determination under section 103.400 whether reasonable cause exists to believe that a discriminatory housing practice has occurred or is about to occur. . . ." At the same time, the Fifth Amendment to the U.S. Constitution ensures that parties are afforded due process under the law, which, in this case, means that the law cannot be applied in an unreasonable, arbitrary, or capricious fashion. That is, HUD's Secretary must have a systematic method by which institutions are identified for investigation.

Given the prohibitions of the Act under Section 810, coupled with the constitutional prohibitions against arbitrarily selecting objects of investigation, my colleagues and I designed and implemented an empirical approach to identify lending institutions for investigation. Our method relies heavily upon straightforward measures of lending activity that account for both characteristics of the applicant and the geographic area for which the loan was sought. These measures illuminate both the performance of one institution against another as well as the institution's performance in minority and majority areas. Most important, the measures are objective, the mechanism by which the measures are combined is unbiased, and the methods are applied equally to all institutions selected as part of the universe.

Our analysis therefore sought to determine which institutions manifest lending activity that reflects: disparate treatment of applicants belonging to different racial or national origin groups; and/or policies, implicit or explicit, that may have had an adverse impact on applicants of different racial or national origin groups.

Cluster analysis was used as one way to identify groups of institutions manifesting similar lending behavior. We began with the assumption that each observation (lending institution) is different from every other institution. Then, in an iterative fashion, institutions that were most similar on the selected measures were joined together to form a group. This process continued, forming additional groups, until all cases were joined into a single, heterogeneous group. Somewhere along the continuum between individual cases and a single, heterogeneous group is a reasonable solution identifying several groups of institutions that are homogeneous on the selected measures. There is no hard and fast rule governing the selection of the best solution.

In cluster analysis the variables that are included or excluded from the analysis are critical, because they form the basis for the homogeneous groups. We selected the following variables for conducting the analysis (see table 19.7)[9]:

- Average dollar amount of applications for credit
- Average income of applicants for credit
- Percentage of all loan applications under $30,000
- Average percentage black population in census tracts in which applications for credit were approved
- Percentage of applicants for credit who were black
- Ratio of market share for approved loans in black versus white census tracts

Table 19.7 CHARACTERISTICS ANALYZED BY INSTITUTIONAL GROUP

Characteristic	Group					
	1 (n = 6)	2 (n = 3)	3 (n = 5)	4 (n = 13)	5 (n = 3)	6 (n = 1)
Characteristics Used in Cluster Analysis						
Average loan amount ($000) (approved)	32.94	56.72	62.29	61.91	102.72	51.31
Average income of applicants ($000) (approved)	29.37	43.91	41.18	41.12	70.25	32.06
Percentage of approved applications under $30,000	63.92	12.97	12.00	11.12	6.03	7.50
Average census tract percentage black (approved)	37.54	25.76	34.88	10.17	24.50	71.85
Percentage black of applicants	42.35	24.31	36.73	9.57	11.24	83.33
Ratio black: white market share (approvals)	2.90	1.47	2.55	.30	.94	21.50
Ratio black: white market share (total)	3.09	1.18	2.12	.29	.87	19.00
Other Characteristics						
Percentage of approved apps under $50,000	86.18	47.83	44.02	37.28	25.77	56.30
Average time (total in days)	70.28	85.25	75.85	74.64	56.96	86.09
Average time (white applicants)	66.57	79.87	71.50	75.83	58.30	75.77
Average time (black applicants)	78.50	95.56	81.60	70.93	67.46	87.96
Average time difference (black–white)	11.94	15.69	10.11	-6.94	9.16	12.19
HMDA rating score (approvals)	59.10	37.23	37.52	17.33	26.00	67.37
HMDA rating score (denials)	68.60	N.A.	48.48	32.58	41.91	67.27
HMDA rating score (ratio—denial:approval)	1.18	N.A.	1.29	2.12	1.76	1.00
Ratio—average census tract percentage black; approved:denied	1.49	N.A.	1.39	1.93	1.24	1.15
Percentage of applications denied (white)	18.66	N.A.	6.96	6.94	13.54	8.33
Percentage of applications denied (black)	38.45	N.A.	17.72	32.73	36.90	12.00
Ratio—percentage denied (black:white)	2.35	N.A.	2.24	5.00	1.72	1.44
Percentage applications for FHA loans	4.19	58.66	40.09	33.36	2.80	79.41
Supervisory agency—OCC	66.7	0.0	0.0	0.0	0.0	0.0
Supervisory agency—Federal Reserve	16.7	100.0	60.0	15.4	0.0	0.0
Supervisory agency—FDIC	16.7	0.0	20.0	7.7	33.3	100.0
Supervisory agency—OTS	0.0	0.0	0.0	38.5	0.0	0.0
Supervisory agency—HUD	0.0	0.0	20.0	38.5	66.7	0.0

Note: N.A. denotes that the institution reported no loan applications denied.

- Ratio of market share for all applications in black versus white census tracts.

Denial rates, and differential denial rates between applicants belonging to different racial or ethnic groups, were not used to distinguish one institution from another in the cluster analysis. We made this decision because differential denial rates can be caused by both discriminatory and nondiscriminatory practices. Therefore, the inclusion of these rates in the analysis would serve only to confuse the issue. Denial rates were, however, used to support the selection of institutions for closer review or investigation and were reflected in the difference between the market share of all loans and approvals.

Thirty-one institutions were subjected to the cluster analysis. Several institutions were excluded because they did not report census tract numbers for any of their loan applications. These institutions should be investigated for potential reporting violations under HMDA, focusing on whether civil rights violations may have been masked as a result of the non-reporting of data.

Our analysis of the cluster analysis results led us to conclude that, maximally, there are six groups of institutions of varying size: group 1 (number of institutions, 6); group 2 (number of institutions, 3); group 3 (number of institutions, 5); group 4 (number of institutions, 13); group 5 (number of institutions, 3); and group 6 (number of institutions, 1). The group summaries for the cluster variables are provided next.

Cluster Variables (*see table 19.7*)

Average Loan Amount ($000)

The institutions in group 1 approved, on average, the smallest loans (mean = $32.9; std. dev. = 7.7); institutions in groups 2, 3, 4, and 6 approved loans that were, on average, similar to the citywide average. Group 5 institutions approved, by far, the largest loans (mean = $102.7; std. dev. = 14.6).

Average Income ($000)

The average income of applicants follows the same pattern as average loan amounts. That is, group 1 applicants were, on average, of lowest income (mean = $29.4; std. dev. = 3.6); groups 2, 3, 4, and 6 had comparable but higher incomes, and group 5 had, on average, the highest income applicants (mean = $70.3; std. dev. = 10.7).

Percentage of All Loan Applications under $30,000

Data on the percentage of all loan applications under $30,000 show that institutions in group 1 were more likely to have approved a substantial portion of their loans under $30,000 (mean, 63.92 percent; standard deviation, 18.4). Conversely, none of the other groups averaged more than 1 in 8 approved loans for under $30,000, and group 5 averaged about 1 in 16 (mean, 6.03 percent; standard deviation, 4.20). Note that the standard deviation in group 5 was the smallest of all groups, showing the uniformity with which these institutions accept a small percentage of applications under $30,000.

Average Percentage Black in Census Tracts in Which Loans Were Approved

The one institution in group 6 approved applications in census tracts that were, on average, nearly 72 percent black—more than double the citywide percentage black. Group 1 and group 3 institutions approved loans in census tracts that were, on average, comparable to the citywide average (mean [group 1], 37.54 percent; standard deviation [group 1], 10.4; mean [group 3], 34.88 percent; standard deviation [group 3], 9.7). Institutions in group 4 approved loans in census tracts with the smallest percentage of blacks (mean, 10.17 percent; standard deviation, 4.4). The standard deviation calculated for group 4 indicates that there is little variation across institutions in the racial composition of census tracts in which loans were approved.

Racial Makeup of Applicants

A very similar pattern is observed with data on the applicant's race. Applicants in group 6 were most often black (mean, 83.3 percent), and the mixture of applicants to institutions in groups 1 and 3 was similar to the citywide percentage black (mean [group 1], 42.3 percent; standard deviation [group 1], 13.1; mean [group 3], 36.73 percent; standard deviation [group 3], 5.9). Conversely, institutions in group 4 were less likely to have received applications from black applicants (mean, 9.6 percent; standard deviation, 7.1).

Market Share Analysis: Total Applications and Approved Loans

Data on market share for approvals show that institutions in groups 1, 3, and 6 were more likely to have substantially greater market share in black areas than white areas. Institutions in groups 2 and 5 held relatively equal market share in white and black areas. Conversely, the institutions in group 4 tended to hold less than one-third the market share in black areas as they held in white areas. A similar pattern holds for total market share, although the differences reflect generally higher denial rates in black areas than in white areas.

SUMMARY

The cluster analysis allowed us to identify six groups of institutions that appeared similar within groups, but very different across groups. Group 1 institutions (the "better" institutions) tended to make numerous loans of lower value to black applicants and black areas. As a group, these institutions held greater market share, both total and approvals, in black areas than in white areas. Group 2 institutions were unique in that, although they shared many other characteristics with each other, they reported no denials. Group 3 institutions (the "middle-class" institutions) tended to make larger loans to higher-income applicants. At the same time, they reached minority communities and applicants.

Group 4 institutions manifested the greatest problems. They originated relatively large loans to higher-income applicants; a small percentage of the loans were under $30,000. These institutions had poor penetration into the minority mortgage market, both in terms of approvals and applicants "coming to their door" from minority communities.

Group 5 institutions ("boutique" institutions) were distinguished by the fact that they appeared to cater to the highest-income applicants looking for the largest loans; these institutions made the smallest percentage of loans under $30,000. Their penetration into the minority mortgage market was subpar, but not the worst.

The institution in group 6 was unique among all institutions. The vast majority of applicants were black and were seeking mortgages for properties in black areas. The income and loan amount profile was about average, but there was a very small percentage of loans under $30,000.

Variables Related to, but Not Used to Form, Cluster Groups (*see table 19.7*)

SUPERVISORY AGENCY

Two-thirds of the institutions in group 1 were supervised by the Office of the Comptroller of the Currency (OCC), one institution was supervised by the Federal Reserve, and one by the Federal Deposit Insurance Corporation (FDIC). All institutions in group 2 were supervised by the Federal Reserve. Three institutions in group 3 were supervised by the Federal Reserve, one by FDIC, and one by HUD. Five institutions in group 4 were supervised by the Office of Thrift Supervision (OTS), and five were supervised by HUD. Two of the institutions in group 5 (both mortgage companies) were supervised by HUD, and one institution was supervised by FDIC. The institution in group 6 was supervised by FDIC.

Percentage of All Loan Applications Under $50,000

Data on the percentage of all loans originated for amounts under $50,000 show that institutions in group 1 predominated, with, on average, applications for loans under $50,000 constituting 86.2 percent of total loan approvals (standard deviation, 10.3). More than half of the loan approvals for the institution in group 6 (mean, 56.3 percent) were under $50,000. Percentages of loan applications for under $50,000 in groups 2 (47.8 percent), 3 (44.0 percent), and 4 (37.3 percent) were similar; institutions in group 5 had the lowest average percentage of such loan applications (mean, 25.8 percent; standard deviation, 12.1).

Average Time to Process Loan Applications

Average loan processing time varied substantially across groups. Group 5 institutions had the shortest average times (mean, 57.0 days; standard deviation, 20.2). Institutions in groups 1, 3, and 4 had similar times, averaging between 70 and 76 days to process applications. The institutions taking the longest average time were in group 2 (mean, 85.2 days; standard deviation, 9.9) and group 6 (mean, 86.1 days).

Difference in Processing Time for Black and White Applicants

In terms of disparate treatment, a factor more important than average days to process loan applications is the difference in average processing time for black and white applicants. On this indicator, all groups (with the exception of group 4 institutions) took, on average, about two weeks longer to process black applicants than they did to process white applicants (range: mean [group 5], 9.2 days longer; mean [group 2], 15.7 days longer). In contrast, group 4 institutions took, on average, 5 days fewer to process black applicants (note, though, that the standard deviation was large compared with the magnitude of the mean).

Average HMDA Rating for Approved and Denied Loan Applications

HMDA ratings reflect not only the racial composition of census tracts in which loans were approved (or denied) but also the median value of homes. High average scores indicate approvals (or denials) in minority and/or low housing value census tracts; low average scores indicate approvals (or denials) in higher housing value and/or white census tracts. Group 4 institutions averaged substantially below the other groups for approvals (mean, 17.3; standard deviation, 6.7). With respect to HMDA ratings for denials, there was less variation across groups, owing largely to the higher scores in groups 3, 4, and 5. This trend indicates that for these three groups, institutions were denying loans in census tracts that were of lower housing value and/or lower percentage minority than tracts in which they approved loans.

Average HMDA Rating Ratio for Denied versus Approved Loan Applications

Ratios close to 1.0 demonstrate parity in the racial composition and/or housing value for tracts in which loan applications were approved and denied. If a ratio is greater than 1.0, the institution denied loans in census tracts that were of lower value and/or had a higher percentage of blacks. Institutions in groups 1 and 6 showed a pattern of relative parity (denials and approvals came from areas that were similar in terms of race and housing value). Conversely, groups 3 and 5 denied loans in areas that were of lower value and a higher percentage of blacks than areas in which loans were approved. Group 4 institutions had the greatest disparity, with denials in census tracts that were twice as black and/or had a low housing value (mean, 2.12) as was the case with approvals.

Average Percentage Black in Census Tracts for Denied versus Approved Loan Applications

We next calculated a ratio that excludes from consideration the housing value indicator and focuses singularly on the actual percentage of blacks in census tracts from which applications occurred. The institution in group 6 showed the greatest parity (mean, 1.15). Unlike the HMDA rating scores, groups 3 and 5 (mean [group 3], 1.39; mean [group 5], 1.24) showed less disparity than group 1 institutions (1.49). Institutions in group 4 denied loan applications in census tracts that had nearly twice the percentage of blacks as tracts in which loans were approved (1.93). These figures must be viewed with caution. If an institution selectively pre-screens applicants from minority communities allowing only credit-worthy people to apply, the ratio will not reveal the totality of the institution's disparate treatment of applicants.

Ratio of Percentage Black versus Percentage White Denial Rates

A ratio of 1.0 reflects equality in denial rates between black and white applicants; ratios greater than 1.0 reflect black denial rates that are higher than white denial rates. Regardless of group, the average of all institutions was 3.0, meaning that black applicants were three times as likely to be denied loans as white applicants. Applicants to the institution in group 6 fared, on average, best, with a denial ratio of 1.44; next closest were institutions in group 5, with a denial ratio of 1.72. Institutions in groups 1 and 3 denied black applicants more than twice as frequently as white applicants. Group 4 institutions averaged black denial rates that were 5 times as great as white denial rates.

Percentage of Applications for FHA Loans

Institutions in groups 1 and 5 were least likely to accept applications for FHA loans; in both cases, fewer than 1 in 20 applications were for FHA loans. Applicants to the institution in group 6 were most likely to make use of the FHA insurance, with nearly 8 in 10 making FHA applications. Between 33 percent and 59 percent of applicants to institutions in groups 2, 3, and 4 sought FHA-insured loans.

Analysis of Rank-Order Scores on Cluster Variables

Working under the assumption that we did not have the resources to conduct in-depth investigations of the 18 institutions in, at the least, groups 3 and 4, we developed a companion method to identify the "worst of the worst." In general, the method calls for the assignment of rank-order scores for each cluster variable for each institution.[10] Rank scores ranged from 1 to 31, with 1 being the lowest rank score.[11] Then, for each institution an average rank score was calculated. The average, like each individual rank score, can range from 1 to 31, with 1 being the lowest rank score.

Table 19.8 shows data on the five institutions with the lowest average rank scores.[12] Note that *all of these institutions were identified by the cluster analysis as exhibiting similar lending behavior and were members of group 4*. Each lending institution highlighted in table 19.7 considers all of Philadelphia as its primary lending territory.

SUMMARY

Using data from the 1990 HMDA data file, this investigation analyzed data on more than 9,000 purchase money mortgage applications for

Table 19.8 AVERAGE RANK ORDER SCORES FOR INSTITUTIONS WITH THE POOREST PROFILES ON CLUSTERING VARIABLES

Institution Number	Rank Score
Institution #1	
Average loan amount of application	5
Average income of applicants	7
Percentage applications under $30K	6.5
Percentage black (census tract)	8
Percentage black (applicants)	9
Ratio of market share (approved loans)	6
Ratio of market share (all applications)	5
Average rank score	6.64
[Ratio black:white denial rate]	7
Percentage FHA (33.5%)	14
Institution #2	
Average amount	8
Average income	10
Percentage applications under $30K	3
Percentage black (census tract)	5
Percentage black (applicants)	12
Ratio of market share (approved loans)	5
Ratio of market share (all applications)	6
Average rank score	7.00
[Ratio black:white denial rate]	2
Percentage FHA (45.3%)	12
Institution #3	
Average amount	13
Average income	8
Percentage applications under $30K	2
Percentage black (census tract)	9
Percentage black (applicants)	13
Ratio of market share (approved loans)	8
Ratio of market share (all applications)	7

properties in the city of Philadelphia. Analysis of these data enabled us to identify those institutions with profiles we believe are most likely to indicate patterns and practices of lending activity violative of Section 805 of the Act. In addition to an exhaustive analysis of the 1990 HMDA data, we also obtained CRA statements and evaluations from depository institutions covered under CRA; conducted interviews with realtors, loan counselors, and community advocates in low-income and minority areas in Philadelphia; and obtained and reviewed the results of preapplication mortgage testing conducted by the Philadelphia Commission on Human Relations.

Table 19.8 AVERAGE RANK ORDER SCORES FOR INSTITUTIONS WITH THE POOREST PROFILES ON CLUSTERING VARIABLES (continued)

Institution Number	Rank Score
Average rank score	8.57
[Ratio black:white denial rate]	5
Percentage FHA (21.3%)	17
Institution #4	
Average amount	12
Average income	15
Percentage applications under $30K	11
Percentage black (census tract)	10
Percentage black (applicants)	8
Ratio of market share (approved loans)	7
Ratio of market share (all applications)	10
Average rank score	10.43
[Ratio black:white denial rate]	29
Percentage FHA (51.9%)	11
Institution #5	
Average amount	11
Average income	17
Percentage applications under $30K	8
Percentage black (census tract)	4
Percentage black (applicants)	15
Ratio of market share (approved loans)	9.5
Ratio of market share (all applications)	9
Average rank score	10.50
[Ratio black:white denial rate]	4
Percentage FHA (98.5%)	2

Note: Italics denote variables not part of the cluster analysis, but important to this table.

Analysis of the data helped us identify three institutions that consistently ranked below their peers along the following dimensions:

- Average dollar amount of applications for credit
- Average income of applicants
- Percentage of all loan applications under $30,000
- Average census tract percentage black in areas in which institutions approved applications
- Percentage of applicants for credit who were black
- Ratio of market share (approved loans) in black versus white census tracts
- Ratio of market share (all applications) in black versus white census tracts.

In addition to poor performance on these measures, each of the three institutions denied black applicants at least three times more frequently than white applicants. Also, each of these institutions received a high percentage of their applications for FHA-insured loans; HUD supervises two of the three.

While analyzing the HMDA data, we uncovered many instances of potential reporting violations that may have civil rights implications. Several institutions failed to report the following: (1) census-tract location for any loan applications; (2) race of applicants; or (3) race information on many denied applications. Several other institutions reported no denied applicants during the entire calendar year. While there are legitimate circumstances under which these data elements could be missing, the institutions identified were sufficiently different from the rest that inquiry is warranted.

I believe we have developed an effective approach for identifying institutions that are potentially involved in pattern and practice lending discrimination.[13] The approach takes into account both individual and geographic characteristics, as well as lending behavior that may have a racially disparate impact (i.e., an indication of de facto minimum loan amounts). Furthermore, the approach is broad based and sufficiently systematic to deflect any claims that the Secretary is using his power under the Fair Housing Act in an arbitrary or capricious manner.

Notes

None of the views in this paper necessarily reflect the views or opinions of the U.S. Department of Housing and Urban Development or the Federal Government.

1. Several studies have compared single indicators (for example, denial rates) for many institutions within an area.

2. The denial rate is computed as: # denied / (# denied + # approved). Using this formula, the 1990 denial rate for applications on one-to-four-family owner-occupied home purchases was 14.7 percent.

3. In 1990 the U.S. Bureau of the Census reported that 36.4 percent of householders were black (U.S. Bureau of the Census 1991a).

4. In 1990 the Census Bureau reported that 4.3 percent of householders were Hispanic (U.S. Bureau of the Census 1991a).

5. In 1990 the Census Bureau reported a median household income of $24,603 and a median family income of $30,259 (U.S. Bureau of the Census 1991a).

6. In 1990 the Census Bureau reported a median housing value of $49,452 (U.S. Bureau of the Census 1991a).

7. The use of $30,000 as a substantively significant break in the data reflects what my colleagues and I learned during our interviews with realtors, loan counselors, and community advocates in Philadelphia's minority communities. Several realtors reported that one of the biggest problems they faced for their low-income and minority clients was the business posture of many local lenders that loans of $30,000 (or $50,000) or less were not rational, given the cost of processing the loans.

8. In Philadelphia in 1990, the median household income of white households was $28,645; the figures for black, Hispanic, and Asian households were $20,349, $21,617, and $21,814, respectively. Similarly, the percentage of the white civilian labor force that was unemployed was 5.6 percent, compared with 12.6, 15.7, and 7.1 percent for blacks, Hispanics, and Asians, respectively. White households were also more likely to live as owners, as opposed to renters, than were black, Hispanic, and Asian households. More than two-thirds (66.8 percent) of white households were owner-occupied, compared to 56.7 percent of black households, 46.2 percent of Hispanic households, and 42.1 percent of Asian households (U.S. Bureau of the Census 1991b).

9. The way in which the variables selected were constructed would require modification if the method were applied in another area.

10. Although the ratio of denials to blacks versus whites was not explicitly considered in the delineation of groups, it is displayed in table 19.8 for each institution (in italics).

11. Note that rank scores in table 19.8 may be other than whole numbers if there is a tie in rank. For example, if two institutions tied for "worst" on a given indicator, rather than numbering them 1 and 2, they each received a rank score of 1.5.

12. One institution had a lower rank-order score than the five listed in table 19.8. Because this institution has only one branch in Philadelphia, in a racially identifiable location, information on this institution was omitted from the table for reasons of confidentiality.

13. Some of our approaches were less revealing than others, and, in hindsight, would be unnecessary to replicate in other geographic areas. In addition, some of the indicators used in Philadelphia would have to be adjusted in other areas. In a city like Philadelphia, with 25 percent of the housing stock valued at this level or below, this is an appropriate cutoff; moreover, our interviews with key witnesses showed this to be a frequently cited cutoff for local lenders. However, in a city with substantially higher-priced housing (e.g., Boston, New York, Los Angeles, San Francisco), a different value may be more relevant.

References

Adams, C., D. Bartelt, D. Elesh, I. Goldstein, N. Kleniewski, and W. Yancey. 1991. *Neighborhoods, Division, and Conflict in a Postindustrial City*. Philadelphia: Temple University Press.

Bartelt, D. 1984. "Redlines and Breadlines: Depression Recovery and the Structure of Urban Space." Temple University Institute for Public

Policy Studies Working Paper. Philadelphia: Temple University Press.

Bartelt, D., D. Elesh, I. Goldstein, G. Leon, and W. Yancey. 1987. "Islands in the Stream: Neighborhoods and the Political Economy of the City." In *Neighborhood and Community Environments*, vol. 9, edited by Irwin Altman and Abraham Wandersman. New York: Plenum Press.

Berry, B., and J. Kasarda. 1977. *Contemporary Urban Ecology.* New York: Macmillan Publishing Co.

Borowski, N. 1991. "Black Segregation Up in Philadelphia, Census Shows." *Philadelphia Inquirer*, April 11, p. 1.

Bradbury, K., D. Case, and C. Dunham. 1989. "Geographic Patterns of Mortgage Lending in Boston, 1982–1987." *New England Economic Review* 4 (September/October): 2–30.

Canner, G., and D. Smith. 1991. "Home Mortgage Disclosure Act: Expanded Data on Residential Lending." *Federal Reserve Bulletin* 77, November: 859–81.

———. 1992. "Expanded HMDA Data on Residential Lending: One Year Later." *Federal Reserve Bulletin*, 78 November: 801–24.

Chudacoff, H. 1975. *The Evolution of American Urban Society.* Englewood Cliffs, N.J.: Prentice-Hall.

Dedman, B. 1988. "The Color of Money: Home Mortgage Practices Discriminate against Blacks." *Atlanta Journal-Constitution*, May 1–16.

Goldstein, I. 1985. "The Wrong Side of the Tracts: A Study of Residential Segregation in Philadelphia, 1930–1980." Ph.D. Diss., Temple University. Philadelphia.

———. 1987. "Mortgage Lending Patterns in Philadelphia, 1987–1989." Temple University Institute for Public Policy Studies Working Paper. Philadelphia: Temple University.

———. 1991. "Segregation in Philadelphia Holds Firm." In *Making Home Ownership A Reality—Not Just A Dream* (65–68). Philadelphia: Philadelphia Commission on Human Relations.

Goldstein, I., and A. Shlay. 1988. "Getting the Credit We Deserve: An Analysis of Residential Lending in New Castle County, Delaware 1984–1986." Temple University Institute for Public Policy Studies Working Paper. Philadelphia: Temple University.

Hula, R. 1991. "Neighborhood Development and Local Credit Markets." *Urban Affairs Quarterly* 27: 249–67.

Jackson, K. 1985. *Crabgrass Frontier: The Suburbanization of the United States.* New York: Oxford University Press.

Munnell, A., L. Browne, J. McEneaney, and G. Tootell. 1992. "Mortgage Lending in Boston: Interpreting HMDA Data." Federal Reserve Bank of Boston Working Paper 92–07. Boston Federal Reserve Bank of Boston, October.

Shlay, A. 1985. *Where the Money Flows: Lending Patterns in the Washington, D.C.-Maryland-Virginia SMSA.* Chicago: Woodstock Institute.

———. 1987a. *Credit on Color: The Impact of Segregation and Racial Transition on Housing Credit Flows in the Chicago SMSA from 1980–1983*. Chicago: Woodstock Institute.

———. 1987b. *Maintaining the Divided City: Residential Lending Patterns in the Baltimore SMSA*. Baltimore, Md.: Maryland Alliance for Responsible Investment.

Shlay, A., and I. Goldstein. 1993. "Proving Disinvestment: The CRA Research Experience." Temple University Institute for Public Policy Studies Working Paper #1. Philadelphia: Temple University Press.

Squires, G. 1992. *From Redlining to Reinvestment*. Philadelphia: Temple University Press.

Squires, G., and W. Velez. 1987. "Neighborhood Racial Composition and Mortgage Lending: City and Suburban Differences." *Journal of Urban Affairs* 9: 217–32.

U.S. Bureau of the Census. 1991a. "Census of Population and Housing, 1990." Summary Tape File #1. Washington, D.C.

———. 1991b. "Census of Population and Housing, 1990." Summary Tape File #2. Washington, D.C.

Chapter Twenty

FAIR LENDING MANAGEMENT: USING INFLUENCE STATISTICS TO IDENTIFY CRITICAL MORTGAGE LOAN APPLICATIONS

David Rodda and James E. Wallace

Both the Fair Housing Act of 1968,[1] as amended, and the Equal Credit Opportunity Act of 1974,[2] as amended, prohibit discrimination in mortgage lending based on race or ethnicity. The Federal Reserve Bank of Boston study of mortgage lending, however, concluded that "even after controlling for financial, employment, and neighborhood characteristics, black and Hispanic mortgage applicants in the Boston metropolitan area are roughly 60 percent more likely to be turned down than whites" (Munnell et al. 1992: 2—also known as the "Boston Fed" study). The Boston Fed study has drawn its share of criticism, but its basic findings have been confirmed by research at the Federal National Mortgage Association (Fannie Mae) (Carr and Megbolugbe 1993) and at the Office of the Comptroller of the Currency (OCC) (Glennon and Stengel 1994). Conclusions similar to those of the Boston Fed study were reached in the U.S. Department of Justice investigation of Decatur Federal Savings and Loan in Atlanta (see Sisken and Cupingood, chapter 16, this volume; also Canner and Smith 1991, 1992; and Canner, Passmore, and Smith 1994).

Criticisms of the Boston Fed study have focused on the use of single-equation models for estimation, and on the potential for conclusions to be the result of data errors. A continuing literature describes the econometric difficulties of using a single-equation model to measure discrimination (Yezer, Phillips, and Trost 1994; Phillips and Yezer 1995). Drawing on work by Maddala and Trost (1982), Rachlis and Yezer (1993) showed that single-equation models of the lending decision may suffer from selection bias. To correct for selection bias, one would need to estimate the probability of applying for a mortgage loan on a sample that included households that could have, but chose not to, apply.

In addition to selection bias, a single-equation model suffers from simultaneous equation bias. A household that expects an application with a high loan-to-value (LTV) ratio to be rejected may choose to borrow less. Some version of LTV, however, is typically treated as an exogenous variable in a single-equation model. A completely unbiased approach would model the choice of loan size as a separate equation in a system of simultaneous equations. Unfortunately, we do not have enough truly exogenous data to identify such a system of equations, nor do we have sufficient information on eligible nonapplicants to solve the selection bias problem. Thus, in spite of the potential biases engendered by single-equation models, the appropriate data are not available, and decision makers, like lenders and regulators, must make choices based on existing information.

Another type of criticism of the Boston Fed study focuses on data errors. Liebowitz and Day (1993) claimed in the *Wall Street Journal* that the Boston Fed data contained many typographical errors. Horne (1994) reported that in a careful review of the loan folders of 95 applications in FDIC-regulated banks, 57 percent had some data error that affected variables included in the Boston Fed model. Obviously, we are likewise concerned about data quality in the Boston Fed data. It is important to note, however, that the results have lately been confirmed by work on new data.

In a recent OCC working paper, Stengel and Glennon (1995) compared the results of generic models to single-equation models separately customized for three nationally chartered banks. They found that customizing the specification according to the underwriting of each bank substantially improved the goodness of fit. Moreover, evidence of disparate treatment, which was significant in two of the three banks in the generic model specifications, was confirmed by the customized model in only one of the three banks. Our interpretation of Stengel and Glennon's (1995) results is that customizing the model specification to the lender is important. The study also shows that a statistical model can identify questionable applications, which in turn can highlight data errors or unusual characteristics (applicant or underwriting) not captured by the model.

The Stengel and Glennon (1995) study is particularly relevant to our work because the authors were able to fine tune the model specifications to localize apparently disparate treatment in one of the three banks. We propose a similar process of careful data inspection and model specification with the help of influence statistics to focus on those situations in which discrimination appears to have occurred. If disparate treatment in mortgage lending has occurred and the model adequately captures the underwriting process, influence statistics can identify an efficient set of candidate cases for further investigation to understand the extent and nature of the disparate treatment.

Influence statistics, like other single-equation models, cannot prove that discrimination occurred. They can be very useful, however, by helping managers and regulators to more efficiently search for cases of disparate treatment. Influence statistics will often identify a relatively small set of cases that materially affect the minority coefficient in a loan approval model. Lenders can review these cases to determine whether they appear to be caused by data errors, factors omitted from the model, or disparate treatment of minority applications. If it appears that there is disparate treatment, a review of influential cases can help to determine whether such treatment is pervasive or concentrated in a few institutions or special situations. Such investigations can profoundly affect the choice of appropriate remedies pursued by managers. Further, influence diagnostics might profitably be used not only for existing databases but also for ongoing monitoring of new applications.

The rest of this chapter is organized as follows. We first review the methodology of the logistic regression model and influence statistics. This methodology is then applied to the public-use sample of the data used in the Boston Fed study. To provide a baseline, we reestimate the Boston Fed model using the Boston Federal Reserve's specification for our sample. After verifying the size and significance of the minority coefficient, we show that those results are robust to alternative specifications involving neighborhood effects. Influence statistics identify a small set of critical cases that are responsible for the minority coefficient being significant. After observing that the most influential cases are minority denials with LTV ratios at or below 80 percent, separate models are run on low- and high-LTV cases. These results indicate that apparent discrimination is concentrated among the 33 percent of minority applicants with low loan-to-value ratios. The estimated minority coefficient for these cases was substantially and significantly greater than the coefficient for minority applications with high loan-to-value ratios. Indeed, whereas the available samples are too small to permit us to reject the possibility of substantial discrimination in approving minority applications with high loan-to-value ratios, there was no statistically significant minority effect for these applications. This suggests that for this data set, effective remedies or additional analyses should concentrate on low loan-to-value applications. The chapter concludes with a summary of findings and suggests how influence statistics could be used with pending mortgage applications to efficiently identify cases that would be highly influential in affecting the minority coefficient, possibly indicating disparate treatment.

METHODOLOGY

For a given mortgage rate, a mortgage lender would be expected to maximize profits by approving good credit risks and denying bad credit risks. The Boston Fed study organized the information from the mortgage application, credit report, and appraisal report into five categories: ability to support the loan, risk of default, potential default loss, loan characteristics, and personal characteristics. Measures of the ability to support the loan include earned and unearned income, net wealth, liquid assets, housing expense-to-income ratio (front-end ratio), and total debt payments-to-income ratio (back-end ratio). Risk of default is estimated by borrower credit history, length and continuity of employment, and probability of unemployment as measured by level of unemployment in the industry or local area. Potential default loss is indicated by the LTV ratio and measures of the trend and variance in local property values. Given that different types of properties and different types of loans have traditionally exhibited different levels of risk, the astute underwriter will be expected to adjust the criteria for approval for loan and property characteristics. Finally, personal characteristics include such factors as age, sex, education, marital status, and minority status. Although the law prohibits denying a mortgage based on age, sex, marital status, or minority status, it is difficult to conceal these factors from the underwriter. Therefore, such factors may have some influence on the probability of mortgage denial.

Economic theory and mortgage lending experience have shown that variables representing the five standard categories potentially play a role in the mortgage lending decision. There is no clear guidance, however, about exactly which variables to include or which functional form is most appropriate for a model of the decision. The general approach is to capture the essential features that are legal in the mortgage decision process, then determine if the remaining variation in denials is associated with minority status. Any factor that has an impact on the mortgage decision and is also correlated with minority status could affect the minority coefficient if that factor is omitted from the model. Unfortunately, the potential list of such factors is much longer than the list of available variables. Therefore, the approach is to keep the functional form simple and try a variety of specifications within available data to minimize the possibility that the minority coefficient is significant due to some missing variable. To that end, a logistic regression model is used in which the dependent variable is the probability of mortgage denial, and the independent variables represent the categories listed previously.

Influence Statistics

The methodology up to this point follows closely the approach used in the Boston Federal Reserve study. Our innovation is the use of influence statistics to identify specifically which cases appeared to have minority status as a highly important factor in the mortgage decision based on the impact of those cases on the minority coefficient. Note that the critical cases are not limited to minority denials but could include both minority and nonminority applications that have a large impact on the minority coefficient.[3] The influence statistic used, called the DBETA for the minority indicator variable, measures how much the minority coefficient would change from the deletion of each loan application relative to the coefficient's error of estimate. If the minority coefficient is the same in a regression with a particular application as it is in a regression without that application, then that application has no influence on the minority coefficient. If the minority coefficient does change substantially, however, then that application plays an important role in the determination of the estimated minority coefficient. The DBETA measures the influence or change in minority coefficient for each application. Ranking the applications according to their influence on the minority coefficient provides an efficient set of applications for further investigation into the potential existence and nature of disparate treatment.

Algebraically, let b be the maximum likelihood estimate of the coefficient vector; let $\hat{V}_b$ be the estimated covariance matrix of b; and let b_j^1 be the maximum likelihood estimate of the coefficient vector when the jth observation is excluded.[4] The difference between b, estimated with all the observations, and b_j^1, estimated without the jth observation, is called Δb_j^1. It would be costly to reestimate b_j^1 by excluding each observation, one at a time, and maximizing the likelihood function. Instead, Pregibon (1981) devised a one-step approximation for Δb_j^1:

$$\Delta b_j^1 = \hat{V}_b x_j (r_j - \hat{p}_j)/(1 - h_{jj}), \tag{20.1}$$

where x_j are the exlanatory values for the jth observation, r_j is 1 if the jth observed response is denial, 0 otherwise, $\hat{p}_j = \frac{\exp(b'x_j)}{1 + \exp(b'x_j)}$ is the predicted probability that the jth application is denied, and $h_{jj} = \hat{p}_j(1 - \hat{p}_j)x_j'\hat{V}_b x_j$ is the jth diagonal element of the hat or projection matrix. Then the DBETA for the ith explanatory variable and the jth observation is:

$$\text{DBETA}i_j = \frac{\Delta_i b_j^1}{\hat{\sigma}(b_i)}, \qquad (20.2)$$

where $\hat{\sigma}(b_i)$ is the standard error of the ith component of b, and $\Delta_i b_j^1$ is the ith component of the one-step difference, Δb_j^1.

The distinction between outlying residuals and influential observations is important. Not all outliers are influential, and not all influential observations are outliers. The key difference is that influential observations make a difference to coefficient estimates, whereas outlying residuals might only affect the variance. An outlying observation with a large residual has a dependent value that cannot be closely predicted given the set of explanatory variables. Excluding such an observation would improve the overall fit of the regression equation without necessarily changing the estimated coefficients of any of the explanatory variables. This would be the case if the residual reflected random error that can happen in any stochastic process. In other words, the observation affected the variance of the model but not the estimated coefficients.

Highly influential observations are not necessarily distant outliers that should be suspected as oddities. They could contain distinctive information. They stand out because they have a considerable impact on the coefficient of an explanatory variable. A priori, it is not obvious whether an influential observation represents a legitimate case of apparent discrimination, a coding error, or the result of model misspecification. Omitted variables or interaction terms are common causes of misspecification. Whether or not the high-influence statistic has a large residual, however, it raises a warning flag indicating that this single observation makes a big difference to a coefficient and deserves closer examination.

The most common use of influence diagnostics is to identify unusual cases that have a substantially larger than average (in absolute terms) influence on estimated coefficient. For this purpose, it is best to measure the influence of each single observation. A logical extension is to measure the importance of the most influential applications as a group to determine if deleting the most influential cases collectively has a significant impact on the minority coefficient. A few cases with extreme DBETA values, either positive or negative, do not necessarily have a large impact on the minority coefficient, for two reasons. The most influential cases may not carry enough weight to materially affect the result, or they may simply involve a combination of offsetting positive and negative effects that largely cancel out.[5]

When a small set of cases is found to substantially affect the size of the coefficient when left out of the regression, this suggests that further investigation should focus on this set of cases. If only one or two observations were responsible for the significant minority coefficient, we obviously would discount the estimate; there would simply be too great a chance that the responsible observations were flukes. Although possible, it is rare that so few observations could be so influential.

The investigation should proceed as follows. First, be sure that the cases that affect the results are not caused by coding errors (Belsley et al. 1980). Presumably, the internal records of a mortgage lender are becoming more reliable as they become increasingly automated, suggesting that direct use of the model by a particular lender with in-house data would be less vulnerable to data error. At least the errors should be easier to detect and correct. Nevertheless, the DBETA influence measure might highlight some applications that have been corrupted by undetected coding errors.

The next step is to look for decisive factors that affected the lending decision but are not reflected by the variables included in the model. For example, the applicant may be an employee of the lender and, thus, qualify for a special program not offered to the general public. Incorporating the variables that had been omitted may significantly change the set of critical cases and improve the model. A practical problem for most lenders is that much of the information in the loan application is not coded into electronic form. This means that the regression model is restricted to a very limited set of variables compared to the variables possibly used by the human decision makers. Moreover, there is considerable local market information that might not even be reported in the appraisal report, but which an experienced underwriter could consider before making a lending decision.

To detect possible minority disparate treatment, it is important to include all the economic variables that could vary by minority status. Researchers at the Boston Federal Reserve undertook a thorough investigation to determine which variables are used by underwriters that could vary by minority status. To supplement the data required by the Home Mortgage Disclosure Act (HMDA), financial institutions were asked to provide 38 additional variables. Even so, the amount of data available to an underwriter far exceeds the information used by the Boston Federal Reserve in the regression model. This is not to suggest that the underwriter necessarily uses all of that information. Rather, the underwriter can choose which subset of information to review depending on the particular situation of the applicant, property, and market.

Despite the large potential for omitted variables, it is surprising how few of the additional variables collected by the Federal Reserve Bank of Boston made a significant improvement in the fit of the model. Perhaps some of these variables would improve customized models for individual lenders, as Stengel and Glennon (1995) found. More research and experience at the individual lender level is needed, but the possibility of model misspecification due to omitted variables will always exist.

Once the coding and specification issues have been resolved, the next step is to use the highly influential cases from the revised model to investigate the existence and nature of disparate treatment. A careful review of these cases may indicate common factors linking the influential cases together. For example, it may turn out that many influential cases originated at a particular branch office, indicating that one or a few underwriters at that branch need retraining. Another possibility is that the influential cases may be concentrated in a particular category of loans, indicating that disparate treatment may occur more frequently in these types of loans. Influence statistics can efficiently focus the search effort into identifying a sample of loan folders with a higher likelihood of reflecting disparate treatment compared to a randomly selected sample of folders.

The vector of influence statistics for the full sample can be correlated with other variables in the database to identify more subtle conditions that appear related to disparate treatment. These correlations can provide valuable indications about the nature of the apparent disparate treatment. There is useful information in the full DBETA vector that can verify the relationships hinted at in the small set of highly influential cases inspected more thoroughly. As described below, exploration using influence statistics on the Boston Fed data shows that apparent discriminatory effects are concentrated in the low loan-to-value minority applications. This relationship was noticed while investigating the small set of highly influential cases. The relationship was further supported by correlations for the full sample and was confirmed by running separate regressions for low- and high-LTV cases.

Once the extent and nature of the apparent disparate treatment have been determined, managers and policymakers can choose the most appropriate remedial action. Apparent discrimination, for which no common loan type or borrower or branch characteristic is found, may require fundamental procedural changes and careful monitoring. A concentrated set of disparate treatment cases may be dealt with by retraining the staff involved or underwriting changes for certain types of loans. Whatever the remedial approach, the regulators will look more favorably on lenders that are proactive.

Finally, influence statistics can play an important role in the ongoing monitoring of new cases. As a new application comes in, it can be examined to see how much influence it would have if the decision were made to deny that application. If the application turns out to be highly influential, it can be referred to a higher level for review. Although this appears to lengthen the review process, management can reduce the amount of oversight provided for the cases that are not highly influential.

APPLICATION TO BOSTON FED DATA

How do influence statistics work using real data? The data used here were collected by the Federal Reserve Bank of Boston in 1991, supplementing 1990 HMDA data with a survey of 38 variables thought to be critical to the lending decision. The public-use version of this database excludes some observations and certain information about location and neighborhood characteristics to protect confidentiality. For example, the percentage of minority people in a tract has been turned into an indicator variable: 1 if greater than 30 percent, 0 otherwise. The percentages of boarded-up buildings, tract vacancy, tract income, and applicant age are similarly treated: 1 if greater than the MSA median, 0 otherwise. Also, some of the cases with extremely large loans or incomes were suppressed for confidentiality. Of the 3,062 cases reported in the Boston Fed study, the public-use data set contains 2,932 cases.

To analyze underwriting decisions for a consistent set of loans, we only considered applications for conventional mortgages for owner-occupied buildings of up to four units (excluding condominiums).

All refinancing, home improvement, and multifamily applications were dropped. In addition, all Federal Housing Administation (FHA), Veterans Administration (VA), and construction loan applications were deleted. If the category "other financing" exceeded the loan amount or income was not positive, then the case was dropped. Finally, if the term of the loan was a year or less, or the term was 40 years or more, then the application was dropped.

In addition to these considerations for consistency, cases with missing values in the model's explanatory variables and cases with non-positive income were omitted. After these deletions, the data set contained 2,686 cases (2,050 whites and 636 minorities) in which the white denial rate was 9.2 percent and the minority denial rate was 27.7 percent. For comparison, the Boston Fed final sample had 3,062 cases (2,340 whites and 722 minorities) in which the white denial rate was 10.3 percent and the minority denial rate was 28.1 percent.

A modest attempt was made to check for data consistency, with indicator variables created to flag cases of inconsistency. One common inconsistency was between annual applicant income from HMDA and the annualized amount of monthly total income for applicant and coapplicant reported in the supplemental survey by the lender. Researchers at the Boston Fed found that in most cases of inconsistently reported income, the income reported on HMDA was incorrect. Sixteen percent of whites and 25 percent of minorities had income measures that differed by more than 10 percent. The base model includes the indicator variable for income inconsistency between reported annualized income and the income reported in the HMDA data.

A related inconsistency was that the ratio of housing expense to income did not match the reported monthly housing expenses divided by income. Also, the purchase price was sometimes substantially different from the appraised value. Ten percent of whites and 16 percent of minorities had appraised values that differed from purchase price by more than 15 percent. No great effort was made at choosing the "correct" amount, but a variable designating each type of inconsistency was included in some specifications to ensure that the minority coefficient was not picking up this effect. Also, a few applications had appraised values that were far below the purchase price and even below the loan amount, creating an LTV greater than 1.0. We suspect that the appraised value is incorrectly reported, so the purchase price was used in place of the appraised value, and the LTV recalculated.

Table 20.1 shows the results of the Boston Fed study and our replication using the public-use sample and before screening for extreme

Table 20.1 DETERMINANTS OF PROBABILITY OF DENIAL OF MORTGAGE LOAN APPLICATION

Variable	Original Boston Fed Study[a]: Coefficient (std. error)	Reestimation on Subsample: Coefficient (std. error)
Constant	−6.61 (.39)	−7.71 (.55)
Ability to Support Loan		
Housing expense/income	.47 (.15)	−.018 (.011)
Total debt payments/income	.04 (.006)	.07 (.009)
Net wealth	.00008 (.00007)	.00013 (.00007)
Risk of Default		
Consumer credit history	.33 (.03)	.29 (.04)
Mortgage credit history	.35 (.12)	.40 (.13)
Public record history	1.20 (.17)	1.09 (.19)
Probability of unemployment	.09 (.03)	.08 (.03)
Self-employed	.52 (.19)	.61 (.20)
Potential Default Loss		
Loan/appraised value	.58 (.18)	1.93 (.53)
Denied private mortgage insurance	4.70 (.49)	4.59 (.50)
Rent/value in tract	.68 (.19)	
Loan Characteristics		
Purchasing two- to four-family home	.58 (.16)	.45 (.18)
Personal Characteristics		
Minority	.68 (.14)	.78 (.15)
Number of Observations	3062	2686
Log Likelihood		−738
Percentage of Correct Predictions (cutoff used is 50%)	89%	89%
False-positive rate		26%
False-negative rate		10%

a. Munnell et al. (1992: 27).

values. The variables are all the same, except rent/value in tract, which was not provided in the public-use data. The estimated coefficients are generally similar, including the minority coefficient. One of the differences is housing expense/income, which we found to be not significant and negative compared to the significant and positive coefficient in the original study. The housing expense to income ("front-end") ratio and the total debt payments-to-income ("back-end") ratio are somewhat collinear. In the Boston Fed study, these were both positive and significant, whereas our results show a larger coefficient for the back-end ratio offset by a negative and insignificant coefficient for the front-end ratio. The other difference is that the coefficient for LTV ratio is three times larger in our results.

Both models predicted "correctly" 89 percent of the time (where a predicted denial probability greater than 0.50 is counted as a denial—see table 20.1). Note that since 85.5 percent of the applications were approved, a simple "prediction" that every application would be approved would be "correct" 85.5 percent of the time. Of course, the models presented attempt the greater challenge of maximizing the percentage correct while minimizing the false positives and false negatives. Unfortunately, the original Boston Fed study did not report any goodness-of-fit statistics other than percentage correct, so it is difficult to compare the fit of our reestimations with their reported models.

Although many different specifications and variable forms were tried, our preferred specification uses a series of indicator variables in place of an index for both consumer credit and mortgage credit. The index was set up by the Boston Federal Reserve so that higher values were linked to longer delays in payment. The linear index form, however, does not fit quite so well as the more flexible indicator variable form we used.

Similarly, experimentation showed that low-LTV applications (less than 80 percent) should be an indicator variable. The high-LTV applications were identified by a variable that measured the excess in percentage points of the LTVs over 80 percent. The deviation approach is based on the idea that underwriters take increasing notice of applications with LTVs above 80 percent. Indeed, secondary market purchasers typically require mortgage insurance for loans with LTV over .80. On the other hand, no exceptional notice is given to an application with an LTV of .65 compared to one with an LTV of .75. A similar strategy was used with the front- and back-end ratios. The front-end ratio of housing expense to income was represented by a variable that measured the deviation from the benchmark 28 percent. The back-end ratio of total debt payments to income was represented by a variable that measured the deviation from 34 percent. A chi-square test using the log likelihoods shows that our preferred specification fits the sample of 2,686 observations better than the original Boston Fed study specification on the same data (*p*-value = .001). Table 20.2 provides the mean and standard deviation for variables included in the models.

Neighborhood Measures

A major concern in this field of research is that the minority coefficient may capture some neighborhood effects and not simply minority status. Since minority families tend to live in neighborhoods with high concentrations of minority households, an indicator of individual racial status is highly correlated with a measure of the percentage of minorities in the neighborhood. Of course, denial of a mortgage application based on neighborhood (i.e., redlining) is discriminatory. However, the minority percentage may be serving as a proxy for some other neighborhood characteristic that is not discriminatory. Table 20.3 compares three models showing the impact of including neighborhood measures. All of the modeling is done on the same database after the exclusions and corrections mentioned earlier. The first column of results is the base model without neighborhood measures. The format of many of the variables is so different from the replication model in table 20.1 that it is hard to make comparisons. The minority indicator variable is the same format, however, and the coefficient, .60, is at the lower end of the range of results presented in the Boston Fed study. Overall, the base model fits better than the replication model, with a slightly higher percentage correct and lower false-positive and false-negative rates. The next column adds to the base model a variable that indicates whether the unit is in a census tract with more than 30 percent minority population. Given a correlation of .54 between MINORITY and MINORTRC, it is not surprising that the minority coefficient declines to .53 when MINORTRC is introduced. The minority coefficient is still significant, but the neighborhood measure is not.

The third column of table 20.3 uses as a neighborhood measure an indicator of whether the unit is in a census tract with a greater proportion of boarded-up buildings than the MSA median. The correlation between MINORITY and BOARDUP is .19, and the minority coefficient only increases to .63.[6] None of the neighborhood measures that were available had significant coefficients as long as the minority variable was included. Neighborhood variables, especially in the

Table 20.2 DESCRIPTIONS AND STATISTICS FOR VARIABLES USED IN MODELS

Name	Description	Mean	Std. Deviation
Dependent Variable			
DENY	1 if mortgage application was denied	364 denied	2,322 approved
PRED	Predicted probability of denial	.14	.23
Explanatory Variables			
BACKD34	Deviation of total debt payments/income from 34%	2.40	4.57
LOW_LTV	1 if loan-to-value ratio less than 80%	.55	.50
LTVLES80	LTV − 80% if LTV greater than 80%	.036	.053
ADJUSTBL	1 if adjustable rate mortgage	.32	.47
INCONSS1	1 if calculated annual income differed from reported income by more than 10%	.18	.39
	Credit History (omitted category is clean record)		
INSUFFCH	1 if insufficient credit history (during past two years)	.039	.19
DELINQC	1 if delinquent credit (60 days past due)	.08	.27
SERDELNQ	1 if seriously delinquent (90 days past due)	.09	.29
	Mortgage History (omitted category is clean record)		
INSUFFMH	1 if insufficient mortgage history (during past two years)	.69	.46
ONELATEM	1 if one or two late mortgage payments	.017	.13
TWOLATEM	1 if more than two late mortgage payments	.010	.10
PUBLREC	1 if any public record of credit problems	.075	.26
PMI_DEN	1 if private mortgage insurance sought and denied	.026	.16
UNVERIF	1 if unverifiable information on application	.05	.22
SELF_EMP	1 if applicant self-employed	.11	.31
SF2_4	1 if purchasing single-family two- to four-unit building	.13	.34
OLD_NUM	1 if applicant age above median for MSA	.46	.50
UNMARRY	1 if marital status of applicant is unmarried (single, divorced or widowed)	.38	.48
MINORITY	1 if race reported is other than white (636 minority, 2,050 white)	.24	.43
MINORTRC	1 if unit in census tract with more than 30% minority population	.12	.33
BOARDUP	1 if unit in census tract with percentage boarded-up buildings above the median for MSA	.48	.50
DFBMINOR	Influence statistic: DBETA on MINORITY coefficient (minimum = −.13, maximum = .13)	0	.02

Table 20.3 ALTERNATIVE SPECIFICATIONS WITH NEIGHBORHOOD EFFECTS ON PROBABILITY OF DENIAL

Explanatory Variable	Base Model: Coefficient (std. error)	Add MINORTRC: Coefficient (std. error)	Add BOARDUP: Coefficient (std. error)
Constant	−4.17	−4.17	−4.09
	(.30)	(.30)	(.30)
BACKD34	.14	.14	.14
	(.01)	(.01)	(.01)
LOW_LTV	−.43	−.43	−.44
	(.23)	(.23)	(.23)
LTVLES80	3.90	3.88	3.83
	(1.85)	(1.85)	(1.85)
ADJUSTBL	−.51	−.50	−.52
	(.17)	(.17)	(.17)
INCONSS1	.57	.57	.57
	(.18)	(.18)	(.18)
INSUFFCH	.66	.64	.68
	(.33)	(.34)	(.34)
DELINQC	.78	.78	.80
	(.24)	(.24)	(.24)
SERDELNQ	1.25	1.25	1.26
	(.21)	(.21)	(.21)
INSUFFMH	.23	.23	.24
	(.20)	(.20)	(.20)
ONELATEM	1.19	1.20	1.19
	(.45)	(.45)	(.45)
TWOLATEM	1.35	1.36	1.32
	(.54)	(.54)	(.54)
PUBLREC	1.40	1.41	1.39
	(.21)	(.21)	(.21)
PMI_DEN	4.49	4.48	4.54
	(.51)	(.51)	(.51)
UNVERIF	3.11	3.11	3.13
	(.25)	(.25)	(.25)
SELF_EMP	.67	.67	.66
	(.22)	(.22)	(.22)
SF2_4	.37	.34	.40
	(.20)	(.21)	(.20)
OLD_NUM	.39	.39	.39
	(.16)	(.16)	(.16)
UNMARRY	.45	.44	.45
	(.16)	(.16)	(.16)
MINORTRC		.18	
		(.23)	
BOARDUP			−.21
			(.16)

Table 20.3. ALTERNATIVE SPECIFICATIONS WITH NEIGHBORHOOD EFFECTS ON PROBABILITY OF DENIAL (continued)

Explanatory Variable	Base Model: Coefficient (std. error)	Add MINORTRC: Coefficient (std. error)	Add BOARDUP: Coefficient (std. error)
MINORITY	.60	.53	.63
	(.17)	(.19)	(.17)
No. of cases	2686	2686	2686
Log likelihood	−626	−626	−625
Percentage correct[a]	91%	91%	91%
False-positive rate	22%	22%	22%
False-negative rate	8%	8%	8%
Hosmer-Lemeshow[b] p-value	0.37	0.55	0.57

a. Percentage denied: Overall, 13.6 percent; minorities, 27.7 percent; nonminorities, 9.2 percent.

b. Hosmer-Lemeshow (1989) goodness-of-fit statistic, $\hat{C}$, is defined as:

$$\hat{C} = \sum_{k=1}^{10} \frac{(o_k - n_k'\overline{\pi}_k)^2}{n_k'\overline{\pi}_k(1 - \overline{\pi}_k)},$$

where n_k' is the total number of cases in the kth group.

$o_k = \sum_j r_j$ is the sum of observed responses in the kth group, and

$\overline{\pi}_k = \sum_j \frac{\hat{p}_j}{n_k'}$ is the average of the estimated probabilities.

The p-value is the probability that $\chi^2_8 > \hat{C}$ (Hosmer and Lemeshow 1989: 140–45). Essentially, the Hosmer-Lemeshow statistic sums up the squared Pearson residuals over 10 equal-sized groups to form a chi-squared statistic. The larger the p-value, the more likely that the differences between the observed and estimated expected frequencies are due solely to chance. In other words, the systematic variation is captured by the model, and the remaining variation is random. Larger p-values represent a better fitting model. One of the main advantages of the Hosmer-Lemeshow statistic over the percentage correct is that the Hosmer-Lemeshow statistic measures goodness-of-fit for low-, middle-, and high-probability events based on the expected probability of the event occurring, whereas the percentage correct only measures the fit of the model relative to a single arbitrary cutoff, usually 50 percent. However, in this case the Hosmer-Lemeshow statistic seems excessively sensitive, showing an improvement in model fit after the inclusion of a variable that has a standard error larger than the estimated coefficient.

dummy variable format, may fail to capture the neighborhood factors that underwriters and appraisers consider important. Although the minority coefficient might be biased without better controls for neighborhood characteristics, the neighborhood measures that were available were too limited to provide a conclusive test.

APPLICATION OF INFLUENCE STATISTICS

The influence statistic on the minority coefficient ranges from -.13 to +.13 centered on zero. We have chosen to designate as extreme those cases with a DBETA larger in absolute value than .10. The standard deviation of the minority DBETA is .02, so the extreme cases exceed two standard deviations.[7] The 30 cases with the most influence on the minority coefficient are listed in table 20.4. Twenty-five of the

Table 20.4 INFLUENCE STATISTICS FOR 30 MOST INFLUENTIAL CASES (ORDERED BY DESCENDING VALUE OF DBETA ON MINORITY COEFFICIENT)

Case No.	Minority	Deny	Predicted Probability of Denial	DBETA on Minority Coefficient
2412	1	1	.08	.134
147	1	1	.07	.132
2287	1	1	.06	.130
2800	1	1	.06	.128
1782	1	1	.12	.123
2892	1	1	.05	.122
1550	1	1	.14	.118
836	1	1	.06	.118
2646	1	1	.07	.111
2678	1	1	.05	.111
879	1	1	.23	.110
1664	1	1	.08	.110
2851	1	1	.17	.110
687	1	1	.10	.108
1382	1	1	.13	.106
2161	1	1	.07	.102
922	1	1	.34	.101
2199	1	1	.08	.101
2829	1	1	.04	.099
609	1	1	.33	.099
2170	1	1	.29	.096
257	1	1	.31	.096
1367	1	1	.05	.095
972	1	1	.08	.094
2305	1	1	.08	.094
526	0	1	.19	−.103
1855	0	1	.13	−.106
2234	0	1	.11	−.112
2152[a]	1	0	.81	−.124
1217	0	1	.07	−.126

[a]Only influential approval. Note that private mortgage insurance was denied, but the loan was approved anyway.

cases turned out to be minority denials with highly positive DBETA values. Another 4 nonminority denial cases and 1 minority approval have extreme negative DBETA values. The predicted probability of denial is low for all the influential cases except for the lone approval. Note that the mean probability of denial for the 30 influential cases (15 percent) is nearly the same as for the overall sample (14 percent) but is well below the mean predicted probability of denial among minority denials (60 percent).

Table 20.5 provides additional information about the 30 most influential cases. Shown immediately below the influential minority denials are the means for the 25 influential minority denials and the means for all minority denials. For most factors, the influential minority denials appear to be better qualified than the average minority denial. The largest difference is that the mean loan-to-value (LTV) for influential minority denial cases is .71 compared to .84 for all minority denials. Indeed, 22 of the 25 (88 percent) influential minority denials have an LTV at or below .80, compared to only 26 percent for all minority denials. In a later section, we explore the relationship between high influence and low loan to value using correlations on the full sample.

Now consider the impact on the minority coefficient of removing the cases with a DBETA value of less than −.10 or greater than .10. Table 20.6 provides the distribution of the DBETA on the minority coefficient divided between approved and denied applications. The first row shows that all 18 cases with DBETA exceeding .10 are denied minority applications. Figure 20.1 further highlights these extreme cases. Here the DBETAs on the minority coefficient are plotted against the Pearson residuals. The Pearson residual normalizes the difference between the observed outcome and the predicted probability by the standard deviation for the binomial distribution. Horizontally the plot is centered on zero, with denials that the model had projected to be approvals on the right, and the reverse on the left. Influence is measured along the vertical dimension, with cutoff lines added to show which cases are removed. The key point shown in the plot is that the critical cases of high influence on the minority coefficient are not simply large residuals. We cannot, and should not, disregard these cases as being outlier oddities, but, instead, should investigate them further to determine why they rely so heavily on racial status. Furthermore, identifying cases that materially affect the minority coefficient is much more efficiently accomplished with the influence statistic on the minority coefficient than through analysis of cases with high residuals. One would have to examine 168 cases with the largest

Table 20.5 CHARACTERISTICS OF 30 MOST INFLUENTIAL CASES
(ORDERED BY DESCENDING VALUE OF DBETA ON MINORITY COEFFICIENT)

Case No.	Minority	Deny	Housing Expense to Income	Debt Payment to Income	Annual Income ($1,000s)	Loan-to-Value Ratio	1 if Less than 2 Years on Job	Credit History (1, Best; 6, Worst)
2412	1	1	.34	.39	114	.80	0	1
147	1	1	.28	.39	56	.75	1	1
2287	1	1	.19	.25	31	.45	1	1
2800	1	1	.36	.36	23	.40	1	5
1782	1	1	.28	.44	46	.79	0	3
2892	1	1	.27	.33	79	.80	1	1
1550	1	1	.27	.42	77	.75	0	5
836	1	1	.27	.38	55	.80	0	1
2646	1	1	.25	.36	41	.58	0	3
2678	1	1	.33	.38	36	.80	0	2
879	1	1	.32	.40	26	.40	0	6
1664	1	1	.19	.37	72	.70	0	1
2851	1	1	.36	.46	19	.71	1	2
687	1	1	.34	.37	27	.77	0	5
1382	1	1	.20	.29	56	.80	0	6
2161	1	1	.18	.37	72	.81	0	5
922	1	1	.22	.30	35	.67	1	1
2199	1	1	.35	.40	32	.78	0	1
2829	1	1	.14	.32	107	.55	0	2
609	1	1	.30	.36	58	.51	0	6
2170	1	1	.26	.32	49	.75	0	6
257	1	1	.15	.37	56	.78	0	6
1367	1	1	.32	.39	49	.89	0	3
972	1	1	.29	.36	69	.95	0	1
2305	1	1	.16	.39	52	.80	0	3
Means of influential minority denials			.26	.37	53	.71	.24	3.1
Means of all minority denials			.29	.40	55	.84	.30	3.8
526	0	1	.14	.15	49	.80	0	6
1855	0	1	.25	.32	62	.79	1	4
2234	0	1	.27	.39	57	.94	0	5
2152	1	0	.19	.22	24	.95	1	2
1217	0	1	.14	.20	88	.97	0	1

Table 20.6 CROSS-TABULATION OF DBETA ON MINORITY COEFFICIENT BY "APPROVED" VS. "DENIED"

DBETA	Approved	Denied
.10 to .13	0	18 (all minority)
.05 to .10	8	40
−.05 to .05	2301	255
−.10 to −.05	12	47
−.13 to −.10	1	4
	2322 +	364 = 2,686

Figure 20.1 PLOT OF DBETA ON MINORITY COEFFICIENT BY PEARSON RESIDUALS

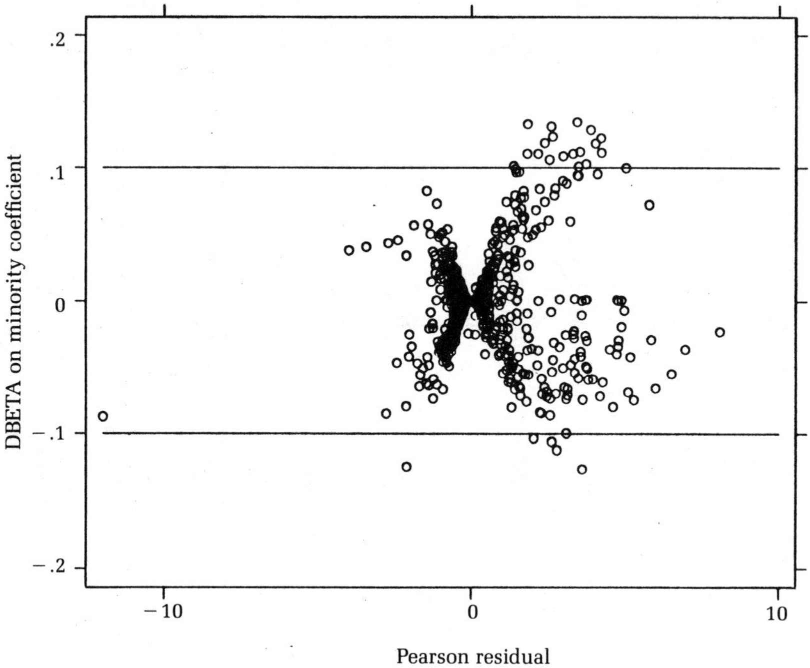

Notes: Pearson residual: mean = −.028; standard deviation = 1.034. DBETA on minority coefficient: mean = 0; standard deviation = .02. The Pearson residual for the jth observation is

$$\chi_i = \frac{r_j - \hat{p}_j}{\sqrt{\hat{p}_j(1 - \hat{p}_j)}},$$

where r_j is the observed ordered response (0 or 1), and $\hat{p}_j$ is the predicted probability that the jth application is denied.

model residuals to encounter the 23 cases with the highest influence on the minority coefficient. It is also worth noting that these critical cases are not those with the greatest leverage on the overall model. Their influence is focused on the minority coefficient.

Ideally, we would look at the loan folders of the extremely influential cases and determine if there are any coding errors and changes in model specification that would improve the model. For example, perhaps some of the low loan-to-value ratios are actually coding mistakes. Or perhaps the cases with the worst consumer credit history could be divided between recent, unexplained credit problems and older or explainable problems. Then rerunning the models with the new variables might show that the minority coefficient was picking up the effects of an omitted credit variable. Once the model has been revised, then the search can turn to uncovering patterns of apparent discrimination. If the number of folders to investigate is only 20 or 30, a lender is more likely to do the research and to find the patterns that are common to the cases of apparent disparate treatment. For this data set we did not have access to the original data files, so we proceeded under the assumptions that the data were coded correctly and that the model was correctly specified.

To gain a better sense of the significance of the extremely influential cases as a group, we experimented by dropping an increasing number of influential observations until the minority coefficient became no longer statistically significant. Of course, dropping a set of randomly chosen minority denials will also reduce the minority coefficient. However, since the critical influence cases are specifically chosen based on their impact on the minority coefficient, we expect that deleting the high-influence cases will have a much larger effect. Running the same three models presented in table 20.3 without the critical cases shows the impact that they have on the model as a group (see table 20.7). The only difference is that out of 2,686 cases, 23 with extreme influence on the minority coefficient have been deleted. We chose to delete 23 because that is the smallest number of extreme influence cases that make the minority coefficient not statistically significant at the 10 percent level of significance. The impact on the minority coefficient is dramatic. In the base model the minority coefficient drops from .60 (p-value of .0004) to .30 (p-value of .10). For comparison, if we had dropped the 23 minority denials with influence closest to the average influence for minority denials, the minority coefficient would decrease to .45, which is still significant at the 1 percent level. The point is that using influence statistics can make

Table 20.7 ALTERNATIVE SPECIFICATIONS ON PROBABILITY OF DENIAL AFTER DROPPING 23 MOST INFLUENTIAL CASES

Explanatory Variable	Base Model: Coefficient (std. error)	Add MINORTRC: Coefficient (std. error)	Add BOARDUP: Coefficient (std. error)
Constant	−4.30	−4.29	−4.23
	(.31)	(.31)	(.32)
BACKD34	.14	.14	.14
	(.01)	(.01)	(.01)
LOW_LTV	−.61	−.62	−.63
	(.24)	(.24)	(.24)
LTVLES80	5.20	5.19	5.15
	(1.90)	(1.90)	(1.90)
ADJUSTBL	−.59	−.58	−.59
	(.18)	(.18)	(.18)
INCONSS1	.57	.57	.57
	(.19)	(.19)	(.19)
INSUFFCH	.77	.75	.78
	(.35)	(.35)	(.35)
DELINQC	.66	.66	.67
	(.25)	(.25)	(.25)
SERDELNQ	1.33	1.33	1.34
	(.22)	(.22)	(.22)
INSUFFMH	.17	.17	.18
	(.21)	(.21)	(.21)
ONELATEM	1.27	1.28	1.27
	(.46)	(.46)	(.46)
TWOLATEM	1.41	1.42	1.39
	(.55)	(.55)	(.55)
PUBLREC	1.47	1.47	1.46
	(.22)	(.22)	(.22)
PMI_DEN	4.81	4.81	4.86
	(.56)	(.56)	(.57)

the search for the best candidates of apparent disparate treatment more efficient.

Columns 3 and 4 of table 20.7 show that the same dramatic decline in the minority coefficient occurs when neighborhood variables for high-minority tracts or boarded-up buildings are included. For this data set we can drive down the minority coefficient even more by deleting a few more high-influence cases. There is nothing magical about the breakpoint of 23 influential cases. A model deleting the 29 most influential cases (using an absolute value cutoff of .095) has a minority coefficient of .21 with a *p*-value of .27. The decline in value and significance of the minority coefficient after deleting fewer than 30 select cases suggests that the underwriting model for this smaller

Table 20.7 ALTERNATIVE SPECIFICATIONS ON PROBABILITY OF DENIAL AFTER DROPPING 23 MOST INFLUENTIAL CASES (continued)

Explanatory Variable	Base Model: Coefficient (std. error)	Add MINORTRC: Coefficient (std. error)	Add BOARDUP: Coefficient (std. error)
UNVERIF	3.28	3.28	3.30
	(.26)	(.26)	(.26)
SELF_EMP	.78	.79	.77
	(.23)	(.23)	(.23)
SF2_4	.43	.40	.45
	(.21)	(.22)	(.21)
OLD_NUM	.52	.51	.52
	(.17)	(.17)	(.17)
UNMARRY	.52	.52	.52
	(.17)	(.17)	(.17)
MINORTRC		.16	
		(.25)	
BOARDUP			−.15
			(.17)
MINORITY	.30	.24	.33
	(.18)	(.20)	(.19)
No. of cases	2,663	2,663	2,663
Log likelihood	−569	−569	−568
Percentage correct	92%	92%	92%
False-positive rate	22%	22%	22%
False-negative rate	7%	7%	7%
Hosmer-Lemeshow p-value[a]	0.24	0.27	0.48

a. See table 20.3, note *b* for a description of the Hosmer-Lemeshow goodness-of-fit statistic (Hosmer and Lemeshow 1989: 140–45).

set of influential cases differs in important ways from the rest of the sample.

The entire vector of DBETA values can be correlated with other variables to learn more about situations conducive to possible disparate treatment. The correlations showed that the LTV ratio is negatively correlated with the minority DBETA. Low-LTV loans are more likely to receive apparent disparate treatment than high-LTV loans. To test this idea, we split the sample into low-LTV cases (with LTV less than or equal to .80) and high-LTV cases. Regressions were run on the low- and high-LTV subsamples, including the high-influence cases that were dropped before. The object was to see if cases of apparent disparate treatment could be localized in low loan-to-value applications.

The left half of table 20.8 shows the low-LTV results, and the right half shows the high-LTV results.[8] The results indicate that discriminatory denials are clearly concentrated among applications with low loan-to-value ratios. The estimated minority coefficient for these cases is 1.26 (with a *p*-value of 0.0001). This is more than five times the estimated coefficient for high loan-to-value applications—a statistically significant and substantial difference. Indeed, the estimated minority coefficient for low loan-to-value applications is both relatively modest (0.24) and not significantly different from zero (*p*-value of 0.27). The 95 percent confidence interval of the minority coefficient in high loan-to-value applications runs from −0.19 to 0.67. Thus, given the available sample, we can neither reject the hypothesis that there is no disparate treatment in high LTV applications nor the hypothesis of substantial disparate treatment. It is, however, clear that disparate treatment is much more severe among low loan-to-value applications.

This finding has important implications both for our understanding of discriminatory effects and for potential actions to redress them. The revised specification does not support a hypothesis of general or systemic prejudice, but, rather, locates clearly discriminatory effects among low loan-to-value applications. The mechanisms behind this may, of course, involve variables other than the low loan-to-value ratio. However, the obvious suggestion is that underwriters may be discounting the security provided by low-LTV minority applicants and that both regulators and managers could most effectively address the discriminatory treatment found in the Boston Fed study by taking steps to improve risk assessment for low loan-to-value mortgages and to remedy any racially or ethnically based assessments of risk.[9]

One of the features of influence statistics most valuable to lenders is that the statistics can be used to flag certain new applications still being processed that, if denied, would appear to receive disparate treatment. The process is simple enough to allow applications to be checked before a final decision is made, enabling higher-level reviews to avoid mistakes in underwriting. The approach deletes the extremely influential cases such that the minority coefficient is not significant, and then tests each new application to see if including it would increase the minority coefficient. If a new application is seen as being highly influential (similar to the influential cases that had been deleted), then this new application can be referred for higher levels of review. Again, it is important that the number of applications flagged for review be quite small, so that managers can focus attention on the few extreme cases. The nonflagged new applications can be added to

Table 20.8 PROBABILITY OF DENIAL, MODELED SEPARATELY FOR HIGH- AND LOW-LTV CASES ON FULL SAMPLE

Explanatory Variables	Low-LTV Cases (LTV ≤ .80): Coefficient (std. error)	High-LTV Cases (LTV > .80): Coefficient (std. error)
BACKD34	.10	.19
	(.02)	(.02)
LOAN/VAL	1.04	2.54
	(.88)	(1.00)
ADJUSTBL	−.26	−.68
	(.27)	(.23)
INCONSS1	.67	.45
	(.28)	(.24)
INSUFFCH	.16	1.07
	(.55)	(.44)
DELINQC	.23	1.00
	(.47)	(.29)
SERDELNQ	1.10	1.37
	(.36)	(.27)
INSUFFMH	−.10	.59
	(.28)	(.32)
ONELATEM	.97	1.24
	(.62)	(.71)
TWOLATEM	1.19	2.01
	(.72)	(.85)
PUBLREC	.89	1.64
	(.39)	(.27)
PMI_DEN	5.08	4.38
	(1.13)	(.57)
UNVERIF	3.27	3.05
	(.36)	(.36)
SELF_EMP	.49	.80
	(.31)	(.33)
SF2_4	.65	.37
	(.36)	(.25)
OLD_NUM	.61	.36
	(.26)	(.21)
UNMARRY	.37	.50
	(.26)	(.21)
MINORITY	1.26	.24
	(.27)	(.22)
No. of cases	1,471	1,215
Log likelihood	−269	−338
Percentage correct	94%	89%
False-positive rate	24%	18%
False-negative rate	6%	10%
Hosmer-Lemeshow *p*-value[a]	.92	.61

a. See table 20.3, note *b*, for a description of the Hosmer-Lemeshow goodness-of-fit statistic (Hosmer and Lemeshow 1989: 140–45).

the data set and the oldest cases aged out, so that the model coefficients are gradually updated in line with the latest underwriting guidelines. The real-time review feature means that influence statistics help managers not only to uncover the mistakes of the past but to avoid mistakes in the future.

CONCLUSIONS

Lenders and regulators need a strategy for identifying cases of disparate treatment in mortgage lending. Although no completely unbiased method has been found to determine disparate treatment, lenders and regulators must make judgments based on available data and techniques. This chapter has demonstrated that influence statistics can be used to identify those cases that contribute the most to a statistical indication of apparent disparate treatment. When applied to Boston Fed study data, the influence statistics method highlighted 30 cases out of 2,700, which were applications by minorities that did not appear to fit the underwriting criteria used on applications by whites. This number of critical cases is small enough so that managers can review the original loan folders to see if the decisions represent a general pattern or are concentrated in some way.

It is important to note that these results do not mean that the Boston Fed study's finding of discrimination is based on only 30 cases. All of the cases contribute to the estimate of the minority coefficient, which measures the average gap between minorities and whites after controlling for differences in the other independent variables. Moreover, disparate treatment could be affecting many minority applicants not highlighted by a ranking of the influence statistics. Nevertheless, influence statistics can provide a useful starting point for an investigation of disparate treatment.

Highly influential cases can be examined for common patterns. For example, in the Boston Fed study data, 19 of the 23 most influential cases had LTVs at or below .80. Further investigation showed that there was no statistical indication of disparate treatment among high-LTV cases, but that there was a strong minority effect among low-LTV cases, despite their generally perceived lower risk. Additional research is needed to determine if these features of the Boston data are replicated in other data sets.

Influence statistics can help managers or regulators identify both specific cases and patterns among these cases that may have been associated with disparate treatment in the past. Exploring these cases can help assess the form in which the apparent disparate treatment occurs and point to appropriate remedies. If discrimination appears widespread, remedies would include reviews of procedures, and general education and training of staff. If discrimination appears to be restricted to a particular category of loans or underwriting factors, remedial efforts can be focused much more specifically on efforts to understand and correct the problem.

Moreover, it is possible to use the mortgage lending model to check decisions on pending applications to determine if any of them would be highly influential if denied. In this way, lenders not only learn from the mistakes of the past but use that knowledge combined with the computer model to avoid cases of apparent disparate treatment in the future.

Notes

1. Fair Housing Act, Title VIII of the Civil Rights Act of 1968, as amended, 42 U.S.C. 3601 *et seq.*

2. Equal Credit Opportunity Act of 1974 (ECOA), as amended, 15 U.S.C. 1691 *et seq.*

3. It can be shown, however, that given the usual pattern of relatively low denial rates overall and minority applications representing a relatively small fraction of total applications, one would expect minority denials to have the highest weight in affecting the minority coefficient on denials.

4. Belsley, Kuh, and Welsch (1980) developed the idea of influence statistics for OLS models. Pregibon (1981) extended the concepts for logistic regression. The notation follows the SAS Institute presentation (*SAS/STAT User's Guide* [1990: 1094]). Both SAS and Stata software were used in the application to Boston Fed data.

5. One of the potential problems with the DBETA version of influence statistics is that the influential points could be *clustered* together, meaning close together in *k*-dimensional space, assuming *k* explanatory variables. DBETA measures the impact of removing any single observation. Suppose there were several high-leverage points positioned close to one another. The impact of removing a single point in that cluster would be far less than if the other points in the cluster were not so close. In effect, the DBETA measure of influence may miss the situations in which a single observation is not highly influential but a small group of observations are influential. Perhaps this could happen in mortgage lending if the discriminatory decisions all occurred because one underwriter thought loans to minority households in a particular neighborhood were risky. It is then possible that the DBETA ranking of any single application in that cluster would be low enough to escape notice.

6. Note that the Hosmer-Lemeshow (1989) goodness-of-fit statistic shows that the models with neighborhood measures fit better than the base model even though the log likelihood and percentage correct are unchanged. The models with neighborhood mea-

sures fit somewhat better in the top two deciles. The expected probabilities for these two groups are virtually the same, but the sorting by decile shifts a few denials into the top category and suggests that the Hosmer-Lemeshow statistic can be sensitive to changes in grouping.

7. Moreover, the extreme cases exceed the Belsley et al. (1980: 28) benchmark of $2/\sqrt{n}$, or .038, but this guide was designed for ordinary least squares.

8. The results presented in table 20.8 used the values in the loan-to-value variable provided in the Boston Federal Reserve public-use data set, rather than the recoded variable used in earlier exhibits that adjusted for LTVs above 1.0. We wanted to guarantee that the findings for the split sample were not driven by our imputations. The variable SET__LTV uses the purchase price in place of the appraised value in the few cases where the loan-to-value listed in the public use data set exceeds 1.0. The variable LOAN/VAL is the loan-to-value as listed in the public use data set. In fact, using the LOAN/VAL variable rather than the imputed SET__LTV increased the minority coefficient for the low-LTV equation from 1.04 (standard error, 0.24) to 1.26 (standard error 0.27).

9. The mechanisms involved still need to be explored. For example, underwriters might discount minority loan-to-value ratios if they expect minority property values to fluctuate more than nonminority properties due to changes in the racial mix of the neighborhood. The underwriters might be concerned that neighborhood transitions could lead to higher default rates among minority borrowers. A more mundane version of the discounting would arise if low-LTV loans denied to minorities were often for low dollar amounts. Lenders might feel that the fixed costs of handling a loan were not adequately covered even though the default risk is slight.

References

Belsley, D., E. Kuh, and R. Welsch. 1980. *Regression Diagnostics: Identifying Influential Data and Sources of Collinearity*. New York: John Wiley & Sons.

Canner, G.B., and D.S. Smith. 1991. "Home Mortgage Disclosure Act: Expanded Data on Residential Lending." *Federal Reserve Bulletin* 77 (November): 859–81.

———. 1992. "Expanded Data on Residential Lending: One Year Later." *Federal Reserve Bulletin* 78 (November): 801–24.

Canner, G.B., W. Passmore, and D.S. Smith. 1994. "Residential Lending to Low-Income and Minority Families: Evidence from the 1992 HMDA Data." *Federal Reserve Bulletin* 80 (February): 79–108.

Carr, J.H., and I.F. Megbolugbe. 1993. "The Federal Reserve Bank of Boston Study on Mortgage Lending Revisited." *Journal of Housing Research* 4(2): 277–314.

Glennon, D., and M. Stengel. 1994. "An Evaluation of the Federal Reserve Bank of Boston's Study of Racial Discrimination in Mortgage Lending." Office of the Comptroller of the Currency, Working Paper 94-2. Washington, D.C.: Office of the Comptroller of the Currency.

Horne, D.K. 1994. "Evaluating the Role of Race in Mortgage Lending." *FDIC Banking Review* 7(1): 1–15.

Hosmer, D.W. and S. Lemeshow. 1989. *Applied Logistic Regression*. New York: John Wiley & Sons.

Liebowitz, S., and T. Day. 1993. "A Study That Deserves No Credit." *Wall Street Journal*, September 1, p. A14.

Maddala, G.S., and R.P. Trost. 1982. "On Measuring Discrimination in Loan Markets." *Housing Finance Review* 1(3) July: 245–68.

Munnell, A.H., L.E. Browne, J. McEneaney, and G.M.B. Tootell. 1992. "Mortgage Lending in Boston: Interpreting HMDA Data." Federal Reserve Bank of Boston Working Paper No. 92-07. Federal Reserve Bank of Boston, October.

Phillips, R.F., and A.M. Yezer. 1995. "Self-Selection and Measurement of Bias and Risk in Mortgage Lending: Can You Price the Mortgage If You Don't Know the Process?" Paper presented at the annual meetings of the American Real Estate and Urban Economics Association, January 5–7, Washington, D.C.

Pregibon, D. 1981. "Logistic Regression Diagnostics." *Annals of Statistics* 9: 705–24.

Rachlis, M.B., and A.M.J. Yezer. 1993. "Serious Flaws in Statistical Tests for Discrimination in Mortgage Markets." *Journal of Housing Research* 4(2): 315–36.

SAS Institute Inc. 1990. *SAS/STAT User's Guide*, vers. 6, 4th ed., vol. 2. Cary, N.C.: SAS Institute.

Stengel, M., and D. Glennon. 1995. "Evaluating Statistical Models of Mortgage Lending Discrimination: A Bank-Specific Analysis." Office of the Comptroller of the Currency, Economic and Policy Analysis Working Paper 95-3, Washington, D.C.: Office of the Comptroller of the Currency, May.

Yezer, A.M.J., R.F. Phillips, and R.P. Trost. 1994. "Bias in Estimates of Discrimination and Default in Mortgage Lending: The Effects of Simultaneity and Self-Selection." *Journal of Real Estate Finance and Economics* 9: 197–215.

Chapter Twenty-One

A PRACTICAL MODEL FOR INVESTIGATING MORTGAGE LENDING DISCRIMINATION BY FINANCIAL INSTITUTIONS

Richard W. Cole

The Federal Reserve Bank of Boston's comprehensive 1992 study of mortgage lending discrimination (Munnell et al. 1992, 1996) has been applauded by mortgage lenders, enforcement agencies, regulators, and minority communities for having conclusively documented a disturbing pattern of mortgage lending discrimination by banks and mortgage companies in the Boston metropolitan statistical area (MSA). The first Federal Reserve study to address this area of discrimination was conducted in 1989, using Home Mortgage Disclosure Act (HMDA) data exclusively; that study was severely criticized for failing to consider a number of factors used by lenders in making residential mortgage lending decisions (Bradbury et al. 1989). Primarily as a result of substantial lender participation in developing a statistical model that identifies and analyzes 38 factors involved in mortgage lending decisions, the 1992 Federal study (known as the "Boston Fed" study) has been described as ending the debate on whether discrimination exists in the mortgage lending industry.

But the Boston Fed study had its limitations. It identified only one individual lending institution with statistically significant racial disparities in its lending patterns, resulting in a referral to the Department of Justice for investigation. The study did not address applicant flow or the reasons for the substantial number of applicant withdrawals and their potential relationship to race. In addition it did not scrutinize the role of private mortgage insurers in producing the higher denial rates for minorities. However, the most important conclusion of the study was that in reviewing the overall pattern of residential mortgage lending by 131 lending institutions in the Boston MSA, there was a significantly higher rejection rate for black and Hispanic applicants for residential mortgages as compared to similarly situated white applicants (Munnell et al. 1992, 1996).

The Boston Fed study's analysis of lending data for the year 1990 for applicants with the same economic and property characteristics revealed that blacks and Hispanics were 60 percent more likely than whites to be denied mortgages. The minority denial rate was 17 percent compared to an 11 percent denial rate for white applicants (a ratio of roughly 1.6 to 1). In a surprising result, the study also found that 80 percent of total applicants failed to meet all the requirements of the secondary market and that lenders exercised discretion in determining which of the 80 percent with some application defects were approved for a loan (Munnell et al. 1992, 1996).

Some financial institutions that participated in the Boston Fed study and were later targeted for investigation by the Massachusetts Attorney General's office, based on the results of the study, argued that it was unfair to reach any conclusion about their lending practices because the study was based on an analysis of the general pool of minority and white applicants for all lending institutions in the Boston MSA, and not a comparison of any one institution's minority and white applicants. They maintained that each institution used broad discretion in approving loans. They also contended that although the study identified individual loans that may have been inappropriately denied, only careful analysis and comparison of their own institution's practices regarding its white and minority applicants could fairly determine whether there was any statistical or other valid evidence of a pattern of discrimination.

This chapter addresses these potential concerns by recommending certain investigation or review protocols for law enforcement agencies and regulators who are committed to eliminating disparate treatment discrimination as well as practices that have a discriminatory effect in the mortgage lending industry.[1] Two areas of mortgage lending practices by financial institutions should be examined to evaluate whether a pattern of discrimination exists. First, all information related to applicant flow should be reviewed; and second, the post-application mortgage approval process should be investigated.

ANALYSIS AND REVIEW OF APPLICANT FLOW DATA AND PRACTICES

A major problem highlighted, although not addressed by the Federal Reserve study, was the extremely low number and percentage of blacks and Hispanics who applied for a residential mortgage loan from banks and mortgage companies in the Boston MSA in 1990. The Boston Fed study analyzed data from 131 lending institutions in the Boston MSA that received at least 25 mortgage applications from borrowers of all races and that served the cities and towns of the Boston MSA. The study found that only 1,210 blacks and Hispanics out of 18,838 total applicants applied for a residential mortgage loan in 1990 (6.4 percent of the total applicant flow) (Munnell et al. 1992, 19, 21).

It is critically important to identify why virtually all the financial institutions that serve and are often based in cities with large minority populations have an extraordinarily low number of minority applicants as compared to white applicants. For example, in the Boston MSA in 1990, the black and Hispanic populations in Boston comprised 36.38 percent of the total population; in Cambridge 20.29 percent; in Brockton 19.28 percent; in Lynn 17.20 percent; in Chelsea 36.41 percent; and in Framingham 11.84 percent. (According to the U.S. Bureau of the Census, about 15 percent of the overall Boston MSA in 1990 was minority.) Although many of the larger banking institutions are primarily based in Suffolk County, which includes Boston and is 33.44 percent black and Hispanic, the size of the resident minority population was in striking contrast to the minority applicant flow for most of those institutions in 1990. Almost all had less than 6 percent black and Hispanic loan applicants.

The mortgage lending industry has argued that any lack of access to mortgage lending is not caused by intentional discrimination, since it would be illogical for a lender to disregard the strong economic incentives and profits that can be earned by encouraging qualified minorities to obtain mortgage loans. The industry maintains that even if the number of minority applicants may appear to reflect that a lending institution is uninterested or even resistant to doing business with blacks and Hispanics or in minority communities, such an impression is inaccurate since these figures are misleading and can be explained by factors unrelated to discrimination by financial institutions. It has been stated that no rational lender would turn down a perfectly good application simply because the applicant is a member of a minority group. On the other hand, community residents have complained that they have been victims of discrimination.

A number of reasons or perceptions, even if inaccurate or invalid, may cause a financial institution to take a passive approach to providing loans to minorities. First, there may be a perception that the institution's efforts will be wasted since a much lower percentage of minority applicants will actually be approved for loans than white applicants because of constraints imposed by the secondary market, the demands of private mortgage insurers, and declining property values in minority communities. Second, there may be a belief that minority loans will be smaller and therefore less economically worthwhile for originators paid by commission, particularly when compared to the time expended in obtaining loan approvals. Third, there may be a perception that an inordinate amount of time will be expended in ensuring that appropriate documentation is obtained for minority applicant approval as compared to that for white applicants. Fourth, there may be a subjective belief that many more minority borrowers than whites will be unwilling or unable to pay the mortgage loans that are granted.

Community advocates argue that the denial of minority applicants is often based not on objective evidence but on "subjective doubt," which is based on impermissible stereotypes. It is difficult to prove such discrimination because direct statements of the intent to discriminate or of bias or prejudice do not occur. Instead, discrimination must be inferred from the circumstances.

A prima facie case of discrimination may be proved by indirect evidence through statistics. Similar to the recognized probative value of statistics in employment discrimination cases, three related probability analyses of minority applicant flow may permit the inference that a lending institution is engaging in a pattern of discrimination. This statistical evidence may be considered when determining the legitimacy of the reasons offered by a financial institution for its low minority applicant flow. In employment discrimination cases, a prima facie case of discrimination is proven if statistical measures determine that the racial composition of an employer's work force significantly deviates from that of the qualified labor pool in the relevant labor market area. "In many cases the only available avenue of proof is the use of racial statistics to uncover clandestine and covert discrimination by the employer or union involved."[2]

Comparing HMDA applicant flow data and 1990 U.S. Census population data may identify institutions with a discriminatory lending record. A statistical analysis of a lending institution's record of minority applicants, compared to the number and percentage of income-eligible blacks and Hispanics residing in the census tracts within the institution's designated service area, could result in the inference that an institution is engaged in a pattern of discrimination. Discrimination may be proven by statistical evidence if a significant disparity exists between the percentage of blacks and Hispanics in the general population residing in the census tracts in the lender's designated service area who can reasonably be considered as income eligible to apply for a mortgage loan, as compared to the actual percentage who applied. Consistent with judicial rulings in employment discrimination cases, if the measured difference is greater than two or three standard deviations, it would be highly probative in proving that lending decisions were not made without regard to the race of the applicant.[3]

In addition, to measure whether the low number of minority applicants could be explained by lower-income levels, the percentages of income-eligible blacks, Hispanics, and whites residing in the census tracts within the designated service area of a financial institution in each income bracket could be compared to the percentages of blacks, Hispanics, and whites who filed applications with the lending institution in 1990 (or any other year). For many institutions, the results are likely to show a statistically significant difference in the percentage of blacks and Hispanics as compared to whites who applied for mortgage loans within each income bracket, resulting in the inference of discriminatory practices by the lending institution.

A third statistical approach would be to compare the percentage of market share a lender has of black and Hispanic loan applications within its CRA (Community Reinvestment Act) designated (or effective) service area to the percentage market share held by other mortgage lending institutions serving the same or similar geographic areas or census tracts. If the mortgage lender being examined has a disproportionately smaller percentage of the market share of minority loan applicants than one or more other mortgage lenders, it would reflect prima facie evidence of discriminatory operations at the institution at the pre-application and origination stage of its mortgage lending process.

These three separate statistical tests would be relevant and probative in proving discrimination by any financial institution regarding its accessibility to blacks and Hispanics.

For many financial institutions located in urban centers, it is highly unlikely that the low percentage of minority applicants could be occurring by chance, especially since the proportion of income-eligible minorities in the general population in most urban areas is substantially above actual applicant flow levels. The probable explanation for the difference is that lending institutions have discriminated against minorities in their overall accessibility, their pre-application counseling, and their outreach and advertising programs. Based on these statistical approaches, it is highly improbable that, for many institutions, these statistical differences could have occurred by chance.

Indirect evidence, whether historical, comparative, or individual, may support the results of a statistical analysis finding significant disparities in treatment of minorities. This indirect evidence of discrimination may include:

- A lending institution's systematic use of different rules or standards for prospective applicants who are black or Hispanic as compared to white applicants
- Differential treatment of prospective minority applicants as compared to white applicants (for example, by providing less pre- or post-application loan counseling information and services to blacks and Hispanics as compared to whites, or by furnishing more assistance or encouragement to white applicants to obtain the documentation to explain problem areas such as items of poor credit history or instability of income as compared to blacks and Hispanics
- The lending institution's record of and general practices and policies concerning recruitment and employment of racial and linguistic minorities
- The failure to follow generally recognized, effective outreach and advertising practices of financial institutions that have a much higher number of minority applicants
- The mortgage lender's compensation structures
- The lender's record of fair lending and diversity training of its staff

A number of factors should be examined to determine if an institution's policies or practices contribute to the failure to attract minority applicants, including the following:

- The lending institution's designation of the communities it serves and whether it includes contiguous minority communities or neighborhoods
- The mortgage lender's effective service area (where it actually originates loans) and whether it fails to serve the minority communities or census tracts designated under the CRA
- The number of full-service branches, loan offices, and lending services located in minority communities and census tracts (so applicants can readily apply for loans and submit the necessary documents), and comparing it to other lenders serving similar geographic areas
- The record of branch or office closings in minority communities or census tracts
- The methods used for outreach and marketing to the communities in which the financial institution does business, including the nature and extent of its advertising of products and marketing in the minority communities it serves (as compared to concentrating its advertising and outreach to primarily white communities)

- The outreach to real estate brokers serving minority as compared to white communities
- The extent to which the institution has developed or has loan products to attract and to satisfy the needs of minority communities, and how its products compare to those offered by other lenders serving the same or similar geographic areas
- Its record of minority hiring including the number and percentage of minority loan originators and underwriters employed by the institution
- Whether the institution engages in comprehensive, ongoing fair lending and diversity training of staff to serve the credit needs of minorities
- Whether minorities are inappropriately being discouraged or turned away before filing an application (determined by reviewing inquiry logs kept by the institution, by interviewing the prospective customers, or by contacting real estate agents and brokers who serve the minority community)
- Whether the lender has minimum loan requirements that will likely serve to disproportionately affect the provision of loans to blacks and Hispanics
- Whether loan originators work on straight commission, thereby providing a disincentive to serve individual borrowers seeking smaller loan amounts
- Whether larger commissions or financial incentives are provided to mortgage originators and account executives to solicit additional minority applicants
- Whether the lending institution sponsors regular community education mortgage seminars in minority communities to increase knowledge of and interest in mortgage loans among residents
- Whether translated materials about the lender's application process is available for those who do not speak English fluently, and who reside in the CRA designated service area

Testers could also be sent to lending institutions to identify problems more precisely and to determine if minorities are discouraged from applying for a mortgage loan or are counseled differently than similarly situated prospective white applicants.

ANALYSIS AND REVIEW OF DISCRIMINATION IN THE UNDERWRITING AND LOAN APPROVAL PROCESS

Separate from the review of the pre-application practices of a lending institution, it is also critical to engage in a careful evaluation of post-application practices and policies to determine if discrimination exists at this stage of the mortgage lending process.

The Justice Department Model for Analyzing Residential Mortgage Lending Discrimination

One method for determining whether an institution has engaged in a pattern of mortgage lending discrimination in loan application processing is to adopt the U.S. Department of Justice (DOJ) model, which was successfully used against Decatur Federal Savings and Loan Association in Atlanta in 1992.[4] This approach requires an extremely costly, comprehensive, resource-intensive review of an institution, including the retaining of experts and the training of individuals who must expend an enormous commitment of time to carefully and painstakingly review every mortgage file in the institution. Then, for each file, every factor, such as income, employment, credit history, loan-to-value ratio, and neighborhood characteristics, used by the lender in making the residential lending decision must be identified and accurately recorded and the data entered into a computer. This methodology then requires experts to identify and apply weights to all the variables used by that institution to make loan decisions, through a logit multiple regression analysis. Investigators must also comprehensively review all documents from the financial institution that are at all relevant to its mortgage lending policies and practices. Finally, the model requires the use of this expensive computer software program (developed by expert consultants retained by DOJ in its Decatur Federal lawsuit), to statistically analyze the data to determine if race was a significant factor in mortgage loan underwriting by the lender.

In February 1993 then Acting Assistant Attorney General of the Civil Rights Division, James P. Turner, in testimony before a Senate Committee, maintained that DOJ's model was the only reliable method available to analyze data collected from mortgage lenders to determine whether individual lenders have engaged in a pattern or practice of discrimination against black or Hispanic applicants (Turner 1993). Apparently, DOJ was unwilling at that time to rely on the model used by the Federal Reserve Bank of Boston for its statistical analysis in its 1992 study (Munnell et al. 1992, 1996).

Most state enforcement agencies and regulators are unable to adopt this model because the price, as well as time and resources required, are prohibitive. More pointedly, exclusive reliance on DOJ legal enforcement, no matter how effective in combating discrimination on an individual institutional basis such as in the Decatur suit, precludes broad-based, coordinated enforcement efforts by federal and state agencies and regulators. Effective elimination of discrimination in mortgage lending cannot realistically be expected to depend solely on DOJ's limited ability to investigate and pursue these complex, time-consuming legal cases and on the relatively small legal staff DOJ assigns to these matters.

The Federal Reserve's Statistical Model for Investigating Lending Practices of Institutions

A second technique for determining whether a financial institution has engaged in a pattern of discrimination in its mortgage lending on the basis of race is to rely upon the Federal Reserve Bank of Boston's statistical model (Munnell et al. 1992, 1996). The model includes detailed data collection, examination of all rejected minority loan files and a selective sampling of white loan files. Through identification of and entry of thirty-eight variables from each file a statistical analysis of the data is performed to determine if race is a factor in the lender's mortgage lending decisions. (The Boston Fed model identified and applied thirty-eight standard factors used across the industry in mortgage loan decisionmaking. It does not require the application of a logit regression analysis on an institution-by-institution basis, as the DOJ Decatur model does.)

A new federal law, which would modify the HMDA requirements to mandate that all financial institutions receiving a minimum number of mortgage applications must report information similar to that voluntarily disclosed by lenders for the Boston study, would significantly reduce investigators' burden of data collection and recording. Of course, investigators would then have to rely upon the financial institution's own collection and recording of data from individual files, a process often fraught with errors, as has been pointed out in regard to HMDA data reporting.

Otherwise, in investigating or reviewing the mortgage lending practices of a financial institution, a similar process of file review, analysis, and data entry must occur. In this model, documentation of a financial institution's overall lending practices must also be reviewed and evaluated. To successfully complete this review, the Federal Reserve or a similar computer software program would have to be made accessible or purchased by states, which is not currently the case. Some private companies now offer such software capabilities for significantly less cost than the three hundred to five hundred thousand dollar cost of the DOJ model. Some state Attorneys General offices are now exploring such a purchase. Additional cost would be incurred, however, to review the files and to input the data.

If a statistically significant disparity is identified between rejected black and Hispanic applicants as compared to whites, one would be able to conclude that an illegal pattern of lending discrimination is present. A more comprehensive review of lending practices would corroborate this statistical finding. However, a pattern of discrimination against any individual institution cannot be proved through either the DOJ's or the Federal Reserve's statistical model if the financial institution does not have a sufficient pool of rejected minority applicants to compare with a sample of similarly situated white applicants.

Alternative Method for Detecting Discriminatory Patterns

A significantly less expensive and less resource-intensive review of a financial institution's mortgage lending practice, similar to that used in employment discrimination cases, is a reliable alternative to either the DOJ or the Federal Reserve models. This model first requires review and analysis of the files of all minority applicants who were denied a mortgage by the financial institution. Each rejection must then be placed into one of three categories:

- Minority applicants who were denied a mortgage even though they satisfied the secondary market or lender's underwriting guidelines, the standards of private mortgage insurance, and other requirements (reflecting a strong case of discrimination)
- Minority applicants who failed to meet the standards so as to have precluded the application of discretion or flexibility available to the lending institution to approve the mortgage, as dictated by the secondary market or private mortgage insurers or by the eligibility requirements for the special products offered by the institution
- Minority applicants who failed to meet all secondary market standard or eligibility requirements for the special products made available by the lender, but who could have been approved for a loan within the discretion of the institution. (The Boston Fed study [Munnell, et al. 1992, 1996] found that 80 percent of all loan applicants fell into this category.)

For those black and Hispanic applicants who were rejected and who fell within the third category just cited, the lending institution should be asked to identify all white applicants who were approved but had similar characteristics. Otherwise a cursory review of a sample of approved white applicant loan files will be necessary to identify those whites who were similarly situated. This more limited group of comparable minority and white applicant files (or a random sampling of similar white applicants) should then be carefully reviewed and analyzed to identify whether blacks and whites in similar circumstances were treated similarly. The investigators should focus on the reasons the institution offered the rejected borrower for its denial, by reviewing the adverse action notice form in the file. Using this method, a state law enforcement agency or regulator should be able to determine if the institution has applied different approval standards for blacks and Hispanics as compared to whites; if white applicants have been extended special consideration, assistance, or counseling; if average processing time was longer for blacks and Hispanics; or if white applicants have been encouraged to provide more documentation to address concerns of the lender not extended to similarly situated black or Hispanic applicants.

If evidence from this review indicates a difference in treatment, individual minority applicants should be contacted and interviewed to learn if any felt they had been discouraged, mistreated or had received disparate treatment from the financial institution's personnel. This information should provide further insight into the financial institution's loan processing and loan approval practices to minorities and the manner in which discretion was applied.

Combined with the statistical evidence regarding applicant flow, evidence of the bank's overall lending practices and business interest in the minority community, the absence of internal systems to ensure fair lending, the institution's employment record toward minorities, its staff training programs, and other relevant information, this comparative review of rejected minority applicant files and selected white applicant files can be helpful in proving either individual cases of or a pattern of discrimination.

Adopting this approach would significantly increase the effective review of financial institutions' mortgage lending practices. Although not nearly so comprehensive an investigative model as that of DOJ or even the Federal Reserve Bank of Boston model, the approach still accomplishes the goal shared by enforcement agencies, regulators, minority communities, as well as the lending industry itself: that of detecting and eradicating discrimination in the residential mortgage industry.

Notes

1. The views expressed in this chapter are solely those of the author and do not necessarily reflect the views of the Attorney General or the Office of the Attorney General of Massachusetts.

2. *International Bro. of Teamsters* v. *United States*, 431 U.S. 324, 337–344. (1977).

3. *Hazelwood School District* v. *United States*, 433 U.S. 299, 308–309, n.14 (1977).

4. *United States of America* v. *Decatur Federal Savings and Loan Association*, N.D. Ga., No. 1-92 CV2128 (Sept. 17, 1992).

References

Bradbury, Katherine L., Karl E. Case, and Constance R. Dunham. 1989. "Geographic Patterns of Mortgage Lending in Boston, 1982–87." *New England Economic Review* (September/October): 3–30.

Munnell, Alicia H., Lynn E. Browne, James McEneaney, and Geoffrey M. B. Tootell. 1992. "Mortgage Lending in Boston: Interpreting HMDA Data." Federal Reserve Bank of Boston Working Paper 92-7. Boston: Federal Reserve Bank of Boston, October.

Munnell, Alicia H., Geoffrey M. B. Tootell, Lynn E. Browne, and James McEneaney. 1996. "Mortgage Lending in Boston: Interpreting HMDA Data." *American Economic Review*. Forthcoming.

Turner, James P., Acting Assistant Attorney General Civil Rights Division, Department of Justice. 1993. Testimony before the Committee on Banking, Housing and Urban Affairs, United States Senate, concerning mortgage lending discrimination (presented on February 24, 1993). 103rd Cong., 1st Sess. 534.

REVIEWING LOAN FILES FOR MORTGAGE LENDING DISCRIMINATION

Zina Gefter Greene

Whether looking at Home Mortgage Disclosure Act[1] (HMDA) patterns, rejection rates, testing, or through the loan files, discrimination is generally found by comparing treatment of minorities to non-minorities in like circumstances. In reviewing HMDA patterns, one needs to compare like census tracts, differentiated only by race. In testing, one should examine minority and non-minority testers with the same financial characteristics, and compare their treatment. The same is true in reviewing loan files—discrimination is found by comparing treatment of like situated minority and non-minority applicants.

The first part of this chapter explains the importance of beginning a loan file review with the bottom line, i.e., external patterns. If HMDA data shows a significantly lower mortgage participation rate of minorities; or a lower participation rate in minority neighborhoods; or if the rejection rates of minorities are significantly higher than non-minorities; or if testing shows evidence of discrimination, one will find evidence in the files that normal market forces are being skewed by actions taken by the lender. Also, external data and testing may produce clues to the types of discrimination found in the loan files.

The second part examines the application process from loan origination to decision-making, identifying where and how discrimination can occur at each stage. The third part examines the loan file for the crucial pieces of information, their location in the file, what to analyze, and how to use a database to look for differential treatment. And part four recommends a three part remedy: individual remedy to victims; neighborhood remedy to minority neighborhoods; and affirmative action to correct and overcome the effects of past discrimination.

This chapter reprinted courtesy of The John Marshall Law School.

PREPARING FOR REVIEW OF LOAN FILES

Discrimination rarely occurs in isolated instances. One will rarely be able to just grab a file and say, "Here it is, I have found discrimination." Throughout an analysis, one must look for patterns of differential treatment to support individual cases. Thus, the perpetual question is: Are minority applicants treated differently from non-minority applicants? To answer this question, one needs to compare the treatment of minority and non-minority applicants.

When discrimination exists in the loan files, an external pattern usually exists as well. Such patterns emerge when HMDA data are mapped, rejection rates are compared, the LOG as well as a lender's marketing techniques are analyzed, and finally, through testing. All of these patterns provide valuable clues as to what one will find in the files. Proper review of this information will assist in analyzing the files and supporting one's findings.

From HMDA, one can observe whether the lender is not making conventional loans in minority census tracts, while making these loans in similar non-minority tracts. If that is the case, then one knows to look for three sources of evidence. First, one needs to ascertain whether the lenders limit their marketing mainly to non-minority areas. Second, one must test for evidence that minority applicants are discouraged at the loan origination stage. Third, where HMDA shows a significantly higher rejection rate for minorities, one must examine the files to discover if there is a longer processing time for loans, and/or if different standards, requirements, or terms are applied to minorities as compared to non-minorities. Analyzing rejection rates reveals if discrimination is occurring uniformly among minority applicants or if discrimination occurs more frequently in minority census tracts. This analysis helps determine how to select a sample of loan files and whether to focus on minority census tracts as well as on minorities in general. Testing experience shows that black applicants in black neighborhoods face the greatest level of discrimination.

Testing is important for many reasons. First, testing is important because if discrimination occurs, it is reasonable to assume that the bulk of it occurs where there is no record: before an applicant submits an application. Second, testing provides quick evidence of different treatment based on underwriting standards; it is here that the standards are bent for white applicants and held rigid for minority applicants. Commonly, these standards include items such as debt ratios, minimum house or loan size, adequacy of cash reserves, and/or source of cash. Differential application of underwriting standards is commonly used to discourage minorities from filing applications.

It does not take a sledgehammer to discourage an applicant. A mere suggestion that he might not qualify is enough to send an applicant to another lender. Thus, in reviewing testing results, the auditor compares messages conveyed to whites as compared to minorities. Are the applicants encouraged to apply? Are the applicants told that they qualify? If they don't, why? Are minorities encouraged to apply for FHA loans, while whites are encouraged to apply here? Does the loan originator ask for financial information or does the test applicant have to offer it? Does the loan originator provide helpful information to make the applicant look better (e.g., gift letters, file on pay day, etc.) or just tell the applicants that they do not qualify.

Analyzing data on the LOG, if such is required by the regulatory agency, can be used to determine whether the rate of applications to inquiries by minorities is substantially different than it is for non-minorities. This process can indicate that discouragement is taking place. Testing, however, is far more effective for finding discouragement because it identifies the form discrimination takes. Also, the LOG, maintained by the lending institution, may be kept improperly.

THE MORTGAGE LENDING PROCESS

In a complicated process, there are many ways to discriminate and many forms that discrimination may take. To find discrimination in the loan files it is helpful to know the loan process and to know where, within that process, discrimination may occur. The process begins with a loan originator and ends with an underwriter, the absolute decision-maker. The underwriter (individual or committee) sets the tone for the entire office and influences the actions of everyone in the office. The underwriter also influences the selection of the outside resources including the sources of credit information, appraisers and private mortgage insurers. Even as we rapidly move to the day when a computer will assist with the decision, the programming decisions in the computer and all exceptions to the rule will be made by an underwriter.

Loan Origination

The loan originator is the "in-take" worker, the person who works with realtors and/or directly with individuals who need a mortgage. The originator generally confirms that the applicant meets the lender's criteria, answers questions, provides advice, and often assists the borrower in preparing the loan application. A borrower applies for a specific type of loan (e.g., conventional, ARM, FHA); specifies the amount of downpayment he will make; and requests specific terms and rates. In determining what terms and rates to ask for, the borrower frequently requests, or the loan originator volunteers, advice.

The loan originator does not make the lending decision. However, the originator knows from experience which type of applications the lender usually accepts and rejects. Thus, the loan originator: (1) takes and provides information; (2) makes recommendations, including loan types and terms; and (3) makes a decision whether to encourage or discourage a borrower to complete an application and pay the filing fee. The decision whether or not to encourage filing an application is based on the loan originator's judgment as to the likelihood that the loan will be approved.

Loan originators are evaluated, and usually paid, according to the value of their production rate, i.e., the dollar value of the loans they bring to closing. Under such circumstances, they may spend extra time with potentially good applicants who are nearly eligible, showing them how to look better on paper. Once an applicant files an application, the originator, as well as a loan processor, spends a great deal of time and effort putting together the myriad of exacting verifications necessary to satisfy the bank, the regulators and the secondary market. A completed loan package, ready for submission to the decision makers and/or the secondary market, is often quite substantial. Every "i" must be dotted and every "t" crossed.

Therefore, loan originators are going to spend as little time as possible with an applicant they believe is likely to be denied. If the underwriter frequently denies minority applicants or applicants in minority neighborhoods, loan originators will respond accordingly, and discourage minority applicants. A loan originator has every incentive to avoid applicants where experience shows a greater likelihood of denial. They will therefore withhold information and assistance, apply bank standards without any common exceptions, suggest other alternatives (e.g., FHA), and otherwise discourage these applicants from submitting an application. This prejudicial treatment may be done consciously or subconsciously; but it is generally without any outward signs of discrimination or disrespect.

Loan Processing

Loan processing is the stage between the lender's receipt of an application and closing, rejection or withdrawal of an application. This stage includes ordering a credit check and an appraisal of the property; properly verifying job, income, savings, and other "facts" in the application; following up on conditions that may have been set for approvals; and assuring that the paper trail required by federal regulators and the secondary market are met. Time is of the essence in loan processing because most sale contracts have a specified time limit for the buyer to receive a commitment and/or close on the sale.

A lender who does not want to give a mortgage can move slowly in processing the application, hoping that the delays will discourage the applicant and that he/she will withdraw. One way to slow down an application is to request additional information a little at a time, coming back over and again to ask for a little more information. A second way is to submit insufficient information to mortgage insurers, e.g., PMI, FHA or VA—guaranteed to kill time or get a denial.

Credit Check

Lenders obtain their credit information from one of three sources. First, they can order a report from a small, local credit agency. This method is generally the cheapest, the least complete, and rarely meets secondary market requirements.

Second, lenders can order a report from one of the three national credit bureaus: TRW, Equifax Inc., or Trans Union Corp. These firms operate independently from the lenders and generally follow uniform standards for reporting information. However, the information these agencies report is information they receive from creditors. All creditors do not report to all of the bureaus. Also, credit bureaus do not request data or verify it, but handle approximately four million changes in data a month, provided to them by creditors and public records (e.g., liens, bankruptcies). Therefore, each of the credit bureaus is likely to have different information, as well as frequent errors, particularly human errors in entry or retrieval.

Finally, the lender can order a report from a mortgage credit verification firm. These firms which will gather data from one or more of the national credit bureaus, verify the data, and do additional research. This method is the most thorough one available.

In selecting the source of credit information, lenders have some control over the information they receive and the cost of obtaining that information. However, it is the manner in which they use the information that discrimination is more likely to occur. Obviously all lenders look for perfect credit, i.e., no late payments, no claims, judgments or liens. Some lenders make provision for exceptions to perfect credit in their underwriting standards, including the opportunity for applicants to explain, in writing, errors or lapses in otherwise good credit. Others do not have written provisions for exceptions, but make exceptions nonetheless. Differential treatment by race may occur in the way lenders select credit sources, when and to whom they provide opportunity for explanation, and when and under which circumstances they make exceptions for less than perfect credit or accept non-traditional credit sources (e.g., rent, utilities, etc.).

The Appraisal

The appraisal determines the value of the collateral. A low appraisal is frequently used to reject applicants applying for a mortgage in a minority neighborhood. An appraised value that is less than the selling price increases the loan-to-value ratio and either disqualifies the applicant or increases the required downpayment. Despite a major overhaul of the official Appraisal Handbook in 1979 (based on a fair housing law suit against the Appraisal Institute by HUD and the Justice Department), appraisals in minority neighborhoods are still a leading source of discrimination.

Appraisals are an important area for audit because the lender selects the appraiser, and is equally culpable if the appraiser discriminates in determining value. *Lenders are now required to make appraisals which are below the selling price available to applicants, upon request. Some lenders may, despite a low appraisal, use a different reason for denial to avoid drawing attention to the appraisal, reducing the likelihood the customer will request a copy of the appraisal.* Thus, in reviewing loan files, all low appraisals should be pursued whether or not they are the stated "cause" for rejection.

The Underwriting Decision

The underwriter (the person or committee who weighs the facts and makes the decision) *must respond to the borrower's request*, that is the request for a particular type of loan, amount of down payment, the rate, the term, and the loan origination fee (points). The loan originator who pre-qualifies the applicant generally recommends a specific loan type and terms. This recommendation is based on the originator's past experience with the underwriter. If the underwriter's terms are generally shorter, rates are higher, or standards are stricter for minorities, the loan originator will make such recommendations at the time of application. Rates and terms for new mortgages are frequently published and thus unlikely to vary; however, expect to find variations by race in loan-to-value ratios, rates, terms, and fees in refinancings.

The underwriter may make exceptions to the rules, bending them slightly or substantially. Making exceptions to secondary market standards could be a problem with selling the loan. However, banks can discriminate by establishing loan standards far in excess of secondary market requirements and in doing so, leave considerable room for "selective" exceptions by race of applicant or neighborhood. Typical of areas where excessive standards and exceptions are combined to discriminate are: minimum loan or property value; maximum age or minimum size of property; length of employment; basic ratios; shorter terms; higher capital requirements; or higher loan costs. Having standards in excess of the secondary market easily permits exceptions for the "right" applicant.

The underwriter has discretion to set additional requirements for making the loan. This discretion could include obtaining Private Mortgage Insurance (PMI), changes in downpayment or terms, or submitting additional information. The extent to which minority applicants face additional or more stringent requirements compared to similarly situated non-minority applicants is an important area for audit.

Private Insurers

A common condition where loan-to-value ratios exceed eighty percent is to require that the amount of the loan in excess of eighty percent be insured. Private mortgage insurers insure the difference between a seventy-five to eighty percent loan-to-value ratio which is saleable in the secondary market and the loan-to-value ratio of the buyer (often ninety to ninety-five percent in conventional mortgages).

The larger the community, the more private mortgage insurance companies. A lender often has a wide variety of insurers from which to choose. Each insurer has published standards for applicants. Thus, a lender that is looking for an easy way to deny a loan to an otherwise eligible applicant can send the application to a private mortgage insurer whose standards for applicants are in excess of that normally required by the lender. When the application is subsequently rejected, the lender simply informs the applicants that they were rejected for PMI. The fact that there may be several other insurers in the community who would approve the application is simply not mentioned. Or, a lender can send an incomplete application to the insurer, leaving out, for example, the letters of explanation for a credit fault.

Test results at the loan origination stage found that the minority applicants were often discouraged by being told that they would need "two" approvals and that "they were hard to get." One can assume that PMI was the second approval because the testers were asking for conventional loans with a ten percent downpayment. However, "two, hard to get" approvals were never mentioned to any of the similarly situated white applicants. Instead, they were all urged to apply.

FINDING DISCRIMINATION IN THE LOAN FILES

Selection of Files

Discrimination cannot be established by looking only at loan files of minority applicants. Too often examiners have compared rejected minority applications to bank standards and have found no evidence of discrimination. An audit must look at comparable non-minority and minority applicants because discrimination is based on different treatment of like situated individuals based on race or other protected status. Even more important, an audit of the loan files should compare files in minority census tracts to comparable non-minority census tracts. Testing experience shows that black applicants in black neighborhoods face the greatest level of discrimination.

Finally, if there is any likelihood that this data will be used in a court of law, the loan files should be selected in a statistically defensible manner. Thus, a statistician or economist should be involved in all aspects of the selection and analysis. You can expect to get into a battle of the experts on endless minutiae.

Applications not originated by the subject lender should not be part of the sample. Such applications generally have a cover letter from a mortgage broker; the loan processing form has very little information;

the application goes through in a few days (compared to the normal 30–60 days); and someone other than the bank orders the appraisal.

Reducing Files to a Manageable Size

The loan files are foreboding in size; however, they can be reduced for an audit by focusing on a few pieces of paper. These include the application, the loan processing log, and the appraisal. Remove all of these pages and then review the credit report. If there are any negatives on the credit report, examine the report and any explanatory letters provided by the applicant. The rest of the material can be set aside. One caveat, *you* need to select the materials to review so always request the *complete* file.

The Loan Processing Form

The loan processing log, originated on paper or computer-generated, is generally an accurate diary of the lender's processing and the underwriter's decisions. It logs each action, the date and the reason or explanation for such actions. It generally contains the name, address, and census tract of the applicant, the date of application, loan-to-value ratio, income and debt ratios, and how they are computed. It logs the request date and the results of the credit report, the appraisal, and the verifications. It logs the recommendation of the loan originator, the date it goes to the underwriter, the underwriter's decision and the date of the decision. It also logs requests for more information (with date requested and date received) and special requirements such as mortgage insurance and the results.

Before using the loan processing log, certain pieces of information should be verified directly from the application. These are: the date of application; the race/sex of applicant(s); the income and sources (is all income listed on the application included in determining the ratios?); and the requested loan type and terms. Sometimes conflicting information will be evident even from a casual comparison of the basic information. If racial information is not provided on the application, the lender is in violation of regulatory requirements.

The loan processing form is the principle source of information for finding differential treatment by race in loan processing and underwriting. The information on these forms indicates whether there is differential treatment between minorities and non-minorities in "requests for terms" (length of loan, rates, points); determining total income and ratios; processing time; application of standards (exceptions to the rule or more loosely defined rules); requirements for PMI; and response to credit problems (e.g., opportunity to explain negative credit rating or errors). Also, one should note whether the appraisal is too low to support the loan.

Using the Lender's LOG

If the lender is required to maintain an Application/Inquiry LOG, information in the loan file should be checked against this LOG. Examine whether all the sample applications are listed; if the lender's application numbers are consecutive based on date of application; and if the application dates match the LOG dates. Evidence of failure to maintain the LOG according to the regulations may provide evidence of wilful intent to discriminate.

Creating a Database

The best way to analyze the files is to create a database for each file, including: file number; race/sex; census tract; minority characteristics of census tract; number of days from the date the application is signed to the date of the decision (final approval, rejection or withdrawal—not closing); ratios; negative factors such as discounting income, credit problems, low appraisal; and the PMI required and obtained. If there are low appraisals, particularly if they are only for minorities or only in minority neighborhoods, you may go back in and add data from the appraisals or create a separate appraisal file.

The purpose in creating the file is to isolate differences by race, or to rank order, by race. For example, the number of days from application to decision (not closing) can be rank ordered by race to determine whether there is a statistically significant difference in length of processing time between minority and non-minority applicants. Using a database for a group of loan files from a midwest bank, I found that: (1) all the minority applicants were in the upper fiftieth percentile in length of time for a decision; (2) minority applicants averaged more than twice the number of days to decision or withdrawal than non-minority applicants; (3) PMI was required at higher loan-to-value ratios for minorities than for non-minorities; and (4) minority applicants always "requested" shorter terms for refinancings.

Reviewing Appraisals

Evidence of discrimination in appraisals shows, initially, in the lender's selection of appraisers. Generally, there will be a high correlation between properties that receive low appraisals and specific appraisers. Using the database, list applications where the appraisal was lower than the sale price or estimated value (whether or not that was the reason given for a denial), by race of applicant, census tract and the name of the appraiser. The evidence may be astounding. Often, most, if not all, of the undervalued properties are in predominantly minority neighborhoods and find select appraisers doing all the low appraisals. In one bank, we found that one appraiser did every "too low" appraisal for minority applicants. In the few cases in which a minority applicant was approved, the bank had hired a different appraiser.

On the appraisal form, evidence of discrimination can be found in the selection of houses as comparables—their location, condition, and the financial "adjustments" for variations from the comparables (e.g., differences in number of bathrooms, central air conditioning, square footage, garage, carport, or patio). It also shows in "adjustments" assigned for functional or economic obsolescence and reasons for those adjustments. Often, homes in minority neighborhoods are given negative adjustments while homes in adjacent, non-minority neighborhoods are not. Sometimes reasons are not given, even though they are required. One does not have to be trained in appraisal techniques to see substantial differences in the "adjustments" assigned in minority neighborhoods compared with adjustments in similar, non-minority neighborhoods.

It is important to remember that the lender hires the appraiser. It makes no difference if the appraiser is a minority. When the appraiser was trained, however, can make a considerable difference. Appraisers trained in the past ten years have used a substantially revised appraisal manual which stresses that race of a neighborhood is not a criteria for value. This was not the case before 1980.

All appraisal manuals published before 1980, many of which are still in use, stress the importance of social (racial) harmony and conformity, and the eventual decline of every neighborhood as evidenced by infiltration of inharmonious (minority) groups. Therefore, if the lender wants a low appraisal, they hire an "old-school" appraiser whom they know and expect will come in with a low appraisal. That appraiser is rewarded for the low appraisals with consistent work—all the work in the minority neighborhoods.

Where an analysis of the appraisals shows a likelihood of discrimination, you can hire an appraiser to reappraise those properties which came in low. A professional appraiser can appraise property for any given time in the past.

Credit

There are two predominant patterns in credit discrimination. First, the lender will buy the cheapest form of credit record for minority applicants if the lender knows he is going to deny the application. Often that is the local credit source, a source that will not even be acceptable to the secondary market. Therefore, it is important to list the credit source on the data file and see if there is any correlation between the credit source and ultimate denial, for any reason. That could provide evidence of intent to deny.

The second pattern, one that is easily evident, is that the lender does not provide an opportunity for the minority borrower to explain why there was a problem with credit. Or if they do provide the opportunity, the lender accepts the explanation of the non-minority applicants but not the same/similar explanation of the minority applicants. A colleague approached me a year ago and informed me that it was true, the credit on minorities was not good. He had in fact gone through dozens of rejected applications of minorities and discovered flawed credit. "Did you go through an equal number of white applicants with flawed credit to see how they were treated?" I asked. "No," he said.

Discrimination will rarely be found if minority treatment is not compared to non-minority treatment. It is in consistently different treatment that you will find discrimination, whether examining external data such as HMDA or rejection rates, or looking at testing results, or inspecting the loan files.

Private Mortgage Insurance (PMI)

There are three patterns of discrimination among lenders requiring PMI. The first pattern occurs in the variation of standards for requiring PMI. I have seen minority applicants required to have PMI with loan-to-value ratios as low as seventy-six percent and non-minority applicants not required to have PMI with loan-to-value ratios as high as eighty-nine percent. The second pattern of discrimination arises in the selection of insurers. The third pattern emerges in the sending of insufficient data regarding the applicant when requesting insurance.

Adding PMI to the database and comparing it with race of applicant, census tract, insurer, loan-to-value ratio and reason for rejection will give evidence of inequitable treatment if it exists. If minority rejection rates are frequently based on rejections of PMI, examine whether applicants are being steered to insurers with more stringent standards, or if certain insurers need to be looked at for possible discrimination. Finally, one will want to see if all the necessary information has been sent to the insurer, or if the insurer is rejecting the application for insufficient information or for lack of an explanation for credit problems.

Where denials are based on rejections by PMI insurers, one can review the reasons given by the insurer, as well as the lender's PMI standards book to see if there are other insurers who would have accepted the applicant. If one is in a small community where there are only a few insurers, and if rejections for PMI are significant, there are ways to change PMI standards. In Des Moines, Iowa, for example, the mortgage lenders met with the leading insurer and negotiated changes in the PMI's standards which permitted far greater minority participation. After all, PMIs cannot exist without referrals from lenders.

Conclusion

It is difficult, if not nearly impossible to take a single file and "prove" discrimination. "Smoking guns" are rarely found. Testing shows that, for the most part, lenders are particularly nice to minority applicants and their suggestions to minority applicants to go elsewhere are put in a helpful, positive light. It is only when one compares the treatment of similarly situated non-minority applicants who are encouraged to stay at an institution and apply for a mortgage that indications of discrimination begin to surface.

Whenever one produces a single file and tries to convince a judge or jury that discrimination occurred in this particular case, the lender can pull in all kinds of experts to show why this particular case should have been denied. The real issues, however, remain whether minority and non-minority applicants are held to the same standard and whether applicants in minority neighborhoods are held to a higher or different standard than similar applicants in non-minority neighborhoods. Thus, it is crucial in examining the loan files to inspect an adequate sample of loan files and reveal that differential treatment is a regular occurrence.

SEEKING REMEDY

Since 1978–1979, when I served the U.S. Comptroller of the Currency as the first Director of Civil Rights and prepared the Comptroller's

Fair Housing Home Loan Data System, I have been challenged by both the pervasiveness and the senselessness of mortgage lending discrimination. It is senseless because it is a voluntary and intentional reduction by a lender of the lender's own market. Can you identify any other consumer product which is not marketed just as aggressively to minorities as to non-minorities of similar income?

Yet, despite its senselessness, HUD-funded "testing" in 1988 showed that black and white testers—all with signed contracts, the same loan-to-value and income to debt ratios, and with similar characteristics—were treated differently based solely on race. We tested in a community where the number of applications were down that summer and where lenders were hustling for applicants. Nevertheless, loan originators in *all* the banks and savings and loans that we tested clearly discouraged black applicants from submitting applications, while actively encouraging similarly situated white applicants to apply. Similar results have been found in subsequent testing by fair housing/lending organizations.

To "look for" and "find" discrimination is threatening to lenders and to their regulators, yet it must be done. Individual remedies to victims of discrimination is long overdue and should be actively pursued. In addition to individual remedy, neighborhood remedy and affirmative marketing should be the tripod of any agreement or plea for remedy.

Once a pattern of differential treatment in one or more areas of mortgage lending is identified through reviewing the loan files, all minority persons who might have suffered discrimination based on that pattern should be individually compensated. Individual compensation would be an appropriate remedy even if the reason for reviewing the loan files is generated by a single plaintiff. Once differential treatment is made evident, then an effort should be made to compensate all individuals who were affected.

Second, repeated acts of discrimination in minority neighborhoods are not only acts against the individuals who apply, but are egregious acts against the entire minority community for they serve to substantially lower property values by removing common forms of mortgage financing. When it becomes difficult to obtain financing within a community, housing and other property values drop and mortgage rates increase. A remedy for entire minority neighborhoods deserves special recognition and specific guidelines. One possible remedy would be a large cash contribution by the lender over several years to endow community-based organizations committed to economic development, health or education in such neighborhoods.

Finally, all findings of discrimination or settlements should require aggressive marketing as part of the remedy, with substantial mortgage targets and adequate monitoring to assure that the lender reaches the underserved minority applicants and all minority neighborhoods. A marketing campaign is not only invigorating, but also good for business. By successfully marketing mortgages to minorities and to minority neighborhoods, the lender's experiences will change, new markets will be found, and, just as we see through lenders' experience with low-income populations in meeting CRA requirements, new beliefs may follow.

Note

1. 12 U.S.C. §§ 2801-2810 (1992).

Chapter Twenty-Three

THE ROLE OF PRIVATE, NONPROFIT FAIR HOUSING ENFORCEMENT ORGANIZATIONS IN LENDING TESTING

Shanna L. Smith and Cathy Cloud

The National Fair Housing Alliance (NFHA) is a private, nonprofit corporation founded in 1988 to help provide national leadership on fair housing issues. The mission of NFHA, which represents virtually all of the private, nonprofit fair housing agencies in the nation, is to promote "the policy of the United States to provide, within constitutional limitations, for fair housing throughout the United States." The Alliance believes that by vigorous, positive, and focused action, its members can work together to achieve fair housing through outreach, education, litigation, conciliation, and research into the nature, extent, and effects of housing discrimination. NFHA is dedicated to developing and implementing strategies to reduce, and eventually eliminate, racially and ethnically segregated housing patterns, and to making all housing accessible regardless of race, color, religion, sex, familial status, disability, or national origin.

To these ends, NFHA's staff and member agencies have pioneered the testing, investigation, and litigation of mortgage lending discrimination. Based upon these experiences, this chapter focuses on the purpose of mortgage lending testing, the types of testing used to measure lending discrimination and to investigate individual allegations of lending discrimination, and the resolutions reached with lenders stemming from fair lending investigations. In addition, the discussion emphasizes the need for full application mortgage lending testing and the essential role of such testing in identifying a lender's discriminatory practices and policies.

PURPOSE OF MORTGAGE LENDING TESTING

Testing is a controlled method of documenting differences in treatment, availability, terms and conditions, and price that can be attributed to a particular protected characteristic, such as race, ethnicity, familial status, or disability. Testing is the best tool available to obtain objective information about the practices of housing, mortgage, and insurance providers. By separating out random acts of behavior from practices and procedures that reflect discriminatory behavior, testing benefits both victims of discrimination as well as providers of housing.

Mortgage lending testing is the latest type of testing utilized by fair housing enforcement agencies. The tests conform, for the most part, to standard testing methodology and are usually conducted at the preapplication stage of the mortgage lending process. Although this stage represents only a small portion of the entire mortgage lending process, much can be learned from tests done at this time. Loan officer behavior can reflect what that person knows about the process, including what is acceptable and unacceptable to underwriters, mortgage insurers, secondary market investors, and other personnel. Tests conducted at the loan origination stage can also provide a paper trail for monitoring or regulatory agency investigators to follow. Currently, there is no such paper trail, which makes it relatively easy for a loan officer to engage in discriminatory practices. For example, if a potential customer is discouraged from applying for a loan, there is no documentation to indicate that an inquiry was ever made. If potential applicants are discouraged at this stage by, for example, the loan officer indicating that the application may not be approved or because of the application fee, they are unlikely to follow through with a written application.

Testing can also protect lenders who are in compliance with the law. While providing evidence to support allegations of discrimination, testing also weeds out those complaints based on behaviors or policies that have been misinterpreted as discriminatory. Tests are conducted for two primary purposes:

1. To measure the extent of discrimination in a particular marketplace or by a particular segment of the industry (generally referred to as auditing); or
2. To provide evidence to support or refute an allegation of discrimination (generally referred to as complaint- or enforcement-based testing).

Although the private fair housing sector endorses testing to measure discrimination, fair housing practitioners typically concentrate their limited resources on testing for enforcement purposes. NFHA's primary concern is the victims of discrimination: individuals, families, neighborhoods, and cities. Measurement of discrimination is important in many policy contexts, but behavior and policy changes are the critical objectives of fair housing enforcement. Therefore, auditing by private fair housing agencies is generally used to develop a "pattern or practice" case of discrimination against larger owners, managers, lenders, or insurers.

Whereas blatant discrimination still occurs in the housing and lending markets, discrimination by lending institutions is typically subtle and sophisticated. Testing results are therefore used to expose as mere pretense the alleged legitimate business reasons given by a lender for denying a loan to a minority or female purchaser, for example, or to an individual seeking a home in a minority or integrated neighborhood.

Not all lending complaints can or should be tested. Often a common-sense examination of the reason for rejection can provide enough information to make testing unnecessary to demonstrate discriminatory conduct.[1] For example, when a lender rejected a loan for a home located in an African-American neighborhood, stating it was not possible to make a 95 percent loan-to-value ratio loan because the property's value exceeded the predominant value of other homes in the neighborhood, the fair housing agency was suspicious because the subject property fell well within the average price range of homes in that neighborhood. The agency determined that the buyers were creditworthy and that the house had been appraised properly. After eliminating every other legitimate business reason for denying the loan, it was concluded that the racial composition of the neighborhood was the real reason for loan denial.

Testing can be used by lenders for staff quality control of their mortgage loan application process, from their application intake personnel to their secondary market investors. Since lenders can be held legally liable for discriminatory treatment of applicants—whether by the lender's employee or the contract appraiser, mortgage insurer, or secondary market investor—it is critical for lenders to take the necessary steps to ensure fair treatment of every mortgage loan application.

Ultimately, loan processing that is designed to be nondiscriminatory will result in more loans to racial and ethnic minorities, as well as to other minority groups such as women and those with disabilities, in addition to more people who are purchasing homes in minority and integrated neighborhoods.

TYPES OF MORTGAGE LENDING TESTING

An *audit* is usually designed to test specific practices of mortgage lenders at the loan origination stage. On the other hand, *enforcement-based* testing is used to determine if the alleged business reason for the loan denial is valid or if the lender's policies and practices have a discriminatory impact upon individuals or neighborhoods belonging to the protected classes.

Mortgage lending tests evaluate discrimination based on race or other characteristics of the applicant, or on the racial composition of the neighborhood in which a property is located. Loan originators' practices can reflect a lending institution's policies as well as the loan officer's personal prejudices. Loan originators may discourage applicants because of assumptions, for example, about minority or female applicants, or applicants with disabilities. They may also discourage applicants because they know their institution does not make loans in particular neighborhoods.

The Fair Housing Act does not require a showing of intent to discriminate to prove disparate impact. Every federal circuit court that has addressed the issue has held that we need only show the disparate effect of a policy or practice to prove housing discrimination.[2] Lenders believe their underwriting standards are objective, necessary, and based on maintaining the financial soundness of the institution. However, in reviewing underwriting guidelines, we have found standards and policies that clearly have a disparate, discriminatory impact on minority and female applicants, as well as on minority and integrated neighborhoods, and are not necessary for sound fiscal management.

The federal courts have decided that a plaintiff in a fair housing/lending case does not have to prove that the defendant acted with a racially discriminatory motive. In the *United States* v. *Black Jack* case (1975), the court said: "Effect, and not motivation, is the touchstone, in part because clever men may easily conceal their motivation."[3] To make a prima facie case of discrimination, one need only show that the defendant's actions had a discriminatory effect.[4]

Some lenders will engage in clever practices to avoid doing business with minorities or making loans in minority neighborhoods. In Indiana, for instance, a lender established a minimum square footage requirement on loans for single-family homes. Upon close review it was discovered that this requirement excluded a large subdivision built in the 1950s whose residents were African American.

What Prompts Mortgage Lending Testing?

AUDITS

Mortgage lending audits are prompted by a number of things including, but not limited to:

- Results of evaluations of Home Mortgage Disclosure Act (HMDA) data indicating a lender is failing to make loans in neighborhoods that are racially or ethnically identifiable, or indicating high rejection rates for minority or female applicants
- Information from real estate agents indicating that a lender refuses to make loans in minority neighborhoods or makes loans on less favorable terms or conditions in these neighborhoods
- Information about particular policies or practices that have a disparate impact on members of the protected classes or neighborhoods
- Requests from lenders for assistance in evaluating their employees' compliance with fair lending practices

ENFORCEMENT-BASED TESTING

Enforcement-based testing is designed to evaluate the validity of the reason for loan denial or the change in terms or conditions of the loan.[5] It generally involves an individual mortgage loan applicant; however, enforcement-based testing can be conducted when a neighborhood organization or other group identifies a policy or practice that has a negative impact on potential or current homeowners.

Enforcement-based testing is prompted by allegations of lending discrimination. Complaints are lodged by buyers, sellers, real estate agents, neighborhood organizations, testers, fair housing organizations, and municipalities. In addition, employees who are required or requested to engage in discriminatory conduct can file complaints under the Fair Housing Act or anonymously notify a fair housing organization about a particular practice. To date, lending discrimination lawsuits have been brought by buyers, sellers, real estate agents, neighborhood groups, and fair housing agencies. These plaintiffs have alleged that the racial composition of the neighborhood, race of the buyer, or a lender's policies and practices have been used in a discriminatory manner to deny, delay, or provide inferior terms and conditions for mortgage loans.

As a result of these lawsuits, federal judges in Indiana and Ohio have established the prima facie or "threshold" case standards for mortgage lending discrimination. (*Thomas* v. *First Federal Savings*

Bank of Indiana 1987;[6] *Old West End Association et al.* v. *Buckeye Federal Savings and Loan* 1987). The definitions established by the courts for both applicant and neighborhood discrimination follow.

Applicant Discrimination (*Thomas* v. *First Federal Savings* 1987) Court-established definitions for applicant discrimination include:

- The applicants are members of a protected class;
- Applicants applied and were qualified for a loan from the defendant;
- The loan was rejected despite their qualifications; and
- The defendant continued to approve loans for applicants with qualifications similar to those of the applicants.

Neighborhood Discrimination (*Old West End Association, et al.* v. *Buckeye Federal* 1987) Court-established definitions for neighborhood discrimination include:

- The housing sought to be secured is in a minority neighborhood;
- An application for a loan to purchase the housing located in a minority neighborhood was made;
- An independent appraisal concluded that the value of the housing equaled the sale price;[7]
- The buyers were creditworthy; and
- The loan was rejected.

It is not possible to test every complaint of lending discrimination. Therefore, it is important to know how to identify discriminatory practices when evaluating the complaint and how to conduct a thorough record search during discovery. We venture to say that too often the reason federal regulators fail to identify discriminatory practices, even though they have access to loan files, is that they lack sufficient knowledge of what to look for.

Our experience with mortgage lending discrimination lawsuits and administrative complaints has underscored that no two cases are exactly alike. Plaintiffs' attorneys have found sufficient documentation to demonstrate disparate treatment of minority loan applicants and/or of loan applications for homes in minority neighborhoods. These cases have involved discriminatory use of credit bureau and appraisal reports, income-to-debt calculations, and underwriting guidelines of the lender, private mortgage insurer, and secondary market investor.

How Far into the Loan Application Process Has Testing Gone?

Whereas most testing has been restricted to the preapplication stage, fair housing organizations in Ohio have tested underwriting standards, appraisal practices, and successfully completed full mortgage loan applications.

In the lawsuit *Lamb v. Citizens National Bank of Bluffton* (1989), filed in Lima, Ohio, two full applications tests were completed.[8] Lamb and the testers alleged they had been denied mortgage loans because the properties that would secure the loans were located in African-American neighborhoods. Both testers were creditworthy and met all financial and credit requirements of the lender, but their applications were rejected. The lender agreed to settle this suit for monetary damages; affirmative relief included a set-aside of money for mortgage loans in Lima's African-American neighborhoods and expansion of the lender's service area to include Lima.

Lending testing can identify where in the mortgage lending process discrimination is occurring. Discriminatory practices have been uncovered in each stage of the lending process through testing or review of the records during discovery. During the preapplication stage, testing or auditing can uncover evidence of disparate treatment by evaluating the following information given to testers: interest rates, points, debt ratios, credit history, terms of application, documentation requirements, types of credit products offered and recommended, helpful qualifying information, quality of treatment, processing time and procedures, referral to other lending institutions, probable (or not) qualification of applicant; and closing costs and procedures. During this testing sequence, the tester inquires about the loan products available and the terms or conditions to apply for the loan. The testing can identify both applicant-based and neighborhood-based discriminatory practices.

Testing of underwriting standards and appraisers is triggered by complaints from loan applicants, sellers, or real estate agents. Testing is designed based upon the reason for the loan rejection or change in terms and conditions as stated in the adverse action notice. For example, in a case where a minority loan applicant is rejected because of a recent change in employment and the lender explains that its underwriting policies require one year of employment at the same job, the test would be structured to have a white applicant inquire about a loan and volunteer information about employment changes. If the loan officer makes accommodations for the white tester's employment situation, that constitutes evidence of differential treatment. This type of test is designed to determine if the loan officer applies underwriting standards equally. If the loan officer does apply this standard equally, the fair housing organization may decide to challenge the standard and whether the standard itself has a discriminatory impact on minority and female loan applicants.

When a loan is rejected based upon the appraised value of the property, there are several ways to test and investigate whether the racial composition of the neighborhood was a factor in the appraisal. One first needs to determine if the value appears to be inconsistent with comparable homes or if there was a deviation from standard appraisal practices. For example, fair housing agencies have contracted for an independent appraisal to be conducted on the subject property to demonstrate that the original appraisal was out of line. The second appraisal can provide enough evidence to proceed with an administrative complaint or lawsuit. The appraiser can also be tested by having a "seller" in a minority/integrated neighborhood contact the appraiser about appraising the seller's house, explaining that the seller wants to know the value before putting it on the market or seeking refinancing. Or a "seller" in a predominantly white neighborhood can explain that he or she is looking at an investment property in a minority/integrated neighborhood and wants the property appraised before making an offer. These methods are used to test how an appraiser treats property located in racially or ethnically identifiable neighborhoods. The challenge for the fair housing agency is to find owners willing to let the agency use their properties for the tests. Finding properties in the minority and integrated neighborhoods is generally not hard; however, finding white owners in white neighborhoods who are willing to cooperate in a test can be difficult.

Testing of mortgage insurers and secondary market investors is possible, but so far we have only had discussions with lenders regarding structuring such a test. Lenders are becoming more concerned about the fair lending practices of mortgage insurers and secondary market investors because the lender can be held legally liable for the discriminatory practices of these entities.

WHAT HAS TESTING UNCOVERED?

Pilot Projects

Two pilot testing projects (audits) provided much of the basis for the mortgage lending testing programs in effect today. These projects, in

Louisville and Chicago, have been reported in other documents (see Center for Community Change 1989 and Cloud and Galster 1993). Some of the results of the Chicago project are highlighted here to emphasize the usefulness and power of mortgage lending testing.

The Chicago Fair Housing Alliance tested 10 institutions: 2 banks, 3 savings and loan institutions, and 5 mortgage companies. This was an experimental program, and different types and numbers of tests were conducted at each institution. The testers were women, most in their thirties, who posed as being married with one or two children, with three or more years with the same employer. All were given financial characteristics that qualified them for a conventional 30-year loan at the predominant interest rate (plus three points) offered on the day of their visit. Even though the program was conducted primarily to test the methodology, some evidence of differential treatment was found at 7 of the 10 institutions tested. This treatment took three primary forms:

1. The African-American testers frequently had difficulty getting a loan officer to sit down with them and discuss credit products and terms.
2. When African-American testers did meet with a loan officer, their debt ratios were usually not calculated, and they were not given an assessment as to their likelihood for qualifying for a loan.
3. When African-American testers did receive information about their qualifications, they were not given as much helpful information as their white counterparts on how to qualify and apply.

Examples of differential treatment can be found in the following scenarios:

- At two locations, loan officers refused to meet with potential minority testers until they had completed an application and brought in a check for the application fee.
- At one location the African-American tester was told the institution did not make loans to first-time homebuyers.
- One African-American applicant seeking a mortgage under $40,000 was told the institution did not make loans under that amount. The loan officer actually said, "It's legal for us to do that." The tester was referred to a mortgage company that made Federal Housing Administration (FHA) loans (no minimum loan amount). The daily rate sheet provided to the tester, however, listed FHA loans as a credit product offered by the tested institution.

These results were consistent with the findings of the earlier-mentioned mortgage lending testing program in Louisville, conducted by the Center for Community Change under a Fair Housing Assistance Program grant.

National Enforcement Testing Program

In 1993, The National Fair Housing Alliance (NFHA) received funding from the Department of Housing and Urban Development under the Fair Housing Initiatives Program (FHIP) to conduct mortgage lending testing in several cities across the United States. The majority of tests were conducted in Chicago and Oakland, with additional tests conducted in Atlanta, Dallas, Denver, Detroit, Richmond, and Norfolk.

There were thirty-five lending institutions at which at least two multi-part (two to five parts) tests were conducted. These tests were conducted at the loan origination stage of the mortgage lending process and included pre-qualification, home purchase, and refinance transactions.

In these tests, there was found consistent and recurring evidence of discrimination against African-American and Latino testers and persons seeking financing for homes in predominantly minority neighborhoods. For tests in which a determination of differential or similar treatment could be made, African-American and Latino persons experienced discrimination in 67.5 percent of the tests, while white persons were treated less favorably in only 3.4 percent of the tests. In 28.6 percent of the cases, testers were treated similarly.

Discriminatory patterns of differential treatment include:

- requiring a credit check, completion of an application, or presentation of other documentation prior to scheduling an appointment with African-American and Latino persons while not imposing the same pre-appointment requirements on white persons;
- quoting more restrictive qualification standards and ratios to African-American and Latino persons;
- making exceptions to qualification standards for white persons while not making the same level of exceptions for African-American and Latino persons;
- requiring higher levels of escrow and reserve payments of African-American and Latino persons at the time of closing than for white persons;
- providing constructive advice (i.e., paying down debt, obtaining gift letters, explaining credit flaws) to white persons on how to

circumvent a potential barrier to qualification while not providing the same advice or quality of advice to African-American and Latino persons.

As of this writing, the National Fair Housing Alliance has filed complaints of discrimination with HUD against four large national mortgage lending institutions. Additional complaints will be filed in 1996.

Enforcement-Based Testing Results

Testing of several complaints in Toledo, Ohio, has identified policies that have a disparate impact on minorities and minority neighborhoods, practices designed to discourage minorities and women from applying for loans, and practices designed to reduce services and close branch offices in minority neighborhoods.

The most simple policies to test are those involving prescreening factors: minimum mortgage amount policies, race of applicant, sex of applicant, location of property, and tiering of interest rates. Although many lenders state that they do not have a minimum loan amount, testing uncovered information that loan applications below $40,000 are steered to FHA or other "special" loan programs rather than to the conventional market. Other lower-priced loan applicants are discouraged from even applying.

Minimum Loan Standards, Sex Discrimination, and Property Location

If a complainant indicates that the loan officer completed an application form without accepting the application fee, a test can be designed to provide the information necessary to complete the application form, but stopping short of providing the fee and signing the application. The following case identifies this type of discrimination and illustrates the necessity of being able to complete mortgage loan applications.

A single white female in Toledo, Ohio, attempted to purchase a duplex in a largely Mexican-American neighborhood. She met with a loan officer for two hours and completed a loan application, but the loan officer never asked for an application fee. The loan officer later telephoned to tell her she was not qualified for the loan, and expressed hesitancy about making a loan to a single woman raising a child. The applicant went to a second lender who also completed a loan application, but did not request an application fee. This loan officer also told her she would not qualify. She telephoned another lender, who asked her where the property was located and then said he would have to drive by it before he could make an appointment for her to apply. The fourth loan officer completed the application, took the application fee, processed her request, and offered her the mortgage loan. She told this loan officer about her experiences with the other lenders. The loan officer suggested that she contact the Fair Housing Center in Toledo, which she did. The Fair Housing Center assisted her in filing a complaint with the U.S. Department of Housing and Urban Development (HUD). Because there were no surviving bank documents to support her claim, HUD was skeptical that she had even been to the lenders. The Fair Housing Center then checked the woman's credit report and learned that one of the lenders had made an inquiry into her credit close to the time she claimed to have visited the lender's office. This proved that she had been at the institution and that the lender had destroyed documents and made false statements to HUD. It also supported her claim that the lender intentionally discriminated against her because of her sex, familial status, the racial composition of the neighborhood, and cost of the housing she sought.

The HUD conciliation in this case included a monetary settlement of $13,500. Other provisions required the lender to:

- Post a large sign in its offices stating that a copy of the mortgage loan application will be available upon request (making it more difficult, one hopes, for lenders to destroy applications)
- Participate in fair lending training sessions in 1992 and 1993 provided by the Fair Housing Center
- Establish a monetary incentive to induce loan officers to process applications for lower-priced housing
- Advertise loan products in both the African-American and Hispanic press
- Participate in quarterly meetings with the Fair Housing Center to discuss how to increase lending opportunities in minority and ethnic neighborhoods
- Provide a copy of the HMDA loan/application register report to the Fair Housing Center at the same time it is filed with the federal regulator

Since this conciliation, the lender has placed fair housing brochures in all of its banking centers and is opening a new branch in an area serving the African-American community. This case is particularly shocking, however, because it occurred in Toledo, Ohio, which has a reputation for vigorously investigating lending complaints. It is also amazing that the federal regulator never made an inquiry into this lender's practices, even though a HUD conciliation agreement was signed.

Tiered Rates

Tiering of interest rates for loans below $40,000 or for other lower-priced loans is also a problem for minorities. Lenders or mortgage brokers increase the interest as the amount of the mortgage loan decreases. In effect, low- and moderate-income homebuyers pay a premium to secure a mortgage. Tiered interest rates have a disparate, discriminatory impact on minority and female buyers attempting to purchase homes and on other buyers attempting to purchase homes in minority or integrated neighborhoods. Testers checking for tiering make inquiries about loan products and interest rates for homes from a variety of neighborhoods and varying prices.

Geographic Discrimination (Redlining)

Other testing has been conducted on policies established and published in the lender's Community Reinvestment Act (CRA) statement. Lenders delineate their service area in their CRA statement. Some lenders define the service area to exclude minority or integrated neighborhoods. Other lenders include these neighborhoods, but still fail to provide service.

Testing demonstrates whether the lender actually refuses to do business in these neighborhoods or makes exceptions that have discriminatory effects. Testers posing as potential homeowners in these areas make loan application inquiries; testers from white neighborhoods located outside of the service area also make inquiries. The tests are evaluated for differing treatment, and any policy to exclude minority neighborhoods from the service area definition is also evaluated for disparate, discriminatory impact.

Although some lenders include minority neighborhoods in their service area definition, testing is designed to determine if the same quality of service and information is provided to loan applicants. Testing has shown, for example, that a lender may require a higher down payment (more than 5 percent or 10 percent) to make a loan in a specific neighborhood. The tests are also designed to identify low appraisal practices when the applicant is seeking refinancing or a home equity line of credit.

Testing was conducted at a specific branch of a lender, located in an African-American neighborhood, after an employee reported that the lender instructed employees to steer potential customers to two other branch locations. Testing supported the allegation. We learned that the lender wanted to close this branch and was using the drop-off in new accounts and the low deposit base to justify its intentions to its federal regulator.

HOW MANY TESTS ARE ENOUGH TO PROVE DISCRIMINATION?

There is no single answer to the number of tests, if any at all, that are needed to prove a case of lending discrimination. In many instances, one test is enough to demonstrate discrimination when investigating an individual complaint. Several tests (three or more) may be necessary to support a claim of a pattern or practice of discrimination. Likewise, no testing may be necessary to prove the discriminatory impact of a policy, or just one team of testers may effectively demonstrate that a policy is applied differently depending upon the applicant's race or the racial composition of the neighborhood.

Some people advocate performing enough tests to be statistically significant in defining a pattern. However, most lenders do not have a large enough volume of mortgage loan applications to conduct dozens of tests without significantly increasing the risk of detection. In addition, if the lender has few applications from minorities, sending in even five testers over a 60-day period may make the loan officers suspicious. Since federal courts across the nation have clearly established the standard of proof for lending/housing discrimination cases, performing dozens of tests for statistical purposes is an unnecessary risk to prove discrimination. As stated early in this chapter, the purpose of enforcement testing is to change behavior, policies, and practices that adversely affect minorities, females, and minority and integrated neighborhoods. To prevail legally or during conciliation, it has not been necessary to prove that the lender repeatedly engaged in discriminatory practices. The courts have said that one act of discrimination constitutes a violation of the federal Fair Housing Act. It is foolhardy to encourage any practice that would raise this standard.

The legal standard for prevailing in a fair housing case is to convince a judge or jury by a "preponderance of the evidence" that discrimination has occurred (i.e., the weight of this evidence must "tip the scales" in favor of the plaintiff). One is not required to demonstrate that discrimination occurred repeatedly in order to prove a violation of the law. In fact, a pattern or practice case may require only one discriminatory policy or as few as three individual instances of discrimination.[9]

No rule establishes the number of tests needed to establish a violation of the Fair Housing Act. If a case can be successfully made without testing, then the fair housing organization should not take any unnecessary risks. However, if testing is the best method available to document the claim, then testing should be attempted.

SETTLEMENTS IN FAIR LENDING INVESTIGATIONS USING TESTING

Settlements reached with lenders that include testing are generally similar to settlements that do not include testing. Most lending complaints are fortified by the evidence gathered during discovery. Combining this evidence with testing results can maximize the affirmative relief and damages sought by the complaining party. If the records support the claim of discrimination, then testing merely helps remove any doubt that discrimination occurred.

Settlements involving tested cases have resulted in loan commitments for the neighborhoods affected by the discriminatory policies and practices. In addition to providing monetary damages to the victim and establishing set-asides of mortgage dollars for the affected neighborhoods, settlements have included reductions in interest rates for the complaining party and changes in underwriting policies. In the previously mentioned settlement where the lender had refused to open new accounts at a branch located in an African-American neighborhood, the lender agreed to a $250,000 renovation of the branch, affirmative advertising, and consultation with the fair housing group about the future of the branch.

In another case, a prescreening complaint settlement included monetary damages to the complainant and reporting by the lender. The redlining complaint where full application testing was completed (*Lamb* v. *Citizens National Bank of Bluffton*) included a substantial monetary settlement for the complainant plus the requirement that the lender offer loans in the minority area originally excluded from its service area definition, with a specific dollar amount set-aside for mortgage loans in minority neighborhoods.

NEED FOR FULL APPLICATION MORTGAGE LENDING TESTING AND CURRENT RISKS IN LENDING TESTING

It would be naive to think that the only people who engage in lending discrimination are loan originators. In fact, in several lawsuits filed in the Midwest, the loan officer has played no role in the act of discrimination. These lawsuits identify appraisers and underwriters for the lender, mortgage insurers, and secondary market investors as the instigators of the discriminatory conduct. To thoroughly investigate these participants in the loan application process, full application mortgage lending testing must be performed. The institutionalized nature of discrimination and the often subtle practices used to discourage, delay, or deny applicants can be successfully revealed using this type of testing.

As private fair housing practitioners, we understand the use of testing and its limitations. The greatest risk in any testing is that the tester will be identified. This risk is significantly reduced in lending testing because the tester generally uses either his or her own identity or an identity that can be verified.

Currently the only legal risk involved in lending testing is having a tester sign a completed loan application form. The mortgage loan application includes the following language:

> **Certification:** I/We certify that the information provided in this application is true and correct as of the date set forth opposite my/our signature(s) on this application and acknowledge my/our understanding that any intentional or negligent misrepresentation(s) of the information contained in this application may result in civil liability and/or criminal penalties including but not limited to, fine or imprisonment or both under provisions of Title 18, United States Code, Section 1001, and liability for monetary damages to the Lender, its agents, successors or assigns, insurers and any other person who may suffer any loss due to reliance upon any representation which I/we have made on this application.

Although the risk is minimal that a lender would file a complaint with the U.S. Attorney's Office for prosecution or that the federal government would prosecute such a complaint, it is still a risk. Our position is that this law was enacted to reduce the risk of fraudulent transactions. The purpose of testing is to discover if discriminatory treatment is occurring in the lending process, not to defraud the lender. In our testing, testers who signed mortgage loan applications were rejected; if they had been accepted, they would have declined the loan.

It should be the goal of the government, including federal regulators, to eliminate discriminatory lending practices. Therefore, the government should advocate making full application lending testing legal. The U.S. Attorney General could assist in achieving this goal by issuing an opinion that exempts qualified fair housing organizations and government agencies from enforcement of this law when they are conducting testing. The U.S. Congress could also pass legislation that exempts testers from this law.

WHO PERFORMS LENDING TESTS AND WHAT TRAINING DO THEY RECEIVE?

Testers are recruited from a wide variety of backgrounds. They are of all races and ages; of both sexes; and from low-, moderate-, and high-income neighborhoods. Some testers have immaculate credit and employment histories; some have blemishes on their credit reports. We also recruit people who will provide the "tester house." These are people who allow us to use their houses during a test, but do not want to be the actual tester.

Training lending testers generally takes two full days. We review fair housing laws with the testers, explain their rights and responsibilities, and tell them that their purpose in testing is to be objective fact finders. Testers participate in role-playing sessions that enable the trainer to evaluate how the tester "thinks on his or her feet." Testers are drilled in preparing written narratives, their powers of observation are tested, and they participate in a practice test. To train testers, an individual should be experienced in fair housing investigations and should have personally conducted various types of testing. In addition, one must be able to evaluate testers' objectivity and listening skills. To conduct training, NFHA uses a training manual, forms, and other materials that are the exclusive property of NFHA. Occasionally, newly trained testers will accompany an experienced tester to observe testing in action. Tester house owners are given instructions about how to respond to telephone inquiries, prepare narrative reports, and handle mail they may receive during a test.

Testers prepare written narratives shortly after completing each test. Although NFHA also uses test report forms, we have found that the detail in the written narratives often provides the clearest picture of the loan application experience. Testers do not make determinations about whether or not discrimination occurred, and they do not discuss their test with other testers.

Evaluating the test reports for discriminatory conduct is the next step. It is crucial that the evaluator have experience in fair housing law enforcement and knowledge of mortgage lending. Lack of knowledge of what specific behaviors, policies, and practices constitute violations of the fair housing laws can cause incidents of discrimination to be overlooked or discrimination to be found where none exists. Certainly, both results are equally hazardous to the lender and the community.

RECOMMENDATIONS FOR FUTURE SYSTEMIC AND INDIVIDUAL MORTGAGE LENDING TESTING

Systemic Testing

A joint systemic program between private, nonprofit fair housing enforcement agencies and the government could provide critical evidence about institutionalized lending discrimination. This evidence could then be used to change behavior, policies, and practices, and to make amends to victims of discrimination.

HUD, the Department of Justice (DOJ), and federal regulators should make funds available to conduct systemic testing of statewide, interstate, and nationwide lenders and mortgage companies. Such testing should cover a variety of loan types, including home purchases, home improvement, home equity lines of credit, and refinancing. Enforcement should be the primary use of the test results. The testing should identify how certain policies affect minority and integrated neighborhoods as well as minority and female applicants. Patterns of discrimination based upon creditworthiness, length and type of employment, cost of housing, and other factors should be included in the testing characteristics.

This testing should be performed under contract with qualified, private, nonprofit fair housing organizations because they have a long and credible history of recruiting and training testers, they have first-hand knowledge of the neighborhoods in their metropolitan areas, and they can perform tests in the most cost-effective and efficient manner.

Private foundations should also support enforcement-based testing. More than a decade of studies have supported the contentions of fair housing practitioners and neighborhood groups that lending discrimination is real. It is time to fund activities that eliminate practices that have significantly contributed to the decline of the quality of life and the decimation of the housing stock in America's minority and integrated neighborhoods.

Individual or Complainant-Based Testing

The number of lending discrimination complaints filed nationwide is very low. This is owing in large part to HUD's failure to publicize ways for people to recognize and report suspicious lending experiences. It is also partly because local fair housing agencies are inadequately staffed to handle lending discrimination complaints and, therefore, do not seek out these cases.

Private foundations and federal, state, and local governments should make funds available to increase the testing and investigative skills of nonprofit fair housing enforcement organizations in the area of lending. Funds should be used to hire and train individuals who specialize in mortgage lending testing, investigation, and CRA issues. Funds should also be set aside for litigation of verified complaints. These funds should be used to pay discovery costs, expert witness fees, and retainer fees for attorneys.

At a minimum, HUD should require every city that receives Community Development Block Grant funds to complete its analysis of "impediments to housing" study and then fulfill its requirement to "affirmatively further fair housing" by establishing a fair housing program that provides comprehensive education, enforcement, and research activities.

HUD should establish a special task force of investigators in mortgage lending who would be part of HUD's Systemic Case Branch. The annual performance evaluations of this staff should not be linked to the number of cases closed, but, rather, to the quality of the investigations performed—and the quality of the relief secured. Other members of the Systemic Case Branch should focus on investigating interstate real estate sales companies, homeowners insurance companies, and interstate and nationwide rental management companies.

FEDERAL REGULATORS' PROPOSAL TO CONDUCT FAIR LENDING EXAMINATIONS AND TESTING

Every federal regulator should be required to include experienced staff from DOJ or HUD in every fair lending examination conducted for the next three years. During this period, the regulator should create a special team of fair lending examiners to carry out the fair lending examination. Team members should be trained by the DOJ/HUD staff as well as private, nonprofit fair housing practitioners and attorneys experienced in mortgage lending. This is necessary because, as indicated earlier, federal regulators have a history of not finding lending discrimination despite having complete access to loan files.

In 1993, the Office of the Comptroller of the Currency (OCC) announced that it would conduct more fair lending investigations and engage in testing to uncover discriminatory practices by the institutions it regulates. Although this represents a greater commitment than in the past, one must question how an agency that has failed to identify past discrimination, or even follow up on HUD complaints or litigation filed against the lenders it regulates, suddenly has staff with the necessary qualifications to identify lending discrimination. In addition, OCC's position to exclude DOJ from its fair lending examinations indicates a lack of commitment both to finding discrimination and to enforce the Fair Housing Act.

Testing by regulators can be useful and important, but regulators already have enough information at hand to uncover discriminatory practices. Instead, regulators should fund prescreening testing. They have complete access to loan files that hold almost every piece of information needed to identify incidents of discrimination. Fair lending litigation experience proves that records review alone can uncover numerous incidents of discrimination. This was clearly evidenced in *United States* v. *Decatur Federal Savings and Loan Association* (1992), as well as in *Old West End et al.* v. *Buckeye Federal* (1987), *Saunders* v. *Diamond Savings and Loan* (n.d.), and *Walton* v. *Centrust Mortgage Company* (1991).[10]

If regulators wish to participate in testing, they should contract with qualified nonprofit fair housing enforcement agencies that are experienced in testing. These local groups have a better understanding of the dynamics operating in the community, and they are in a position to secure qualified testers and tester houses. Cooperating with experienced fair housing groups can provide both prescreening and full application testing. Full application testing will provide information about appraisal practices and the application of underwriting guidelines by mortgage insurers and the secondary market investors.

SUMMARY

In summary, private, nonprofit organizations have tested just the tip of the iceberg in lending discrimination and are aware of the enormous task ahead in eliminating discriminatory lending practices. With financial assistance from the federal government and private foundations, coupled with cooperative investigatory and testing efforts, it is possible to greatly increase mortgage loans to minority or female applicants, as well as within integrated and minority neighborhoods. Testing will remain a viable and valuable tool in this effort.

Notes

1. There was no testing in the following mortgage lending cases: *Old West End Association et al.* v. *Buckeye Federal Savings and Loan*, 675 F. Supp. 1100, 1103 (N.D. Ohio 1987); *Briceno* v. *United Guaranty Residential Insurance Company*, 3:89 CU 7325 (N.D. Ohio); *McMillian* v. *Huntington National Bank*, C 85-7530 (N.D. Ohio); and *Peck/Demuth* v. *First Federal of Delta*, case #C85-7602, unreported, 1985.

2. See cases cited in notes 93–108 and accompanying text in Schwemm (1990: §10.4[1]).

3. *United States* v. *Black Jack*, 508 F.2d 1179, 1185 (8th Cir. 1974), *cert. denied* 422 U.S. 1042 (1975).

4. *Robinson* v. *12 Lofts Realty, Inc.*, 610 F.2d 1032, 1036-37 (2nd. Cir. 1979).

5. If the lender changes the applicant's original request for the terms or conditions of a loan, this can be interpreted as rejecting the loan. If the changes in the terms or conditions discriminate against the loan applicant or the neighborhood where the housing is located, a fair housing complaint can be filed.

6. *Thomas* v. *First Federal Savings Bank of Indiana*, 653 F. Supp. 1130, 1338 (N.D. Ind. 1987).

7. This standard was modified in the memorandum and order in a motion for summary judgment in the *Steptoe* v. *Savings of America* case (*Steptoe* v. *Savings of America*, 800 F. Supp. 1542 [N.D. Ohio 1992]). The order was filed on August 25, 1992. Briefly, the court said it would waive the appraisal standard in *Buckeye Federal Savings* (1987) when the appraisal is the reason for the loan denial. This decision eliminates the opportunity for a lender to intentionally undervalue an appraisal to avoid a lawsuit.

8. *Lamb* v. *Citizens National Bank of Buffalo*, 3:89 CU 7502 (N.D. Ohio).

9. See Schwemm (1990: §26.2[2], notes 27–33 and accompanying text).

References

Center for Community Change. 1989. "Mortgage Lending Discrimination Testing Project." Washington, D.C.: Author/U.S. Department of Housing and Urban Development.

Cloud, C., and Galster, G. 1993. "What Do We Know about Racial Discrimination in Mortgage Markets?" *The Review of Black Political Economy* 22 (1, Summer).

Schwemm, R. 1990. *Housing Discrimination: Law and Litigation*. New York: Clark Boardman Callaghan.

Chapter Twenty-Four

PREAPPLICATION MORTGAGE LENDING TESTING PROGRAM: LENDER TESTING BY A LOCAL AGENCY

Rachel Lawton

Commissioners and staff of the Philadelphia Commission on Human Relations (henceforth, the Commission) have been concerned for the past several years about what the Home Mortgage Disclosure Act (HMDA) data have revealed about the mortgage lending pattern in Philadelphia. Quite simply, it is the same pattern that repeats itself in study after study across the United States: mortgage lending is taking place in predominantly white census tract areas, with disproportionately little lending occurring in minority census tract areas. This reality is particularly disturbing because, historically, minority and ethnic neighborhoods have been redlined by lenders according to race and ethnicity. Lack of capital entering these areas, owing to discrimination, has helped to create today's inner cities. Even though fair housing laws have eradicated the legislative foundation and support for such practices, affected neighborhoods have yet to recover.

With that in mind, and with support from a U.S. Department of Housing and Urban Development (HUD) Incentives Fund grant, the Commission sponsored a conference in 1991 whose purposes were to examine the federal fair housing laws, mortgage lending patterns and practices in Philadelphia, and low-income credit needs. Representatives from every major facet of the mortgage lending process were present at the conference: community groups, brokers, lenders, secondary mortgage market institutions, and private mortgage insurers. Among the speakers were Ira Goldstein, now with HUD, who presented an HMDA analysis of Philadelphia from 1987 to 1989 (see also Goldstein's chapter 19, this volume); Joe Rich, of the U.S. Department of Justice; and Shanna Smith, of the National Fair Housing Alliance (NFHA) (see also Smith and Cloud's chapter 23, this volume). The Commission's intent was to assemble as many key players as possible to explore the issues in a professional forum. Many of these groups are often antagonistic and blame each other when certain loans are not forthcoming. It was hoped that by facilitating discussion and communication among the participants, the flow of mortgage money into low-income and minority neighborhoods would increase.

In the wake of that conference, and in consideration of the fact that HMDA does not require lenders to keep a record of loan inquiries, the Commission applied for and received another HUD Incentives Fund grant to conduct both a preapplication mortgage lending testing program and another fair lending conference for the 1991–92 contract year. The Commission believed that approaching fair lending from both an enforcement and an educational perspective would be effective and revealing, which it was. This chapter describes the lending testing program we conducted and its results.

GOALS—PREAPPLICATION MORTGAGE LENDING TESTING PROGRAM

The goals for conducting the testing program were fourfold:

1. To determine whether black testers who inquire about mortgages are treated differently than white testers with regard to the quality, content, and quantity of information and services received at banks, savings and loans, and private mortgage companies.
2. To determine whether lenders are discriminating based upon the neighborhood in which a sale property is located.
3. To initiate complaints when violations occur.
4. To require affirmative steps by lenders to promote fair lending policies, practices, and services in the future.

Four teams of testers were hired, each consisting of one black and one white tester, to conduct five weeks of preapplication mortgage testing from August to September 1992, with the first few days spent in training. Testers were paid $10 an hour for 25 eight-hour days, for a total testing cost of approximately $16,000. Our local unemployment compensation office referred candidates to us; all hired candidates were experienced professionals in various fields who, for one reason or another, had been recently laid off. One of the testers, for instance, had recently retired from HUD's Fair Housing Equal Opportunity Office in Philadelphia, where he had been an accomplished investigator. All testers presented themselves in a credible manner, had good interpersonal and writing skills, and were middle-aged to approaching senior status. Each team consisted of testers of the same sex. One female black-white team and three male black-white teams were hired. One member of each team was required to have a car for use during the testing program and they were reimbursed for expenses.

Lenders were chosen from HMDA data for Philadelphia, the telephone book, and newspaper advertisements. Each targeted lender was tested by each of the four testing teams, but not more frequently than once a week by any one team. The importance of repeated testing was to determine whether discriminatory patterns and practices existed. Because of the degree of difficulty and the complexity in conducting lending testing, an isolated test would, in most cases, be insufficient to charge a lender with a violation of fair lending laws. It was anticipated that each team would be able to test two to three lenders a day, and that approximately 60 lenders would be repeatedly tested during the course of the program.

A computer programmer was furthermore hired for $4,600 to develop a software program to permit entry of all the data into a computer and generation of reports and comparative analyses.

TRAINING

Shanna Smith, of NFHA, conducted two days of preapplication mortgage lending training for the Commission.The eight testers, as well as five Commission personnel—the fair housing supervisor, the testing coordinator, two housing investigators, and a computer specialist—participated in the training. Smith presented clear information on the history and types of rental, sales, and lending testing; applicant- and neighborhood-based mortgage lending discrimination; the mortgage loan process; and procedures for mortgage lending testing. She also explained how to fill out test assignment and report forms. Her effective presentation ensured that even the most uninitiated member of the training group felt comfortable enough to begin the testing program. The second day of training included role playing, with the testers filling out actual test report forms and placing real telephone test calls to lenders. One of the most important features of the training were the materials supplied by NFHA, including all of the forms involved in conducting the training: a financial characteristics worksheet for each tester; a test assignment form; a telephone contact report form; and a detailed, five-page test report form. NFHA also supplied each participant with a *Mortgage Lending Testing Training Manual*, a

NFHA publication, which explained in detail all of the areas covered in the program.

DEVELOPING TESTER PROFILES AND MATCHING THEM TO REAL PROPERTIES

The commission identified primarily low- to moderate-income white, integrated, and minority neighborhoods from which the testers were to choose properties to allegedly buy. The actual properties were chosen from a Philadelphia Multiple Listing Service (MLS) book that was a year old. The theory was that these properties would probably have already been sold, so the testers would not risk showing a lender an agreement of sale on a property that had recently gone to settlement. The MLS book also provided the testers with pictures and other information about the properties that would be important during questioning. The eight testers participated in choosing the properties they would "buy," with prices ranging from $39,000 to $104,000. Each team's properties listed for about the same price. Once each tester had chosen a prospective property, he or she also participated in drawing up an agreement of sale. These agreements helped ensure that when the testers inquired about mortgages, they would be perceived as serious clients with a short period of time in which to choose a lender and apply for a loan.

Due to the cooperative relationship between the Commission and the Philadelphia Board of Realtors, and because brokers were aware that the Commission had demonstrated sensitivity to the role of brokers in the mortgage lending process (by including a broker on the agenda of the first mortgage lending conference), several brokers volunteered their offices as agents for the seller on the agreement of sale. This was an important step in creating a successful preapplication mortgage lending testing program, because there were insufficient numbers of people selling their own homes to prevent lenders from becoming suspicious if presented with hundreds of "For Sale by Owner" forms over a period of only a few weeks. We also could not risk falsifying brokers' names and addresses, because the testers could encounter experienced loan officers who might realize the offices did not exist. Blank agreement of sales forms were given to the Commission by a supportive broker, with each agreement stating that the tester (buyer) was looking for a 30-year, fixed-rate conventional mortgage and was prepared to make a 10-percent downpayment.

Lastly, the testers developed their own financial profiles. For testing purposes, each tester was going to buy his or her property with an alleged spouse. Employers, job titles, salaries, combined incomes, assets, and various debts were all computed so that each tester would qualify, but not by a wide margin, for the mortgage loan he or she was seeking. In hindsight, having the testers participate in choosing their properties, preparing their agreements of sale; and developing their financial profiles proved to be more than just a training tool. It also helped them to feel more like active participants in the testing program and less like temporary hired help—in addition to aiding their recall of the data—all of which probably improved the quality of their work.

RESULTS

Banks, savings and loans, and private mortgage companies both inside and outside Philadelphia were tested. Due to the fact that many lenders have offices only outside the city, Philadelphians often have to leave the city to apply for more competitive mortgage rates. Each testing team was given a specific geographical quadrant of the city and suburbs to test during a given week, and the areas were rotated each week. The numerical results of the tests are as follows:

274 Total number of individual tests over four weeks
192 Individual tests in which there was a matched test by a team member
96 Completed tests
68 Lenders tested (multiple branches of 11 of these lenders were tested)
11 Generated complaints to date; all complaints were also filed with HUD
5 Complaints resolved to date (3 by consent orders with publicity and 2 by settlement agreements with no publicity)

Of the 11 complaints filed, the following is a breakdown of the allegations:

- One complaint involving "steering," in which the lender allegedly refused to consider a loan in a predominantly black neighborhood in Philadelphia and suggested that the tester apply at another lender, while not rejecting an inquiry from a tester seeking a loan

in a predominantly white, upper-class neighborhood in Philadelphia.
- Two complaints involving terms and conditions, in which black testers allegedly were treated differently than white testers with regard to services and treatment.
- Three complaints involving lender policies that require borrowers to put 20 percent down to qualify for a mortgage. This type of policy is discriminatory because it has an adverse impact on minorities. There is a greater percentage of low-income minorities than whites who cannot afford to put 20 percent down on a property in Philadelphia.
- Five complaints where lenders refused to lend under the following amounts: $45,000; $50,000; $60,000; and $100,000. These policies are discriminatory because they have an adverse impact on minorities. In the Philadelphia metropolitan area, a greater percentage of minorities than whites live in housing that requires mortgage loans of less than $45,000.

On the whole, the lenders' responses to the complaints were professional, courteous, and cooperative. Most retained attorneys immediately or referred the matter to their legal departments. Of the three consent orders signed, the following are two samples of what respondents agreed to:

1. *Philadelphia Commission on Human Relations* v *St. Edmond's Savings and Loan Association*—Docket No. H92120892 HUD#03-93-0268-1

   Allegation: "The Respondent discriminated on the basis of race and/or color in lending, guaranteeing loans, accepting mortgages, or otherwise making available funds for the purchase or acquisition of a housing accommodation, including but not limited to requiring prospective customers to put 20% down on the properties they are purchasing."

   Consent Order: The respondent agreed to change its underwriting criteria to allow applicants the opportunity to put a minimum of 5 percent down on the purchase price of a home.

   In addition, the respondent agreed to advertise this fact in community newspapers that serve both the majority and minority populations in its service area; to inform local real estate agencies and community organizations of the policy change; to furnish the Commission with copies of advertising and notices that indicate the 5-percent down-payment mortgage policy; to advertise loan products in both majority and minority community newspapers; and, finally, to arrange for all loan officers and other employees responsible for distributing information or taking mortgage lending applications to receive fair lending training from the Philadelphia Commission on Human Relations. Copies of consent orders signed to date, as a result of the preapplication mortgage lending conference, are available from the Commission upon request.

2. *Philadelphia Commission on Human Relations* v *People's Mortgage Company, Inc.*—Docket No. H92110886 HUD#03-93-0085-1
   Allegation: "The Respondent discriminated on the basis of race and/or color in lending . . . including but not limited to: refusing to give mortgages under $60,000, which would eliminate many of the minority census tract neighborhoods in Philadelphia from qualifying . . . ."
   Consent Order: The respondent agreed to immediately eliminate any policy that establishes a minimum loan amount and to arrange for its staff to receive fair lending training from the Philadelphia Commission on Human Relations.

The two settlement agreements negotiated by the Commission were with banks, one large and one small. The large bank settled with the Commission after being sent summaries of the nine tests conducted at various branches. A review of all the tests at that bank suggested that blacks may be treated less courteously and given less information on loan products than whites. Both banks agreed to fair lending training.

Of the six cases that remain open, all but one are against private mortgage companies. Many of these mortgage companies serve as brokers for a small number of lenders whose home offices can be anywhere in the country. Respondents have commonly replied to our charges by explaining that they are forced to base their policies on the policies of national lenders who require a certain percentage down or a minimum loan amount to qualify. Other arguments have stated that it simply is not economically feasible to process loans under $50,000.

Although we continue to investigate these various allegations, one point is clear: these small mortgage companies, who serve as brokers for various national lenders, are but single examples of a far-reaching problem. Behind them are potentially thousands of lenders around the country whose underwriting criteria eliminate a disproportionate number of minorities from access to the most competitive mortgage rates.

Note

As of February, 1996, all eleven PCHR complaints have been settled. Six were settled by Consent Orders that include publicity clauses. Four were settled by Settlement Agreements with no publicity and one went to HUD and was conciliated in Sept. 1994. See Appendix 24A, following.

APPENDIX 24A CONCILIATION AGREEMENT

THE UNITED STATES DEPARTMENT OF HOUSING AND URBAN DEVELOPMENT
(hereinafter referred to as HUD)

COMPLAINANT: Philadelphia Commission on Human Relations

RESPONDENT: Sunrise Mortgage Company

EFFECTIVE DATE: Date signed by the Director, Office of Fair Housing and Equal Opportunity, U.S. Department of Housing and Urban Development, Mid-Atlantic Region

HUD FILE NO.: 03-93-05661-8

PCHR DOCKET NO: H-5889

WHEREAS, this Conciliation Agreement is a result of allegations that the Respondent discriminated in the provision of loans to purchase or refinance dwellings as defined under Section 802 of the Fair Housing Act (the Act), 42 U.S.C. 3600 *et seq.*; and

WHEREAS, complaints were filed with HUD and the Pennsylvania Human Relations Commission (PHRC), alleging a violation of the Act and the Pennsylvania Human Relations Act; and

WHEREAS, a determination has not been made, but the parties wish to amicably resolve this matter;

IT IS THEREFORE agreed that a Conciliation Agreement be entered into under the following terms and conditions:

1. "Complainant," as used herein, shall mean the Philadelphia Human Relations Commission, their representatives, agents, attorneys, successors and assigns. "Respondent," as used herein, shall mean itself, its officers, directors, shareholders, partners, agents,

attorneys, employees, affiliates, subsidiaries, successors and assigns.

2. It is understood that this Agreement does not constitute an admission of guilt by the Respondent of any violation of the fair housing laws, either state or federal.
3. This agreement shall apply to all activities conducted by the Respondent dealing with residential real estate-related transactions as defined under Section 805 of the Act.
4. The Respondent agrees to suspend its minimum loan amount policy. In order to comply with this term, the Respondent agrees to affirmatively seek investors that will purchase mortgages valued under $50,000 (the alleged discriminatory loan minimum raised by the Complainants).
5. The Respondent acknowledges that it has been advised that the practice of "price testing" or "overage" may have a discriminatory effect under the Act and the Equal Credit Opportunity Act (ECOA). Should a complaint be filed, HUD may accept the complaint. Among other things, the Respondent would have to demonstrate that there is a compelling, legitimate business necessity for this practice and that there is no less discriminatory alternative. The Respondent acknowledges that it may be required to submit documentation regarding cost and profitability of each of its loan products to support any "business necessity" claim.
6. The Respondent agrees that within the terms of this Agreement, the Respondent and all employees engaged in the activities defined in paragraph 3 shall obtain a minimum of four hours of instruction on the provisions and requirements of all applicable state and federal fair housing laws. The first training session shall occur within 60 days of the effective date of this Agreement. The instruction shall be conducted jointly by representatives of the Philadelphia Commission on Human Relations and the HUD's Office of Fair Housing and Equal Opportunity at the Respondent's main office.
7. The Respondent shall, with the assistance of the U.S. Department of Housing and Urban Development and the PCHR, within ninety (90) days of the effective date of this Agreement, develop a policy on non-discrimination in residential mortgage lending. The policy shall be reviewed and approved by the HUD Regional Office of Fair Housing and Equal Opportunity. This policy shall be provided to each of the Respondent's employees.
8. All employees involved in real estate related transactions shall, within seven (7) days of the Respondent's completion of its non-

discrimination policy, sign an acknowledgement that he/she has received, read and will comply with the Respondent's policy of non-discrimination and that he/she understands that failure to do so may result in legal action and/or dismissal. All future employees shall be provided a copy of this policy and sign said acknowledgement at the time of employment. The Respondent shall keep a copy of each signed acknowledgement on file, and mail a copy of all such acknowledgements to HUD's Office of Fair Housing and Equal Opportunity on the anniversary of the effective date of the Agreement.

9. No later than June 1st of each year (beginning in 1995) during the term of this Agreement, the Respondent shall contact the Complainant and HUD's Office of Fair Housing and Equal Opportunity in writing to obtain information concerning changes in state and federal fair housing laws.
10. The Respondent agrees to outreach, for purposes of marketing its products, to local fair housing groups and real estate brokers doing business in the minority and low income areas of this region. The Complainant agrees to assist by providing a list of real estate brokers doing business in minority and low income areas. The Respondent's outreach will commence within 90 days of the effective date of the Agreement.
11. The Respondent agrees to make available, for a period of two years from the time an application was taken, the complete loan application file including FNMA forms 1003, 1008 and all other application information. These loan application files will be available for inspection by HUD only and at the Respondent's main office.
12. The Respondent hereby waives, releases, and convenants not to sue the Complainant with respect to any and all claims arising out of, or in any way relating to, these facts or circumstances occurring between the Complainant and the Respondent for and in consideration of the Complainant's waiver of right (hereinafter stated), and in settlement of this matter with HUD.
13. The Complainant, for and in consideration of the Respondent's policy change, affirmative actions and reporting requirements under this Agreement, in full settlement of this matter, hereby waives, releases and covenants not to sue the Respondent with respect to any and all claims arising out of, or in any way, relating to, these facts or circumstances occurring between the Complainant and the Respondent.
14. It is agreed and understood that the Secretary may review compliance with this agreement and as part of such review may re-

quire documentation concerning compliance, may examine witnesses, and inspect the premises upon reasonable notice.

15. This Agreement shall remain in effect for three (3) years from the date the Regional Director, U.S. Department of HUD, Office of Fair Housing and Equal Opportunity, affixes his signature. If HUD determines that the provisions of this Agreement are not being implemented, the Secretary of HUD will advise the Department of Justice to initiate court action to enforce the terms of this Agreement under Section 810(c) of the Act. HUD has the sole authority to determine compliance.
16. The Complainant reserves the right to publicize this Agreement. Any Press Release that pertains to this Agreement will clearly state that there is no admission of guilt by the Respondent. The Press Release shall also state that HUD has made no finding with respect to whether the Respondent's actions violated the Fair Housing Act. Any Press Release regarding this case will also be written in such a way as to educate and inform the general public about fair housing issues and concerns. The Respondent will have the opportunity to review any Press Release regarding this case prior to its release. A draft Press Release, written by the Complainant and reviewed by the Respondent, is attached to this Agreement as Appendix A.

CONCILIATION AGREEMENT SUSPENDS MINIMUM LOAN AMOUNT POLICY

In a Conciliation Agreement entered into with the Philadelphia Commission on Human Relations (PCHR) and the U.S. Department of Housing and Urban Development (HUD), Sunrise Mortgage Company of Huntingdon Valley (Sunrise) agreed to suspend its minimum loan amount policy in providing loans to purchase or refinance homes in Philadelphia.

The Conciliation Agreement does not constitute an admission of guilt by the Respondent of any violations of fair housing laws and specifically states that HUD has made no determination that Sunrise was in violation of the Fair Housing Act.

The PCHR filed complaints against Sunrise after conducting a series of tests that showed that Sunrise refused to accept mortgages under $50,000, a policy alleged to have an adverse impact on minorities because there is a greater percentage of minorities living in housing requiring loans of less than $50,000 than there is of whites in the Philadelphia area.

As part of the Conciliation Agreement, Sunrise agreed to obtain from the PCHR and HUD's Office of Fair Housing and Equal Opportunity training for all employees on fair housing laws and was advised that its practice of "price tiering" or "overage" may have a discriminatory effect under the Fair Housing Act and the Equal Credit Opportunity Act.

Chapter Twenty-Five

THE CHEVY CHASE CASE

The text following reproduces the 1994 complaint and consent decree in the case of United States v. Chevy Chase Federal Savings Bank and B. F. Saul Mortgage Company, *in which the U.S. Justice Department alleged that Chevy Chase Federal violated the federal Fair Housing Act and the Equal Credit Opportunity Act by redlining African-American neighborhoods for mortgage lending. As a result, approximately 97 percent of the bank's loans in the Washington, D.C., metropolitan area from 1976 through 1992 were in predominantly white areas. The case was the first federal lending discrimination suit to focus solely on a bank's refusal to market its services in minority neighborhoods. At the time, Chevy Chase Federal was the largest savings institution based in the Washington, D.C., area.*

In its claim for monetary damages, the Justice Department required Chevy Chase Federal to pay $11 million to the redlined areas through a special loan program and the opening of bank branches and mortgage offices. The bank was to pay at least $7 million by offering special home mortgage loans at below-market rates to all residents of majority black areas in Washington, D.C., and Prince George's County, Maryland, resulting in approximately $140 million in special financing for the communities. The bank furthermore agreed to:

- *Open three mortgage offices in majority African-American neighborhoods in Washington, D.C., and one bank branch in the Anacostia section of the District of Columbia;*
- *Evaluate other sites for bank branches in the redlined communities;*
- *Take all reasonable steps to obtain a market share of mortgage loans in African-American neighborhoods that is comparable to the bank's market share in white neighborhoods;*
- *Extensively advertise the bank's services and target sales calls to real estate professionals in African-American areas; and*
- *Continue efforts to recruit African Americans for loan production positions and provide training to its loan staff in affirmative marketing programs.*

IN THE UNITED STATES DISTRICT COURT
FOR THE DISTRICT OF COLUMBIA

UNITED STATES OF AMERICA,
c/o U.S. Department of Justice
P.O. Box 65998
Washington, DC 20035-5998

U.S. Attorney's Office
555 4th Street, N.W.
Washington, DC 20001
Plaintiff,

v.

CHEVY CHASE FEDERAL SAVINGS BANK,
8401 Connecticut Avenue
Chevy Chase, Maryland
and
B. F. SAUL MORTGAGE COMPANY,
8401 Connecticut Avenue
Chevy Chase, Maryland
Defendants.

COMPLAINT

The United States of America alleges:

1. This action is brought by the United States to enforce the provisions of Title VIII of the Civil Rights Act of 1968 (the Fair Housing Act), as amended by the Fair Housing Amendments Act of 1988, 42 U.S.C. §§3601-3619, and the Equal Credit Opportunity Act, 15 U.S.C. §§1691-1691f.

2. This Court has jurisdiction of this action pursuant to 28 U.S.C. §13450, 42 U.S.C. §3614, and 15 U.S.C. §1691(h).

3. Defendant, Chevy Chase Federal Savings Bank (hereinafter "Chevy Chase") is a federally chartered savings and loan association doing business in the District of Columbia and in the States of Maryland and Virginia. Chevy Chase offers the traditional services of a financial depository institution, including the receipt of monetary deposits, the financing of residential housing, business, commercial and consumer loans, and other types of credit transactions. As of March 31, 1993, Chevy Chase had over $3.8 billion in total deposits,

and consolidated assets of $4.7 billion, making it the largest savings institution based in the Washington, D.C., metropolitan area.

4. Defendant B. F. Saul Mortgage Company was established in 1975, and has been a wholly owned subsidiary of Chevy Chase since 1984. The institution is responsible for effectuating the development of real estate-related transactions for Chevy Chase. The mortgage company solicits and originates real estate-related financing transactions, both residential and commercial, in the District of Columbia and in the States of Virginia and Maryland.

5. Chevy Chase commenced operations in 1969 as a Maryland chartered savings institution, and began operating as a federally chartered institution on April 8, 1986. Chevy Chase is subject to the regulatory authority of the Office of Thrift Supervision, and its deposits are insured by the Federal Deposit Insurance Corporation.

6. Chevy Chase is subject to federal laws governing fair lending, including the Fair Housing Act, the Equal Credit Opportunity Act, and the Community Reinvestment Act of 1977 (12 U.S.C. S§2901-2906). The Community Reinvestment Act and its implementing regulations require Defendant Chevy Chase to help to meet the credit needs of the entire community in which it operates, including the credit needs of low- and moderate-income neighborhoods.

7. Although Chevy Chase first began its operation in Chevy Chase, Maryland, it subsequently has expanded its business, and that of its mortgage subsidiary, to substantial portions of the Washington, D.C., metropolitan area.

8. A major component of the expansion of defendants' business has been the establishment of branches of Chevy Chase and offices of the B. F. Saul Mortgage Company. New branches and mortgage offices are designed to better serve existing customers and to attract new customers to the services of the institutions. Persons who become depository account customers of Chevy Chase are likely to inquire of the institution when they desire mortgage or other credit transactions, and the proximity of mortgage offices enhances business opportunities for the institutions.

9. The offices of the B. F. Saul Mortgage Company, in addition to servicing customers referred by Chevy Chase branches, actively solicit residential real estate-related financing business from real estate professionals and builders, particularly those real estate professionals and builders that operate in the area near the B. F. Saul Mortgage Company offices. The companies also have relied upon newspaper and radio advertising to increase the effectiveness of the business marketing programs.

10. By 1994, Chevy Chase has grown to a network of seventy-eight branch offices, and the subsidiary B. F. Saul Mortgage Company has grown to a network of twenty mortgage offices.

11. Residential housing data for the Washington, D.C., metropolitan area show significant patterns of racial segregation. According to the 1990 Census, over 74.3 percent of the African American population of the Washington, D.C., metropolitan area resides in the District of Columbia and Prince George's County; African Americans constitute 65.1 percent of the population of the District of Columbia. African American residents of the Washington, D.C., metropolitan area are concentrated in majority African American census tracts encompassing well-defined, predominately African American neighborhoods. Approximately 90.3 percent of the 395,213 African American residents of the District of Columbia reside in 126 majority African American census tracts, most of which are located in the Northeast, Southeast, and Southwest quadrants of the city; the vast majority (85.9 percent) of the District's white residents live in the Northwest quadrant. Approximately 76.7 percent of the African American residents of Prince George's county live in majority African American census tracts, most of which are concentrated in the central and southern portions of the county.

12. In expanding their business, defendants have acted to meet the savings and lending needs of the identifiably white residential areas of the Washington, D.C., metropolitan area and have intentionally avoided the servicing of identifiably African American residential areas.

13. As of June 29, 1993, the date the Department of Justice notified the defendants of its investigation, which led to the commencement of this action, seventy (70) of the then existing seventy-four (74) branches of Chevy Chase were located in census tracts in which a majority of the residents are not African American (hereinafter referred to as white census tracts). The location of two of the branches in majority African American census tracts was not selected by defendants, but rather the branches were acquired as part of a purchase of another institution. A third branch located in a majority African American residential area was first opened by the defendants at a time that the census tract was white. The remaining branch located in a majority African American census tract is outside of the Washington, D.C., metropolitan area.

14. As of June 29, 1993, seventeen (17) of B. F. Saul's then existing eighteen (18) mortgage offices were located in white census tracts.

The only office located in a majority African American census tract was opened in May 1993.

15. Although the defendants have considered and applied various standards in selecting locations for branches and mortgage offices (such as customer-deposit statistics, location of competitors, and the location of other businesses that may attract customers), the branch location factors have not been applied uniformly throughout the metropolitan area. Race has remained a factor in the selection of branch and mortgage office location, and the consideration of race has caused the absence of Chevy Chase branches and B. F. Saul Mortgage Company offices in African American neighborhoods.

16. The consideration of race in the business practices and customer solicitation efforts of the defendants is also evident from the service area boundaries that defendants have established under the Community Reinvestment Act. In 1986, Chevy Chase determined to include the entire District of Columbia within its delineated area, but in 1989 decided that the District of Columbia would not be served and thus dropped the District of Columbia in its entirety from the Chevy Chase delineated area. At the time the District of Columbia was dropped, Chevy Chase operated a branch within the District of Columbia. In 1992, after receiving criticism from the Office of Thrift Supervision for the decision to exclude the District of Columbia from its delineated area, Chevy Chase added a portion of the District to its delineated area; the portion chosen has the highest percentage of white residents of any area of the District of Columbia.

17. Employees of the B. F. Saul Mortgage Company have actively and aggressively solicited real estate-related financial transactions through real estate professionals and builders serving white residential areas, but intentionally have avoided seeking such business from real estate professionals serving African American residential areas. In 1980, the company established a policy not to seek financial transactions secured by District of Columbia properties located south of Calvert Street, N.W., or east of Connecticut Avenue, N.W. The portion of the District of Columbia that was designated for company business is the area with the highest percentage of white residents. While exceptions to this policy were made in some circumstances, the extent of the policy and the racial impact of the policy are revealed by the business that the company has transacted in the District of Columbia. From 1976 through 1993, only 21.1 percent of the mortgage loans that the defendants originated in the District of Columbia were secured by properties located in majority African American census tracts, and

78.9 percent were secured by properties located in white census tracts.

18. Other business practices utilized by the defendants, at least until the United States began its investigation, furthered the objective of servicing white residential areas and not servicing residential areas in which African Americans reside. As examples:

A. Defendants have utilized a commission structure to compensate the mortgage company's loan officers/originators and thus have provided an incentive to solicit and originate mortgage loans on higher-priced homes, and not on lower-priced homes in the Washington, D.C., area. Census statistics demonstrate that, on the average, residential properties in African American neighborhoods of the Washington, D.C., metropolitan area sell for lower prices than properties in white residential areas.

B. The B. F. Saul Mortgage Company has employed few African Americans in the position of loan officer/originator. Since 1985, the company has employed approximately 234 persons in these positions, of whom 5 (2.1 percent) were African American.

C. In advertising its mortgage products through the media, defendants have rarely or never utilized newspapers, radio stations, or other media that are oriented to the African American community in the Washington, D.C., area.

19. The policies and practices described in the preceding paragraphs have achieved the intended racial impact, as demonstrated by statistics revealing the number of home mortgage applications received by defendants from residents of African American neighborhoods of the Washington, D.C., metropolitan area, and by the number of home mortgage loans made by the defendants to residents of African American neighborhoods of the metropolitan area. Examples of those statistics are stated in paragraphs 20 through 24 below.

20. During 1991, Chevy Chase and the B. F. Saul Mortgage company received 3,515 mortgage loan applications from the Washington, D.C., metropolitan area. Of these applications, 3,432 (97.6 percent) were received from applicants in white census tracts, and 83 (2.4 percent) were received from applicants residing in majority African American census tracts.

21. During 1993, Chevy Chase and the B. F. Saul Mortgage Company received 7,311 mortgage loan applications from the Washington, D.C., metropolitan area. Of these applications, 6,947 (95.0 percent) were received from applicants in white census tracts, and 364 (5.0 percent)

were received from applicants in majority African American census tracts.

22. During 1988, Chevy Chase and the B. F. Saul Mortgage Company originated 2,050 mortgage loans in the Washington, D.C., metropolitan area. Of these loans, 1,998 (97.5 percent) were secured by properties located in white census tracts, and 52 (2.5 percent) were secured by properties located in majority African American census tracts.

23. During 1991, Chevy Chase and the B. F. Saul Mortgage company originated 2,744 mortgage loans in the Washington, D.C., metropolitan area. Of these loans, 2,691 (98.1 percent) were secured by properties located in white census tracts, and 53 (1.9 percent) were secured by properties located in majority African American census tracts.

24. During 1993, Chevy Chase and the B. F. Saul Mortgage Company originated 6,524 mortgage loans in the Washington, D.C., metropolitan area. Of these loans, 6,206 (95.1 percent) were secured by properties located in white census tracts, and 318 (4.9 percent) were secured by properties located in majority African American census tracts.

25. Exhibit C [not included here] contains maps depicting the location of properties secured by mortgage loans initiated by the defendants in the Washington, D.C., metropolitan area in the years 1978, 1985, and 1990–1992, as well as the racial composition of the neighborhoods in which the properties are located.

26. The racial disparities in the defendants' loan application and loan origination rates cannot be explained by differences in demand for mortgages in majority white areas as compared with majority African American areas. An analysis of the defendants' share of the total mortgage loans made in white and majority African American census tracts shows that defendants have a significantly greater market share in white census tracts than in majority African American census tracts. For example, from 1990 through 1992, the defendants' share of all purchase money mortgages originated in white census tracts ranged from 1.5 percent to 2.1 percent. During that same period, the defendants' share of such mortgages originated in majority African American census tracts ranged from 0.2 percent to 0.4 percent. These disparities in the market share of loan originations are statistically significant—the units of standard deviation range from 2.9 to 4.8—and cannot be explained by random, nonracial variations in the defendants' marketing and loan solicitation practices.

27. Certain mortgage products, such as loans insured through the Federal Housing Administration (FHA) or the Veterans' Administra-

tion (VA), are in greater demand in African American residential areas than in white residential areas. While the defendants offer both FHA and VA loans, they rarely advertise the availability of such loans and have made only a small number of such loans. Most of the loans made have been directed to the white, rather than the African American, community. For example, from 1985 through 1992, defendants originated 2,312 FHA and VA loans in the Washington, D.C., metropolitan area, 2,243 (97.0 percent) of which were secured by properties located in white census tracts, and 69 (3. 0 percent) of which were secured by properties located in majority African American census tracts.

28. The defendants have also originated the vast majority of their home improvement loans and non-occupancy (investor loans) in majority white areas. For example, in 1992, the defendants originated a total of 26 home improvement loans in the Washington, D.C., metropolitan area of which 23 (88.5 percent) were secured by properties located in white census tracts, and 3 (11.5 percent) were secured by properties located in majority African American census tracts. From 1985 through 1992, the defendants originated a total of 198 non-occupancy loans in the Washington, D.C., metropolitan area, of which 189 (95.5 percent) were secured by properties located in white census tracts, and 9 (4.5 percent) were secured by properties located in majority African American census tracts.

29. The vast majority of defendants' residential construction and commercial loans also support properties and businesses in white residential areas, with little corresponding support for properties and businesses located in African American residential areas. For example, according to the minutes of Chevy Chase's loan committees, the defendants made at least 502 residential construction and commercial loans from the late 1970s to the early 1990s in the four most populous jurisdictions in the Washington metropolitan area (Montgomery County and Prince George's County, Maryland, Fairfax County, Virginia, and the District of Columbia). More than 90 percent of those loans were made in the very heavily white jurisdictions of Fairfax County and Montgomery County, 29 (5.7 percent) were made in the majority African American District of Columbia, and 18 (3.5 percent) were made in the majority African American Prince George's County. Also, virtually all of the loans made in the District of Columbia were in predominantly white areas of the District.

30. From 1976 through 1992, the defendants made approximately 29,846 mortgage loans totaling $3,739,116,000 to borrowers in the Washington, D.C., metropolitan area. Of the total number of loans, 28,888 (96.8 percent) were secured by properties located in white

residential areas, and 958 (3.2 percent) were secured by properties located in African American residential areas. Of the total dollar amount, $3,627,977,000 supported properties in white census tracts, and $111,138,000 supported properties in majority African American census tracts.

31. The totality of the policies and practices described herein amount to a redlining of African American residential neighborhoods of the Washington, D.C., metropolitan area as off limits for the defendants' business. The policies and practices are intended to deny, and have the effect of denying, an equal opportunity to residents of African American neighborhoods, on account of the racial identity of the neighborhood, to obtain mortgage financing and other types of credit transactions. The policies and practices causing the racial impact are not justified by business necessity.

32. The defendants' actions as alleged herein constitute:

a. Discrimination on the basis of race in making available residential real estate-related transactions in violation of Section 805 of the Fair Housing Act, 42 U.S.C. §3605(a);

b. The making unavailable or denial of dwellings to persons, because of race, in violation of Section 804 (a) of the Fair Housing Act, 42 U.S.C. §3604(a);

c. Discrimination on the basis of race in the terms, conditions, or privileges of the provision of services or facilities in connection with the sale or rental of dwellings, in violation of section 804(b) of the Fair Housing Act; and

d. Discrimination against applicants with respect to credit transactions, on the basis of race, in violation of the Equal Credit Opportunity Act, 15 U.S.C. §1691(a)(1).

33. Defendants' policies and practices as alleged herein constitute:

a. A pattern or practice of resistance to the full enjoyment of rights secured by the Fair Housing Act, as amended, 42 U.S.C. §3601, *et seq.*, and the Equal Credit Opportunity Act, 15 U.S.C. §1691e(h); and

b. A denial of rights granted by the Fair Housing Act, as amended, to a group of persons that raises an issue of general public importance.

34. Persons who have been victims of defendants' discriminatory policies and practices are aggrieved persons as defined in 42 U.S.C. §3602(i), and have suffered damages as a result of the defendants' conduct as described herein.

35. The racially discriminatory policies and practices of defendants were, and are, intentional and willful, and have been implemented with reckless disregard for the rights of residents of African American neighborhoods.

WHEREFORE, pursuant to Federal Rule of Civil Procedure 38(b), the United States requests that a jury decide defendants' liability under the Fair Housing Act and the Equal Credit Opportunity Act for the pattern or practice of racial discrimination alleged herein and the amount of damages owed to the victims of defendants' discrimination. Furthermore, the United States requests that the Court issue an appropriate injunctive order, including a prospective remedial plan, to correct the effects of defendants' past discrimination and bring the defendants into compliance with federal fair lending law, and assess appropriate civil money penalties as to each defendant.

WHEREFORE, the United States prays that the Court enter an ORDER that:

(1) Declares that the totality of the policies and practices of defendants constitute a violation of Title VIII of the Civil Rights Act of 1968, as amended by the Fair Housing Amendments Act of 1988, 42 U.S.C. §§3601-3619, and the Equal Credit Opportunity Act, 15 U.S.C. §§1691-1691f;

(2) Enjoins defendants, their agents, employees and successors, and all other persons in active concert or participation with them, from discriminating on account of race in any aspect of their business practices;

(3) Requires defendants to develop and submit to the Court for its approval a detailed plan that: (a) defines a service area for defendants' business without regard to race and provides policies and procedures to ensure all segments of the defined area are served without regard to race, and (b) remedies the vestiges of defendants' discriminatory policies and practices;

(4) Awards such damages as decided by a jury that would fully compensate the victims of defendants' discriminatory policies and practices for the injuries caused by the defendants;

(5) Awards punitive damages in an amount to be determined by a jury to the victims of defendants' discriminatory policies and practices; and

(6) Assesses a civil penalty against each defendant, in order to vindicate the public interest.

The United States further prays for such additional relief as the interests of justice may require.

IN THE UNITED STATES DISTRICT COURT
FOR THE DISTRICT OF COLUMBIA

UNITED STATES OF AMERICA,
Plaintiff,

v.

CHEVY CHASE FEDERAL SAVINGS BANK
and
B. F. SAUL MORTGAGE COMPANY,
Defendants.

CONSENT DECREE

I. INTRODUCTION AND SUMMARY

This decree is entered, upon consent of the parties, to resolve claims of the United States that Chevy Chase Federal Savings Bank and the B. F. Saul Mortgage company (hereinafter referred to as the Bank and Mortgage Company) violated the Fair Housing Act, 42 U.S.C. §§3601-3619, and the Equal Credit Opportunity Act, 15 U.S.C. §§1691-1691f by discriminating on the basis of race in home mortgage financing and other types of credit transactions in the Washington, D.C., metropolitan area. The United States contends that the Bank and Mortgage Company have considered the racial composition of residential areas in determining where to market their products, and have avoided doing business in areas where African American persons reside. The United States further alleges that the challenged practices and policies are intended to deny, and have the effect of denying, an equal opportunity to residents of African American neighborhoods, on account of the racial identity of the neighborhood, to obtain mortgage financing and other types of credit transactions. The totality of the policies or practices challenged are commonly referred to as redlining.

In June 1993, the United States began the investigation that resulted in this lawsuit. Before and after that date the Bank and Mortgage Company initiated an aggressive effort to market their products to African American residential areas. Most notably, the Bank and Mortgage Company have opened three Chevy Chase Bank branches and four B. F. Saul Mortgage Company offices in African American residential neighborhoods of the Washington, D.C., metropolitan area, and have engaged in an aggressive campaign to solicit business in African American neighborhoods. Those efforts will be continued and expanded by the terms of this Consent Decree.

By this decree, the Bank and Mortgage Company have committed to a remedial plan by which they will take all reasonable actions to obtain a market share of mortgage loans in African American neighborhoods that is comparable to the Bank and Mortgage Company's market share in white residential areas. The Bank and Mortgage Company's plan to achieve this objective includes opening another three mortgage offices in African American residential neighborhoods of the Washington, D.C., metropolitan area in the near future, which will provide some banking services by automated teller machines (ATMs). The Mortgage Company also will expand significantly its outreach efforts to market loan products in African American neighborhoods. Promptly upon receipt of regulatory approval from the Office of Thrift Supervision, the Bank will open a branch in the Anacostia area of Washington, D.C., and the Bank expects to open additional branches in African American residential neighborhoods of Washington, D.C., and Prince George's County, Maryland, during the term of this consent decree.

The Bank and Mortgage company will invest $11,000,000 in the African American community of the Washington, D.C., metropolitan area during the five-year consent decree period to settle the claims of the United States for the damage caused by the alleged redlining, and in furtherance of their commitment to better serve this community. This investment will be undertaken through a combination of subsidized lending programs directed to Washington, D.C., metropolitan area African American neighborhoods and the opening of new bank branches and mortgage offices in these neighborhoods. Specifically, over five years the Bank and Mortgage Company will provide at least $7,000,000 in lending subsidies for the special home mortgage loans, which may be increased depending on the number of bank branch/mortgage office locations to be opened during the consent decree period.

Chevy Chase and the Mortgage Company adamantly deny that any act or omission on their part as alleged in the government's complaint or this consent decree as violative of federal law was motivated in any way by discriminatory intent or racial bias. The Bank and Mortgage Company have agreed to the undertakings set forth in the Consent Decree to settle the government's claims against them and because they believe the affirmative lending actions and practices described will enable them to better serve the African American community.

This Consent Decree is entered into solely for the purposes of resolving the claims against Chevy Chase and the Mortgage Company in the present proceeding involving their lending practices in the Washington, D.C., metropolitan area. The Court has not made any finding or determination that there has been a violation of the law. The entry of this consent Decree is not to be considered an admission or finding of any violation of law by Chevy Chase or the Mortgage Company.

Since this lawsuit is being resolved without a public trial, the United States believes the public interest is furthered by explaining, in Part II of this Decree, the factual allegations on which the United States relies in claiming the violations of the Fair Housing Act and the Equal Credit opportunity Act. Part III of the Decree will describe the remedial steps taken by the Bank and Mortgage Company since June of 1993. Part IV will describe the remedial plan to be implemented in the future. Part V will describe the special loan programs which will provide compensation to the alleged redlined areas. The remaining Parts describe record keeping, reporting requirements, modification of the decree, jurisdiction retention, dismissal procedures, and costs.

II. DESCRIPTION OF THE ALLEGED LEGAL VIOLATIONS

Chevy Chase began operating from a single facility in 1969, and the B. F. Saul Mortgage Company was established as a wholly owned subsidiary in 1975. Chevy Chase has grown into the largest savings and loan association in the Washington, D.C., metropolitan area. By June of 1993, when the United States initiated its investigation, Chevy Chase operated seventy-four branches, and the Mortgage Company operated eighteen offices.

The expansion of the Bank and Mortgage Company's business has taken place in a metropolitan area with segregated living patterns. According to the 1990 Census, over 74.3 percent of the African American population of the Washington, D.C., metropolitan area resides in the District of Columbia and Prince George's County; African Americans constitute 65.1 percent of the population of the District of Columbia. African Americans are concentrated in majority.African American census tracts encompassing well defined, predominantly African American neighborhoods. Approximately 90.3 percent of the 395,213 African American residents of the District of Columbia reside in 126 majority African American census tracts, most of which are located in the northeast, southeast, and southwest quadrants of the city; the vast majority (85.9 percent) of the District's white residents live in the northwest quadrant. Approximately 76.7 percent of the African American residents of Prince George's County live in majority African American census tracts, most of which are concentrated in the central and southern portions of the county. The Bank and Mortgage Company have marketed their loan products in a number of ways. The Community Reinvestment Act requires Chevy Chase to define the area it intends to serve, and the Bank and Mortgage Company's business intentions are further revealed through branching decisions and loan office location decisions.

The Bank and Mortgage Company also market loan products through outreach by loan officers and other employees to real estate professionals and builders, and to the community at large by advertising. The Bank and Mortgage Company have provided instructions to loan-production employees regarding the areas to which they should devote their efforts, and also have indirectly influenced loan production in some residential areas by the manner in which the Bank and Mortgage Company compensate loan production employees, by the manner in which the Bank and Mortgage Company advertise their products, and by employee recruitment and retention.

In defining a Community Reinvestment Act delineated area, the Bank and Mortgage Company's treatment of the District of Columbia has varied. In 1986, Chevy Chase included the District of Columbia in its delineated area, although it had no branches in the District and made few loans outside of heavily white residential areas. In 1989, the institution eliminated the District of Columbia in its entirety from its delineated community, even though, by that time, it had a branch in the heavily white upper northwest area of the District. When that decision was criticized by federal regulators, the institution, in 1992, added the heavily white upper northwest corner of the District to the delineated area. At the time the United states began its investigation, Chevy Chase was still operating under this delineation, which included only the most heavily white portion of the District of Columbia. Chevy Chase did include all of Prince George's County in its delineated community.

If this lawsuit had proceeded to trial, the United States would have presented evidence from real estate professionals demonstrating that the Bank and Mortgage Company rarely solicited loan-production business from professionals serving African American residential areas, but actively solicited such business from professionals serving white residential areas. At least one witness would testify that in 1980, the company established a policy for its own employees not to seek financial transactions in the District of Columbia south of Calvert Street, N.W., or east of Connecticut Avenue, N.W. The area accepted for business is the most heavily white residential area of the District of Columbia. Exceptions to this policy were made for residential areas into which white persons were moving, such as Capitol Hill and DuPont Circle. The policy allegedly remained in effect until 1992.[1]

Loan officers of the Bank and Mortgage Company have been paid on a commission basis, which encourages them to direct mortgage production toward residential areas with higher housing values. This policy has contributed to the overall failure to service African American residential areas, since the properties in many of the African American neighborhoods sell for a lower amount than properties in white residential areas. Prior to the initiation of the United States' investigation, the Bank and Mortgage company had employed few African Americans in loan production positions. And the Bank and Mortgage Company had rarely, if ever, used minority-directed media to advertise the availability of mortgage loans and other products offered by the Bank and Mortgage Company.

At the time the investigation began, in June 1993, Chevy Chase was serving the public through a system of seventy-four branches. Four of the seventy-four bank branches operating in June 1993 were located in majority African America census tracts; one was located in a majority African American census tract in Annapolis, Maryland, and the three remaining branches were located in African American areas in the Washington, D.C., metropolitan area. Two of these branches located in African American census tracts in the D.C., area were acquired in purchasing another institution. The other branch, which opened in 1976, is located in a census tract that was white at the time of the 1970 census and majority African American at the time of the 1980 census. In sum, prior to the United States' notice of an investigation, Chevy Chase had never opened a branch in an identifiably African American neighborhood in the Washington, D.C., metropolitan area.[2] The location of mortgage offices reveals a similar pattern.

The Bank and Mortgage Company did not open a mortgage office in a majority African American census tract until May of 1993.

Further evidence of redlining—and the overall impact of the challenged practices—is revealed by the location of properties secured by loans actually made by the Bank and Mortgage Company. Data submitted by the Bank and Mortgage Company pursuant to the Home Mortgage Disclosure Act (HMDA) show that from 1985 through 1993, the Bank and Mortgage Company made the vast bulk of their home mortgage loans in majority white census tracts of the Washington, D.C., metropolitan area; in no year was the percentage of loans in white census tracts less than 95 percent of the total.[3] During 1993, the Bank and Mortgage company originated 6,524 mortgage loans in the Washington, D.C., metropolitan area. Of these loans, 6,206 (95.1 percent) were secured by properties located in majority white census tracts, and 318 (4.9 percent) were secured by properties located in majority African American census tracts.

The Bank and Mortgage Company's loan applications also showed the same disparities. Only 5.7 percent of the loan applications received from 1988 to 1992 were from majority African American census tracts. Moreover, during 1993, the institutions received 7,311 mortgage loan applications from the Washington, D.C., metropolitan area. Of these applications, 6,947 (95 percent) were received from applicants in majority white census tracts, and 364 (5 percent) were received from applicants in majority African American census tracts.

The racial disparities in the Bank and Mortgage Company's loan applications and originations cannot be explained by differences in demand for mortgages in white areas and majority African American areas. The Bank and Mortgage Company's performance, when analyzed in relation to records of the total number of mortgage loans made by all providers, reveals that the Bank and Mortgage Company have a significantly greater market share in the white census tracts than in majority African American census tracts. For example, from 1990 through 1992, Chevy Chase's share of all purchase money mortgages originated in majority white census tracts ranged from 1.5 to 2.1 percent. During the same period, the institution's share of such mortgages originated in majority African American census tracts ranged from 0.2 percent to 0.4 percent. The disparities are statistically significant and cannot be explained by non-racial variations in the institutions' marketing and loan solicitation practices.

The redlining practices were not limited to home financing. The vast majority of the Bank and Mortgage Company's residential construction and commercial loans also support properties and businesses in white residential areas, with little corresponding support for properties and businesses located in African American residential areas. The Bank and Mortgage Company made at least 502 residential construction and commercial loans from the late 1970s to the early 1990s in the four most populous jurisdictions in the Washington, D.C., metropolitan area (Montgomery County, Prince George's County, Fairfax County, and the District of Columbia). More than 90 percent of those loans were made in the very heavily white jurisdictions of Fairfax County and Montgomery County; 5.7 percent were made in the District of Columbia, virtually all in white areas; and 3.5 percent were made in Prince George's County.

III. PROACTIVE LENDING INITIATIVES BY THE BANK AND MORTGAGE COMPANY

The United States recognizes that the Bank and Mortgage Company have voluntarily taken a number of steps toward improving fair lending performance since early to mid 1993, and the receipt of the United States' investigation-notice letter in June 1993.

Throughout this period the Bank and Mortgage Company have taken steps to help meet the credit needs of African American neighborhoods. Advertising efforts directed to African American neighborhoods have been increased. Advertisements have been placed in three newspapers directed to African American citizens: *Capitol Spotlight*, *New Dimensions*, and *Washington Informer*. The advertising initiative also has included the use of radio stations directed to the African American community. The Bank and Mortgage Company have increased efforts to solicit business from real estate professionals and builders serving African American residential areas. A recent survey in May 1994 undertaken by an independent consultant found that the Mortgage Company now has the highest name recognition among such real estate professionals.

In late 1993, the Mortgage Company retained an independent consultant to conduct a mystery shopper program to test for racial discrimination, and no discrimination in the treatment of applicants was reported.

In January 1994, the Mortgage Company revised the method of compensating loan officers in an effort to increase loan originations in residential areas with lower housing values. The revised method provides for a commission payment of 10 basis points more than the standard commission of 50 basis points for all loans of $60,000 or less in the Washington, D.C., metropolitan area. In addition, the Mortgage Company has established a special salary plus commission compensation structure for four Washington, D.C., originators. The Mortgage Company has also increased substantially the number of African American employees in loan-production positions.

In February 1994, Chevy Chase revised its Community Reinvestment Act delineated community so as to include the District of Columbia in its entirety. Chevy Chase has opened three new branches in African American residential areas.

Chevy Chase and the Mortgage Company have increased their lending initiatives in the Washington, D.C., metropolitan area. In March 1993, they offered a $25,000,000 special lending program featuring below-market fixed-rate mortgages to low- and moderate-income individuals throughout the Washington, D.C., metropolitan area. This fund was fully subscribed within 60 days. In December 1993, they committed $20,000,000 to the D.C. Community Development Fund for home buyers and invested $30,000 in the Washington, D.C., advertising campaign to publicize the program. In December 1993, they committed $1,000,000 to the $4,500,000 Prince George's County Revitalization Loan Fund that provides loans to small businesses in Prince George's County. In May 1994, they announced an addition of $100,000,000 to the Community Development Loan Fund for low- and moderate-income borrowers, and $50,000,000 in support (of) revenue bond programs to government jurisdictions, which include for the first time Prince George's County and the District of Columbia Mortgage Revenue Bond Program.

The Mortgage Company has also increased significantly the number of applications and home mortgage loan originations from African Americans during 1993. Specifically, between 1991 and 1993 the Mortgage company increased the number of home mortgage loan applications received from African American borrowers from 249 to 1074, and increased the number of home mortgage loans made to such borrowers from 162 to 884.

In addition, Chevy Chase is aggressive in offering other types of credit to the African American communities in the Washington, D.C., metropolitan area. Chevy Chase's commitment to lending to African American borrowers is exemplified by the bank's credit card lending record, which shows that the bank has aggressively made credit card loans available to residents of majority African American census tracts in its community. Indeed, Chevy Chase has the second highest market share in credit card lending to lower income and minority groups of any lender in the Washington, D.C., metropolitan area.

The United States agrees that the above-described actions are positive remedial steps that address the issues which were the subject of the United States' investigation and complaint. These successful actions are hereby incorporated by reference in the remedial plan described in Part IV.

IV. REMEDIAL ORDER

A. General Injunction

Defendant Chevy Chase Federal Savings Bank and defendant B. F. Saul Mortgage Company, and all officials, employees, agents and successors of the Bank and Mortgage company, are hereby enjoined from engaging in any act or practice that discriminates on the basis of race in any aspect of residential real estate related transactions or in the extension of other types of credit. The Bank and Mortgage Company shall take the steps necessary to ensure racial fairness in the marketing, solicitation, and processing of home mortgages, and other forms of financing, such as commercial loans and residential construction loans, and other credit offered by the institutions, and in the provision of services or facilities in connection with any such credit transactions. The Bank and Mortgage Company are further enjoined from imposing, on the basis of race, different terms or conditions for the availability of credit. Fair Housing Act, 42 U.S.C. §§3604 and 3605; Equal Credit Opportunity Act, 15 U.S.C. §1691(a)(1).

B. Community Reinvestment Act Delineated Community

As noted in Part III, in February 1994 Chevy Chase revised its delineated territory to include the District of Columbia, in its entirety. During the period that the Consent Decree remains in effect, Chevy Chase will continue to include all portions of the District of Columbia and Prince George's County, Maryland, in its delineated territory.

C. Marketing Program

The Bank and Mortgage Company shall implement an aggressive marketing program designed to improve performance in meeting the credit needs of African American residential areas of the Washington, D.C., metropolitan area. The Bank and Mortgage Company will take all reasonable steps to ensure that home mortgage loans are marketed and made available in African American residential areas to an extent comparable to white residential areas. The success of the remedial plan will be judged by its effectiveness in achieving a market share of home mortgage loans in majority African American census tracts that is reasonably comparable to the Bank and Mortgage Company's market share in white residential areas during the period of time that this decree is in effect. This provision should not be interpreted as requiring the Bank and Mortgage Company to make bad loans. Rather, the provision requires aggressive marketing and outreach as a remedy for the alleged past discrimination, and envisions that the expected applicants will be treated without regard to race. So long as all reasonable steps have been taken to achieve this goal, the Bank and Mortgage Company will be considered to be in compliance with this provision of the decree.

The Bank and Mortgage Company will retain discretion to implement other actions that they believe appropriate to achieve the remedial goal, without prior approval of the United States or this Court except as otherwise provided in this order. All provisions of the Consent Decree are to be implemented consistent with the safety and soundness of the institution. The initial plan of the Bank and Mortgage Company for achieving the remedial goal is as follows:

1. Additional Bank Branch and Mortgage Office Locations

In addition to the new branches and mortgage loan offices described in Part III, the Bank and the Mortgage Company will take further action to provide banking and lending services to African American communities. Subject to the approval, where necessary, of the Office of Thrift Supervision, the Bank and Mortgage Company will open additional bank branch and/or mortgage office locations in African American neighborhoods in the Washington, D.C., metropolitan area during the consent decree period. The mortgage offices will effectuate home mortgage lending in the African American communities in which they are established and will also provide certain banking services through automated teller machines (ATMs). Specifically, the Bank and Mortgage Company already have opened a branch/mortgage office on Riggs Road and plan to open a similar facility in the Anacostia section of southeast Washington, D.C., promptly upon receipt of regulatory approval from the Office of Thrift Supervision. The Bank will exercise its best efforts to open this branch by year-end 1994. In addition, the Mortgage Company will open a mortgage office in or around the Seat Pleasant area of Prince George's County, Maryland, by June 1995. Additionally, the Mortgage Company will open another mortgage office in a majority African American census tract in D.C., outside of the northwest quadrant, by January 1996.

The Bank shall continue to evaluate sites for branches in majority African American census tracts that the United States contends were redlined. By March 1, 1995, the Bank shall present its evaluation of branching possibilities to the United States, and the parties shall jointly consider whether the overall goals of the decree can be better served by additional branches or by utilizing in the special loan fund the money that would have been committed to new branches.[4]

The prior approval of counsel for the United States shall be obtained for the precise location of the mortgage offices and branches. If the United States fails to object to a location within thirty days of receipt of a request for approval, the request shall be deemed to be approved. Any branch the bank seeks to open pursuant to this decree shall be subject to the normal regulatory approval of the office of Thrift Supervision.

The new branches and mortgage offices opened pursuant to the terms of this decree shall remain open during the life of this decree.

2. *Criteria for Future Locations of Branch Banks and Mortgage Offices*

The Bank and Mortgage Company will follow an objective set of criteria to evaluate future branch and mortgage office openings, closings, and other significant changes in services, and these criteria will incorporate the Bank and Mortgage Company's Community Reinvestment Act obligations, as well as the remedial design of this decree. The institutions will pay particular attention to how any proposed changes would affect the Bank and Mortgage Company's ability to meet the credit needs of low- and moderate-income neighborhoods, especially neighborhoods in predominantly African American census tracts. The Bank and Mortgage company will promptly provide to counsel for the United States a copy of any applications or notices to open or close any branches or mortgage offices during the period in which this decree is in effect.

3. *Advertising*

The Bank and Mortgage Company will further augment an advertising program, as described in Part III, designed to attract qualified applicants for home mortgages from African American residential areas of its community, as defined pursuant to the Community Reinvestment Act. The advertising program will include special provisions to target residents of predominantly African American neighborhoods.

a. The Mortgage Company shall continue to advertise in media directed to the African American community as described in Part III. During the term of this decree it will place a total of at least 960 column-inches of advertising during each one-year period of the Consent Decree in newspapers or other publications oriented towards African Americans in the Washington, D.C., metropolitan area. It may vary the size and frequency of advertisements and the choice of publications for this advertising campaign, as long as the above overall average is met for each one-year period. These advertisements will be for home mortgage products, and will mention the availability of FHA and VA loans and may also include references to other loan products that have comparable advantages.

b. The Mortgage Company will create special point-of-sale materials (e.g., posters, brochures, etc.) to advertise products and services of interest to African American home buyers and place the materials in bank branches and mortgage offices in predominantly African American neighborhoods.

c. The Mortgage Company will develop a brochure describing its special products for first time homebuyers, community homebuyers program, its FHA and VA loan programs, and/or comparable programs. The Mortgage Company will distribute at least 2,500 of these brochures per year during the Consent Decree period through direct mail and appropriate channels such as real estate professionals serving African American residential areas of the Washington, D.C., area.

d. All advertisements for home mortgage loan products will contain an equal housing opportunity logotype, statement, or slogan as described in the Fair Housing Advertising regulations of the United States Department of Housing and Urban Development, 24 C.F.R. Part 109. The lender will follow the guidance of Tables I and II of Appendix I to 24 C.F.R. Part 109 in selecting appropriate type size as well as a slogan, statement, logotype, and other standards for advertising.

e. All of the Mortgage Company's advertising that uses human models in video, photographs, drawings, or other graphic techniques will reasonably represent African American as well as white residents and other minorities of the area which the Bank and Mortgage Company serve. Models, if used, will portray persons in an equal social setting and indicate to the general public that the Bank and Mortgage Company's products are available on a nondiscriminatory basis.

f. The Mortgage Company will place a total of at least 360 thirty-second spots per one-year period of the Consent Decree on at least three radio stations oriented to the African American communities in the Washington, D.C., metropolitan area. All of this advertising will be for home mortgage products, and the Mortgage Company's advertising program will include advertising of the availability of FHA and VA loans and other comparable loan programs. The Mortgage Company may vary the frequency of the spots and choice of stations for its advertising campaigns, as long as the above overall total is met for each one-year period.

g. In all radio and television advertisements and promotions for home mortgage loans, the statement "Equal Housing Lender" will continue to be audibly stated. In the alternative, if a television advertisement or promotion for home mortgage loans includes a written statement appearing on the screen, the nondiscrimination statement may so appear; the nondiscrimination statement must continue to meet the requirements set forth in Appendix I to 24 C.F.R. Part 109 and must appear on the screen as long as any other written statement appears.

4. Ascertaining Credit Needs of African American Neighborhoods

The Mortgage Company will conduct additional ascertainment efforts to further understand the home mortgage credit needs of the African American community. In this regard, representatives of the lender will meet each year with members of at least three African American community or civic groups to examine current Mortgage Company loan products, services, and advertising, and discuss ideas for improvements, if improvements are necessary.[5]

5. Other Efforts to Solicit Business in African American Residential Areas

a. The Mortgage Company will continue to target real estate agents and builders active in neighborhoods in predominantly African American census tracts within its delineated community for sales calls. The lender will maintain a list of the names and addresses of the real estate agents, builders, and developers on whom it intends to make sales calls, including those entities the Mortgage Company currently calls on pursuant to the initiatives discussed in Part III.

b. Each loan officer will maintain a log of all sales calls on a real estate agent or agency, builder, or other person or organization contacted for the purpose of soliciting loan applications in targeted African American neighborhoods.

c. The Mortgage Company will authorize a position for a supervisor who will be responsible for overseeing the activities of all loan officers regarding soliciting and originating home mortgage loans in predominantly African American neighborhoods in the Washington, D.C., metropolitan area and special loan programs that are geared toward low- and moderate-income neighborhoods. The individual will additionally develop a program to provide loan officers with expertise in these special loan programs, and in targeting low- and moderate-income neighborhoods. The supervisor will also prepare annual reports on these activities, and serve as a resource to loan office managers and loan officers to encourage the origination of more home mortgage loans to African American borrowers.

d. The Mortgage Company will retain the lending incentives discussed in the compensation package for loan officers described in Part III for the duration of the decree.

6. Recruitment of Personnel

a. The Bank and Mortgage Company will continue their efforts to recruit African American candidates for positions with the companies with particular emphasis on loan-production positions, such as Loan Officer, Underwriter, Loan Processor, Staff Appraiser, Assistant Branch Manager, and Branch Manager.

7. Special Programs

a. The Mortgage Company will regularly conduct seminars for real estate agents or agencies active in African American neighborhoods of the Washington, D.C., metropolitan area whereby the institution apprises the agents of products offered, including the programs set out in this decree, and otherwise furthers business contact with the agents. At least six such seminars will be conducted by the B. F. Saul Mortgage Company each year at locations reasonably convenient to the agents' business operations during the consent decree.

b. The Mortgage Company will regularly conduct programs such as the Community Homebuyers Program developed by Fannie Mae in the African American neighborhoods of the Washington, D.C., metropolitan area. The Mortgage Company's programs, such as the Homebuyers Program, will instruct participants about such topics as managing credit, controlling the household budget, preparing for and applying for a home mortgage loan. The company will use its best efforts to present this Program at least twelve times per year during the consent decree period.

c. The Mortgage Company will hire a new credit counselor who will be responsible to assist borrowers that do not meet the institution's underwriting standards.

8. Non-discriminatory Treatment of Home Mortgage Loans

a. The Bank and Mortgage Company will develop procedures that outline guidance for bank branch personnel to follow regarding all inquiries for home mortgage loans. Such guidelines shall include, among other things, that bank branch personnel record the name and race of each person who inquires about home mortgages and shall provide each person with a copy of a home mortgage loan application and assist the customer in setting up an interview with a loan officer at a mortgage office, bank branch, or other mutually convenient location.

b. The B. F. Saul Mortgage company will solicit information necessary to allow for fair evaluation of applications and will assess completed applications from African American customers in the same manner and under the same underwriting criteria that it applies to white customers.

c. The Mortgage Company will continue its Second Review Committee review of each initially rejected loan. The members of the Mortgage Review Committee will certify by signature that he/she concurs with or has elected to change (for reasons noted) the initial decision.

9. Training

a. The Mortgage Company will continue to provide training to all of its staff with significant involvement in home mortgage lending to ensure their activities are conducted in a nondiscriminatory manner.

b. The Mortgage Company will provide training to its loan origination staff on its affirmative marketing programs, including targeted sales calls, and will monitor their activities.

c. Within 45 days after the entry of this Consent Decree, the Mortgage Company will conduct comprehensive training sessions on the applicable provisions of this consent Decree for every Loan Originator, Underwriter, Staff Appraiser, Loan Processor, Assistant Branch Manager, and Branch Manager.

d. The Bank and Mortgage Company will continue to conduct regular compliance training of staff with significant involvement in home mortgage lending on the Community Reinvestment Act, the Fair Housing Act, the Equal Credit Opportunity Act, and this Consent Decree. This training will continue to include scheduled training sessions, staff meetings, compliance newsletters, videotapes, regulatory updates, and/or comparable methods. The lender will incorporate cultural diversity and sensitivity training into its training programs given to all managers and customer-contact employees. The lender may contract with outside consultants to provide any of this training.

e. The Mortgage Company will continue to contract with a qualified organization during the consent decree period to periodically test for racial discrimination in its home mortgage lending. The Mortgage Company will review the testing results with the relevant individual employees and will use the results to determine how to address any concerns with individual employees and whether changes in training are necessary.

V. SATISFACTION OF THE UNITED STATES' CLAIMS FOR MONETARY RELIEF

The Bank and Mortgage company will invest $11,000,000 in the neighborhoods that the United States contends were redlined. This investment will satisfy the claim of the United States for monetary damages, and the monetary remedy will be enforceable by the United States as would be any other court order or judgment.

At least $7,000,000 of the investment will be provided in the form of special mortgage loans offered to residents of majority African American census tracts that the United States contends were redlined. The financing will be offered at interest rates, or on terms, that are more advantageous to the borrower than normally would be provided, and thereby the lender will subsidize each transaction. Each $1,000,000 of subsidy provided by the Mortgage Company will provide approximately $20,000,000 in special financing for the community.

Persons living in the defined census tracts who desire to participate in the financing program for home mortgage loans up to $203,150 will, if they otherwise qualify for financing, have an option of (1) obtaining a mortgage loan (including both purchase money and refinancing) at an interest rate that is one percent below the rate that the Bank and Mortgage Company otherwise would charge or (2) a one-half percent below-market interest rate and a grant in the amount of two percent of the loan which would be applied to the downpayment requirement, and a $400.00 waiver of fees.

The Mortgage Company will underwrite the loans for this special program in accordance with the underwriting guidelines of Fannie Mae's *Enhanced FannieNeighbors with Community Home Buyers Program (including the 3/2 Option)* or other programs with similarly flexible underwriting guidelines. FannieNeighbors Mortgages are conventional, fixed-rate mortgages secured by single family residences in designated neighborhoods. The program offers various flexibilities that are designed to allow a minimum down payment of five percent; the borrower is permitted to obtain two percent of the down payment through gifts, thus necessitating that the borrower provide only three percent from his or her own funds. Under this program Fannie Mae will waive the standard requirement that the borrower have reserves equal to two mortgage payments at the time of closing. The program also allows closing cost flexibilities. Any initially rejected applications will be reviewed by the Mortgage Company's Second Review Committee.

The precise amount of the subsidy to be provided by the Mortgage Company pursuant to this special program will be related to the number of branches to be opened. For planning purposes, however, the Bank and Mortgage Company shall make an initial investment of $7,000,000 over the five year period of the consent decree, thereby allocating approximately $28,000,000 in special loan products for each of the five years. The total monetary amount will be made available for loans secured by properties in defined census tracts of the District of Columbia and Prince George's County, Maryland. The money will be apportioned between the District and Prince George's County in relation to the United States' estimate of the manner in which the alleged underlying violation affected each community. The initial estimated distribution will be as follows:

a. Approximately $20,000,000 each year, for five years, will be allocated for loans secured by properties in the District of Columbia census tracts identified in Attachment A [not included] and

b. Approximately $8,000,000 each year, for five years, will be allocated for loans secured by properties in the Prince George's County census tracts identified in Attachment B [not included].

For the duration of this program, the balance from each year's fund which has not been loaned by the anniversary date of the program, will be added to the next year's fund. If by the fourth anniversary of this decree, the Bank has not completed its projected investment in bank branches/mortgage offices, the additional funds will be supplied in the final year of the special program so as to ensure that the $11,000,000 investment has been fully made within the consent period. If, at the end of five years, that amount has not been fully invested in the community, the Bank and Mortgage Company shall make a contribution to a charitable or community organization(s) dedicated to the improvement of housing or home ownership in the targeted census tracts in an amount equal to the remaining balance in the compensation program.

VI. RECORD-KEEPING AND REPORTING REQUIREMENTS

a. The Bank and Mortgage Company will retain all records relating to its obligations under this Consent Decree, including its advertising, mortgage production, branching, special programs, recruitment, and compliance activities.

b. The Bank and Mortgage Company will provide the United States annually for the duration of the Consent Decree on magnetic tape in standard EBCDIC format the Home Mortgage Disclosure Act data provided by it to the FFIEC within 30 days of providing such data to the FFIEC.

c. The Bank and Mortgage Company will report their progress under this Consent Decree to the Civil Rights Division of the United States Department of Justice on an annual basis for a period of five years. All reports will be submitted to the United States within 30 days after the close of the annual time period and will include the following information:

i. A report on advertising conducted pursuant to this Consent Decree, including the media names, types, and frequencies. The report will include representative copies of all advertising.

ii. A report on lending efforts conducted pursuant to this Consent Decree. The report will discuss the program to target African American neighborhoods as set forth in Part IV and will include a list of the individuals determined to be active in content of the Consent Decree and request the Court sign the Order to enter the attached Consent Decree.

Notes

1. The Bank and Mortgage Company note that during the period 1988–1992, the Mortgage Company extended 641 loans for $139.4 million to residents of the District of Columbia within the geographic area south of Calvert Street and east of Connecticut Avenue.

2. In 1989 and 1990 Chevy Chase applied to open a branch in Fort Washington, Maryland. According to the 1990 Census the population in the census tract in which Chevy Chase planned to open the branch was 52% African American.

3. White census tracts are defined as those tracts where African Americans do not constitute 50 percent or more of the population. Minorities may constitute a majority in some such census tracts.

4. The Bank and Mortgage Company may also seek the consent of the United States to a delay of the scheduled opening of a mortgage office if they plan to incorporate a mortgage office with a branch opening.

5. While this settlement provides remedies for African American communities, the defendants will ascertain the home mortgage credit needs of other minority communities in the Washington metropolitan area and aggressively solicit and originate home mortgage loans in those communities.

Chapter Twenty-Six

PATTERNS OF RESIDENTIAL MORTGAGE ACTIVITY IN PHILADELPHIA'S LOW- AND MODERATE-INCOME NEIGHBORHOODS: 1990–91

Paul S. Calem

Changes in the requirements of the Home Mortgage Disclosure Act (HMDA) that became effective in 1990 multiplied the types and amount of information collected by federal regulatory agencies from residential mortgage lenders. The original HMDA, enacted in 1975, required that institutions report the geographic distribution, by census tract, of their home purchase and home improvement loans. Since 1990, respondents also have had to report the disposition of each residential loan application, along with the census tract location of the subject property, the race and income of the applicant, and the loan amount. The expanded set of data collected under HMDA during 1990 and 1991, combined with data on neighborhood economic, demographic, and housing stock characteristics from the 1990 United States Census, offers an unprecedented opportunity for studying mortgage lending patterns.

This chapter exploits this opportunity by examining mortgage lending patterns across low- and moderate-income neighborhoods in Philadelphia from 1990 to 1991. Regression equations relating census-tract application and origination activity to census variables are estimated; likewise, logit equations are used to relate the disposition of applications (approved or not approved) to census variables, applicant income, applicant race, and loan amount.

Following the approach of my earlier paper (Calem 1993), I highlight the impact of the Delaware Valley Mortgage Plan (DVMP), a low- and moderate-income lending program in Philadelphia, by estimating separate equations for plan lenders and non-DVMP institutions. This chapter goes beyond the previous study, however, by examining the geographic distribution of mortgage loan applications and by analyzing approval and denial patterns, in addition to looking at mortgage origination activity.[1]

The estimation results indicate that much of the variation in mortgage lending activity across low- and moderate-income tracts in Philadelphia is tied to socioeconomic characteristics of the tracts. The results suggest that census tract variables are proxies for the size or quality of neighborhood properties or general condition of the neighborhood, for housing affordability, and for household mobility. Furthermore, it is suggested that these factors influence mortgage activity.

Other factors held constant, I find that both DVMP and non-DVMP lenders are less likely to approve a loan application if the subject property is in a minority tract. Minority status of an applicant, on the other hand, does not exhibit a strong independent effect on likelihood of approval.[2]

In various other aspects, DVMP and non-DVMP institutions differ substantially. For instance, for DVMP institutions, application activity is as strong or stronger in minority neighborhoods than in nonminority neighborhoods. As a result, there is no substantial disparity between minority and nonminority tracts with respect to the loan origination activity of DVMP institutions.[3] For the non-DVMP group, application and origination activity each bear a strong inverse relationship to the neighborhood's percentage minority population.

This chapter is organized as follows. The next section provides a brief description of the Delaware Valley Mortgage Plan,[4] followed, in the third section, by development of the model on which the empirical specifications are based, as well as a description of the data and empirical procedure. The fourth section presents a logit analysis of the disposition of loan applications. The fifth section examines patterns of application and origination activity. The sixth and final section contains concluding comments.

THE DELAWARE VALLEY MORTGAGE PLAN

This study distinguishes between two groups of lenders: banks that participate in DVMP and those that do not.[5] Calem (1993) described how DVMP substantially influenced the loan origination patterns of participating institutions from 1984 to 1989. The present study covers the period from 1990 to 1991 and highlights the impact of DVMP on loan approval patterns and application activity, in addition to examining origination activity.

DVMP is a community reinvestment program that was initiated in 1977 by a coalition of banks as a result of discussions between bankers and community leaders on how to increase homeownership in disadvantaged sections of Philadelphia. The three main elements of the program are flexible lending criteria, "second-chance" review of applications slated for rejection, and aggressive marketing and outreach on the part of participating lenders.[6]

According to the terms of the DVMP, a low- or moderate-income household applies for a mortgage under the plan at a participating institution.[7] The creditworthiness of the applicant and collateral value of the property are then evaluated by the bank according to standards consistent with plan guidelines, which instruct lenders to be flexible.[8] For instance, under DVMP credit guidelines, applicants with no credit history are to be given an opportunity to document their creditworthiness by providing records of rent and utility payments.[9] Under DVMP property guidelines, appraisals are to be based only on the structural condition of the subject property and the condition of other properties on the immediate block. Broader neighborhood factors are excluded from property evaluations.

DVMP is governed by a credit committee, which meets weekly to review proposed rejections; a policy and planning committee, which meets quarterly to review policies, procedures, and performance; and an executive committee, which meets at least quarterly and provides leadership. These committees are composed of representatives of each member institution. All committee meetings are attended by representatives of the Greater Philadelphia Urban Affairs Coalition, a nonprofit organization that provides staff support and oversight to DVMP.

An application under the program cannot be rejected without first being reviewed by the credit committee, which may request the rejecting bank to reconsider its decision and approve the loan. If the bank continues to decline the application, another member can choose to adopt the application for consideration.[10] This review process ensures that credit decisions remain consistent with DVMP guidelines, and it allows applicants a second chance, since specific lending policies differ across banks.[11]

Participating banks vigorously promote the plan by marketing to neighborhood real estate agents, by advertising, and by maintaining relationships with community organizations. Applicants for DVMP loans typically are referred to the plan by a real estate broker, community development corporation, or neighborhood organization.

Almost all DVMP mortgages are conventional, as opposed to federally insured.[12] Private mortgage insurance may be required if the loan-to-value (LTV) ratio exceeds 80 percent.[13] There is no DVMP pricing policy; rates and fees on loans under the program are left to the discretion of individual institutions. In many instances, lenders choose to offer below-market interest rates or fees on DVMP loans.

MODEL AND EMPIRICAL PROCEDURE

The equations to be estimated are based on the following simple representation of an urban mortgage market. There are two lenders in the market, indexed by $i = 1, 2$ (corresponding to DVMP and non-DVMP institutions). The market is divided geographically into a number of neighborhoods (tracts), indexed by j, each of which is distinguished by its particular socioeconomic characteristics and locational amenities or disamenities. Housing stock attributes may vary across tracts, but all houses within a given tract are identical.[14] Each neighborhood contains the same number of houses.[15]

Suppose that the pool of mortgage applicants can be divided into K categories, represented by attribute vectors $Z_1, Z_2, \ldots, Z_K$. Let A_{ij} denote the set of applicants at bank i for loans to purchase properties in tract j, and let N_{ij}^k denote the number of applicants in A_{ij} that have the attributes Z_k. I assume that N_{ij}^k depends on: (1) factors specific to bank i, including the bank's loan terms and its credit policies (as perceived by the public); (2) applicant type k; (3) the price of a house in the tract, denoted P_j; (4) the quantity of housing services provided by a house in the tract, that is, house size and quality, denoted by the vector $QNTY_j$; and (5) the overall condition of the neighborhood, represented by a vector of neighborhood attributes $NBRHD_j$. Thus,

$$N_{ij}^k = f_i^k(P_j, QNTY_j, NBRHD_j) \tag{26.1}$$

Implicitly, I am positing that P_j, $QNTY_j$, and $NBRHD_j$ suffice to determine the distribution of future resale values. I am likewise positing that each applicant in A_{ij} would compare P_j, $QNTY_j$, and $NBRHD_j$ to the prices and attributes of houses in other tracts in the city prior to choosing tract j. Hence, loan demand N_{ij}^k as represented by equation (26.1) depends implicitly on housing prices and characteristics of neighborhoods and housing elsewhere in the city.

As an example, suppose that two tracts, say tracts 1 and 2, contain houses of similar size and construction, but tract 1 is in generally poorer condition with relatively large areas covered by vacant and abandoned properties or poorly maintained housing units. With prices equal across the two tracts, potential homebuyers presumably would prefer tract 2; demand in tract 1 would grow as the price in tract 1 declines below the price in tract 2.[16]

Next let p_{ij}^k denote the probability that an applicant in A_{ij} having attributes Z_k will be approved for a loan. Like N_{ij}^k, p_{ij}^k would depend on bank-specific credit policies; applicant type; the house price P_j; house size and quality $QNTY_j$; and the condition of the neighborhood $NBRHD_j$.[17] For example, if the current house price P_j and the condition of the neighborhood and property are such that there is substantial risk of a decline in the value of the property, the bank will be inclined to deny the loan. Thus,

$$p_{ij}^k = g_i(Z_k, P_j, QNTY_j, NBRHD_j). \qquad (26.2)$$

Now let N_{ij} denote the total number of applicants in A_{ij}, and let $\hat{p}_{ij}$ denote the approval rate at bank i for loans to purchase properties in tract j. Thus,

$$N_{ij} = \sum_{k=1}^{K} N_{ij}^k \text{ and } \hat{p}_{ij} = \sum_{k=1}^{K} [N_{ij}^k p_{ij}^k]/N_{ij}, \qquad (26.3)$$

where the summation is over categories of applicants. From equations (29.1) and (29.2), it follows that one can express N_{ij} and $\hat{p}_{ij}$ as functions of P_j, $QNTY_j$, and $NBRHD_j$;

$$\begin{aligned} N_{ij} &= f_i(P_j, QNTY_j, NBRHD_j) \text{ and} \\ \hat{p}_{ij} &= h_i(P_j, QNTY_j, NBRHD_j). \end{aligned} \qquad (26.4)$$

Note that total demand in tract j equals $\hat{p}_{1j}N_{1j} + \hat{p}_{2j}N_{2j}$.

Next let S_j denote the supply of houses for sale in tract j. I assume that S_j is a function of P_j, $QNTY_j$, and $NBRHD_j$. For example, residents may be less inclined to place their homes for sale if current housing prices and the characteristics of the neighborhood and its housing stock are such that neighborhood properties are viewed as good investments. In addition, I assume that S_j depends on demographic factors influencing the propensity of the tract's residents to relocate, as represented by the vector of demographic variables $MOBILE_j$. Thus,

$$S_j = S(P_j, QNTY_j, NBRHD_j, MOBILE_j). \qquad (26.5)$$

Finally I assume that each neighborhood real estate market is in equilibrium, with price at the level P_j that equates demand and supply. By equations (26.4) and (26.5), the equilibrium price P_j^* is a function of $QNTY_j$, $NBRHD_j$, and $MOBILE_j$. In theory, equilibrium house prices across neighborhoods would be determined simultaneously since, as noted previously, potential homebuyers would make comparisons across tracts. Thus, implicitly the equilibrium price in any one tract depends on property and neighborhood attributes in all other tracts. I can safely ignore this fact, however, because it has no bearing on the empirical analysis.[18]

Substituting P_j^* for P_j in equation (26.2) yields

$$p_{ij}^k = g_i^*(Z_k, QNTY_j, NBRHD_j, MOBILE_j). \tag{26.6}$$

Equation (26.6) provides the basis for our empirical study of loan approval patterns. As indicated by equation (26.6), whether or not an applicant at bank i is approved for a loan in tract j will depend on applicant-specific characteristics (such as income and loan amount) and on socioeconomic attributes and housing stock characteristics of the census tract.

Substituting P_j^* and P_j in equations (26.4) yields

$$N_{ij} = f_i^*(QNTY_j, NBRHD_j, MOBILE_j) \tag{26.7}$$

and

$$\hat{p}_{ij} = h_i^*(QNTY_j, NBRHD_j, MOBILE_j). \tag{26.8}$$

Multiplying (26.7) and (26.8), yields the following relationship between total originations in tract j, denoted L_{ij}, and tract variables:

$$L_{ij} = h_j^* f_i^*, \tag{26.9}$$

Equations (26.7) and (26.9) form the basis for this study's empirical analysis of application and origination patterns. As indicated by these equations, tract application and origination activity will depend on socioeconomic characteristics and housing stock attributes of the tract.

Data

I estimated empirical equations based on equations (26.6), (26.7), and (26.9), relying on two data sources. Data on neighborhood economic, demographic, and housing stock characteristics are obtained from the 1990 U.S. Census. Mortgage application and origination data are from the period 1990–91 and were collected from mortgage lending institutions by federal banking authorities as required under HMDA.[19] HMDA data include the disposition (approved or not approved) of each residential loan application received by the respondents, the loan amount applied for, the applicant's income and race (or ethnicity, for Hispanics), the loan type (conventional or federally insured), and the census tract location of the subject property. This study is restricted to examining loans for the purchase of one- to four-family, owner-occupied properties.

Several non-DVMP institutions were dropped from the sample because they failed to identify the census tract locations of a substantial proportion of their loans in Philadelphia. Several institutions also consistently reported loans that appeared to be outliers with respect to loan size, in comparison to other loans made within the same tract in the same year. These institutions may have been misreporting census tract locations and were likewise dropped from the sample. The procedure employed to identify these institutions is fully described in the accompanying appendix.[20]

This study's analysis of mortgage lending patterns is confined to tracts having at least 30 owner-occupied units. The focus is also restricted to low- and moderate-income tracts; specifically, to tracts with median family income below $36,665 and median house value below $82,000.[21] The income and house value restrictions are for several reasons. First, low- and moderate-income tracts may be subject to distinct factors influencing mortgage activity. Second, the distribution of mortgage credit across low- and moderate-income tracts is an important component of the overall community reinvestment performance of depository institutions.[22] Third, restricting the sample to a more economically homogeneous set of tracts marginally improves the goodness-of-fit of the estimated equations. Fourth, during 1990 to 1991, most activity in the city's residential real estate market was in low- or moderate-income tracts.[23]

Table 26.1, parts *a* and *b*, present descriptive statistics profiling the activity of several categories of HMDA reporting institutions in Philadelphia. Table 26.1*a* reports each group's deposit share in the city, its deposit share in low- and moderate-income tracts, its share of mortgage originations in the city, and its share of originations in low- and moderate-income tracts. Table 26.1*b* reports each group's loans in low- and moderate-income tracts as a proportion of the group's citywide total and each group's deposits in low- and moderate-income tracts as a proportion of the group's total deposits in Philadelphia. Note that originations in low- and moderate-income tracts accounted for more than two-thirds of citywide mortgage originations during 1990 to 1991. Table 26.1*b* also shows that, relative to other HMDA reporters in Philadelphia, DVMP institutions originated a much larger proportion of their total home purchase loan portfolio in low- or moderate-income neighborhoods during 1990–91.

Table 26.1 HMDA-REPORTING INSTITUTIONS IN PHILADELPHIA: 1990–91

a.

Type of Institution	Deposit Share[a]		Share of Mortgage Originations[b]	
	All Tracts	Low- and Moderate-Income Tracts	All Tracts	Low- and Moderate-Income Tracts
DVMP banks	59.9	60.2	20.2	27.1
Non-DVMP banks and mortgage subsidiaries[c]	15.7	7.3	38.0	36.2
Savings and loans	17.0	30.3	17.5	15.3
Other mortgage companies	NA	NA	22.0	19.5
Credit unions	7.3	2.3	2.3	1.8

b.

Type of Institution	Number of Mortgages in Low- and Moderate-Income Tracts as Percentage of Group Total	Dollar Deposits in Low- and Moderate-Income Tracts as Percentage of Group Total
DVMP banks	83.6	13.6
Non-DVMP banks and mortgage subsidiaries	60.0	13.4
Savings and loans	54.7	49.8
Other mortgage companies	55.7	NA
Credit unions	49.0	7.8

a. Deposit shares are based on an institution's total deposits on June 30, 1990, plus its total deposits on June 30, 1991, at all of its Philadelphia branches and at its branches in low- and moderate-income tracts, respectively.

b. Origination shares are based on an institution's total originations over the period 1990–91.

c. Includes commercial banks, savings banks, and mortgage subsidiaries of bank holding companies.

Empirical Procedure

Throughout this study's empirical analysis, I distinguished between DVMP and non-DVMP institutions, estimating separate equations for the two groups of lenders.[24] To analyze loan approval patterns, I estimated logit specifications based on equation (26.6), relating the disposition of loan applications to characteristics of the census tract where the subject property is located and to applicant-specific variables. To analyze application and origination patterns, I estimated regression equations based on equations (26.7) and (26.9), relating tract application or origination activity to neighborhood variables.

I measured tract origination (or application) activity by the total number of originations of (or applications for) loans to purchase properties located in the tract during 1990 and 1991, divided by the total number of owner-occupied units (OOUs) in the tract as counted by the 1990 Census. This measure is referred to as loans (applications) per OOU. I divided by the number of OOUs in order to measure mortgage activity relative to the potential size of the house resale market. For instance, if 3 mortgages are originated in one neighborhood containing 100 OOUs, and 30 mortgages are originated in another neighborhood containing 1,000 OOUs, I considered the two areas as equally active with respect to originations.[25]

The census tract variables employed in the study as explanatory variables are listed and defined in table 26.2, along with each variable's mean value across low- and moderate-income tracts in Philadelphia. Also listed in the table, together with their sample means, are three application-specific variables employed in the study's logit equations: income, loan amount, and a dummy variable identifying minority applicants.[26]

Census Tract Variables

With the exception of lowPOPDEN, the census tract variables listed in table 26.2 are employed as proxies for $QNTY_j$, $NBRHD_j$, and/or $MOBILE_j$.[27] I included lowPOPDEN to control for the possibility that new housing construction during 1990 and 1991 may have had a disproportionate impact on mortgage demand in tracts that previously had been undeveloped. This variable also controls for the possibility that the study's measures of application and origination activity (applications per OOU and loans per OOU) may be biased upward in tracts with comparatively few OOUs.

The demographic variables AGE 35–44, AGE 45–54, AGE 55pl, and MINPOP are included as proxies for the mobility of neighborhood residents.[28] For instance, relative to other urban homeowners, owner-occupants under age 35 may be more mobile; that is, more apt to sell their homes and relocate. These demographic variables may also act as proxies for the size or condition of neighborhood properties. For example, homeowners in the over-55 age category may do more to maintain or improve their properties because they have more savings or because they have fewer competing expenses.[29]

Table 26.2 NEIGHBORHOOD DEMOGRAPHIC AND ECONOMIC VARIABLES

Census Tract Variable	Description	Mean[a]
LOANS/OOU	Total number of HMDA-reported mortgages, 1984–89, divided by number of owner-occupied units	0.018
APPLICATIONS/OOU	Total number of HMDA-reported applications, 1990–91, divided by number of owner-occupied units	0.023
OOU	Number of owner-occupied units	1,168
TRINC	Census tract median income	$24,555
MINPOP	Percentage of minority (Asian, Hispanic, or African-American) population	59.5
AGE 35–44	Percentage of households headed by individual aged 35–44	19.8
AGE 45–54	Percentage of households headed by individual aged 45–54	15.0
AGE 55pl	Percentage of households headed by individual aged 55 or over	42.0
HSGRAD	Percentage of households headed by high school graduate	58.1
UNEMP	Percentage of labor force unemployed	13.5
$UNEMP^2$	Square of tract unemployment rate	233.6
RENT250	Percentage of tract rental units with monthly rent under $250	16.3
PCTRENT	Percentage of tract housing units that are rental (as opposed to vacant or owner-occupied)	31.4
PRE 50	Percentage of tract housing stock built before 1950	76.6
POST 70	Percentage of tract housing stock built after 1970	6.3
POST 80	Percentage of tract housing stock built after 1980	2.8
lowPOPDEN	Dummy variable identifying low-density tracts (1990 population density less than 3,495)	0.05
Applicant Variable		
APPINC	Applicant's family income	$29,664
AMOUNT	Loan amount applied for	$39,242
MINAPP	Dummy variable identifying minority applicants	0.49

a. Mean value across Philadelphia low- and moderate-income tracts.

The tract unemployment rate, UNEMP, and its square, $UNEMP^2$, are proxies for the mobility of neighborhood residents and for general neighborhood quality. Unemployed residents may be more apt than others to seek to sell their homes and relocate. On the other hand, neighborhood deterioration and disamenities are more likely to be found in areas of high unemployment.

Tract median income and HSGRAD likewise are proxies for mobility as well as for house size and general condition of the neighborhood. For example, educated household heads may be more mobile, as suggested by Ioannides (1987). Alternatively, in lower-income areas and in areas where a comparatively small percentage of households is headed by a high school graduate, related economic and social difficulties may lead to neighborhood disamenities. In addition, houses in such neighborhoods may be smaller, of lower quality, or not as well maintained.

The housing stock variables PRE50, POST70, POST80, RENT250, and PCTRENT are proxies for house size or quality and/or neighborhood condition. More recently constructed housing is apt to be in better condition and therefore of higher quality than older housing. Low rental values are an indicator of a less desirable housing stock or of neighborhood disamenities.[30] Neighborhoods where rental units comprise a relatively small percentage of the housing stock may be in better condition because owner-occupants may have greater incentive to maintain or improve their properties or neighborhoods than landlords or tenants.[31]

Limitations of Empirical Analysis

This study's empirical analysis is subject to several obvious limitations. First, the logit equations omit many application-specific variables—such as the loan-to-value ratio and whether or not the applicant exhibited past credit problems—because this information is unavailable. Such variables are crucial to the lender's credit decision, but are not recorded in HMDA data.[32] Such omitted variables may also be correlated with included variables; hence, one must be cautious when interpreting the results. Second, because of colinearity among some of the explanatory variables, the study's estimation results may understate the significance of some of these variables. Third, the study's regression equations are essentially reduced forms; in general, one cannot infer whether the impact of a particular census tract variable on application or origination activity is due to its impact on mortgage supply or demand.

APPLICANT APPROVAL PATTERNS

To investigate loan approval patterns at non-DVMP institutions, I estimated separate logit equations for minority and white applicants, because a statistical test rejected pooling. For DVMP institutions, however, I estimated a single equation because a statistical test did not reject pooling of applicants.[33] For DVMP institutions, I estimated

$$\begin{aligned}\text{DENY} = {} & \alpha_0 + \alpha_1\text{APPINC} + \alpha_2(\text{APPINC})^2 + \alpha_3\text{AMOUNT} \\ & + \alpha_4\text{CONVEN} + \alpha_5\text{MINAPP} + aX\end{aligned} \tag{26.10}$$

across the entire pool of applicants. The dependent variable in equation (26.10), DENY, takes a value of 1 if the loan application is denied, and 0 otherwise.[34] Applicant-specific explanatory variables include a dummy variable (MINPOP) identifying minority (African-American, Hispanic, or Asian-American) applicants; applicant income (APPINC); the square of applicant income; loan amount; and a dummy variable (CONVEN) identifying applications for conventional (as opposed to federally insured) loans. I also controlled for the neighborhood characteristics listed in table 26.2, represented by the vector X. For non-DVMP institutions, I estimated equation (26.10) separately for white and minority applicants after deleting the dummy variable MINAPP.

I also estimated a single logit equation of the form:

$$\begin{aligned}\text{DENY} = {} & \alpha_0 + \alpha Z + aX + \beta_0\text{MINAPP}^*(1 - \text{DVMP}) \\ & + \beta Z^*\text{MINAPP}^*(1 - \text{DVMP}) \\ & + bX^*\text{MINAPP}^*(1 - \text{DVMP}) + \gamma_0\text{DVMP} \\ & + \gamma Z^*\text{DVMP} + cX^*\text{DVMP},\end{aligned} \tag{26.11}$$

pooling all applicants. In equation (26.11), Z denotes the vector of applicant-specific variables APPINC, $(\text{APPINC})^2$, AMOUNT, and CONVEN; X continues to represent the vector of census tract characteristics; DVMP is a dummy variable identifying applicants at DVMP instituitons; and Z*MINAPP*(1 – DVMP), X*MINAPP*(1 – DVMP), Z*DVMP, and X*DVMP are vectors of interaction terms.

Results

The results from estimations of equations (26.10) and (26.11) are presented in tables 26.3 and 26.4, respectively.[35] Column I of table 26.3

Table 26.3 LOGIT EQUATION ESTIMATES
(Chi-square statistics in parentheses)

	Dependent Variable: Application Denied = 1; Otherwise = 0		
	I DVMP All Applicants	II Non-DVMP Minority	III Non-DVMP White
Explanatory Variable	(898 denied 1,769 approved)	(437 denied 1,604 approved)	(391 denied 2,715 approved)
UNEMP	−.0535 (1.84)	.0412 (0.69)	−.0136 (0.06)
$UNEMP^2$	.0021 (4.16)[b]	−.0012 (0.80)	.0006 (0.22)
TRINC	3×10^{-5} (2.61)	-4×10^{-5} (2.83)[c]	5×10^{-5} (6.64)[a]
HSGRAD	−.0046 (0.30)	−.0053 (0.20)	−.0347 (9.95)[a]
MINPOP	.0082 (11.6)[a]	.0087 (7.19)[a]	.0099 (7.17)[a]
RENT250	−.0058 (1.36)	.0062 (1.03)	−.0031 (0.24)
PCTRENT	.0244 (7.72)[a]	−.0146 (2.20)	.0255 (5.69)[b]
PRE50	.0113 (5.20)[b]	−.0011 (0.06)	.0068 (2.40)
POST70	.0442 (7.37)[a]	.0131 (0.64)	−.0035 (0.04)
POST80	−.0734 (10.2)[a]	−.0118 (0.16)	.0100 (0.10)
APPINC	-1×10^{-6} (0.01)	-4×10^{-5} (9.14)[a]	-7×10^{-5} (24.8)[a]
$APPINC^2$	-1×10^{-10} (0.62)	6×10^{-10} (10.9)[a]	6×10^{-10} (13.3)[a]
AMOUNT	-1×10^{-5} (11.4)[a]	-4×10^{-6} (0.77)	-8×10^{-7} (0.06)
MINAPP	.0908 (0.49)	—	—
CONVEN	.2363 (0.89)	.3747 (9.76)[a]	.4775 (14.4)[a]
Likelihood ratio	118.3	73.7	124.3

Note: See equation (26.10) in text.
a. Statistically significant at 1-percent level.
b. Statistically significant at 5-percent level.
c. Statistically significant at 10-percent level.

Table 26.4 LOGIT EQUATION ESTIMATES
(Chi-square statistics in parentheses)

	Dependent Variable: Application Denied = 1; Otherwise = 0 (1,726 denied, 6,088 approved)		
Explanatory Variable	I Independent Effect	II Interaction With MINAPP* (1 − DVMP)	III Interaction With DVMP
INTERCEPT	−.9705	.5109	−2.847
	(0.30)	(0.05)	(1.82)
UNEMP	−.0136	.0548	−.0384
	(0.06)	(0.55)	(0.32)
$UNEMP^2$	.0012	−.0024	.0008
	(0.61)	(1.42)	(0.22)
TRINC	5×10^{-5}	-9×10^{-5}	-3×10^{-5}
	(6.640)[a]	(8.90)[a]	(0.31)
HSGRAD	−.0347	.0400	.0301
	(9.95)[a]	(6.07)[b]	(4.66)[b]
MINPOP	.0099	−.0013	−.0010
	(7.17)[a]	(0.80)	(0.06)
RENT250	−.0031	.0093	−.0030
	(0.24)	(1.11)	(0.14)
PCTRENT	.0255	−.0402	.0011
	(5.69)[b]	(7.62)[a]	(0.01)
PRE50	.0068	−.0079	.0043
	(2.40)	(1.49)	(0.42)
POST70	−.0035	.0166	.0477
	(0.04)	(0.50)	(4.13)[b]
POST80	.0100	−.0217	−.0834
	(0.10)	(0.26)	(4.67)[b]
APPINC	-7×10^{-5}	-3×10^{-5}	7×10^{-5}
	(24.8)[a]	(1.89)	(14.6)[a]
$APPINC^2$	6×10^{-10}	-1×10^{-11}	-5×10^{-10}
	(13.3)[a]	(0.00)	(4.31)[b]
AMOUNT	-8×10^{-7}	4×10^{-6}	-1×10^{-5}
	(0.06)	(0.70)	(5.66)[b]
CONVEN	.4775	−.1028	−.2393
	(14.4)[a]	(0.35)	(0.73)
Likelihood ratio = 689			

Note: See equation (26.11) in text.
a. Statistically significant at 1-percent level.
b. Statistically significant at 5-percent level.
c. Statistically significant at 10-percent level.

provides the findings from estimation of equation (26.10) for the group of DVMP institutions; columns II and III provide the findings for minority and white applicants, respectively, at non-DVMP institutions.[36] Column I of table 26.4 provides the estimated coefficients α_0, α and a; column II provides the estimated coefficients β_0, β and b; and column II provides the estimated coefficients γ_0, γ and c, obtained from estimation of equation (26.11).

In several instances where tract variables are statistically significant, the signs on these variables suggest that they proxy for the overall condition of the neighborhood and that disrepair or disamenities adversely affect likelihood of approval. For example, DVMP institutions are more likely to deny an application if the subject property is located in a tract characterized by a high unemployment rate or in a tract with a high proportion of rental housing. Also, the denial rate for white applicants at non-DVMP institutions is positively related to the proportion of rental housing in the tract where the subject property is located.[37]

In other instances, the signs on statistically significant variables suggest that they are proxies for affordability of neighborhood housing (as determined by the size and condition of neighborhood properties), and that affordability has a positive impact on approval rates. For example, the denial rate for white applicants at non-DVMP institutions is positively related to tract median income. At DVMP institutions, a loan is more likely to be denied if the subject property is located in a tract where a larger proportion of the housing stock is of post-1970 construction. The most plausible interpretation of these relationships is that where house prices are lower, buyers are able to afford a more substantial down payment, increasing the likelihood of approval.

At non-DVMP institutions, likelihood of approval clearly is higher for federally insured loans. The estimated coefficient on CONVEN is positive and statistically significant for both white and minority applicants at these institutions.[38]

Comparison of DVMP and Non-DVMP Lenders

At both DVMP and non-DVMP institutions, likelihood of approval is negatively and significantly related to MINPOP, other factors held constant. MINAPP, on the other hand, does not exhibit a strong, independent effect on likelihood of approval. For instance, one cannot reject pooling of applicants at DVMP institutions, and the estimated coefficient on MINAPP*(1 − DVMP) in equation (26.11) is not statistically significant.[39]

At DVMP institutions, loan amount bears a positive and statistically significant relationship to likelihood of approval; applicant income, however, is not statistically significant. In contrast, applicant income and income squared are statistically significant variables for non-DVMP lenders, whereas loan amount is not. This distinction may reflect differences in the mix of applicants between the two groups of lenders or differences in credit policies.[40]

Another noticeable distinction between the two groups of lenders is that the variables PRE50, POST70, and POST80 are more strongly related to likelihood of approval in the case of DVMP institutions. For DVMP institutions the estimated signs on these variables are consistent with the view that these variables are proxies for the quality of the housing stock.[41]

APPLICATION AND ORIGINATION PATTERNS

To analyze the geographic distribution of home purchase loan applications and originations across low- and moderate-income tracts in Philadelphia, I estimated cross-sectional regression equations of the form

$$(\text{DEP}) = \alpha_0 + aX. \tag{26.12}$$

The dependent variable in equation (26.12), DEP, denotes tract application or origination activity (APPLICATIONS/OOU or LOANS/OOU). The explanatory variables in equation (26.12) are the census tract characteristics listed in table 26.2. Separate equations are estimated for the group activity of DVMP institutions and for that of non-DVMP institutions.

Results

The results from the regression with APPLICATIONS/OOU as the dependent variable are presented in table 26.5; the results from the regression with LOANS/OOU are in table 26.6. Columns I and II of each table present the findings for DVMP and non-DVMP lenders, respectively.

The estimation results suggest that the size or quality of neighborhood properties or the general condition of the neighborhood influ-

Table 26.5 REGRESSION EQUATION ESTIMATES
(*t*-statistics in parentheses)

	Dependent Variable: APPLICATIONS/OOU	
	I DVMP	II NON-DVMP
Explanatory Variables	(N = 218, R^2 = .36)	(N = 218, R^2 = .54)
INTERCEPT	.0842	.0847
	(5.83)[a]	(4.48)[a]
UNEMP	.0011	−.0008
	(2.41)[b]	(1.35)
$UNEMP^2$	-3×10^{-5}	1×10^{-5}
	(3.48)[a]	(0.76)
MINPOP	4×10^{-5}	−.0001
	(1.44)	(2.95)[a]
TRINC	1×10^{-8}	7×10^{-7}
	(0.06)	(2.69)[a]
AGE 35–44	−.0007	-8×10^{-5}
	(3.70)[a]	(0.33)
AGE 45–54	−.0007	−.0011
	(3.16)[a]	(4.12)[a]
AGE 55pl	−.0007	−.0005
	(5.14)[a]	(3.09)[a]
HSGRAD	−.0004	.0002
	(4.43)[a]	(1.41)
RENT250	4×10^{-6}	6×10^{-5}
	(0.01)	(0.81)
PCTRENT	−.0003	-2×10^{-5}
	(3.13)[a]	(0.16)
PRE50	2×10^{-5}	−.0002
	(0.33)	(2.74)[a]
POST70	3×10^{-5}	−.0001
	(0.29)	(.091)
POST80	.0002	1×10^{-5}
	(0.95)	(0.05)
lowPOPDEN	.0072	.0400
	(2.49)[b]	(8.54)[a]

a. Statistically significant at 1-percent level.
b. Statistically significant at 5-percent level.

ence application and origination activity. For example, the application and origination activity of non-DVMP lenders are positively related to TRINC and negatively related to PRE50, while DVMP institutions process comparatively few applications for loans to purchase properties in tracts characterized by high unemployment. Similarly, DVMP

Table 26.6 REGRESSION EQUATION ESTIMATES
(t-statistics in parentheses)

Explanatory Variables	Dependent Variable: LOANS/OOU — I DVMP ($N = 218$, $R^2 = .30$)	Dependent Variable: LOANS/OOU — II NON-DVMP ($N = 218$, $R^2 = .49$)
INTERCEPT	.0523	.0616
	(4.61)[a]	(3.57)[a]
UNEMP	.0009	−.0003
	(2.59)[a]	(0.63)
$UNEMP^2$	-3×10^{-5}	3×10^{-7}
	(3.60)[a]	(0.03)
MINPOP	-8×10^{-7}	−.0001
	(0.04)	(3.95)[a]
TRINC	3×10^{-8}	4×10^{-7}
	(0.21)	(1.74)[c]
AGE 35–44	−.0005	7×10^{-5}
	(3.40)[a]	(0.34)
AGE 45–54	−.0004	.0008
	(2.34)	(3.04)[a]
AGE 55pl	−.0004	−.0003
	(4.12)[a]	(1.76)[c]
HSGRAD	−.0002	-7×10^{-5}
	(3.22)[a]	(0.60)
RENT250	4×10^{-6}	8×10^{-5}
	(0.09)	(1.17)
PCTRENT	−.0002	-6×10^{-5}
	(2.41)[b]	(0.61)
PRE50	2×10^{-5}	−.0002
	(0.43)	(3.00)[a]
POST70	4×10^{-5}	−.0003
	(0.45)	(2.42)[b]
POST80	.0001	.0002
	(0.73)	(0.64)
lowPOPDEN	.0072	.0080
	(3.15)[a]	(2.30)[b]

a. Statistically significant at 1-percent level.
b. Statistically significant at 5-percent level.
c. Statistically significant at 10-percent level.

institutions process comparatively few applications for loans to purchase properties in tracts where rental units comprise a large proportion of the housing stock.

The mobility of neighborhood residents also appears to be an important factor influencing mortgage application and origination activity, for both DVMP and non-DVMP institutions. For example, application and origination activity are inversely related to the percentage of households headed by an individual over age 45, and this relationship is even stronger if the household is headed by an individual over age 55. The most natural interpretation of this finding is that older households have tended to be less mobile.[42]

Comparison of DVMP and Non-DVMP Lenders

The application and origination activity of non-DVMP lenders is much more closely tied to tract racial composition than that of DVMP institutions. For the non-DVMP group, application and origination activity bear a statistically significant, inverse relationship to percentage minority population in a neighborhood, whereas no such relationship is found for the DVMP lenders.[43]

The application activity of DVMP institutions bears a strong inverse relationship to HSGRAD. Other factors held constant, tracts where a smaller percentage of households are headed by a high school graduate tend to have more affordable housing. Thus, it appears that the application patterns of DVMP institutions are related to the affordability of neighborhood housing. No comparable relationship is observed for non-DVMP institutions.

These findings provide evidence that DVMP is having a substantial impact. In particular, the marketing and outreach activities of DVMP banks, and their flexible lending policies, have generated an increase in the number of minority applicants, and have enabled an expanded number of minority households to qualify for loans. Attempts by DVMP institutions to make mortgages more affordable (by offering below-market rates to many applicants) may have had a similar effect.[44]

CONCLUSION

This chapter has analyzed mortgage lending activity across low- and moderate-income tracts in Philadelphia over the period 1990 to 1991, relying on data collected under the newly expanded HMDA and on data from the 1990 U.S. Census. The analysis distinguishes between institutions that participate in DVMP and those that do not, in order to highlight the impact of this low- and moderate-income lending program. Logit equations were estimated relating the disposition of applications to applicant-specific characteristics and census tract variables, and regression equations were estimated relating application and origination activity to census tract variables.

The estimation results indicate that much of the variation in mortgage lending activity across low- and moderate-income tracts in Philadelphia is tied to socioeconomic characteristics of the tracts. The results suggest that census tract variables act as proxies for the size or quality of neighborhood properties or general condition of the neighborhood, for housing affordability, and for household mobility, and that these factors influence mortgage activity. These conclusions are based on interpretation of the signs on variables that are statistically significant in the estimated equations.

This study found that both DVMP and non-DVMP lenders are less likely to approve an application if the subject property is in a minority tract, other factors held constant. Minority status of an applicant (MINAPP), however, was not found to exhibit a strong, independent effect on likelihood of approval.

DVMP and non-DVMP institutions differ markedly with respect to application and origination activity in minority neighborhoods. For DVMP institutions, application activity is as strong or stronger in minority neighborhoods than in nonminority neighborhoods. As a result, there is no disparity between minority and nonminority tracts with respect to the loan origination activity of DVMP institutions. For the non-DVMP group, application and origination activity each bear a strong inverse relation to the percentage minority population (MINPOP). Furthermore it appears that the application activity of DVMP institutions is positively influenced by affordability of neighborhood housing. No comparable relationship is observed for non-DVMP institutions. These findings indicate that DVMP is having a considerable impact, widening the scope of mortgage activity in Philadelphia's low- and moderate-income neighborhoods and generating an increase in the number of minority households applying and qualifying for loans.

Notes

1. Calem (1993) compared the mortgage origination patterns of DVMP and non-DVMP institutions across low- and moderate-income tracts in Philadelphia 1984 to 1989. The

analysis indicates that the mortgage activity of DVMP institutions is distributed more broadly, reflecting the impact of the program.

2. The finding that an applicant's minority status does not exhibit a strong independent effect on likelihood of loan approval is surprising, because at the aggregate national level, and consistently at the metropolitan statistical area (MSA) level, minority applicants are rejected two to three times more frequently than white applicants (see Canner and Smith 1991, 1992). Moreover, a study based on a survey of banks in Boston found a statistically significant disparity in approval rates between whites and minorities, even after controlling for a wide range of applicant and loan variables, such as LTV ratio and applicant credit history (see Munnell et. al. 1992, 1996).

3. These results are consistent with the analysis in Avery, Beeson, and Sniderman (1993), who found at the national level that differences across categories of lenders with respect to mortgage origination patterns primarily reflect differences in application activity.

4. For a more complete discussion of the DVMP, see Calem (1993).

5. The nine institutions that participated in DVMP over the period covered by this study are Meritor Savings Bank, Fidelity Bank, Provident National Bank, Mellon Bank, CoreStates Bank, Continental Bank, Meridian Bank, Beneficial Mutual Savings Bank, and Germantown Savings Bank.

6. A fourth important element of the DVMP program is financial counseling for prospective mortgage applicants and postpurchase counseling of borrowers.

7. A household qualifies for the program only if family income and mortgage amount do not exceed specified maximum values.

8. Unlike lending consortia operating in other cities, which finance community development or affordable housing projects through joint pools, DVMP focuses on home purchase lending, and each loan under the program is originated by a single bank.

9. Just how flexible a lender should be, and what specific standards to employ, are left to the discretion of individual institutions.

10. For an informative look at the DVMP review process, see Steve Cocheo, 1992.

11. Further monitoring is conducted by the policy and planning committee, which oversees each institution's overall performance. In addition, the executive committee conducts an annual membership review, which involves an evaluation of each member's commitment to the goals and policies of DVMP.

12. In the study sample, only 3 percent of the minority applicants and 4 percent of the white applicants at DVMP institutions applied for an FHA- or VA-insured loan. This compares to 54 percent of minority applicants and 39 percent of white applicants at non-DVMP institutions.

13. Thus, participation by private mortgage insurers has contributed to the success of the program. The DVMP works with insurers on approval issues to help increase the availability of mortgage insurance.

14. The assumption that all houses within a given tract are identical is made for expositional purposes only. The model can readily be generalized to allow for several types of houses in a tract.

15. The assumption that each neighborhood contains the same number of houses is made simply for convenience.

16. With prices equal, potential homebuyers would prefer tract 2 because of the disamenities in tract 1, so long as the risk of a substantial decline in property values in tract 2 is no greater than in tract 1; it seems reasonable to presume that this would be the case.

17. If bank i illegally redlines minority neighborhoods, then p_{ij} also would depend separately on neighborhood racial composition.

18. Empirically, each tract j is small, with a unique set of characteristics. Hence, the distribution $F_j(X)$ of a vector of property and neighborhood characteristics X across all tracts other than j can be identified with the citywide distribution of X. Thus $F_j(X)$ would be captured by the constant term in the study's cross-sectional logit and regression equations.

19. The set of HMDA reporters includes commercial banks, savings banks, savings and loan institutions, credit unions, mortgage subsidiaries of bank or other depository institution holding companies, and other mortgage companies that are independent companies and subsidiaries of firms other than depository institutions. Mortgage subsidiaries of bank holding companies have been covered under HMDA since 1988, whereas other mortgage companies have been covered only since 1990.

20. In addition, for the logit estimations, we deleted observations that were outliers with respect to loan amount or income—in particular, applications for loans exceeding $300,000 and applications with applicant income greater than $100,000 or less than $5,000. For the logit estimations, we also deleted several non-DVMP institutions that appeared to be misreporting applicant income or loan amount. These institutions were identified by a procedure analogous to that described in the accompanying appendix.

21. The $36,665 family income threshold equals 85 percent of median family income in the Philadelphia MSA. The $82,000 house value threshold is imposed to exclude "gentrifying" neighborhoods or other tracts where median family income is less than $36,665 but sales to middle- or upper-income home buyers are the primary determinant of mortgage activity.

22. The federal Community Reinvestment Act (CRA) calls on every bank and thrift to serve the credit needs of its entire community in a manner consistent with safe and sound banking practices. CRA obligates regulators to monitor banks' community reinvestment activities. It also requires regulators, when ruling on certain applications by a bank or its holding company, to consider the bank's record of community lending.

23. The study's estimation results are robust to deleting all tracts having fewer than 50 OOUs. In addition, the results are robust to expanding the set of tracts to all tracts with median household income less than or equal to $41,959 (MSA median income) and median house value less than or equal to $90,000.

24. Statistical tests to determine whether DVMP and non-DVMP institutions should be pooled consistently rejected pooling at the 1-percent significance level.

25. We scaled by the size of the resale market to avoid heteroscedasticity and multicollinearity problems in the empirical analysis.

26. Correlations among the explanatory variables were checked and, not surprisingly, several pairs of variables were found to have correlation coefficients exceeding 50 percent. Aside from mathematically related variables such as UNEMP and UNEMP^2 or AGE 45–54 and AGE 55pl, these pairs include: UNEMP and TRINC (−.81); UNEMP and HSGRAD (−.65); UNEMP and MINPOP (.61); UNEMP and PCTRENT (.55); UNEMP and RENT250 (.54); TRINC and HSGRAD (.66); TRINC and MINPOP (−.59); TRINC and RENT250 (−.60); TRINC and PCTRENT (−.55); PCTRENT AND RENT250 (.59).

27. Census tract economic and demographic variables have been found in previous studies to correlate with mortgage activity. In fact, the urban economics literature contains an assortment of studies, most dating from the 1970s, exploring the influence of neighborhood variables on mortgage activity. For surveys, see Benston (1979), Canner (1982), and Schweitzer (1993); see also Bradbury, Case, and Dunham (1989), which examines the geographic distribution of mortgages in Boston from 1982 to 1987; and

Canner, Gabriel, and Woolley (1991), which explores the factors influencing whether a household relies on conventional or FHA mortgage financing.

28. Empirical evidence indicates that residential mobility is related to household demographic characteristics. See, for example, Ioannides (1987).

29. MINPOP also captures the effect of racial discrimination, if present.

30. Clearly, inclusion of median sales price in 1990 as an explanatory variable would be inappropriate, because of endogeneity of that variable. Rental values, I presume, are exogenously determined. For instance, consider the extreme case that in a given tract during a given year, potential home sellers (and/or homebuyers) are forced into the rental market because banks are redlining a neighborhood. The impact on rental values would be negligible, so long as the number of houses (tenants) added to the rental market is small relative to the preexisting supply (and/or demand) in that market. Readers who remain skeptical regarding exogeneity of RENT250 should note that the empirical findings reported in the following are robust to omission of this variable. Dropping RENT250 has little impact on the signs or statistical significance of other variables in the estimated equations.

31. For elaboration on this latter point, see Henderson and Ioannides (1983).

32. We partly controlled for each applicant's LTV ratio, since we included loan amount along with tract characteristics that influence neighborhood house prices. It would be preferable, however, to directly control for LTV ratios.

33. To test whether separate estimation of equation (26.11) for minority and white applicants is more appropriate than pooling, likelihood ratio tests were performed. For non-DVMP institutions, pooling of applicants was rejected at the 1-percent significance level. For DVMP institutions, pooling of white and minority applicants could not be rejected.

34. More precisely, DENY takes a value of 1 if the loan application is either denied, withdrawn, or otherwise canceled.

35. For the sake of brevity, I only report results pertaining to variables that are statistically significant in at least one estimated equation. The variables that are not statistically significant in any of the logit estimations are AGE 35–44, AGE 45–54, AGE 55pl, and lowPOPDEN.

36. These results are robust to inclusion of the square of the loan amount in each estimated equation.

37. Other such instances include: (a) the denial rate for white applicants at non-DVMP institutions is inversely related to HSGRAD, and (b) the denial rate for minority applicants at non-DVMP institutions is inversely related to tract median income. The latter two findings are consistent with an adverse impact of neighborhood disamenities on approval rates, but also may indicate a positive relationship between house size and quality and approval rates.

38. The lack of significance of CONVEN in the estimated equation (26.10) for DVMP institutions may be due to the fact that there were few applicants for federally insured loans.

39. At non-DVMP institutions, minority applicants are more likely to be approved for a loan if the subject property is in a more moderate-income tract, whereas nonminority applicants are more likely to be approved if the subject property is in a low-income tract, for example. On average, however, minority status of an applicant is not strongly related to likelihood of approval.

40. On average, applicants at DVMP institutions are lower income, apply for smaller loans, and are more predominantly minority.

41. Thus, PRE50 bears a statistically significant, inverse relationship to probability of approval at DVMP institutions; POST80 bears a statistically significant, positive relationship. The observed inverse relationship between POST70 and likelihood of approval at DVMP institutions might be due to comparative affordability of houses constructed prior to 1970.

42. I also found that for DVMP institutions, application and origination activity increased with UNEMP, within a moderate range of values of UNEMP.

43. To formally test this distinction between the two groups of institutions, I also estimated cross-sectional regression equations of the form $(DEP)_{ij} = \alpha_0 + D + aX + bDX$, where $(DEP)_{ij}$ is application or origination activity in tract i of group j (DVMP and non-DVMP, respectively); X is as in equation (29.12); D is a dummy variable equal to 1 for the group of DVMP institutions, and DX is the interaction of each variable in X with D. As expected, the estimated coefficient on DMINPOP was positive and statistically significant at the 1-percent level in both of the APPLICATIONS/OOU and ORIGINATIONS/OOU regressions.

44. As argued in Calem (1993), it seems unlikely that the distinct lending patterns of the two groups of institutions reflect the spatial configuration of their branches, rather than the impact of DVMP. Potential applicants are not limited to branches in their neighborhood when shopping for a loan. The vast majority of branches of financial institutions in Philadelphia are conveniently located in the central city area or on a major thoroughfare. The number of branches that are accessible only to particular neighborhoods is very small in comparison. Furthermore in terms of branch coverage (branches per capita or per square mile), both DVMP and non-DVMP lenders are disproportionately represented in nonminority neighborhoods. To determine whether these lending patterns result from a disproportionate number of branches of non-DVMP lenders in the somewhat distinct, predominantly white, northeast section of Philadelphia, we added a dummy variable for those tracts to our empirical equations. Inclusion of this variable did not affect our results in any substantial way.

References

Avery, Robert B., Patricia E. Beeson, and Mark S. Sniderman. 1993. "Cross-Lender Variation in Home Mortgage Lending." Federal Reserve Bank of Cleveland Working Paper 9219. Cleveland, Ohio: Federal Reserve Bank of Cleveland.

Benston, George, J. 1979. "Mortgage Redlining Research: A Review and Critical Analysis." In *The Regulation of Financial Institutions*. Conference Series 21, Federal Reserve Bank of Boston. (101–43). Boston: Federal Reserve Bank of Boston.

Bradbury, Katharine L., Karl E. Case, and Constance R. Dunham. 1989. "Geographic Patterns of Mortgage Lending in Boston, 1982–1987." *New England Economic Review* (September/October): 3–30.

Calem, Paul S. 1993. "The Delaware Valley Mortgage Plan: Extending the Reach of Mortgage Lenders." *Journal of Housing Research* 4(2).

Canner, Glenn B. 1982. "Redlining: Research and Federal Legislative Response." Board of Governors of the Federal Reserve System Staff Study 121. Washington, D.C.: Federal Reserve System.

Canner, Glenn B., and Delores S. Smith. 1991. "Home Mortgage Disclosure Act: Expanded Data on Residential Lending." *Federal Reserve Bulletin* 77: 859–81.

———. 1992. "Expanded HMDA Data on Residential Lending: One Year Later." *Federal Reserve Bulletin* 78: 801–24.

Canner, Glenn B., Stuart A. Gabriel, and J. Michael Woolley. 1991. "Race Default Risk, and Mortgage Lending: A Study of the FHA and Conventional Loan Markets." *Southern Economic Journal* 58 (July): 249–62.

Cocheo, Steve. 1992. "Giving Home Loans a Second Opinion." *ABA Banking Journal* 84(2, October): 85–90.

Henderson, J. Vernon, and Yannis M. Ioannides. 1983. "A Model of Housing Tenure Choice." *American Economic Review* 73: 98–113.

Ioannides, Yannis M. 1987. "Residential Mobility and Housing Tenure Choice." *Regional Science and Urban Economics* 17: 265–87.

Munnell, Alicia H., Lynn E. Browne, James McEneaney, and Geoffrey M.B. Tootell. 1992. "Mortgage Lending in Boston: Interpreting HMDA Data." Federal Reserve Bank of Boston Working Paper 92-07. Boston: Federal Reserve Bank of Boston.

Munnell, Alicia H., Geoffrey M. B. Tootell, Lynn E. Browne, and James McEneaney. 1996. "Mortgage Lending in Boston: Interpreting HMDA Data." *American Economic Review*. Forthcoming.

Schweitzer, Robert. 1993. "Discrimination in Mortgage Lending: Past and Present." Newark: University of Delaware, Department of Finance. Draft.

APPENDIX 26A IDENTIFICATION OF "UNRELIABLE" RESPONDENTS

To distinguish respondents that appear to be consistently misreporting census tract locations, the following procedure was employed:

1. For every census tract in Philadelphia, for each year 1990 and 1991, the average loan size was computed for each institution lending in the tract that year, as well as the mean loan size across all institutions for that tract and year. (This was done for all tracts, not only low- and moderate-income tracts.)
2. For each tract and for each year, all outliers were identified; an *outlier* was defined to be an institution with an average loan

amount more than two standard deviations higher or lower than the tract mean for that year.

3. For each institution j, for a given year i, S_j^i denoted the number of times the institution was identified as an outlier, and N_j^i denoted the total number of observations of institution j in year i (an observation corresponds to a census tract and year in which the institution originated at least one loan).
4. Next, S_j^i was assumed to be the number of "successes" out of N_j^i draws from binomial distribution with "success" probability π.
5. The hypothesis $\pi \leq .1$ was then tested; if this hypothesis was rejected at the 5-percent level, institution j was dropped from the sample for the year in question. The interpretation of this test is that .1 is an acceptable "error" rate for HMDA respondents; if an institution's probability of misrepresenting is greater than .1, that institution should be dropped from the sample.[1]

1. For one institution in the sample, $\pi \leq .1$ was rejected in 1990 at the 5-percent level and in 1991 at the 10-percent level. I opted to drop the institution from the sample in both years.

Part Three

FUTURE DIRECTIONS

Chapter Twenty-Seven

FUTURE DIRECTIONS IN MORTGAGE DISCRIMINATION RESEARCH AND ENFORCEMENT

George Galster

To attempt to set forth future directions on any topic is a particularly intimidating task. The author must assume either clairvoyance or uncommon personal persuasiveness. Making neither assumption, I undertake in this final chapter to provoke debate about how the research, advocacy, and regulatory communities can work effectively to eradicate unlawful discrimination from our mortgage lending markets. This essay was initially prepared for the May 1993 U.S. Department of Housing and Urban Development (HUD) conference on "Home Mortgage Lending and Discrimination." I subsequently added an epilogue to reflect some of the key issues that have emerged since then.

In evaluating emerging trends in research and enforcement related to mortgage discrimination, I apply a purposely myopic perspective and employ only two criteria. The first criterion is whether any particular research approach or regulatory innovation is likely to provide practical assistance in (1) assessing the magnitude of a specific type of discriminatory behavior in a marketplace (and thus also the need for renewed enforcement efforts); (2) identifying particular individuals or institutions engaged in discrimination; and/or (3) developing effective policies to eradicate mortgage discrimination.[1]

The second criterion is whether an initiative can command support from the multiple constituencies involved in the issue at hand: social science researchers, community groups and civil rights activists, financial institution regulators, and lenders themselves. Operationally, this means that an initiative should satisfy the preeminent concern of each constituency, that being: (1) the methodological standards of researchers; (2) the practical applicability and programmatic effectiveness of advocates; (3) the operational simplicity and cost-effectiveness of regulators; and (4) the predictability, fairness, and business soundness of lenders. My assessment, inevitably subjective and often speculative, is based on both the application of social science research principles and on the institutional and political realities of these groups. Whenever possible, I attempt to identify the tough methodological and implementation problems associated with emerging initiatives. At the outset, I should stress that a consensual "magic bullet"—a demonstrably scientific, cost-effective, politically feasible research or enforcement initiative—has not emerged in the contemporary arena. However, I argue that two initiatives primarily—preapplication paired testing and mortgage scoring—hold promise of being such magic bullets, and that they deserve major intensified study.

This chapter is organized into three main sections. The first of these addresses how best to assess the nature and extent of illegal discrimination in mortgage and related markets. The second section considers how individual violators can best be pinpointed, presumably as a prelude to enforcement or compliance actions. The third major section looks at how studies of institutional context, deterrence versus education approaches, and future research can aid in developing ways to more effectively eliminate lending discrimination. The section also demonstrates how the analysis in the prior sections suggests that two initiatives—preapplication testing and mortgage scoring—warrant special merit in the pantheon of future directions in both research and enforcement.

WHAT IS THE NATURE AND EXTENT OF DISCRIMINATION IN MORTGAGE AND RELATED MARKETS?

Several recent comprehensive reviews of the literature have already addressed the nature and extent of discrimination in mortgage and related markets (see Galster 1992; Wienk 1992; Cloud and Galster 1993; Yinger, chapter 2 in this volume). I, therefore, focus here on emerging research trends and their potential for filling the gaps in our knowledge about mortgage discrimination. Filling such gaps is a prerequisite to allocating enforcement resources efficiently. I subdivide this literature into six subsections. The first two subsections analyze direct tests of differential treatment discrimination at the preapplication and underwriting stages of the mortgage process. The third subsection involves tests of adverse impact discrimination. The fourth subsection examines indirect indicators of the combined effect of all sorts of discrimination in mortgage lending. The fifth subsection suggests several areas closely related to the mortgage market where additional research is required. The sixth subjection considers research into the causes and consequences of mortgage discrimination.

Direct Investigations of Discrimination at Preapplication Stage

Paired testing has emerged as the principal research method for directly investigating differential treatment on the basis of race when prospective applicants initially contact a lender to obtain information (Barry Leeds and Associates 1993; also Smith and Cloud, chapter 23, this volume). Pilot studies employing this methodology have been conducted in several metropolitan areas, and most recently in Philadelphia (Philadelphia Commission on Human Relations 1993).[2] These pilot studies have been extremely valuable, pathbreaking experiments and have advanced the state of knowledge about testing in the field. In spite of their exploratory nature, several tentative conclusions can be drawn from the studies. First, testing is a device that can elicit useful information, even if it is restricted to transactions that occur prior to submitting an application. Second, instances of preapplication discrimination appear to occur in a small fraction of transactions, except perhaps when tests are conducted at institutions evincing prior suspicious behaviors. Third, when differential treatment occurs, it seems to involve providing black testers with less information, less-frequent instances of prequalifying, and a lower degree of sales effort. These conclusions must be advanced with caution, however, since the test projects were experimental in nature. Indeed, test reports, where they exist, fall short of social scientific standards of clarity, replicability, and statistical validity. Several operational aspects of preapplication testing require further investigation before we can be completely confident of the method's research efficacy (Galster 1993).

Detecting Subtle Differential Treatment

Some analysts have raised concerns that behaviors evinced by loan officers are so subtle that testers would be unable to detect them (Board of Governors 1991: 33–37) or that testers would only be able to provide unreliable, highly subjective accounts of their experiences (Riedman 1993). I believe it is likely, however, that a series of objective questions posed on tester debriefing forms could capture discouragement in unambiguous ways. One example is a checklist of the type of information provided by the loan officer. Was the tester invited to fill out an application? Was the tester prequalified for the loan? Was the tester given hints as to how to increase the chance of qualifying?

Extensive self-testing commissioned by lenders suggests that their findings are robust (Barry Leeds and Associates 1993).

A second aspect of such concerns is that no single variable may be sufficient to suggest an overall pattern of discouragement. This probably is true, but there is no reason why a cluster of debriefing items from testers' records could not be statistically analyzed for such patterns. Indeed, factor analysis and canonical correlation analysis are but two statistical means of detecting clusters of responses that, after interpretation, might clearly be indicative of multidimensional discouragement.

Sample Design

The key question regarding sample design is the way in which the researcher chooses to allocate a given number of tests over the mortgage lenders in the metropolitan area under investigation. Given that 40 percent of metropolitan areas have fewer than 25 lenders and 70 percent have fewer than 40 (Board of Governors 1991: table 1), it is often feasible to test all institutions. Elsewhere, a subset might be selected. This selection might be random, or the probability of an institution's being selected could be proportional to its share of the market. The selection might also be purposive with, say, the top five lenders in each institutional category being selected, or—a strategy that might be employed by activists or regulators—only those institutions might be selected for which there existed a prior suspicion of wrongdoing.

The obvious weakness of the purposive strategy is its inability to generalize findings to any other institutions in the local market. On the other hand, the universal or the randomized sampling strategies might produce ambiguous results, especially if sample sizes are modest and few institutions are tested more than once. In such cases, the (expected) low overall incidence of differential treatment will be unable to distinguish between whether all institutions discriminate (though infrequently) or a few discriminate always and the rest never.[3]

Sample Size

As in any empirical work, expanding the size of the sample increases the power of the statistical tests to distinguish among random, chance, and systematic results. The power is not constant for any given sample size, however, but varies according to the frequency of the behavior being observed and the interracial differences in the frequencies of such behaviors. For example, to reject (at a 5-percent significance level) the null hypothesis of no interracial differences when white testers are discouraged 45 percent of the time and black testers are discouraged 50 percent of the time requires 772 paired tests. Respective white and black testers' frequencies of 10 percent and 5 percent, on the other hand, imply only 213 paired tests (Board of Governors 1991).

Unfortunately, a priori one can estimate little about what incidences and interracial differences in treatment one is likely to find in lending tests. The Federal Reserve Board's best guess for the lending market as a whole is a difference in discouraging treatment of no more that 15 percentage points and a frequency of discouragement of no more than 25 percent for black testers (Board of Governors 1991: 64–65). This means that about 2,100 paired tests should be contemplated if one is to be confident of detecting a difference in treatment of at least 5 percentage points at a 5-percent level of significance in a general sample of lenders that includes more than only suspicious institutions.

Of course, these estimates may be wildly exaggerated if the sample includes only institutions suspected of discriminatory behavior. The Chicago lending test suggested more dramatic difference in treatment, for example (Galster 1993). Once again, these results have unfortunately not been reported in a way that permits tests of statistical significance.

DISCOVERY

The validity of the test for both research and enforcement is compromised by the discovery (or even suspicion) of its existence by the institutions being tested. Discovery is more likely (1) the more the tests are repeated in the same institutions; (2) the more similar and/or unusual the tester pair scenarios are; (3) the smaller the institution is in terms of loan originations and number of loan officers; (4) the more predominantly white the racial compositions of the areas in question are; and (5) the more fabricated the documents and histories the testers provide are (especially when subject to potential verification by the institutions).

Would, say, 200 paired tests of a wide-ranging sample of institutions be likely to avoid detection? I believe so, at least in the large metropolitan areas. A smaller group of institutions (the 10 largest, for example) would, of course, increase the number of repeat tests needed at each, and given the increasing centralization of loan originations, these repeat tests could arouse suspicion. The Federal Reserve has noted that 20 visits (10 pairs) per institution is a reasonable operational estimate for a pilot study, presumably without discovery (Board of Governors 1991: 71). Of course, if the sample design focuses on presumed violators, a smaller number of repeat tests would achieve the requisite statistical power and thus would provide even less chance of discovery.

Tester Scenario

There has been much discussion of and a modicum of empirical experimentation with regard to how testers should approach loan officers (Board of Governors 1991: 47–49). One issue involves whether a specific property should be mentioned. Testers can approach a loan originator by saying that they wish to know in general how large a loan they might qualify for, because they are considering buying a home (perhaps in a particular neighborhood) and wish to know in what range of affordability they can search. Alternatively, testers can posit a contract for a particular house and seek to obtain information about whether they could obtain a mortgage for it. A criticism of the former approach is that testers will not be treated as seriously without a sales contract in hand and therefore will elicit only limited, superficial behavior that will be unlikely to mimic behavior toward "real" prospects. Another criticism is that unless the geographic area of the intended purchase is clearly specified, the potential for eliciting discriminatory responses based on redlining is eliminated. The criticism of the latter approach is the difficulty of establishing valid contracts, an issue discussed later in this subsection.

Another scenario issue is whether testers should begin by attempting to set up appointments over the telephone (and manually or electronically record information conveyed) or merely walk in unannounced at offices. In my opinion, the two-step telephone/personal interview test is preferable, inasmuch as it catches those (perhaps rare) cases of discrimination at the first stage, maximizes the productive use of testers' time at the second stage, and allows for the unambiguous identification of the testers' race by the loan officer and, thereby, for the possibility of discrimination on that basis.

If the sales contract scenario is employed in lending tests, the issue arises as to whether the sale should be by the owner or through an agent. The former scenario is operationally simpler because it does not require the collaboration of real estate agents and can use homes not currently for sale. Its shortcoming is that such transactions are rare in most markets, and therefore the appearance of many such reputed sales during the testing period might arouse suspicion. In addition, loan originator behavior regarding such transactions may differ from that when real estate agents, who are familiar to the organizations, are involved. On the other hand, recruiting real estate agents to participate in a study (by, for example, signing dummy sales contracts on homes currently off the market) would be risky because it might increase the chances of the tests being discovered.[4] Agents might be reluctant to participate because their livelihood depends on a close working relationship with lenders, although providing guarantees of anonymity should assuage fears in this vein. Another strategy might be to set up a temporary dummy real estate company, complete with office space, yellow pages listing, and a staff to answer the telephone. This company would handle all of the testers' transactions (or some of them, if a few "for sale by owner" units were also used), and would be cited by testers if questioned by lenders. Such a plan would overcome the shortcomings just cited, but at considerable expense and operational complexity.

Analytical Design

The standard analytical approach in testing has been to consider the differences in treatment (if any) of the pair of testers as the unit of observation, while controlling as many characteristics of the teammates as possible. Each pair can thus be scored (for individual items of treatment or for the test as a whole) as either "white favored," "minority favored," or "neutral." Both the frequencies of these results and the amount of difference evinced (in certain ratio-level variables such as length of interview, time of processing application, points charged, etc.) can be tabulated, and paired differences-of-means tests performed (see Yinger 1986).

An alternative is to view each individual visit by a tester as a unit of observation (Board of Governors 1991: 56–61). Here the nonracial controls of the experiment are provided not by careful matching of testers but by multivariate statistical analysis of the results. That is, each visit provides a unit of observation of a model where the dependent variable is a measure of behavior toward the individual tester (measured in discrete or continuous terms), and the independent variables control for characteristics of the tester, the loan officer, the property in question, the circumstances of the test, and so forth.

Unlike the paired method, such a model cannot provide an estimate of the overall frequency of systematic discrimination in the sample or even of whether particular visits demonstrated disparate treatment; it can only estimate whether, across the tests, race accounted for a different probability or amount of a particular treatment, ceteris paribus. In addition, a larger sample of tests is required to provide adequate degrees of freedom for the statistical procedures. Nevertheless, the nonpaired method offers two advantages. Because it can accommodate a wider variation in tester characteristics and scenarios, it complements testing involving real tester identities (thereby permitting a deeper probe into the application process) or testing with strong concerns over discovery arising out of excessively similar tester pairs.

A final design question relates to whether paired testing can continue the investigation to and past the point of filing an application. The main worry has been the potential legal liability associated with falsifying financial records and the difficulty of creating false financial histories that such a depth of testing would necessitate. Experiments in full application testing have been conducted in Lima, Ohio (Smith and Cloud, chapter 23, this volume), although it is unclear whether the issues just cited have been resolved. Related questions about how such full application tests might be designed to investigate discrimination in home appraisals or underwriting of private mortgage insurance also remain unanswered.

The preceding concerns about paired testing are valid, and few firm conclusions can be offered about the best methodologies until we have considerably more field experimentation with testing of lenders. Nevertheless, I am confident that clever design of tester questionnaires and debriefing procedures is capable of objectively detecting even subtle forms of discouragement. The limited evidence also suggests to me that there is an intersection of test scenarios and sample sizes such that researchers can be confident of detecting rather small, yet statistically significant, differences in treatment in a wide-ranging sample of institutions without having the tests discovered. Whether this is the case for a single institution is problematic, unless that institution is already suspected of questionable behaviors, an issue discussed later in the context of enforcement. Tests would seem more efficacious if they could involve both telephone contacts and (attempts to obtain) personal interviews, and if they could avoid reliance on "for sale by owner" contracts or the guise of merely "shopping around for a mortgage" with no particular home in mind. Neither of these operational requirements seems onerous. How deeply testing might probe into the lending/appraisal/insurance process is speculative. Nevertheless, mortgage testing clearly is a priority area for future research, which, as amplified in the sections following, should yield important enforcement payoffs.

Direct Investigation of Mortgage Underwriting Process

The current statistical technique of choice for uncovering illegal differential treatment of otherwise comparable mortgage applications is a logit analysis of application file data.[5] The models attempt to identify all the factors that influence the underwriter's decision to approve or deny each applicant in the sample. Once all these myriad factors (property characteristics, applicant's debt, income, credit history, etc.) are statistically controlled, if the race of an applicant (or the race of the neighborhood in which the property was located) proves a statistically significant predictor of denials, there is a prima facie case of racial discrimination. This methodology was most recently applied in the 1992 *United States* v. *Decatur Federal Savings and Loan* case (Hancock 1993; Siskin and Cupingood, chapter 16, this volume) and in the Federal Reserve Bank of Boston study of over 300 lenders known as the "Boston Fed" study, by Munnell et al. 1992, 1993).

Although certainly a promising avenue of research, logit analyses of application file data face several challenges. As already discussed by Yinger in this volume, these include, in brief:

- *Data availability.* To operationalize this method requires access to a large number of confidential loan application files held by private institutions that are typically under no obligation to relinquish them to researchers.
- *Functional form.* Logits typically specify predictor variables as having separable, quasi-additive effects.[6] One potential way to overcome this is by specifying a number of interaction terms (such as negative credit history, but high down payment), but the number of control variables typically is so large that degree-of-freedom problems mount. There is also concern over how to specify the impact of "killer variables"—conditions that automatically yield denial, regardless of the potentially compensatory aspects of the application. In such cases, should the impact of these other aspects on the decision be mathematically forced to zero to obviate biasing their coefficients?
- *Aggregation bias.* Inasmuch as the research sample includes lending institutions that promulgate distinct lending standards, an attempt to estimate a single logit relationship may badly misrepresent the decision rule of individual lenders. Similar aggregation questions can be raised concerning pooling of loan types (conventional or Federal Housing Administration [FHA]/Department of Veterans Affairs [VA], purchase or refinancing) or terms (fixed or adjustable rate).
- *Testing for redlining.* Operationalizing and testing for differential treatment of an applicant based on protected characteristics of the property's neighborhood needs further development. For example, Munnell et al. (1993) used a race-stratified logit to compare pre-

dicted denials to actual denials in sets of neighborhoods defined by building ages, race, or income parameters. Whether particular subsets or intersections of subsets of such broadly defined neighborhood categories were redlined was not investigated.

- *Endogeneity of explanatory variables.* The logit models have assumed that the terms of a prospective mortgage are predetermined before the underwriting decision is made. Inasmuch as terms are a function of counteroffers and negotiations, this assumption is violated; inasmuch as counteroffers and negotiations are related to race, the estimated parameter estimates for race will be biased.[7]
- *Omitted variables.* There is some question whether all the idiosyncratic features of a mortgage application and their potential synergistic interactions can be identified easily, coded appropriately, and included in the logit model. Maddala and Trost (1982), for example, argue that loan amount is typically omitted, thereby overstating the importance of race.
- *Implicit restrictions on the logit parameters.* Yinger (chapter 2, this volume) has shown that the standard logit model assumes that the estimated impacts of applicant, property, and loan characteristics on the probability of denial can be interpreted as the effect of the loan's anticipated rate of return on this probability. Yet, if these estimated effects themselves reflect differential treatment or adverse impact forms of discrimination at other stages of the lending process, the standard approach will probably yield an underestimate of racial discrimination.
- *Repeated observations.* Applicants may reappear in the sample multiple times if they are denied at least once and reapply. It is even more methodologically troublesome that both applicants and lenders may change their behavior once a prior denial has occurred.[8]

Despite these concerns, I believe that additional research can be productively conducted using this methodology, even if all the preceding wrinkles are not ironed out. Order-of-magnitude levels of current underwriting discrimination have been provided for only one area (Boston) and only for home purchase mortgages. It clearly would be useful for enforcement purposes to better understand such discrimination's geographic scope,[9] as well as to discern whether it infects home improvement and home equity lines of mortgage credit (Lehman 1993a) and is more prevalent in commercial banks, savings and loans, or mortgage companies.

Identifying Adverse Impact Discrimination

The foregoing discussion has dealt with discrimination defined as illegal difference in treatment based on race. Given the precedent that has been established in other contexts such as housing and employment, discrimination can also be defined in terms of adverse impact—evenhanded treatment that results in adverse consequences for protected classes. As Wienk (1992) and Kushner (1992) have noted, there are few legal precedents for judging which rules applied by lenders, if any, have illegal disparate impacts.[10]

To my knowledge, no studies have attempted to quantify statistically such adverse impacts and to ascertain the degree to which different standards would reduce such impacts while retaining fiduciary responsibility. A valuable step has been taken by the New York State Banking Department, however (Kohn et al. 1992; Kohn 1993). Their examination of 10 savings banks found that 4 banks promulgated standards (such as high minimum down-payment ratios and loan sizes) that could adversely affect minorities, females, and lower income and predominantly minority neighborhoods. They were also critical of all 10 institutions' failure to offer FHA-insured mortgages and of 6 institutions' inadequate outreach activities in local communities. The recent Philadelphia paired testing study (Philadelphia Commission on Human Relations 1993) surprisingly turned up many more instances of adverse impact policies than differential treatment.

More research with a clear enforcement payoff is warranted in the area of adverse impact. To my knowledge, quantitative research has never been conducted to estimate what the profile of the "appropriate pool of potential borrowers from protected classes" looks like or to determine how particular underwriting criteria (such as debt-to-income ratios) differentially affect various groups. There also is a need to better specify the origin of these underwriting standards, to ensure they are based on sound models that are predictive of delinquency and default probabilities. This would be a precursor to asking whether current standards are more restrictive than necessary (Kohn et al. 1992; Kohn 1993).

Investigating Other Discriminatory Transactions Related to Mortgage Market

As comprehensively documented by Greene (chapter 22, this volume), differential treatment discrimination can occur in many other activities that are inextricably linked to the lending process. In brief particular concerns that warrant further research are:

- *Home appraisals.* Even though there is ample historical evidence that appraisers were trained to evaluate properties on the basis of a neighborhood's racial composition (Schwemm 1993; Cloud and Galster 1993), the contemporary record lists few court cases and only circumstantial evidence (Schwemm, chapter 12, this volume). Little statistical research has been conducted in this area (Schaefer and Ladd 1981).
- *Private mortgage insurance.* Case histories (Lehman 1993b) and tantalizing regression evidence provided as a spin-off of the Boston Fed study (Munnell et al. 1992, 1993) suggest worrisome racial patterns.
- *Home casualty insurance.* ACORN's (1992) pioneering investigation into racial differentials in the types of insurance held by homeowners, policy cancellation rates, and other features cries out for more methodologically sophisticated follow-up studies. At this writing, the Urban Institute is completing a testing study of this issue.
- *Real estate broker mortgage steering.* Evidence from the national Housing Discrimination Study (Turner, Struyk, and Yinger 1991) shows that brokers tend to steer minority homeseekers toward government-insured mortgages.

As explained by Yinger (chapter 2, this volume), discrimination in transactions occurring prior to the final underwriting decision can lead to a disproportionate number of minorities being legitimately denied credit from the underwriter's perspective. Yet, the race coefficient in a logit of denial probabilities need never prove significant. Likewise, such discrimination would not be revealed by paired tests of lenders at the preapplication stage or by careful examination of lenders' underwriting guidelines. In principle, there is no reason why multivariate statistical modeling, paired testing, and underwriting policy examination could not be adapted to investigate these transactions related to mortgage lending; the need appears urgent.

Indirect Methods for Identifying Discrimination

All the research methods just discussed attempt to identify particular acts of differential treatment or particular policies that promulgate adverse impact by directly analyzing the acts or policies. By contrast, several other methods—including market segmentation models, analysis of Home Mortgage Disclosure Act (HMDA) data, the marginal default probabilities model, and the average default rate model—attempt to deduce indirectly the existence of unspecified forms of discrimination by identifying its symptoms. In my opinion, none of these four indirect methods warrants further research; two have run the course of their usefulness, and two are severely flawed conceptually. Each is considered in turn next.

Market Segmentation Models

Market segmentation models attempt to determine whether lenders encourage or insist that (putatively) riskier borrowers, such as minorities, apply for government-insured (and thus less risky) mortgages. In the most thorough investigation of the phenomenon to date, Canner, Gabriel, and Woolley (1991) analyzed a 1983 survey of consumer finance data and found that the average minority household seeking a mortgage in a minority neighborhood is only about one-third as likely to obtain a conventional loan as a comparable white household in that same neighborhood, even when controlling for several objective measures of default risk. Similar patterns were reported in 1990 HMDA data (Canner and Gabriel 1992) and in HUD's FHA data (Canner et al. 1993).

These results are consistent with a hypothesis of lender bias, but, as Canner and colleagues have admitted (1991: 120), the findings are also consistent with "differences in preferences for FHA vs. conventional financing among different racial-ethnic groups, the effect of steering by real estate agents, (or) market specialization by mortgage bankers." This leads me to a pessimistic prognosis of future research using this approach. Even highly sophisticated multivariate models will be unable to make unambiguous conclusions from any racial differentials observed in the categories of mortgage loans held.

Analysis of HMDA Data

The most common indirect research approach compares publicly available HMDA data on amounts of loans for census tracts varying by racial composition (for a review, see Galster 1991; Canner and Gabriel 1992; Wienk 1992). With two notable exceptions (Hula 1991; Perle, Lynch and Horner 1993), these studies have shown racial differentials in applications and approvals, even when numerous other features of the tracts are controlled. Unfortunately, such aggregate data cannot precisely show the number and characteristics of loan applications from these areas, and thus cannot discern whether the differential was due to lack of demand, legal supply constraints, or illegal supply constraints (Benston 1981; Canner et al. 1991; Galster 1991). The fundamental problem with HMDA data is that they do not include crucial information needed to sort out competing hypotheses.

Consider, first, the disproportionately low number of applications from African Americans and Hispanics. Four (not mutually exclusive) hypotheses readily suggest themselves. First, these applicants could afford a mortgage for a home, but simply are not aware of their qualification. This could be termed a failure of information or marketing. Second, they may be unsure of whether or not they can afford a mortgage, and when they try to obtain information from a prospective lender, they are misinformed or otherwise discouraged from applying. This is lender discrimination at the preapplication stage. Third, they may correctly believe that they cannot afford the size of mortgage required to purchase their desired property (for one personal financial reason or another) and thus do not apply. This is a problem of personal financial management, lack of personal productivity, macroeconomic conditions, or discrimination in the labor market. Finally, they may correctly believe that they can afford a sizable mortgage, but choose not to apply for one—either because they do not see advantages of homeownership, such as high property appreciation (Avery and Buynak 1981) or they cannot find a home to purchase superior to the one they currently occupy. This could be due to historical unfamiliarity with homeownership, relatively low property appreciation in minority neighborhoods, or discrimination in the housing market, which limits housing choices.

Now consider the higher rate of loan denials for black and Hispanic applicants. Again, four hypotheses are plausible. First, applications may be treated more harshly by lenders merely because they are from minority applicants or because the property in question is located in a minority-occupied neighborhood. This is the hypothesis of racial discrimination by differential treatment of applications. Second, applications from minorities may be evaluated according to similar standards as those for whites, but the standards are arbitrary, inflexible, and serve no sound business interest. This is known as racial discrimination through adverse impact. Third, applications from minorities may be treated evenhandedly in light of fair, flexible standards with sound business rationales, but they do not pass muster as often as those from whites. Even with identical incomes, blacks and Hispanics on average are less likely to have as large a down payment, as long a job tenure, as good a credit history, or as low a debt/income ratio as whites (Munnell et al. 1992, 1993). They also may be more likely to have property value declines (Avery and Buynak 1981). This situation is due to a complex legacy of interracial, socioeconomic inequalities in America. Fourth, minority applicants may have been approved, were it not for appraisers who discriminatorily undervalued the properties in question or mortgage insurers who discriminatorily refused to grant insurance.

It is my belief that all of these hypotheses have some validity. The problem is that the HMDA data tell us nothing about the degree to which any of the hypotheses are responsible for what we observe. This is why I cannot recommend additional research using such data (unless they are vastly reinforced with additional information)—owing to little enforcement policy payoff. Because HMDA data do not identify the source of the problem, we are left with no guidance on how to invest our scarce resources to better meet the credit needs of minorities.

Marginal Default Probabilities Model

Van Order, Westin, and Zorn (1993) have introduced a provocative method for deducing any discriminatory lending practices that make it more difficult for qualified minority applicants to obtain mortgages. The upshot is this: discrimination should result in the riskiest non-minority approved applicant being viewed as riskier than the riskiest minority approved applicant. That is, of the marginally acceptable applicants, one should observe a lower risk profile for minorities because discrimination has served to weed out some of their riskier compatriots (who would have been approved had they not been minorities).

The initial attempt to operationalize this logic involved estimating race-specific default risk models based on ex post facto default experience, then applying these models' coefficients to the generation of "risk scores." Cross-racial comparison of the higher-risk tails of the distributions of risk scores provides the test. Lack of desired data clearly hampered the execution of this creative approach: borrower race (instead of ZIP code racial proxies), credit history, employment stability, and property-specific value changes are the most glaring examples.

But even if these empirical shortcomings could be solved, Yinger (chapter 2, this volume) has argued that the conceptual approach is fatally flawed for at least four reasons. First, it is unlikely that one could ever observe a clear break in the distribution of risk scores, given that many underwriters (at institutions articulating different standards) would not assess reputedly equal scores as equal. Second, the underwriting process is a smoothly probabilistic exercise for applicants, as opposed to one in which all applicants below some threshold are denied and all above it are approved. Third, lenders can discriminate on observed characteristics. Although they may believe that (observed) race predicts (unobserved) rate of return and thereby exact a race penalty, there is no reason to be confident that the penalty they exact correctly adjusts for the differential. The marginally approved minority might still, therefore, evince a lower rate of return than the marginally approved nonminority. Fourth, inasmuch as lenders can discriminate against borrowers with prospective defaults, default rates will not be decent proxies for borrower risk.

Average Default Rate Model

A variant of the argument just described has received major attention in the press (e.g., Brimelow 1993; Brimelow and Spencer 1993; Roberts 1993) and has even gained the imprimatur of Nobel Laureate Gary Becker (1993). The model states that if underwriters were discriminating, they would be granting mortgages to less-qualified, riskier whites while denying them to relatively more creditworthy minorities. Thus, we should observe a lower default rate on average for minorities than whites.

This argument is wrong for several reasons (Cross 1993; Yinger, chapter 2, this volume), the primary reason being that average default rates are an unreliable indicator of lending discrimination. First, it is possible for there to be rampant discrimination while the pools of minority and white mortgage holders remain comparable to what they would be in a nondiscriminatory world. It is unlikely that all lending officers in all financial institutions discriminate all the time. Thus, having been rejected once due to discrimination, minorities often apply for and receive a loan elsewhere. Furthermore, as explained earlier, discrimination may incorrectly assess the risk of minorities and unwittingly approve some who are riskier than whites.

The second reason this argument is incorrect is because it erroneously assumes that in a nondiscriminatory world, pools of both whites and minorities who were successful in obtaining mortgages will subsequently demonstrate equal average rates of default on their mortgages. On the contrary, because of inequality between the races, in occupations, income, indebtedness, and assets (even in a nondiscriminatory world), minority mortgage holders typically will be distributed more heavily in the categories of borrowers who are at a higher risk of defaulting.

Defaults occur most often when either the borrower's income falls, unforeseen expenses arise, or home value declines. Minority borrowers generally confront higher chances of being laid off during recessions, have fewer assets to fall back on in time of financial exigencies, and are more likely to live in central city areas that have suffered deflation of property values. Minority mortgage holders, therefore, will tend to have higher default rates than the pool of white mortgage holders in a world devoid of lending discrimination. It may well be that discrimination on the margin would reduce the observed average default rates of the minority borrower pool. However, what the argument neglects to consider is that discrimination might simply be lowering average minority default rates to a level on par with average white default rates. In other words, what would have been a higher average minority default rate in a hypothetical, nondiscriminatory world may have been equalized by the offsetting effects of lending discrimination to produce the rates observed in the actual world.

The point is that interracial comparisons of average (or marginal) default rates are unreliable indicators of the presence or absence of discrimination in any mortgage market. This approach is indelibly flawed and should be debunked and abandoned forthwith.

Research on Causes and Effects of Mortgage Lending Discrimination

Although not directed toward finding out how much mortgage lending discrimination exists in a particular market, another area of concern warrants more research: the causes and effects of lending discrimination. As I have suggested elsewhere (Galster 1992), more modeling and empirical testing of alternative hypotheses about why lenders might discriminate is needed. The debate between those who see an irrational motive (Benston 1979) and those who see an economically rational motive (Lang and Nakamura 1993) remains unsettled. I need only echo Yinger's (chapter 2, this volume) eloquent rationale for exploring these alternative causes more thoroughly: it determines what sorts of enforcement efforts will be most efficacious. Whether the cause is the irrational prejudices of individual loan officers, the conscious, profit-enhancing policies of statistical discrimination, or unconscious habits of institutionalized racism, modeling and testing matter for enforcement purposes.

Other than vignettes, we also have little understanding of the scope and seriousness of harms wrought by such discrimination. Yet, given increasingly shrill cries from some quarters over regulatory burdens imposed by fair lending and Community Reinvestment Act (CRA) requirements, I believe it is crucial to quantify the magnitude of discriminatory harms that these regulations are designed to prevent.

Several areas of investigation seem appropriate in this regard. Does mortgage discrimination:

- Reduce minorities' rates of homeownership?
- Yield less favorable terms and conditions and/or inferior products for minority borrowers?
- Force minority applicants to invest more time, energy, and out-of-pocket expense in reapplying to alternative lenders?

Efforts should be directed toward obtaining the answers.

HOW CAN INDIVIDUAL DISCRIMINATION BE IDENTIFIED?

I now turn to the issue that, although closely related to assessing the nature and extent of discrimination, is more directly related to fair lending enforcement. Areas requiring further research need to be identified so that those most concerned about ensuring fair lending for all—particularly federal and state regulatory agencies and community-based and nonprofit organizations—can better identify violators and target them for education or sanctions. Four such areas are analyzed below: enforcement testing, statistical analysis of mortgage application files, enhanced file examination strategies, and analysis of publicly available data.

Enforcement Testing by Regulatory Agencies and Civil Rights Groups

Regulatory Agencies

Citing the methodological concerns raised previously here, federal financial institution regulatory agencies have for years refused to adopt (even on an experimental basis) paired testing as a means of carrying out their mandate to ensure compliance with civil rights laws (Riedman 1993), although the Office of the Comptroller of the Currency (OCC) has conducted a paired testing experiment (Spayd 1993), whose results are about to be announced to the public at this writing. There is little doubt that some other federal agencies are moving toward acceptance, even advocacy, of testing: witness HUD's longtime sponsorship of housing testing studies and its recent funding of enforcement testing for mortgage discrimination through the Fair Housing Initiative Program; the Department of Justice's use of testing evidence in filing housing pattern and practice suits and its growing interest in employment testing; and the Equal Employment Opportunity Commission's (EEOC's) recent approval of testing in employment cases.

Current regulatory procedures are incapable of detecting discrimination at the preapplication stages of transactions because periodic examinations focus only on written documents and have no means of investigating conversations between loan originators and prospective applicants that create no documentation (Board of Governors of the Federal Reserve 1991: 7–8). The gap in regulatory enforcement is clear.

Whether testing can effectively fill this gap is not clear. The answer depends upon the pattern of discrimination across institutions and, if it is concentrated in only a few institutions, on whether they can be identified for targeted testing. If discrimination at the preapplication stage is rare (or nonexistent) at lending institutions, testing would be an ineffective regulatory tool. Every institution would need to be tested many times to ensure statistically significant results, yet this would likely lead to detection by the institutions, as well as unreasonably high operation costs. On the other hand, if only a few institutions discriminate but do so virulently, a modest amount of testing would hold more promise of detecting the discrimination. This presumes, of course, that the violating institutions could be identified by some criteria before conducting the targeted testing. Perhaps consumer complaints, patterns of HMDA data, or suspicious underwriting behaviors revealed in prior examinations could provide these indicators, but, as explained later in this chapter, this is questionable. Another option (albeit more costly) would be to do a broad-based sampling of tests, with each institution receiving several. Those with unusually high incidences of differential treatment could be the focus of subsequent targeted tests.

Needless to say, no definitive answer can be given to the question of the cost-effectiveness of testing as a regulatory tool until more testing fieldwork is done to ascertain the scope and depth of discrimination at the preapplication stage and the costs of conducting such tests. Indeed, this consideration, combined with an assessment of weaknesses in the current examination procedures and the great promise of the testing technique, led the Consumer Advisory Council of the Federal Reserve Board of Governors to recommend in June 1991 that the Federal Reserve sponsor a systematic, social-scientific study of testing at the preapplication stage of lending. Unfortunately, the

Federal Reserve rejected this recommendation in September 1991, leaving it in the tenuous position of admitting to a gap in its oversight procedures, yet refusing to experiment with a method for closing it. I hope that this unconscionable position is reversed quickly; ignorance is bad public policy. The recent OCC actions to experiment with regulatory applications of paired testing represent a positive step in closing this gap.

Civil Rights Groups

Regardless of whether paired testing is used as a tool by regulators, it could be employed by civil rights groups to obtain evidence in legal proceedings alleging lending discrimination. The recent tests of the Philadelphia Commission on Human Relations (1993), reported at the 1993 HUD conference on "Home Mortgage Lending and Discrimination," are illustrative. The potential usefulness of the method for litigation purposes may well be greater than in either the research or the regulatory applications. For example, researchers' concerns about statistical significance may be less important than the "preponderance of evidence" adjudged by the court, thereby diminishing concerns about sample design, sample size, and risk of discovery. Similarly, regulators' interests in the cross-institutional pattern and severity of discrimination become irrelevant when one institution is targeted in litigation.

Having said that the value of testing for litigation purposes may be independent of its value for research and regulatory purposes, I do not mean to imply that those three efforts are anything but complementary. Indeed, advances in the method spurred by research initiatives may have clear payoffs in regulatory and litigation arenas and vice versa. A growing body of case law establishing evidentiary standards for lending testing may persuade lending regulators to look more kindly upon the method. Accordingly, all advances in lending testing should be supported by interested researchers, regulators, and civil rights groups, regardless of the tests' particular application.

Statistical Analysis of Application Files

An individual institution's mortgage application files can, in principle, be subjected to the same sorts of logit multivariate statistical analyses as described earlier. One could attempt to model the institution's articulated underwriting standards and then ascertain whether, having controlled for such standards, there was any statistically significant relationship between the probability of the applicant being denied and that applicant's race or some other protected classification. Such an analytical approach was employed by the Justice Department in the *Decatur Federal Savings* (1992) case, for example (see Siskin and Cupingood, chapter 16, this volume). As a spinoff from the Boston Fed study's use of this method, subsequent analysis by the Massachusetts Attorney General's Office for specific institutions in Boston has resulted in consent decrees being reached with ten lenders (Commonwealth of Massachusetts 1993).[11]

Although the statistical analysis of application files clearly shows promise, a number of thorny issues must yet be confronted, including:

- *Statistical specification.* All the technical questions raised previously in the context of research applications concerning correct functional form, definition of variables, inclusion of variables, and restrictions on parameters apply here as well. Presumably, each institution has distinct underwriting standards, so a different logit model would need to be estimated for each institution.
- *Resource limitations.* Substantial costs would be involved in collecting, cleaning, and computerizing all the additional information required to operationalize logit models, estimate the parameters, and interpret the results. Whether examiners have the time or expertise to conduct such analyses is questionable (Riedman 1993).
- *Sample size limitations.* Relatively few lenders generate a large enough volume of mortgage applications to make this statistical approach feasible. Riedman (chapter 23, this volume) estimated, for example, that only 90 of the 3,600 national banks regulated by the OCC have adequate sample sizes to support a model like that used by the Boston Fed study to analyze black-white discrimination, and only 120 of 3,600 could support Hispanic-Anglo discrimination analyses. What about the other institutions with small, idiosyncratic portfolios?
- *Statistical power of models.* Bauer and Cromwell (1994) have produced provocative simulations of how a stylized, seven-variable statistical model might work in identifying discrimination in individual institutions. They indicated that if the institution were systematically increasing borderline minority applicants' probability of denial by 0.20, statistical models would likely fail to uncover statistically significant racial differential in more than half of the simulated analyses conducted, even when sampling 500 files each time.[12] On the other hand, when the incremental probability of denying those on the approval borderline on purely racial grounds rises to 0.60, a repeated sampling of only 200 files would be suffi-

cient to identify discrimination in 89 percent of the trials. For any size sample, Bauer and Cromwell (1994) estimated that the probability of the model indicating discrimination when, in fact, there was none, is between 0.04 and 0.10. Regardless of the precision of the Bauer and Cromwell estimates, the statistical power to identify individual violators will be crucially shaped by the frequency and severity of discriminatory actions at specific institutions, juxtaposed against the size of the loan file sample being analyzed.

Enhanced File Examinations

Since 1993, the constituent regulatory agencies comprising the Federal Financial Institutions Examination Council (FFIEC) have engaged in intensive efforts to modify the procedures used by their fair lending compliance officers during their periodic lender examinations (Lindsey 1993). More modifications doubtless are still forthcoming, but three enhancements have emerged: (1) using preliminary statistical analyses to target institutions and particular files, (2) focusing on reasons for denial, and (3) uncovering racial differentials in discretionary aspects and quality of assistance. Although each of these enhancements represents a creative attempt to improve examinations, I have doubts about their ultimate efficacy. Each is considered next.

Preliminary Statistical Analyses to Target Institutions and Files

HUD and federal regulators are experimenting with systems whereby HMDA-type data for each institution could be used as the basis for either identifying which institutions look particularly "suspicious" or which files in an institution to be examined are worthy of particular attention (Heyman 1993; also Chud and Bonnette, chapter 18, this volume; and Goldstein, chapter 19, this volume). Given all the potentially misleading features of the HMDA data already noted, however, the efficiency and equity of such HMDA-based targeting schemes remain questionable. Although HMDA data apparently can be cluster-analyzed to produce groups of lenders with similar profiles, there is no external validation that the variables or weights defining the profiles are related to discrimination. Other HMDA patterns appear contradictory. Avery, Beeson, and Sniderman (chapter 3, this volume) found, for example, that interracial differences in denial rates for individual institutions' alternative loan products were rarely consistent. Finally, it is unclear how lenders currently manipulate their HMDA data or might do so if particular indicators were eventually employed as targeting devices.[13]

Difficult questions remain to be answered by new statistical procedures to identify particular application files in need of more intense scrutiny by examiners. Basically, all the new procedures being discussed appear to specify a logit-type model in which many variables are omitted for reasons of cost and simplicity. Parameters of the models are used retrospectively to "reunderwrite" applications. Those from different races with equal simulated probabilities of denial but unequal treatment in actuality, and/or those minorities with a low simulated probability of denial who were denied nevertheless, and/or those nonminorities with a high simulated probability of denial who were approved nevertheless could be selected for more scrutiny. Once such files have been isolated, the problem remains one of examiner subjectivity. Because all relevant variables were not in the original logit, examiners must still estimate how the given excluded underwriting factors were evaluated by the lender and, more importantly, whether they were evaluated consistently for all races. If the logit is used to generate mispredicted cases, which cases are so aberrant that they warrant inclusion in the scrutiny sample? If "essentially similar" files are identified by the logit, how close must their simulated probabilities of denial be? Even if files with identical simulated denial probabilities but different denial actions are identified, what is the criterion for assessing whether the difference in treatment was due to chance?

Subjectivity is not an inherent evil, but I believe that excessive subjectivity undermines the current and prospective examination process. If examinations are to deter illegal acts or serve as educational devices, the evaluative standards must be objective, precise, and predictable from the lenders' perspective; and if regulators are to have credibility in the eyes of advocacy groups and congressional overseers, they must have restricted opportunities for being too lenient on violators. Also, the tedious comparisons used as input into the subjective judgments inhibit the cost-effectiveness of the examination.

Reason for Denial

The new comparative file review process recently instituted at the OCC (Riedman 1993) seeks to compare the stated reasons for adverse actions with the corresponding so-called objective data for those applicants. This presents a number of problems. First, examiner subjectivity must be taken into account, as just described. Second, it is artificial to conceive of one or two reasons for denial as the basis for an underwriting decision, because it is the confluence of both negative and positive (compensating) features in an application that determines outcome. The reason for denial might equally be phrased "Negative factor X present" or "Inadequate compensatory factors present to offset X." Thus, examiners will inevitably be drawn back into the mire of multidimensional differences between comparison files. Riedman's (1993: 20) suggestions that simple guidelines could suffice here must be treated with extreme skepticism.

Discretionary Acts and Quality of Assistance

The OCC hopes to uncover cases of discrimination in which more assistance was provided to white applicants over black applicants in terms of explaining blots on credit histories or providing additional support materials. Although this is a worthy objective, it is unclear how attainable it is. How will "comparable" applicants be identified? Remember, the preliminary logit presumably identifies files of applicants who have practically identical qualifications; here one would seek files that started with equal (dis)qualifications and were subsequently rendered unequal. Could files be tampered with by the institutions to minimize the "thicker file phenomenon." What would examiners consider to be prima facie evidence of discriminatory assistance?

Undoubtedly, examiners face an extremely difficult task in identifying which files to consider and in developing effective rules for interpreting differences in the files analyzed. But even if such hurdles were overcome, the power of the examination to identify violators might still be quite modest. Bauer and Cromwell's (1994) study also simulated the effects of a stylized examination process. The examiner was to compare the proportion of rejected minority applicants whose qualifications dominated those of accepted whites with the proportion of rejected white applicants whose qualifications dominated those of accepted African Americans. If the institution under examination was penalizing borderline minority applicants with a 0.40 or higher probability of denial,[14] an examination based on a sample of 25 minorities and 25 whites would indicate discrimination only 36 percent of the time. Even if the sample were increased to an unwieldy 125 minorities and 125 whites, in only 50 percent of the examinations would discrimination be indicated.

Analysis of Public Data

I have previously argued that extreme caution should be taken when considering how well publicly available (primarily HMDA) data can target fair lending violators, primarily because so many factors can influence the apparent patterns in the data that have nothing to do with illegal activities. Nevertheless, it seems clear that community groups, regulatory agencies, and, perhaps, the Justice Department, have and will continue to examine publicly available data for suspicious patterns.

Elsewhere, I have suggested (Galster 1991) that such data might be of circumscribed value in at least three applications. First, since the omission of control variables from public data tends to create a bias toward a finding of discrimination, absence of a clear racial pattern can often be taken as an indicator of a clean bill of health.[15] Second, because public data implicitly control for the demand potential in a neighborhood, analyzing how an institution's share of the market varies across racial areas can be instructive. Finally, a multifaceted approach in which, for example, HMDA data on denial rates, application volumes, and market shares, office locations, and mortgage product types are considered as a whole can provide potentially useful indications of problem institutions.

That said, however, I see the need for more rigorous research into the efficacy of such methods that rely on public data to identify discriminators so that these methods do not falsely indict institutions that do not discriminate. Perhaps future studies could correlate more definitive indicators (such as results from paired tests and logit analyses of application files) with various public data indicators. Nevertheless, I remain skeptical of the prospective payoffs from further research is this area.

REMEDIES FOR ENDING LENDING DISCRIMINATION

Beyond the questions of the scope of lending discrimination in a particular market and of who specific violators might be, is the issue of which research initiatives hold the most promise for ending such violations. I first consider two overarching issues: appropriate institutional context for an enhanced enforcement effort and whether deterrence or education is more effective. I then consider two methodological initiatives—paired testing and mortgage scoring—that, I believe, are prospective magic bullets. I am convinced that these techniques would command widespread support and would so enhance the enforcement community's arsenal that the identification and eradication of lending discrimination would leap forward.

Overarching Issues

Institutional Context

Debate has continued about which institution(s) should have responsibility over antidiscrimination activities in the lending field. Some recently have argued that civil rights supervisory power should be stripped from members of the FFIEC and assigned, instead, to HUD. Others argue that HUD has shown insufficient initiative and competence in the area of fair housing enforcement to be entrusted with this extra task. Some suggest the creation of a new Fair Housing and Lending Commission by executive order. This commission might be structured much like EEOC and would assume responsibilities previously carried out by HUD's Fair Housing and Equal Opportunity division. Still others advocate elevating the fair lending enforcement function within existing FFIEC agencies. I advocate no single position here. Rather, I believe it is appropriate to conduct more rigorous, institutional-historical studies that might aid thinking about this issue beyond the pale of polemics and ideology that has frequently clouded such deliberations.

Deterrence versus Education

Closely related to institutional context is the issue of how best to change potential violators' behavior. Clearly, the FFIEC's past emphasis has been on education coupled with compliance monitoring. Although many community-based organizations also actively work to educate lenders, their primary impact has been felt through deterrence, as manifested specifically by CRA challenges and legal suits. Unfortunately, we know precious little about which approach (or combination of approaches) is more successful in combating discrimination.

There currently seems to be a political consensus that more punitive deterrence needs to be added to the equation: witness the recent legal requirements mandating that probable cause cases uncovered by FFIEC examiners be referred to the Justice Department (see Reidman 1993). The difficulty with this trend is its subjectivity. Deterrence necessitates a clear understanding on the part of potential violators about what constitutes an illegal act. Unfortunately, as previously emphasized, the examiners are forced to make highly subjective interpretations of evidence, even with the enhanced examination procedures. Furthermore, the FFIEC agencies themselves seem reluctant to promulgate detailed guidelines about what precisely constitutes an actionable finding. This is understandable, considering that only a handful of court cases have gone to trial and had an opinion rendered about the veracity of the evidence (Cloud and Galster 1993). It is this recurrent theme of needing quantifiable, clear-cut evidence from which illegal acts can be ascertained that motivates my choice of the following two strands as preeminent foci for future research efforts.

Two Prospective "Magic Bullets"

Paired Testing

It is crucial to investigate lending practices at the preapplication stage. Academics and regulatory agency representatives have worried for over a decade that this part of the transaction process could involve substantial discrimination that has so far gone undetected (Schafer and Ladd 1981; Canner 1982). Indeed, there is reason to suspect that discrimination may be more likely to occur before rather than after an application is filed. If an institution wanted to discriminate, it clearly would be more likely to escape detection if it initially discouraged prospective minority applicants instead of leaving a paper trail of rejected applications. Even if the management of an institution did not want to discriminate, the behavior of loan originators toward customers may be less closely monitored than that of underwriters toward written documents subject to supervisory review. Thus, there may be more room for originators to exercise personal prejudices and to be motivated to save costs and time on presumably less-qualified applicants at the preapplication stage, with both these rationales for discrimination going unchecked by management (Board of Governors 1991: 29–32).

There appear to be no prospective substitutes for obtaining information equivalent to that revealed by paired tests. Studies of, for example, lender advertising practices or office locations might provide suggestive (but not definitive) indicators of discriminatory patterns, much in the manner of HMDA data. In addition, carefully specified, multivariate statistical analyses of the treatment afforded completed applications can often detect discrimination in underwriting practices. However, no alternative type of evidence can provide unambiguous indications of discriminatory behavior at the preapplication stage. Thus, I believe it is imperative that we strive to overcome the remaining methodological hurdles and to answer the remaining operational questions related to paired testing investigations of mortgage markets.

More testing initiatives clearly command the support of several relevant constituencies; for others, the case is less clear. Researchers have found paired testing to be a scientific and powerful tool. Activists have spearheaded the use of paired testing in lending, as they did in the housing field; with new financial support from HUD, their efforts are likely to intensify. Regulators have previously eschewed testing, but the OCC's recent conducting of a pilot study of examination testing represented a laudable break with precedent. Lenders may still look askance at paired testing conducted by examiners or community groups, but they are beginning to recognize the power of the technique; self-testing has also been endorsed by the American Bankers Association.

Mortgage Scoring

I propose that we work toward developing a model that allows underwriters to best rate applicants objectively and quantitatively according to their ex ante expected profitability (or rate of return). This model would, by necessity, be based on detailed historical data on the delinquency and default performance of a large number of borrowers, so that all the appropriate characteristics of the applicants and the desired property can be accounted for. Once statistically estimated, the parameters of this model would be used by underwriters as a template for scoring each mortgage applicant. Assuming that the model was a robust predictor of profitability, only those applicants meeting some minimum standard would be approved; no discretion would be allowed on the part of the underwriter. Different vendors could supply alternatives of such models, much as they do for credit card application scoring systems today. Individual institutions could develop their own model or choose from a vendor, whichever approach served their corporate policies most effectively.

The main requirement would be that all models would need to be based demonstrably on historical, statistically validated performance criteria that did not utilize legally protected categories as predictors. This singular requirement merits emphasis and expansion. I anticipate that the new developments in mortgage scoring will move far beyond the underwriting criteria currently employed by lenders. Some of these current criteria may be validated or modified, others may be soundly rejected, while still others might be newly developed. Indeed, it is my hope that creative research in this area could produce underwriting criteria that would reduce the adverse impact associated with the current, non-validated underwriting criteria.

Such an analytical development could offer the opportunity for marked advances in both research and enforcement. In research it would relate to many issues:

- The use of the mortgage score as an independent variable in a logit model of loan denials would finesse the problem of omitted underwriting variables and determine whether the variables were good predictors of profitability.
- In analogous fashion, a mortgage scoring model could be used to test the implicit restrictions in the standard model's specification, as urged by Yinger (chapter 2, this volume).
- By rigorously establishing the "business necessity" criterion, we could better assess whether or not certain current underwriting standards had a justifiable adverse impact.

In the examination process, the mortgage scoring model would obviate most of the shortcomings of current and proposed schemes:

- Small and large institutions could be judged by the same criteria.
- No subjectivity by the examiner is needed; either the scores were correctly generated and decisions were consistently based on those scores or not.

All constituencies should be able to support additional research aimed at understanding what factors predict loan profitability. Academics will have their penchant for rigorous, statistically validated models satisfied. Activists might use these new research products to bring adverse impact challenges and should be more confident that regulatory examinations have succeeded in eliminating differential treatment in racial underwriting. Regulators will see their examination processes as more credible, simple, and cost-effective. Lenders will perceive more predictability and fairness in the examination process and should have more confidence in the performance of their underwriters and their portfolios.

In a broader sense, the mortgage scoring model might well help us answer one of the important, yet longstanding, questions in the field: Is enhanced lending to minorities or predominantly minority-occupied areas antithetical to safety and soundness considerations? The conventional answer of yes has been a major obstacle to fair lending and community reinvestment efforts; nevertheless, without sufficient analyses of mortgage performance, this conventional wisdom has not been tested adequately. Clearly, all constituents in the issue have a major interest in ascertaining this answer.

Although the benefits would be immense, I do not mean to minimize the concerns often associated with this initiative. The first concern is that an inflexible mortgage scoring system might have an unintended adverse impact on minority applicants, whose applicants are reputedly more idiosyncratic and require more "flexibility" to approve. Although a valid concern, there is no reason to believe a priori that all such scoring schemes would have a worse adverse impact than current underwriting standards; as noted previously, the opposite is likely. Even if such schemes were to have such an unavoidable impact in the short run, it would suggest to me that additional efforts would be warranted in consumer education and credit counseling, rather than a return to a judgmental underwriting system that too often has penalized minorities by differential treatment and has been virtually impossible for examiners to detect. If the rules of the underwriting game are made plain to everyone, everyone will have a better opportunity to develop strategies for success.

The other concern is technical: Can such a robust mortgage scoring model be estimated? Several worries readily come to mind. The endogeneity of loan terms and conditions and the default decision is complex to model, as are alternative borrower and lender strategies occurring after default but before foreclosure (Ambrose and Capone 1993). The sample upon which historical performance correlates is based is truncated (Barth, Cordes, and Yezer 1979). Predicting ex ante large declines in applicants' income and in the value of their property, both crucial determinants of default (Quercia and Stegman 1992), is exceedingly difficult. Borrowers' credit scores at the time of loan origination have declining ability to predict default as the loan seasons (Holloway et al. 1993). Many of the functional form, variable interaction, and other technical issues related to logit models of underwriting discussed earlier are relevant here. These are difficult, perhaps insuperable, problems. Nevertheless, I believe that the potential payoffs are so great that future research should be focused here. Even if a full-blown mortgage scoring system of underwriting were not achieved, the benefits noted previously still would be partially realized.

CONCLUSION

In assessing current and emerging initiatives, I have tried to identify those that would both command sizable support from academics, activists, regulators, and lenders and would significantly improve our ability to end discrimination in mortgage and related markets. Although my analysis suggests a number of areas deserving of further research, two areas seem paramount in light of these two criteria:

paired testing and mortgage scoring. Paired testing is especially attractive because it appears workable, commands widespread support, uniquely fills a glaring weakness in the examination process, and offers a powerful tool for gathering courtworthy evidence. By contrast, how far we can move down the road toward a valid, nonadverse-impact mortgage scoring model is less clear. However, multiconstituency support for mortgage scoring should be even stronger than for paired testing because the potential payoffs for all are so dramatic.

EPILOGUE

Few targets of prospective research have moved so dramatically as has the field of mortgage lending discrimination. Since 1993, when the preceding discussion was written, the field has been flooded by scholarly research, enforcement, and regulatory initiatives, many following directions I advocated at that time. I am thus in the bittersweet position of simultaneously having my writings vindicated and rendered outdated. This epilogue briefly traces the major strands of response along the research lines I recommended in 1993, together with my current ruminations on the future directions of the topic.

In 1993 I urged further studies of differential treatment in the mortgage underwriting process using statistical analysis of loan application files. Subsequently, major works have appeared by, for example, Rachlis and Yezer (1993), Horne (1994), and Yezer, Phillips, and Trost (1994), which attacked the data and methods of the 1992 Boston Fed study, while others have replicated its results and rebutted criticisms—for example, Carr and Megbolugbe (1993) and Browne and Tootell (1995). The Federal Reserve Bank of Chicago study (Hunter 1995) and Rodda and Wallace (chapter 20, this volume) have made valuable analytical advances based on the Boston Fed data that offer the potential to better direct enforcement efforts. Details of these studies are provided by Yinger (chapter 2, this volume).

I also suggested that additional work was needed in identifying adverse impact. The potential impact of allowing certain renter groups to become homeowners by changing underwriting standards has since been investigated by Savage and Fronczek (1993), and is currently the subject of an Urban Institute study sponsored by the U.S. Department of Housing and Urban Development (HUD). Berkovec et al.'s (1995) studies of the default and loss performance of the Federal Housing

Administration portfolio have provided valuable insights into the business necessity of various underwriting standards.

Indirect methods for investigating lending discrimination was another subject I discussed, although my skepticism did not prevent further work from emerging. Schill and Wachter (1993) managed to find a new slant on analyzing HMDA data that provided insightful tests of redlining. And HUD, at this writing, is sponsoring a small grants competition aimed at generating creative research with HMDA data that bridges both academic and enforcement concerns. The marginal default probability model approach was further refined by Berkovec et al. (1995) and has produced considerable controversy.

Finally, I argued that research on two fronts would offer the biggest mutual returns to scholarly and enforcement communities: paired testing and mortgage scoring. On the former front, there has been a dramatic upsurge in the level of enforcement testing activity conducted by private fair housing organizations under the aegis of HUD's Fair Housing Initiatives Program. Unfortunately for the scholarly community, the techniques, results, and statistical issues surrounding enforcement testing are typically shrouded by the veil of legal proceedings.

On the latter front, the Federal Home Loan Mortgage Corporation (Freddie Mac) and the Federal National Mortgage Association (Fannie Mae) have taken great strides toward developing an automated underwriting system. Fannie Mae's approach is to create an artificial intelligence algorithm that mimics the underwriter's decision process. Freddie Mac has moved to the operational prototype stage of a computerized mortgage scoring system developed from their econometric models of loan performance. Applicants whose characteristics produce a sufficiently high score are to be given short turnaround approval without ever having to be scrutinized by a human underwriter.

The current state of mortgage discrimination research and enforcement is characterized, in my view, by a dramatic incongruity: the Department of Justice and fair housing groups have proceeded apace with suits against lenders at the same time that the research community has returned to a more skeptical stance about the severity of the problem. Since 1993, the Justice Department has settled landmark mortgage discrimination suits against Chevy Chase Federal Savings Bank (1994), First National Bank of Vicksburg (1994), Blackpipe State Bank (1995), and Northern Trust Co. (1995).

As if to belie these intensifications of enforcement activity, the research that has emerged since 1993 has swung the pendulum of opinion away from the strong consensus that coalesced in the year following the Boston Fed study. The previously cited critiques by Rachlis and Yezer (1993), Horne (1994), and Yezer et al. (1994) have raised doubts about the veracity of the Boston Fed study, and the claims of Berkovec et al. (1995) about the reputed absence of prejudice-based discrimination as deduced from their default model have been especially effective in raising doubts about the nature and severity of mortgage lending discrimination.

Thus, what I now see as major foci of research are: (1) testing that probes potential differential treatment at both the preapplication and underwriting stages of the lending process; (2) studies that benchmark differential treatment in office location and advertising; and (3) studies that investigate disparate impacts of dimensions of lender behavior, from (human or automated) underwriting standards to office location to loan product development. The first focus is urgently needed to clarify the severity of differential treatment discrimination in prescreening and underwriting and thus to provide the appropriate political momentum for enforcement efforts. Studies that would prove invaluable in this regard could either involve paired testers with fictitiously matched financial profiles (who, presumably, were given waivers from federal fraud statutes) or unmatched testers with actual profiles (who are subsequently matched by multivariate statistical techniques). The second focus on better understanding other sorts of differential treatment, such as lenders' branch office location and marketing practices, is fertile ground for more work in light of the suit against Chevy Chase Federal. We need to identify more rigorously, for example, a standard for equal treatment with regard to outreach and marketing activities so that differential treatment can be assessed.

The third focus, to study disparate impacts of lender behavior, also has clear immediacy, given that HUD will be monitoring progress toward secondary mortgage market purchasing goals of Freddie Mac and Fannie Mae in underserved areas, and will soon begin drafting regulations to clarify fair lending violations under Section VIII of the 1968 Civil Rights Act. The challenge will be to pursue research in all these directions that bridges the needs of social scientific rigor, legal precision, enforcement effectiveness, and regulatory practicality.

Notes

The views expressed in this chapter are the author's and do not necessarily reflect those of The Urban Institute.

I wish to acknowledge several people whose comments were instrumental in preparing this work: Calvin Bradford, Lynn Browne, Cathy Cloud, Glenn Canner, Charles Finn, Deb Goldberg, John Yinger, and Tony Yezer. Brian L. Lee and Diane Hendricks provided professional assistance in preparing the manuscript.

1. My conclusions differ somewhat from those reached by Yinger (chapter 2, this volume) because of the application of different criteria.

2. See also the summary of pilot studies in Galster (1993: chap. 7).

3. This is true even if the results are statistically significant.

4. Smith and Cloud (chapter 23, this volume) downplay this concern.

5. Note that I have critiqued less sophisticated methodologies employing publicly available HMDA data elsewhere (Galster 1991, 1992).

6. Even though the marginal impact of one variable on the probability of denial depends on the values assumed by other variables, this effect is forced by the specification of the cumulative normal function in the logit.

7. For a seminal discussion of endogeneity and an attempt to model structural equations of mortgage terms, see Barth et al. (1979). Also see Black and Schweitzer (1985).

8. I am indebted to John Yinger and Leonard Nakamura for these points.

9. However, note that, at least according to HMDA data, Boston appears quite typical (Avery, Beeson, and Sniderman, Chapter 3, this volume).

10. See the case descriptions in Cloud and Galster (1993).

11. According to personal correspondence between the author and staff at HUD and the MA. Attorney General's Office, Shawmut Morgage Company of Boston was the subject of a Department of Justice Federal Trade Commission investigation during March, 1993. This investigation was triggered by the Federal Reserve Board referral that itself appeared to have been spawned by review of the Boston Fed study data. A complaint and consent decree were filed simultaneously on Dec. 13, 1993.

12. It was assumed that 50 percent of all sample applicants were minorities.

13. I am indebted to Peter Zorn for this point.

14. This is a parameter that, when applied to the simulated data, produces interracial denial rates comparable to those observed from HMDA data.

15. This claim has been employed, for example, in Schill and Wachter's (1993) tests for redlining using HMDA data.

References

Acorn (Association of Community Organizations for Reform Now). 1992. *A Policy of Discrimination? Homeowners Insurance Redlining in 24 Cities*. Washington, D.C.: ACORN.

Ambrose, Brent, and Charles Capone. 1993. "Borrower Workouts and Optimal Foreclosure of Single-Family Mortgage Loans." Paper presented at American Real Estate and Urban Economics Association conference, June 1–2, Washington, D.C.

Avery, Robert, and Thomas Buynak. 1981. "Mortgage Redlining: Some New Evidence." *Economic Review of Federal Reserve Bank of Cleveland* 17: 18–32.

Avery, Robert, Patricia Beeson, and Mark Sniderman. 1992. "Cross-Lender Variation in Home Mortgage Lending." Federal Reserve Bank of Cleveland Working Paper 9219. Cleveland: Federal Reserve Bank of Cleveland, December.

Barry Leeds and Associates, Inc. 1993. "Testing for Discrimination during the Preapplication and Post-Applicant Phase of Mortgage Lending." Paper presented at conference on "Home Mortgage Lending and Discrimination: Research and Enforcement," sponsored by U.S. Department of Housing and Urban Development, May 18–19, Washington, D.C.

Barth, James, Joseph Cordes, and Anthony Yezer. 1979. "Financial Institution Regulations, Redlining, and Mortgage Markets." In *The Regulation of Financial Institutions*. Conference series 21 (101–43). Boston: Federal Reserve Bank of Boston.

Bauer, Paul, and Brian Cromwell. 1994. "A Monte Carlo Examination of Bias Tests in Mortgage Lending." Federal Reserve Bank of Cleveland Economic Review 30(3): 27–40.

Becker, Gary. 1993. "The Evidence against Banks Doesn't Prove Bias." *Business Week*, April 19: 18.

Benston, George. 1979. "Mortgage Redlining Research: A Review and Critical Analysis." In *The Regulation of Financial Institutions*. Conference Series 21 (144–95). Boston: Federal Reserve Bank of Boston.

———. 1981. "Mortgage Redlining Research: A Review and Critical Analysis." *Journal of Bank Research* 12: 8–23.

Berkovec, James, Glenn Canner, Stuart Gabriel, and Timothy Hannan. 1995. "Discrimination, Default, and Loss in FHA Mortgage Lending." Paper presented at the Allied Social Sciences Association Meetings, January, Washington, D.C.

Black, Harold, and Robert Schweitzer. 1985. "A Canonical Analysis of Mortgage Lending Terms." Urban Studies 22: 13–19.

Board of Governors of the Federal Reserve System. 1991. "Feasibility Study on Application of the Testing Methodology to the Detection of Discrimination in Mortgage Lending." Washington, D.C.: Federal Reserve Staff Analysis Paper, June.

Brimelow, Peter. 1993. "Racism at Work?" *National Review*, April 12: 42.

Brimelow, Peter, and Leslie Spencer. 1993. "The Hidden Clue." *Forbes*, January 4: 48.

Canner, Glenn. 1982. "Redlining: Research and Federal Legislative Response." Study 121. Washington, D.C.: Board of Governors of the Federal Reserve System.

Canner, Glenn, and Stuart Gabriel. 1992. "Market Segmentation and Lender Specialization in the Primary and Secondary Mortgage Markets. *Housing Policy Debate* 3(2): 241–329.

Canner, Glenn, Stewart Gabriel, and John Woolley. 1991. "Race, Default Risk, and Mortgage Lending: A Study of the FHA Conventional Loan Markets." *Southern Economic Journal* 58(July): 249–62.

Canner, Glenn, Stuart Gabriel, Timothy Hannan, and James Berkovic. 1993. "FHA Defaults and Race." Paper presented at conference on "Home Mortgage Lending and Discrimination: Research and Enforcement," sponsored by U.S. Department of Housing and Urban Development, May 18–19, Washington, D.C.

Carr, James, and Isaac Megbolugbe. 1993. "The Federal Reserve Bank of Boston Study on Mortgage Lending Revisited." *Journal of Housing Research* 4(2): 277–313.

Cloud, Cathy, and George Galster. 1993. "What Do We Know about Racial Discrimination in Mortgage Markets?" *Review of Black Political Economy* 22: 101–20.

Commonwealth of Massachusetts. 1993. "Harshbarger Obtains Agreement with Banks to Settle Lending Bias," Boston, Mass.: Office of the Attorney General News Release, Dec. 2.

Cross, Stephen. 1993. "Discrimination Studies: How Critical are Default Rates?" Paper presented at conference on "Home Mortgage Lending and Discrimination: Research and Enforcement," sponsored by U.S. Department of Housing and Urban Development, May 18–19, Washington, D.C.

Galster, George. 1991. *A Statistical Perspective on Illegal Discrimination in Lending*. Washington, D.C.: American Bankers Association.

———. 1992. "Research on Discrimination in the Housing and Mortgage Markets: Assessment and Future Directions." *Housing Policy Debate* 3(2): 639–83.

———. 1993. "Use of Testers in Investigating Discrimination in Mortgage Lending and Insurance." In Michael Fix and Raymond Struyk, eds. *Clear and Convincing Evidence*. Washington, D.C.: Urban Institute Press.

Hancock, Paul. 1993. "Federal Efforts to Enforce Fair Lending Laws." Paper presented at conference on "Home Mortgage Lending and Discrimination: Research and Enforcement," sponsored by U.S. Department of Housing and Urban Development, May 18–19, Washington, D.C.

Holloway, Thomas, Gregor MacDonald, and John Straka. 1993. "Credit Scores, Early Payment Mortgage Defaults, and Mortgage Loan Performance." Paper presented at American Real Estate and Urban Economics Association (AREUEA) Conference, June 1–2, Washington, D.C.

Horne, David. 1994. "Evaluating the Role of Race in Mortgage Lending." *FDIC Banking Review* 7(Spring/Summer): 1–15.

Hula, Richard. 1991. "Neighborhood Development and Local Credit Market." *Urban Affairs Quarterly* 27: 249–67.

Hunter, William. 1995. "Discrimination in Mortgage Lending." *Chicago Fed Letter* 195: 2–4.

Kohn, Ernest. 1993. "The New York State Banking Study: Research on Mortgage Discrimination." Paper presented at conference on "Home Mortgage Lending and Discrimination: Research and Enforcement," sponsored by U.S. Department of Housing and Urban Development, May 18–19, Washington, D.C.

Kohn, E., C., Foster, B. Kaye, and N. Terris. 1992. *Are Mortgage Lending Policies Discriminatory? A Study of 10 Savings Banks*. New York: New York State Banking Department, Consumer Studies Division.

Kushner, James. 1992. "Federal Enforcement and Judicial Review of the Fair Housing Amendments Act of 1988." *Housing Policy Debate* 3: 537–600.

Lang, William, and Leonard Nakamura. 1993. "A Model of Redlining." *Journal of Urban Economics* 33: 223–34.

Lehman, Jane. 1993a. "Second-Mortgage Industry Assailed." *Washington Post*, February 20: E3.

________. 1993b. "Borrower Data to be Disclosed." *Washington Post*, March 6: E140.

Lindsey, Lawrence. 1993. Statement before the U.S. House of Representatives Subcommittee on Consumer Credit and Insurance of the Committee on Banking, Finance, and Urban Affairs. Washington, D.C.: Board of Governors of the Federal Reserve, February 18.

Maddala, George, and Robert Trost. 1982. "On Measuring Discrimination in Loan Markets." *Housing Finance Review* 1: 245–68.

Munnell, Alicia, Lynn Browne, James McEneaney, and Geoffrey Tootell. 1992. "Mortgage Lending in Boston: Interpreting the HMDA Data." Federal Reserve Bank of Boston Working Paper 92-07. Boston: Federal Reserve Bank of Boston, October.

________. 1993. "Is It Redlining or Discrimination?" Paper presented at American Economic Association Meetings, Jan. 8, Anaheim, Calif.

Perle, Eugene, Kathryn Lynch, and Jeffrey Horner. 1993. "Model Specification and Local Mortgage Market Behavior." *Journal of Housing Research* 4: 225–44.

Philadelphia Commission on Human Relations. 1993. "Use of Testing to Identify Potential Discrimination: Lender Testing by a Local Agency." Paper presented at conference on "Home Mortgage Lending and Discrimination: Research and Enforcement," sponsored by U.S. Department of Housing and Urban Development, May 18–19, Washington, D.C.

Quercia, Roberto, and Michael Stegman. 1992. "Residential Mortgage Default: A Review of the Literature." *Journal of Housing Research* 3(2): 341–79.

Rachlis, Mitchell, and Anthony Yezer. 1993. "Serious Flaws in Statistical Tests for Discrimination in Mortgage Markets." *Journal of Housing Research* 4: 315–36.

Riedman, Larry. 1993. "Perspectives from a Regulatory Agency." Paper presented at HUD's "Discrimination and Mortgage Lending Research and Enforcement Conference," May, Washington, D.C.

Roberts, Paul. 1993. "Banks in the Line of Fire." *Washington Times*, March 12: F1.

Savage, Howard, and Peter Fronczek. 1993. *Who Can Afford to Buy a House in 1991?* U.S. Bureau of the Census Current Housing Report H121-93-3. Washington, D.C.: U.S. Bureau of the Census.

Schafer, Robert, and Helen Ladd. 1981. *Discrimination in Mortgage Lending.* Cambridge, Mass.: MIT Press.

Schill, Michael, and Susan Wachter. 1993. "A Tale of Two Cities: Racial and Ethnic Geographic Disparities in Home Mortgage Lending in Boston and Philadelphia." *Journal of Housing Research* 4(2): 245–76.

Spayd, Liz. 1993. "White House Targets Mortgage Loan Bias." *Washington Post*, May 6: B12.

Turner, Margery, Raymond Struyk, and John Yinger. 1991. *The Housing Discrimination Study* (volumes). Washington, D.C.: Urban Institute and U.S. Department of Housing and Urban Development.

United States of America v. *Decatur Federal Savings and Loan Association.* 1992. N.D. Ga. No. 1-92 CV 2128 (Sept. 17).

United States of America v. *Shawmut Mortgage Company*. 1993. D. Mass. No. 93-CV-2453.

United States of America v. *Chevy Chase Savings Bank*. 1994. D.D.C. No. 9-1-1825 JG.

United States of America v. *First National Bank of Vicksburg*. 1994. W.D. Miss. No. 5:94 CV 6(B)(N).

United States of America v. *Blackpipe State Bank*. 1994. D.S. Dakota. No. 93-5115.

United States of America v. *Northern Trust Company*. 1995. D. Illinois. No. 95-C 3239.

Van Order, Robert, Ann-Margaret Westin, and Peter Zorn. 1993. "Effects of the Racial Compositon of Neighborhoods on Default, and Implications for Racial Discrimination in Mortgage Markets." Paper presented at American Economics Association Meetings, Jan. 8, Anaheim, Calif.

Wallace, James, and David Rodda. 1995. "Fair Lending Management: Using Influence Statistics to Identify Critical Mortgage Loan Applications." Paper presented at American Real Estate and Urban Economics Association (AREUEA) Mid-Year Meetings, May 30–31, Washington, D.C.

Wienk, Ron. 1992. "Discrimination in Urban Credit Markets: What We Don't Know and Why We Don't Know It." *Housing Policy Debate* 3(2): 217–40.

Yezer, Anthony, R.F. Phillips, and Robert Trost. 1994. "Bias in Estimates of Discrimination and Default in Mortgage Lending: The Effects of Simultaneity and Self-Selection." *Journal of Real Estate Finance and Economics* 9(3, November): 197–215.

Yinger, John. 1986. "Measuring Racial Discrimination with Fair Housing Audits." *American Economic Review* 76: 88–93.

LIST OF TABLES AND FIGURES

Tables

Figures

ABOUT THE EDITORS AND CONTRIBUTORS

John Goering has designed and conducted fair housing research at the Office of Policy Development and Research at the U.S. Department of Housing and Urban Development since 1978 and is the author of numerous articles on this issue. He was the supervisor of the first national assessment of American Indian housing needs, among many other research projects.

Ron Wienk has had numerous policy research positions, including research associate at the Urban Institute, senior fair lending advisor at the Office of the Comptroller of the Currency, and research analyst at the U.S. Department of Housing and Urban Development. His publications include "The Persistence of Segregation in Urban Areas: Contributing Causes," co-authored with Marjorie Austin Turner, in *Housing Markets and Residential Mobility* (Washington, D.C.: Urban Institute Press, 1993).

Kent B. Alexander is the U.S. Attorney for the Northern District of Georgia. Formerly he was counsel with King & Spalding in Atlanta, Georgia, and represented Decatur Federal Savings & Loan in the 1992 mortgage lending discrimination lawsuit brought by the Department of Justice.

Robert B. Avery is a senior economist at the Board of Governors of the Federal Reserve System. He is the author of two books and numerous articles in economics, finance, and statistics.

Patricia E. Beeson is an associate professor of economics at the University of Pittsburgh and a Research Associate of the Federal Reserve Bank of Cleveland. Her current research interests center on issues of regional growth and decline.

James A. Berkovec is a principal economist at Freddie Mac and was formerly an economist at the Board of Governors of the Federal Reserve System. Dr. Berkovec's area of specialization is applied econometrics, especially analyses of housing and mortgage markets.

Hal Bonnette is an Equal Opportunity Specialist in the Office of Fair Housing and Equal Opportunity (FHEO) in the Department of Housing and Urban Development (HUD). For the past two years, he has focused almost exclusively on mortgage lending investigations.

Paul S. Calem joined the staff of the Board of Governors of the Federal Reserve System in February 1995. His ongoing and published research covers topics in banking market structure and competition, bank capital regulation, and community reinvestment and fair lending.

Glenn B. Canner is senior economist, Division of Research and Statistics, Board of Governors of the Federal Reserve System. Dr. Canner specializes in the area of micro-consumer issues and banking regulation at the Board.

Ann Chud is Chief, Systemic/Secretary-Initiated Case Branch in the Office of Investigations, Office of Fair Housing and Equal Opportunity, at the U.S. Department of Housing and Urban Development. She has also served on the Interagency Task Force on Fair Lending Policy's subgroups on policy, enforcement, and targeting.

Cathy Cloud is the Enforcement Program Director of the National Fair Housing Alliance in Washington, D.C., responsible for the implementation of nationwide fair housing enforcement programs. She currently coordinates national mortgage lending and homeowners insurance discrimination investigations.

Richard W. Cole is Chief of the Civil Rights Division and an Assistant Attorney General at the Office of the Attorney General of Massachusetts. Since he became a member of the Masachusetts Bar in 1974 he has been counsel in a number of leading civil rights and public interest law cases in state and federal court.

Leonard A. Cupingood is a statistician and vice president of the Center for Forensic Economic Studies and a member of the Department of Mathematical Sciences at Villanova University. He has expertise in the development and application of statistical models to employment discrimination cases and fair lending practices.

Stuart A. Gabriel is a professor of finance and business economics and co-director of the Minority Program in Real Estate Finance and Development in the Graduate School of Business Administration of the University of Southern California. He has published extensively on housing and mortgage markets and finance, urban and regional economics and policy, and population mobility.

George Galster is a program director and principal research associate at the Urban Institute. He has published widely on the topics of racial discrimination, segregation, neighborhood dynamics, urban poverty, and community lending patterns.

Ira J. Goldstein is the Mid-Atlantic Enforcement Center Director for HUD's Office of Fair Housing and Equal Opportunity (FHEO). He has published several articles on community reinvestment and lending discrimination.

Zina Gefter Greene is on the board of the Washington, D.C. Housing Finance Agency. She is also a consultant to lawyers and non-profit organizations in the areas of housing finance and mortgage lending discrimination.

Timothy H. Hannan is an economist in the Division of Research and Statistics at the Board of Governors of the Federal Reserve System. His area of specialization is industrial organization and the economics of the banking industry.

Rachel Lawton is the assistant director of the Compliance Division of the Philadelphia Commission on Human Relations. She has supervised several fair housing testing programs, including rental, sales, and pre-application mortgage lending testing.

Richard Ritter is a private fair lending consultant in Washington, D.C. He was formerly Special Litigation Counsel in the Justice Department's Civil Rights Division and headed the Justice Department's first insurance redlining investigation.

David Rodda is an economist at Abt Associates, specializing in the areas of fair lending and housing finance.

Stephen L. Ross is an assistant professor in the department of economics at the University of Connecticut. His research interests are urban economics, espeically urban labor markets, local public finance, and race and discrimination in urban housing and credit markets.

Robert G. Schwemm is the Ashland Oil Professor at the University of Kentucky College of Law, where he has taught since 1975. Professor Schwemm has written and lectured extensively on fair housing litigation.

Bernard R. Siskin is a senior vice president of the Center for Forensic Economic Studies, and is a former chairman of the Department of Statistics at Temple University. He specializes in the application of statistics in litigation and has written and lectured extensively on the topic.

Shanna L. Smith is the executive director for the National Fair Housing Alliance (NFHA) and has worked for the Alliance since the fall of 1990. She has testified frequently on mortgage lending and homeowners insurance discrimination issues before committees of the U.S. Senate and House of Representatives.

Mark S. Sniderman is senior vice president and director of research of the Federal Reserve Bank of Cleveland. His research department responsibilities include overseeing the production of various research publications and directing the Bank's economic and monetary policy analysis.

Geoffrey M.B. Tootell is an assistant vice president and economist at the Federal Reserve Bank of Boston. He is one of the co-authors of the Boston Fed study on mortgage discrimintion.

Robert Van Order is Chief Economist of Freddie Mac. Prior to joining Freddie Mac, Van Order served as Director of the Housing Finance Analysis Division at the U.S. Department of Housing and Urban Development (HUD).

James E. Wallace is a Vice President and Principal Associate at Abt Associates. His research focuses on housing policy analysis, evaluation of HUD programs, and management of large-scale research studies.

John Yinger is professor of economics and public administration at the Maxwell School, Syracuse University, and Associate Director for the Metropolitan Studies Program at the Maxwell School's Center for Policy Research. He is a specialist in state and local public finance, racial and ethnic discrimination in housing, and urban economics.

INDEX

D

N